OBJECT AND SELF:
A DEVELOPMENTAL APPROACH

OBJECT AND SELF:
A DEVELOPMENTAL APPROACH

Essays in Honor of Edith Jacobson

Edited by

SAUL TUTTMAN

CAROL KAYE and MURIEL ZIMMERMAN

INTERNATIONAL UNIVERSITIES PRESS, INC.

New York

Library of Congress Cataloging in Publication Data

Main entry under title:

Object and self, a developmental approach.

    Includes bibliographies and index.
    1.   Psychoanalysis — Addresses, essays, lectures.
2. Self — Addresses, essays, lectures. 3. Interpersonal
relations — Addresses, essays, lectures. 4. Psychology,
Pathological — Addresses, essays, lectures. 5. Jacobson,
Edith. I. Jacobson, Edith. II. Tuttman, Saul.
III. Kaye, Carol, 1925–   IV. Zimmerman, Muriel.
[DNLM: 1. Ego. 2. Object attachment. 3. Psychoanalysis.
WM 460.5.02 012]
RC506.024   150'.19'5   80-39875
ISBN 0-8236-3700-X

Manufactured in the United States of America

CONTENTS

Part III
APPLICATIONS

CONTRIBUTORS

E. James Anthony, M.D.
Blanche F. Ittleson Professor of Child Psychiatry; Director of the Eliot Division of Child Psychiatry, and Director of the Edison Child Development Research Center, at Washington University School of Medicine, St. Louis, Mo.; Training Analyst, St. Louis Psychoanalytic Institute; President, Association for Child Psychoanalysis.

Jacob A. Arlow, M.D.
Past President, American Psychoanalytic Association; Formerly Editor-in-Chief, *Psychoanalytic Quarterly*.

Sidney J. Blatt, Ph.D.
Professor in Departments of Psychology and Psychiatry; Chief, Psychology Section in Department of Psychiatry, Yale University, New Haven, Conn.; Faculty, Western New England Institute for Psychoanalysis; Member, Western New England Society for Psychoanalysis.

Susan K. Deri, Dipl. Med. Psychol.
Formerly, lecturer, Graduate School of Psychology of City College, New York; Faculty Member, National Psychological Association for Psychoanalysis; Training and Supervising Analyst, Institute for Psychoanalytic Training and Research, New York.

Theodore L. Dorpat, M.D.
Clinical Professor of Psychiatry, University of Washington; Training Analyst, Seattle Psychoanalytic Institute.

Norbert Freedman, Ph.D.
Professor of Psychiatry, Director of Psychology and Research

Training in Psychiatry, Downstate Medical Center, State University of New York; Past President, Training and Supervising Analyst, Institute for Psychoanalytic Training and Research, New York.

GEORGE GERO, PH.D., M.D.
Supervising and Training Analyst, New York Psychoanalytic Institute.

PETER L. GIOVACCHINI, M.D.
Clinical Professor, Department of Psychiatry, University of Illinois College of Medicine; Co-Editor, *Adolescent Psychiatry*.

ARNOLD GOLDBERG, M.D.
Attending Psychiatrist, Institute for Psychosomatic and Psychiatric Research and Training, Michael Reese Hospital and Medical Center, Chicago, Ill.; Clinical Professor of Psychiatry, Pritzker School of Medicine, University of Chicago; Training and Supervising Analyst, Chicago Institute for Psychoanalysis.

ANDRÉ GREEN
Past Chief of the Clinic of the Chair of Psychiatry (Paris); Past Director of the Paris Psychoanalytic Institute; Formerly Co-Editor, *The International Journal of Psycho-Analysis*, Co-Editor, *Nouvelle Revue de Psychanalyse*.

CAROL KAYE, PH.D.
Faculty and Training Analyst, Director of Referral and Treatment Center, Institute for Psychoanalytic Training and Research, New York.

OTTO F. KERNBERG, M.D.
Medical Director, New York Hospital-Cornell Medical Center, Westchester Division, and Professor of Psychiatry, Cornell University Medical College; Training and Supervising Analyst, Columbia University Center for Psychoanalytic Training and Research, New York.

PETER H. KNAPP, M.D.
Professor of Psychiatry, Associate Chairman of the Division of Psychiatry, and Chief, Psychosomatic Medicine, Boston University Medical Center; Training Analyst, Boston Psychoanalytic Society and Institute.

FREDERIC J. LEVINE, PH.D.
Associate Professor, Department of Mental Health Sciences, Hahnemann Medical College and Hospital, Philadelphia, Pennsylvania.

HELEN BLOCK LEWIS, PH.D.
Adjunct Professor of Psychology, Yale University; Supervising and Training Analyst, Institute for Psychoanalytic Training and Research, New York.

LESTER LUBORSKY, PH.D.
Professor of Psychology in Psychiatry, School of Medicine, University of Pennsylvania, Philadelphia, Pennsylvania; Member, Philadelphia Association for Psychoanalysis; Past President, Society for Psychotherapy Research.

STANLEY ROSENMAN, PH.D.
Past Adjunct Professor, Department of Psychology, The City College of the City University of New York; Senior Member, National Psychological Association for Psychoanalysis, New York Center for Psychoanalytic Training, and Council of Psychoanalytic Psychotherapists; private practice of psychotherapy.

DAVID L. RUBINFINE, M.D.
Private practice of psychoanalysis.

SHULA SHICHMAN, M.A. (TEL AVIV UNIVERSITY)
Doctoral candidate, Department of Social Psychology, Teacher's College, Columbia University, New York.

SAMUEL SLIPP, M.D.
Clinical Professor of Psychiatry, New York University School of Medicine, New York; Medical Director, Postgraduate Center for Mental Health.

ANN SKENDALL TEELE, PH.D.
Senior Psychologist, Boston University Hospital Inpatient Service; Instructor, Department of Psychiatry, Boston University School of Medicine; Fellow, Massachusetts Psychological Association.

SAUL TUTTMAN, M.D., PH.D.
Clinical Assistant Professor of Psychiatry, New York University

School of Medicine; Past President, Training and Supervising Analyst, Institute for Psychoanalytic Training and Research, New York.

VAMIK D. VOLKAN, M.D.

Professor of Psychiatry, University of Virginia Medical Center; Medical Director, Blueridge Hospital, University of Virginia, Charlottesville, Va.; Faculty Member, Washington Psychoanalytic Institute.

MURIEL ZIMMERMAN, PH.D.

Clinical Assistant Professor, Department of Psychiatry, Cornell University Medical College and New York Hospital; Training and Supervising Analyst, Institute for Psychoanalytic Training and Research, New York.

ACKNOWLEDGMENTS

We are grateful that Martin Azarian, President of International Universities Press, encouraged and supported the unfolding of this volume as a tribute to Edith Jacobson, all of whose volumes were published by I.U.P. We appreciate that he and every contributor to this project participated enthusiastically, inspired by Jacobson's work and personality.

The secretarial help and dedication of Vicki Ellis, Claudia McGeary, and Mercy Russell is acknowledged with thanks.

Most importantly, we are indebted to Lottie M. Newman, who served as manuscript editor of this volume, and who edited Jacobson's books as well as those of other outstanding analytic authors. Her knowledge of psychoanalytic theory and literature, and her outstanding editorial skills, have provided aid of the highest caliber. Mrs. Newman's contributions have been invaluable and her devotion to psychoanalytic scholarship is inspirational.

PREFACE

A few years ago Dr. Edith Jacobson's friends, colleagues, and students honored her in New York City on the occasion of her eightieth birthday.[1] This volume grew out of that celebration. Jacobson's ideas inspire an ongoing exploration of all aspects of the developmental drama. She encouraged an integration of object relations theory and ego psychology within a traditional framework utilizing both topographic and structural hypotheses and considering the drives and affects in the context of external reality. Her multidimensional view of the evolution of the self—in relation to others—is clinically based, theoretically sophisticated, and eminently humanistic.

The goal of this volume is to survey Jacobson's work and its implications within a historic context and to offer new essays on object relations theory. The introductory chapter offers an overview of the history of object relations theory. The relevant ideas of Freud, Melanie Klein, and other early pioneers, developmental and ego psychologists are considered.

Part I consists of papers which explore: the meaning and implications of Jacobson's concepts on the self and the object world as well as her ideas about affect states (Arlow, Gero, Tuttman, Kernberg).

Part II consists of papers dealing with issues of theory and treatment. These papers, apparently diverse, have deliberately been encompassed within one section to emphasize the mutual influence of theoretical assumption, therapeutic practice, and clinical findings. The first group of papers is predominantly concerned with theoretical issues (Goldberg, Dorpat, Deri, Anthony, Lewis, Freedman, Zimmerman, Green, Blatt and Schichman, Slipp); the second

---

[1]At a meeting sponsored by the Institute for Psychoanalytic Training and Research, January 21, 1977, at which Arlow, Gero, and Tuttman spoke. At this celebration, Edith Jacobson was present and addressed the gathering.

1

group deals more specifically with problems in treatment (Rubinfine, Giovacchini, Volkan).

Part III is devoted to various applications of object relations theory. Two papers deal with methodology. Research findings are presented which offer data about object relations in a form compatible with testing hypotheses. The goal is to subject dynamic subtleties to experimental study without destroying the complexities of such material (Knapp and Teele, Levine and Luborsky). The other paper in this section examines the Narcissus myth from a developmental object relations viewpoint (Rosenman).

In summary, the essays in this volume strive to examine contemporary issues in developmental object relations theory in the tradition of Edith Jacobson. That is: to explore concepts in terms of their historical perspective and practical ramifications; to scrutinize cautiously the implications of observations and hypotheses; to root theory in a solid clinical foundation; to remain cognizant of the multifaceted lines of development throughout the phases of life; and to search the broad spectrum of theoretical models of value and application.

The most meaningful dedication to Edith Jacobson will emerge from the efforts of those psychoanalysts and students who strive today and tomorrow, inspired by the quality of her commitment and her work.

1

A HISTORICAL SURVEY OF THE DEVELOPMENT OF OBJECT RELATIONS CONCEPTS IN PSYCHOANALYTIC THEORY

SAUL TUTTMAN, M.D., PH.D.

The overall purpose of this introductory paper is to highlight the evolving trends in psychoanalytic thinking which are pertinent to object relations theory up to the time of Edith Jacobson's major contributions. The work of a few representatives of each trend is offered. Although the ideas of neo-Freudians (like Sullivan) and nonanalytic psychologists (like Piaget and Werner) are relevant to object relations theory, the focus here is circumscribed by the specific purpose of this volume; namely, to review the theoretical climate in which Jacobson worked, to appreciate and survey her contribution, and to offer new essays on object relations based upon her legacy and in her memory.

Although Freud did not systematically develop a theory of object relations, he was repeatedly led to formulations about the "self"[1] and about involvement with the world of real and fantasied objects.

Freud's earliest attention to object relations evolved in the context of a determination to formulate an "objective" scientific psychology. That is, his intention was to develop a psychology that is a natural science. The goal was expressed in "Project for a Scientific Psychology" in 1895 (Freud, 1950b). In this work, he referred to the importance of a *caretaking person* in providing gratification for the helpless infant. The special parental object plays a role in the un-

---

[1]Hartmann (1956) noted the ambiguity in Freud's use of the term *das Ich* and suggested that, in the prestructural theoretical writings (that is, before 1923), *das Ich* should be translated as "the self," of one's own person. He felt that Freud's concept of narcissism might be better understood today as "the libidinal cathexis of one's own person, as opposed to that of the objects" (p. 288).

folding and developing of an interest in the world, first in terms of pleasure and later from the viewpoint of reality. Throughout Freud's writings, the general theory focuses upon intrapsychic tension management. Before developing the structural concepts, he emphasized the instincts and their vicissitudes in terms of his psychosexual theory. As he developed structural formulations, he consistently dealt with issues involving object relations; however, he did not devote himself to the metapsychological integration of object relations theory.

Freud's Concepts of Object Relations

Freud (1905a) offered these definitions: "I shall...introduce two technical terms. Let us call the person from whom sexual attraction proceeds the *sexual object* and the act towards which the instinct tends the *sexual aim*" (pp. 135–136). Ten years later, he elaborated: "The object of an instinct is the thing in regard to which or through which the instinct is able to achieve its aim [satisfaction]....It [the object] is what is most variable about an instinct and is not originally connected with it, but becomes assigned to it only in consequence of being peculiarly fitted to make satisfaction possible" (1915a, p. 122).

In other early papers, Freud explored drives in relation to self and object.[2] He emphasized the investment of psychosexual energies in the self and the manifestations of libidinal fixations in autoerotism and masturbation, in perversion and hypochondriacal preoccupation, and in basic character formation. He noted how fixation points correlate with the kind and degree of neuroses or psychoses as well as with the quality of object relations. For example, in a section of *Three Essays on Sexuality*, Freud (1905a) dealt with deviations having to do with object choice or *Objektfindung*. This term refers to the choice of a person (i.e., "his father") or to a type of object (i.e., "homosexual object choice"). Freud stressed the instinctual aim rather than the object. Nevertheless, aims of instincts which involve objects are also an aspect of object relations. A subject manifesting oral needs might find satisfaction in sucking or biting. Depending upon the individual's history, the object involved might be a particular person, part of a person, inanimate thing, a symbol, or an ideal (such as

---

[2]Freud did not distinguish between the cathexis of actual individuals and of mental representations of objects.

mother, breast or penis, the sacrament of communion, or words). In the anal phase pleasure may come from controlling the object or expressing aggression. The aim characteristic of the genital phase would involve sharing satisfaction with a person by offering and accepting love.

Freud (1911) studied the role of object relations in psychopathology. He proposed that Schreber's delusions and psychotic regression involved a loss of reality contact connected with a withdrawal of cathexis from objects[3] and things from the external world generally. "The end of the world is the projection of...internal catastrophe; his subjective world has come to an end since his withdrawal of his love from it" (p. 70). In the Schreber paper and other work on psychoses (1924a, 1924b), Freud's notions may have been precursors of the concept of the representational world. He described an inner world of organized self and object images which exists under conditions of normal development, but which is abandoned in psychosis, where, first, there is cathectic withdrawal and regression to an autistic state, and then there is an attempted restitutional reconstruction.

Freud (1911) hypothesized that the pathologically prolonged autoerotic phase of patients like Schreber leads them to a homosexual choice since such objects are similar to themselves. When the efforts to repress and sublimate fail, paranoid trends erupt. The "weak spot in their development is to be looked for somewhere between the stages of auto-erotism, narcissism and homosexuality and ...their disposition to illness...must be located in that region" (p. 62). These ideas appear to have been forerunners of concepts about narcissistic problems and compensatory strivings.

In *Totem and Taboo* (1912a), Freud examined infantile omnipotence fantasies and explored the psychosexual stages at which the self is cathected as the first libidinal object. Here was the beginning of the concept of narcissism. In 1914, he defined "narcissism" as a perversion in which the subject's own body becomes the sexual object. He distinguished between self-love (ego libido) and love of others (object libido) and their reciprocal relation. Schizophrenic withdrawal and megalomania were attributed to a pulling back of

---

[3]Today we would probably stress withdrawal of cathexis from the mental representations of object (Sandler and Rosenblatt, 1962; Jacobson, 1964).

libido from objects into the ego. In this paper, two kinds of object choices were described: the *narcissistic,* where a person loves someone like himself; and the *anaclitic,* where he is attached to someone like the nurturing and protecting figure upon whom he was dependent. This idea and those that followed connect the beginnings of developmental psychology and object relations. Freud (1915a) stated, "Under the dominance of the pleasure principle a further development now takes place in the ego. In so far as the objects which are presented to it are sources of pleasure, it takes them into itself, 'introjects' them (to use Ferenczi's [1909] term[4]); and, on the other hand, it expels whatever within itself becomes a cause of unpleasure" (pp. 135–136). Freud also introduced the term *incorporation* in this paper. By 1917, he wrote of the "object relationship" and referred to another mechanism of great importance to object relations theory: *identification,* which he described as the archaic way by which the ego chooses an object and incorporates that object into itself. In discussing mourning and melancholia as reactions to object loss, he concluded that the lost object is incorporated and regressively replaced by means of an identification. The process of identification was further elaborated as the earliest form of emotional bond with another person which precedes true object ties. Freud (1921) distinguished identification from object cathexis in the following formula. "In the first case [identification] one's father is what one would like to *be,* and in the second [object cathexis] he [one's father] is what one would like to *have*" (p. 106).

In 1923, Freud described the character of the ego as a precipitate formed from identifications which replaced abandoned early object cathexes. This substitution of object ties by identifications "has a great share in determining the form taken by the ego" (p. 28), and these identifications make an essential contribution toward the building up of the character of the ego. In this paper, the critical attitudes and the ideal strivings were proposed to be components of a newly described agency he called the *superego.* The transformation of an erotic object tie into an identification implies the abandonment of sexual aims and the transforming of object libido into narcissistic libido. These concepts (introjection, projection, identification) con-

---

[4]See below for more detailed discussion of Freud's and Ferenczi's collaboration regarding this concept.

tributed to the foundation of object relations theory.

Freud also focused upon reality contact and psychopathology from an object relations viewpoint, in the following sense. An investment in the outer world means a concern with reality, whereas a fixation or regression involving narcissistic investments reflects intense self-absorption and, where extreme, an autistic state which may involve a loss of reality along with the abandonment of objects.

In *The Ego and the Id,* Freud (1923) described the internalization of objects and the crucial role this process plays in the development of ego and superego. Whereas in "early" Freud, objects were sought to fulfill instincts, from 1923 on, objects were understood as providing sources for identifications which come to constitute ego and superego qualities. Thus, Freud's emphasis shifted to the impact of object relationships upon the development of internal psychic structures. Among other important matters, he discussed the relationships between object choice and sexual attributes and interests, the significance of the oedipal conflict and its resolution for the sexual identity of the self and for object choices.

In reply to Rank's (1924) contention that birth trauma was of singular importance in primal anxiety, Freud redefined his theory of anxiety and outlined a developmental sequence of the basic danger situations: fear of losing the loved object, fear of losing the important object's love, and castration anxiety. *Inhibitions, Symptoms and Anxiety* (1926) raised significant issues which are very relevant for object relations theory. The early mother-infant situation generates anxiety when the infant loses perception of mother. Somewhat later, when the child experiences maternal anger, the possibility of losing her love arouses anxiety. Freud also described mental anguish when objects are mourned; he distinguished pain when a valued object is actually lost from anxiety, which is the reaction to the danger entailed in the possible loss of a beloved or needed object. Thus, the central issue of object loss is acknowledged. This idea has become a basic premise of object relations theory. Balint, Guntrip, Fairbairn, Mahler, and Spitz developed major formulations on this point. Toward the end of his life, Freud (1940a) concluded that the child's attachment to the mother is the first and strongest object relationship. Indeed, this unique bond becomes the prototype for all later love relations and has an unalterable impact. While Freud himself did not investigate the details of this crucial relationship, both child and adult analysts have subsequently contributed to this important area.

Although the term "oedipus complex" first appears in Freud's formal writings in 1910, the concept evolved gradually and it had become accepted by 1908. This complex, in Freud's opinion, plays a basic role in the structuring of the personality and in determining the fundamental object choices. The oedipus complex involves the loving and hostile wishes that the child experiences toward his parents. Like the story of *Oedipus Rex,* the *positive* form of the complex involves a death wish toward the parent of the same sex who is experienced as a rival since the child has sexual desire for the parent of the opposite sex. The *negative* form involves love for the parent of the same sex, and jealousy and hatred for the other parent.

Freud (1925a) acknowledged that, with his early seduction theory, he "had in fact stumbled for the first time upon the Oedipus complex" (p. 34). The complex became clearer to Freud in the course of his self-analysis. Work with his patients also contributed to his recognition of his love for his mother as related to jealousy of his father for whom Freud also felt deep affection. In a letter to Fliess written in 1897, Freud (1950a) stated: "we can understand the riveting power of *Oedipus Rex*...the Greek legend seizes on a compulsion which everyone recognizes because he feels its existence within himself" (p. 265). Furthermore, Freud (1905a) asserted that the validity of Oedipus was universal: "Every new arrival on this planet is faced with the task of mastering the Oedipus complex" (p. 226). Later, the complexities of this triangle situation were elaborated: "a boy has not merely an ambivalent attitude towards his father and an affectionate object-choice towards his mother, but at the same time he also behaves like a girl and displays an affectionate feminine attitude to his father and a corresponding jealousy and hostility towards his mother" (Freud, 1923, p. 33). The son's ambivalence toward father involves the interplay of heterosexual and homosexual components rather than a simple rivalry. In 1923, Freud proposed as the high point of the Oedipus complex's dominance — for both sexes — the phallic stage of libidinal development, generally occurring between the ages of three and five. Although the early versions of the oedipal theory were based upon the development of the little boy, Freud (1931) recognized eventually that, for the female, unlike the case of the boy, the oedipal situation involves a change of love object from mother to father; furthermore, there is some question that the phallus is the only anatomical object of importance for the psychological development of women.

Freud attributed basic functions to the oedipus complex: the choice of love object, since the object cathexes, identifications, and incest prohibitions are the outcome of the complex; mature genital psychological functioning and phallic primacy result from the resolution of the oedipal crisis by identification; the structuring of the personality (such as superego and ego-ideal formation) are important consequences of the successful resolution of oedipal conflicts. These important intrapsychic changes occur in healthy development. "If the ego has in fact not achieved much more than a *repression* of the complex, the latter persists in an unconscious state in the id and will later manifest its pathogenic effect" (1924c, p. 177).

According to Freud's view, the "threat of castration," by the father, is the determining factor in bringing about the decline of the complex in the young boy. This results in renunciation of the incestuous wishes and the abrupt end of the complex. Freud (1925b) also concluded, "Whereas in boys the Oedipus complex is destroyed by the castration complex, in girls it is made possible and led up to by the castration complex" (p. 256; italics omitted). He elaborated, "Renunciation of the penis is not tolerated by the girl without some attempt at compensation. She slips — along the line of a symbolic equation, one might say — from the penis to a baby. Her Oedipus complex culminates in a desire, which is long retained, to receive a baby from her father as a gift — to bear him a child" (1924a, pp. 178–179).

Laplanche and Pontalis (1967) in their summary of the oedipal concept make the important point, namely, that the complex need not be considered reducible to an actual situation — to the actual influence exerted by the parental couple over a child. It brings into play a proscriptive agency (the prohibition against incest) which bars the way to naturally sought satisfaction and forms an indissoluble link between *wish* and *law*. One can analyze "which social roles or even which institutions incarnate the proscriptive agency and which social modes spontaneously express the triangular structure constituted by the child, the child's natural object and the bearer of the law" (p. 286). In concentrating on the triangular relationship itself, the unconscious desires of both parents, and the parental relations as well as the subject and his instincts are important.

Despite contemporary controversies regarding female sexuality, the universality or significance of the oedipus complex, penis envy, and castration anxiety, a review of the history of object relations theory would be incomplete without acknowledging these formulations and hypotheses of Freud which are concerned with biological and social forces, the role of parent-child interaction in fantasy and reality, intrapsychic and interpersonal factors. All of these are of interest to object relations theorists who are concerned about object choice, identifications, and the development of the sense of self and the object world. Although Freud stressed the role of the oedipal situation in healthy and pathological development, there are many analysts who believe that conflicts originating in the dyadic, pre-oedipal period can be treated effectively without focusing upon triadic or oedipal concerns. Thus, in the course of this survey of object relations theorists, a difference in emphasis will be discernible. Often it is the analyst whose patient population consists of the very young or the more severely disturbed who stresses the dyadic problems; whereas the analyst who treats primarily neurotic patients continues to emphasize the significant role of the oedipus complex and of triangular relationships.

In summary, Freud provided the foundations for a theory of object relations. He explored: the oedipus complex and object choice (1905a); the relations with objects as a basis for reality contact of pathological withdrawal and loss of the representational world (1911); types of object choices in relation to early development (1914); concepts of internalization in depression, mourning, and normal development (1915a, 1917b, 1923); and the impact and reactions to object loss in early life (1926). Finally, also important to object relations theory is Freud's concept of splitting of the ego (1940a, 1940b). He stated that splitting and fetishism are a means of dealing with psychic trauma; furthermore, he observed that splitting is universally present in psychoneuroses as well as in psychoses. Thus, Freud provided the roots for an object relations theory, although he did not offer an integrated formulation. Many issues remained ambiguous and unexplored.

Subsequent workers have spelled out the impact of the mother-child relationship on the development of the ego, the structure which mediates the person's relation to reality. Central to this "reality" are the important objects in the person's life. In addition, the implications of this crucial human bond for the analytic situation have been investigated.

Following this summary of Freud's major formulation dealing with object relations, I will present a brief survey of the relevant work of Ferenczi, Abraham, and Federn. They were among the important pioneers who elaborated and extended Freud's concepts, thereby providing the broad foundations upon which object relations theory was to develop.

Pioneering Contributions of Ferenczi, Abraham, and Federn to Freudian Object Relations Concepts

Ferenczi's work, in conjunction with Freud's, led to clarification of such basic concepts as *introjection* and *transference*. Ferenczi (1909) was the first analyst to define these terms. In addition, he actually explored the importance of the therapeutic dyad as a primary force in successful treatment. He stressed the crucial role of early maternal care in emotional development. He introduced the term *introjection* (1909), stating, "the paranoic expels from his ego the impulses that have become unpleasant, [while] the neurotic helps himself by taking into the ego as large as possible a part of the outer world, making it the object of unconscious phantasies. . . . One might give to this process, in contrast to projection, its name of *Introjection*" (p. 47). Although there were many ambiguities in this formulation, Freud adopted the term and utilized the idea more explicitly and in relation to incorporation and identification (1915b).

In close working relationship, Freud and Ferenczi elucidated the term and concept *transference*. Freud described such phenomena as early as 1895 when referring to Anna O.'s treatment with Breuer (see Breuer and Freud, 1893–1895). In the Dora case (1905b) Freud asked, "What are transferences? They are new editions or facsimiles of the impulses and phantasies which are aroused and made conscious during the progress of the analysis; but they have this peculiarity, which is characteristic for their species, that they replace some earlier person by the person of the physician" (p. 116). It was Ferenczi who then (1909) used the term *transference*. In 1909, he recognized that in analysis — as also in hypnosis — the patient unconsciously makes the doctor play the role of the loved or feared parental figures. Three years later, Freud (1912b) spelled this out in "The

Dynamics of Transference."

Despite the controversial nature of his experiment with technique dealing with difficult patients who had suffered early psychic trauma, "It was Ferenczi who first emphasized the great importance to healthy infant development of sufficient, loving body contact with the mother, as well as the dangers of too intense stimulation of the baby by adults" (Lorand, 1966, pp. 23–24). Ferenczi also suggested that a thorough analysis of the analyst was essential for successful treatment (Thompson, 1950). In another paper (1913), Ferenczi described the stages in the gradual evolution of a sense of reality of young children. He pointed out how significant persons prepare the child to cope with reality and how, in turn, the reality stage achieved determines the attitudes and expectations regarding objects (pp. 226–227).

As teacher of Michael Balint and the first analyst of Melanie Klein, Ferenczi generated a heritage which still influences an evolving object relations theory. He made major contributions to concepts of internalization and transference. He was concerned about the consequences of inadequate mothering in early life as manifested in: the development of a sense of reality, the patient's psychopathology, and the psychoanalytic treatment situation. His work involved studying: transference and countertransference factors, the role of regression in treatment, and the effects of abstinence or nurturance within the framework of the therapeutic alliance. All of these matters deal with object relations issues.

Karl Abraham's writings were further impetus to the development of object relations theory. Perhaps his most important contribution (1924) was an elaboration of developmental steps[5] in the evolution of object love which parallel libidinal phases. The emphasis was on instinct theory when he proposed that character develops in accordance with the following psychosexual stages: oral (subdivided into early passive-sucking and later active-biting or cannibalistic-sadistic); two anal-sadistic stages; and the genital (beginning with the phallic and finally the mature genital). According to Abraham, the fully developed personality has overcome pregenital ambivalence, thus permitting an enhanced capacity whole-

---

[5]Despite the psychosexual framework, there are implicit object relations concepts in Abraham's schema. Erikson's work (1950) related Abraham's stages to a series of object ties and social developmental phases (see below).

heartedly to express and discharge libidinal energy. Sublimatory capacities are enhanced, and there is less need for reaction formations. Autoerotism prevails during the earliest oral period and so, Abraham believed, no object love exists at that time. This is followed by a predominantly narcissistic period during which total incorporation of objects is the characteristic mode of relating. Abraham's anal phases involve partial or ambivalent love with incorporation. Finally, maturity is arrived at when postambivalent genital object love is possible.

Abraham's ideas about manic-depressive states (1911, 1924) developed in the course of an intimate working relationship with Freud. An understanding of mourning and melancholia (Jones, 1955, pp. 329–333) also evolved as a result of their exchanges. Each contributed to a mutually developed formulation.

Abraham (1911) believed that psychotic despair is always the result of the loss of a love object. Schizophrenia may emerge when trauma induces regression to reactivate an early infantile narcissistic fixation. Similarly, he related melancholia to a regression to very early oral stages. Intense ambivalence and hatred lead to guilt. Although all depression was considered to involve the loss of someone's love, just as mourning follows the death of a beloved, in melancholia the loss activates unconscious hate and murderous rage. Self-hatred is also involved. Abraham (1924) believed that the oral regression is to an ambivalent archaic state in which the patient tries to destroy introjected objects in reestablishing the object-free primary narcissistic state. He concluded that the patient's superego treats his ego as the patient unconsciously wishes to treat the lost object. This dynamic relates to Freud's (1917b) finding that the self-reproach of the depressed may be an attack against the introjected object. Abraham elaborated by proposing that accusations which had been made originally by a "real" object, now internalized, might be experienced as within the self and then turned against the self. Abraham also recognized the likelihood that primal depression of infants may be a precursor of later-life melancholia.

Thus, Ferenczi and Abraham, in conjunction with Freud, elaborated and clarified issues dealing primarily with internalization. Also these early co-workers of Freud's stressed the importance of early-life dyadic interaction with mother. They did not distinguish objects from their mental representations, nor were the stages in development of a sense of self in relation to objects elaborated. Much about internalization processes remained unclear. Nevertheless, they contributed formulations which strengthened a foundation upon which further work on a theory of object relations could be developed.

Paul Federn explored a new pathway also relevant to a future understanding of object relations. He made careful observations of psychotic patients (when they were undergoing states of unreality, depersonalization or detachment, excitement or depression). He devised the terms "ego feeling" (*Erlebnis*) and inner and outer "ego boundaries"[6] (relating to the awareness of an inner "mental" self when the inner boundary is cathected and the awareness of external objects when the outer boundaries are energized). Federn referred to body boundaries in a sense which fits in with Schilder's (1935) work on body image.

Federn (1952) focused upon his awareness of being by conscious introspection. He reported personally experiencing various ego states (such as awakening from sleep or falling asleep; functioning under the influence of medications and stages of anesthesia; and reacting during fatigue, depression or illness).

Federn described the psychodynamics and the phenomenology of alienation and depersonalization in pathology, which he contrasted with the ongoing vivid self-feelings in health.

Although Federn appreciated Freud's concepts and terminology, he applied them in a distinctly personal way. For example, his use of the term "narcissistic cathexes" refers to the energizing of ego boundaries. He did not mean by that a sexualized investment in the ego, but what might now be thought of as neutralized energy (Hartmann, 1950). Federn's original formulations provided a unique viewpoint. I find his ideas particularly helpful in understanding and treating the most severely disturbed patients' subjective states and their relationships with objects. His paper on "Healthy and Pathological Narcissism," written more than 50 years ago, although ignored to this day, contains perspectives of great contemporary relevance and application. Perhaps Federn's lack of a developmental framework plus his need to utilize Freud's terminology

[6]Jacobson (1964) believed that Federn's concept of mental boundaries could be best understood in terms of the establishment of differentiations between mental representations.

to cover very different and original ideas has led to confusion about Federn's concepts so often encountered in the reactions of colleagues and students. An integration of his theories with those of ego psychologists and object relations theorists might further understanding. Thus far, there has been limited attention devoted to Federn's work.

Building upon the pioneering efforts of Freud and his early co-workers, individual analysts selected and elaborated upon different aspects of Freud's work, thereby extending analytic theory and practice. The balance of this paper will survey representative contributions within the following framework.

Melanie Klein's role in the evolution of one major aspect of object relations theory and the origins of the British school are presented. Following this, developments in the British school, which focus upon treatment of the more disturbed patient, are illustrated by reference to the work of Fairbairn, Guntrip, and Balint. Then the contributions of ego psychology to object relations theory are considered. This section includes the theoretical concepts of Hartmann, Anna Freud, and others whose work is based upon reconstructive analytic treatment of neurotic patients, as well as on the studies based upon direct observation of children by analysts (e.g., Spitz, D. Burlingham, A. Freud, and others). Finally, the integrative contribution of those who have been influenced by the ongoing work in ego psychology but who also worked with children or regressed patients (Erikson, Winnicott, and Mahler) are described.

Melanie Klein's Role in the Evolution of Object Relations (and the Origins of the British School)

Prior to 1920, encouraged by her first analyst, Ferenczi, Melanie Klein began to work with children in Budapest. At the Psychoanalytic Congress in 1920, she met Freud and Abraham (Lindon, 1966). Abraham invited her to continue her work in Berlin. She did so and entered analysis with him. Undoubtedly, her analysis deeply influenced her theoretical focus and areas of concern. The concepts of Freud, Ferenczi, and Abraham had an impact upon her thinking. The work on internalization, projection, transference, as well as the references to the crucial role of early caretaker-infant relationship, impressed her.

She considered herself a Freudian analyst who applied classical treatment methods to very young children. Early in her work, she noted that the young child patient expresses fantasies and anxieties in play, and she offered active interpretations along the lines of Freud's analyses of dreams. When she reported her findings, the descriptions of archaic part object, horrifying, unrealistic, aggressive fantasies generated much resistance and skepticism. Ernest Jones was impressed with her work. He encouraged her to settle in England in 1926 where she primarily treated adults, developed her concepts further, and concentrated on teaching, supervising, and writing.

Melanie Klein was a very significant influence upon what was to become the British School of Object Relations. Over the years much controversy occurred concerning the validity and applications of her findings and theory. Schisms developed within the British Psycho-Analytical Society and a spectrum of viewpoints emerged— even among those who accepted an object relations framework. Many psychoanalysts, especially in England, South America, and France have been influenced by her formulations. Today her followers make up one branch of the British school of object relations.

Melanie Klein (1932) concluded that mood fluctuations and the earliest reality sense were caused by projective and introjective processes which she deemed to be active from birth. Similarly, fantasy formation is an ego function operating from the very beginning of life. Klein described (1937) the presence of an archaic sense of reality consisting of fantasies about primitively felt part objects. This reality sense is experienced as the result of the active need to protect the "good self" and the "good object" by externalizing the "bad" by projection. Deeply impressed by Freud's (1920) *Thanatos* formulations, Klein (1932) saw early life conflicts as intensified by clashes between life and death instincts. Furthermore, Klein (1937) suggested that the young child's subjectively triggered relationships with parents are distorted by archaic pregenital and genital part-object fantasies. These observations of the mental life of youngsters as reported in play reflect an earlier timetable than Freud's for the oedipus complex and superego development. Klein characterized early mental life as a world in which various figures—or parts of them—once external come to be introjected and are then felt to exist and function within the child's body. Perceptions are distorted by the press of libidinal and aggressive impulses. Reparation is important in renewing and preserving objects. Envy, jealousy, and gratitude (1957) contribute significantly to pathological and normal development. A major Kleinian construct involves developmental *positions*. This term refers to "a specific configuration of object relations, anxieties and defenses which persist throughout life" (Segal, 1964, p. ix). The Kleinians describe two positions: the *paranoid-schizoid* position "is the earliest phase of development. It is characterized by the relation to part objects, the prevalence of splitting in the ego and in the object and paranoid anxiety." The *depressive* position "is ushered in when the infant recognizes his mother as a whole object. It is a constellation of object relations and anxieties characterized by the infant's experience in attacking an ambivalently loved mother and losing her as an external and internal object. This experience gives rise to pain, guilt and feelings of loss" (Segal, 1964, pp. 105–106).

Klein acknowledged that her theoretical development was also influenced by Rado's (1928) early object splitting, Glover's (1932, 1943) ego nuclei, and Fairbairn's (1941) understanding of the schizoid state.

The infant, according to Klein, strives to protect the valued object from his own envious, sadistic wishes. Finally, though still within the first year of life, given adequate care, a sense of stable, reliable objects is established. However, when good-object abandonment is fantasied or experienced, there ensues a threat of profound loss, mourning, and the dread of a possible dissolution of the inner world. This is related to the depressive position.

Melanie Klein stressed that the infant reacts with anxiety to his own aggressive projections which are expressed as oral sadism in early life. As a result, percepts of primitive part objects are experienced as devouring, cannibalistic, and destructive (such as the "bad" breast). Thus, the infant is inundated by persecutory fears, dread of annihilation, and envy. Klein also proposed libidinally tinged percepts of pleasure-giving, gratifying "good" objects (such as the "good" breast). In reaction to these, feelings of gratitude and efforts at reparation ensue.

Klein did not agree with Freud's and Abraham's sequence of object stages related to psychosexual stages (that is, from autistic to narcissistic to object love); rather she proposed that object relations begin with the earliest experience with mother. Klein stressed splitting and projective identification in normal development and in pathology. Splitting "can involve the ego and the object. The earliest splitting is between the good and the bad self and the good and the bad object. The deflection of the death instinct involves a splitting of the part felt to contain the destructive impulses from the part felt to contain the libido" (Segal, 1964, p. 107).

Projective identification "is the result of the projection of parts of the self into an object. It may result in the object being perceived as having acquired the characteristics of the projected part of the self but it can also result in the self becoming identified with the object of its projection" (Segal, p. 105). Since this process involves a forceful projection by the subject, person A, *into* the recipient, person B; the subject may succeed in actually invoking responses from B as though A's projected inner object really functions as if emanating from the recipient! This has implications for interpersonal dynamics, group functioning, and countertransference reactions in the analyst. Hoedemaker (1967) offered impressive clinical examples. Rosenfeld (1966) utilized Kleinian concepts in the analytic treatment of psychotics and drug addicts. Bion's formulations about "the container," "bizarre objects," schizophrenic thought, "attacks on linking," as well as his seminal work on group dynamics (1967) all have a Kleinian base.

Many have criticized and questioned her theory as being ambiguous, unscientific, and arbitrary.[7] Nevertheless, an impressive number of her ideas pervade contemporary formulations, including the work of her critics. The major criticisms deal with the following: (1) the centrality she gave to Freud's most speculative idea — the death instinct — and her stress on the aggressive drive; (2) her timetable—"compressing" into the earliest period of life ego functioning as well as unconscious fantasies and object relations purported to exist from birth, superego and oedipal development during the first year, the innate knowledge of the genitals; (3) treatment which does not focus upon resistances, intrapsychic structures, diagnostic considerations, or psychodynamics.

Klein has frequently been "accused" of: ignoring external reality; neglecting environmental factors; compressing preoedipal and oedipal factors; failing to differentiate endopsychic objects from "real" external objects and object representations; neglecting sequential stages of ego and superego development; and failing to consider

---

[7]Among these are Glover (1945), Bibring (1947), Brierley (1951), Zetzel (1953, 1956), Rapaport (1959), Guntrip (1961), Jacobson (1964), Modell (1968), Kernberg (1969), and Yorke (1971).

neurophysiological and maturational processes and possibilities. Her interpretations have been questioned as overly active, symbolic, and intrusive. Despite these criticisms, Melanie Klein was the first to apply analysis to children. She was the first to elaborate a specific theory of early object relations and to spell out the role of aggression in early development. Her concepts of splitting, projective identification, paranoid-schizoid and depressive positions are helpful to many clinicians. She offered insights into early defensive operations and pioneered in providing psychoanalytic help for regressed patients.

Klein originally presented her ideas before the introduction of more precise structural concepts like "mental representation" (Hartmann, 1950), the "representational world" (Sandler and Rosenblatt, 1962), and ego psychological elaborations, such as the distinction between the various mechanisms of internalization (Jacobson, 1964; Schafer, 1968). In recent years, Kleinians have offered more systematic and integrative formulations (e.g., Segal, 1964; Rosenfeld, 1966; Bion, 1967; Meltzer, 1967). Her concepts appealed primarily to those who worked with more severely disturbed patients.

Mahler and Furer (1968) credit Klein with having first described the rapidly alternating primitive identificatory mechanisms of early life. Friedman (1975) also acknowledged that "Historically Melanie Klein was an important figure in directing psychoanalytic attention to early object relations. . . it has taken time for some of her views to be integrated with the views of the ego psychological school" (p. 138). Winnicott (1962b) and Zetzel (1956) reviewed her contributions and expressed deep respect for her understanding of unconscious processes and aspects of object relations despite their reservations about certain of her theoretical formulations.

Guntrip (1969) considered Klein's work to be decisive in changing "the mode of psychoanalytic thinking. . . wherein object relations replace instincts as the focal point" (p. 406).

Before Klein, the human psyche was regarded as an apparatus for experiencing and controlling biological instincts originating outside the ego. . . . After Klein, it became possible to see the human psyche as an internal world of a fully personal nature, a world of internalized ego-object relationships, which partly realistically and partly in highly distorted ways reproduced the ego's relationships to personal objects in the real outer world. . . in Klein's work. . . object relations first begin to replace instincts as the focal point of theory. This is making possible a subtle but enormously important change of 'atmosphere' in psychoanalytic thinking; from a *mechanistic* to the *personal*, from the study of mental phenomena, the clash of psychic forces, to the study of the human being's struggle for self-realization as a person in personal relationships [pp. 407–408].

Neither Fairbairn, Guntrip, nor Winnicott accepted Klein's metapsychology — especially her commitment to the death instinct. Nevertheless, each acknowledged the important influence of her ideas upon their understanding.

Developments in the British School of Object Relations

Fairbairn, the Scottish psychoanalyst, who worked in Edinburgh in relative isolation from colleagues, was a Freudian analyst who had successfully treated a number of schizophrenic and regressed patients in the 1930s and 1940s (Guntrip, 1975, p. 146). Jones (1952) summarized Fairbairn's new ideas: "Instead of starting, as Freud did, from stimulation of the nervous system proceeding from excitation of various erotogenic zones and internal tensions arising from gonadic activity, Dr. Fairbairn starts at the centre of the personality, the ego, and depicts its strivings and difficulties in its endeavour to reach an object where it may find support" (p. v). Though conservative, especially in practice, Fairbairn gradually evolved his unique theory of object relations. Despite disagreement with some of Melanie Klein's ideas, he credited her with providing a perspective and new insights which directly led to his new formulations. His impact upon analytic theory, until quite recently, has been primarily through his writings and those of his student, Harry Guntrip (1961, 1969, 1975).

Fairbairn attempted to develop an overall model for psychoanalytic object relations theory. Rinsley's (1979) excellent summary and critique provide a synopsis of Fairbairn's theory of endopsychic structures and need not be repeated here. However, in the context of a historical survey, certain aspects of Fairbairn's ideas and their evolution must be singled out.

Fairbairn began his career as a classical analyst in the 1920s. By 1931 he expressed an interest in ego analysis. He presented to the British Psycho-Analytical Society a case study of a patient which included dreams. He was impressed how the cast of characters in the dreams so clearly personified various aspects of the patient's ego or total self (Fairbairn used these terms interchangeably). For example, the patient's descriptions of figures in his dreams clearly represented aspects of himself (i.e., "the critic" was his superego manifestation; the "mischievous boy" was id phenomena; "the little girl," an aspect of the dreamer's self-feelings). Fairbairn concluded that, though the case data showed the existence of structural units within the patient which corresponded to ego, id, and superego, "the same data seem equally to indicate the impossibility of regarding these functioning structural units as *mental entities*. . . . Perhaps the arrangement of mental phenomena into functioning structural units is the most that can be attempted by psychological science" (1952, p. 216). Thus, as early as the 1930s, Fairbairn searched for a nonmechanistic psychology of self. He did not offer a revised theory, however, until he learned about Klein's analysis of internalized objects and her concept of object splitting. He was also impressed by Freud's (1940a) view that ego splitting occurs universally in the psychoneuroses and psychoses. In 1954, Fairbairn concluded, "Psychology may be said to resolve itself into a study of the relationship of the individual to his objects, whilst, in similar terms, psychopathology may be said to resolve itself more specifically into a study of the relationships of the ego to its internalized objects" (p. 60).

Earlier in this paper I have reviewed Freud's concepts concerning the infant's narcissistic condition and the gradual development of an attachment to objects via instinctual and aggressive cathexes and affective reactions. In Freud's metapsychology, the id forces cannot be adequately managed by the ego and the internalized parental restraints help the ego master id impulses. To Fairbairn, "the schizoid patient is not primarily concerned with the control of impulses in object relationships. . . but with whether he has an ego capable of forming object relations at all. He finds object relations so difficult, not merely because he has dangerous impulses, but because he has a weak, undeveloped, infantile, and dependent ego" (Guntrip, 1966, p. 233).

At first, Fairbairn proposed that the schizoid's withdrawal from objects resulted from fear that unsatisfied needs, not met by the object, would arouse so much greed and devouring fantasies that such love would become even more dangerous than the hate of the object.

Later, after Fairbairn discarded impulse psychology, he concluded, in agreement with Guntrip, that ego weakness, the inability to cope with the outer world, overwhelms the infantile ego. "The schizoid is split in his growing emotional life by the inconsistency of his primary parental objects and becomes prey to loss of internal unity, radical weakness, and helplessness." While still partly struggling to relate in the outer world, he also partially withdraws. This leads to detachment and a search for refuge in a fantasy world. "This is not a problem of impulse control but of ego splitting" (Guntrip, p. 233). Fairbairn developed his theory of endopsychic structure using Freud's superego formation as a model; however, Fairbairn focused upon early schizoid concerns rather than on melancholia and depression, and he stressed the personal, experiential object relations aspects which develop in the context of a parent-child relationship. He dealt with a psychodynamic ego, using its instinctive endowments and conducting personal object relationships. The emphasis shifts from impulse theory to ego developmental failure and the schizoid problem.

Normally, in early life, according to Fairbairn, the infant unconsciously splits and internalizes subjectively experienced components of important external figures. The first objects so treated are the frustrating aspects of needed persons (i.e., the "bad" mother) with the aim of gaining control over them. This results in an unconscious inner presence of a "needed-exciting" object and a "frustrating-rejecting" object. The libidinal ego becomes attached to the "needed-exciting" internal object. Both this aspect of the ego and the inner object are repressed by the "I" (or "central ego") for fear of rejection if needs are acknowledged and expressed. Similarly, the split-off "anti-libidinal ego" attached to the inner "frustrating-rejecting" object attacks the "needed-exciting" object and "libidinal ego." (Fairbairn called this unconscious intrapsychic process the "internal saboteur.")

As dependency decreases, the ego need not continue to resort to splitting. The individual develops from the early stages of dependence through transitional and finally to a mature dependency stage. Complete independence is never achieved, in Fairbairn's view. Health is defined in psychosocial terms, dealing with the wholeness of self in loving interaction with objects. Fairbairn did not consider genital attraction the only path toward mature object relations.

When splitting is no longer necessary and internalized objects have been successfully externalized, the ego becomes outer-directed and there is a natural interest in ongoing relations with others.

Guntrip (1976) contended that Fairbairn's early belief in a "whole pristine unitary ego" in the beginning of life blocked him from understanding that "bad" relations with the mother who failed to relate could account for failures in ego development. Guntrip concluded that "the schizoid core develops in an infant who is left without adequate object relations, left alone in a psychic vacuum in which he can only develop an 'out of touchness' which erupts in later life as an inability to relate because he was not related to in the beginning. . . . At its worst, the child is totally enclosed within himself—an autistic, infantile schizophrenic" (p. 375). Such individuals have the greatest difficulty relating to others. Guntrip and Fairbairn eventually concluded that the schizoid's "ego weakness" relates to a sense of profound helplessness, a feeling of diffuseness, confusion, and fragility; and a lack of confidence in the ability to cope with others.

Shortly before his death, Fairbairn (1963) contended that libido is a function of the ego and the ego is fundamentally object seeking. Modell (1968) commented, "Fairbairn's theory was not intended to supplement Freud's theory but to supplant it. As an alternative to Freudian theory, Fairbairn's theory has won very few supporters, although many psychoanalysts, and I inlcude myself in this group, have profited greatly from his understanding of the schizoid patient" (pp. 4–5).

In summary, to Fairbairn, the ego is central and active from early life. Its relationship with objects is primary. Libido is not considered to be pleasure-seeking (in the sense of energy using erotogenic zones to release inner tension); rather, libido is looked upon as object-seeking. Fairbairn thought of developmental processes in terms of the vicissitudes of objects, not the vicissitudes of instincts. This viewpoint polarized the British object relations school. At one end, there is the Kleinian branch, influenced by Freud's instinct theory and stressing primitive fantasy. At the other end, stand Fairbairn's followers, minimizing instinctual forces and pleasure-seeking and stressing the centrality of an "I" or ego as the core phenomenon of the psyche. His theory is not based upon instinct or an organization of functions. Rather, the emphasis is on an original state of infantile dependence and the struggles of a vulnerable ego, oriented toward external reality, and motivated to seek out and develop secure relationships. A "middle group" within the British object relations school also emerged. The theories of Winnicott, major spokesman of their viewpoint, will be surveyed in the section on integrative conceptions.

Michael Balint was another contributor to this "middle group." The basis for Balint's work goes back to shortly after World War I. Ferenczi observed in some of his patients a reactivation during treatment of vivid infantile traumas which had probably originally involved significant child-rearing persons. The patients expressed these memories and feelings in the transference, craving comfort, understanding, and reparation. Ferenczi wondered if the usual analytic neutrality might not further traumatize those who had experienced indifferent or neglectful parents. In those instances where classical technique did not yield therapeutic results, he experimented with a more indulgent stance, which he called "relaxation technique" (Ferenczi, 1932). Freud, who had supported Ferenczi's investigations, became distressed about arousing incessant cravings, frustrations, and regressions (Peto, 1967). This clash between Ferenczi and Freud seems to have constricted further study of the problems relating to regression in analysis until the work of both Balint and Winnicott. After Ferenczi's death, Balint pursued this subject in relative isolation. He remained in contact with several of Ferenczi's former patients. Balint (1968) noted his teacher's final realization of the hazards and failings in this approach; however, Balint also reported that there were significant theoretical gains: the special "object relationship" between patient and analyst could be examined under the condition of neutrality, as contrasted with other attitudes; the issues of countertransference and the importance of the analyst's feelings and communications opened a new area for consideration (Ferenczi, 1932). When Balint moved to England, he continued his study of the effects of regression in treatment, carefully exploring both the dangers and the potential value. He conceived of regression as benign and potentially beneficial when the analyst provides an accepting atmosphere in which the patient feels safe enough to regress "for the sake of recognition," shared experiencing, and understanding. When the patient strives to satisfy libidinal aims in the treatment situation, there is danger of a "malignant regression." Balint

(1968) felt that his notion of malignant regression was quite similar to the "regression that overwhelms the ego" concept of Kris (1952).

Balint (1968) concluded that psychological development, impeded by inappropriate stimulation or lack of understanding on the part of the caretaker when the infant is in an undeveloped and dependent state, results in an internal sense of "basic fault." These patients come to a point in treatment where they experience "something distorted or lacking in the mind, producing a defect that must be put right." Unless there had been a "harmonious, interpenetrating mix-up" between significant other and self (but all of this before there was a verbal or conceptual understanding or a sense of differentiation); unless the parent "fit" the need (as the amniotic fluid and the fetus, the sea and the fish, the air and the lungs); unless there had been a spontaneous, need-gratifying, nonconscious flowing between — unless these conditions were met, there would result a "basic fault" and its consequent pathology. Words and explanations are useless since they are meaningless in such a preverbal framework. Meaningful therapeutic engagement can occur only when the patient finds the situation safe enough to allow the overwhelming, disquieting reactivation of the faulty psychophysiological matrix before boundaries and words. But if the patient originally could not rely upon the crucial "support systems" of early life, there would be dread and avoidance[8] of reexperiencing such frustrated dependency needs which have remained deeply unfulfilled and hidden ever since that archaic, most vulnerable period. Thus, the task of the analyst treating a patient with such a history must be to create a trusting therapeutic alliance which encourages the dissolution of resistances to the period of the "basic fault." At this point, acceptance, acknowledgment, and recognition are essential. This view contrasts with the Kleinian concept of active verbal interpretations of the material involving the greatest anxieties (although Bion's [1967] concept of the "container" may be related to nonverbal acceptance).

Describing his theory of object relationships, Balint (1968) maintains that the "individual is born in a state of intense relatedness to his environment, both biologically and libidinally" (p. 67). Prenatal conditions are usually "harmoniously mixed-up" in that self

---

[8]Sechehaye's (1951) "pretransference resistance" and Khan's (1974) "dread of surrender to resourceless dependence" as well as Winnicott's ideas are all related to Balint's concepts.

and object interpenetrate each other. There are as yet no objects, no delineation of boundaries. Birth is traumatic. Objects (including the ego) emerge from the mix-up after birth and then there are firm contours and sharp boundaries. Out of the primary love of the original, harmonious, limitless expanse and fusion with substances, the modes of relating to the emerging sense of self and objects emerge. Libido may be withdrawn to the ego in a narcissistic manner, or it may be transferred primarily to the emerging objects. Another form of cathexis "results in the development of the ocnophilic and the philobatic structures of the world" (1968, p. 68).

In the ocnophilic mode, the primary cathexis adheres to emerging objects which are experienced as safe and comforting while spaces between objects are felt to be threatening and horrid. In contrast, "in the philobatic world, the objectless expanses retain the original primary cathexis and are experienced as safe and friendly, while the objects are felt as treacherous hazards" (1968, p. 68). Both of these reactions, Balint believed, are instances of the basic fault. The ocnophil clings to objects and introjects them in an effort to overcome insecurity. The philobat overcathects his own ego functions in order to develop skills and maintain himself alone, requiring little help from objects.

Thus Balint developed an object relations concept of normal and pathological development and an approach to treatment. He did not develop a metapsychological theory, nor did he provide a new concept of the mental apparatus. He implied the dyadic nature of early personality development and the crucial role of recapitulating aspects of that dyadic interaction in analysis, stressing the object relations aspects of the process. Some of his notions of the developing styles of relating fit in with Mahler's observations which will be described later. Balint's distinctions between benign and malignant regression and his focus upon treatment of such conditions are of great value and are similar to the ideas and concerns of Winnicott.

Object Relations Theory from the Viewpoint
of Ego Psychology and Developmental Studies

I have reviewed Freud's formulations concerning the "ego" in the context of object relations. Freud (1917b) described the ego as the repository of abandoned objects, and in 1921 also referred to early-life identifications involving an emotional tie to another person. Throughout Freud's writings, there are seminal thoughts about object relations and ego psychology, ideas which inspired Heinz Hartmann, Spitz, Jacobson, Mahler, and others.

Over the years, Freud offered many important yet unelaborated ideas about the ego. Hartmann studied, organized, and expanded these earlier ego formulations. He has had an important influence upon the development of contemporary ego psychology, especially in the United States. When Hartmann began his work, psychoanalytic treatment was based primarily on Freud's psychosexual theory. Many practitioners found this system limited in accounting for clinical data and in providing effective treatment. The psychology of the self and important interactions with others were not adequately explained by drive theory alone. Hartmann's (1939, 1964) contributions clarified normal ego development and offered a fuller comprehension of the nature of developmental failure and its pathological consequences. This understanding helped psychoanalysts develop more effective therapeutic measures regarding psychoanalytic treatment, especially of the more severely disturbed patient.

I will focus upon those aspects of his contributions primarily applicable to object relations theory. Hartmann's role has been important in encouraging developmental observation—a crucial emphasis in the scientific evolution of psychoanalytic thinking. He (1950) introduced the term "self" to refer to the whole person (both body and psychic organization). The psychic self contains, among other components, the ego and the psychic representations (of oneself and of objects). Hartmann also introduced the term "self representation" as contrasted with "object representation." Furthermore, he (1956) distinguished between two inherent meanings of the term *das Ich* in Freud's writings: (1) the ego as subject; the experience of being and feeling "the self"; and (2) the psychic structure of the system "ego," the agency which mediates inner and outer reality.

Hartmann (1939) viewed the ego as an organ of "adaptation," that is, there are inborn apparatuses (such as perception, thinking, motility, and language) which emerge from an "undifferentiated matrix."[9] This repertoire of adaptational resources usually develops

[9]A concept utilized and further developed by Jacobson (1964) and Schur (1966).

in a "conflict-free sphere," except under serious traumatic circumstances. In an "average expectable environment" the individual
gradually acquires the capacity to act upon himself and to elicit
helpful environmental responses. Hartmann (1952) described the
earliest stages of ego development from several angles: "as a process
of differentiation that leads to a more complete demarcation of ego
and id and of self and outer reality; as a process that leads from the
pleasure to the reality ego; as the development of the reality principle; as the way leading from primary narcissism to object relationships; from the point of view of the sequence of danger situations; as the development of the secondary process, etc." (pp.
165–166).

Hartmann emphasized the crucial role of the mother in providing the neonate with psychological as well as physical nurturance,
thereby facilitating maximal adaptational potential. His concept of
"neutralization" is applicable here: as the growing capacity to neu-
tralize drive energy, along with the increasing ability to delay drive
discharge,

> . . . places energy for ego building (structuralization) and expanding ego
> functions at the disposal of the infant. The hungry infant of three months
> has already achieved some capacity to neutralize drive energy. Thus, he
> uses the sensation of hunger in conjunction with memory traces of past
> gratification to summon his mother by his cry, which, by then, has
> changed from the objectless cry of the neonate to a purposeful one. Ob-
> ject relations are built by transferring energy—which was formerly in-
> vested only in the drives—to the ego, for negotiation with the environ-
> ment [Blanck and Blanck, 1974, p. 34].

In contrast to earlier writers, who had stressed only the sublimation of libido, Hartmann included the neutralization of aggression, emphasizing its role in countercathexis, defense, and resistance. In all of this, he stressed the stabilizing power of good object relations which enable the ego effectively to mediate between the
drives and reality.

According to Hartmann, object relations also advance developmentally from an initial stage of primary narcissism (in which there
are no objects), followed by an anaclitic stage (in which the object is
experienced solely as need fulfilling), to a stage of object constancy
(where an ongoing cathexis of the mental representation of the object
persists regardless of need or the object's presence). When object

images are constant, the self representation also is continuous.

Hartmann's emphasis on the caretaker's role in interaction with the growing infant has encouraged more detailed and specific study of the developmental dyad. This emphasis has stimulated further concern with object relations.

Rapaport (1959), in surveying the history of ego psychology, concluded that "the theory of object relations remained outside the scope of psychoanalytic ego psychology and the psychosocial implications of reality and object relations" (p. 12) until Hartmann and Erikson, who developed the concept of epigenesis.[10]

Gedo and Goldberg (1973) offered an example of the epigenetic concept. "We can define orality as an instinctual drive that undergoes changes from its original primitive state to more mature neutralized forms, from archaic aims and object to those more appropriate in later life; and from a stage of unintegrated discharge to one of increasingly complex synthesis within the totality of the personality." They added that such considerations "apply to any developmental sequence of functions we may choose to examine: object relations, the situation of danger, the regulation of behavior" (pp. 17–18).

Ferenczi had first used the related term "lines of development" when referring to ontogenetic development of successive stages of mental functioning. Anna Freud (1965) has used this concept as an *integrative* approach to the development of psychic functions that had previously been described in isolation.

Anna Freud's (1936) early work focused upon the ego's defense mechanisms. She systematized her father's formulations (1926) about conflict, anxiety, and adaptation. Based on her observations of young children in analysis, she considered defenses as a means of maintaining functioning rather than succumbing to conflict. In some cases, defenses permit the ego to bind anxiety and avoid displeasure. This can help the ego avoid anxiety and channel instincts so as to provide some gratification, "thereby establishing the most harmonious relations possible between the id, the superego, and the forces of the outside world" (p. 176).

Child analysis and studies based on the direct observation of

[10]Epigenesis (a term borrowed from embryology) was implicit in many of Freud's writings (1905a). It refers to the "interaction of the organism with the environment in a sequence of specific phases" (Gedo and Goldberg, 1973, p. 8).

children by analysts have contributed to the development of ego psychology. These data, in addition to hypotheses devised primarily from reconstructive analytic work with neurotic patients, plus the related theoretical formulations of Hartmann (1939, 1964), Kris (1952, 1975), A. Freud, Spitz, and others shifted the emphasis in psychoanalytic thinking away from the id to how the ego utilizes instinctual processes and how the ego itself is shaped by the child's early experiences with objects.[11]

Anna Freud and Dorothy Burlingham (1939–45) studied children's reactions to bombing in London during World War II. They observed that if mothers or acceptable surrogate figures remained available and calm, young children were not traumatized. Anxiety occurred under two conditions: concern over loss of the anaclitic object triggered separation anxiety or a physically present but *anxious* mother imparted dread to the child. Modell (1968) proposed a parallel in the borderline and schizophrenic transference to the analyst. "The patient believes that his safety in the world depends upon the sustained relationship to the analyst. An illusion is created" (p. 34).

Many proponents of object relations theory contend that the therapist-patient dyad parallels the earliest, most important developmental dyad, that of caretaker (usually mother) and infant. Related to this issue is the question of whether or not there is a possibility of working in treatment with preverbal experience. While Anna Freud acknowledged the importance of the preverbal period, she noted the controversy and practical and theoretical problems related to analyzing such early psychic material in treatment:

> Instead of exploring the disharmonies between the various agencies within a structured personality, the analyst is concerned with the events which lead from the chaotic, undifferentiated state toward the initial building up of a psychic structure. This means going beyond the area of intrapsychic conflict, which had always been the legitimate target for psychoanalysis, and into the darker area of interaction between innate endowment and environmental influence. The implied aim is to undo or to counteract the impact of the very forces on which the rudiments of personality development are based.
>
> Analysts who work for this aim assure us that this can be achieved [1969, pp. 38–39].

[11]The converse also seems to apply, namely, the quality of ego functioning strongly influences the capacity for object relating.

She expressed her doubt about dealing with the area of primary repression. She also discussed another controversy of relevance to object relations theory and treatment:

There is, further, the question whether the transference really has the power to transport the patient back as far as the beginning of life. Many are convinced that this is the case. Others, myself among them, raise the point that it is one thing for preformed, object-related fantasies to return from repression and be redirected from the inner to the outer world (i.e., to the person of the analyst); but that it is an entirely different, almost magical expectation to have the patient in analysis change back into the prepsychological, undifferentiated, and unstructured state, in which no divisions exist between body and mind or self and object [pp. 40–41].

Thus, Anna Freud clearly expressed her doubts regarding Melanie Klein's treatment philosophy, which involves the analysis of the earliest part-object fantasies composed of archaic projections and introjections going back to the beginning of life. Does this imply that Anna Freud questions Balint's and Winnicott's efforts to "work through" in treatment, via the "holding environment" offered by the "good-enough" analyst, reactivations of the preverbal "basic fault" and to facilitate the emergence of a "truer self"?

René Spitz did not rely solely upon the patient's verbal or pre-verbal communications to study epigenetic issues — including those involving relationships. He reported his observations of infant development. In addition to examining normal infants in relation to their caretakers, he observed the effects of change provided by circumstances somewhat like an experimental design where variables are systematically modified so as to test hypotheses. Spitz studied hospitalized infants. He also followed neonates, born to incarcerated women, when their babies were separated from their mothers some months after birth in accord with prison regulations. He expressed his determination to study the reciprocal dyad of mother-infant by means of direct observation. He said, "we shall present our findings and ideas on object relations — their beginnings, development, stages, and certain anomalies" (Spitz, 1965, p. 3). As a result of his investigations, he described hospitalism and anaclitic depression (1945, 1946, 1950). He concluded that a lack of contact with mother has profound consequences for the development of ego functions as well as for object relations. Since infants of six months of age show signs of anaclitic depression when separated from their mothers, he concluded that there is, by that age, the mental awareness of an object upon whom the baby is dependent.

Although he believed that there is a synthetic tendency from the beginning of life, it is not until the third month that the "smiling response" to a human face appears. This is the first sign of the establishment of a libidinal object. Spitz (1965) proposed that "organizers of the psyche" are factors which relate to internal shifts introducing new levels of developmental integration and these may be noted by an outside observer via "indicators."

Spitz proposed that the "smiling response" is the first indicator reflecting sufficient psychic organization, the probable presence of memory traces, and some discriminatory perception of the external object. By about eight months of age, there is an indication of "stranger anxiety." This represented to Spitz the baby's contemplated loss of the object in a context of beginning verbalization. Head-shaking along with "no" is an indicator of the third organizer, which reflects the child's identification with the aggressor, the mother who prohibits and frustrates. At this level (fifteen to eighteen months or so) there are semantic distinctions and communication. Interchange between objects occur and internalization takes place.

Spitz's conception of the very beginnings of perception relate to the "oral cavity." The earliest coenesthetic sensing of the neonate and the earliest interaction between newborn and mother are carefully explored by Spitz, who describes how signals are filtered through the infant's innate stimulus barrier. At the same time, the mother provides a protective screen which serves as an external auxiliary ego (p. 43). Spitz (1965) described this first dyadic interaction between the affect-laden, self-centered baby and the baby-directed mother. The infant nurses and sucks the nipple while seeing the mother's face. This nursing experience does more than gratify. "It initiates the transition from exclusive contact perception to distance perception. It activates the diacritic perceptual system, which gradually replaces the original and primitive coenesthetic organization" (p. 75).

In such terms, Spitz described the beginnings of a crucial shift in perception from an autistic contact, need-gratifying sensing to an object-related discriminatory awareness. In the context of an object relationship, the foundations of psychic reality develop. Utilizing a biological (or to be more specific, embryological) epigenetic model, Spitz provided detail observation-based data and formulations to clarify important aspects of the development of the psyche in the context of mother-child interaction. Great respect is paid to the importance of object relations — and the precursors of object relations — in making survival, reality contact, and adaptive ego functioning possible.

The Integrative Concepts of Erikson, Winnicott, and Mahler

In Erikson's view, developmental stages become channels of socialization rather than merely constricting biological pathways. Of course, these are mediated via human relationships. Erikson has attempted to build an epigenetic bridge involving the intrapsychic and the social world. He related his sequence of phases of psychosocial development to libidinal stages, but his schema goes beyond Freud's and Abraham's psychosexual stages from birth to maturity and encompasses the "whole life cycle" (Erikson, 1950).

> We cannot even begin to encompass a human being without indicating for each of the stages of his life cycle the framework of social influences and of traditional institutions which determine his perspectives on his most infantile past and on his most adult future [Erikson, 1958, p. 20].

In each phase, from birth to death, there are unique developmental tasks (1946) to be solved. The possible solutions at any phase emerge from the influences of and interactions with the prior phases. In this manner experiences and solutions of past phases contribute to solutions in subsequent phases. Erikson (1956) formulated solutions (polarized as successful versus unsuccessful) for each phase's specific tasks so as to express the degree of mastery attained. The dichotomy of solutions for each psychosocial crisis are: basic trust vs. mistrust; autonomy vs. shame and doubt; initiative vs. guilt; industry vs. inferiority; identity vs. identity diffusion; intimacy vs. isolation; generativity vs. stagnation; integrity vs. despair.

Erikson (1950) assumed a "mutuality," coordination, or "cogwheeling of the life cycles" between the caretaker who also has phase-specific needs (and who serves as a representative of society) and the needy developing individual. Thus caretakers are societal "carriers." There are social institutions and traditions which support the viability of the developing personality's struggle with phase-specific conflicts. Erikson concluded that typical solutions vary from society to society, while epigenetic phase sequences are assumed to be universal. Thus, Erikson added a social and interpersonal dimension to the psychosexual stages. In 1959, he concluded:

> The limited usefulness of the *mechanism of identification* becomes at once obvious if we consider the fact that none of the identifications of childhood...could, if merely added up, result in a functioning personality ....*Identity formation*, finally, begins where the usefulness of identification ends. It arises from the selective repudiation and mutual assimilation of childhood identifications, and their absorption of a new configuration, which, in turn, is dependent on the process by which a *society...identifies the young individual* [pp. 112–113].

Among the many paradoxes about Donald Winnicott is the following: from the beginning, his psychoanalytic contributions in England were "politely disregarded" (Khan, 1975). He presented his paper "The Use of an Object and Relating Through Identification" in New York in 1968 and met with much criticism (Guntrip, 1976). Today, both in the United States and abroad, he appears to be the most appreciated spokesman of the "middle group" of the British school of object relations.

His personal recollections and the report of his widow (Claire Winnicott, 1978) suggest that he had an unusually secure and "most facilitating" family background and early life. Yet, his work focused upon patients whose problems involved profound isolation, constriction, depression, withdrawal, and hate. He met such challenge with an unusual capacity for empathy, creative and playful responsiveness, and impressive clinical skill.

Following his medical training, he specialized in pediatrics and for more than twenty years, as head of a London hospital clinic, he examined and observed the emotional and physical state of thousands of infants and youngsters in interaction with their mothers. In the course of these experiences, he asked himself what preceded this first object relationship. He wrote (1952):

> I found myself saying...(about ten years ago [1942])...'There is no such thing as a baby'...if you show me a baby you certainly show me also someone caring for the baby, or at least a pram with someone's eyes and ears glued to it. One sees a 'nursing couple'...today I would say that before object relationships the state of affairs is this: that the unit is not the individual, the unit is an environment-individual set-up....By good-

enough child care, technique, holding, and general management the shell becomes gradually taken over and the kernel...can begin to be an individual....The human being now developing an entity from the centre can become localized in the baby's body and so can begin to create an external world at the same time as acquiring a limiting membrane and an inside. According to this theory there was no external world at the beginning although *we as observers* could see an infant in an environment...we think we see an infant when we learn through analysis at a later date that what we ought to have seen was an environment developing falsely into a human being, hiding within itself a potential individual [pp. 99–100].

Winnicott's papers reflect his developmental focus, observational approach, and object relations orientation as well as some Kleinian influence. He was analyzed by Strachey and Riviere and supervised by Melanie Klein. Winnicott acknowledged the importance of Freud's psychology, Fairbairn's ideas, and the formulations of ego psychology. Nevertheless, his work is quite original. Khan (1975) said, "For him facts were the reality, theories were the human stammer towards grasping the facts. He had a militant incapacity to accept dogma. Winnicott was a non-conformist by upbringing; nothing was given and absolute. Each man had to find and define his own truth. What was given was the experiential spectrum. And it was towards making sense of his long encounters with the clinical realities that he devoted all his energies" (1975, p. xi). He began his psychoanalytic work at a time of great stimulation and conceptual debate within the British Psycho-Analytical Society. Freud had recently developed the structural hypothesis (1923) and the theory of anxiety (1926). Anna Freud and Melanie Klein had begun their work with children, and Klein had recently arrived in London and was having a dramatic impact on analytic thinking. Fairbairn was offering new formulations. Ferenczi's experiments provided alternative approaches to treatment.

Balint's "basic fault" is an idea very much related to Winnicott's (1965) description of the disruption of the infant's beginning ego development when maternal relating fails. The concepts of "good enough mothering," "the holding environment," the importance of "transitional objects" (1951), the function of play (1971), the use of objects (1969), and the "true self and the false self" (1960) all are formulations developed by the former English pediatrician turned psychoanalyst.

To Winnicott, the interrelation between infant and caring mother makes up a unit which becomes the first and most important object relationship. In this regard the theories of Winnicott and Mahler overlap. The "maturational processes" and the inherited potential depend upon the "facilitating environment" (1965) which involves the "good enough mother." Even before the infant's birth, "primary maternal preoccupation" (1956) anticipates the coming new unit in which the complete dependency of the neonate and the maternal provisions will be crucial. An ever-changing, need-gratifying balance between "space" and "holding" provides the matrix[12] which will permit transitions, the possibilities for development of a true self in the context of a developing ego. In addition to the provision of love and nurturance, the arousal of aggression and anger in response to frustration will encourage ambivalence and destructive fantasies. The survival of the important external object when it is hated is most reassuring to the child (1969). Although this survival challenges the infantile sense of omnipotence, the object's ongoing presence reassures the child that anger need not be deadly; that outside objects are *real* and indeed external and remain alive and reliable enough even when attacked. Playing (1971) provides further opportunity for creatively and symbolically exploring the self and the world. The capacities for concern (1963) and to be alone (1958) have a chance to develop. Winnicott's ideas concerning both early development and the treatment experience are the reflections of a creative, intuitive clinician.

Although he did not conceptualize along metapsychological lines and did not reconstruct theory, important object relations concepts were elaborated and an invigorating thrust to psychoanalytic technique was stimulated by Winnicott's cryptic, paradoxical style, poignant observations, and inspiring creativity,

One aspect of Winnicott's appreciation of creative playfulness involves a spontaneous, inner-generated, fun-loving serendipity. This is exploratory self-expression within ample psychological space in which potential flows. Another aspect involves the serious struggle to find a means for the patient and analyst to reach the underlying anguish, despair, emptiness, and anxiety relating to early-life deficiency or trauma. His use of the squiggle drawing technique, his

---

[12]See below for the related ideas of Mahler on separation-individuation.

spatula "game" in interviewing baby and mother, his exploration of the holding environment and transitional objects all relate to the creative adventure of discovering the true self in childhood and in creative treatment. In a paper "Playing: The Search for the Self" (1971) he wrote:

I shall need the sequence:
(a) relaxation in conditions of trust based on experience;
(b) creative, physical, and mental activity manifested in play;
(c) the summation of these experiences forming the basis for a sense of self.

Summation or reverberation depends on there being a certain quantity of reflecting back to the individual on the part of the trusted therapist (or friend) who has taken the (indirect) communication. In these highly specialized conditions the individual can come together and exist as a unit, not as a defence against anxiety but as an expression of I AM, I am alive, I am myself [Winnicott, 1962]. From this position everything is creative [p. 56].

Deri (1979) summarized Winnicott's developmental steps as: the stage of dual union (Hermann, 1936); the stage of hallucinatory wish fulfillment; the stage of playing; and, finally, the stage of creativity in adult life. To me this reflects Winnicott's stress on object relations and the crucial role of play.[13]

Mahler, in the same tradition as Spitz, believed that observation of the first year of life "touches on the essence of reconstruction and on the problem of coenesthetic empathy, both so essential for the clinical efficiency of psychoanalysis" (1971, p. 404). She does not agree with Anna Freud's position regarding the implausibility of reconstruction and interpretation of the preverbal period. Yet, Mahler does not concur with what many analysts consider to be the Kleinian tendency; that is, actively and quickly to offer interpretations on an intuitive basis, going back to the beginnings of life. In her early work, Mahler carefully studied tics and psychoses in children. More recently, she has developed observational techniques to study young toddlers interacting with their mothers in a special nursery school setting. In addition, she designed experiments which permit the study of mothers' personalities and dynamics as well as the reactions

[13]Examples of his therapeutic techniques may be found in Milner (1969), Winnicott (1972, 1977), Guntrip (1975). For summaries of his work, see Khan (1975), Friedman (1975), Guntrip (1976).

of their youngsters both to mother and her absence. Her work serves
to integrate biology, developmental psychology, social-interpersonal
factors, and intrapsychic processes.

Mahler and Furer (1968) proposed three main phases of
development: autistic, symbiotic, and separation-individuation
phases along the path from nonawareness to a sense of identity. During approximately the first three months of life, there is an autistic
orbit and no awareness of self as separate from environment or from
others. Toward the conclusion of this phase, according to Mahler,
the infant dimly senses the "need-gratifying agent" as apart from the
vaguely formed body image. She called this second developmental
period (extending from about the third to ninth month) the "symbiotic." Since memory traces of previous caretaking are probably
registered mentally by this time and the symbiotic object (fused
mother-infant) is probably perceived as a unit, Mahler felt that this
is the beginning of an ego. "The more nearly optimal the symbiosis,
the mother's 'holding behavior' has been; the more the symbiotic
partner has helped the infant to become ready to 'hatch'. . . the better
equipped has the child become to separate out and to differentiate
his self representations from the hitherto fused symbiotic self-plus-
object representations" (1968, p. 18). From the ninth month on, as
locomotion and coordination increase, more physical separation
from mother is possible. Concomitantly, perceptual maturing and
greater attention to the outer world permit comparisons of mother's
face with other objects. The toddler has begun the separation-
individuation phase, the first subphase of which she called *differentiation.* Mental differentiation and separation of self representation
from the fused self-object phenomenological unit occurs. The *practicing* subphase follows: energy tends to become invested in
motorically exploring and reacting to the outside as well as to learning and experiencing the self. This sequence may extend from about
the tenth to the sixteenth month. There is a shift away from the symbiotic orbit and mother to a more autonomous self engaged in exploring the world. At about this stage, the toddler may experience
the threat and fear of object loss and abandonment. This makes for
vulnerability and a regressive dedifferentiation of the developing
sense of separation and selfness. The mother's phase-specific reactions are again crucial. In part, her responses will be determined by
her own developmental history including her babyhood and mem-

ories of the mothering she experienced (Benedek, 1959). The match-
ing, interacting needs and rhythms of mother and child play a vital
role. During the period of about one and one-half to three years, internalizations gradually lead to ego identifications. There is an
awareness and pleasure in being separate and increasingly autonomous. Language and thought develop and object constancy develops. The *rapprochement* subphase ensues and, under good-enough
conditions, the firmly established self and object representations are
maintained regardless of pressure or frustration, and a stable sense
of identity persists.

When the vicissitudes do not permit optimal development,
Mahler (1971) described the pathological consequences:

> . . .the ambivalence conflict is discernible during the rapprochement
> subphase in rapidly alternating clinging and increased negativistic be-
> haviors. This may be in some cases a reflection of the fact that the child
> has split the object world, more permanently than is optimal, into "good"
> and "bad." By means of this splitting, the "good" object is defended
> against the derivatives of the aggressive drive.
>
> These mechanisms, coercion and splitting of the object world, are
> characteristic in most cases of borderline transference [p. 413].

Mahler's references to splitting and part objects are quite
reminiscent of Melanie Klein. In fact, Mahler recognized this although her developmental "timetable" is somewhat different:

> We may assume that confluence and primitive integration of the scat-
> tered "good" and "bad". . .part images of the self, as well as split "good"
> and "bad" part images of the mother, do not occur before the second year
> of life. This is attested to by the normal emotional ambivalence (and
> behavioral ambitendency) that is clinically discernible at this age. . . .
>
> [F]rom twelve to eighteen months on, during the process of
> separation-individuation, are the rapidly alternating primitive identifica-
> tion mechanisms possible and dominant. We owe their description to
> Melanie Klein (1932) [1968, p. 46].

Mahler et al. (1975) stated that issues about separation-
individuation subphases make up "a major organization of intrapsychic and behavioral life" (p. 4). Mahler and Kaplan (1977)
emphasized that by means of "predominantly observational study of
the preverbal and primary process phases of development, the
subphase-related progress in object relations could be fairly reliably

studied through its *referents*—furnished by observation of interactive behaviors of the mother-child unit over the course of time, polarized by the two partners of the dual unit" (p. 72). They described the relative ease in noting progress in object relations in contrast with difficulties in observing the growth of a cohesive, separate, whole self representation since the subjective states of infants may elude the observer and behavioral referents are scarce.

Through Mahler's detailed descriptions of the dyadic early-life phases, we have an opportunity to study the importance of object relationships in the development of (1) self and object representations and the sense of identity and reality, (2) ego and superego formation, (3) mental health and psychopathology.

Mahler's work—along with the contributions of other object relations theorists and ego psychologists—leads to the conclusion that maturational processes involve a crucial interaction: the developing ego enhances the personality's capacity to utilize objects for further internalization and personality structuring and to relate to objects for satisfaction and security. At the same time, it is through the availability of caretaking objects, the interaction with objects, and the internalization of object representations that ego development is possible.

Conclusion

I have reviewed object relations concepts by summarizing the relevant work of analysts representative of each of the major trends of psychoanalytic thought within the Freudian framework. These concepts provided a background for the integrative contributions of Edith Jacobson regarding the development of the self and the object world. A more complete survey of object relations theory would include the concepts of several other analysts,[14] the work of H. S. Sullivan and others who stressed cultural and interpersonal approaches, the theories of developmental psychologists (like Piaget and Werner), and the ethological formulations (of Bowlby, Harlow, Lorenz, etc.). Since the purpose of this paper is the review of psychoanalytic thinking underlying Jacobson's work, the efforts of those who followed her are not presented here.

[14]Especially Greenacre, Kernberg, Kohut, Kris, Lichtenstein, Loewald, and Modell.

Historical perspectives are useful in evaluating theories and in highlighting unresolved issues. There is no overall psychoanalytic theory of object relations which adequately accounts for the role and interactions of: drives, ego, superego, reality experiences and their elaboration, the subjective experiences of patients, and the clinical observations of analysts. Some analysts contend that a unified object relations theory is attainable and desirable (Modell, 1968), whereas others see no need for an overall theory of object relations. Gedo and Goldberg (1973) suggested that a hierarchical approach, in an epigenetic framework, could provide a variety of models, each applicable to specific phases of development. In this context, object relations would be one line of development. There is the question of the validity, utility, and limitations of an object relations perspective.

There remain many unanswered questions about the nature of internalization and inner mental representation. There are neurophysiological and psychological aspects of cognition, among them the processes and timing of: image formation, memory banking, and the establishment of mental representations. Related hypotheses are supported or modified in the light of data obtained by a variety of techniques from different sources. Some object relations theory is based upon the primary process material of very young children or psychotic behavior and verbalizations expressed in treatment. Other constructs result from observations of "normal" children or reconstructions based upon the associations and memories of neurotic patients. Those who seek "indicators" of the growing child's psychic state by observation elicit one kind of "objective" data — nonetheless filtered through the "observer bias" of the researcher. For example, Spitz, Hartmann, and others considered eighth-month stranger anxiety to be indicative of the awareness and internalization of a caring object; in contrast, Décarie (1965, 1974) explored alternative hypotheses to account for the same manifest behavior without resorting to the psychoanalytic concept of mental representation.

Another kind of "subjective" data is derived from the free associations of patients who provide manifestations of their experiential world in treatment situations. Such productions are usually influenced by prior interpretations and the state of transference-countertransference. Freud suggested that a variety of sources and kinds of data could be exploited to develop greater understanding. It

is my impression that recently it has become the trend[15] to inter-
relate data and integrate theory rather than to accentuate factions,
unidimensional concerns or predilections. There remain controversies about: the role and primacy of drives or instincts, the value of
metapsychology, the possibility of reconstructing early preverbal experience in treatment, and the timing of the development of ego
functioning.[16]

That branch of object relations theory which emphasizes developmental ego psychology stresses the executive functions of the
ego. For example, in Hartmann's view, the ego has autonomous,
adaptive capacities to cope with outer reality. Treatment, from that
vantage point, focuses upon the developmental aspects of the
caretaker-infant unit and the role of this dyad in the unfolding of
such capacities and in the establishing of mental representations and
intrapsychic structures. Erikson added a psychosocial perspective to
this schema. One limitation of the viewpoint described thus far is
absence of concern with the precognitive state prior to differentiated
mental representations of self and object. Generally, the more classical analysts and ego psychologists do not undertake treatment of
problems emanating from preverbal phases. They cautiously and
systematically utilize interpretation to analyze resistances and
defenses—focusing upon intersystemic and intrasystemic conflicts.
In contrast, those of the British school of object relations claim to
work with the archaic, undifferentiated, preverbal period. They consider the predyadic and earliest dyadic experiences crucial to
successful resolution of severe characterological and psychotic
problems.

There are differences in technique and emphasis among those
who are devoted to different branches of object relations theory.
Kleinians actively interpret the most archaic fantasies. They offer
deep interpretations, contending that this approach establishes a
meaningful alliance and reaches otherwise disabling anxieties. In
contrast, analysts following Balint or Winnicott, though treating
similar types of patients, utilize a "holding environment" to facilitate

---

[15]Unfortunately, the work of Kohut, although of considerable value, does not
go along with this trend (Levine, 1977; Tuttman, 1978).

[16]That is, do ego functions, dealing with awareness and fantasied inner objects,
exist from the beginning of life or is there a gradually emerging adaptive potential
and the evolution of mental representations.

the working through of the preverbal "basic fault" in a treatment dyad paralleling the caretaker-infant unit.

A related distinction between psychoanalytic object relations theoreticians may be conceptualized in terms of a continuum: from a structuralist viewpoint to a phenomenological position. At one pole are analytic notions dealing with objects, real and fantasied, as sources for internalization which lead to the development of psychic structures and the repertoire of ego and superego functions. The opposite position reflects the conviction that the experiencing person strives for closeness with others and that this subjective need ("object-seeking") is a central and basic motivation of human beings. Both viewpoints are important and both contribute to psychoanalytic understanding within an object relations perspective (Tuttman, 1978, 1979).

Finally, the role of reality in object relations and psychoanalytic theory has an interesting history. Originally, Freud conceived of defenses as directed against reencountering memories of particular reality experiences which would rearouse painful affects. He believed that these traumatic, unacceptable memories involved important object relationships. When Freud discovered that his patients' reports of infantile seduction were fantasies, reality lost its central position in his theory. Instead, his interest shifted to a focus upon instinctual drives which, he came to believe, motivated the fantasies. Psychoanalytic theory then became involved in the study of internal forces with which the instincts come into conflict, and the defensive organization.

The concepts of secondary process and conciousness (Freud, 1900), the reality principle (1911), and the later structural ideas (1923, 1926) ushered in another shift of focus — this time to ego psychology. The importance of reality gradually became central once again in psychoanalytic theory. Freud then proposed that the ego, utilizing defenses at its disposal to curb and channel instinctual drives, becomes concerned with adaptation and reality relationships. Now he had developed a theory of the ego which takes into account both the drives and the relation to reality.

Although Freud acknowledged the importance of the mother's influence during infancy, he left it to later workers to examine in detail the crucial role of the early caretaking objects in the development of personality. In the contributions surveyed in this paper, it is generally acknowledged that object relations play a very significant part in the evolving of ego and superego; furthermore, the identifications and object choices which result from early-life interaction with objects determine the style of reality relations (between self and object) in the adult world. Thus, object relations again become central in psychoanalytic thinking — only this time, the role of objects in the development of the self and the importance of self and object mental representations in reality relations are emphasized.

As one seeks historical perspectives in any area of psychoanalytic theory, some facts become apparent. The vast majority of psychoanalytic insights and hypotheses as well as the central formulations of the treatment method, and innumerable ingenious speculations are essentially the product of a single, prolific mind. This unusual historical situation arouses both awe and ambivalence in analytic theorists and practitioners. Freud's assertions are frequently distorted, taken out of context, or overlooked. They are often either revered or negated. Which analyst does not wish to make immortal contributions? Who does not seek the narcissistic gratification of fame? If one cannot be a father conquistador, perhaps one settles for the role of reformer, modifier, or critic. Some gain stature by representing the traditional as stalwart protector of the orthodox. Others seek prominence as proponents of heterodoxy. A powerful father figure often sires heirs who are either dependent and compliant or rebellious and oppositional. Such factors tend to create dynamics of conflict and polarization which are not conducive to a working through of theory in terms of perspectives and integration of concepts.

Data are collected from varying clinical populations. Observations are processed in the contexts of different theoretical frameworks. Inevitably, contrasting viewpoints emerge which come to be presented in polarized form. These clusters of ideas develop into contrasting schools of thought. Advocates of each position evolve their own rationale and issues become vested and politicized. Cants and special terminologies grow. The trends are reinforced when data from particular patient populations of "favored" pathologies or developmental stages are exploited to reinforce the formulations of a specific conceptual stance. Theoretical debate is a double-edged sword. On the one hand, it leads to productive dialogue and stimulating controversy; on the other hand, it can result in a rigidification of ideas and a lack of communication.

Prior to the work of Jacobson, object relations theorists tended to offer islands of thought, each constructed from one or another aspect of analytic theory. Among the wealth of ideas, there was no overall perspective or context which took into account the diversity, complexity, and interrelationship of factors. Jacobson attempted to bridge these islands by means of a unifying, developmental schema.

There remain many unresolved problems dealing with object relations theory too numerous to explore here. Perhaps an object relations framework offers some unique opportunities as a context for psychoanalytic thinking.

Most symptoms of psychopathology involve subjectively experienced and objectively perceived identity problems and difficulties in the perception of self and object and in relationships with others. Consequently object relations concepts are useful and pertinent in understanding pathology and planning treatment.

Object relations theory highlights two aspects of the analytic treatment model: first, the "observer"-monitoring function of the analyst seeking a historical perspective. This offers the patient an opportunity to align himself with a more objective view of himself and others. At the same time, the analyst's empathic stance facilitates the patient's shared exploration of his vivid, inner subjective world and how it feels. I have previously (1978, 1979) described the applicability and functions of these therapeutic stances.

A focus on mental representations of the self and the world of objects provides a vantage point which offers both rich intrapsychic and endless interpersonal aspects; furthermore, the realm of object relations deals with structural considerations while also exploring the phenomenological world. That is, object relations theory involves metapsychological structures (i.e., the world of internal mental representations and the identifications which make up the psychic institutions). At the same time, object relations theory deals with the human world of subjectivity and the existential. Thus, an object relations perspective provides a meeting place for object and subject and the opportunity to study their origins and qualities.

References

Abraham, K. (1911), Notes on the psycho-analytic investigation and treatment of manic-depressive insanity and allied conditions. In: *Selected Papers on Psycho-Analysis*. London: Hogarth Press, 1948, pp. 137–156.

———— (1924), A short study of the development of the libido, viewed in the light of mental disorders. *Ibid.*, pp. 418–502.

———— (1925), Character-formation on the genital level of the libido. *Ibid.*, pp. 407–417.

Balint, M. (1959), *Thrills and Regressions*. New York: International Universities Press.

———— (1968), *The Basic Fault*. London: Tavistock.

Benedek, T. (1959), Parenthood as a developmental phase. *J. Amer. Psychoanal. Assn.*, 7:389–417.

Bibring, E. (1947), The so-called English school of psychoanalysis. *Psychoanal. Quart.*, 16:69–93.

Bion, W. R. (1961), *Experiences in Groups*. London: Tavistock.

———— (1962), *Learning from Experience*. London: Heinemann.

———— (1967), *Second Thoughts*. London: Heinemann.

———— (1977), *Seven Servants*. New York: Jason Aronson.

Blanck, G. & Blanck, R. (1974), *Ego Psychology: Theory and Practice*. New York: Columbia University Press.

———— (1979), *Ego Psychology II*. New York: Columbia University Press.

Breuer, J. & Freud, S. (1893–1895). Studies on hysteria. *Standard Edition*, 2. London: Hogarth Press, 1955.

Brierley, M. (1951), Problems connected with the work of Melanie Klein. In: *Trends in Psycho-Analysis*. London: Hogarth Press, pp. 57–89.

Décarie, T. G. (1965), *Intelligence and Affectivity in Early Childhood*. New York: International Universities Press.

———— (1974), *The Infant's Reaction to Strangers*. New York: International Universities Press.

Deri, S. (1979), Transitional phenomena. In: *Between Reality and Fantasy*, ed. L. Barkin, S. A. Grolnick, & W. Muensterberger. New York: Jason Aronson, pp. 43–60.

Erikson, E. H. (1946), Ego development and historical change. *The Psychoanalytic Study of the Child*, 2:359–396.

———— (1950), *Childhood and Society*. New York: Norton.

———— (1956), The problem of ego identity. *J. Amer. Psychoanal. Assn.*, 4:101–164.

———— (1958), *Young Man Luther*. New York: Norton.

———— (1959), *Identity and the Life Cycle* [*Psychol. Issues*, Monogr. 1]. New York: International Universities Press.

Fairbairn, W. R. D. (1941), A revised psychopathology of psychoses and psycho-neuroses. In: *Psycho-Analytic Studies of the Personality*. London: Tavistock, 1952, pp. 28–58.

———— (1952), *Psycho-Analytic Studies of the Personality*. London: Tavistock.

———— (1954), *An Object-Relations Theory of the Personality*. New York: Basic Books.

———— (1963), Synopsis of an object-relations theory of the personality. *Int. J. Psycho-Anal.*, 44:224–225.

Federn, P. (1952), *Ego Psychology and the Psychoses*. New York: Basic Books.

Ferenczi, S. (1909), Introjection and transference. In: *Sex in Psychoanalysis*. New York: Basic Books, 1950, pp. 35–93.

———— (1913), Stages in the development of the sense of reality. *Ibid.*, pp. 213–239.

———— (1932), *Final Contributions to the Problems and Methods of Psychoanalysis*. New

York: Basic Books, 1955.

Fraiberg, S. (1969), Libidinal object constancy and mental representation. *The Psychoanalytic Study of the Child,* 24:9–47.

Freud, A. (1936), The ego and the mechanisms of defense. *The Writings of Anna Freud,* 2. New York: International Universities Press, 1966.

———— (1965), Normality and pathology in childhood. *The Writings of Anna Freud,* 6. New York: International Universities Press.

———— (1969), *Difficulties in the Path of Psychoanalysis.* New York: International Universities Press.

———— & Burlingham, D. (1939–45), Infants without families. *The Writings of Anna Freud,* 3. New York: International Universities Press.

Freud, S. (1900), The interpretation of dreams. *Standard Edition,* 4 & 5. London: Hogarth Press, 1953.

———— (1905a), Three essays on the theory of sexuality. *Standard Edition,* 7:125–243. London: Hogarth Press, 1953.

———— (1905b [1901]), Fragment of an analysis of a case of hysteria. *Standard Edition,* 7:3–122. London: Hogarth Press, 1953.

———— (1908), On the sexual theories of children. *Standard Edition,* 9:205–226. London: Hogarth Press, 1959.

———— (1910), A special type of choice of object made by men. *Standard Edition,* 11:163–175. London: Hogarth Press, 1957.

———— (1911), Psycho-analytic notes on an autobiographical account of a case of paranoia (dementia paranoides). *Standard Edition,* 12:3–82. London: Hogarth Press, 1958.

———— (1912a), Totem and taboo. *Standard Edition,* 13:1–161. London: Hogarth Press, 1955.

———— (1912b), The dynamics of transference. *Standard Edition,* 12:97–108. London: Hogarth Press, 1958.

———— (1914), On narcissism. *Standard Edition,* 14:67–102. London: Hogarth Press, 1958.

———— (1915a), Instincts and their vicissitudes. *Standard Edition,* 14:109–140. London: Hogarth Press, 1957.

———— (1915b), Observations on transference-love. *Standard Edition,* 12:157–171. London: Hogarth Press, 1958.

———— (1917a), The development of the libido and the sexual organizations. *Standard Edition,* 16:320–338. London: Hogarth Press, 1963.

———— (1917b), Mourning and melancholia. *Standard Edition,* 14:237–260. London: Hogarth Press, 1957.

———— (1920), Beyond the pleasure principle. *Standard Edition,* 18:7–64. London: Hogarth Press, 1955.

———— (1921), Group psychology and the analysis of the ego. *Standard Edition,* 18:67–143. London: Hogarth Press, 1955.

———— (1923), The ego and the id. *Standard Edition,* 19:3–66. London: Hogarth Press, 1961.

———— (1924a), Neurosis and psychosis. *Standard Edition,* 19:149–153. London: Hogarth Press, 1961.

———— (1924b), The loss of reality in neurosis and psychosis. *Standard Edition,* 19:183–187. London: Hogarth Press, 1961.

———— (1924c), The dissolution of the oedipus complex. *Standard Edition,* 19:173–179. London: Hogarth Press, 1961.

_____ (1925a), An autobiographical study. *Standard Edition,* 20:3-74. London: Hogarth Press, 1959.

_____ (1925b), Some psychical consequences of the anatomical distinction between sexes. *Standard Edition,* 19:243-258. London: Hogarth Press, 1961.

_____ (1926), Inhibitions, symptoms and anxiety. *Standard Edition,* 20:77-175. London: Hogarth Press, 1959.

_____ (1931), Female sexuality. *Standard Edition,* 21:221-244. London: Hogarth Press, 1961.

_____ (1940a [1938]), An outline of psycho-analysis. *Standard Edition,* 23:141-207. London: Hogarth Press, 1964.

_____ (1940b [1938]), Splitting of the ego in the process of defence. *Standard Edition,* 23:271-278. London: Hogarth Press, 1964.

_____ (1950a [1892-1899]), Letter 71 (October 15, 1897). Extracts from the Fliess papers. *Standard Edition,* 1:263-266. London: Hogarth Press, 1966.

_____ (1950b [1895]), Project for a scientific psychology. *Standard Edition,* 1: 283-410. London: Hogarth Press, 1966.

Friedman, L. J. (1975), Current psychoanalytic object relations theory and its clinical implications. *Int. J. Psycho-Anal.,* 56:137-145.

Gedo, J. E. & Goldberg, A. (1973), *Models of the Mind.* Chicago: University of Chicago Press.

Glover, E. (1932), A psycho-analytical approach to the classification of mental disorders. In: *On the Early Development of Mind.* New York: International Universities Press, 1956, pp. 161-186.

_____ (1943), The concept of dissociation. *Ibid.,* pp. 307-323.

_____ (1945), Examination of the Klein system of child psychology. *The Psychoanalytic Study of the Child,* 1:75-118.

Guntrip. H. (1961), *Personality Structure and Human Interaction.* New York: International Universities Press.

_____ (1966), British school of psychoanalysis: II. The object-relations theory of W. R. D. Fairbairn. In: *American Handbook of Psychiatry,* ed. S. Arieti. New York: Basic Books, vol. 3, pp. 230-239.

_____ (1969), *Schizoid Phenomena, Object-Relations and the Self.* New York: International Universities Press.

_____ (1975), My experience of analysis with Fairbairn and Winnicott. *Int. Rev. Psycho-Anal.,* 2:145-156.

_____ (1976), A short history of the British school of object relations and ego psychology. *Bull. Menninger Clin.,* 40:357-382.

Hartmann, H. (1939), *Ego Psychology and the Problem of Adaptation.* New York: International Universities Press, 1958.

_____ (1950), Comments on the psychoanalytic theory of the ego. In: *Essays on Ego Psychology.* New York: International Universities Press, 1964, pp. 113-141.

_____ (1952), The mutual influences in the development of the ego and the id. *Ibid.,* pp. 155-181.

_____ (1956), The development of the ego concept in Freud's work. *Ibid.,* pp. 268-296.

_____ (1964), *Essays on Ego Psychology.* New York: International Universities Press.

_____ Kris, E., & Loewenstein, R. M. (1946), Comments on the formation of psychic structure. *The Psychoanalytic Study of the Child,* 2:11-38.

Hermann, I. (1936), Clinging—going-in-search. *Psychoanal. Quart.,* 45:5-36, 1976.

Hoedemaker, E. W. (1967), The psychotic identifications in schizophrenia. In:

Psychoanalytic Treatment of Schizophrenic and Characterological Disorders, ed. L. B. Boyer & P. L. Giovacchini. New York: Science House, pp. 189–208.

Jacobson, E. (1964), *The Self and the Object World.* New York: International Universities Press.

Jones, E. (1952), Preface to W. R. D. Fairbairn, *Psycho-Analytic Studies of the Personality.* London: Tavistock.

———— (1955), *The Life and Work of Sigmund Freud,* vol. 2. New York: Basic Books.

Kernberg, O. F. (1969), A contribution to the ego psychological critique of the Kleinian school. *Int. J. Psycho-Anal.,* 50:317–333.

Khan, M. M. R. (1974), *The Privacy of the Self.* New York: International Universities Press.

———— (1975), Introduction to D. W. Winnicott, *Through Paediatrics to Psychoanalysis.* New York: Basic Books, 1975.

Klein, M. (1932), *The Psychoanalysis of Children.* New York: Delacorte Press, 1975.

———— (1937), Love, guilt and reparation. In: *Love, Guilt and Reparation & Other Works.* New York: Delacorte Press, 1975, pp. 306–343.

———— (1957), *Envy and Gratitude.* New York: Basic Books.

———— (1961), *Narrative of a Child Analysis.* New York: Basic Books.

———— & Riviere, J. (1937), *Love, Hate and Reparation.* London: Hogarth Press.

Kris, E. (1952), *Psychoanalytic Explorations in Art.* New York: International Universities Press.

———— (1975), *Selected Papers.* New Haven: Yale University Press.

Laplanche, J. & Pontalis, J.-B. (1967), *The Language of Psycho-Analysis.* New York: Norton, 1973.

Levine, F. (1977), Review of Kohut's *Restoration of the Self. J. Philadelphia Assn. Psychoanal.,* 4:238–246.

Lindon, J. A. (1966), Melanie Klein. In: *Psychoanalytic Pioneers,* ed. F. Alexander, S. Eisenstein, & M. Grotjahn. New York: Basic Books, pp. 360–372.

Lorand, S. (1966), Sándor Ferenczi. In: *Psychoanalytic Pioneers,* ed. F. Alexander, S. Eisenstein, & M. Grotjahn. New York: Basic Books, pp. 14–35.

Mahler, M. S. (1971), A study of the separation and individuation process. *The Psychoanalytic Study of the Child,* 26:403–24.

———— & Furer, M. (1968), *On Human Symbiosis and the Vicissitudes of Individuation.* New York: International Universities Press.

———— & Kaplan, L. (1977), Developmental aspects in the assessment of narcissistic and so-called borderline personalities. In: *Borderline Personality Disorders,* ed. P. Hartocollis. New York: International Universities Press, pp. 71–85.

———— Pine, F., & Bergman, A. (1975), *The Psychological Birth of the Human Infant.* New York: Basic Books.

Meltzer, D. (1967), *The Psychoanalytic Process.* London: Heinemann.

Milner, M. (1969), *The Hands of the Living God.* New York: International Universities Press.

Modell, A. H. (1968), *Object Love and Reality.* New York: International Universities Press.

Peto, A. (1967), Dedifferentiated fragmentations during analysis. *J. Amer. Psychoanal. Assn.,* 15:534–550.

Rado, S. (1928), *Psychoanalysis of Behavior.* New York: Grune & Stratton.

Rank, O. (1924), *The Trauma of Birth.* New York: Basic Books, 1952.

Rapaport, D. (1959), An historical survey of psychoanalytic ego psychology. In: *Identity and the Life Cycle.* [*Psychol. Issues,* Monogr. 1]. New York: International Universities Press, pp. 5–17.

Rinsley, D. (1979), Fairbairn's object-relations theory. *Bull. Menninger Clin.*, 43: 489–514.

Rosenfeld, H. (1966), *Psychotic States*. New York: International Universities Press.

Sandler, J. & Rosenblatt, B. (1962), The concept of the representational world. *The Psychoanalytic Study of the Child*, 17:128–145.

Schafer, R. (1968), *Aspects of Internalization*. New York: International Universities Press.

Schilder, P. (1935), *The Image and Appearance of the Human Body*. New York: International Universities Press, 1950.

Schur, M. (1966), *The Id and the Regulatory Principles of Mental Functioning*. New York: International Universities Press.

Sechehaye, M. (1951), *Symbolic Realization*. New York: International Universities Press.

Segal, H. (1964), *Introduction to the Work of Melanie Klein*. New York: Basic Books.

Spitz, R. A. (1945), Hospitalism. *The Psychoanalytic Study of the Child*, 1:53–74.

_____ (1946), Hospitalism: a follow-up report. *The Psychoanalytic Study of the Child*, 2:113–117.

_____ (1950), Anxiety in infancy. *Int. J. Psycho-Anal.*, 31:138–143.

_____ (1965), *The First Year of Life*. New York: International Universities Press.

Symposium (1954), The widening scope of indications for psychoanalysis. *J. Amer. Psychoanal. Assn.*, 2:567–620.

Thompson, C. (1950), Introduction to *The Selected Papers of Ferenczi*. New York: Basic Books.

Tuttman, S. (1978), Kohut symposium. *Psychoanal. Rev.*, 65:624–629.

_____ (1979), Regression: is it necessary or desirable? *J. Amer. Acad. Psychoanal.*, 7:111–133.

Winnicott, C. (1978), D. W. W.: a reflection. In: *Between Reality and Fantasy*, ed. L. Barkin, S. A. Grolnick, & W. Muensterberger. New York: Jason Aronson, 1978, pp. 15–34.

Winnicott, D. W. (1951), Transitional objects and transitional phenomena. In: *Collected Papers*. New York: Basic Books, 1957, pp. 97–100.

_____ (1952), Anxiety associated with insecurity. *Ibid.*, pp. 97–100.

_____ (1956), Primary maternal preoccupation. *Ibid.*, pp. 300–305.

_____ (1958), The capacity to be alone. In: *The Maturational Processes and the Facilitating Environment*. New York: International Universities Press, 1965, pp. 29–36.

_____ (1960), Ego distortion in terms of true and false self. *Ibid.*, pp. 140–152.

_____ (1962a), Ego integration in child development. *Ibid.*, pp. 56–63.

_____ (1962b), A personal view of the Kleinian contribution. *Ibid.*, pp. 171–178.

_____ (1963), The development of the capacity for concern. *Ibid.*, pp. 73–82.

_____ (1965), *The Maturational Processes and the Facilitating Environment*. New York: International Universities Press.

_____ (1969), The use of an object and relating through identifications. In: *Playing and Reality*. New York: Basic Books, 1971, pp. 86–94.

_____ (1971), *Playing and Reality*. New York: Basic Books.

_____ (1972), Fragment of an analysis. In: *Tactics and Techniques in Psychotherapy*, ed. P. Giovacchini. New York: Jason Aronson, pp. 455–694.

_____ (1977), *The Piggle: An Account of a Psychoanalytic Treatment of a Little Girl*, ed. I. Ramzy. New York: International Universities Press.

Yorke, C. (1971), Some suggestions for a critique of Kleinian psychology. *The Psy-*

choanalytic Study of the Child, 26:129–155.
Zetzel, E. R. (1953), The depressive position. In: *The Capacity for Emotional Growth.*
New York: International Universities Press, 1971, pp. 63–81.
_____ (1956), Concept and content in psychoanalytic theory. *Ibid.,* pp. 115–138.

Part I
THE CONTRIBUTIONS OF EDITH JACOBSON

2

THE CLINICAL BASE OF
EDITH JACOBSON'S CONTRIBUTION

Jacob A. Arlow, M.D.

The contribution of Edith Jacobson to psychoanalysis is unique. It is measured not only by the great number of her valuable scientific writings, but also in terms of her exemplary devotion to her patients, students, and colleagues. One can only surmise to what extent she has helped and given comfort to so many over the lengthening span of her years.

The name of Edith Jacobson is, of course, most significantly linked to the psychology and treatment of depression and depressive conditions. On this subject, she is regarded as the foremost authority in the field of psychoanalysis. Depression is a broader subject than the psychopathological entity we encounter clinically; the subject is really unpleasure in the mental life of man (Brenner, 1975)—the anguish, the pain, misery, despair, frustration, and humiliation that are the sad and inexorable dimension of the human condition. Those who have known these feelings in their most agonizing and disruptive forms have been the center of Jacobson's interest and research. These difficult cases form the clinical base for her theoretical conclusions. For this reason, I have chosen to concentrate on her clinical contributions and to discuss how she interpreted and conceptualized the data in order to arrive at her theoretical formulations.

A fresh reading of her papers illuminates how—in the spirit of the true physician—for Jacobson, her patients' pain and suffering served as the point of contact, the area of affective communion where empathic identification provides the necessary access to the patient's inner life and clears the path to trust, to hope, and to cure. The cases she studied most deeply and described in greatest

55

detail are not the usual type of patients who present themselves for treatment. She chose and learned from the more difficult ones: those who had known real trauma, genuine suffering and deprivation—people in desperate straits whose hold on themselves and their world was tenuous. The relationship between the self and the object world was always in the forefront of Jacobson's thinking.

It is, therefore, most appropriate to begin with a clinical contribution of major significance. Written in English shortly after she came to this country, it is a paper characterized by perception, intuition, and compassion. But beyond all of these considerations, it strikes one for the modest, awesome heroism it portrays. The paper is entitled "Observations on the Psychological Effects of Imprisonment on Female Political Prisoners" (1949). I have chosen to present this paper in some detail not only because it is a classic of its kind, but because in it one can see, as in the case of Freud's early writings, adumbrations of much that was to come later from Jacobson's researches. The early impressions and insights documented here were refined, expanded, elaborated, and made more precise in later contributions as her understanding of the issues deepened with time.

In her introductory statement, Jacobson describes the conditions under which the data for her study were obtained. She gives a balanced account of conditions in a German Nazi civilian prison. Almost as an aside, she adds that there was a peculiar situation which was "indeed, not favorable for scientific research [but] actually of great advantage to the study even though [these conditions] may reduce the value and the validity of the findings in some respects. The fact that the observer shared her life with a group of prisoners offered a rare opportunity to observe first-hand and to watch the psychic reactions to prison confinement more closely than is possible under other circumstances" (p. 342). For those who have never seen the interior of a prison, much less been confined in one, it is almost impossible to imagine what it could be like to be incarcerated for almost three years by the Third Reich—that lawless state where guarantees of protection in the courts of justice simply did not exist. Prisons are a vicious caricature of life. They distort, exaggerate, and project in bold relief all the qualities—usually the worst ones—that are possible in both prisoner and keeper. The conditions of prison life are like an experiment in externally imposed distortion of object relations and self-esteem. It was in such a setting and under such conditions that Jacobson produced a study of unparalleled dimension. This work alone would merit her the most eloquent tribute.

Jacobson begins with the trauma of arrest, which shatters the individual's illusion of omnipotence. The reality of the trauma is significant, since response to trauma runs as a theme through Jacobson's work. The first example she gives is that of a young woman, a severe moral masochist, who, although already out of danger, convinced her friends that she should return to Germany— where she was promptly arrested at the frontier. The arrest proved shattering. In prison, she committed suicide.

The catastrophe of arrest leads to stupefaction, blurred thinking, anxiety, and finally to depression. Sudden isolation from the object world, particularly for prisoners who are immediately put into solitary confinement, is devastating. The throttling of normal discharge of libidinal and aggressive energies leads to intense instinctual tension, causing the ego to collapse. Thus weakened, the ego succumbs to the overwhelming assault of the intruding instinctual drives. It is inundated by wild impulses. The resulting paralysis of function is not unlike that typical for the outbreak of a psychosis. "The stupor of the ego can even lead to a temporary loss of the sense of time and locality" (p. 344), an observation Jacobson developed later in her works on depression (1953), psychosis (1957a), and depersonalization (1959a).

During questioning, the prisoner is exposed to a realistic attack which he is able to withstand better than the internal, instinctual dangers. This often causes the stupor to recede. Female prisoners seemed better able to withstand cross-examination than did men. When being beaten, men seemed to be overwhelmed by castration fear, which proved disorganizing. One of the striking features of prison experience is how this newly imposed reality fosters a regression to more infantile levels of behavior. "There were women who on the first day of captivity would cry incessantly for their mothers, others who would moan for their deserted children, frequently in transparent unconscious reversion of their own infantile wish for protection" (p. 345). Thus, object loss and separation were combined with mourning as the precipitating elements for regression (see also Jacobson 1953, 1965, 1967).

After hours or days the chaotic state of mind changes to one of desperation, then to a quiet depression, leading finally, as the personality begins to reorganize, to recuperation and a new equilibrium.

During the period of imprisonment pending trial, neurotic symptoms come to the fore. Jacobson noted that the prisoners tended to forget names, streets, and persons, probably motivated by a wish to conceal damaging facts and to protect friends and colleagues, a deterioration of ego function induced by realistic motives, a theme which appears later in Jacobson's work on denial and repression (1957a). Depersonalization was common and persistent in prisoners at this stage. "Such conditions are . . . reactions of the threatened ego which defends itself by denying the reality of the situation" (p. 347). In her subsequent work, Jacobson returned many times to the defensive use of denial and depersonalization in the face of realistic threat and trauma (1957a, 1959a, 1967).

All the prisoners who were studied developed functional disturbances of varying degrees. These were not physical consequences of incarceration, but psychosomatic phenomena. Jacobson observed and was impressed by the cessation of menses in women prisoners. She noted that menstruation frequently recurred shortly before the prisoners were released.[1]

In the period before trial, anxieties heightened and the prisoners often accused those whom they regarded responsible for having been captured. In turn, such feelings often gave way to self-accusation, particularly concerning friends or members of the family toward whom the prisoners might have felt ambivalent. In this context, an impulse to betray one's friends and associates often came to mind. This impulse made a deep impression on Jacobson who subsequently (1971a) was able to elucidate the dynamics of the paranoid urge to betray.

"With most political prisoners the feeling of serving a cause helped to relieve guilt feelings, to restore their self-esteem and to regain a collected, composed and courageous front" (p. 349). Thus, long before the surge of interest in self-esteem regulation and the

---

[1]Jacobson (1946b) presented a fascinating study of sterility, a study which was carefully documented from both the physical and psychological points of view. In a meticulously detailed presentation, she demonstrated how a case of sterility, presumably based on definite organic findings, was cured by means of psychoanalytic treatment. This paper is one of the pioneer studies in psychophysiological relationships.

narcissistic personality disorders, Jacobson was keenly aware of the vicissitudes of self-esteem as related both to conflict with the demands emanating from the superego and with ambivalence toward love objects. The political cause for which these prisoners were arrested was connected with a collective ego ideal whose erotization deeply influenced the subject's self-esteem (see also 1961). Normal and pathological moods were structured on the basis of the dynamics of this interaction (1957b). In this connection, Jacobson made an astute sociological observation: she suggested prisoners from a higher social background were driven into political activity by the influence of unresolved infantile conflicts. Their philosophy, then, did not equip them with sufficient strength to meet the traumatic situation of imprisonment. A childhood rebellion displaced against the ruling regime was without a sufficiently supportive, stable group identification. Most of these individuals were moral masochistic characters who did not hold up well in the face of political persecution, in contrast to working-class revolutionaries.

After the trial, most of the prisoners — even those who had received heavy sentences — returned from the court in a gay mood because of the sudden lifting of the emotional burden. This led, in a short time, to a brief, hypomanic state such as is sometimes felt immediately after the loss of a loved one (1953, 1954c).

The psychology of the prison guard did not elude Jacobson. She noted that the infantile impulsiveness of the delinquent prisoners threatened the defenses of the guards and roused in them their own primitive, antisocial tendencies. For the keeper, the criminal represents a dangerous, unconsciously long-fought temptation. Interestingly, these tendencies were more marked in elderly, unsatisfied women guards, who were particularly sadistic. Some were inclined to establish strange, personal, homosexually tinged relationships with convicts whom they consciously despised. These relationships offered a partial sharing of forbidden instinctual gratification. Such identifications provoked guilt feelings, which were gotten rid of by rude treatment of the prisoners (1954a). The instinctualization of superego functioning and the superego's vacillation between its erotic and aggressive instinctual investment were patent in these observations. By way of contrast, the attitude of most prison officials toward political prisoners was less ambivalent. They were not troubled by such intensely instinctualized superego involvement as in the case of the delinquent prisoners.

The deprivation of object relations resulted in regression to an infantile emotional level. This kind of reaction occurred sooner and was more intense in those convicts who were isolated from their fellow prisoners as compared with those who had not been. Convicts kept in isolation were more prone to develop serious depressions. They attempted to find refuge in daydreams and fantasic illusions, many of which were concerned with what life would be like after they had been freed. Because of the unrealistic nature of these fantasies, the reality of freedom often became a great burden, and many of the former prisoners broke down after gaining their freedom. From these experiences Jacobson concluded that confinement can have little curative effect on delinquents; on the contrary, captivity can only drive such individuals further into antisocial behavior because of the artificially imposed disturbance in object relationships. Jacobson noted that a program of prison reform should provide for "a minimum of primitive gratification, such as appetizing food, the possibility of normal sexual gratification, decent dayrooms and greater freedom of movement" (p. 367). It is striking to observe that in the recent flurry of civil rights interest, recommendations of this sort have been most prominent in the programs for prison reform.

A number of special qualities are typical of Jacobson's approach to interpreting psychoanalytic data as she makes the transition from clinical observation to hypothesis formation and theory building. Methodologically, she relies on the concepts of conflict, regression, defense, and energic shifts. When using energy concepts, she is one of the more parsimonious of analytic writers and therefore more convincing and successful. Ordinarily, considerations of energic transformation, when applied to clinical data, fall short of being impressive. Jacobson applies such concepts in a way that lends credibility. She does this by two means. First, as mentioned above, she is extremely parsimonious in the use of energic theory. Secondly, she assembles her data in a detailed, meticulously organized fashion, oriented precisely toward the thesis she wishes to establish. Her clinical analyses are enriched and illuminated by an apposite confrontation with metapsychological theory.

One of the distinctive features of Jacobson's clinical analyses is her use of the concept of regression. Alongside the well-known con-

cepts of instinctual regression, she introduced the novel and significant concept of regression of the self, i.e., the backward dissolution
of the organized self representations and of the superego into their
antecedent identifications and to their earlier levels of function
(1954b). In this process, the fate of the specific identification, crucial
in the organizing of the self and superego, becomes central. The role
that identifications play in the organization of the self and the superego really expresses how experience with the real world of people—
the object world—impinges on the organization of the personality.
These conceptualizations became possible because, in her clinical
work, Jacobson devoted the most careful attention to the fate of the
specific identifications that had been effected earlier in life. Only
careful attention to the details of the data brings such relationships to
light. And it is this kind of careful observation we find in Jacobson's
contributions. Patients who have severe disturbances in their relations with the object world frequently misperceive and misidentify
objects because in their past they characteristically had used the
primordial object relations in an effort to resolve their inner conflicts
(1946c, 1967). The object of the external world, Jacobson demonstrated, may be the token of any number of self representations, recent and archaic, as well as of parents and siblings, usually related to
specific experiences and conflicts earlier in life. The more disturbed
the patient, the more archaic is the projection of the regressively
reactivated identification onto the current objects in the patient's experience (1954a). This is exemplified, for example, in Jacobson's
study of patients with a paranoid urge to betray (1971a). These patients usually were gifted individuals, sincere, with high ideals and
with exaggerated, grandiose rescue fantasies, in all of whom narcissistic instability was pronoucned. Part of the urge to save the
world constituted a reaction formation against hostility toward siblings, especially in those patients fixated at the sadomasochistic
level. In their case histories, Jacobson demonstrated a typical pattern of a childhood experience of shifting loyalties and conflicts between parents. Vacillations of loyalty from one parent to another
presaged later shifting allegiances. The urge to betray went further
than the concept of shifting allegiances because in the act of betray-
ing, a sadistic wish for vengeance from the past was gratified on
some object in current reality. Such instability of loyalty reflects an
ambivalent attitude toward the ego ideal, i.e., toward the parent

with whom the patient had identified in the structuring of the ego ideal (1961).

A practical clinical application of these findings can be seen in the experience of certain patients who consult with two therapists at the same time. I was struck by this observation when I read the paper, because it brought to mind the angry reaction of many collagues who have dismissed patients when such a pattern of seeing several consultants at one time came to light. Jacobson, however, was able to trace out the dynamic origin of this unusual behavior in relation to therapy. She demonstrated that it represented an attempt to play one parent against another.

Much of Jacobson's work is devoted to the problem of identification. In the case of certain neurotic interactions in marriage (1956), mutual identification is one of the basic problems. Jacobson described marriages between psychotic partners, both suffering from manic-depressive psychosis. The coin of such relationships is the exchange of practical for moral support, a kind of symbiotic relationship in which the partner — a mixed superego and ego-ideal figure — is overvalued in the hope of forcing him or her to bestow love and praise. It corresponds to a narcissistic object choice — a mixture of object relations and identification. The relationship may shift suddenly in such cases, upsetting the equilibrium when the object no longer fulfills the appropriate role which the identification gratified. The origin of such regressive identification is, of course, most often to be found in the mother-child relationship — a feature commonly found in certain types of female homosexuality as well. In this connection, Jacobson makes a technical point well worth repeating. Despite the highly narcissistic coloring of such unions effected between two psychotic manic-depressive partners, the complaints each raises about the other partner are worth listening to; more often than not, they turn out to be an accurate assessment of the situation.

Jacobson explored the wide-ranging role of identification in psychopathology in every clinical investigation she undertook. A brief survey of how she assesses various conditions from the point of view of identification is most instructive. The relatively familiar state of depersonalization is a defensive reaction (1959a). Jacobson (1949) already appreciated this fact in connection with the political prisoners who denied the unpleasant reality in which they found themselves. Later reflection on the data, plus the opportunity to analyze several cases, deepened her understanding of this condition. Depersonalization develops when the ego is threatened by regressive processes leading to drive defusion and to an overwhelming upsurge of pregenital drives. In such circumstances, when the superego is weak and contradictory, a conflict ensues between the advanced "normal" identifications and the archaic preoedipal identifications. The patient is, as it were, confronted with a choice of behavior based upon images of the self emanating from different stages of his life. A narcissistic conflict ensues as the patient, in effect, tries to disown or deny the undesirable aspects of his ego or self image. In the case of the political prisoners, this conflict was most poignant because under the conditions of confinement, the temptation to identify with the criminal element reevoked temptations connected with forbidden gratification of preoedipal impulses from the past.

How Jacobson assessed the differential significance and role of identification in various psychopathological entities can be seen in the following observations. In regard to the psychoses, Jacobson (1954a) demonstrated how by tracing out the fate of the specific identifications, one could not only explain much of the psychopathology, but also discover guidelines for treatment. The elaboration of the technical approaches unfortunately cannot be considered at this time. As a point of departure, one may study how Jacobson (1953, 1954a, 1961, 1966, 1967) reviews the role of identification in depression. Under normal circumstances following grief, the individual effects a realistic identification with the lost object. He makes himself over, as it were, in keeping with certain qualities, usually ideal ones, identified with the object. Ambivalence yields to reconciliation and emotional growth. The process of mourning is successful. In the case of the melancholic, however, matters eventuate differently. He cannot give up the object. He *identifies* with it and denies his loss by treating himself as if he were the object. The schizoid, on the other hand, *becomes* the object in the sense that he behaves in imitation of or, more correctly, in duplication of the object. The as-if personality is overwhelmed by identifications. He cannot maintain a stable self image. Based on a regression to preoedipal fantasies of oral incorporation, the as-if patient keeps fusing self image with object imagoes. In schizophrenia, the fate of identification is even more complicated. The regression is more severe; it proceeds from resembling the object to magical union *with* the object, a union that may undergo many changes and transformations. The schizophrenic, for example, may in fantasy destroy the object and replace it with the self, or through another form of identification may annihilate the self and replace it with the object. In either instance, one can perceive how the ever-present danger of suicide eventuates in this unusual shift of identification.

Although this presentation of Jacobson's views of the fate of identification in mental life is schematic and abbreviated, one has to be impressed by how closely these formulations rely on and derive from clinical observations. They are not encumbered by a super-structure of unprovable speculation such as characterizes the primordial identification fantasies from the first few months of life used by Melanie Klein (1921–45) or by formulations of theories of special types of energy which are hard to substantiate, as suggested by Kohut (1971, 1977).

The emphasis I have accorded Jacobson's analysis of identification stems from my conviction that it is essential to her entire outlook on psychoanalysis, central to her views about regression, and to her concepts of object relations. Identifications, by and large, are the bridge between the self and the object world. The traffic on this bridge proceeds in both directions—in the course of normal develop-ment, through separation and individuation to the phase where a coherent self is organized largely on the basis of identifications. In the process of regression, whether in psychopathological formations as in psychoses, or in the usual course of dream representations dur-ing sleep, the organized self may dissolve or become fragmented into the various component identifications from which it was con-structed. Whatever the mechanism from the instinctual or ego side, be it projection, incorporation, internalization, or imitation, the tangible, clinical mechanism for the transformation of the psyche in-to a coherent self, separate from the object world, is the mechanism of identification.

Problems of the self are closely related to fluctuations in self-esteem (1975). In this regard, Jacobson's work paralleled and con-nected with that of Annie Reich (1973), who was her close friend and frequent collaborator. One of the most devastating blows to self-esteem follows upon the loss of a parent or other love object in child-hood. The appreciation of this type of trauma runs like a scarlet thread through Jacobson's work. Early loss upsets the normal progression of identificatory processes, taxing the child with florid family romance fantasies and with a predisposition to mobilize the mechanism of denial against a hostile fate (1943, 1965). Jacobson observed that the surviving or remaining parent is blamed, while the dead or abandoning parent is glorified. This work anticipates much that has been recently written about problems of adoption. Perpetual hope for the impossible — for union with the lost parent — is matched by perpetual disappointment. The narcissistic injury is overwhelming. All of Jacobson's patients in this category, i.e., those who had early losses, were depressed, indicating, one can assume, an identification with the ambivalently loved and hated lost object. One eventuality of this situation that Jacobson mentions, and that struck me from my own experience while I was consultant to an orphans' home, was the tendency on the part of the orphans to deny the significance of the loss of the parent, combined with an identification with a fantasied substitute parent figure. Several of the boys and a male patient I had in analysis rejected or denied the need for a father and took pride in the fact that they were "their own man." They owed nothing to father figures; they were, in fact, their own progenitors. In fantasy, however, they were forever seeking aggrandized, glorified father imagoes, either to identify with them or to wreak upon them the childhood vengeance for having abandoned them so early in life.

At least one mention has to be made of how these observations can be applied to problems of therapy. There is one paper which, for me, epitomizes all the qualities of perceptiveness, conceptualization, and compassion typical of Jacobson's work. This paper (1943) relates to the role of the oedipal complex in the development of depressive mechanisms. Jacobson traced the development of the patient's difficulties through many traumas, failed hopes, disappointments, frustrations, and ineffective defenses against the background of the patient's persistent fantasies and identifications. The analysis culminated in a four-hour session in which the interplay of oedipal and preoedipal factors became eminently clear.

It is unfortunate that one has to omit a number of delightful clinical studies, precise, penetrating, and novel. These include: "The Exceptions" (1959b); "A Child's Laughter" (1946a); and "Development of the Wish for a Child in Boys" (1950). In view of the fact that I have covered only a small corner of the realm of Jacobson's contributions, it is plain that such an effort would require another full formal presentation. Reading her work gives one a sense of immediate enrichment and indebtedness which all of us have felt over the years.

References

Brenner, C. (1975), Affects and psychic conflict. *Psychoanal. Quart.,* 44:5-28.
Jacobson, E. (1943), Depression: oedipal conflicts in the development of defense mechanisms. *Psychoanal. Quart.,* 12:541-560.
_____ (1946a), The child's laughter. *The Psychoanalytic Study of the Child,* 2:39-60.
_____ (1946b), A case of sterility. *Psychoanal. Quart.,* 15:330-350.
_____ (1946c), The effect of disappointment on ego and superego development. *Psychoanal. Rev.,* 33:129-147.
_____ (1949), Observations on the psychological effects of imprisonment on female political prisoners. In: *Searchlights on Delinquency,* ed. K. R. Eissler. New York: International Universities Press, pp. 341-369.
_____ (1950), Development of the wish for a child in boys. *The Psychoanalytic Study of the Child,* 5:139-152.
_____ (1953), Contribution to the metapsychology of psychothymic depression. In: *Affective Disorders,* ed. P. Greenacre. New York: International Universities Press, pp. 49-83.
_____ (1954a), Contribution to the metapsychology of psychotic identification. *J. Amer. Psychoanal. Assn.,* 2:239-262.
_____ (1954b), The self and the object world. *The Psychoanalytic Study of the Child,* 9:75-127.
_____ (1954c), Transference problems in the psychoanalytic treatment of severely depressed patients. *J. Amer. Psychoanal. Assn.,* 2:595-606.
_____ (1956), Interaction between psychotic partners. In: *Neurotic Interaction in Marriage,* ed. V. W. Eisenstein. New York: Basic Books, pp. 125-134.
_____ (1957a), Denial and repression. *J. Amer. Psychoanal. Assn.,* 5:61-92.
_____ (1957b), Normal and pathological moods. *The Psychoanalytic Study of the Child,* 12:73-113.
_____ (1959a), Depersonalization. *J. Amer. Psychoanal. Assn.,* 7:581-610.
_____ (1959b), The "exceptions." *The Psychoanalytic Study of the Child,* 14:135-154.
_____ (1961), Adolescent moods and the remodeling of psychic structures in adolescence. *The Psychoanalytic Study of the Child,* 16:164-184.
_____ (1965), The return of the lost parent. In: *Drives, Affects, Behavior,* vol. 2, ed. M. Schur. New York: International Universities Press, pp. 193-211.
_____ (1966), Problems in the differentiation between schizophrenic and melancholic states of depression. In: *Psychoanalysis—A General Psychology,* ed. R. M. Loewenstein, L. M. Newman, M. Schur, & A. J. Solnit. New York: International Universities Press, pp. 499-520.
_____ (1967), *Psychotic Conflict and Reality.* New York: International Universities Press.
_____ (1971a), The paranoid urge to betray. *Bull. Menninger Clin.,* 35:72-76.
_____ (1971b), *Depression.* New York: International Universities Press.
_____ (1975), The regulation of self-esteem. In: *Depression in Human Existence,* ed. E. J. Anthony. Boston: Little, Brown, pp. 169-181.

Klein, M. (1921–45), *Contributions to Psycho-Analysis*. London: Hogarth Press, 1948.
Kohut, H. (1971), *The Analysis of the Self*. New York: International Universities Press.
_____ (1977), *The Restoration of the Self*. New York: International Universities Press.
Reich, A. (1973), *Psychoanalytic Contributions*. New York: International Universities Press.

3

EDITH JACOBSON'S WORK ON DEPRESSION IN HISTORICAL PERSPECTIVE

George Gero, Ph.D., M.D.

A long time ago, when I was a resident at the Psychiatric Clinic in Heidelberg, the nosological system of mental illness, as established by Kraepelin, was relatively simple. Only two groups of psychosis were recognized: manic-depressive illness and schizophrenia, or, as it was then called, dementia praecox. The diagnosis of both forms of mental disturbance instantly incorporated the prognosis. The process was predictable: the manic-depressive went through a cycle, but ended relatively well; dementia praecox involved a progressive deterioration.

At that time, however, it was also recognized that there were still other simpler depressions which did not fit into the cyclothymic type. Among these cases, two forms were differentiated: reactive depression and endogenous depression. Reactive depression was caused by some loss, defeat, or disappointment. But when a person became depressed without any obvious cause, the assumption was that he or she was the victim of some mysterious process. The trailblazing discoveries of Sigmund Freud, although not accepted by academic psychiatry, radically changed these oversimplified views.

The discovery of mental processes which exist beyond conscious awareness made it possible, for instance, to detect that the loss of a love object does not necessarily mean that a beloved one has actually died. A love object dies when, because of inner conflicts, the depressed person's love dies. Or, to give a different type of example: a person may have plenty of money in the bank, but as a symptom of his depression, he becomes convinced that he has lost his fortune. He thus suffers from *Verarmungsangst,* fear of impoverishment.

The discovery of the existence of unconscious mental life

opened up the understanding of neurotic suffering. Severe depression is one of the most crippling forms of neurotic illness, and it is in this area of investigation that Edith Jacobson gained significant insights. In order to appreciate her contributions to the understanding of depression, however, some reference to the previous work on this subject is necessary.

The basic text which opened up the exploration of depressive illness was, of course, Freud's study on "Mourning and Melancholia" (1917). Comparing melancholia with a normal reaction, namely, mourning, one finds both similarities and differences between the two. Both reactions follow a loss, the loss of a love object or the loss of some abstraction which has taken the place of such an object, for instance, one's country, liberty, or an ideal. Profound mourning causes the loss of interest in the outside world and an inhibition of activity in the everyday tasks of life.

Melancholia, on the other hand, does not necessarily follow an actual loss. More often, it is caused by a disappointment or rejection, perhaps betrayal by a love object, or by an ambivalence conflict which destroys the love, although not the love object. The painful affect, which is so characteristic of melancholia, has much in common with mourning—the same indifference toward the outside world and the accompanying inhibitions regarding normal daily pursuits.

There is one feature of melancholia, however, that does not exist in normal mourning. This is the self-accusations of the melancholic patient. While this characteristic was a well-known observation in clinical psychiatry, no attempt was made to find an explanation for this bizarre symptom. It was Freud's genius to recognize that only by understanding the self-accusations of the melancholic can the deepest mysteries of this painful disease be revealed.

The analysis of the melancholic self-accusations led Freud to a discovery, the significance of which goes far beyond the understanding of a simple nosological entity. What Freud unearthed was nothing less than the superego. While he did not at this point use the specific term, he clearly described the essential features of the superego: "We see how...one part of the ego sets itself over against the other, judges it critically, and, as it were, takes it as its object" (p. 247). Freud, enlarging upon the discovery, concldued that this agency, which he then called "the conscience," can ultimately become diseased itself.

One approach to the understanding of the melancholic self-accusation is that a "diseased" superego torments the ego. The question remains, however, what caused the critical agency to be transformed into such a cruel entity.

The other interpretation which Freud offers was even more unexpected. He suggests that the self-accusations seem to be directed against another individual, one whom the melancholic patient loves or once loved or should love. This means that by some mysterious process the love object is worked into the patient's ego, like a foreign body which becomes fully absorbed into the fabric of the organism. This mysterious process Freud called "identification."

Identification was recognized by commonsense psychology as a process of partly conscious emulation of an admired person. In this sense, identification is a common and healthy process which contributes to the building blocks of the individual's personality. But what Freud discussed is the transformation of an ego by incorporating the representation of another person — a process which occurs entirely outside of conscious awareness.

Identification itself, as mentioned before, is a normal process. What concerns the analyst are the conditions which transform a normal process into a malignancy, such as in the case of the self-accusations of the melancholic. This is one area in which Edith Jacobson's work contributed most importantly.

Freud's explanation was that when a disappointment or a rejection shatters a love relationship, the libido is withdrawn from the object. For unknown reasons no new object is found. Instead, the love object is incorporated into the ego, and the hatred which originally was directed against the rejecting love object now turns against the ego.

At the time of its publication, Freud's essay presented entirely novel ideas. Nonetheless, it left many problems unresolved. No one was more aware of this fact than Freud himself. He stated that the empirical material upon which he based his study was insufficient to answer further questions. For instance, the problem of how a conflict with a love object can result in an identification with its fateful consequences is not adequately explained. The work of Edith Jacobson brought significant new insights and offered previously undetected solutions to this question.

It is interesting to note that at the end of his paper, Freud expresses the expectation that the melancholic process will spontaneously end. He explains that once the fury of self-hatred has spent itself, the love object is abandoned and viewed as valueless. In direct contrast to this view, Edith Jacobson has shown that denigrating the object does *not* end the process because the patient becomes merged with the devalued object.

It is clear that Freud is thinking of cases of depression which fit more into the cyclothymic manic-depressive types of melancholia, and that he adheres to the Kraepelinian diagnosis-prognosis expectation, according to which the most likely result is that the melancholia will turn into mania. In his study, Freud emphasizes that melancholia or depression takes on various clinical forms, such as the severe chronic depressions which do not fit into the cyclothymic group and where there is no tendency for spontaneous termination of the depressive state. Such cases necessitated new theoretical models. The study of this type of case enabled Edith Jacobson to advance new, original ideas. Before I speak specifically about her work, however, I must refer to the work of another great analytic investigator, Karl Abraham.

Abraham's work (1924) followed and elaborated upon Freud's discoveries. He suggests that in the melancholic patient there is a regression to the oral-cannibalistic phase. He viewed the developmental phases of sexual instincts as running through a rigid predetermined pattern. In accordance with then-current theory, Abraham considered only the sexual instinct. Yet it is obvious that he saw the instinctual constellation as a mixture of sexual and aggressive components; the earlier the phase, the more violent is the instinctual response. According to this theory, the nature of object relations is automatically determined by the phase of libidinal development, independent of the actual environmental response to the child. Thus, Abraham felt that in the oral-cannibalistic phase, the child's intention is to destroy the object.

Paradoxically, in interpreting his clinical case material, Abraham does not adhere to his theory. He emphasizes, for instance, the enormous importance of early disappointment in the etiology of melancholia, basically a disappointment in the mother. Abraham cites incidents from his patients' histories which illustrate how such disappointments arose. There is, of course, the ubiquitous disappointment which even the most loving mother cannot avoid inflicting on her child, or rather on the male child, namely, the oedipal disappointment. But Abraham does not seem to recognize that the most important predisposing factors for severe depression are the frustrations caused by maternal neglect during the first year of life.

The specific frustrations in the nursing situation which are inflicted on the infant by an uncaring mother unleash oral-sadistic biting impulses. Typical clinical findings in the life history of severely depressed patients reveal, not through conscious memory but rather transmitted in the family chronicle, that the infant was often left screaming with hunger. The mother was either too insensitive to respond to the infant's need or too insistent upon maintaining a rigid schedule of feeding. Typically, in these patients, dreams of cannibalistic fantasies are openly expressed and sometimes also conscious fantasies.

Such cases demonstrate that the intensity of the aggressive component in the oral phase is influenced by the mother's attitude. It is true that in the nursing situation the infant "eats" the mother. The memory traces of this experience lead to what Bertram Lewin (1950) so beautifully described as the oral triad, namely, satiation at the breast; eat or being eaten; and sleep.

But this is a happy situation which does not automatically become aggressive. Abraham feels that when the infant enters the second oral phase, passing from sucking to biting, this activity has the aggressive intent of hurting the mother. However, it is highly questionable whether one can interpret the biting of a teething infant as directed against an object, since we do not know how much awareness of an object one can assume at such an early phase.

Similarly, a fantasy of incorporation is not necessarily aimed at the destruction of an object, but rather can mean a safekeeping of that object. The expression "I love you so much I could eat you up" illustrates the libidinal function of eating as well as the aggressive one. The phenomenon of introjection emphasizes that the model in the unconscious for introjection or incorporation is the cannibalistic act. It took courage to suggest that even in the unconscious mind of the most "civilized" person, a cannibal can be hidden.

What is the meaning of the introjective mechanism in the depressive patient? Freud's answer was that because of a disappointment in love the object is given up but incorporated into the ego, and thus becomes the heir to both love and hatred. Abraham, on the other hand, interpreted the reaction of the melancholic patient to a severe disappointment as a *violent* act, aimed at destroying the object. This interpretation leaves the question of the meaning of the introjection open, if one assumes, as Abraham does, that the object is destroyed. Probably the answer is that introjection is a restitutive process — an attempt to reintroject the object. If one takes the regression literally and assumes that in the regressive process the early infantile oral-cannibalistic impulses are reactivated, one must remember that these impulses of diffuse discharge phenomena are caused by frustration, and become object-directed only later when an object is more clearly perceived.

We must keep in mind that it is not without reason that introjection is considered a defense mechanism, but against what does introjection defend? Clearly, against the impulse to destroy the object. Shifting the object from the outside to the inside deflects the aggressive impulse and at the same time saves the object.

Aside from his contribution to the theory of depression, Abraham made excellent clinical observations about depressed patients, such as noting that beneath the surface of the apparent humility in melancholic patients, there is certain demanding attitude, a claim for self-importance, even some aspect of grandiosity. Another insight was the finding that in the depressive male patient castration anxiety is predominantly connected with the mother. This is because the rage against the frustrating mother and the oral-sadistic impulses against the breast bring about projective expectations — fear of retaliation by the mother.

Abraham remarks that in no other neurosis beside depressive illness does the compulsive tendency to repeat an experience operate so strongly. I myself observed a recurring fantasy in a depressive patient in which he saw himself rejected by a powerful cold woman (unknown to him) who dismissed him as a worthless person. The fantasy brought tears to his eyes. He experienced a tremendous longing for the woman's love. As a matter of fact, this was what love meant to him: the masochistic fixation upon the rejecting woman. This observation validates Freud's comment that while the depressive patient loses the object, the love — in the form of longing — remains.

The advent of ego psychology, the discovery of the superego

and its pathology, the consideration of early object relations, the differentiation between self and object representation — all these revelations provided new conceptual tools with which to analyze the data of clinical observation. Edith Jacobson was a master in the usage of these tools.

One excellent example of her ability can be found in the chapter on recurring depressive states (1971). In a fascinating case study, she illustrates the genesis of a depression caused by experiences of disillusionment and abandonment at an early infantile stage. We understand that the effect of early frustrations and disappointments is so devastating only if a person tends to respond to them with uncommonly intense hostility. In this case, the primal childhood depression was precipitated by specific traumatic events, which were followed by severe disappointment in both parents at the beginning of the oedipal period. Edith Jacobson demonstrates that such general disillusionment in a phase when the boundaries between object and self images are not yet firmly established and when the infantile love relationships still have preoedipal narcissistic characteristics may lead to severe pathology in the development of both object relations and narcissism.

What is new here is a deeper understanding of the self-esteem regulation. We always knew that a characteristic phenomenon of depression is the collapse of self-esteem, but Edith Jacobson helped us understand the etiology of this collapse. A healthy self-esteem in the child presupposes a feeling of acceptance and love from the parents, and a mutual love and respect for them. If the parents encourage the child's autonomy, he will learn to derive satisfaction and a positive self-esteem from his own independent activities.

Jacobson's patient did not develop a mature level of self-esteem. Her love objects represented idealized parental images with which she identified through participation in their superiority. Only through their love and recognition of her could she maintain her self-esteem. Since her self-esteem depended totally upon the high value of her love objects, disappointment caused not only their devaluation but simultaneously a devaluation of her own self-esteem.

In the analysis of narcissistic personalities, I have repeatedly observed that while on the one hand they wish the analyst to be a powerful, even omnipotent figure in order to participate in his power, on the other they are also too ready, because of their ambivalence, to discover his real or imagined weaknesses, and then tear him down.

Jacobson's patient overvalued and idealized the love objects. The wishful self images and the ego ideal were too high to be reached. Because such a narcissistic coloring of the personality does not change fundamentally, the depression is repeated whenever a new disappointment destroys a new relationship and causes a denigration of the love object in which the self image participates.

In this case study, Jacobson made another equally important contribution. She showed that a better analysis of the intricacies of the introjective process allows a clearer understanding of the self-reproaches of the depressive patient. Rado (1928) had been the first to point to the double introjective process in melancholia: "The 'good object', whose love the ego desires, is introjected and incorporated in the super-ego. There...it is endowed with the prescriptive right... to be angry with the ego—indeed, very angry" (pp. 434–435). Jacobson modifies Rado's statement by making the important distinction between the introjection of the deflated, bad, worthless parents into the self image and of the inflated, good, punishing ones into the superego. The child can still hope to gain love, praise, security from the punitive godlike parents, but he can no longer expect anything from the devalued parents.

I can confirm this important finding from my own clinical experience. As long as the analyst is perceived in the transference as the powerful parental figure, he may be accused of withholding love, and the patient will react to such a transference disappointment with rage; but when the analyst is devalued and thus powerless, the reaction of the patient is a feeling of utter hopelessness.

Reading this case history of Jacobson's in which at times during the treatment the patient's productions and behavior appear clearly psychotic, one cannot help but admire Jacobson's courage, determination, and conviction that she could help this patient. I believe that the ultimate success of the therapy was as much dependent upon this quality of Jacobson's personality as it was upon her profound understanding of the pathological process.

While Freud and Abraham interpreted melancholia as resulting from object loss and the introjection of the love object into the ego, Jacobson presents a somewhat different view. Her concept is that in the depressive state a constant fluctuation takes place between libidinal and aggressive cathexes of the object. The depressive patient retains the infantile conception of a helpless self, drawing its strength from a powerful ideal love object. Because the melancholic patient is so dependent on a strong love object, he must build up the love object by a continuous illusory overestimation and an equally illusory under- or overestimation of himself. If the denial mechanism breaks down, either because of a disappointment in the love object or because the patient meets with a failure, two things can happen: (1) the patient may go into a manic state; or (2) in order to repair the narcissistic injury and build up self-esteem, the patient will disparage the love object. Now the whole aggressive cathexis will be shifted to the object image and the libidinal cathexis to the self image.

Jacobson makes an interesting observation, a kind of postscript to the well-known phenomenon of individuals wrecked by success. She states that manic-depressives may react to success in love and work in the same way as to failure, that is, with a manic state or a depression. The type of reaction depends upon what success means to them — either an aggressive self-assertion by derogation and destruction of the love object or a present from the powerful love object. The inability of manic-depressive patients to accept success is not always or not only an expression of their moral masochism and guilt conflict.

Jacobson believes that the manic-depressive patient is desperately afraid of a lasting self-inflation. Such a self-inflation might lead to the loss of the love object because the libidinal cathexis is withdrawn from the love object and the hostility is unleashed against it. I can understand this statement only if I assume that the relationship to the love object was very ambivalent to begin with, that the love object was also a hate object, and that the self-inflation was a hostile act of competition with the love object. There is obviously a difference between a healthy self-esteem, which can be maintained without killing a competitor, and one where the self-image is weak and dependent upon the magical participation in a powerful individual. .

Jacobson follows the step-by-step sequence of this ambivalent struggle with the love-hate object. This struggle reaches its tragic climax when the patient is so depleted in libido that he cannot recathect the object sufficiently. It is my experience that such a depletion of libido occurs when sexual conflicts and inhibitions are especially strong. Of course, one might respond that in a severe depressive mood no one is very interested in sex. That is obviously true, but the fact remains that sexual conflicts and inhibitions antedate the depressive state and undoubtedly contribute heavily to the difficulty in achieving libidinal cathexis of the object. It is equally true, however, that the presence of sexual conflicts does not explain why in the depressive state a merging between the devalued object and the devalued self takes place.

Jacobson's rich and extensive experience with depressive patients allowed her to formulate a clear idea of the expected transference reactions of these patients during analysis. She describes these reactions in sequence: "the initial, spurious transference success; the ensuing period of hidden, negative transference with corresponding negative therapeutic reactions, i.e., waxing and more severe states of depression; the stage of dangerous, introjective defenses and narcissistic retreat; and the end phase of gradual, constructive conflict solution" (1971, p. 287).

The knowledge of this probable progression in the transference reaction could be especially helpful for younger, less experienced colleagues who, when enjoying the flowering of the positive transference, ought also to be aware of what is in store for them.

The new theory of depression which Jacobson developed is based on a different type of patient than that previously described by psychoanalysts. The so-called borderline cases or narcissistic personalities present a somewhat different pathology than the classic neurotic type in which the ego is less disturbed. Jacobson postulates that these patients seek solutions to their emotional and instinctual conflicts in a regressive escape which involves not only instinctual regression, but a severe regressive process in the whole personality organization due to constitutional and environmental factors, such as early emotional deprivation and instinctual overstimulation or frustration. These patients are evidently predisposed to such a profound regressive process by an arrested, defective ego and superego development.

The main operational concept of classical psychoanalytic theory and practice is the concept of conflict — conflict between the instinctual drives and the opposing forces of ego and superego. At present, another cause of pathogenesis is increasingly being emphasized, namely, developmental defect. Developmental defect means that because of reasons which we do not yet fully understand, a normal ego and superego development in the child is not reached. A defect remains which may be covered up, becoming visible only under stresses of later life. The relation between the original defect and the later illness is the same as between infantile and adult neurosis. The infantile neurosis can remain latent and become acute when stresses or critical life situations, such as adolescence or marriage, reactivate it. With this new concept of developmental defect a change in the chronology of the genesis of mental illness became apparent. The modern theory claims that the more severe the pathology, the earlier is its origin in development.

Such a shift in chronology necessitates a better understanding of the early stages of the development of the mind, as well as the forging of new conceptual tools to describe these findings. That is just what Edith Jacobson did in her book *The Self and Object World* (1964). In order to understand her theory of depression, one must study this book. In it, she develops her views about the fate of the child's relationship to the primary love object and examines the earliest stages of mental development.

Finally, I would like to say a few words about those aspects of Edith Jacobson's personality which were responsible for her success with depressive patients. It was her warmth, her patience, her empathy, which enabled her to follow the inner drama of her patients with infinite understanding. But she had another quality which was so helpful in this demanding work. Dealing with severely depressive patients, listening to their unending complaints and despair, being the target of their hostility without becoming bored or even desperate oneself, we know demands supreme inner resources of optimism and cheerfulness — qualities which she had in abundance.

During my very long friendship with Edith Jacobson, I often had the opportunity to admire her courage. In fact, she was one of the most courageous people I ever met, and the following story will prove my point.

In 1976 the *Psychoanalytic Quarterly* published an English translation of one of her early papers entitled "Ways of Female Superego Formation and the Female Castration Conflict" (1937). Although it is 40 years old, it is an extremely topical paper. She discusses Freud's theory which states that women do not develop a strict superego.

Why then, Jacobson asks, do women so frequently fall victim to melancholic illness, in which one can observe the attacks of a mercilessly cruel superego? And she adds that the formation of the female superego is much more complex than hitherto assumed.

This beautiful paper is specifically about women and is very modern in tone, as the following fragments from it illustrate:

...We can observe in the course of the last decades a change in the psychic structure in women at all social levels. This finds expression in their love life as well as in the organization of their egos and superegos... there is very clearly a trend toward an expansion of the formerly rather limited female love life and the onset of the growth of the ego that is richer in sublimations of a more independent and more stable...superego....In any case, the liberation of women from old ties must result in a characteristic new form of feminine nature, which we cannot simply conceive of in terms of a 'masculinization' of females....However, we question how far feminine progress actually aims at a phallic development. I should regard such an interpretation as faulty, at least in many cases [p. 526].

The Women's Liberation Movement should be extremely grateful to Edith Jacobson for this revolutionary paper, and the following revelation makes this work even more of an amazing accomplishment. This paper was written in jail when Edith Jacobson was imprisoned by the Nazis. To write a work which is so full of vitality and optimism, without knowing what might await her—that indeed requires incredible courage.

References

Abraham, K. (1924), A short study of the development of the libido. In: *Selected Papers on Psycho-Analysis*. London: Hogarth Press, 1927, pp. 418–501.

Freud, S. (1917), Mourning and melancholia. *Standard Edition*, 14:237–260. London: Hogarth Press, 1957.

Gero, G. (1936), The construction of depression. *Int. J. Psycho-Anal.*, 17:423–461.

―――― (1953), An equivalent of depression: anorexia. In: *Affective Disorders*, ed. P. Greenacre. New York: International Universities Press, pp. 117–139.

Jacobson, E. (1937), Ways of female superego formation and the female castration complex. *Psychoanal. Quart.*, 45:525–538, 1976.

―――― (1964), *The Self and the Object World*. New York: International Universities Press.

―――― (1971), *Depression*. New York: International Universities Press.

Lewin, B. D. (1950), *The Psychoanalysis of Elation*. New York: Norton.

Rado, S. (1928), The problem of melancholia. *Int. J. Psycho-Anal.*, 9:420–438.

4

THE SIGNIFICANCE OF EDITH JACOBSON'S
SELF AND OBJECT WORLD
IN CONTEMPORARY
OBJECT RELATIONS THEORY

SAUL TUTTMAN, M.D., PH.D.

In the 1950s, Edith Jacobson became increasingly concerned with problems of self-awareness and disturbances in the feeling of identity. She concluded:

> The rising interest in the problem of identity is probably caused by the widening scope of psychoanalysis and the growing number of borderline or even psychotic patients who call on the psychoanalyst for help. In such patients, we can observe processes of regression that lead to a grave deterioration of object relations and of superego and ego functions, with dissolution of those essential identifications on which the experience of our personal identity is founded [1964, p. xii].

The purpose of this paper is to summarize, in developmental sequence, Edith Jacobson's integrative concepts of the emergence of the sense of self and of the "object"[1] world and her application of this framework in an effort to comprehend psychopathology. Hers was the first attempt to trace, within a strictly psychoanalytic framework, the development of the self—a term introduced into psychoanalysis by Hartmann (1950) to signify the whole person as a subject in contrast to the surrounding world of objects. In this attempt Jacobson used all of the metapsychological viewpoints, stressing the inter-

---

[1]The term "object" (to represent a person who is the object of one's drives and feelings with which it is cathected or invested) may be construed, although its use was not so intended, in terms of its unfortunate nonhuman connotations; nevertheless, this word so permeates the psychoanalytic literature that it would add confusion to change terminology at this time.

action of all the factors. Thus, one could say that she described the developmental line (A. Freud, 1965) of the self and its mental representations.

I shall present her views under the categories of drive-energic factors, structural concepts, and their reciprocal impact on the development of object relations. Jacobson assumed the burden of communicating complex, multifaceted interactions. To do so in a simple yet comprehensive manner was a most ambitious undertaking. This paper is offered in the hope that a "distillation" and summary will encourage students and a new generation of analysts to undertake the difficult but rewarding task of a thorough exploration of her original writings.

Drive-Energic Factors in Normal and Pathological Development

The most speculative and hypothetical areas of her project deal with the neonatal state. We have limited data regarding the phenomenology and psychophysiology of the earliest period of life, and available techniques for scientific study were even more limited when Jacobson approached the issues of the vicissitudes of psychic energy and drive during the phases of early infancy.

When she deals with later phases of development, however, we feel the depths of Jacobson's solid clinical practice and the empathic subtlety of her understanding. Both are brilliantly applied to produce a remarkable and unique blending of metapsychological theory and clinical judgment which enlighten our view of normative development and psychopathology.

Influenced especially by Freud, Hartmann, and Schur, Jacobson (1964) envisioned

> . . . an initial psychoeconomic state, characterized by a low level of tension and by a general, diffuse dispersion of as yet undifferentiated psychophysiological energy within the primal undifferentiated self. Under the influence . . . of intrinsic factors and of external stimuli, the undifferentiated forces would then begin to develop into the libidinal and aggressive psychic drives. . . . [During the earliest stages of the primal self] most of this undifferentiated energy . . . is diffusely discharged in small amounts on the inside, at first exclusively through physiological channels. But after birth the pregenital erogenous zones and, to an increasing degree, the whole sensory and motor systems, the "primary autonomous"

core of the future ego, become periodically hypercathected; processes of drive discharge toward the outside begin to develop, which become observable in pregenital (sexual and aggressive) activity and in biologically prepatterned, primitive affectomotor and instinctive reflex motor reactions, easily recognizable as the forerunners of feelings, thinking, and of motor and other ego functions. In the course of structural differentiation the libidinal and aggressive drives would undergo processes of fusion and partial neutralization. These neutralized drives, together with part of the libidinal and aggressive drives, would become vested in the new systems, the ego and the superego, and could be utilized for the building up of emotional and thought processes and the corresponding ego and superego functions [pp. 14–15].

Jacobson suggested that psychic life probably originates in physiological processes which are probably relatively independent of external sensory stimulation.

From birth on, however, the discharge processes expand with the opening up of biologically predetermined...pathways for discharge in response to external stimulation...and to pleasurable or unpleasurable sensory experiences....Evidently these phenomena are no more than genetic forerunners of the emotional and thought processes and of the complex functional activities whose development sets in with the beginning of ego formation....[During] the first infantile stages, the predominant expression of...emotional and fantasy life is still "psychophysiological," the so-called "affective organ language" which encompasses...not only the "silent" inner physiological processes...but also visible vasomotor and secretory phenomena and manifestations in the realm of oral and excretory functions....[This] affective organ language survives, to some extent, even in the emotional life of normal adults in anxiety states and in other manifestations of "resomatization" of affects (Schur, 1955) [p. 11].

In that manner, Jacobson correlated "the original psychoeconomic state and the earliest type of drive discharge within the self to the psychophysiological forerunners of adult affective and ideational expression" (p. 11). She concluded that such correlations are confirmed by observations of patients with psychosomatic disorders who show signs of severe narcissistic regression. In psychosomatic conditions, she proposed, in accord with Schur's formulation (1955), "a pathological partial retransformation of ideational and emotional into somatic, physiological expressions, which are then perceived only as painful body sensations" (p. 12).

"In psychoses, the depressed or catatonic stuporous states appear to be pathological versions of the infant's dozing states." Drive qualities of pathological, regressed conditions also differ from the original infantile state in that these disordered patients show evidence of destructive and self-destructive processes — both psychological and physiological, "of which we find no signs in the normal state of sleep and in the healthy, early infantile childhood state" (p. 12).

Considering energic regression, Jacobson pondered the possible relationship between the reversion of psychic energy following ECT treatment or psychosurgery, where there appears to be a complete absence of libidinal or aggressive drive manifestations. Similarly, could the concept of energic regression apply to aging and physical decline? "All such processes might involve a decrease in the cathexes of the periphery, of perceptive and motor functions, resulting in a rise of the cathexis of the body organs, with concomitant regressive drive defusion to the point of prevalence of destructive drive energy, which must again be discharged through physiological channels in the body" (p. 17).

Jacobson compared the psychosomatic state (i.e., a profound energic regression involving inner body organs) and the hysterical condition in which peripheral cathexes are sustained and reinforced by sensory and motor investments in the organs (at the site of the symptom) at which there is a "partial retransformation of normal affective, ideational, and functional motor discharge into primitive affectomotor and physiological discharge processes finding expression in the hysterical conversion" (p. 17).

Precursors of Self and Object Images

Jacobson described the beginnings of identification and object images, utilizing the then recent contributions made by Spitz, Schur, Greenacre, and Mahler. The precursors to infantile orality experiences involve the subtle interplay between mother and infant. Stressing in this context the importance of the *instinctual drives* (which are regulated by the pleasure principle), Jacobson distinguished between these drives and the *instinctive patterns* (innate, prepatterned affectomotor responses), which serve survival and "provide for the discharge of psychic ('instinctual') drive energy" (p. 34).

Jacobson emphasized that oral eroticism is not limited to the feeding situation but extends to skin and mucous membranes, acoustic and visual, propioceptive and kinesthetic sensations.

> . . . we do not know precisely at which time the psychic apparatus becomes capable of retaining memory traces of pleasure-unpleasure experiences; but there is no doubt that long before the infant becomes aware of the mother as a person and of his own self, engrams are laid down of experiences which reflect his responses to maternal care in the realm of his entire mental and body self.
>
> . . . [Probably] the child's and his mother's drive-discharge patterns in general become tuned in to each other during the infant's first months of life. . . . For this reason, disturbances of the psychophysiological equilibrium, resulting in anxiety, may be caused by separation of the infant not only from the breast but from the "whole mother," before the child can discriminate her from other persons [pp. 34–35].

Jacobson concluded that the combined oral-visual experience of the breast-primal cavity (Spitz, 1955) makes up the first image of the gratifying mother, a primitive image around which memory traces left by subsequent libidinal arousal and pleasure will cluster. In like fashion, the buildup of self images of the gratified (or deprived) self will also tend to absorb engrams of all kinds of stimuli and satisfactions (or deprivations).

Jacobson offered a concrete summary of her position that drive theory is most helpful in conceptualizing the mother's influence on the infantile development of the ego, the self and object images: "when a mother turns the infant on his belly, takes him out of his crib, diapers him, sits him up in her arms and on her lap, rocks him, strokes him, kisses him, feeds him, smiles at him, talks and sings to him, she offers him not only all kinds of libidinal gratifications but simultaneously stimulates and prepares the child's sitting, standing, crawling, walking, talking, and so on, i.e., the development of functional ego activity" (p. 37).

Jacobson describes a series of processes and stages in answer to the question: how does development progress from (1) the primitive, infantile, amorphous matrix in which self and object are fused to (2) the transitonal, reversibly fluid boundary state of beginning ego and superego identifications of the self as distinct from others, and to (3) the emergence of a coherent, ongoing sense of self delineated and apart from an awareness of others?

In early life, there seems to be very little discrimination between

the infant's pleasurable sensations and the objects from which they
are derived. Thus in the first place ego and superego identifications
require the gradual maturation of the perceptive function for discriminations. Second, unpleasurable experiences of frustration and
separation from the love object probably induce fantasies of reunion
(via incorporation) to reestablish the lost unit: "These earliest
wishful fantasies of merging... are certainly the foundation on
which all object relations as well as all future types of identification
are built" (p. 39).

"Thus, the hungry infant's longing for food, libidinal gratifications, and physical merging with the mother, which is the precursor
of future object relations, is also the origin of the first primitive type
of identification... achieved by refusion of self and object images.
This... will be accompanied by a temporary weakening of the perceptive functions and hence by a return... to an earlier, less differentiated state" (p. 40). This type of identification dominates the preoedipal and early oedipal mental life and, to some extent, persists
through life. The adult ego makes use of the intimacy of sexual experience and of introjective and projective mechanisms (involving
fusion of self and object images) in the development of subtle, empathic understanding of others, especially those we love. This applies to both temporary and more lasting identifications. However,
such temporary fusions in adult life (induced in the service of the
ego) do not normally weaken the boundaries between the images of
self and objects, whereas in the early infantile stage firm enough
boundaries have not yet been established.

Although the fluidity of self and object images may result in
regressive refusion and subsequent progressive delineations
throughout life, child analysts report conscious merging fantasies
with love objects up to the age of three in normal development; however, the continued dependency of the child on the mother—despite
full awareness of himself and love objects as individual entities— "is
still bound to prevent the complete separation of maternal and self
images" (p. 41).

Beyond this symbiotic fusion basis for identifications, a more
active process of primitive identification involves imitation. The
mother can "induce affects in the baby by way of her own affective
expression...[resulting in a] mutual 'tuning-in'" (p. 42).

"The child's expanding motor activities, his learning to walk and to talk and to behave like the parents, his cleanliness training, which is expressive of a beginning instinctual control — all these accomplishments certainly mark the progress of ego formation" (p. 43).

At first the imitations are "as if," empathic, magical fantasies indicative of a primitive merging and sensual fusion for the purposes of gratification. Wishful fantasies and insufficient capacity for reality perception facilitate the fluidity of boundaries and drastic cathectic shifts. These early identifications involve primitive introjective and projective mechanisms.

As the second year of life begins, there are signs of a gradual transition toward individuation and ego autonomy. Vital factors are (1) the concept of a future, a new time category; and (2) the developing ability (a) to distinguish and compare single features of differing objects and (b) to discriminate between features of objects and self. The aim of the narcissistic strivings change. Body growth and ego maturation support the child's effort for realistic achievements "which no longer revolve exclusively about wishes to control magically the love objects on which he depends" (p. 49). Furthermore, his efforts also seem to be more independent of the instinctual needs. The identifications are more selective and involve partial introjections. This new kind of identification represents a compromise between the symbiotic need and a developing tendency to loosen dependency by way of aggressive, narcissistic, independent expansive ego functioning.

The preoedipal child identifies "with the mother, both as the aggressor (A. Freud, 1936, 1949) and as the person who imposes instinctual restrictions (A. Freud, 1936)" (p. 50). This leads to a new process of identification which is characterized by realistic content and aims, in contrast to the earlier magical fantasies of fusion and imitation. The child begins to develop the qualities of the admired object. These characteristics, along with narcissistic, ambitious strivings, develop into wishful self images. Wishful self images plus emerging realistic self representations form a developing sense of identity. The wishful images provide direction for potential change in the future, while the self representations relate to the present. Well-defined self representations and true object relations protect the growing child from relapses into the world of magic fantasies of fusions and early identifications.

Jacobson stresses the crucial role of parental influence in stimulating the growth of the ego by supporting "control, partial inhibition, partial fusion, neutralization and utilization of sexual and aggressive drives.... [Parental influences] contribute greatly to the psychosexual development and the maturation of feelings, thinking, acting, and the sense of reality, and promote the establishment of aim-inhibited personal and social relations and of solid identifications with the love objects" (pp. 54–55). She stresses parental love (which promotes stable, enduring libidinal cathexes both of the objects and of the self) as the "best guarantee for the development of object and self constancy, of healthy social and love relations, and of lasting identifications, and hence for a normal ego and superego formation" (p. 55). She adds, however, the crucial role of parental demands along with instinctual and emotional frustrations and prohibitions in the development of an independent and self-reliant ego.

> They teach the child to relinquish not only his preoedipal and oedipal sexual drives but also his early infantile magic expectance of support, protection, and wish fulfillment from without. On his way to this goal, the child passes through experiences of continual deprivations, hurt, frustration, and disappointments in his parents, which arouse intense feelings of ambivalence [p. 55]. [These ambivalence conflicts can be utilized by the ego:] at first the child wants to take in what he likes and spit out what he dislikes; to ascribe to his self what is pleasant and to the "strange" outside object what is unpleasant. In other words, he tends to turn aggression toward the frustrating objects and libido toward the self. Hence frustrations, demands, and restrictions, within normal bounds, reinforce in principle the process of discovery and distinction of objects and self; they throw the child back upon his resources and stimulate progressive forms of identification with the parents, which open the road to realistic independent achievements....
>
> Yet overgratifications, no less than severe frustrations, tend to induce regressive fantasies of reunion between self and love object... [and] may therefore delay the child in establishing firm boundaries between the objects and the self, and hence may interfere with ego and superego formation and with normal...individuation [p. 56].

In surveying parental attitudes, Jacobson refers to the work of Benedek (1959) and Greenacre (1958) who described the symbiotic pull between parents and children in their mutual interactions and their possible consequences. Jacobson states in a telling sentence:

"Even in the earliest symbiotic stage of the mother-infant relationship, the best emotional climate is indeed one in which the mother prepares the process of the child's individuation by a kind of maternal love that is aware of the differences between her own and the child's needs and roles, and tries to gratify both" (p. 57).

The parents' fantasies of merging with the child—to keep him passive and dependent or to extend themselves—ignore the child's individual needs and may increase the potential danger to preoedipal ego and superego precursors by further blurring the indistinct demarcation between maternal and self images in the child. Other factors contribute to parental attitudes which may fixate developing object relations at a primitive narcissistic level, e.g., masochistic, self-abnegating, overgratifying, overprotective parental attitudes or hostile, neglectful parental approaches. Aside from these influences, constitutional deficiency, weakness or retarded maturation of the child's infantile ego may compel the child to lean heavily on the mother, and such factors may impede development.

Generally, Jacobson suggests that around two years of age, "the child's ego maturation, his ability to walk and to talk, the everwidening scope of his perceptive and locomotor functions, his increasing manual accomplishments, his weaning and cleanliness training, etc., have advanced enough to bring about the startling discovery of his own identity, the experience of 'I am I'" (p. 59).

Of course, this is not the completion of a stable self concept but represents an important peak in the ongoing process of self delineation and awakening of identity. Jacobson proposes that the distinction between objects probably proceeds more rapidly than the distinction between self and objects since perception of the external world is easier than self perception; furthermore, the child normally has less instinctual motivation for the fusion of different objects than for his own remerging with mother. Feelings of rivalry and competition may be the strongest incentives for learning to distinguish his own needs, gratifications, frustrations, and possessions from those of other persons. Feelings of envy, acquisitiveness, and possessiveness lead to many frustrations and disappointments. Eventually, the child learns to differentiate wishful from realistic self and object images. Jacobson summarizes this aspect of the saga:

So far I have described how the child's finding of his identity, although dependent on the maturational growth of his ego, gains tremendous sup-

port from his beginning emotional relations to his first love objects and
especially from his preoedipal envy and rivalry conflicts. . . . [The] discovery of his identity, which is so greatly promoted by aggressive forces,
is a prerequisite for his gradual transition from the stage of primitive fusions and identifications with his love objects to the level of true object
relations and of only partial and selective identification with them. . . .
[She adds the important point that emotional investments in other persons as objects who are different from himself can be established only
after he has experienced his own identity;] and since active strivings to
acquire likenesses to others are also motivated by the discovery of differences from them, these strivings cannot develop either until the child has
become aware of such differences [pp. 62–63].

Enduring selective identification processes set in only when
vacillations between self- and object-directed cathexes have subsided
to the point of permitting relatively lasting emotional investments in
self and objects.

These processes call on the libidinal resources of the child, which are the
indispensable ferment needed to forge "total" concepts from the opposing
images of good and bad love objects and of a good and bad self.
   . . . Facilitating the gradual fusion of good and bad maternal images
into a unified "good" but also sometimes "bad" mother, these shifts certainly assist the development of tension tolerance and of those feelings of
pleasurable anticipation which introduce the category of time and secure
the establishment of lasting emotional relations with the mother, i.e., of
object constancy [p. 63].

Following this important development, it becomes possible to
experience rival figures as more human and less naïvely polarized
(all "good" or "bad"). This is not "an easy achievement for the child"
(p. 64).

To recapitulate, two important psychological tasks are crucial
preliminaries for reality-oriented object relationships and identity
feelings:

   1. The boundaries between self and object must become firmly
established. Specifically, the core "mother-me" symbiotic matrix becomes the delineated mental representation of me and the specific
mental image "mother."

   2. Equally important, the naïve, primitive mental representations "all good mother," "all good me," "all bad mother," "all bad me"
must be modified so that these extreme and polarized psychic

images are replaced by the less polarized and more realistic "good and bad me" and "good and bad mother."

In Jacobson's view, the child's sense of identity may be promoted by the early mental differentiation from the hated rivals rather than by his closeness to mother. This delineation induces partial identifications with rivals rather than with the main love object. The libidinal wishes for union, closeness, and becoming like the mother remain important; nevertheless, the youngster's identification processes increasingly center about admired rival figures.

Jacobson proposes that "the child's object relations and identifications evolve hand in hand and exercise a mutually beneficial influence on each other. . . . Identifications seem actually to serve the absorption and neutralization of aggression, which can be vested increasingly in countercathectic formations and be discharged in ego functions" (p. 65). She considers identifications to be more successful if the child's object relations predominantly involve libidinal forces. These subsequently enable the ego to gain strength, better tolerate frustration, and build up sublimations. Enduring "selective identifications [for the boy] with the predominant rival, the father, cannot be established before the child's loving feelings toward him are sufficiently strengthened to permit relations with him, too, as with a total 'good and bad' person" (p. 66).

Blanck and Blanck (1974), Kernberg (1976), Masterson (1976), Volkan (1976), and I (Tuttman, 1979) have reiterated Jacobson's contention that the more the youngster comes to experience the full-range "totality" (good and bad) and the uniqueness of others and of the self, the easier can the realistic differences between self and others be distinguished and tolerated and *likenesses* be enjoyed.

Jacobson stresses that "the establishment of object and self constancy must be regarded as a very important prerequisite for both a healthy process of identification and normal superego formation" (p. 66). She concludes her summary of the discovery of one's identity by describing the role of love and the inherent ambivalence. Underlying the successfully emerging sense of self runs the theme:

"I don't need you; if you don't want to do it for me, I can do it myself; and if you don't want to give it to me, I can give it to myself." While identifications display the child's touching dependency on his parents, they bring him closer step by step to the state of independence and to the time when the parents will become dispensable. Moreover, the selectivity of identifications increasingly expresses the child's rebellious struggle for the development and maintenance of his own independent identity, since it means: "In this respect I like you and want to be like you, but in other respects I don't like you and don't want to be like you; I want to be different, in fact, myself!" [p. 66].

By such examples, Jacobson vividly illustrates how the consolidation of self and object representations occurs as increased drive fusion and neutralization develop during ego formation. Only when identifications become selective, enduring, and consistent can they be integrated, become a part of the developing ego

> . . . permanently modify its structure, and support the organization and stabilization of the ego's defense system. This advances ego formation and. . . concomitantly the process of identity formation to the point where the child becomes aware of having a coherent self that has continuity and remains the same despite and in the midst of changes. . . . Only the identifications which originate in enduring emotional object investments, and which result in gradual, consistent structural changes showing a definite direction, can fortify the inner feeling of continuity of the self [p. 68].

In contrast with this healthy evolution of a stable self, a lack of balance between libido and aggression can be observed in the tragic early histories of those who become psychotic. Oversevere hostility conflicts in early life can lead to a collapse of object relations and the simultaneous breakdown of identifications. In such patients, Jacobson noted "fears of accepting and acquiring likenesses to others, in conjunction with an inability to perceive and tolerate differences from them, and to relate to them as separate and different individuals. Likeness and difference are equally frightening, because likeness threatens to destroy the self and difference the object" (p. 69).

The Sense of Sexual Identity

Greenacre (1958) describes how the sense of one's self finds reinforcement via the visual "taking in" of a similar person. During the early oedipal phases, there is an increasing awareness of one's own genitals and the sex organs of others. Such preoccupations lead to a sense of sexual identity, "a most significant component of personal identity" (Jacobson, 1964, p. 70). Greenacre (1958) also emphasized the comparative invisibility of the sexual organs—especially of the female genitals—in contrast to the facial features.

Jacobson stresses the inhibiting influence of castration anxiety and oedipal conflicts on the establishment of realistic genital images. Both sexes, she contends, conceive of the female genital as an undeveloped organ. "Moreover, the prohibition of manual genital play, i.e., of 'touching' is certainly responsible for the child's usual overcathexis of visual perception, particularly with regard to seeing the genitals of others as well as his own" (p. 71).

Jacobson describes the various disturbances that may result in relation to the sense of sexual identity in boys and girls. Her explanation goes far beyond issues about visual (voyeuristic, exhibitionistic) and tactile interests and restrictions, castration anxieties and social taboos, primal scene fantasies and adult emphases upon categorical stereotypic physical and mental "male" and "female" qualities. She adroitly pursues the observation that women with "phallic" attitudes or "maternal" men and even certain types of manifest homosexuals of either sex do not always develop conspicuous disturbances in their feelings of personal identity. "I found that their sexual and ego development had been determined mainly by identifications with a loving but dominant, active 'phallic' mother" (p. 72). Although identification with such a distorted maternal image had led to manifest homosexuality, "it had permitted their egos to develop sufficient stability, functional ability, and secondary autonomy to accept and eventually to integrate their sexual deviation well enough to build up a comparatively consistent and coherent concept of their self" (pp. 72–73). On the other hand, Jacobson notes that profound identity problems in latent or manifest homosexuals rest on severely masochistic identifications with mothers who presented themselves as victimized, suffering, and castrated. Yet, she concludes with an insight that carries her beyond the accepted views of her time:

> . . . identity formation and the feelings of personal identity are not quite as dependent upon the heterosexual position as one might imagine: they are largely influenced by the extent to which consistent and enduring identifications leading to secondary autonomy and independence of the ego can be established, even if they lead to sexual pathology [p. 73].

The preoedipal child vacillates between heterosexual and homosexual, active and passive—playfully assuming various roles in fantasy and alternative actions and attitudes. Merging fantasies and the plasticity of role playing and wish fulfillment are still operant. Learning about and accepting sexual differences stabilize growing identifications. Despite complex vicissitudes, the little girl gradually comes to accept the mother as her main model. The little boy ardently desires to become part of a male group, tending to deny his dependency on mother. "His growing self assertion as a superior male toward the other sex, combined with his heterosexual strivings, promotes phallic-masculine attitudes to the mother and other females. The recognition of anatomical likeness to his father, oedipal jealousy, competition, and concomitant admiration now definitely center his identification around the father. . . Toward the end of the oedipal phase, the influence of sexual prohibitions and castration fear reinforce affectionate attachments and drive neutralization in general." In the course of maturation, the images of the executive organs become increasingly cathected with "more or less neutralized libidinal and aggressive forces at the expense of the genital and the pregenital erogenous zones. Desexualized thought and feeling processes gradually win out over sexual fantasies and impulses" (pp. 75–76). As the autonomous ego functions mature, ego identifications, object relations, as well as self and object mental representations are built up.

The Development of the Superego

As the child develops ego interests,[2] he increasingly experiences more independent functioning and, in the process, turns aggressive forces increasingly away from love objects and toward the self.

Hurts and failures are inevitable in the course of beginning independent strivings and explorations. "What he once experienced as disappointments and frustrations, hurts for which he blamed the parents alone, he now begins to regard partly as injuries that he has inflicted upon himself" (Jacobson, p. 78). The real hurt is accompanied by feelings of inferiority and self-criticism. Thus there is the onset of self-directed aggression and potential "secondary masochism."

[2]According to Kanzer (1962), these object-directed pursuits are in contrast to self-interests.

The internalized parental demands and criticisms, "beginning with the establishment of reaction formations and culminating in the constitution of the superego," add an aggressive as well as libidinal cathexis to the self representation. The child's competitive comparisons with his rivals promote

> ...his testing of external objects and of his own self, and hence teaches him to distinguish the omnipotent fantasies about his love objects and himself from the real objects and his real (potential and actual) self.... [The] normal pursuit of ego interests presupposes sufficient awareness of the differences between grandiose narcissistic strivings and corresponding wishful self images on the one hand, and realistic ego goals based upon sound notions of the own self's potentials..., on the other. ...The capacity for such a distinction develops under the influence of both failures and successes, of narcissistic hurt and expression, of criticism and self criticism as well as of encouragement, approval and self approval, that is to say, of both libido and aggression [pp. 79–80].

Jacobson's formulations about the superego have paved the way for a deeper understanding of self-esteem regulation, socialization processes, the evolution of civilized ethical standards, and related pathological states.

It all "begins with the acceptance of 'sphincter morality'" (p. 119) and, during the oedipal period, centers about castration anxiety, incest taboo, the law against patricide and the need for love and approval.

Under the influence of oedipal restraints, psychic energy can be liberated for aim-inhibited interests, physical and cultural activities, and intellectual concerns.

Special identifications which go back to infantile processes are crucial to the establishment of superego components: "not all infantile identifications arise under the influence of the child's sexual and ambivalence conflicts; ...we can also observe identifications which, developing directly from the child's close intimacy with his love object, remain centered about it and hardly acquire any reactive and defensive qualities" (p. 90).

A different variety of identifications results from the child's competitive and narcissistic expansive urges. Wishful fantasies of becoming like the aggrandized images of love objects and rivals lead to increasingly aggressive identification fantasies. Prohibitions and fears limit the expression of these fantasies.

Neutralizing and displacing the child's forbidden sexual, aggressive, and narcissistic strivings to acceptable aims and objects, they [the instinctual identifications with parental love objects] acquire entirely new, in part reactive and defensive, qualities, and bring about remarkable modifications of the psychic structures...[thereby serving the] building up of superego and ego and of aim-inhibited pursuits [p. 91].

...closely interrelated with the identifications,...we observe processes of a different nature which, serving primarily the solution of the child's instinctual conflicts, transform the primitive, wishful images of the self and the love objects into a unified ego ideal and, by internalization of the parental moral prohibitions and demands, establish, to use Hartmann's and Loewenstein's [1962] terms, the "direction-giving," the "enforcing," and the "self-critical" superego functions [p. 93].

[Jacobson adds,] it is my impression that the direction-giving functions work with a higher degree of more or less neutralized libido than the "enforcing" functions which, as this very term indicates, seem to operate with a greater amount of aggression....The qualities of the different superego functions depend not only on the degree of neutralization but even more on the proportions between libido and aggression [p. 94].

She proposes that the preponderance of libidinal over aggressive forces is crucial for the ego's capacity for neutralization, which in turn is vital for the establishment of nonsadistic, adaptive superego functioning. To Jacobson, the superego is a unique human acquisition since it is "the one area in the psychic organization where, by virtue of a reactive reversal of aims, the child's grandiose wishful fantasies can find a safe refuge and be maintained forever to the profit of the ego" (p. 94).

The infantile, magic, wishful self and object images begin to form the primitive kernel of an ego ideal even before the resolution of the symbiotic phase. At this early stage, love and identification can scarcely be differentiated; since the primitive object relations entail the operation of continuous introjective and projective mechanisms, these processes are first intermingled." Jacobson regards "the first pregenital reaction formations, which already begin to constitute internalized parental demands and prohibitions, as forerunners of the superego" (p. 95).

...the most drastic changes in the cathexis of the self and object representations are brought about, first, by the curbing of pregenital and sadistic strivings, then by the castration threat, and finally by superego formation.

...Conflict-born and founded on countercathectic processes, the anal reaction formations for the first time turn the child's aggression drastically from his love objects to his self. Contrary to the processes of sublimation..., reaction formations as such do not displace libido or aggression from forbidden onto aim-inhibited interests...they represent essentially changes in the child's attitudes toward his own instinctual strivings and in general toward himself, and consequently also toward the object world [pp. 96–97].

Jacobson describes the development of attitudes—defined as "characteristic features...manifest...in all mental areas: in a person's ideals and ideas, his feelings, and his behavior" (p. 97)—by detailing reaction formation as it applies to bowel control and other early life concerns.

Unique in psychoanalytic writings is her style which combines a "commonsense" reality interwoven with vivid descriptions of intrapsychic and interpersonal processes. She combines great clinical sensitivity to unconscious dynamics and a lucid description of metapsychological theory.

In but a few pages, the reader finds himself better able to understand the implications for child care. She makes clear the effects of parents who are not consistent and strong enough or not loving and empathic. She spells out the consequences when the child's disillusionment does not occur at an appropriate phase-specific point in development. She clarifies distinctions between empathy, helpful feelings, pseudoconcern, and neurotic pity.

"Centered about the incest taboo and the law against patricide, they [moral codes] begin at this stage [the end of the oedipal phase] to become independent of the parents and to displace the conflicts between parents and child onto the inner, mental stage. Then only can we observe a gradual depersonification and abstraction of the ego ideal, combined with the development of consistently demanding, directive, prohibitive, and self-critical superego functions" (p. 119). A self-critical and enforcing regulatory psychic institution capable of maintaining a personal moral code has evolved!

Exploring the important distinctions between castration fears and guilt feelings, Jacobson states:

...castration fears, though signaling external danger, are not primarily induced by threats from without. They originate in the child's own sadistic wishes which are attributed to the parental images and then ascribed to — and possibly confirmed by — the real objects.

Thus, inasmuch as castration fears are magic retaliation fears of threatening parental images, they arise, likewise, from endopsychic tensions. The difference [between castration fears and guilt feelings] is that castration fear develops within the ego as a result of conflicts between ego and id, whereas superego fear is expressive of conflicts between the superego and ego [p. 121].

This new institution, the superego, utilizes guilt feelings as a signal (far less ferocious usually than the primitive, instinctual, precursor underlying imagery). These toned-down guilt feelings of the superego take over the "signal function of the castration fear, yet combine it effectively with such guiding and self-critical functions which are a safeguard against castration, since they offer definite directions as to how to prevent punishments" (p. 122).

Jacobson does not consider the delineation of the superego as a specific psychic agency arbitrary. "Freud's final systemic distinctions are based on significant inner experiences. It is not accidental that in times of conflict we may hear the voice of temptation, the id; the voice of reason, the ego; and the voice of conscience, the superego" (p. 123).

Ego and superego develop hand in hand, one agency's maturation facilitating growth in the other: "the rapid advance of ego development, with structural ego modifications and changes in the nature of object relations and identifications accomplished by the oedipal defense struggle" (p. 125), permits superego maturation. Self and object constancy and general drive neutralization are particularly important in enhancing an effective functional superego, which in turn will achieve mastery over "the incestuous problem and further promote the process of ego maturation, the growth and organization of personal relations and identifications, and the establishment of a solid defense system" (p. 126).

Superego formation "appears to presuppose an advance of the ego from the stage of concretistic object and self imagery to that of a more conceptual, abstract, and discriminating understanding of the parental personalities. . . . Only at this stage can selected ideal, directive, prohibitive, disapproving, and approving parental traits and attitudes and parental teachings become constructively correlated and gradually blended into a consistent, organized set of notions" (p. 126). Selective internalizations of conceptualized standards and partial identifications then become coordinated.

Jacobson does not believe that the superego is experienced only during conflict. Although one's "conscience" may be silent, it provides a pleasurable feeling to have a good conscience. "Harmony between ego and ego ideal can produce a very enjoyable elated affective state" (p. 128).

Jacobson credits the mature autonomous superego with many functions: (1) signaling fears; (2) expressing self-critical and self-rewarding affects; (3) guiding and enforcing principles and demands; (4) motivating via guilt feelings; (5) modifying the ego's cathectic conditions and discharge processes; (6) influencing self-esteem stabilization by regulating narcissistic and object cathexes; (7) governing factors on behalf of mood regulation.

> [The interaction of superego and ego functions accomplishes] a partial victory of the reality principle, not only over the pleasure principle, but also over exaggerated "idealism" and thus over the superego. Only then do the superego functions work with more neutralized energy. In fact, the final maturation of both the ego and the superego sets in only after the tempest of instinctual conflicts during adolescence has subsided. Then we observe a gradual moderation of youthful idealism and illusions,... more reasonable goals and... the ability to... evaluate the outside and inside reality correctly, reasonably, and with greater moral tolerance, and to act according to such judgment.
>
> Thus, whereas self perception always represents an ego function, the self evaluation of an adult person is not exclusively a superego function [p. 130].

Her concluding remarks about superego formation relate to the beginning of latency, which signifies "the termination of the period of infantile repression, with consolidation and integration of all preoedipal and oedipal countercathectic formations into an organized unit. This result demonstrates, indeed, the remarkable influence which the processes of identification in the superego and ego exercise on the development of a coherent, consistent defense organization. But during this phase, the representation of the self and object world also gain definite, lasting configurations" (p. 135).

Summary and Conclusion

Although Jacobson's work regarding the psychological establishment of the self and the object world goes beyond the periods of life explored thus far (including a discussion on latency and adolescent development), this summary will not include those important phases since the essential concepts and principles are contained in her focus on crucial earlier stages.

It is my belief that Edith Jacobson's contribution is the most encompassing and integrative work dealing with human development within the context of modern ego psychology—utilizing the formulations of Freud, A. Freud, Hartmann, and Schur; and selectively applying some of Erikson's ideas. In addition, the observational studies and concepts of Spitz and Mahler play an important role. Jacobson's efforts offer the only major over-all theoretical approach which considers both the topographic and structural framework, including physiological and social variables along with object relations theory constructs. Here we have a unique blending of intrapsychic and interpersonal forces which provide a rich metapsychological matrix. Her model helps us comprehend psychopathology. And from her work we can derive guidelines which have applications to child care, education, and therapeutic endeavors.

Jacobson remained loyal and yet critical regarding Freud's pioneering work. She was quick to scrutinize and yet maintained respect for the traditional, continually seeking the implications and ramifications of every theoretical construct. Despite her predilection for concept, she never strayed far from the clinical base. Despite the intricacies and complexities of her writings, there remains a vivid everyday reality and practical, human perspective.

In my opinion, it may have been unfortunate that she was not more responsive to the work of Melanie Klein and some of Paul Federn's ideas. Searles (1965) may be correct in hypothesizing that her interest in "individuation" was at the price of more emphasis on the symbiotic phase and holistic concerns. Nevertheless, I am confident of one thing: whatever the future offers in the way of insight regarding psychoanalytic matters, Edith Jacobson's work will continue to have a far-reaching impact. Few others in the history of psychoanalysis have made such significant contributions.

References

Benedek, T. (1959), Parenthood as a developmental phase. *J. Amer. Psychoanal. Assn.*, 7:389–415.

Blanck, G. & Blanck, R. (1974), *Ego Psychology.* New York: Columbia University Press.

Federn, P. (1952), *Ego Psychology and the Psychoses.* New York: Basic Books.

Freud, A. (1965), *Normality and Pathology in Childhood.* New York: International Universities Press.

Freud, S. (1914), On narcissism: an introduction. *Standard Edition,* 14:67–102. London: Hogarth Press, 1957.

——— (1917), Mourning and melancholia. *Standard Edition,* 14:237–260. London: Hogarth Press, 1957.

——— (1923), The ego and the id. *Standard Edition,* 19:3–66. London: Hogarth Press, 1961.

——— (1925), Negation. *Standard Edition,* 19:235–239. London: Hogarth Press, 1961.

——— (1926), Inhibitions, symptoms and anxiety. *Standard Edition,* 20:77–175. London: Hogarth Press, 1959.

——— (1940), An outline of psycho-analysis. *Standard Edition,* 23:141–207. London: Hogarth Press, 1964.

Greenacre, P. (1948), Anatomical structure and superego development. In: *Trauma, Growth, and Personality.* New York: Norton, 1952, pp. 149–164.

——— (1958), Early physical detrminants in the development of the sense of identity. *J. Amer. Psychoanal. Assn.,* 6:612–627.

Hartmann, H. (1939), *Ego Psychology and the Problem of Adaptation.* New York: International Universities Press, 1958.

——— (1950), Comments on the psychoanalytic theory of the ego. *The Psychoanalytic Study of the Child,* 5:74–96.

——— (1952), The mutual influences in the development of ego and id. *The Psychoanalytic Study of the Child,* 7:9–30.

——— (1960), *Psychoanalysis and Moral Values.* New York: International Universities Press.

——— Kris, E., & Loewenstein, R. M. (1946), Comments on the formation of psychic structure. *The Psychoanalytic Study of the Child,* 2:11–38.

——— (1949), Notes on the theory of aggression. *The Psychoanalytic Study of the Child,* 3/4:9–36.

——— & Loewenstein, R. M. (1962), Notes on the superego. *The Psychoanalytic Study of the Child,* 17:42–81.

Jacobson, E. (1953), The affects and their pleasure/unpleasure qualities in relation to the psychic discharge processes. In: *Affects, Drives, Behavior,* ed. R. M. Loewenstein. New York: International Universities Press, pp. 38–66.

——— (1954a), The self and the object world. *The Psychoanalytic Study of the Child,* 9:75–127.

——— (1954b), Contribution to the metapsychology of psychotic identification. *J. Amer. Psychoanal. Assn.,* 2:239–262.

——— (1964), *The Self and the Object World.* New York: International Universities Press.

Kanzer, M. (1962), Ego interest, egoism and narcissism. Abstr. in Panel: Narcissism, rep. J. H. Bing & R. O. Marburg. *J. Amer. Psychoanal. Assn.,* 10:593–605.

Kernberg, O. F. (1972), Early ego integration and object relations. *Ann. N. Y. Acad. Sci.,* 193:233–247.

——— (1975), *Borderline Conditions and Pathological Narcissism.* New York: Jason Aronson.

_____ (1976), *Object Relations Theory and Clinical Psychoanalysis.* New York: Jason Aronson.

Mahler, M. S. (1952), On child psychosis and schizophrenia: autistic and symbiotic infantile processes. *The Psychoanalytic Study of the Child,* 7:286–305.

_____ (1957), Problems of identity. Abstr. in Panel: Problems of identity, rep. D. L. Rubinfine, *J. Amer. Psychoanal. Assn.,* 6:131–142, 1958.

_____ (1958), Autism and symbiosis: two extreme disturbances of identity. *Int. J. Psycho-Anal.,* 39:77–83.

Masterson, J. (1976), *Psychotherapy of the Borderline Adult: A Developmental Approach.* New York: Brunner/Mazel.

Schur, M. (1953), The ego in anxiety. In: *Drives, Affects, Behavior,* ed. R. M. Loewenstein. New York: International Universities Press, pp. 67–103.

_____ (1955), Comments on the metapsychology of somatization. *The Psychoanalytic Study of the Child,* 10:119–164.

Searles, H. F. (1965), Review of Edith Jacobson's *The Self and the Object World. Int. J. Psycho-Anal.,* 46:529–532.

_____ (1979), *Countertransference and Related Subjects.* New York: International Universities Press, pp. 45–70.

Segal, H. (1964), *Introduction to the Work of Melanie Klein.* New York: Basic Books.

Spitz, R. A. (1955), The primal cavity: a contribution to the genesis of perception and its role for psychoanalytic theory. *The Psychoanalytic Study of the Child,* 10:215–240.

_____ (1953), Aggression: its role in the development of object relations. In: *Drives, Affects, Behavior,* ed. R. M. Loewenstein. New York: International Universities Press, pp. 126–138.

_____ (1957), *No and Yes: On the Genesis of Human Communication.* New York: International Universities Press.

Tuttman, S. (1979), Regression: is it necessary or desirable? *J. Amer. Acad. Psychoanal.,* 7:11–133.

Volkan, V. (1976), *Primitive Internalized Object Relations.* New York: International Universities Press.

5

AN OVERVIEW OF
EDITH JACOBSON'S CONTRIBUTIONS

OTTO F. KERNBERG, M.D.

The purpose of this paper is to provide an overall summary and critique of the work of Edith Jacobson. As far as I know, there are only two, and quite restricted overviews of her work available at this time, one dealing exclusively with her contributions to depression (Mendelson, 1974), and the other very brief and condensed (Blanck and Blanck, 1974). I believe that the most important contribution of Edith Jacobson to psychoanalysis is her development of a comprehensive, developmental, and psychostructural model that includes an integrated object relations theory, a sophisticated model that provides a clearly circumscribed, yet broad frame of reference for the psychoanalytic understanding of the entire spectrum of psychopathology and of normal development.

Starting out in 1937 with the exploration of superego formation in women, Jacobson then analyzed the relationship between depressive syndromes and ego and superego formation, and the relationship between normal and pathological affects on the one hand, and structural development on the other, throughout the years 1943 to 1954. In 1954, she arrived at an integrating frame for the development of self and object representations in her fundamental paper, "The Self and the Object World" (1954d). Throughout the following ten years, she systematically explored depressive syndromes in the light of the influences of normal and pathological object-relations-derived structures on the ego and the superego,

Expanded and modified version of a presentation at a scientific session in honor of Edith Jacobson of the New York Psychoanalytic Society and Institute, September 27, 1977. This paper also appeared in the *Journal of the American Psychoanalytic Association*, 27:793–819, 1979.

103

mapped out the vicissitudes of depressive affects and moods in this context, applied her model to the study of normal and abnormal adolescence, and clarified an entire constellation of early defense mechanisms intimately connected with the vicissitudes of self and object differentiation and predating the definite integration of the tripartite intrapsychic structures of ego, superego, and id (1956, 1957a, 1957b, 1959, 1961). In *The Self and the Object World* (1964) she summarizes her main propositions and discusses, carefully, point by point, her theoretical contributions, which have expanded the boundaries of metapsychology and clinical psychopathology. After further clarification of her evolving new concepts regarding psychosis (1966), and the treatment of psychotic disorders (1967), Jacobson updated all her work on depression in the light of her definite theoretical frame in the book on *Depression* (1971). In order to highlight her integrative conceptual framework, I shall first summarize some of the salient features of Jacobson's work and then evaluate her contributions.

Summary of Edith Jacobson's Work

I shall examine Jacobson's contributions under three headings: (1) affect theory; (2) depression; (3) object relations theory.

Affect Theory

Jacobson started out from the classical psychoanalytic debate whether affects represented fundamentally discharge processes — Freud's (1915) second theory of affects and Rapaport's (1953) firm conviction — or whether affect represented central, subjective states potentially including but not identical to discharge phenomena — Freud's (1894) first theory of affects and Brierley's (1937) assumption. In discussing Freud's, Brierley's, and Rapaport's classical contributions to this subject matter, Jacobson (1953a) concluded that affects had to be considered as discharge processes, but also as dispositions originating within each of the overall psychic structures. She thus combined Freud's second theory of affects with his third and last theory (Freud, 1926), considering at least some affects as dispositions originating within the ego and not only the id. However, Jacobson herself soon felt that this effort to preserve Freud's second and third theories led to unsatisfactory classifications of affect; while temporarily leaving aside the ultimate question of the relationship between instinctual drives and affects, she rapidly moved into the developmental study of affects and their clinical characteristics.

She first clarified that a theory of affects as discharge processes should not be confused with the conception of affects as processes of tension reduction (1953a). On the contrary, she suggested, there are pleasurable tensions as well as unpleasurable discharge phenomena, and the function of the pleasure-unpleasure principle is to produce an optimal oscillation between the polarities of tension and relief, thus contributing ultimately to the constancy principle by means of an ever-changing, dynamically maintained optimal tension. Within this conception, discharge processes encompass both mounting and falling tensions, and affects are conceived as both tension and discharge processes. The reality principle influences the pleasure-unpleasure axis with the ultimate objective of maintaining an optimal tension state in the face of external reality. However, Jacobson observed, certain pathological structures within the ego and the superego related to self and object representations might bring about such a severe distortion in this regulatory process, that—particularly in psychotic depression—the pleasure principle might have to be sacrificed entirely to adjust by means of a pathological "optimal" tension to a distorted intrapsychic reality. This observation contributed to drawing Jacobson's attention to the relationship between affect theory and self and object representations.

Another major observation by Jacobson was that even within a theoretical frame of affects considered as discharge processes, the discharge of affects, so prominent in the case of primitive affect states, becomes a much less conspicuous phenomenon in the case of complex, integrative, sophisticated affects which may combine aggressive and libidinal drive derivatives in various proportions and which are represented in the higher level affects or feelings. Feelings are more than discharge states; they represent overall drive investments in the self and in object representations as well as in external objects, an obvious enrichment of mental life rather than excessive or insufficient tension to be regulated. Thus, for example, self-esteem—a crucial and complex libidinal affect investment of the self—cannot be considered simply a drive-determined, affective discharge process.

The most definite finding that anchored her clinical theories of affect in the vicissitudes of self and object representations was the study of moods (1957b). Moods, she proposed, are diffuse, temporarily fixed affect states that involve the entire world of self and object representations and reflect a major impact of a sudden influx of libidinal or aggressive drive derivatives upon intrapsychic life in the form of generalized but regulated and regulating affect states. Moods are general affective colorings of the entire experience of the self and the world of objects, a potential protection from disorderly discharge processes, on the one hand, and a potential danger for severe, generalized distortion of all psychic experience, on the other. Jacobson described normal mood processes in the phenomenon of falling in love, in the diffuse elation after a person has overcome a danger or after the unexpected resolution of a tension state, and in the sadness and grief of normal mourning processes.

Jacobson differentiated normal moods from pathological ones, particularly those of neurotic and psychotic depression, by pointing to the predominance of aggressive drive derivatives in the case of pathological depression, and the effects of primitive, pathological, exaggerated superego control in the form of violent mood swings that replace the more focused, cognitively delimited, and circumscribed self-criticism emanating from more mature levels of superego functioning. In this process, she clarified the fundamental role of affect control vested in the superego.

In addition, she differentiated neurotic from psychotic depression (1953b; 1971, chap. 6), in that, in the latter, a pathological refusion of self and object representations takes place within the ego and within the superego, thus bringing about the classical attack of a highly pathological, idealized, yet sadistic superego onto a devalued and fused self-object representation in the ego. At all levels of depression, it turns out that, in addition to qualitative aspects of the affects involved (and the drive cathexes represented by such affective processes), the ultimate quality of the affect, its normality or pathology, and its impact on the entire psychic system depend on the structural arrangements of self and object representations within the ego and the superego. For example, sadness, a component of grief, reflects the mourning for a loved, realistically or neurotically lost object; in severe depression, the capacity for sadness is lost, because the pathological processes of devaluation of the object and its intrapsychic representation (that has been fused with a devalued self representation) interfere with the experience of normal longing for the loved and unavailable object. It is only when psychotic depressed patients begin to improve that some of them are again able not only to feel depressed but to feel sad.

In summary, Jacobson evolved a conceptualization of affective processes that explained their fundamental intrapsychic regulatory functions by means of their investment in self and object representations, and she clarified the mutual relationships between affective discharge and intrapsychic tension, on the one hand, and the vicissitudes of ego and superego structures, particularly their constituent self and object representations, on the other. She drew our attention to the intimate connections between affect differentiation, the vicissitudes of intrapsychic self and object representations, and of ego and superego differentiation (insofar as they integrate affects in the context of object relations).

On the basis of Jacobson's findings — but, I think, in contrast to her view — I now conceive of affects as deriving from constitutionally determined, pleasurable and unpleasurable subjective states that arise first in the undifferentiated psychophysiological self, are then integrated and differentiated in the context of internalized, good and bad object relations, and eventually are the most important contributors to the differentiation of instinctual drives into libido and aggression (Kernberg, 1976b, chap. 3).

A related conclusion, namely, that the psychic apparatus originates from an interactional field in which both instincts and the individual's psychic apparatus differentiate gradually within the dyadic matrix of early object relations, has been suggested by Loewald (1978).

Depression

Jacobson's analysis of depression starts out with a critical assessment of Bibring's formulations. She agrees with Bibring's (1953) statement that depression originates as an intrasystemic affect state of the ego, a state that reflects the discrepancy between a real and a wished-for or ideal self image: in other words, an affect state indicative of narcissistic frustration. However, on the basis of her own observations of depressed adolescent and adult patients, and of the study of normal and pathological affects and moods during the subphases of individuation-separation described by Mahler (1952, 1968), Jacobson (1953b, 1961, 1971) concludes that the origin of depression within the ego does not preclude conflicts prior to such narcissistic frustration and deflation of self-esteem. She stresses the normal reaction to the frustration of oral-dependent needs from mother in terms of the mobilization of hostile and demanding affects, and the fact that clinically one never sees a depressive affect in which there is not an involvement of both libidinal and aggressive drive derivatives, and an interaction between real and ideal self representations and real and idealized object representations, in addition to relationships with actual objects.

In more general terms, Jacobson stresses that the vicissitudes of affects cannot be separated from the vicissitudes of drive derivatives and object relations. Thus, she proposes an ego psychological theory of depression that assumes the origin of depressive affects within the ego; but, insofar as these affects are invested in self and object representations, they will eventually become integrated with superego as well as with ego functions, and provide the superego with its important control function over the ego by means of mood swings. Jacobson then goes on to examine the clinical manifestations and the underlying psychodynamic implications of neurotic, borderline, and psychotic depressions, and differentiates between depression in manic-depressive or affective illness and schizophrenic depression.

On the basis of extensive clinical material, she first reconfirmed Freud's (1917), and Abraham's (1911, 1916, 1924) conclusions regarding the predominance of early oral and sadistic conflicts in depressed patients, and the abnormally intense dependency on ambivalently loved, idealized, and hated objects that are feared to be frustrating and rejecting. She described various stages in the development of psychotic depression, stages that permitted her to identify the predominant object relations and defensive operations involved, and to contribute significantly to the clinical analysis and the metapsychology of the crucial stages in the development and resolution of psychotic depression. The beginning stage is the growing sense of narcissistic frustration derived from partly real and partly fantasied frustrations from real objects.

Jacobson proposed that the main anxieties and conflicts in depression are related to the fear of abandonment from the object, and to a related fear, the development of aggression against the needed and frustrating object (1943, 1946, 1953b, 1954b). The main initial defensive mechanisms activated are an increasing idealization of the needed object, and an effort partially to identify with that object by self idealization achieved in closeness with this object. The denial of frustrating and aggressive aspects of the object is part of this idealization, and denial of the patient's own aggression and frustration also tends to reinforce the idealization.

The failure of these mechanisms leads to a catastrophic devaluation of the object and its representations. Jacobson described the defensive mechanism of devaluation as usually linked to preoedipal aggression; at best, such a devaluation would be partial and temporary, and contribute to a hostile self-affirmation and indirectly to increased autonomy. At worst, the devaluation would reflect such an aggressive destruction of investment in the object and the object representation, that it would immediately lead to an impoverishment of the self. This impoverishment reflects both the loss of the idealized object and the loss of the protective functions of the corresponding intrapsychic object representation. Here begins the differentiation between neurotic and psychotic depression.

In the case of neurotic depression, with relatively minor tendencies toward denial and idealization, and stability of self and object representations, and the maintenance of some reality testing and object investments in other areas, the sense of loneliness and abandonment, perhaps even the sense of unconscious guilt reflecting superego pressures, is relatively tolerable and does not increase further the destruction of the object world.

In contrast, in psychotic depression, further defensive mechanisms and restitutive efforts develop; these lead to more devastating deterioration in internalized object relations. Here, there is at first a masochistic effort to renew the idealization of the love object, combined with efforts sadistically to extract gratification of love and narcissistic supplies from it; simultaneously projection of the aggression onto the object now makes that object strong and powerful and potentially dangerous and bad at the same time: the tendency toward masochistic behavior and self devaluation, together with angry demands directed at the powerful, bad, although potentially ideal object complement each other.

However, as this defensive posture threatens the patient with the open expression of aggression in the context of a sadomasochistic relationship with the ambivalently loved object, additional defenses that are typically psychotic are brought into the picture. There is a renewed devaluation of the object and a pathognomonic double introjection of it into the superego and into the ego. Here Jacobson utilizes Rado's (1928) observation that the depressed patient attempts to recuperate the ambivalently loved object by introjecting it in the form of an ideal, powerful, and sadistic object into the superego, with the implication that the ego's submission to the superego is also an effort to regain the love of the lost object. She stresses, however, that this introjection into the ego and superego also implies a double fusion.

The internalization of the object into the ego is represented by the devalued, deflated aspect of the object, first reflected in a deflated object representation; and later, in the refusion between the deflated self and object representations. The internalization of the object into the superego is followed by the fusion of that idealized, yet sadistic object with sadistic superego forerunners, so that an ideal, yet sadistic, primitive ego ideal attacks the devalued, fused self-object representation. It is this double refusion, within ego and superego, typical for psychotic depression, that interferes with the maintenance of ordinary ego boundaries and reality testing; it thereby reinforces the distorting effects upon reality testing that derive from the depressive mood triggered off by the superego as an expression of its sadistic attacks on the ego.

Thus, in psychotic depression, the superego-ego boundary is still maintained, but reality testing is lost, and a psychotic transformation of all psychic experience takes place together with a total loss of the real object. In schizophrenic depression (1954b, 1954c, 1966) — including both schizoaffective illness and depressed moods in schizophrenia proper — the process of refusion of self and object representations proceeds further. This refusion of self and object representations includes additional fragmentation and fusion of such representations, with the reconstruction of primitive, pathological new units that reflect unrealistic combinations of real and ideal, self and object fragments. At the same time, the dissolution of the constituent identifications of ego and superego brings about a loss of ego and superego differentiation.

In borderline conditions — an intermediary situation between that of psychotic depression and neurotic depression — the intermediary stages of this chain of events are paradoxically stronger and prevent the final psychotic regression. The reason is that the prevalence of denial, sadomasochistic tendencies, idealization, devaluation, and contradictory object relations of borderline patients, together with the relative lack of integration of the superego, permit repetitive cycles of idealization and devaluation, sadomasochistic interactions, a clinging search for new objects, and depressive episodes to go on in an endless, unstable stability.

In addition to idealization, denial, and devaluation, Jacobson (1957a, 1959, 1964) also focused on depersonalization, introjection, and projection as typical defensive operations in borderline conditions. Depersonalization involves an extensive process of ego regression rather than a specific defensive mechanism; it depends upon the mutual denial of contradictory self representations, particularly the need to deny segments of the self experience in radical opposition or contrast to a person's core identity. (It is well known that Jacobson first analyzed this process in her experiences with co-prisoners in Germany; and the intimate connection between intrapsychic and external reality in maintaining normal ego identity is another important aspect in this analysis.) Introjection and projection refer to the modification of the self image after the object image, and the modification of the object image after the self image, respectively. Introjection and projection thus reflect early mechanisms employed to restore the unity between self and object lost with separation-individuation; early global imitation of the object is later followed by partial, selective identifications with it, within the context of an overall ego identity.

One more defensive mechanism — or rather, a complex set of expressions of all these defenses in the patient's interaction with the environment — is the attempt, in early stages of refusion of self and object representations in psychotic depression, and even more so in schizophrenic illness, forcefully to engage in real, although highly pathological interactions with objects in the external world as a final effort to control internal object relations and their vicissitudes under the effects of excessive ambivalence, aggression, and chaotic alternations of idealization, devaluation, projection, and introjection. From this viewpoint, the withdrawal from external reality is not a preliminary step of psychotic regression, but indicates a failure of the first line of psychotic defenses.

Jacobson utilized all these discoveries and formulations in proposals regarding the psychoanalytic approach to the treatment of depression in borderline and psychotic depressed patients (1954c, 1956, 1966, 1967). She stressed the need to warn the patient tactfully of the potential negative consequences and the defensive functions of his idealization, at times when such idealization is predominant. At a later stage, when sadomasochistic transferences predominate, the interpretations of these resistances need to be matched by the analyst's careful monitoring of his countertransference, the need to maintain warmth and dedication to the patient at a point when he is desperately trying to induce, in the analyst, the enactment of powerful and sadistic behavior. At a stage of frank psychotic regression and complete devaluation of the analyst, the ongoing availability of the analyst, even the establishment of parameters of technique which underline the analyst's continuing aliveness and dedication to the patient, may be important aspects of an essentially interpretive approach. The analyst also needs to clarify ego boundaries and reality at points when reality testing is lost. A very important contribution to the understanding and interpretation of the patient's reality is the analysis of the complex interactions of manic-depressive patients with their — often surprisingly similar — spouses.

Object Relations Theory

Jacobson combined her findings in the treatment of adults with affective disorders and adolescents with severe identity and narcissistic conflicts with the findings of Mahler (1952, 1957, 1958, 1968) regarding autistic and symbiotic psychosis in childhood and normal and pathological separation-individuation (findings that Mahler, in turn, had interpreted in the light of Jacobson's formulations) and integrated them into a comprehensive developmental framework. Starting from the metapsychological contributions of Hartmann (1948, 1950, 1952, 1955), Hartmann et al. (1946, 1949), and Hartmann and Loewenstein (1962), particularly from Hartmann's clarification of the differences between the ego and the self, Jacobson then related her developmental model to psychoanalytic metapsychology. Her developmental schemata represent an "intermediary language" between theoretical and clinical psychoanalysis. What follows is a summary of that developmental frame (Jacobson, 1954d, 1964).

Intrapsychic life starts out as a primary psychophysiologial self in which ego and id are not yet differentiated, and in which aggression and libido as overall drives are undifferentiated as well. The first intrapsychic structure is a fused self-object representation which evolves gradually under the impact of the relationship between mother and infant. The first few weeks of life, before such a primary self-object representation is consolidated, constitute the earliest, pre-symbiotic or, to use Mahler's term, autistic phase of development. Pleasurable affects are the first emerging manifestations of the differentiating libidinal drives, and their investment in the fused self-object representation representing the first intrapsychic libidinal investment. Insofar as that fused structure represents the origin of both self and object representations, libidinal investment in the self and in objects is originally one process.

The symbiotic phase of development comes to an end with a gradual differentiation between the self representation and the object representation, which contributes importantly to the differentiation between the self and the external world. At the stage of beginning differentiation, two processes make their appearance: (1) the defensive refusion of libidinally invested self and object representations as the earliest protection against painful experiences, giving rise, when this process is excessively or pathologically maintained, to what later will become psychotic identifications characteristic of symbiotic psychosis in childhood, and of affective psychoses and schizophrenia in adulthood (1954a, 1954b, 1954d, 1957a, 1964, 1966); (2) the differentiation of painful experiences into aggressively invested self and object representations is an early effort to separate and deny the frustrating interactions between self and mother and their intrapsychic representations. A fused, undifferentiated self-object representation invested with aggressive drive derivatives becomes the counterpart of the libidinally invested one, so that, at a certain point, the intrapsychic world of object relations is reflected in "good" and "bad" self representations and similarly "good" and "bad" object representations.

Efforts to restore the ideal, symbiotic relationship with mother now give rise to processes of introjection and projection, geared to replace refusion in fantasy with a mutual modeling of self and object representations, in order to maintain good or ideal relations between self and object representations, and to deny and project bad ones: these bad self and object representations will become the sadistic superego forerunners, the first layer of superego development. The stage of separation-individuation is thus characterized by multiple, differentiated, but not integrated good and bad self and object representations.

The next stage of development consists in the gradual, more realistic integration of good and bad self representations into real self representations, and the integration of good and bad object representations into real object representations. In this process, therefore, partial aspects of self and object representations become integrative or total self and object representations. The completion of the stage of separation and individuation and the establishment of object constancy mark, precisely, this phase of development (Mahler et al., 1975).

A new, additional set of ideal self and object representations develops throughout all this time, particularly during the second and third years of life. As self and object representations become more realistic, the child becomes aware of his own shortcomings as well as of shortcomings and frustrations that stem from the good mother. He builds up ideal self images reflecting such aspired-to changes in himself which would restore the ideal relationship with mother that existed during the symbiotic phase. These ideal self images are complemented by ideal object images, namely, the good or ideal mother lost when the child acquired a more realistic assessment of the relationship between himself and mother. The early reaction formations against instinctual, particularly anal, drive derivatives in the second year of life are controlled by the aspirations and demands incorporated into such ideal self and object representations. It needs to be stressed that, in contrast to the earlier good and bad self and object representations, these later ideal self and object representations are based not on the denial of their respective opposites, but on the realistic integration of good and bad self and object representations; they reflect a more mature and sophisticated form of idealization.

The normal development of idealization processes, however, needs to be examined in the context of the simultaneous development, throughout all this time, of processes of devaluation that complicate the picture. Efforts to deny and to devalue the bad aspects of mother and her representations — and, by the same token, the bad aspects of the self representations — lead to rejection of certain aspects of frustrating or dangerous closeness with mother, foster autonomy, and further differentiate self from objects. Moreover, in order to protect the good relationship with mother, compensating idealizations are built up that reinforce ideal object representations and, by means of introjection, ideal self representations. Miscarriage of all these processes leads to the development of depressive psychopathology, a development I explored in this paper's section on Depression.

The next stage of development, which starts with object constancy and predominates throughout the fourth and fifth years, to be completed with the passing of the oedipus complex and the beginning of latency, consists in the integration of ideal self and ideal object representations into the ego ideal and the incorporation of the ego ideal as part of the superego. It is only then that a clear differentiation between ego and superego occurs, thus completing the integration of the tripartite structure (ego, superego, and id) that was initiated with the separation of ego and id when repression began to predominate over the earlier, primitive defensive mechanisms of introjection, projection, denial, idealization, and devaluation. In addition, the delimitation of ego boundaries initiated by the differentiation of self and object representations gradually consolidated the ego boundaries with external reality as well as with the id; the refusion of self and object representations under pathological conditions is the immediate cause of breakdown of ego boundaries and loss of reality testing.

In the most comprehensive analysis of the superego in the psychoanalytic literature, Jacobson (1954d, 1964) described three overall layers of superego formation. The first, deepest layer is represented by the sadistic forerunners that reflect the internalization of fantastic, sadistically prohibitive, and punishing object images or, rather, "bad," fused self and object representations that were projected onto the frustrating mother and other objects as part of an effort to deny and project the aggressively invested object relations. A second layer is constituted by the integration of the ego ideal, on the basis of the fusion of ideal self representations and ideal object representations, and represents a final effort to reconstitute the original libidinally invested symbiotic relation with mother at a higher level of intrapsychic aspirations and demands. Under optimal circumstances, a mutual toning down of the earliest, sadistic, and later, idealized superego forerunners occurs, repeating within the evolving superego the processes of integration of good and bad object relations that occurred earlier within the ego. Jacobson described how such an integration and toning down in turn permit the internalization of a third layer of superego determinants, namely, the realistic, demanding, and prohibitive aspects of the parents that characterize the later stages and completion of the oedipus complex, and bring about the final constitution of the superego as an integrated structure.

At this point, the superego takes over an important aspect of both protection of the libidinal investment of the self and regulation of self-esteem by means of mood swings. Throughout the next stage of development, the latency period, such dispositions toward mood swings gradually decrease, and processes of depersonification, abstraction, and individualization occur in the superego, bringing about regulation of self-esteem by more focused, delimited, cognitively differentiated affects and demands. Guilt feelings represent the most significant elaboration of depressed moods under the influences of superego integration. The mature superego is characterized by control exerted through mild or modulated mood swings, guilt feelings, and a growing sense of autonomy, while a pathological, excessively aggressive, and primitive superego is characterized by the predominance of severe, depressive mood swings. In addition, feelings of inferiority and shame now reflect the participation of the ego ideal in superego regulation of the ego; the more there is a general defect in superego integration, the more feelings of inferiority and shame predominate over the capacity for experiencing modulated depressed affects (such as sadness) and differentiated guilt feelings.

At the same time, throughout the oedipal and latency periods, the integration of the self representations into an organized self concept proceeds, and ego identity, originally stemming from the integration of good and bad self representations at the time when object constancy was established, is further consolidated. Jacobson (1964) criticizes Erikson (1956) for his excessively broad use of the term "ego identity," and for his deemphasis of infantile stages of identity formation. However, she considers his concept of "identity formation" to be valuable, provided that it includes processes of organization within all structures of the psychic apparatus. She suggests that the objective process of normal identity formation is reflected in the normal subjective feeling of identity. The integration of the self concept within the ego has a powerful influence on the integration of superego forerunners; in turn, superego integration powerfully reinforces the integration of the ego and particularly of the self concept.

The next stage of development is adolescence, and Jacobson described the partial repersonalization, reprojection, and redissolution of the superego that occurs as a key aspect of the adolescent task of reinforcing infantile prohibitions against oedipal strivings, while, the same time, the adolescent needs to identify with an adult model of sexual behavior and to integrate the tender and erotic aspects of sexual drives. Here, the careful study of the nature and extent to which such partial redissolution and reprojection of the superego occur, and the extent to which normal ego identity is still maintained, differentiates normal and neurotic adolescence from their borderline and narcissistic counterparts (1954d, 1961, 1964). Severe identity conflicts in adolescence reflect failure in the stage of development in which good and bad self representations integrate into a total self concept, and the derived failure of integration of idealized and sadistic forerunners of the superego. Under these circumstances, the internalization of the third superego layer of realistic parental images also fails; and parental images are distorted by powerful projective processes, reactivating a chaotic world of all-good and all-bad self and object representations. Failure in the consolidation of the self and of integrative object representations also fosters the continuation of primitive defensive mechanisms such as denial, introjection and projection, idealization and devaluation, and interferes with the integration of the superego, thus creating a vicious circle of lack of differentiation and integration of the tripartite structural system. This is characteristic of borderline conditions and narcissistic psychopathology, and Jacobson studied the effects of such developments on the characteristics of depression in such personality structures. In contrast, the successful integration of the superego and the consequent reconfirmation of ego identity create the background of neurotic psychopathology and normality.

Implications and Critique of Edith Jacobson's Work

I think that Jacobson's developmental model includes the only comprehensive psychoanalytic object relations theory that links earliest development in the realm of affect differentiation, object relations, early defensive mechanisms, and vicissitudes of early instinctual development with the tripartite structural model of the psychic apparatus, and thus provides an integrative developmental frame for psychoanalysis at large. Jacobson's close collaboration with Mahler provided Mahler with an overall frame of reference which was important in the study of autistic and symbiotic psychosis and separation-individuation. In turn, Mahler's revolutionary findings regarding autistic and symbiotic childhood psychosis and the vicissitudes of normal and abnormal separation-individuation provided powerful supportive material for the development of Jacobson's overall model. The clinical and metapsychological studies of depressive reactions in normal, neurotic, borderline, and psychotic patients provided Jacobson with the clinical evidence which stimulated her theoretical formulations regarding relatively advanced levels of development and the harmonious linkage between early development and that following the consolidation of the tripartite structure.

Several other major efforts to develop an integrated object relations theory ended up with important and self-defeating shortcomings. Thus, Sullivan's (1953) efforts to develop a conception of the psychic apparatus as reflecting interpersonal interactions failed to provide any structural model of development, could not integrate drive theory, and generally underestimated the complexity of unconscious, intrapsychic development. Erikson (1956, 1959, 1963), within an ego psychological frame, attempted to trace the development of ego identity and, in studying the sequence of introjection, identification, and ego identity, arrived at a developmental model— his stages of psychosexual development. However, as Jacobson herself pointed out (1964, chap. 2), he underestimated the importance of early determinants of identity formation, overestimated the importance of adolescent conflicts in determining the vicissitudes of ego identity, and never evolved a complete developmental outline that would simultaneously spell out the vicissitudes of drive derivatives, affects, object relations, structure formation, and defensive organization.

One most interesting object relations theory that is in sharp contrast to Jacobson's is Fairbairn's (1952, 1963). Fairbairn was aware of the dyadic origins of internalized object relations, and attempted to link the vicissitudes of split-off parts of the self and of internal objects (to use his terminology) in the light of overall intrapsychic structure formation. His analysis of splitting mechanisms as a central, unifying, defensive operation in early development — the pathology of which would be most apparent in schizoid personalities — seems to me an important contribution to the study of the psychopathology of borderline conditions (Kernberg, 1975a). However, Fairbairn, in contrast to Jacobson, collapsed his structural development into the first year of life, neglected important intermediary stages of structure formation, and, above all, dogmatically rejected psychoanalytic instinct theory.

Melanie Klein (1934, 1940, 1945, 1946) also focused sharply on earliest development, on early internalization of object relations, and on early defense mechanisms and instinctual developments. However, as Jacobson (1964) has critically pointed out, Melanie Klein failed in not differentiating self from object representations and their development, arbitrarily pushed intrapsychic developments even further than Fairbairn into the first half of the first year of life, and neglected almost totally the relationship between normal and abnormal early development on the one hand, and the consolidation of the definite tripartite structure, on the other (Kernberg, 1969, 1976b, chap. 4).

Against this background of failure in the alternative attempts to establish a satisfactory object relations theory, Jacobson's work stands out as a unique contribution to the integration of internalized object relations within the structural theory, extending the work of Hartmann, Kris, and Loewenstein.

I now turn from the implications of Jacobson's work for metapsychology to those for psychopathology. Her contributions and those of others related to her general theoretical frame, particularly Mahler's work, have already had a definite impact on the applications of psychoanalytic theory and technique to various psychopathological conditions, and to psychiatric theory in general. I shall briefly review these contributions, following the developmental line of Jacobson's theoretical frame of reference.

The first stage of development, preceding the establishment of the fused self-object representation, is reflected—when prolonged or permanent—in the autistic syndromes of childhood. It may well be that organic factors are important in codetermining the lack of establishment of the original, fused self and object representation as an intrapsychic structure in many cases, and that a regressive destruction or deterioration of such intrapsychic structure may determine or codetermine an autistic syndrome in other cases. Object relations theory thus offers a common, final pathway for organically and psychologically determined early pathology: Mahler's contributions in this area are well known (1968).

Regarding the second stage of development, an excessive prolongation of the symbiotic phase, or a defensive regression in terms of a refusion of self and object representations (what Jacobson has called psychotic identifications), characterizes symbiotic childhood psychosis and schizophrenia in adulthood. In addition to Mahler's (1952, 1968) fundamental work in this area, the contributions of Searles (1965) regarding schizophrenic transferences, of Lewin (1950) and of Jacobson herself regarding depressive psychosis illustrate how the refusion of self and object representations determines loss of reality testing and typically psychotic interactions in the transference.

Jacobson (1954c, 1956, 1966, 1967, 1971) has explored the diagnostic and therapeutic consequences of pathological refusion of self and object representations in depressive psychosis and schizophrenia. She has pointed out that schizophrenic refusion involves fragmentation and pathological reorganization of fragments of self and object representations into new units, while the tripartite intrapsychic structure completely disintegrates and all higher-level internalized object relations disintegrate as well. Therefore, the schizophrenic patient assumes new, partial, pathological identity fragments. In contrast, in depressive psychosis, the refusion of self and object representations occurs within the ego and within the superego, without a dissolution of an integrative superego structure as such. This has fundamental consequences for the maintenance of certain aspects of the relationship with reality, and for the enactment in the transference of a primitive object relation between an all-powerful, sadistic, fused self-object representation in the superego and a deflated, devalued, fused self-object representation in the ego.

In the next stage of development, when self and object representations are differentiated from each other but not yet integrated into total object representations and a comprehensive self concept, the spectrum of pathology of borderline personality organization becomes predominant. Here, Mahler (1971, 1972) has described the relationship between abnormal separation-individuation, particularly of an abnormal rapprochement subphase, and the pathological development of splitting mechanisms and primitive object relations that characterize the borderline conditions. This is also the area where I (1975a) applied Jacobson's work in great detail and attempted to describe systematically the constellation of primitive defensive operations, primitive object relations, and particular condensation of pregenital and genital conflicts under the overriding influence of aggression characteristic of these cases. My theoretical frame of reference and, in fact, my theory of technique and actual therapeutic strategy with borderline cases and narcissistic pathology derive from Jacobson's work (Kernberg, 1975b, 1976a, 1976b). I would like to stress particularly the therapeutic implications of her findings in the sense of a careful analysis, in the transference, of primitive, dissociated, part-object relations in order to foster, by interpretive means, the integration of contradictory, conflictual self representations into an integrative self and of conflictual, contradictory object representations into integrative conception of objects.

In broader terms, Jacobson's formulations permit us to understand why patients may have sharply defined intrapsychic conflicts and defenses and stable, highly pathological ego structures without presenting an integrated tripartite structure, and how, in these cases, the interpretation of impulse and defense is reflected in the interpretation of mutually contradictory and conflictual internalized object relations.

It needs to be stressed that many of the clinical manifestations of borderline conditions in the psychoanalytic situation; the understanding of their pathological object relations, severely narcissistic conflicts, and disintegrated or dissociated identifications; and the vicissitudes of reality testing in these cases — all were clarified in the pioneering contributions of Stone (1954), Frosch (1964, 1970, 1971), and Greenson (1954, 1958). I think that Jacobson's work provided an integrative frame for these observations, and a theoretical and clinical set of tools for further clarifications and treatment of these conditions.

The next stage of development is represented by the full integration and consolidation of the superego, and the consequent further integration of the ego and reinforcement of the repressive barrier with the id. Here the pathology of neurotic conditions and nonborderline character pathology represents the main psychopathology. Classical psychoanalytic theory and its enrichment with modern ego psychology have provided the basic theoretical, clinical, and technical understanding in this area.

To conclude, a few words about the impact Jacobson's work has had on the psychoanalytic field in general. Her writings have a complex, terse, highly elaborated nature. Her original proposals are embedded in a careful analysis of the implications of her findings for psychoanalytic theory and technique, and she deals extremely respectfully and carefully with potential objections and alternative formulations. All of this makes the study of her work difficult, and militates against an easy extraction from it of an "exportable," simple scheme. Therefore, Jacobson has not, as far as I can see, been the object of one of those transitory fashions that, from time to time, develop within the psychoanalytic field, and seem to clarify all complex issues by means of a few simple generalizations. However, by the same token, her influence on psychoanalytic theory formation has been profound and definite, and it is still growing. Throughout her work, she has demonstrated the profound vitality and the exciting developments that psychoanalysis offers today and promises for the future. I am convinced that the object relations theory developed by Edith Jacobson in the last twenty-five years has been one of the fundamental lines of progress in psychoanalytic theory and technique.

References

Abraham, K. (1911), Notes on the psycho-analytic investigation and treatment of manic-depressive insanity and allied conditions. In: *Selected Papers on Psycho-Analysis.* London: Hogarth Press, 1927, pp. 137–56.

———— (1916), The first pregenital stage of the libido. *Ibid.,* pp. 248–79.

———— (1924), A short study of the development of the libido, viewed in the light of mental disorders. *Ibid.,* pp. 418–501.

Bibring, E. (1953), The mechanism of depression. In: *Affective Disorders,* ed. P. Greenacre. New York: International Universities Press, pp. 13–48.

Blanck, G. & Blanck, R. (1974), *Ego Psychology.* New York: Columbia University Press.

Brierley, M. (1937), Affects in theory and practice. In: *Trends in Psycho-Analysis*. London: Hogarth Press, 1951, pp. 43–56.

Erikson, E. H. (1956), The problem of ego identity. *J. Amer. Psychoanal. Assn.*, 4:56–121.

_____ (1959), *Identity and the Life Cycle* [*Psychol. Issues*, Monogr. 1]. New York: International Universities Press.

_____ (1963), *Childhood and Society*, 2nd ed. New York: Norton.

Fairbairn, W. D. (1952), *An Object Relations Theory of the Personality*. New York: Basic Books.

_____ (1963), Synopsis of an object relations theory of the personality. *Int. J. Psycho-Anal.*, 44:224–225.

Freud, S. (1894), The neuro-psychoses of defence. *Standard Edition*, 3:45–61. London: Hogarth Press, 1962.

_____ (1915), Repression. *Standard Edition*, 14:146–158. London: Hogarth Press, 1957.

_____ (1917), Mourning and melancholia. *Standard Edition*, 14:243–258. London: Hogarth Press, 1957.

_____ (1926), Inhibition, symptoms and anxiety. *Standard Edition*, 20:87–172. London: Hogarth Press, 1957.

Frosch, J. (1964), The psychotic character. *Psychiat. Quart.*, 38:81–96.

_____ (1970), Psychoanalytic considerations of the psychotic character. *J. Amer. Psychoanal. Assn.*, 18:24–50.

_____ (1971), Technique in regard to some specific ego defects in the treatment of borderline patients. *Psychiat. Quart.*, 45:216–220.

Greenson, R. R. (1954), The struggle against identification. *J. Amer. Psychoanal. Assn.*, 2:200–217.

_____ (1958), On screen defenses, screen hunger, and screen identity. *J. Amer. Psychoanal. Assn.*, 6:242–262.

Hartmann, H. (1948), Comments on the psychoanalytic theory of instinctual drives. *Psychoanal. Quart.*, 17:368–388.

_____ (1950), Comments on the psychoanalytic theory of the ego. In: *Essays on Ego Psychology*. New York: International Universities Press, 1964, pp. 113–141.

_____ (1952), The mutual influences in the development of the ego and the id. *The Psychoanalytic Study of the Child*, 7:9–30.

_____ (1955), Notes on the theory of sublimation. *The Psychoanalytic Study of the Child*, 10:9–29.

_____ Kris, E., & Loewenstein, R. M. (1946), Comments on the formation of psychic structure. *The Psychoanalytic Study of the Child*, 2:11–38.

_____ _____ _____ (1949), Notes on the theory of aggression. *The Psychoanalytic Study of the Child*, 3/4:9–36.

_____ & Loewenstein, R. M. (1962), Notes on the superego. *The Psychoanalytic Study of the Child*, 17:42–81.

Jacobson, E. (1937), Wege der weiblichen Über-Ich-Bildung. *Int. Z. Psychoanal.*, 23:402–412.

_____ (1943), Depression. *Psychoanal. Quart.*, 12:541–560.

_____ (1946), The effect of disappointment on ego and superego formation in normal and depressive development. *Psychoanal. Rev.*, 33:129–147.

_____ (1952), The speed pace in psychic discharge processes and its influence on the pleasure-unpleasure qualities of affects. *Bull. Amer. Psychoanal. Assn.*, 8:235–236.

_____ (1953a), The affects and their pleasure-unpleasure qualities in relation to the psychic discharge processes. In: *Drives, Affects, Behavior*, ed. R. M. Loewenstein. New York: International Universities Press, pp. 38–66.

_____ (1953b), Contribution to the metapsychology of cyclothymic depression. In: *Affective Disorders*, ed. P. Greenacre. New York: International Universities Press, pp. 49–83.

_____ (1954a), Contribution to the metapsychology of psychotic identification. *J. Amer. Psychoanal. Assn.*, 2:239–262.

_____ (1954b), On psychotic identifications. *Int. J. Psycho-Anal.*, 35:102–108.

_____ (1954c), Transference problems in the psychoanalytic treatment of severely depressed patients. *J. Amer. Psychoanal. Assn.*, 2:595–606.

_____ (1954d), The self and the object world. *The Psychoanalytic Study of the Child*, 9:75–127.

_____ (1956), Interaction between psychotic partners. In: *Neurotic Interaction in Marriage*, ed. V. W. Eisenstein. New York: Basic Books, pp. 125–134.

_____ (1957a), Denial and repression. *J. Amer. Psychoanal. Assn.*, 5:61–92.

_____ (1957b), Normal and pathological moods. *The Psychoanalytic Study of the Child*, 12:73–113.

_____ (1959), Depersonalization. *J. Amer. Psychoanal. Assn.*, 7:581–610.

_____ (1961), Adolescent moods and the remodeling of psychic structures in adolescence. *The Psychoanalytic Study of the Child*, 16:164–183.

_____ (1964), *The Self and the Object World*. New York: International Universities Press.

_____ (1966), Problems in the differentiation between schizophrenic and melancholic states of depression. In: *Psychoanalysis—A General Psychology*, ed. R. M. Loewenstein, L. M. Newman, M. Schur, & A. J. Solnit. New York: International Universities Press, pp. 499–518.

_____ (1967), *Psychotic Conflict and Reality*. New York: International Universities Press.

_____ (1971), *Depression*. New York: International Universities Press.

Kernberg, O. F. (1969), A contribution to the ego-psychological critique of the Kleinian school. *Int. J. Psycho-Anal.*, 50:317–333.

_____ (1975a), *Borderline Conditions and Pathological Narcissism*. New York: Jason Aronson.

_____ (1975b), Transference and countertransference in the treatment of borderline patients. *J. Nat. Assn. Priv. Psychiat. Hosp.*, 7:14–24.

_____ (1976a), Technical considerations in the treatment of borderline personality organization. *J. Amer. Psychoanal. Assn.*, 24:795–829.

_____ (1976b), *Object Relations Theory and Clinical Psychoanalysis*. New York: Jason Aronson.

_____ (1977), Structural diagnosis of borderline personality organization. In: *Borderline Personality Disorders*, ed. P. Hartocollis. New York: International Universities Press, pp. 87–121.

Klein, M. (1934), A contribution to the psychogenesis of manic-depressive states. In: *Contributions to Psycho-Analysis, 1921–1945*. London: Hogarth Press, 1948, pp. 282–310.

_____ (1940), Mourning and its relation to manic-depressive states. *Ibid.*, pp. 311–338.

_____ (1945), The oedipus complex in the light of early anxieties. *Ibid.*, pp. 339–390.

———— (1946), Notes on some schizoid mechanisms. *Int. J. Psycho-Anal.*, 27:99–110.

Lewin, B. D. (1950), *The Psychoanalysis of Elation.* New York: Norton.

Loewald, H. W. (1978), Instinct theory, object relations and psychic structure formation. *J. Amer. Psychoanal. Assn.*, 26:493–506.

Mahler, M. S. (1952), On child psychosis and schizophrenia. *The Psychoanalytic Study of the Child*, 7:286–305.

———— (1957), Problems of identity. Abstr. in Panel: Problems of identity, rep. D. L. Rubinfine. *J. Amer. Psychoanal. Assn.*, 6:131–142, 1958.

———— (1958), Autism and symbiosis. *Int. J. Psycho-Anal.*, 39:77–83.

———— (1968), *On Human Symbiosis and the Vicissitudes of Individuation.* New York: International Universities Press.

———— (1971), A study of the separation-individuation process and its possible application to borderline phenomena in the psychoanalytic situation. *The Psychoanalytic Study of the Child*, 26:403–424.

———— (1972), On the first three subphases of the separation-individuation process. *Int. J. Psycho-Anal.*, 53:333–338.

———— Pine, F., & Bergman, A. (1975), *The Psychological Birth of the Human Infant.* New York: Basic Books.

Mendelson, M. (1974), Jacobson. In: *Psychoanalytic Concepts of Depression*, 2nd ed. New York: Spectrum, pp. 72–88.

Rado, S. (1928), The problem of melancholia. *Int. J. Psycho-Anal.*, 9:420–438.

Rapaport, D. (1953), On the psychoanalytic theory of affects. In: *The Collected Papers of David Rapaport*, ed. M. M. Gill. New York: Basic Books, 1967, pp. 476–512.

Searles, H. F. (1965), *Collected Papers on Schizophrenia and Related Subjects.* New York: International Universities Press.

Stone, L. (1954), The widening scope of indications for psychoanalysis. *J. Amer. Psychoanal. Assn.*, 2:567–594.

Sullivan, H. S. (1953), *The Interpersonal Theory of Psychiatry.* New York: Norton.

Part II

ISSUES OF THEORY
AND TREATMENT

6

MEANING AND OBJECTS

Arnold Goldberg, M.D.

The aim of this paper is to examine an implication of present-day object relations theory in terms of its compatibility with a view of psychoanalysis as a psychology of meaning. There is no doubt that much of the credit for the growth of object relations theory goes to Edith Jacobson, whose fundamental writing on the object world offered psychoanalysis a perspective or viewpoint that a mere concentration on drives and defenses failed to present. In recent years, a shift has occurred in psychoanalysis. This new trend—its major spokesman has been George Klein (1968)—concentrates on analysis as concerned with people's intentions and motives rather than on analysis as a model of forces, energies, and whatever other technological as opposed to humanistic images come to mind. These two seemingly opposing points of view reflect a more fundamental problem of analytic theory.

In a letter to Wilhelm Fliess (August 1, 1899), Sigmund Freud wrote: "I am accustoming myself to regarding every sexual act as an event between four individuals" (1923, p. 33). When asked who these four people were, one senior analyst said they were the man and his mother, and the woman and her father. Yet, reading the whole letter makes it clear that Freud meant the four to be the masculine and feminine components of each partner, thus underscoring Fliess's as well as his own ideas on bisexuality. Another analyst saw the group as consisting of the man and his vision of himself in the woman's eye, and the parallel experience in the woman. When the first analyst was offered these varied perspectives, he had no difficulty accepting all of them. Psychoanalysis happily lives with many ways to look at things and only rarely do the differing views seem to express real disagreements or conflicts of ideas.

Disagreements among scientists usually are a sign of a need for further experimentation or a search for supporting evidence which will aid in a resolution. The persistence of some of the failures to reach agreement occasionally indicates that varied theoretical approaches allow one to see certain phenomena in a different light or even to see via one theory what another one may obscure. A related but different cause of dissension in scientific inquiry is the variability in what McGuire (1976) calls the data base or the very selection of data from a given field. In psychoanalysis, we frequently experience a lack of consensus in a variety of clinical pursuits, either because we still have much to learn, or because we employ different theoretical approaches, or because we are examining different sets of phenomena.

The history of "objects" in psychoanalysis lends itself to an examination of a seemingly innocuous word or concept that has spawned theories, schools, and rivalries. An attempt to disentangle the issues might lead not to a resolution or consensus, but perhaps to a clearer understanding of whether the problem is one that requires further data or more clearly delineated data or different ways of viewing the data.

Review of Definitions

Inasmuch as the literature on objects and object relations almost parallels that of psychoanalysis, a brief review can serve to highlight some essential definitions of objects.

An object per se has always been considered in tandem with a drive and an aim. Thus, the original classification of objects had to do with their relation to libido. Object libido was the force of the sexual instincts directed toward an object. A libidinal object is characterized by and can be described in terms of the structure and vicissitudes of sexual drives and partial drives directed to it. This original classification of Freud, expanded by A. Freud (1952), Hartmann (1952), and Hartmann et al. (1946), conceptualized object relations as the multifold and varied relationships of the ego to the object assessed in terms of instinctual and ego tendencies. Objects are noted as stimulators of the instincts, tied to the instincts, gratifying the instincts when serving for discharge, or binding or damming the instincts when frustrating of discharge.

Two major steps in the rather pure consideration of objects and their tie to instincts were made to deepen and perhaps to complicate the picture. The first was the consideration of object relationships along developmental lines. For this work we are primarily indebted to Anna Freud (1965). The second major advance was the study of the structural framework or dimension of objects; along with countless other contributors, the work of Edith Jacobson is outstanding in this regard.

Jacobson (1964) studied severely disturbed individuals, and, by utilizing the pathology of the psychoses, made a number of stimulating suggestions about the organization of what came to be called "the object world." In a sense, we are all obligated to her for her steadfast insistence on utilizing a psychoanalytic perspective on all of her clinical material. Rather than restrict herself to the treatment of the classical or pure neuroses, she extended her psychoanalytic vision to the most disturbed kinds of patients and thereby showed how our clinical theory must expand to explain the wide range of psychopathology which we encounter, whether or not we employ analytic techniques with these patients. Such a commitment to the psychoanalytic position enabled the theory to encompass the treatment of patients heretofore considered unanalyzable, and opened up an area which still is in the process of development.

In terms of development, we are familiar with the sequence progressing from narcissistic to need-satisfying objects to the stage of object constancy. These stages often are considered in some parallel fashion to those of libidinal development. Whereas Freud (1916–17) saw the development of object relations moving from autoerotic to homoerotic to heteroerotic, further elaborations by others included archaic objects, transitional objects, and the choice of objects in childhood, puberty, and adolescence. Likewise, study was directed to object differentiation. This postulated such concepts as the primary child-mother unit, the undifferentiated self, and activities of both normal and pathological manifestations of separation of objects from the self.

The development of ego psychology suggested the value of defining more specifically the differences between the introjection of an object or object representative into the ego as a functioning unit of the mental apparatus, or into the self (one's own person) or into the "self image" as a mental content to be distinguished from an "object image." This work derived from Freud's original descriptions of object identification. He said that object loss establishes an identification of the ego with the abandoned object, thereby encouraging study of the structural aspects of object relationships. Essentially, this has tended to become a description of the organization of psychological images or representations. The object presentation or *Instanz* is a complex of visual, acoustic, tactile, and kinesthetic impressions, as well as others, linked to a word which thereby acquires meaning. The object presentation is not closed and has numerous associations, but the word *presentation* is closed, although capable of extension. The process of internalization of object presentations forms object representations. Therefore, we can see this organization as primarily a preconscious arrangement. We are indebted to Sandler and Jacobson for their elaborate portrayals of the forms of this systematization. In his most recent statement, Sandler (1977) likens object relationships to wish fulfillments, thereby almost completing the inclusiveness of the concept.

In a review of the contributions of Fairbairn and Guntrip to object relations theory, Alan Sugarman (1977) comments that the theory has enabled psychoanalysis to be less mechanistic and more concerned with the experiential and humanistic aspects of analysis. He includes a variety of interpersonal approaches in his discussion, and concludes that the inner feeling of agents in conflict or opposition often mirrors interpersonal phenomena. This may serve to highlight a subtle but significant *raison d'être* for these theories, i.e., they attempt to categorize and explain by an exchange of phenomena that are intrapsychic in terms of the interpersonal; they attempt to understand what goes on between people according to an entirely inner or personal perspective. Thus, it is not surprising that a sort of miniature theater of the world becomes transferred to the inside of the skull. As Stolorow (1978) says, "object relations theory focuses upon the 'internalization' of interpersonal relations and, in particular, the contribution of early images of the self and others (objects) and their associated affects to the development of normal and pathological personality structure. The suggestion [is] that constellations of self-images, object-images, and affects constitute the basic building blocks in personality development" (p. 32).

The status of object representations presents us with a certain kind of scientific challenge. For one, we need to distinguish the nature of external or real objects from that of internal or preconscious images of objects and, in turn, from that of unconscious phenomena. These latter can qualify as archaic or repressed objects, or as instinctual ties to objects. For this task of clarification, a brief orientation of a different sort is in order. This is a presentation of options for us to consider with the clear proviso that analysts can and should use a variety of tools and methods.

The External vs. Internal Dichotomy: Interpersonal vs. Intrapsychic

A fascinating series of articles (Schafer, 1972; Meissner, 1979) can be followed in the psychoanalytic literature over this issue of internalization. As long as one conceives of things (events, processes, or percepts) being taken from an outside boundary to a locus inside that line, the struggle will remain as to whether these are fantasies or "real" processes, or mere metaphors of some sort. This argument cannot be resolved since we know both that we do not really internalize objects, and that we feel that we do. It might profit us to recall that the eye is not a camera but, as a part of the brain, it constructs what it sees. This dilemma of internalization may be similar to that of the novice in psychoanalysis wondering if libido really cathects people or if we just get interested in them. One answer to this seeming dilemma is that the external-internal dichotomy is a false one or one that we have unwittingly helped to foster.

There are, no doubt, numerous ways to conceptualize this supposed dichotomy, but I shall highlight three.

1. *Opposition.* The consideration of external objects as merely opposed to internal ones is based on a simple transposition of the arena of external events to a somewhat smaller theater inside the head. Although this may seem to be a simplistic and unfair portrayal of thinking in this sphere, we can note that it is prevalent either as a method of illustration of development or as a firmly believed fact. Here is an example (McDevitt, 1975):

> Toward the end of the practicing subphase we see the beginnings of deferred imitation and symbolic play as well as the verbal evocation of the mother in her absence. . . . The child may go to the door and say "bye-bye" or "mama" in anticipation of or during his mother's absence; the junior toddler — especially the little girl — may mother her doll in symbolic play, using this play to comfort herself while her mother is away. She may be heard to say "mama" and "baba" while cradling and rocking

the doll.

These behaviors are significant for several reasons. First, they indicate that the junior toddler is now able to effect mental representations of behavior patterns, thereby implying the evocation of the mother at a time when she is neither present nor perceived. In these behaviors, action becomes detached from its previous motoric context, and rests instead on representation in thought. Second, this is the beginning of identifications that are patterned on a representational model. By re-creating in play an actual experience with the mother, the junior toddler is able to function better during her absence. Third, symbolic play based on identification serves as an intermediate step between the actual mother-child relationship and the transfer of that relationship to the child's inner world. It is striking how often such play appears to be an exact replication of the actual mother-child relation and its significant qualities. . . . This transfer of the mother-child relation to the child's inner world permits a continuing relationship with the love object during the latter's absence [pp. 725–726.].

The assumption that a child who says "mama" has an inner representation of a mother is, of course, speculative, since a child's use of words is limited and "mama" can stand for a variety of things. The use of the term representation here sounds like the author considers it to be an inner image or picture or replication of the person who is gone.

Otto Kernberg (1971) takes a step away from such an immediacy of transfer by stressing that "the examination of the quality of object relationships must include the internal relationships to others, in contrast to a simple observation of the patient's interpersonal behavior. . . . The quality of a person's object relationships is actualized in the prognostically most meaningful way in the quality of the relationship he establishes with the therapist. . . . The quality of the relationship that the patient establishes with the therapist also reveals the quality of the patient's superego" (p. 629).

This suggests a graded step between external and internal, with the added feature that the internal milieu might be more accurately reexternalized in treatment. It also states that abstract psychic structures are "revealed" in the transference. Jacobson and others also have demonstrated the externalization of what we ordinarily claim to be inner structure. Margaret Mahler (1968) furthers this differentiation between internal structures and external objects when she states that the mother is an "object" in the psychoanalytic sense; that is, something through which drive gratification is achieved is far more than an "object" in the merely physical descriptive sense. Yet the nature of the difference again seems to relate more to the use of the object rather than to the internal object belonging to a different realm of psychology. The nature of the difference between an external object and its representation is more in the way of an *added* feature of the external object. There seems to be a need for a further distinction, and for this I turn to another category.

2. *Different Logical Types.* Another way of distinguishing external from internal in terms of psychoanalytic objects is via the device of logical typing. Essentially, this is a hierarchical arrangement, most congenial to mathematicians but familiar to most scientists, whereby one abstracts a certain order from one set of data and types or classifies it. Any map of a territory introduces a set of rules for portrayal, and the rules or codes are examples of higher logical types. The central thesis depends upon Bertrand Russell's theory of logical types, according to which there is a discontinuity between a class and its members. The class cannot be a member of itself, nor can one of the members be the class, because the term used for the class is of a different level of abstraction or logical type than the terms used for the members of the class.

According to this perspective, object representations are of a different level than object relations in the external world. They are maps or codes or commentaries which cannot be directly connected to external phenomena and are devised according to certain principles of organization which need bear no resemblance to actual perceptions. If the principle employed is libidinal gratification, then one *limited* form of organization is seen. As Susan Blanck (1977) has shown, there is often more similarity seen in object representations based on cultural background than on anything else that is readily discernible, inasmuch as these maps are essentially preconscious modes of arrangement from which we derive certain psychological conclusions. In dreams and early memories, we see examples of this coding according to the early ideas about symbol formation when one symbol stood for a host of things or vice versa. In analysis, it becomes commonplace for the analyst to stand for many other persons as well as for many images. The finer discriminations of introjection, identification, and the varied aspects of internalization are examples of this effort. Although many psychoanalysts would grant that logical typing is characteristic of the so-called representational world, they would insist that this by no means exhausts the status of internal objects. That is, in a sense, an unsatisfactory or incomplete explanation and leads us to the third.

3. *Different Domains of Discourse.* This is a somewhat more radical stance, according to which the realm of internal object relationships might bear a resemblance to that of the external world, but essentially they are different universes of discourse. Thus, the internal image is seen via a different theory or set of concepts or spoken of in a different language than is the external. Freud's (1914) very significant premise that the narcissistic object is what one was or what one would like to be or someone who once was a part of oneself seems to go beyond simple transposition and even hierarchical classification to a position of what the object means to the person. This then seems to take us to the realm of psychoanalysis as a psychology of meaning. I think this also allows us to focus on a new form of object representation: that of the self-object (Kohut, 1971). This is a different theoretical stance than that devoted to external observables and is dependent totally on the inner world. It follows from a special mode of observation which allows us entry into that world: that of vicarious introspection.

The discussion of different domains is common enough in our science and stretches from our struggles to resolve the mind-body problem to the vigorous efforts to construct bridging concepts such as identity to "connect" what seemingly is unconnectable. One resolution of this dilemma is to restrict the data obtainable by one particular method employing a particular set of theories. This, for instance, clearly delineates and disconnects the "self" of psychoanalysis from that of sociology or other forms of behavioral science. Leaving aside for the moment the possible argument over the sources of psychoanalytic data, I believe it is clear that empathic observation or introspection will restrict our data and theory. Watching two or more persons interact will, in turn, yield a different sort of description and will depend upon a theory that is most congenial to it. The difference in methods parallels a difference in theories, inasmuch as (contrary to lay opinion) our theories do dictate what we see and our perceptions confirm our theories. So, too, will the words and concepts of a theory depend on the methods. Empathy or vicarious introspection thus yields a set of observations and an ordering of these observations that directs itself to the questions: what is the person experiencing; of what is his world constructed; how does he see himself? In other words, to a psychology of meaning.

The concept of the self-object, another person experienced as part of one's self, would appear to shift considerations of object relationships from external events as well as from internal organization to the arena of meaning. There is no easy way outside of introspection that an observer can tell from mere observation of behavior what one person means to another. When Margaret Mahler insists that trained psychoanalytic observers make inferences from observed phenomena, it is from the realm of logical conclusions that the word "inference" is used. It is a different sense of meaning than that delivered by empathic closures. This is not to say that logical deductions are not or cannot be employed in empathic pursuits, but suggests that perhaps different forms of making sense of observables are to be considered. In vicarious introspection, we feel we are correct in our conclusions by experiences of fitting things together and the revealing of more material that seemed to be hidden. Unfortunately, this topic needs a much more detailed elaboration than is possible here, but is a confirmation of the more radical shift from object relations theory to a theory of meaning.

Clinical Illustrations

This clinical excerpt is offered only to highlight the issue of variability of the concept of object relations as well as that of the nature of the self-object. The patient is a man who was in analysis because of a symptom of perverse behavior. The particulars of this behavior were related to his work as a physician and his specific duty of doing rather frequent physical examinations. On occasion, he would massage the neck of a female patient and carefully manipulate her so that her face would be in contact with his penis. Shortly thereafter, he usually would succeed in having the woman perform fellatio on him. The entire procedure would be conducted without any verbal interchange; the women were anonymous and usually not seen again. I have no doubt that this patient's quality of object relations, at least in this sector of his personality, would be characterized by a host of negative connotations, including primitive, narcissistic, archaic, need-satisfying. The elements of this perverse symptom are worth examining to see if it holds any clues for us to evaluating what it might represent—what it says about the patient and what it means to the patient.

In the beginning phase of the analysis, the patient reported a dream of himself being in two parts—a healthy man and a burdened woman. Shortly thereafter, he had the following dream: "An aged grandmother was in a rocker and she was saying wise things. She then began to suck my penis, on which there was a blister." He connected the grandmother to me, describing me as crotchety, but still as someone with whom he felt he agreed and to whom he could connect. He felt the blister would heal in time. He then said he was fearful of the impending weekend and a resultant depression. The room of the dream reminded him of the recovery room at the hospital and the fear of death that seemed to be there.

The symptom reenacted in the transference reflected parts of himself that became lived out or externalized in the ensuing regression of analysis. One could say the essence of the object relationship was of an injured child being soothed by mother. Indeed, the patient had a significant history of childhood illness and a strong feeling of not being properly comforted. The meaning of the injury was not clear; the fear of depression at being without me was equally troublesome.

This patient had been in analysis previously and had been offered the interpretation that his symptom was an enactment of the "doctor game" about which Ernst Simmel (1926) had written. That analysis and the explanation had done little to ameliorate the difficulty, and in his next analytic experience there seemed little evidence of an oedipal conflict being responsible for the trouble. Throughout this analysis, I had to decipher this symptom to see what it might stand for. As an external bit of behavior, it could *not* simply be a pleasure-seeking pursuit since, as with most perverse behavior, it was ushered in with tremendous anxiety and succeeded by profound shame. As a representative of something, it first had to be desexualized and seen in the transference as reflecting a particular developmental configuration. Finally, only as it came to have a particular and individual meaning for this patient could we grasp the multiple significance it had for him.

Over a period of time, this patient developed a narcissistic transference with a slow but steady diminution of his symptomatology. I would now like to focus on some events that occurred toward the end of his analysis. He had been considering termination and announced that, with his continued feeling of well-being and lack of anxiety, perhaps he should set a date for termination. He felt he had terminated his first analysis too soon; this had been connected with the birth of a sibling when the patient was one and a half years old, and the feeling throughout the ensuing years that he had been forced to grow up too soon. Life was a series of premature departures — of being pushed out before he was ready.

He planned a vacation, entertaining an idea that this would serve as a test of his ability to go it alone. Soon he announced the dates of his vacation and I realized that I, too, would be away for part of the same period of time. I felt this was an unnecessary comment, but I was routinely telling my patients when I would be away and saw no reason to avoid informing this patient. The following day he missed his appointment — not an unusual event. When he next came, he told me that he had overslept and reported a dream in which he told his wife, who was hiding under a tent, to call me about his missing. This was followed by another dream about a man who wanted to do something, and the patient angrily refusing this man.

The patient felt that the second dream had to do with his feeling that he no longer needed analysis. But he then confessed that he had acted out after his last appointment. He had felt terribly excited and then terribly bad. I wondered whether my being gone at the time of his departure could be significant. He said that was unimportant; that the main thing was the intensity of his excitement. He felt restless and was reckless, and even drank to excess, something quite unusual for this man. He felt strongly that he would prefer to handle his emotions according to his old patterns and *not* with understanding. He had an equally strong, belligerent feeling toward me that I could not force him to do things; I failed to understand that he *had* to do things his way. He then, in a more relaxed manner, said that he was really very embarrassed by this revealing of his excitement. I said that the hiding wife (in the first dream) really was himself, and he agreed, saying that he always tried to pretend that he was casual about matters. He said that he was like his mother: a wet blanket. Then he felt that I, too, would make him ashamed of his excitement. He went on to tell me of the day he had received his letter of acceptance to medical school and had run into the kitchen to report the good news to his mother. She barely looked up from her work to mutter how nice that was. He had run from the house and screamed at the sky, but he could not recall if his feelings were of joy or frustration.

In essence, this patient had experienced a relationship with a mother who he felt could not respond to him and to his feelings. In the analysis, the predominant transference was one of a self-object needed to reflect and mirror himself. When this was established, he felt intact; and when it was disrupted, he sexualized the relationship via his perversion. The planned-for termination, to this patient, was a momentous event which frightened him because it ushered in a traumatic state. This state of overstimulation required a narcissistic object to contain it, and at this point the analyst was seen as the mother of old, who was emotionally unavailable. In the same way the patient saw a change from acting out to understanding as a relinquishment of the analyst who had been necessary as a functional part of the self. No doubt the neatest explanation is that of the sexualized, narcissistic configuration, i.e., the grandiose self needing a response of a compliant other who makes no demands and has no individuality; a rather clear-cut narcissistic object. However, this form of summary always is an abbreviated classification because the web of associations leads us to explanations that demand the filling in of the unique life of that singular patient. In fact, this patient earlier in analysis had demonstrated that the analyst, as mother, initially was exciting and later left him on his own to handle his feelings. One can then return to the image and action of the symptom to note that this element as well can be seen there.

At the risk of being repetitious, I shall enumerate the levels at which these analytic data can be comprehended. To begin with, the overt behavior expresses a relationship which immediately calls up a host of descriptive terms. Each of these terms can be classified descriptively; that is, according to development or some other form of ordering; and each, in turn, is a part of an inner code or organization. As the behavior is conceived of via an internal or representational viewpoint, it is also assumed to carry other significance. For example, the overt perversion which is an actualization of a persistent developmental problem with the mother also can be coded in terms of a narcissistic relationship of a self image. If we choose to go beyond this inner coding method, we enlarge our perception to reveal the individual particulars of the behavior for this person in his unique life and we thereby encounter the complexity of a psychology of meaning. Rather than concentrating on the symptoms per se, we must understand that this set of behavior reflected only a sector of this man's personality. He was a husband, father, and a quite accomplished physician, and by no means was his total personality reflective of this earlier described pathological development. But the more we allow ourselves to conceptualize the totality of the patient, the more do we move away from codes or maps to the knotty problem of meaning, and to the conclusion that our understanding of the symptomatic behavior relevant to object relations belongs to that particular realm of discourse.

The illustrative choice of a patient with perverse behavior is designed only to highlight the succession of conceptual steps seen in the movement from object relations to object representations as representative of roles to those roles as indicators of deeper meanings (Goldberg, 1975).

As the patient's termination period began to take shape, he wondered again and again how I felt about his decision to end, and what would be a reasonable date to set for this ending. Again, he acted out. He did so with a patient about whom he simply was unable to determine whether or not she previously had been a willing participant in his perversion or was a totally unknown individual. As his doubt became more and more intense, he decided that only action on his part would resolve his dilemma. He maneuvered her face to the appropriate position, opened his pants, exposed his penis, and she screamed. He was terrified. She was enraged; and he was in trouble. He had been wrong about her; had acted abruptly; and now was mortified and about to begin a series of maneuvers to free himself of the consequences of his action. This involved pleading for forgiveness and a subsequent legal conflict.

The analysis clearly was the stage where the action of the patient belonged and soon we realized that the meaning of his behavior had to do with his doubt over setting a termination date. If one can sexualize an affect, then this surely is an example of this phenomenon. As the issue of doubt was focused upon, we connected it to early childhood doubtfulness about his mother and what she was thinking and, in particular, how she felt about him. It was equally difficult for this woman to respond to her child's excitement and to share with him any of her feelings. She was cold, stern, and un-yielding. He felt that she did not like people to be too happy; that others' pleasure seemed to discomfort her. In the transference, he was intensely curious about my reaction to his elation over termina-tion. Did I care or was I convinced that he would fail? So, too, he had been terribly curious about his mother and what she thought and how she felt. He had been left with doubts about her, and now they emerged in his perversion.

To answer what his perverse act means is to lift it away from the restricted neatness of object relations. It is both a multidimensional, subjective experience and a communication to another. It does not treat another person as an object or thing, but, rather, participates in a web of relationships with both historical and topographic dimen-sions. And so it is in this arena of meaning that we focus our at-tention.

The use of the metaphor of the internal stage or the drama of in-ner persons in interaction runs the danger of psychoanalysis adopt-ing a form of role theory, albeit an internal one, for its under-pinnings. Psychoanalysis never has been content with the position of role theory which concentrates on overt or manifest roles or be-havioral criteria and thereby ignores the unconscious components of behavior. Although we do enrich this theory by including uncon-scious roles, we may still inhibit a comprehension of the range of complexity of the experience. If, for example, a student speaks to a teacher or a patient questions a doctor, we can usually perceive that these so-called obvious roles may conceal the fact that a child-parent relationship also is in gear. In fact, this insight of the implicit role of a participant in any sort of meaningful relationship was the first great revelation of psychoanalytic psychology and over the years has become commonplace. When we add to this very general orientation those particulars of the relationship having to do with development, we take the next great step that analysis has to offer to this picture of the hidden roles being enacted, i.e., just what sort of a child is lurk-ing in the shadows? Yet, not until we investigate the nature of the exchange do we ever feel that we become true analytic investigators. Of course, merely watching the person's interacting never is suffi-cient. Adding the components of language, nuance, gesture, etc., serves to enlarge the range of comprehension. But we ultimately ask just what effect does one person have upon another? What are the feelings involved? How does the one person expect to alter and be altered by the other? In brief, we ask the nature of the personal experience or the subjective meaning of the interchange. The hidden role of the child talking to a parent simply does not reveal the form of data that are of analytic interest; rather, it is an aid to orienting one in the determination of what this person must feel as both student or patient *plus* child in this interaction. Thus, role theory is notoriously limited for psychoanalysis, and to say that the internal drama is the real story of the external one still necessitates that one ask just what the story is and not merely who the actors are. One must take the step demanded by the complexity of this exchange to investigate it as a theory of meaning, which is more comprehensive than that of inner actors who both replicate and complicate the happenings of the external world.

Another clinical example is that of a young woman in analysis who, during the course of treatment, began an extramarital affair with a man who insisted on the introduction of a third person, another woman, into their sexual activity. Again we have a set of behavior which we seek to interpret and understand. The patient initially claimed that she did not mind the intrusion, but this seemed to conceal her shame at this form of deviance. When the shame diminished, she seemingly enjoyed the situation. Her past history was characterized by a life with an unfaithful father and a long-suffering, depressed mother. During a prolonged period of maternal transference, the patient repeatedly expressed a desire to terminate her treatment. She had a dream of going off on a trip with her mother and boyfriend; of leaving the two of them only to be reunited with them in a hotel, and then finally having the mother leave. The wish to terminate was interpreted as an attempt to achieve a separation from mother, something that she had been unable to achieve as a child. She identified with the oft-departing father, who returned repeatedly, as well as with the yearning and lonely mother. The sexual activity could be seen to represent the unresolved and unbreakable threesome of the patient's identifications. In fantasy, as the analyst became the third member of the threesome, the patient found herself unable to be orgastic with her lover. She reported a dream of being in a hotel, going into the kitchen to take out the bones of a fish prepared for her boyfriend. The associations to the smell of the fish led to her inability to achieve orgasm. The interpretation about the bones was directed to her not wanting her boyfriend to be "stuck" with her sexual problems. The bones, however, also referred to her own lack of a penis and her feeling sad over her own small clitoris. More and more she spoke of not having enough to satisfy her mother as well as of her failure to have her mother for herself without the mother longing for the father.

As the analysis worked more on the patient's feelings about herself as a woman, and her concomitant early wish to look more like her father and brother, the issue of penis envy seemed to recede. She told me that she felt that she was not looking for a penis from me, but rather simply wanted to be okay just as she was. This was seen in the transference as the wish for acceptance from both mother and father.

About a year later, the patient reported another dream of herself protecting a little girl who, in turn, was protecting an aquarium. Her first association referred to her earlier dream of the fish; she then recalled the intense childhood shame about her clitoris and her fixation on it for pleasure. Now, however, in her analytic transference, she was alternately the little girl longing for recognition and the hidden masculine component of her psyche.

The triangual perverse action is displayed in the analysis in its many levels of significance. The patient, at the times of wanting to leave analysis, is the father who deserts the mother. When she turns to the analyst for help and support, she expresses the portion of the little girl who needs the mother's protection. In turn, this presentation of the little girl can serve as a defense both against revealing her hidden penis and against the recognition of her vulnerability as a woman, like mother, unable to hold her man. Certainly, each and all these relationships are object relations, but they serve different meanings at different points in analysis and in life.

No doubt, this is a simple, though much abbreviated, segment of a familiar sequence in analysis. The acting-out behavior stood for her early childhood relationships, her unresolved identifications, and the presence of the missing part of her anatomy. In the transference it served to represent these aspects of her psyche, but also showed a deeper set of relationships with mother and father. However, only via the patient's particular and individual assignment of significance to the behavior, the roles, the representations, and the past, do we finally come upon the unique meaning to the patient.

However one may characterize her object relationships, we see that they reveal little about the patient except in the most general way. As a map, they lead one to the proper terrain, but our real exploration remains in the area of individual meaning.

Psychoanalysis is getting more complicated. Although this is true of the advancement of any science that moves from macro- to micro-examination of its data (see Levin, 1977), it is even more true of psychoanalysis because it deals primarily with complexities. It is no longer possible to trace linear conflicts in analysis because our research and our clinical experience have revealed the multiple interrelationships of psychological material. As we have moved away from the singular study of conflict, so, too, has our concern moved to psychoanalysis as a psychology of meaning. The recent wave of changes called for in theory have paralleled a call for an emphasis on meaning. The hoped-for solution to theoretical problems in this quest has, of course, opened up an entirely new set of problems.

To begin with, we rarely have achieved clear definitions of meaning. Nor do we ever claim to equate analysis with the entire universe of meaning. When someone tells us how to get to Brooklyn, we may know what he means; but just as clearly we know that this is a cognitive accomplishment not at all related to the emotional world of psychoanalysis. Only by a return to empathic comprehension of a rather large mass of data can we begin to define and draw the boundaries of our field of inquiry.

Truth and Meaning

The dichotomy between truth and meanings or between facts and opinions became a sharp scientific problem when Freud was able to differentiate between objective reality and psychic reality. The realm of subjective experience could no longer be dismissed as mere opinion, since we increasingly realized that psychic reality was the overriding arbiter of truth or facts. Much of "what really happened" in history became a matter of the person doing the recording. Much of "what is happening" becomes a question of the instrument of perception. And much of truth thus becomes a matter of subjective interpretation.

To maintain the dichotomy between objective and subjective is, for psychoanalysis, a necessity. Therefore, we delineate our interpretive field as one of meaning, as opposed to truth. The realm of meaning is one of personal experience and therefore not of testable or verifiable or falsifiable facts. On the other hand, we maintain an equally firm foothold in objective reality when we study development as an outside observer who is involved in determining an accurate description of real events. Thus, we alternate between truth and meaning, with the latter always being primary.

Anatol Rapaport (1968) defines meaning as the intuitive grasp of wholes. In a discussion of intuition, Kohut (1971) sharply contrasts it with empathy, the former being the result of rapid cognitive activity, while the latter involves affective comprehension based on a controlled merger with another. I suspect Rapaport, as a mathematician, was stressing the total approach, in contrast to the piecemeal, and probably would agree that the crucial issue is the encompassing of the gestalt or of the total field. If we, in turn, concentrate on this point, then we may be able to offer a definition of object relations in terms of the total field or total complex configuration which is empathically grasped. Such an emphasis on the empathic grasp of complex wholes would limit the study of object relations to the internal world; would allow the unconscious component to be included as a part of our comprehension in depth; and would minimize the significance of one or another of the components or elements of the configuration. The essence of this definition is the delivery of meaning to the observer.

Objects as such have no meaning. The limited scheme of objects leading to gratification of the drives or the fulfillment of wishes seems peculiarly restrictive to the richness of psychoanalytic work. The introduction of the concept of the self-object has caused a shift of our understanding to an emphasis on how someone or something is experienced. The experience can and does include drive gratification, but it becomes a larger issue and allows a wider and deeper comprehension of psychological material. Fundamentally, an awareness of another's experience is not achieved by careful and detailed observation and logical conclusions as much as it is by vicarious introspection and empathic closures. Therefore, we must also shift our theoretical stand on object relations from the external field of interpersonal behavior to the inner world, which is fundamentally a different world. Likewise, we must move from a concentration on singular components to one of complex configurations.

The rules or codes for classifying object relations become guides or pointers to our empathic comprehension, but they explain nothing by themselves — they only help to explain what we understand empathically.

I am sure that for some psychoanalysts these points are so obvious as hardly to merit a discussion; but for others, they are a drastic distortion of analytic theory. The present state of analytic work requires repeated efforts at clarifying areas of uncertainty or confusion and this effort is directed to that end.

If a resolution of the problem is to be entertained, it would have to make some sharp distinctions about both the methods and data of psychoanalysis. Piaget and Inhelder (1969) have shown that in the early years of life, sensorimotor activity is the center of cognition; similarly, psychoanalysts probably could say that there is little distinction between behavior and meaning during that period. As the child develops and as he commences internal operations, we, in turn, concentrate on the inner world and often utilize schemes such as the transfer of action to the arena within. This is a time of egocentric manipulation and is not yet at the stage where meaning becomes entirely divorced from behavior. This latter stage depends on man's primary function as a symbolizing animal, one that some say makes humans so unique. In this sense, a symbol is a conceptual vehicle, and thus is the carrier of psychological meaning. It is, of course, a different definition of symbol than Jones would have offered. The journey from action to drive gratification to symbolization is that of the developing sense of object relations, and the endpoint is where analysts seem to concentrate their interest — on the understanding of what things mean. This will naturally soon lead us to conceptualizing a developmental line of meaning, as well as to clarifying the definition of meaning that is most reflective of psychoanalytic psychology. I suggest that, more than any other, this is the focus of psychoanalytic science and should be sharply distinguished as such. As a suggestion, it is offered with no plea for it being a rule or a law, but rather that it be distinguished as one viewpoint among many. The more psychoanalysis grows, the more we see that a unifying theory will be, not the result of reducing everything to a minimum, but rather an achievement of harmony of diverse elements much like that happy equilibrium of ego, id, and superego that Freud envisaged.

References

Blanck, S. (1977), Personal communication.

Freud, A. (1952), The mutual influences in the development of ego and id. *The Psychoanalytic Study of the Child,* 7:42–50.

_____ (1965), *Normality and Pathology in Childhood.* New York: International Universities Press.

Freud, S. (1914), On narcissism: an introduction. *Standard Edition,* 14:67–102. London: Hogarth Press, 1957.

_____ (1916–17), Introductory lectures on psycho-analysis. *Standard Edition,* 15 & 16. London: Hogarth Press, 1963.

_____ (1923), The ego and the id. *Standard Edition,* 19:3–66. London: Hogarth Press, 1961.

Goldberg, A. (1975), A fresh look at perverse behavior. *Int. J. Psycho-Anal.,* 56: 335–342.

Hartmann, H. (1952), The mutual influences in the development of ego and id. *The Psychoanalytic Study of the Child,* 7:9–30.

_____ Kris, E., & Loewenstein, R. M. (1946), Comments on the formation of psychic structure. *The Psychoanalytic Study of the Child,* 2:11–38.

Jacobson, E. (1964), *The Self and the Object World.* New York: International Universities Press.

Kernberg, O. F. (1971), Prognostic considerations regarding borderline personality organization. *J. Amer. Psychoanal. Assn.,* 19:595–635.

Klein, G. S. (1968), Psychoanalysis: ego psychology. In: *International Encyclopedia of the Social Sciences,* 13 & 14:11–31. New York: Free Press.

Kohut, H. (1971), *The Analysis of the Self.* New York: International Universities Press.

Levin, D. (1977), The continuing usefulness of physics as a model for psychoanalytic thought. Unpublished manuscript.

Mahler, M. S. (1968), *On Human Symbiosis and the Vicissitudes of Individuation.* New York: International Universities Press.

McDevitt, J. B. (1975), Separation-individuation and object constancy. *J. Amer. Psychoanal. Assn.,* 23:713–742.

McGuire, M. T. (1976), A descriptive, research-justified data-base for psychiatry: would it change things? Unpublished manuscript.

Meissner, W. W. (1979), Critique of concept and therapy in the language approach to psychoanalysis. *Int. J. Psycho-Anal.,* 60:291–310.

Piaget, J. & Inhelder, B. (1969), *The Psychology of the Child.* New York: Basic Books.

Rapaport, A. (1968), Foreword. In: *Modern Systems Research for the Behavioral Scientist,* ed. W. Buckley. Chicago: Aldine Press.

Sandler, J. (1977), Address on affects. International Psycho-Analytical Association Congress, Jerusalem.

Schafer, R. (1972), Internalization: process or fantasy? *The Psychoanalytic Study of the Child,* 27:411–436.

Simmel, E. (1926), The "doctor-game," illness and the profession of medicine. *Int. J. Psycho-Anal.,* 7:470–483.

Stolorow, R. D. (1978), Review: *Object Relations Theory and Clinical Psychoanalysis.* *Contemp. Psychol.,* 23:32–33.

Sugarman, A. (1977), Object-relations theory: a reconciliation of phenomenology and ego psychology. *Bull. Menninger Clin.,* 41:113–130.

7
BASIC CONCEPTS AND TERMS IN
OBJECT RELATIONS THEORIES

THEODORE L. DORPAT, M.D.

The aim of this paper is to undertake a conceptual analysis of some of the principal concepts and terms in object relations theories. I hope to clarify and explain key concepts, and to analyze critically how some of the main terms are used in psychoanalytic discourse.

The Misconception of "Intrapsychic or Interpersonal"

Object relations theories may be divided into those taking an interpersonal point of view and those taking the so-called intrapsychic point of view. According to Gedo and Goldberg (1973), some object relations theories are concerned with actual human transactions in the real world, whereas others refer to the "intrapsychic object as laid down in the memory system" (p. 60). Kernberg's (1976, pp. 56–59) definition of object relations theory emphasizes the intrapsychic, although it encompasses both of what he calls the intrapsychic and interpersonal "fields." The distinction between the intrapsychic and interpersonal runs through much of contemporary psychoanalytic literature. Langs (1976b), for example, distinguishes between intrapsychic and interactional defenses, resistances, and mechanisms.

I submit that the distinction between intrapsychic and interpersonal is false and misleading, and that it retards progress in the development of object relations theories. Much conceptual confusion and ambiguity surrounds the use of the word *intrapsychic* in psychoanalysis. A review of the literature reveals at least four different usages, which include: (1) inside the mind or psyche, (2) the inner or internal world, (3) inside the head or brain, and (4) psychic reality or subjective meaning. This last meaning of intrapsychic is the only one which I consider valid and useful for psychoanalysis.

149

The word intrapsychic is a spatial metaphor which is commonly and incorrectly interpreted in a literal sense to mean inside the psyche or mind. Used in this way, the subject commits the error of reification, because he speaks of the mind as if it were a space. As usually used, intrapsychic has no existent referents, but only vague verbal referents which are related to an overall fantasy or myth — the myth of the mind as an inner or internal world. Terms such as intrapsychic and inner world can logically refer only to fantasies and not to actual entities or processes. No existent action, event, process, or thing corresponds to the reified metaphors intrapsychic and inner world. Use of the phrases intrapsychic or interpersonal and intrapsychic and interpersonal tends to support the mythical and false view of two worlds, an internal psychic world and an external physical and/or interpersonal world. As Home (1966) explained, in using such terms as intrapsychic, analysts are talking about different metaphysical things created by the mistaken use of language. The major fallacy implicated in the invention of terms for inner psychic processes and entities is reification, which involves talking about thought and affect in terms used appropriately for describing physical events.

Wittgenstein (1945–49), Ryle (1949), Schafer (1976), and others have rejected the idea of hidden or theoretical entities in an inner mental world. Psychoanalytic concepts of the mind or an inner world are no less fantastic and mythical than religious dogmas of a soul separable from the body. The words for soul and mind are not distinguished in French and German. The fallacy of the literal interpretation of spatial metaphors in philosophical and psychoanalytic writings obviously does not account for the prevalence or influence of such myths. Sarbin (1972), studying the historical beginnings of the myth of the mind or soul as an inner world, traced this misconception to the religious and scientific transformations of the Renaissance. He concluded: "It was not until the development and widespread acceptance of religious beliefs about the existence of a separate inner life, a private shadowy stage, that terms had to be borrowed or created to denote happenings in this ghostly world" (p. 129).

My criticism of how psychoanalysts use the word intrapsychic is somewhat different from Schafer's (1976) criticism of such spatial metaphors in psychoanalytic discourse. I do not agree with his recommendation that we banish spatial metaphors from psychoanalytic theory. Conceptual problems in psychoanalytic discourse arise more from the ways words are used than from the words themselves. Confusion about metaphors occurs when their meaning is taken in a literal sense (Meissner, 1976). Spatial metaphors such as *internalization* and *introjection* may be used to refer to psychic process so long as they are not used or interpreted in a literal way.

The conceptual problems and confusion which come about when analysts misuse spatial terms is illustrated in Kohut's (1971) distinction between his theoretical standpoint and that of Mahler and others who use the method of child observation. Writing first about those who use the method of child observation, he said, "This theoretical system is defined by the position of the observer who, equidistant from the interacting parties, occupies an imaginary point *outside* of the experiencing individual. The core area of psychoanalytic metapsychology...is defined by the position of the observer who occupies an imaginary position *inside* the psychic organization of the individual with whose introspection he empathically identifies" (p. 219).

In my opinion, Kohut made an erroneous distinction between his theoretical stance and that of Mahler. The essential features of the investigative methods — the use of empathy and the search for the meaning of the observed behaviors — are the same for both. It is not clear what is meant in his description of his theoretical standpoint when he wrote about taking an "imaginary point *inside* the psychic organization." If "inside" is interpreted in a literal sense, his statement is illogical. How can one imagine being inside the psychic organization when the psychic organization is not a space or like a space?

Equally confusing is Kohut's phrase "*outside* of the experiencing individual" in his description of the child analyst's viewpoint. Does it mean that the analyst who observes children takes a stance similar to the behaviorist in merely observing the activities of the interacting parties without trying to understand their subjective meaning? If so, this is not true, because child analysts do use empathy in trying to understand the meaning of the child's behaviors and relationships.

I do not mean to imply an identity between adult psychoanalysis and psychoanalytically informed observation of children. But the observer's stance of discovering the meaning of the individual's actions through the use of empathy is common to both adult psychoanalysis and the systematic observation of children by child psychoanalysts. This fact has far-reaching implications for the comparison, cross-fertilization, and integration of object relations theories derived from adult psychoanalysis with those formed from psychoanalytic studies of children.

Yet, the word intrapsychic does refer to something of crucial importance to psychoanalysis when it is used to imply or denote *psychic reality*. The concept of psychic reality refers to subjective meaning, especially unconscious meaning (Schafer, 1976, p. 89). Psychoanalytic explanation and interpretation depend on our knowing what a particular action or object means to the subject. The psychoanalyst's concern with psychic reality stands in sharp contrast to the methods and theoretical stance of the behaviorist who seeks to describe and explain human behavior without taking into account subjective meaning.

It does not make sense to speak of object relations, defenses, or any other kind of human activity as taking place in two different worlds, an internal or intrapsychic world and an external physical and/or interpersonal world. Only in fantasy and not in actuality do humans exist in two worlds. One may, however, make a valid and meaningful distinction between relations with objects which are carried out *privately* in conscious or unconscious fantasy from those relations with objects that are conducted *publicly*. We should bear in mind Schafer's (1976, p. 160) idea that "private" is not just another word for "inner," because it expresses an entirely different way of conceptualizing psychic actions.

Object Relations as Actions

What do we mean by *relations?* I propose that we take the term relations to mean human actions. As used here and comprehensively discussed by Schafer (1976), *action* refers to intentional and meaningful behavior. He defined action as "human behavior that has a point; it is meaningful human activity; it is intentional or goal-directed performances by people; it is doing things for reasons" (p. 139). The concept of action includes all private psychic activities such as thinking, as well as public activities such as speaking, which have intentional and symbolic properties. Actions may be performed consciously, preconsciously, or unconsciously. Complex actions combine in one activity a number of actions.

The word actions may be used to describe the activities of one person in an interpersonal relationship. If we view the activities of both parties in a relationship, we may use the term *interactions*. Both actual and imagined object relations involve some kind of action or interaction between the subject and an object. There are, of course, many different specific relations which may occur in a relationship, e.g., loving, hating, controlling, talking.

The relation is the essential and dynamic factor in interpersonal interactions which the subject internalizes and employs for the formation of ego and superego structures. Martin Buber's (1970) statement, "In the beginning is the relation" (p. 69), is true in several senses, including the developmental sense. During ontogenesis the internalization of the relation precedes the time when the young child can differentiate between the subject and the object involved in the relation. As Jacobson (1964) noted, the earliest self and object images are not differentiated from each other. From the infant's point of view, the object is nothing but the prolongation of the infant's activity. Only gradually through a process of *objectivation* does the young child learn to make a distinction between his activity and the object toward which this activity is directed (Fraiberg, 1969, p. 87).

One of the most common misconceptions in object relations writings is one wherein self and object are viewed as substantially separate entities which are somehow brought together in a relationship. The "I" and "you" exist only in the activity of relating. This fundamental truth has been expressed by several philosophers in their attempts to overcome the Cartesian split between subject and object (Buber, 1970; Cassirer, 1967; Dewey and Bentley, 1949). Cassirer (1967) wrote:

> However, if we no longer begin with the "I" and the "you" as two substantially separate entities, but locate them in the meeting point of that reciprocal transaction, which consummates itself in speech or any other culture-form, our perplexities dissipate. In the beginning is the act; always, in the function of speech, in artistic creation, in the process of thought and inquiry there is expressed a specific *activity*. And only in this activity do the "I" and "you" exist with the possibility of simultaneously distinguishing themselves from each other. They exist both within speech, thought, and all measures of artistic expression [p. 109].

In their studies on introjects and introjection, both George Klein (1976, p. 294) and Kernberg (1976, p. 65) describe the "components" of introjected object relations as including a self representation, an object representation in interaction with the self representation, and an affective state. The term "components" is objectionable and misleading because it implies the existence of separable entities or parts which are put together. The items listed as components (self, object, and affect) would be more accurately described as aspects.

All human actions have an object. The term *object* refers to the person, thing, or whatever to which the subject's overt behaviors, thought, and feeling are directed. Subject, action, and object are different but related aspects of a description or explanation of experience. Any description of experience must refer to the totality subject-action-object (Chein, 1972, p. 201). Actions, whether performed consciously, preconsciously, or unconsciously, have an essentially intentional character, and one is always conscious of something, some object (Husserl, 1965, p. 96).

Although Schafer's (1976) writings on action and action language do not explicitly consider the topic of objects, the concept of there being an object involved in all human action is implied in his definition of human action as "intentional or goal-directed performances" (p. 139). One of the defining properties of intentional actions is the idea of the intentional object (Husserl, 1965).

The concept of action also implies an acting subject (the "I" or self-as-agent). This co-definition of subject, action, and object is not empirical; it is conceptual or logical. Subject, action, and object are indissolubly linked, and together constitute any experience.

The object relations perspective I am proposing is this: object relations theories are concerned with human actions; the self and object representations involved in actions; and the transformations of actions into psychic structures. An implicit, if not explicit, consensus obtains in the studies of various psychologists, philosophers, and psychoanalysts that all psychic life, all of our private and public action, are object-relational (Chein, 1972; Fairbairn, 1952; Husserl, 1965; M. Klein et al., 1955).

My aim here is to mention some of the implications of this object relations concept. One can, in principle, analyze any action or complex action from this perspective. All clinical phenomena, e.g., defenses, symptoms, character traits, can be analyzed from the point of view of the actions and the representations of self and objects involved. Later, in the section on affects, I shall discuss the view of Sandler and Sandler (1978) that all wishes imply some kind of object relationship. Every wish "contains" representations of the self and object in interaction. The object relations concept advanced here agrees with the Sandlers' formulation, but goes beyond it. This perspective on object relations is not being presented with the purpose of changing psychoanalytic theory or technique. The object relations concept which emphasizes the basic totality of subject-action-object makes explicit what psychoanalysts have already been doing and talking about.

Object relations theories are the most important and essential part of what George Klein (1976) called the psychoanalytic clinical theory. Object relations theories are derived from and, to a large extent, testable by psychoanalytic clinical methods and by the systematic employment of psychoanalytically oriented child observation. In his discussion of object relation theories among the British school, Sutherland (1963) stressed that clinical data provide the foundations for object relations theories. He pointed to the greater distance between clinical data and theory in the American ego psychology group as contrasted with the British analysts who pioneered in the formation of object relations theories.

Object relations theories are clinical, not metapsychological theories. G. Klein (1976) distinguished between the clinical theory, which is derived from the methods of psychoanalysis, and the metapsychological theory, which is an expression of Freud's philosophy of science. A similar distinction was made by Rapaport (1960, p. 125), who differentiated between a *specific* psychoanalytic theory, which is dependent on psychoanalytic methods, and a *general* psychoanalytic theory, which is little dependent on those methods.

The Psychoanalytic Concept of Object

I have defined object as the person, thing, or whatever to which the subject's overt behavior, thoughts, and feeling are directed. The objection could be raised that this concept of objects is too inclusive. If someone were to complain that this idea means that there is some kind of object involved in everything an individual thinks or does, I would agree. But that is exactly the point.

I have already taken up one reason for proposing this inclusive definition of object — the desirability and logic of linking the object concept with the conception of relations as action. Another reason is that this definition is the only one sufficiently broad to cover all of the different kinds of objects written about in psychoanalysis. Furthermore, my analysis of the way the word object is usually used in psychoanalysis reveals one common factor in the many instances studied. This common factor, or definining property, of psychoanalytic objects is that they are the object of the subject's actions. An object is that which the subject consciously or unconsciously, in thought or in deed, acts upon. A similar concept of object was discussed by Chein (1972), who used the term object "to designate any thing, event, process, situation or what-have-you that is referred to in a sentence by the syntactical object — direct and/or indirect — of a transitive verb" (p. 69).

Many kinds of objects are written about in psychoanalysis, including part objects, whole objects, need-satisfying objects, transitional objects, self-objects, good and bad objects, the self-as-object, objects which possess object constancy. As Fairbairn (1955) explained, object, as used in psychoanalysis, is a comprehensive term employed to cover all the types of objects studied and described by psychoanalysts.

Unless the text provides a definition of what kind of object is being written about, the reader has to supply the specific meaning of a particular object by examining the context in which the term is used.

Abenheimer (1955) objected to the use of the word object on the grounds that the objects with which the individual seeks to establish relationships are persons, and therefore the term object is too impersonal to be appropriate. Fairbairn (1955) countered Abenheimer's objections with the argument that psychoanalysis needs a comprehensive term which could be used to encompass the diverse kinds of both human and nonhuman objects with which psychoanalysis is concerned. Although it is fundamentally with persons that the individual seeks to establish relationships, the vicissitudes of emotional life lead to relations with innumerable animate and inanimate objects, e.g., transitional objects, that are not persons. In my opinion, Fairbairn's arguments for using objects to include both human and nonhuman objects prevail over the view advanced by Kernberg

(1976, p. 58) that the term objects should refer only to the human object.

One's self can be the object of one's actions. In objective self-assessment the self is the object of one's assessment (Kohut, 1971, p. 39). Schafer (1968, p. 80) wrote about the self-as-object (the "me"), and distinguished it from the self-as-agent (the "I"). The self-as-object is the self, for example, that is criticized in self-criticism.

On the Use of "Self"

Much confusion surrounds the word *self*, since it has been used in so many ways in psychoanalysis. As Schafer (1976) explained, self is a multipurpose word like the pronouns I and me. There are many different senses in which self words are used to define or to discuss experience. Self may be used to mean my personality, my actions, my body agency, my continuity, etc.

Schafer (1976) argued persuasively against using the words self and identity as systematic terms in psychoanalytic discourse. "Self and identity are not names of identifiable homogeneous or monolithic entities; they are classes of self-representations that exist only in the vocabulary of the observer" (p. 189). Self and identity are commonly treated as motivational-structural entities on the order of the "ego." In this regard they suffer the same reification that has afflicted Freud's concepts of the ego and superego. Self can be properly used only as a descriptive term to refer to a content of subjective experience.

Merger, Fusion, and Boundaries

Most often the terms *fusion, merger,* and *boundaries* are used as metaphors in object relations theories. Through the use of these words the language we use to describe physical entities has been applied metaphorically to describe different ways in which individuals represent themselves and others. Conceptual problems and confusion occur when these metaphors are erroneously used and interpreted in a literal sense. For example, some authors mistakenly write of self and object representations[1] as if they were some kind of substantive

[1]In psychoanalysis the word representation is generally used to mean an idea

entities which in early development are at first merged, then later become separated and demarcated by actual boundaries. *Representations* (ideas) do not literally merge or fuse, and they are not, literally speaking, separated by boundaries.

Another frequent fallacy, the anthropomorphic fallacy, is committed when one speaks of representations as if they were active agents which could fuse, merge, or perform any kind of action. Persons may merge their self representations with certain object representations, but representations as such cannot (logically) do anything. To explain the correct meanings of these metaphors, I shall examine their clinical or experiential referents. Since my reading of the psychoanalytic literature indicates that the meanings of merger and fusion are interchangeable, I shall use the term merger to stand for both.

The most common usage of merging refers to a type of mental content or experience in which the subject consciously or unconsciously feels joined or united in some way with an object. In empathy, for example, one feels temporarily merged or "at one" with the object of one's empathy. Here merging is used as a metaphor, because the subject's experience of merging himself with his representation of another person does not involve any actual physical merging of substantive entities. Schafer (1968, p. 134) wrote about a patient who during times of stress would merge his self representation with the introject of his "monster" mother, and then perceive himself and act as if he were a "monster." Merging in this case involved a temporary and defensive identification with his "monster" introject.

Kohut (1971) described a merger kind of mirror transference in which the analyst is experienced by the analysand as an extension of the patient's grandiose self. The idealizing transference, according to Kohut, involves a merger of the analysand with the idealized object.

Jacobson (1964, p. 69) noted that one can differentiate normal from pathological fusions between self and objects on the basis of whether or not the regressive fusions are prompted by fantasies of libidinal union between the self and objects, or by severe hostility

---

(Schafer, 1968, p. 60). Another usage, proposed by Sandler and Rosenblatt (1962), has received little acceptance. They consider representations to be schemas, and they distinguish between representations, which are nonconscious, and images, which may be conscious, preconscious, or unconscious.

conflicts. Transient fantasies of libidinal union between the self and objects are usually not pathological, and they do not involve an irreversible loss of boundaries between self and object representations. By contrast, regressive fantasies caused by severe conflicts over aggressive wishes may result in irreparable loss of the boundaries between self and object representations.

In psychoanalysis the word boundaries has several different meanings. Sometimes boundary is used to refer to the border between the subject's body and the environment or to the subject's representation of that border. Most often, though, boundary is used as a metaphor when we, for example, speak of ego boundaries or boundaries between self and object representations. The clinical referent for the metaphorical usage of boundaries is the individual's capacity for forming and/or maintaining conscious, preconscious, or unconscious personally significant distinctions. Some of the more important personal distinctions include the distinction between self and object representations; between representations of the past, present, and future; between what is fantasy and what is reality. Because this metaphorical usage does not refer to the body or to any other physical or spatial entity, the literal misinterpretation of the metaphor boundaries leads to the erroneous use of representations (ideas) as if they were physical or spatial entities demarcated by actual, concrete boundaries.

Pathological boundary problems occur in individuals where there has been a developmental failure of boundary formation, or where the capacity to maintain significant distinctions undergoes a regressive and/or defensive suspension under stress (see Blatt and Wild [1976] for a comprehensive study of boundary defects in schizophrenia).

As noted above, the metaphorical usage of boundaries should be distinguished from the usage in which "boundaries" refer to the body boundary. Developmental psychologists and child psychoanalysts agree that at about one year the infant develops the capacity for distinguishing between himself as a physical body from the bodies of others. At this stage the infant acquires some awareness of his *physical* separateness from others. The term boundaries is used in this context to refer to the subject's representation of an interface between his body and the environment. There is a definite spatial coordinate in this usage; body boundary refers to the subject's representation of the limits of his bodily place in space. Ordinarily one's skin and other body surfaces are experienced and represented as a boundary between one's body and other physical entities.

Object Relations Theory and Structural Theory

As a recent panel report on object relations theory demonstrated (Spruiell, 1978), there is much disagreement and uncertainty about the place of object relations theory in psychoanalytic theory. Guntrip (1971) and others would eliminate structural theory and replace it with an object relations theory. Kernberg (1976) seems to view his object relations theory primarily as an elaboration of the structural point of view. Gedo and Goldberg (1973) favor the construction of object relations theories to cover preoedipal phases or development, and the retention of structural theory as applicable to oedipal and later levels of psychic development.

Gedo and Goldberg (1973) have described the gap in psycho-analytic clinical theory for the segment of psychic development preceding id-ego-superego differentiation. According to them, no satisfying set of concepts has been proposed for the state of the psyche prior to its differentiation into ego, superego, and id structures. In their view, an object relations model can fill this gap in psychoanalytic theory. They designed a hierarchical model of the mind which includes a tripartite model at a higher developmental level (oedipal and higher) and an object relations model at a lower developmental level. They present arguments for limiting the application of the tripartite model to higher developmental level psychopathology such as typically occurs in psychoneurotic patients who do not have significant ego or superego defects. They proposed that an object relations model is needed for conceptualizing psychic development before ego and superego differentiation, and for understanding clinical conditions in which there are major preoedipal components, e.g., borderline conditions, the psychoses, and narcissistic personality disorders.

In an earlier paper (1976) I employed the hierarchical model of Gedo and Goldberg (1973) to distinguish between two kinds of psychic conflict, *structural conflict* and *object relations conflict*. Structural conflict refers to conflict involving the major psychic structures: ego, id, and superego. The structural theory adequately encompasses conflicts between the subject's aggressive, sexual, or other wishes and his own values, prohibitions, and injunctions. Object relations conflicts were defined as conflicts between the subject's wishes and the prohibitions and injunctions that are not experienced as his own, but rather are represented in primary or secondary process representations of some (usually parental) authority.

Since one cannot determine from the manifest content of a symptom or character trait whether it stems from a structural conflict or an object relations conflict, the analyst must make a careful examination of the patient's associations in order to determine what kind of conflict is involved. The content (wishes, prohibitions, affects) of the two opposing parts of the conflict may appear to be the same in both types of conflicts. The crucial difference between the two types of conflict is this: in a structural conflict the subject experiences (or is capable of experiencing, if some part of the conflict is unconscious) the opposing tendencies as aspects of himself. His own prohibitions, values, and injunctions are in conflict with his aggressive, sexual, or other kinds of strivings and wishes. In an object relations conflict, the subject experiences the conflict as being between his own wishes and his representations, e.g., introjects, of another person's moral values or prohibitions.

A case study of an analytic patient who had significant conflicts and fixations at the separation-individuation phase of development was presented. As his analysis progressed, he began to suffer from both separation anxiety and separation guilt. His profound sense of separation guilt was triggered by real or imagined actions characterized by independence from his possessive and controlling mother. Unlike superego guilt, separation guilt is not experienced as stemming from real or imagined transgressions against one's own moral values. The patient did not consider the feelings, ideas, or overt acts that elicited separation guilt to be morally wrong. Rather, he experienced guilt because he felt that his strivings toward individuation and self-gratification would displease his mother. Separation guilt arose out of an object relations kind of conflict in which his wishes for independence were in conflict with prohibitions from his mother introject against independent action.

Since the conflict just described did not involve his own superego values and prohibitions, it was not a structural conflict. Object relations conflicts are psychic conflicts, and they should not be confused with conflicts with another person (interpersonal conflicts). The patient referred to above sometimes became involved in interpersonal conflicts with his actual mother, but such interpersonal conflicts were not necessarily or usually related to the kinds of object relations conflicts described above.

Object relations conflicts imply ego and/or superego defects. Kohut (1971), Gedo and Goldberg (1973), and others have studied the relationship between such defects and the kinds of self-object transferences patients with narcissistic personality disorder develop in psychoanalysis. The narcissistic transference object (or self-object) serves as a substitute for the patient's missing or defective psychic structures. In analysis and in their everyday life, such patients seek self-objects to carry out functions (guiding, controlling, comforting) that persons with more differentiated ego and superego structures are capable of doing for themselves.

In the absence of other persons who serve them as self-objects, such patients employ introjects to control, comfort, and/or punish themselves and to guide their activities in a manner similar to superego functioning. However, the ideals and values of superego functioning are more abstract, and the mode of functioning is more stable and autonomous from id and environmental pressures than in patients who use introjects for moral regulations. Also, superego functioning (moral *self*-regulation) is distinguished from moral regulations mediated either by introjects or by persons who serve as self-objects by the *depersonalized* quality of superego activity (Freud, 1926, p. 139). Superego moral demands are not ordinarily represented or experienced as stemming from representations of one's parents.

Transference and Object Relations

By *transference* we refer to a particular aspect of a person's relationship to another person. All human relationships contain a mixture of transference and realistic reactions (Fenichel, 1941, p. 72). As Freud demonstrated, transference is a repetition, a new edition of an old relationship. There is general acceptance of the view which considers transference a universal aspect of object relations (Loewald, 1960; Szasz, 1963). The analytic situation does not of itself create transference, but it provides conditions for transference to emerge into consciousness to be understood and to be worked through.

Greenson (1967) defined transference "as the experiencing of feeling, drives, attitudes, fantasies and defenses toward a person in the present which do not befit that person but are a repetition of reactions originating in regard to significant persons of early childhood, unconsciously displaced onto figures in the present" (p. 155). Greenson's definition is unobjectionable except that his definition is limited to displacement reactions. In recent years there has been a growing trend toward a more inclusive concept of transference which would include projection and externalization reactions as well as displacement (Langs, 1976b; Sandler et al., 1969). Kohut (1971, pp. 203–238) and others have argued for a broader definition of transference that would include preoedipal, self-object, and transitional object transference.

Sandler et al. (1969) stress that the clinical and technical usage of the term transference has come to cover a wide variety of elements, all of which enter into object relationships in general. They view transference as a multidimensional rather than a unitary or unidimensional phenomenon. One should not regard all aspects of the patient's relationship to the analyst as transference. Greenson and Wexler (1969), Dewald (1976), and others have studied the nontransference or "real" aspect of the analysand's relation to the analyst.

The idea of transference should not be restricted to the way in which the patient distorts his perception of the analyst, but can be taken to include the unconscious and often subtle attempts by the patient to manipulate the analyst in order to evoke a particular type of response in him (Sandler et al., 1973). This type of transference reaction can be viewed as the patient's unconscious attempt to bring about a situation which would be a disguised repetiton of an earlier real or imagined object relationship.

In 1976, Sandler reinforced the link between transference and countertransference from the standpoint of seeing transference as the patient's attempt to manipulate the analyst into reactions which represented for the patient a concealed repetition of old object relations. Countertransference was viewed as a compromise between the analyst's own tendencies and his response to the role which the patient attempts to force upon him. The relationship between transference and countertransference was conceptualized as a specific instance of the general phenomenon of *actualization*.

In analysis and in everyday life, individuals attempt to actualize the particular object relationships inherent in their dominant unconscious wishes and fantasies. This striving toward actualization, J. and A.-M. Sandler (1978) explain, is part of the wish-fulfilling aspect of all object relationships. The many different forms of actualization include delusional actualization, illusional actualization, symbolic actualization, actualization in dreams, and actualization in one's interpersonal relationships.

Sandler's (1976) idea that one kind of transference reaction involves the patient's unconscious manipulations of the analyst, performed in order to actualize some wished-for relationship, is similar, though not identical, to the concept of projective identification. Langs (1976a) committed the error of reification when he defined projective identification as "an interactional effort to put one's own inner contents into someone else" (p. 26). Psychic contents are abstractions, and hence they cannot (logically) be literally put into someone else. Only in fantasy, and not in reality, can one concretely put one's psychic contents into someone else. Primary process thinking is concrete, and so someone using primary process thinking may well *imagine* that he could concretely put his ideas, feelings, and introjects into another individual. Lang's definition describes a common unconscious fantasy operative at the time a person is using the projective identification mechanism, but it does not describe or define a process or an interactional defensive activity. Knowledge of the subject's unconscious fantasy does not inform us about what the subject does to actualize the desired result in the other person. In projective identification, the subject's unconscious fantasy of putting his psychic contents into someone else is acted out through verbal and mainly nonverbal communications consciously or unconsciously designed to provoke or evoke in another person various emotions and attitudes.

A reasonably complete clinical description of a patient's use of projective identification would indicate some mention of the following: (1) the specific content of the patient's unconscious fantasy, e.g., putting this or that affect or idea into someone else; (2) the patient's reasons and motives for the fantasy — the complex action of projective identification may have many and varied aims including the wish to get rid of painful and/or conflictual feelings, the wish to have the analyst understand, manage, and/or contain what the patient feels unable to cope with; and (3) the particular communications and other actions employed by the patient in order to actualize the fantasy — in other words, what the patient said and did to manipulate the analyst.

In summary, contemporary psychoanalysis views transference as a multidimensional phenomenon. Transference is a universal aspect of all object relations. The concept of transference has been broadened to include the many types of object relations stemming from all developmental levels. Recent studies of transference emphasize a previously neglected aspect, the analysand's unconscious manipulations of the analyst, performed in order to actualize some wished-for object relation.

Organ Modes and Object Relations

Guntrip (1971, pp. 87–91) argued that Erikson's (1963) reinterpretation of Freud's oral, anal, and genital scheme of development had converted Freud's libido theory into an object relations theory. Erikson's theories of psychosexual and psychosocial development give a psychodynamic description of the manifold means by which the human infant develops different ways of relating to other persons.

To Erikson, the terms oral, anal, and genital represent orifices or zones of the body that are related to *modes* or ways of relating, first to physical objects, e.g., food, and later also to human objects. His concept of modes provides a conceptual device for understanding and organizing the characterological transformations and developmental vicissitudes of sexual needs. Erikson's theory of organ modes can be generalized to the action patterns of body organs other than the erogenous zones, and to the role of these action patterns in the psychic development. I shall subsequently discuss how psychic defenses are derived from somatic activities.

The term mode does not refer to manifest behavior, although we infer the mode from similarities of form in various manifest actions (Wolff, 1967). The referent of the term mode is the formal properties of action patterns rather than the physiological activities per se. *Taking in* and *rejecting* are oral modes; *holding in* and *letting go* are anal modes; and *invading* is a phallic mode.

In Erikson's view, various modes of basic thought patterns are developmentally derived from the innate physiological patterns of the erogenous zones. The mental attitude and the activity of the bodily zone belong together, making up the response of the person to his world. During development these modes or action patterns become displaced from their somatic origins in erogenous zone activities, first to other somatic activities and then to psychic actions. According to Erikson, each body zone does not stand exclusively for what is generally regarded as its own characteristic mode; every zone can use all the modes. For the infant, the oral zone is at first only the focus of the incorporative or taking-in mode. Later, however, this action pattern is displaced to the responses of other body organs. The infant is soon able to "take in" with his eyes what enters his visual field.

Through maturation and developmental processes organ modes become organized patterns of relating to others and of approaching the world. When psychoanalysts speak of oral, anal, or phallic character traits, they are not referring concretely to body organs. Rather, they are referring to specific patterns of relating. For example, when we talk of a person's anal character traits, we are referring to his characteristic ways of employing the modes of holding in and letting go in his relations with people and things.

Erikson's (1963) concept of organ modes and Piaget's (1967) theories on cognitive development provide us with a method for formulating the development of psychic defenses out of their physiological precursors. Both Piaget and Erikson demonstrate the displacement in childhood development of action patterns or modes, first from one organ activity to another, and later from organ activities to cognitive operation. Thinking, according to Piaget, develops by the internalization of overt sensorimotor actions. For example, the child's imagined visual image of an object is an imitation of his overt sensorimotor action of visually perceiving (looking at) the object.

Let us consider how psychic defenses are developed through this internalization process in which the subject imitates in fantasy various sensorimotor actions. Closing or blinking the eyes as a sensorimotor protection reaction against various visual stimuli, such as bright lights, has been considered one of the precursors of the defense of denial (Hartmann, 1950). Over time, and through many imaginary imitations of closing the eyes, this self-protective reaction becomes internalized and transformed into the defense of denial. The unconscious defensive idea of the subject may be represented as follows: "I will not look at, imagine, or think about this painful matter. Since I do not 'see' it, it does not exist."

As Knapp (1967) demonstrated, the action pattern of "riddance" is another example of a psychic defense developed out of an overt sensorimotor activity. During ontogenesis the mode of riddance is displaced from its origin in such sensorimotor reflexes as coughing, sneezing, and vomiting to cognitive operations, where it becomes the psychic defense of repression. These reflexes protect the body through the riddance of noxious or harmful physical objects. The unconscious or preconscious experiential referent of the riddance mode in repression includes the wish to be rid of some threatening feeling, idea, or percept. George Klein (1976, p. 295) viewed repression as a maneuver directed against a disturbing introjected object relationship. The physiological riddance reflexes and the psychic defense of repression are homologous with respect to the mode of riddance. Both the somatic reflex and the psychic action of repression involve the organism's attempt to protect itself against a disturbing object.

Child psychoanalysts, such as Spitz and Escalona, who have studied early defenses by direct observation of infants, trace a continuous series beginning with biological prototypes and ending in familiar psychic defenses (see Rubinfine, 1959). Greenacre (1958) spoke of physiological activities such as respiration, defecation, and eating as the precursors for the later development of psychological defenses. Freud (1920) connected the development of projection with his concept of *Reizschutz* (stimulus barrier), and since then other analysts have also conceptualized the stimulus barrier as a precursor for the development of psychic defenses.

Affects and Object Relations

A patient's affects often provide the most telling clues as to the patient's transferences and his unconscious object relations. Similarly, the analyst's affective responses to the patient frequently illuminate the nature of the patient's unconscious transferences. Affects and moods are modes of action in which we are attuned in one way or another to the object world. The analyst's rule-of-thumb is "Follow the affect!" For affective states bring disclosure, and they reveal how we are related to others. Affects disclose the nature of our object relations in fundamental ways, and they give us an appreciation of the situation where we find ourselves.

All affects have objects. We are afraid *of* things, angry *with* people, love *someone*. The object of the feeling state may be unconscious. Frequently patients do not know what they are depressed about, whom they are angry with. Then one of the analyst's tasks is to listen for signs indicating the unconscious object of the patient's feeling state.

Numerous psychoanalysts have pointed to the centrality of affects for object relations (Diatkine, 1978; Landauer, 1938; Rangell, 1967; Sandler and Sandler, 1978; Schafer, 1964). Affects are constant factors in our existence, and according to Novey (1961), "no human relatedness is conceivable without affective participation" (p. 22). Kernberg (1976) proposed that primitive units of affect state, object representation, and self representation constitute the basis for the later structuring in internalized object relations. He viewed pleasurable and painful affects as the major organizers of the series of "good" and "bad" internalized object relations. Early in development affect states determine the integration of both internalized object relations and the overall drive systems. Later, affects signal the activation of drive and represent it in the context of the activation of specific internalized object relations.

According to Sandler and Sandler (1978), the part played by affective experience is central in the development of object relations. They regard affects as feeling states which may be pleasurable or unpleasurable, conscious or unconscious. An experience has meaning for the child only if it is linked with feeling. They assume that object relationships represent the fulfillment of important needs in the developing child as well as in the adolescent and adult. Such needs may manifest themselves in the form of wishes. The Sandlers emphasize the importance of including noninstinctual as well as instinctual needs and wishes in their formulation. Every wish involves a self representation, an object representation, and a representation of the interaction between them. They wrote, "The idea of an aim which seeks gratification has to be supplemented by the idea of a *wished-for interaction,* with the wished-for or imagined response of the object being as much a party of the wishful fantasy as the activity of the subject in that wish or fantasy" (p. 288).

Sandler and Sandler (1978) view object relationships as being wish fulfillments in the broad sense. To the extent, then, that the wish contains an object relationship, every form of actualization will represent the fulfillment of a wished-for relationship. Finding an object in reality, in fantasy, or in both which will act in accord with the wish brings about the fulfillment of the wished-for object relationship.

Needs and the specific wishes associated with the needs are aroused by disturbances in the conscious or unconscious affects of the individual. As noted above, wishes of all sorts contain the representations of the self, the object, and of the interaction between the two. The aim of such interactions in reality or in fantasy is to bring about, one way or the other, closeness to the primary affective "good" state or object, and distance from the primary affective "bad" painful state or object. Sandler and Sandler (1978) have provided a view of motivation, psychopathology, and symptoms in which the control of feelings via the direct or indirect maintenance of specific object relationships is of crucial significance.

The Concept of Defensive Splitting

The concept of the defensive splitting is central in the object relations theories of Melanie Klein (1946), Fairbairn (1952), Kernberg (1976), and others. In my review (1979b) of the psychoanalytic literature on the defense of splitting, I presented both logical and empirical evidence in support of the proposition that there is no splitting defense different from or distinguishable from the defense of denial. Before going on with my critique of the concept of defensive splitting, I shall briefly summarize Kernberg's (1976) theory of splitting. The object relations theory he has constructed provides a valuable integration of the previous work of others on object relations, and my only major criticism is that he has confused the concept of splitting with that of denial.

Kernberg (1976) postulated two basically different levels of ego organization, an earlier, primitive level in which splitting is the characteristic defense, and a higher level characterized mainly by repression and related high-level defenses, e.g., undoing, reaction formation, isolation. He accounted for the persistence of the primitive level of defense in adults by postulating trauma early in life, especially during the separation-individuation phase of development. His hypothesis on the splitting defense is derived mainly from his clinical observations of borderline patients. He noted their successive activation of contradictory ego states (or ego splits), and he inferred that these contradictory ego states are formed by the splitting defense. An important technical implication of this theory of the splitting defense is that there must be "an active focus on the mechanism of splitting as a primary defensive operation to be overcome before any further changes can be achieved in such patients" (p. 46).

Kernberg (1976) argued that splitting is the central mechanism for the defensive organization of the ego prior to the development of object constancy. Splitting occurs with other related lower-level defenses such as projection, omnipotence, primitive forms of idealization, and devaluation. Normally at some time in the third year splitting is replaced by repression and other higher-level developmental defenses. Prior to the development of object constancy, the young child constructs unintegrated and disparate good (libidinally invested) and bad (aggressively invested) self and object representations. Object constancy is achieved when the good and bad object representations are integrated into whole object representations, and when the corresponding good and bad self representations become integrated. Defensive splitting, according to Kernberg, involves the active separation of the good and bad self and object representations, thereby maintaining or restoring the unintegrated state of self and object representations which normally occurs only before object constancy is developed.

Kernberg's (1976) formulations on the developmentally earlier and later defensive organizations are essentially correct, except that denial, in my opinion, and not splitting is the central defense in the early period. The same phenomena in early childhood which he has ascribed to defensive splitting can more correctly be attributed to denial and the consequent formation of contradictory attitudes (ego splits). As Rubinfine (1962) demonstrated, denial in young children is orginally directed against disturbing percepts of the earliest object which might evoke aggression, and hence threaten object loss. In this way, denial for the young child plays a special role in preserving need-fulfilling object relations.

The terms *split* and *splitting* are used in two different ways in the psychoanalytic literature. First, they are used as descriptive nouns and adjectives to designate the coexistence of conscious or unconscious attitudes, ego states, and self and object representations that are contradictory to each other. A common clinical example is the contradictory sets of "good" and "bad" self and object representations observed so frequently in borderline patients and others. Freud (1927, 1938) and others have shown that such contradictory attitudes, or ego splits, are brought about by the denial defense. When used in this descriptive way, the words split and splits do not refer to a defense or to any other psychic action or process. In these contexts, split and splits simply refer to the coexistence of contradictory attitudes and ego states.

Second the terms split and splitting have been used illogically as active, transitive verbs to denote a defensive activity in which the subject splits various psychic contents such as affects and representations. Discussions of the splitting defense by Kernberg (1976), M. Klein (1946), and others have committed the fallacy of reification, because it is logically impossible literally to split psychic contents. Physical things, e.g., a piece of wood, can be split, but abstractions such as affects and ideas cannot be split.

An analyst colleague was able to observe and study the relationship between denial defense and the consequent formation of contradictory attitudes in *statu nascendi* (Dorpat, 1979b). An analytic patient said that he did not care about the fact that the analyst was late starting the analytic hour. When the analyst asked for the patient's ideas about "I don't care," the patient's associations revealed that he actually did care about the lateness. He remembered that just before the session started he had felt frustrated about the tardiness. His ruminations that his watch was broken and that he had arrived for the analytic session at the wrong time were further attempts to deny both the fact of the analyst's lateness and his disturbing angry feelings. Through denial he barred from consciousness representations of the "bad" tardy analyst, as well as representations of himself as angry at the analyst. Also, denial assisted him in maintaining a sense of well-being through affirming his relationship with a "good" idealized caretaking object. The patient's denial defense resulted in his two contradictory attitudes of idealization of the analyst and anger over the analyst's mistake.

The damaging effects that the persistence of the splitting defense had upon the development and maintenance of ego boundaries and self and object boundaries was discussed by Kernberg (1976). Here again, one can cite the known pathological consequences of denial to account for the effects described by Kernberg. Modell (1961), for example, described a patient who made a serious suicide attempt during a time when he had defensively dissolved boundaries between his self and object representations. The patient denied any suicidal intention or wish to kill himself at the time of the act. Separation anxiety was the stimulus for his massive use of denial. Denial was linked with a profound ego regression in which he denied his separateness from others and sought through death to achieve an objectless stage and fulfillment of his wish for reunion with his mother. Kernberg (1976) noted that repression, unlike splitting, is characterized by a blockage of discharge. A similar observation was made by Jacobson (1957) in her examination of the difference between denial and repression. Repression leads to an inhibition over motor discharge, whereas denial often (as in Modell's case described above) leads to loss of controls over impulses and to acting out.

Because of the widespread ambiguity, confusion, and reification in the usage of split and splitting, Pruyser (1975) and I (1979b) have recommended banning these words from the psychological vocabulary. As Pruyser indicated, these terms have become bits of jargon used indiscriminately to denote some alleged psychic process or activity which, on close scrutiny, may not be there at all.

Object Relations and Internalization Processes

Psychoanalytic developmental psychology has shifted from a predominantly biological orientation, which emphasized factors such as instincts and drives, to an orientation concerned with the role of the subject's interpersonal relationships in the formation and patterning of his psychic structures. Today psychoanalysis conceptualizes personality development as a resultant of the interaction and intermeshing of innate maturational givens with experiential factors derived principally from the subject's interactions with important persons in his environment (Meissner, 1976). Psychoanalysis adheres to the epigenetic concept of development which views the formation of psychic structures as the products of successive transactions between the individual and his environment (Loewald, 1978). Psychic development does not simply unfold in a predetermined fashion; rather, it requires what Winnicott (1965) called the "facilitating environment." Contemporary emphasis in developmental studies is on the quality of parent-child transactions as determined by the capacities of parents to respond adaptively and empathically to the changing needs of their children.

Kernberg (1976) defined introjection, identification, and ego identity as three sequential processes in the internalization of object relations. I shall discuss the concept of introjection, the least well understood of the internalization processes. Introjection by itself does not bring about ego or superego structural changes, but it does provide new psychic contents which may later be utilized as models for forming selective identifications and modifying ego and superego structure.

In previous papers on introjection (1974, 1979a), I presented case studies of patients with narcissistic personality disorders who had conscious fantasies of the analyst outside of treatment hours, and who used these fantasies for internalizing patient-analyst relations. In the first transformation, patient-analyst relations were introjected through the replication in memory or fantasy outside of treatment hours of patient-analyst relations. The second transformation included the patients' gradual modification and strengthening of ego and superego structures through the formation of selective identifications with the analyst introject. The patient-analyst relation of empathic listening was examined, and I described the various steps taken by a patient in internalizing this action (Dorpat, 1979a). Her gradual internalization of the listening relation strengthened her capacities for introspection and empathy.

There has been an unfortunate ambiguity and lack of consistency in the use of internalization words such as introjection and identification. Introjection, the internalization process which precedes identification, and which provides the contents for identification, has frequently been confused with the process of identification. One reason why introjection and identification have not been distinguished is because they often occur close together, making it difficult for one to observe or to infer two different processes. Here I would like to summarize both the logical and the empirical evidence for the proposition that introjection and identification are different and distinguishable processes. The process of introjection must precede identification for the following reasons. The subject forms identifications from his object representations. One identifies with one's object representations, not with an actual person. Therefore it follows that an introjection, the process which includes the psychic formation of an object representation, must precede the process of identification. The empirical evidence for the distinguishability of introjection from identification proceses may be found in the numerous clinical studies which demonstrate that internalization processes can be arrested at the introjection phase. In other words, individuals may form introjects which are not later used for identification.

Introjection is the process whereby the subject transforms an interpersonal relation into a fantasy action, and constructs a representation of the action, the self, and the other person involved in the relation. Introjection is a complex, predominantly unconscious biopsychological process involving a number of psychic functions such as fantasy, perception, and memory. The product of this process I shall call an *introject*. The essential dynamic factor which is internalized in the process of introjection is the relation between the subject and an object. As Loewald (1970) put it, "What becomes internalized. . . are not objects but interactions and relationships" (p. 59).

This conception of introjects differs from others who view introjects as a type of primitive object representation. For example, M. Klein (1955) considered each unconscious primary process object representation as an introject. Schafer (1968) wrote about introjects as a type of primary process presence.

There are several reasons for rejecting their concepts of introjects as incomplete. First, as I argued earlier, object representations are not discrete, separate entities; they always occur linked with representations of the self and with the particular action involving self and object. Second, clinical observations on introject experiences indicate that the object representation involved is subjectively viewed as an active, powerful agent acting in one way or another on the subject. The object representation is experienced as condemning, punishing, comforting, scolding, praising. Together with George Klein (1976), I regard the word introject as denoting some type of *relational mode* involving a representation of some action, the self, and an object.

The process of introjection has been confused by M. Klein

(1946) and others with *fantasies* of oral incorporation. As Schafer (1968, p. 20) explained, the term incorporation refers to conscious or unconscious fantasies that one has taken a part or all of another person into one's self corporeally. I have found no evidence in my patients or in the psychoanalytic literature that incorporative fantasies contribute in any way to internalization processes. The words introjection and internalization are spatial metaphors which should not be interpreted in a literal sense to mean that some physical object has been taken inside the subject's body (Meissner, 1976; Schafer, 1976). The process of introjection is not an imaginary act of physical incorporation. Cannibalism, whether real, fantasied, ritual, or whatever, does not enhance psychic development, although many persons consciously or unconsciously imagine that it does.

Conclusion

Object relations theories seem to be taking the place of the much-criticized mechanistic metapsychology. In my opinion, this is a sign of progress in psychoanalysis. However, as my paper has attempted to demonstrate, some of the same conceptual problems and fallacies of the older metapsychological theories are now appearing in object relations writing. Further progress in the construction of object relations theories depends not only upon empirical investigations but also upon studies of our concepts and theoretical language.

References

Abenheimer, K. (1955), Critical observations on Fairbairn's theory of object-relations. *Brit. J. Med. Psychol.*, 28:29–41.

Blatt, S. J. & Wild, C. M. (1976), *Schizophrenia*. New York: Academic Press.

Buber, M. (1970), *I and Thou*. New York: Scribner's.

Cassirer, E. (1967), *The Logic of the Humanities*. New Haven: Yale University Press.

Chein, I. (1972), *The Science of Behavior and the Image of Man*. New York: Basic Books.

Dewald, P. A. (1976), Transference regression and real experience in the psychoanalytic process. *Psychoanal. Quart.*, 45:213–230.

Dewey, J. & Bentley, A. F. (1949), *Knowing and the Known*. Boston: Beacon Press.

Diatkine, R. (1978), The development of object relationships and affects. *Int. J. Psycho-Anal.*, 59:277–284.

Dorpat, T. L. (1974), Internalization of the patient-analyst relationship in patients with narcissistic disorder. *Int. J. Psycho-Anal.*, 55:183–188.

———— (1976), Structural conflict and object relations conflict. *J. Amer. Psychoanal. Assn.*, 24:855–874.

_____ (1979a), Introjection and the idealizing transference. *Internat. J. Psychother.*, 7:23–53.

_____ (1979b), Is splitting a defence? *Int. Rev. Psychoanal.*, 6:105–113.

Erikson, E. H. (1963), *Childhood and Society*, rev. ed. New York: Norton.

Fairbairn, W. D. (1952), *An Object-Relations Theory of the Personality.* New York: Basic Books.

_____ (1955), Observations in defence of the object-relations theory of the personality. *Brit. J. Med. Psychol.*, 28:144–156.

Fenichel, O. (1941), *Problems of Psychoanalytic Technique.* Albany, N.Y.: Psychoanalytic Quarterly.

Fraiberg, S. (1969), Libidinal object constancy and mental representation. *The Psychoanalytic Study of the Child,* 24:3–47.

Freud, S. (1920), Beyond the pleasure principle. *Standard Edition,* 18:7–64. London: Hogarth Press, 1955.

_____ (1926), Inhibition, symptoms and anxiety. *Standard Edition,* 20:87–172. London: Hogarth Press, 1955.

_____ (1927), Fetishism. *Standard Edition,* 21:152–159. London: Hogarth Press, 1961.

_____ (1938), Splitting of the ego in the process of defence. *Standard Edition,* 23: 271–278. London: Hogarth Press, 1964.

Gedo, J. E. & Goldberg, A. (1973), *Models of the Mind.* Chicago & London: University of Chicago Press.

Greenacre, P. (1958), Toward an understanding of the physical nucleus of some defensive reactions. *Int. J. Psycho-Anal.,* 39:69–76.

Greenson, R. R. (1967), *The Technique and Practice of Psychoanalysis.* New York: International Universities Press.

_____ & Wexler, M. (1969), The non-transference relationship in the psychoanalytic situation. *Int. J. Psycho-Anal.,* 50:27–29.

Guntrip, H. (1971), *Psychoanalytic Theory, Therapy, and the Self.* New York: Basic Books.

Hartmann, H. (1950), Comments on the psychoanalytic theory of the ego. *The Psychoanalytic Study of the Child,* 5:74–96.

Home, H. J. (1966), The concept of mind. *Int. J. Psycho-Anal.,* 47:43–49.

Husserl, E. (1965), *Phenomenology and the Crisis of Philosophy.* New York: Harper & Row.

Jacobson, E. (1957), Denial and repression. *J. Amer. Psychoanal. Assn.,* 5:61–92.

_____ (1964), *The Self and the Object World.* New York: International Universities Press.

Kernberg, O. F. (1976), *Object Relations Theory and Clinical Psychoanalysis.* New York: Jason Aronson.

Klein, G. S. (1976), *Psychoanalytic Theory.* New York: International Universities Press.

Klein, M. (1946), Notes on some schizoid mechanisms. *Int. J. Psycho-Anal.,* 27: 99–110.

_____ et al. (1955), *New Directions in Psycho-Analysis.* New York: Basic Books.

Knapp, P. H. (1967), Some riddles of riddance. *Arch. Gen. Psychiat.,* 16:582–602.

Kohut, H. (1971), *The Analysis of the Self.* New York: International Universities Press.

Landauer, K. (1938), Affects, passions and temperament. *Int. J. Psycho-Anal.,* 19:388–415.

Langs, R. (1976a), *The Bipersonal Field.* New York: Jason Aronson.

────── (1976b), *The Therapeutic Interaction,* vol. 2. New York: Jason Aronson.

Loewald, H. W. (1960), The therapeutic action of psycho-analysis. *Int. J. Psycho-Anal.,* 41:16–33.

────── (1970), Psychoanalytic theory and the psychoanalytic process. *The Psychoanalytic Study of the Child,* 25:45–68.

────── (1978), Instinct theory, object relations, and psychic-structure formation. *J. Amer. Psychoanal. Assn.,* 26:453–506.

Meissner, W. W. (1976), A note on internalization as process. *Psychoanal. Quart.,* 45:374–393.

────── (1976), Three essays plus seventy. *Int. J. Psycho-Anal.,* 57:127–133.

Modell, A. H. (1961), Denial and the sense of separateness. *J. Amer. Psychoanal. Assn.,* 9:533–547.

Novey, S. (1961), Further considerations on affect theory in psychoanalysis. *Int. J. Psycho-Anal.,* 42:21–31.

Piaget, J. (1967), *Six Psychological Studies.* New York: Vintage Books.

Pruyser, P. (1975), What splits in "splitting"? *Bull. Menninger Clin.,* 39:1–46.

Rangell, L. (1967), Psychoanalysis, affects, and the "human care." *Psychoanal. Quart.,* 36:172–202.

Rapaport, D. (1960), *The Structure of Psychoanalytic Theory* [*Psychol. Issues,* Monogr. 6]. New York: International Universities Press.

Rubinfine, D. L. (1959), Report of panel: Some theoretical aspects of early psychic functioning. *J. Amer. Psychoanal. Assn.,* 7:561–576.

────── (1962), Maternal stimulation, psychic structure, and early object relations. *The Psychoanalytic Study of the Child,* 17:278–282.

Ryle, G. (1949), *The Concept of Mind.* New York: Barnes & Noble.

Sandler, J. (1976), Countertransference and role-responsiveness. *Int. Rev. Psycho-Anal.,* 3:43–47.

────── Dare, C., & Holder, A. (1973), *The Patient and the Analyst.* London: Allen & Unwin.

────── Holder, A., Kawenoka, M., Kennedy, H. E., & Neurath, L. (1969), Notes on some theoretical and clinical aspects of transference. *Int. J. Psycho-Anal.,* 50:633–645.

────── & Rosenblatt, B. (1962), The concept of the representational world. *The Psychoanalytic Study of the Child,* 17:128–145.

────── & Sandler, A.-M. (1978), On the development of object relationships and affects. *Int. J. Psycho-Anal.,* 59:285–296.

Sarbin, T. R. (1972), Anxiety. In: *Essays on Metaphor,* ed. W. Shibles. Whitewater, Wis.: Language Press, pp. 124–140.

Schafer, R. (1964), The clinical analysis of affects. *J. Amer. Psychoanal. Assn.,* 12:275–299.

────── (1968), *Aspects of Internalization.* New York: International Universities Press.

────── (1976), *A New Language for Psychoanalysis.* New Haven: Yale University Press.

Spruiell, V. (1978), Report of panel: Current concepts of object relations theory. *J. Amer. Psychoanal. Assn.,* 26:599–614.

Sutherland, J. D. (1963), Object-relations theory and the conceptual model of psycho-analysis. *Brit. J. Med. Psychol.,* 36:109–121.

Szasz, T. S. (1963), The concept of transference. *Int. J. Psycho-Anal.,* 44:432–443.

Winnicott, D. W. (1965), *The Maturational Processes and the Facilitating Environment.*

New York: International Universities Press.

Wittgenstein, L. (1945–49), *Philosophical Investigations,* 3rd ed. New York: Macmillan.

Wolff, P. H. (1967), Cognitive consideration for a psychoanalytic theory of language acquisition. In: *Motives and Thought,* ed. R. R. Holt [*Psychol. Issues,* Monogr. 18/19]. New York: International Universities Press, pp. 300–343.

8

ACTING OUT AND SYMBOLIZATION

Susan K. Deri, Dipl. Med. Psychol.

"The good order of the world depends on the discipline of language," Confucius (450 B.C.) said. And that is what the acting-out person cannot achieve; he cannot carve out for himself a meaningfully ordered life space or communicate satisfyingly with other people. The world of the acting-out character is well described by another theologian philosopher about 2,500 years after Confucius. Max Picard (1963) says, "Without language space and time are undivided. Without language the world would be in a state of constant eruption and catastrophe. Things would have no continuous existence: they would always be changing. It would be a world of magic. The gods who are not conditioned by language would become idols and monsters" (pp. 40–41). I can only add that this is the confused, magic, threatening world of those who act out. Not only do they feel easily threatened and provoked by the world surrounding them, but they can make the world threatening for the rest of us.

Acting out is related to the pleasure principle, but even though it may be experienced as ego-syntonic at the moment of action, in the long run those moments add up to a painfully endured life. Enduring frustration and passivity are exactly what such persons want to avoid by relying on direct action rather than on symbolic thought and language communication in their endeavors to reach their desired goals and to reach them quickly. Then, by a paradoxical twist due to the inexorable laws governing human fate, the seemingly energetic actor's life becomes a pathetically fragmented juxtaposition of actions and scenes leading nowhere but to frustration and rage. Instead of attaining his aim to be the autonomous master of his fate, the acting-out character turns out to be the passive puppet of the tyranny of his unmodulated infantile impulses.

This brief description of the life of acting-out persons has already emphasized the role of discursive language symbolization — or rather, the lack of it — in the genesis of that particular disorder. It is precisely *dis*order that is brought about by the deficiency of symbol formation. "The order of the world depends on the discipline of language."

Symbolization leads away from internal and external chaos and toward perceptible, articulated order. Symbolization, by establishing delineated structures, brings about *distanced* order from unbounded chaos. If not for the ordering function of symbolization, a function that is intrinsically built into the human mind and perception, we would be living in the "big blooming, buzzing confusion" William James (1911) talks about. The specifically human mode of perception and communication takes place by symbolic means, be it intrapsychic or interpersonal communication. The acting-out individual is deficient in both.

It is obvious from the above that I am using the concept of symbolization in its generic sense, in the sense of the philosophers of symbolization such as Whitehead (1927), Cassirer (1944), and Langer (1942), and to some extent Wittgenstein (1958), not in the psychoanalytic sense of the term, which has a much more restricted meaning.

Only by understanding something about the generic process of symbol formation can we grasp the dehumanizing effects of defects in this most human of all organismic functions. Malignant forms of acting out, those which pervade the full range of a person's performances, deprive him or her of much of what makes a human being specifically human.

There are milder forms of acting out, with the disorder having a more restricted scope. Those are more closely related in their dynamic structure to neurotic conflicts. There is a continuum connecting (1) the most malignant forms of generalized acting out, driven by the pressure of unmodulated, unsymbolized impulses; and (2) more focalized, compulsively repetitive symptomatic actions, driven by the *de*symbolizing effect of repressions, and thus lending themselves to the classical analytic mode of interpretation. The meaning of these symptomatic acts eludes the patient. To the therapist, these actions reveal a meaning and he can therefore, by means of discursive verbal language, transmute the symptomatic act into the organized form of language symbolization, intelligible to the patient. The pressuring impulses invading the motor system thus become bound into perceptible forms of mental content. Formless impulses become by means of language symbolization formed thoughts and intentions that can be contemplated *across* a psychic *distance,* thought *about,* instead of directly discharged in heedless acting out.

Finally, in the continuum of types of acting out, (3) there is play-acting or role-playing which is used, consciously or preconsciously, to *hide* some feelings while discharging others, but in which the person derives exhibitionistic pleasure from performing for an audience. The object relations of these people have an "as if" quality. They can produce verbal talk in profusion, but without authentic communication *to* the other. Speech itself is used to act out the need to be looked at and admired, the words forming a supposedly colorful screen to hide behind. This group is motivated by an interesting combination of consciously self-engineered play-acting, aimed at hiding and charming simultaneously, and a repetitive, compulsive drivenness which stems from the defensive function of the need to charm. These pseudocommunicators pose special, but often not unsurmountable, problems in analysis, *if* the analyst does not fall into the trap of interpreting the copiously flowing "interesting" content, but focuses on the problem of pseudocommunication. Otherwise these patients will terminate their treatment after a while, adding the badge "I have been analyzed" to the rest of their sparkling possessions that they display for their public.

The histrionic quality of this compulsive play-acting connects this syndrome with hysteria, or rather with "hysteroid characters"; while the more malignant primary forms of impulsive acting out impress one more as an uncontrolled psychosomatic pattern of discharge, related to epilepsy or "epileptoid character."

These considerations lead to speculations, on the one hand, about the relationship between epilepsy and hysteria — not a new idea as the diagnostic category of "hysteroepileptic seizure" shows — and, on the other, about a neurological substratum underlying all disorders of impulse control that lead to motor activity rather than to meaningful language communication. On the neurological level there might be a short-circuiting of internal stimuli into channels of motor discharge. In other words, there might exist innate deficiencies in the capacity for symbol formation, just as innate forms and intensities of symbolizing capacities can be assumed in creative artists.

I believe that the capacity for symbol formation has roots in the biological genetic core of the personality—a statement that does not deny the effects of the child's early experiences, mainly those of the early mother-child relationship, upon furthering or thwarting the development of these innate capacities. The assumption of innate roots for the capacity to symbolize implies the corollary assumption regarding an innate proclivity toward acting out, since acting out stands in inverse relationship to the capacity for symbolization.

If we consider in this context the fragmented life patterns of massively acting-out characters, one is reminded of Janet's proposition (which accorded with Breuer's) that hysterical patients are "inherently incapable of holding together the multiplicity of mental processes into a unity and hence arises the tendency to mental disassociation" (Freud, 1910, p. 21). Janet's proposition even would account for the use of massive repression by hysterics who have a deficient capacity for welding together intense and complex stimulations into meaningful symbolic structures. Material that lies beyond their symbolizing capacity to synthesize and contain in an organized mental structure, i.e., in a mental symbol, in a cohesive psychic gestalt—such unassimilable material has to be repudiated from the organized territory of the conscious-preconscious (part of the ego) and banned into the more chaotic unconscious, from where the *de*-symbolized content, with the pressure of unbound energy, erupts from time to time directly into action. In such cases we are confronted with the more focalized acting out, corresponding to lacunae in verbalizable memory. These are the people who act out *instead* of remembering. Analytic work can fill these lacunae in the preconscious with the help of interpretations couched in organized language. This process *translates* proprioceptively not discernible unconscious impulse into delineated and *therefore* perceptible preconscious mental structure. This structure is a mental symbol with a specific gestalt and can therefore be contemplated, thought *about*, instead of acted out. Perception of a unit that has a gestalt implies *distance across* which to look in order to perceive. Unbound pressuring impulses become "tamed" and perceptible by becoming *bound* into symbolic form.

The essence of the mysterious process of binding energy is, I believe, a formative rather than a cathectic process in which instinctual energy in its hypothesized flow becomes attached to—"cathects"—

already formed presentations. This difference is important in order to appreciate the therapeutic significance of symbolization per se. The working-through process with acting-out patients hinges on the energy-binding and distancing function of symbolization. Unthought-about acting out is always indicative of an impoverished storehouse of preconscious symbolic forms.

The preconscious is the locus where intentionality supersedes the more purely "causal," pressured-from-below, principle of mental functioning. The preconscious symbol structures lend something like "free will" or free choice to human beings. The instinct-driven acting-out person has very little of this human freedom. He acts more as a machine propelled by a steam engine.

Symbolization is a process representing phenomena that take place in one region, in a more formalized medium characteristic of another region. Symbolizing activity condenses that which is diffuse, and therefore by itself not perceptible, into a more delineated form, thereby producing order. Symbolization organizes stimulations, whether they originate inside or outside. Symbolization *gives meaning* to phenomena taking place in one region, by registering or translating them into the "language" of another region. Therefore, shaping of the unformed instinctual impulses into meaningfully structured, preconscious, instinct derivatives can be looked upon as intrapsychic or *centrifugal* symbol formation. Instinct derivatives represent the instinctual impulses in an altered but fitting form that makes introspection, perception of the inside, possible; just as the organizing activity built into our external perception performs its order- and meaning-giving function in a *centripetal* direction. The preconscious is the ground on which the symbolic structures derived from either direction meet. Visual perception presents the external world in meaningfully ordered, delineated gestalts, instead of a medley of contiguous lines and surfaces. Delineation implies distance between objects and between the perceiving subject and the object. Acting-out persons disregard this distance; they act—and may perceive—as if the self and the object world were contiguous.

Plato, Kant, Freud, and the gestalt psychologists were aware of different aspects of the basic truth that neither external nor internal reality can be grasped as it *is* without the mediation of some transforming processes. The philosophers of symbolization elaborated this truth into a new, encompassing philosophical system, which is there for us to contemplate and further assimilate into psycho-analysis. A generic theory of symbolization has implications for our style of work, for dream theory, and for the way we couch our inter-pretations. Moreover, such basic questions as the nature of truth and certainty, the problem of causal interpretations, the analyst's preinterpretive perceptual organization of the material, the status of memories on the dimension of historical facts versus fantasy — all these need to be rethought in the light of a generic theory of sym-bolization.

The assimilation of this conceptual framework into psycho-analysis, like the assimilation of gestalt psychology into psycho-analytic theory, yields new ways of looking at and dealing with our clinical observations and our method of work. The attempt to under-stand the *processes* of binding energy and the function of the pre-conscious in terms of symbolic gestalt formation is a case in point — an extremely important point when applied to acting-out patients. Suzanne K. Langer's definition of the brain as a transformer, and the epistemological differentiation between symbols and signs, helped me to see the acting-out disorder from a new angle. Langer (1942) says, "The material furnished by the senses is constantly wrought into *symbols* which are our elementary ideas" (p. 46). "The human brain is constantly carrying on a process of symbolic trans-formation of the experiential data that come to it" (p. 47).

In the acting-out personality the brain-mind does not function as a reliably symbolizing transformer. Observing my acting-out anal-ysands with the mental symbols of symbolization theory in my mind helped me to conceptualize *what* went wrong in the functioning of their "transformer." Their transformer produced signs instead of symbols. Symbols *represent* something absent. Signs *indicate* some-thing present. Symbols evoke thinking *about* something that is sep-arated by a distance, something not directly reachable. Full-fledged symbols operate within the abstract dimensions of time and space. Signs operate within concrete contiguities and immediacy of actions. The acting-out person lives in a concrete action space, while symbols imply delay of action. Symbols evoke the conception of the thing that is absent. *"Le symbole c'est la présence d'une absence"* is a nice definition of the paradoxical function of a symbol (I forgot where I read it). To conceive a thing is different from reacting to it directly and overtly. Signs, on the other hand, act analogously to a conditioned reflex.

The dog does not think *about* food when the bell rings but salivates as if the food were present. Signs announce their object and evoke rigidly preformed, immediate reactions.

For acting-out individuals, certain slight environmental stimuli can act the same way. A facial expression, a movement, a word, or the omission of one can evoke an almost stereotyped and sometimes quite lengthy outburst. "I cannot stop before the whole thing is out" was one patient's description of these seizures. Some patients, the more mature and differentiated ones, in retrospect experience these seizures as ego-alien and humiliating. They suffer from their "demons," to use another patient's expression — their demons which appear at certain signals. These patients feel dehumanized because the driving power of their "seizure" reaction wipes out their control, even though they might be aware of the disproportionate intensity of their reaction to the slightness of the stimulus. In fact, this form of acting out does resemble the function of "sign releasers" as described by Tinbergen (1951) and Lorenz (1937) in their discussion of animal behavior. The fitting releasers elicit *total* instinctive action patterns in animals. Environmental releasers and instinctive behavior patterns are well fitted. This fittedness guarantees that the animal does the right thing at the right time. The valence-character of the environment is organically and unambiguously given for them.

Humans are not endowed with such certainty of choices. They are neither as instinct-bound nor as stimulus-bound as animals. Due to the nature of the human organism, man cannot cope directly, without the mediation of symbols, with the intensity and complexity of inner and outer stimulations. The interpolation of the universe of symbols between the action-prone human being and his surrounding object world is needed in order to safeguard the wholeness of the individual. Symbols achieve this by putting a distance in space and time between the impulse-ridden subject and the world of real objects. Symbols vouchsafe the distance that is indispensable for the integrity of the individual, yet at the same time they also serve as connecting bridges. Symbols connect the subject with his intended, chosen object. This is one aspect of the Janus-face of symbols.

Humans, lacking the coherent instinctive directedness of animals, cannot function wholesomely in a universe of signs. The massively acting-out person whose mental transformer produces signs instead of symbols is a *human manqué* as well as an *animal manqué*.

But man's symbolizing potential can be enhanced by appropriate analytic therapy. These patients do not take easily to psychoanalytic therapy, yet I believe this is the one method that holds out hope for developing their capacity for correct symbolic communication. Many of the new modalities of therapy seem to be based on a hybrid mixture of inadequate symbolization and acting out. In psychoanalysis, the combination of discursive language, which isomorphically represents the order of the world (Wittgenstein, 1958), and the transference, which to some extent is an artificially produced acting-out illness vis-à-vis the analyst, can change symptomatic acting out into organized secondary process action and language communication.

Freud (1914) calls the transference neurosis an "intermediate region between illness and the real life through which the transition from one to the other is made" (p. 154). He also reminds us that "conjuring up a piece of real life...cannot always be harmless and unobjectionable" (p. 152); and that is very true.

The eliciting and handling of the transference are potentially the most effective and also the most dangerous aspects of psychoanalysis. Healing with the help of the transference neurosis resembles the homeopathic principle: to heal illness by inflicting a similar but new illness. There is some acting out in this method. But precisely because of the potential for harmfully acting out — and the danger exists in both participants, the analyst and the patient — the "homeopathic principle" can result in inflicting iatrogenic illness.

The ancient principle of homeopathy was expressed in Delphi through the Oracle of Apollo: "the wounder heals." After having destroyed most of the human and animal population in 300 B.C. by sending the plague through his mice and his sharp arrows, Apollo sent his son Asclepius as healer to Rome. He was called Apollo Medicus but also Apollo Smintheus, which means: the god who sent mice and the plague. Kerenyi (1959) gives numerous examples from Greek mythology which show that the god and hero physicians alternately inflicted wounds and healed them. Physicians lived in a twilight zone between the underworld and the luminous world. Physicians had firsthand knowledge of wounds because many of them suffered from incurable wounds themselves. So did Chiron, the centaur, the primordial mythological physician who taught the use of medical herbs to Asclepius and also to Achilles, but Chiron was not able to heal his own wound.

What does all this tell about us analysts? That we are wounded people and therefore have knowledge of wounds in others. We have to hurt (in both the active and the passive sense of the verb) in order to heal. Yet, sending the plague seems to me too much acting out, even if some healing follows. Gods may be able to afford doing such things, but we humans better watch out to control the transference before it turns into a personal plague.

Acting-out patients who perceive signs in everything do produce malignant transferences that are difficult, and sometimes impossible, to use for healing. Detecting signs in everything lends paranoid features to their world, and this trend can become particularly intense, practically psychotic, vis-à-vis the analyst. They perceive ominous signs in his or her face, voice, in the arrangement of objects on the desk, in other words, in anything. These patients "know" what everything means. There is no "maybe"; no hypothetical thought exists in a world of signs. The paranoid acting-out patient does not have the flexibility of mind to keep up the "double frame" needed for a usable transference or symbolic perception in general. They resemble Goldstein's (1939) brain-injured patients who "lost the ability to live in two spheres." Neither the brain-injured nor the omnipotent acting-out patient can differentiate between the *real* and the *possible*.

Concretistic, magic omnipotence of thought characterizes the thinking of the acting-out patients. They often think in *pictures* and have extremely vivid *visual sense*. Greenacre (1952) repeatedly points out the affinity between heightened cathexis of the visual functions and acting out. Eidetic imagery is frequent in acting-out juvenile delinquents.[1] Picture thinking is less orderly than language thinking. Pictures represent things in static relations. Pictures are poorly suited to communicate, to symbolize, the process of change in time. Visual imagery refers to specific concrete situations. With the help of discursive language symbolization, generalities can be represented. Acting-out patients keep their past in their head in the form of frozen, framed pictures. The task of producing change in these patients encounters particular difficulties because they are not willing to decathect their

[1]As I found when as a student in Hungary I assisted a juvenile court psychiatrist in her correlation study of eidetic imagery and juvenile delinquency.

mental picturebook. They like to exhibit these pictures, some self-created, hardly connected to marginal memories. But they like to display these mental pictures as proofs for the legitimacy of their claims—claims on parents, on analysts, on the whole world—in order to rectify concretely their childhood injuries. This is one way to stay eternally intermingled with the parental imagoes of early childhood.

Without adequate separation, there is no symbolization and vice versa. It is a circular process with no definable point of causal origin. Sartre (1956) said that before language can exist, it is necessary for the *other* to exist. In his words, "Language . . . presupposes an original relation to another subject." Autistic children can neither separate nor symbolize. On the other hand, we know that from the earliest nursing and "holding" situation on, the mother is influential in fostering or thwarting the development of wholesome, creative symbolization in the child. Overindulgence or overfrustration of the child's needs and wishes is equally harmful for the development of his capacity to grow into an individual with proper symbolic means at his disposal. Such a person can enjoy human contact of various degrees of closeness and distance, without the need for clinging or fear of intimacy. Overintrusiveness or aloofness of the mother interferes with such wholesome development. Optimal duration of the mother's absence stimulates the child's capacity to resort to symbolic means of self-expression and of bridging over to the absent other. Rich alternatives for symbolic channelization of needs, i.e., a rich preconscious, result in creative self-sufficiency without the earmarks of anxious narcissistic withdrawal. Early in life it is the mother who hands over the objects of the world to her child. If this task is well done, the world will seem to the growing child, and later to the adult, a place for potential enjoyment, even though pain and frustrations are unavoidable. There will be no greediness for the accumulation of objects and no need for the manic defense of externalized hyperactivity. Symbolization in thought will alternate with alloplastic action. The creation of a two-way dialogue between the person and his environment will result in a fairly harmonious life space. Harmonious dialogue between inside and outside implies the uninterrupted cycle of symbolic intake (perception, internalization) and symbolic output (creation of symbolic forms that reach out from the inside to the outside). If this circularly symbolizing process is unimpeded, the life space will not be shattered into fragmented bits by impulsively driven acting out. The acting-out person craves for unbounded fusion with the outside world, and still expects the wish, the act, and the fulfillment to coincide.

Yet, the blueprint of the human organism necessitates the acceptance of delineated objects separated by space and time. Good symbolization testifies to the acceptance of these conditions, while good symbols are also the only means to establish uninterrupted connectedness. It is exactly in the realm of thoughts that humans can recapture *some* of the limitless fusion with the outside world which they imagine was once experienced. Thoughts, as long as they remain thoughts and are not acted out, do not have to obey the limits of time and space. In the world of ideas, art, music, and religion, humans can transcend the dividedness of so-called real reality.

References

Breuer, J. & Freud, S. (1893–95), On the psychical mechanism of hysterical phenomena. *Standard Edition,* 2:1–18. London: Hogarth Press, 1955.

Cassirer, E. (1944), *An Essay on Man.* New Haven: Yale University Press.

Freud, S. (1910), Five lectures on psycho-analysis. *Standard Edition,* 11:3–56. London: Hogarth Press, 1957.

—————— (1914), Remembering, repeating, and working-through. *Standard Edition,* 12:145–156. London: Hogarth Press, 1958.

Greenacre, P. (1952), *Trauma, Growth, and Personality.* New York: Norton.

Goldstein, K. (1939), *The Organism.* New York: American Book Company.

James, W. (1911), *Some Problems of Philosophy.* London: Congman's Green & Co. Quoted in *The Philosophy of William James.* New York: Modern Library, p. 76.

Kant, E. (1787), *Kitik der reinen Vernunft.* Riga: Johann Friederich Hartknoch.

Kerenyi, A. (1959), *Asklepius: Archetypal Image of the Physician's Existence.* New York: Pantheon Books.

Langer, S. K. (1942), *Philosophy in a New Key.* New York: Mentor Books, 1951.

Lorenz, K. (1937), Über die Bildung des Instinktbegriffs. *Naturwissenschaften,* 25: 289–300; 307–318; 324–331.

Picard, M. (1963), *Man and Language.* Chicago: Henry Regnery.

Sartre, J. P. (1956), *Being and Nothingness.* New York: Philosophical Library.

Tinbergen, N. (1951), *The Study of Instinct.* Oxford: Oxford University Press.

Whitehead, A. N. (1927), *Symbolism.* New York: Macmillan.

Wittgenstein, L. (1958), *The Blue and Brown Books.* Oxford: Oxford University Press.

9

SHAME, GUILT, AND THE
FEMININE SELF IN PSYCHOANALYSIS

E. James Anthony, M.D.

> When a person is too much of a man or too much
> of a woman, the commonsense generally isn't
> there. . . . But neuters have no trouble under-
> standing men and women.
>
> Yasunari Kawabata (1958)

> Man can be analysed, women. . . merely adored.
>
> Oscar Wilde (1895)

There has been much discussion of where the psychoanalyst takes up his position with reference to the human mind that he is analyzing, but it is generally agreed that he should seek a point as neutral as possible: psychodynamically equidistant from ego, superego, and id; psychodynamically equidistant in some transitional space between inner and outer reality; psychodynamically equidistant from the male and female components of personality so as to interfere as little as possible with the expression of paternal and maternal transferences and the bisexual urges of the patient. In this last respect, the situation is a difficult one: however neutral the analyst sets out to be *sub specie aeternatis*, in actual practice he can no more be a psychological neuter than a physical one, and the biases stemming from a lifelong experience of maleness and femaleness will assuredly affect his analytic attitude and behavior toward the sex and sexuality of his patient.

For Freud (1933), the feminine psyche was not only difficult to understand psychoanalytically but difficult to treat psychoanalytically. This did not preclude him from attempting to do both and running into strife with female critics on the way. The fact that he took as the point of his departure the anatomical absence of the penis in womankind was seen by them as reprehensible in two ways: it reduced women to the negative psychological status of mutilated men, and it seemed completely to overlook the positive attributes originating from womanly sources. Since they were genitally lacking, women had to be deeply and pervasively activated and motivated by shame, so that in trying to write a psychology of women, Freud (1933) ended up writing a psychology of shame:

> Shame, which is considered to be a feminine characteristic *par excellence* but is far more a matter of convention than might be supposed, has as its purpose, we believe, concealment of genital deficiency. We are not forgetting that at a later time shame takes on other functions [p. 132].

According to him, genital deficiency led to certain logical consequences: first, it rendered women more narcissistic and more liable to narcissistic object choices than men since they endeavored in this way to counterbalance their sexual inferiority; second, it made women inept as discoverers and inventors and limited their contribution to civilization to plaiting and weaving that meant little more than the symbolic matting together of pubic hair to conceal the missing penis; third, it caused women to be more envious than men in all aspects of mental life and generally less fair in their judgment; and, finally, because in their development, the oedipus complex was not brought to a dramatic close by the fear of castration but only gradually and incompletely resolved, the superego was inadequately formed and consequently left female morality deficient in guilt and overcompensated with shame.

Although feminism was still comparatively nonmilitant at the time of his writing, Freud was aware that his conclusions were sensitive to the charge of masculine chauvinism but made no attempt to excuse his ideas on this ground. Psychoanalysis had schooled him to accept the unacceptable, however unpopular this was. He said, for example: "You may take it as an instance of male injustice if I assert that envy and jealousy play an even greater part in the mental life of women than of men" (p. 125); and, "If you reject this idea as fantastic and regard my belief in the influence of lack of a penis on the configuration of femininity as an *idée fixe,* I am of course defenceless" (p. 132).

As a result of this primary shame of genital deficiency, secondary shames therefore accumulated in the psychological makeup of women conducing to greater vanity, greater jealousy, greater unreasonableness, greater revengefulness, greater long-sufferance, greater secretiveness, and greater passivity and submissiveness. Because of their primary shame, they are also more liable to become chronically discontented, masculinized, and possibly sexually inhibited, all adding to their quota of shame.

As if this was not enough, Freud (1933) had still another shameful fact to recount: women, in his opinion, were not as analyzable as men:

> The woman of. . .[about thirty, as compared with a man of the same age] often frightens us by her psychical rigidity and unchangeability. Her libido has taken up final positions and seems incapable of exchanging them for others. There are no paths open to further development; it is as though the whole process had already run its course and remains thenceforward insusceptible to influence — as though, indeed, the difficult development to femininity had exhausted the possibilities of the person concerned. As therapists we lament this state of things [pp. 134–135].

We can hardly be surprised that Freud ends this essay on femininity with the remark that it "does not always sound friendly" (p. 135). It does not sound "friendly," but then the purpose of psychoanalysis from its inception was not to make friends but to discover truth, however unpalatable this might be. Freud was no partisan. He followed where his intuitions led him and if these were shaped by his culture, his environment, his age, his upbringing, and his sex, our task as analysts is to extract as much from his genius for analysis as we can at the points where it transcended his time, his place, and his personality.

There were two ways in which he made his approach psychoanalytically to the woman: from the point of view of genital difference and from the point of view of the female's tendency to hypercathect her objects to the extent of having problems in relinquishing them. This second factor was as important in understanding both the psychology and treatment of women. One had to consider, in the first place, the girl's prolonged preoedipal attachment to the mother and, secondly, her prolonged oedipal attachment to the father. Both led frequently to standstills during development and psychoanalysis. Furthermore, one could not hope to elucidate the psychology of the woman without recognizing that her development was more difficult and more complicated; that she needed to change her erotogenic zone as well as her object, and that she needed to pass from a masculine to a feminine phase of development. The little "boy" had to become a little girl.

All this implied that there was greater liability for women, as compared with men, to develop preoedipal fixations and to encounter hazards as they worked their way more slowly and gradually through the oedipus complex. Still another problem had to do with bisexuality. Whereas the proportion of male and female in any one individual was subject to considerable fluctuation, Freud suggested that bisexuality was more salient in the female and a contributing factor to their "enigma." There was also more variability and unpredictability:

> . . . the development of femininity remains exposed to disturbance by the residual phenomena of the early masculine period. Regressions to the fixations of the pre-Oedipus phases very frequently occur; in the course of some women's lives there is a repeated alternation between periods in which masculinity or femininity gains the upper hand [p. 131].

Freud is certainly right that the first distinction one makes on meeting a human being is "male or female?" with conscious, preconscious, and unconscious resonances throughout the psyche. This is further enhanced when that human being is on the couch, and the male-female distinction is followed and entangled by the analyst-patient distinction, so that male analyst and female patient may intensify the sufficient-deficient distinction. One would therefore as a male analyst need to analyze within oneself constantly the negative impact of the female patient in generating "fears" over her rigidity and unchangeability, and "lamentations" at her emotional nature — none of which may be at a conscious level. These reactions may be aggravated by the sytle of a particular analyst, his androgynous makeup, and his experience in the analysis of women.

Based on these various ideas of feminine development put forward by Freud, it should be possible to predict the course of treatment in a woman:

1. Because of the more difficult and complicated development of the female in general, the course of analysis is likely to be more

difficult and more complicated.

2. Because of the prolonged preoedipal attachment to the mother, there is likely to be a greater tendency toward preoedipal fixations and dispositions, as well as a more preoedipal configuration than would be the case with the male. This would, in general, make for a longer analysis of the preoedipal phase. More and more, the average woman in analysis tends to present as a predominantly pre-oedipal character.

3. Because the woman's preference for passive behavior and passive aims is carried into the analysis, the treatment may appeal profoundly to her passive, dependent, and submissive needs, and make her disinclined to give it up, tending to prolong the analysis.

4. The problem of termination with a male analyst may be particularly troublesome for a number of women who remain, until a quite late age, tenderly dependent on their fathers, and therefore on their analysts.

5. The powerful masochistic impulses characteristic of many women may lock analyst and patient into a sadomasochistic bind from which both may find it difficult to extricate themselves. For all these reasons, women are more prone to interminable analyses.

6. The cycles of masculinity and femininity during the analysis, described by Freud, and the cycles of drive, fantasy, and dream that alternate during the course of the month in every woman may complicate the ongoing analytic and working-through processes and loosen them up, leaving the analyst at times bewildered by the facile regressions to the preoedipal phase, by the emergence of strong masculine identifications in response to the male analyst, by the reactivation of bitter disappointments stemming from both mother and father, by the waves of passivity that overtake the female patient from time to time, by the sudden abject moments of surrender, and, most puzzling of all, by episodes of shamelessness during which habitual modesties are overwhelmed and vulgarizations, disturbing for the male analyst, may display themselves. Shame follows rapidly in the wake of such exhibitions.

7. The intense ambivalent dependency on the preoedipal mother may sometimes spare the analyst but descend on the husband, who becomes for a time the mother's heir. This displaced struggle with the husband gets early and easily to the forefront of the analysis, and he frequently becomes its first casualty. As Freud says,

"When this reaction has been lived through, a second marriage may easily turn out very much more satisfying" (p. 133). This may also be true of a second analysis.

In spite of these many inherent problems in the analysis of the woman, there are compensations that can make her the better candidate once the management of her shame is mastered. She is, as a rule, less aggressive, less defiant, more dependent, more compliant, and more liable to form a stronger and less wavering object cathexis to the analyst. Her intuitiveness, her empathy, her often charming narcissism, and her subtle interpersonal intelligence add appreciably to her attractiveness as a patient, if not to her analyzability. Even more than the man, she wishes very much to become the patient that her analyst wants, or that she imagines that he wants. She desires very much to love and to be loved in the analysis, so that an erotic transference is more often the rule than with the man. She is much more aware of being disloyal or unfaithful to the analyst when she turns to extra-analytic relationships during the course of analysis. (I am not referring here only to acting out.)

Freud felt that the ultimate difficulty in the analysis of women lay in their refusal to give up their wish for the penis. In a sense, this is their deepest envy and their lasting shame. "At no other point in one's analytic work," he said, "does one suffer more from an oppressive feeling that all one's repeated efforts have been in vain, and from a suspicion that one is 'preaching to the winds', than when one is trying to persuade a woman to abandon her wish for a penis on the ground of its being unrealizable" (1937, p. 252).

Many of Freud's less positive analytic experiences with women can be documented by other analysts, including myself, but over time, I have become convinced that once the initial analysis of shame has been thoroughly and systematically undertaken, paths are opened to further analytic development; and the difficult road to femininity has not exhausted the possibilities for dealing constructively and even creatively with the ramifications of guilt when masturbation and its fantasies have been confessed, when frigid sexual responses have been revealed, when the "genital wound" has been exposed, when the body, as an ugly excremental system has been confronted, when oedipal failure has been recognized, and when homosexuality has been suddenly revealed in a storm of shame. One aspect of the analytic situation must be seen for what it means to the patient — an arena of shame with the analyst as a shaming agent using techniques, however gentle, to touch on the very profundities of shame. With women, the initial analysis of shame is fundamental to the total treatment. Freud himself was very clear as to what he wished to accomplish in the analysis of a woman: "psycho-analysis does not try to describe what a woman is — that would be a task it could scarcely perform — but sets about inquiring how she comes into being, how a woman develops out of a child with a bisexual disposition" (1933, p. 116).

A woman is born psychologically into shame and must develop out of shame before she can become a feminine being. The analysis of shame demands a meticulous and systematic analysis of the pre-oedipal phases as far as we can reach them with the analytic method. The analysis of shame involves on the one side the analysis of paranoia and on the other the analysis of depression, and it is by no means surprising how frequently the analysis of a woman shifts between shame, paranoia, guilt, and depression, especially in the prolonged initial stages. All analyses involve the analysis of the moral system with its essential ingredients of shame and guilt, but in the analysis of women the analysis of shame is the major preliminary step.

Shame and Paranoia

When Freud first wrote of shame (1950 [1892–99]), he referred to it as one of the primary symptoms of defense in the obsessional neuroses and associated it with conscientiousness and self-distrust as reactions to the early "disgraceful" passive seductions that had been experienced. Later (1896), he examined its appearance in the case of a chronic paranoid woman patient who complained that seeing naked women at the public baths filled her with shame. She went on to confess that she had always felt ashamed at the thought of being seen naked. Freud then set about analyzing the shame that seemed to be so central in this particular patient's psychopathology. He described his approach as follows:

> Since I was obliged to regard the shame as something obsessional, I concluded, in accordance with the mechanism of defence, that an experience must have been repressed here about which she had *not* felt ashamed. *So I requested her to let the memories emerge which belonged to the theme of feeling ashamed.*

She promptly reproduced a series of scenes going back from her seventeenth to her eighth year, in which she had felt ashamed of being naked in her bath in front of her mother, her sister and the doctor; but the series ended in a scene at the age of six, in which she was undressing in the nursery before going to bed, *without feeling any shame* in front of her brother. . . it transpired that. . . the brother and sister had for years been in the habit of showing themselves to one another naked before going to bed. I now understood the meaning of her sudden idea that she was being watched as she was going to bed. It was an unaltered piece of the old memory which involved self-reproach, *and she was now making up for the shame which she had omitted to feel as a child* [1896, p. 178; my italics].[1]

Here we have an example of shame linked closely to shyness, to the beginnings of modesty in the little girl, and to the paranoid feeling of being watched when naked. There is also an element of disgust in the reaction. This sense of unpleasure due to the release of premature sexual experience was regarded by Freud (1950) as the makings of his first moral system (1896) in which shame and guilt acted as repressing forces and were focused in the neighborhood of the sexual and excretory organs, thus drawing disgust into the picture.

Freud then went on to examine the conditions under which shame failed to appear, *as in the case of men,* of lower-class people, and of rural persons who were often exposed to disgusting circumstances and therefore had their susceptibilities blunted. In the absence of shame, there was no repression and therefore no neurosis. In these early writings [1896], shame, rather than guilt, was associated with neurotic developments. Shame was seen as a repressing force, a defensive maneuver, and, at the same time, an affective transformation stemming from self-reproach, that also evoked anxiety, hypochondriasis, and *a feeling of persecution.*

The relationship between shame and paranoia was fairly direct, as indicated by the clinical vignette. Shame was a fear that other people might find out what one wished to keep concealed, so that it involved exposure to others. Paranoia was seen as intermediate between neurosis and psychosis and related to the fear that others might be thinking and condemning what had been found out.

Freud also undertook to examine the experience of shame as it

[1]When this vignette was presented to a class of candidates, the women were at once aware of the shame involved, while the men insisted that the patient was mistaking guilt for shame.

occurred in dreams and parapraxes, and here he came up with some new and interesting observations. The most characteristic aspect of a shame dream, he found, was the shameful nakedness of the dreamer associated with a complete absence of shame in those around him. As in the case of *The Emperor's New Clothes,* no one in the crowd or in the procession appeared to notice the Emperor's nakedness except the naïve, innocent child. The adults in the dream and in the fairy tale ignore the shamefulness and react, as Freud (1900) put it, with "solemn and stiff expressions" (p. 243). The situation of the dream appeared to recapitulate the developmental sequence: during a certain period of infancy and early childhood, it was acceptable to be naked and unashamed in the Eden of the nursery with the connivance of the attending adults. The child did not feel ashamed, and the adults did not feel ashamed for the child. They even appeared to enjoy the nakedness of the child and vicariously the child's enjoyment of his own nakedness. By the next stage, the child begins to feel the rudiments of shame, the first tinges of embarrassment, the first elements of shyness, and *pari passu* the attitude of the parents stiffens, especially if strange adults are around. Finally, the child's nakedness is condemned as exhibitionism and wanting in modesty, and the child and his parents share equally in the production of shame. The developmental sequence, as described by Freud (1896), can be summarized as follows:

1. "I am naked; I enjoy my nakedness; everyone enjoys my nakedness, and I feel no shame."
2. "I am naked while undressing in front of my siblings before going to bed; I have no feelings of shame, but the adults look solemn and stiff. My siblings and I enjoy our nakedness."
3. "I am naked while taking my bath and I feel ashamed when others come in. I also feel ashamed when I go into the bathroom and observe others to be naked."
4. "I feel ashamed when I am undressing, even when no one is in the room with me. I feel ashamed because I imagine that they may be watching through the window, and I feel more ashamed because of what they might be saying. They may be condemning and criticizing my shamelessness."

In the origins of shame, what starts lightheartedly as "an affair between children" ends as a very serious business and acts as a "primary symptom of defense" behind which lie a variety of so-

cial anxieties, self-disgust, sexual curiosity, exhibitionism and voyeurism, sadomasochistic fantasies and paranoid anxieties. To what
extent it can be regarded as a "true" formation is still debatable. One
can sense the extent to which the "flood of shame" with its intensive
archaic anxieties can overwhelm the child during development[2] and
interrupt not only his growing consciousness of himself and his body
self, but his total identity. The individual becomes an ashamed character, full of shameful memories that have punctuated his course of
development, starting with an early conscious or screen memory of
primary shamelessness. As an ashamed adult, he is, as Freud put it
so succinctly, "making up for shame which he had omitted to feel as
a child."

Many of the shameful memories that come back to haunt the
adult life of the patient are associated with furtive experiences of
masturbation: while both sexes have feelings of guilt connected with
autosexual practices and the fantasies accompanying them, the
female is more prone to feel ashamed and more prone to inhibit the
activity altogether from deep feelings of shame. Later, masturbation
becomes the bridge between shame and guilt. For many patients,
the whole lost story of early childhood can be written in terms of a
succession of zonal shames that then gradually become a secondary
but still powerful supplement to the moral deterrent of guilt. The
proportion of shame and guilt finally achieved within the moral
system varies with the individual, but Freud would logically conclude that the shame factor was predominant in the female. With
both sexes, it seems that untreated guilt continues unabated through
life, while shame becomes attenuated except in certain predisposed
personalities.

Aristotle, writing on the psychology of shame 2,500 years ago,
already had summed up many of our current notions on this topic.
He differentiated shame from guilt as "a kind of fear of disgrace" and
pointed to the fact that it had strong somatic concomitants, such as

---

[2]Jacobson (1964) tells of a little boy of three who was overheard by his mother
expostulating to himself after he had discovered he had wet the bed: "Oh! Oh! What
happened? Terrible! I ought to be ashamed of myself! No! No! I won't! I will not be
ashamed of myself!"

Piaget (1932) tells of his two-year-old daughter who had been given a purgative
and very carefully informed of its possible effects to obviate any possible shame. In
spite of this the little girl is greatly ashamed "experiencing the same feelings as if the
thing had happened in normal circumstances through her own negligence."

blushing. He also felt that it ran a developmental course, so that shame was an appropriate deterrent in the young but was inappropriate in the old, who ought to have learned by other techniques how to refrain from disgraceful acts for reasons other than shame. If shame persists into mature life, one must regard it as indicative of a "faulty character," lacking in proper self-control. But shame had its season: "It is a feeling not suitable to every age, but only to youth: we do think that the young should be shamefaced, because since they live at the beck and call of passion, they do much that is wrong and shame acts on them as a check."

It is a curious fact that although Freud was deeply interested in the phenomenon of shame in his earlier phase, he paid much less attention to it later on when he became preoccupied with the question of guilt and its relation to the ego and superego in structural theory. There seemed to be no place for shame in structural theory at first until it was linked to the ego ideal and became part of a total superego-ego moral complex.

Lest one is left with the notion that Freud considered shame to be the prerogative of women, let us add two vignettes that negate this. One instance was of a young man who had walked peculiarly since the age of fourteen for which he felt ashamed. The history revealed that his ambulation was modeled on the walk of a dissolute uncle who had developed syphilitic tabes. He reported to Freud that his uncle *was not in the least ashamed* of his gait and he wondered at his own shame. Once again, Freud was able to trace these shameful feelings back to an earlier stage when the boy had contracted gonorrhea that inconvenienced his walking and to an even earlier time when sexual erections had a similar effect. However, Freud felt that "the cause of shame lay deeper." He found that his patient had been enuretic as a child and that his mother had threatened to go to his school and tell everyone about it. *"So that was where his shame belonged"* (1950, p. 275; my italics).

In another case, the patient blushed, sweated, and was deeply ashamed whenever he saw a girlfriend at the theatre. There was an underlying fantasy of his deflowering her associated with the conscious thought: "Now the silly goose thinks that I am ashamed in front of her. If I had her in bed, she would see how little embarrassment I feel with her." Once again, Freud (1950, p. 279) traced back earlier events along the pathway of shame — failures at school, masturbating in the toilet at Interlaken while staring at the Jungfrau through the window, and back to the age of three with his brother in the bathtub, having soapsuds rubbed over his face.

Following these preliminary studies on shame, the theme entered a sort of psychoanalytic limbo and lost its primary place in treatment. Later analysts, especially Jacobson, have attempted to restore its importance by linking it with such topical issues as guilt, depression, inferiority, narcissism, self-esteem, and identity formation. Analysts specializing in the condition of erythrophobia have also reexamined the phenomenon.

Shame and Guilt

One must regard *The Self and the Object World* by Jacobson (1964) as the critical piece of literature that not only disentangled some of the confusions relating to shame and guilt but at the same time linked these two unpleasurable affects to depression and paranoia and eventually to identity. In it, she described a type of schizoid depression in which "the guilt conflicts may be absent or recede in favor of paranoid fears of exposure, while feelings of shame and inferiority, self consciousness and fears or feelings of loss of identity frequently appear as a characteristic triad of symptoms" (p. 198).

One should also take note of the inclusion of a terminal chapter on "Acting Out and the Urge to Betray in Paranoid Patients" in her book on *Depression* (1971), the juxtaposition suggesting that paranoid and depressive tendencies have a psychogenetic relationship to each other and that the two together (as seen in paranoid depressions) are associated with flagrant identity conflicts. We begin to see here the tentative linkage between the development of shame and guilt, the development of ego ideal and superego, and the development of paranoia and depression.[3]

Jacobson did not subscribe to the Kleinian formulation in which a so-called schizoid-paranoid position was genetically linked in the infant with a so-called depressive position, but she was clinically aware of the fact that paranoia and depression were not infrequently seen together, especially in women. The case presented by

[3]I was the discussant at the Therese Benedek lecture given by Jacobson on the topic of "Guilt, Shame, Identity," and it was the interaction with Jacobson on this occasion that helped to crystallize some of the notions presented in this chapter.

Freud of chronic paranoia, referred to earlier, would be a case in point. In such patients, the paranoia involved a depressive mood coupled with intense self-consciousness and shame, but no fixed and systematized delusions. The critical question posed by the clinical association of paranoia and depression was whether it had normal or abnormal infantile antecedents. Jacobson was critical of Klein's assumption of a normal infantile paranoia and depression that were reactivated in the schizophrenias and melancholias of adult life through the intermediary of introjective and projective mechanisms, severe ambivalence conflicts, and regressions to oral, anal, and narcissistic positions. Yet, there was a certain psychoanalytic logic to Klein's postulations: if the basic tenet was true that there could be no adult neurosis without an infantile neurosis, might it not also be true that there could be no adult psychosis without an infantile psychosis; and if there was an infantile psychosis, it would only be contained within the preoedipal period. Why did Jacobson (and other classical analysts for that matter) not see the necessity for an infantile precursor of paranoia? Benedek (1956) and Mahler (1966) have injected depression into the preoedipal phase, but not paranoia; and the depression was not an integral part of normal ontogeny. Postulating a sequence of "psychotic" fixation points, as did Abraham (1924) and Glover (1932), had minimal explanatory value.

Shame breeds shame since the feeling of shame is itself regarded as shameful. This is partly due to the "paranoid" propensity that accompanies shame and generates the feeling that the other person is aware of one's shameful thoughts and actions and, in some mysterious way, has access to one's mind. If pressed about this, the shameful one will deny this as unrealistic, but, at a more irrational level, he will feel that his thoughts are exposed.

The phenomenology of shame has been much described. Patients who are prone to shame reactions are acutely self-conscious, worried about their performance, afraid of being looked at, expecting to be laughed at, and wishing to sink through the floor and hide themselves from the penetrating gaze of the other.[4] Shame is a reaction to face-to-face encounters, when one is mainly in visual contact

---

[4]In his analysis of the gaze, Sartre (1950) speaks of the destructive, dehumanizing quality of the process of looking at and its capacity to transform the person into a thing.

with the observing other upon whom one projects one's ideal and from whom one expects odious comparisons. The face-to-face situation is evocative not only of shame, but also of paranoid projections. The anlayst, as the archetypal "measure of all things," seems constantly to be using shaming techniques through his interpretations. One cannot live up to him, one cannot stand up to him; and the result is an increasing tension between the patient's ego and the idealized ego projected onto the analyst. The threat, implicit in the analytic situation, is narcissistic hurt and abandonment. No one, reasons the patient, would want to remain with her once they knew what a shameful person she was and what shameful things she did. At a less manifest level, the wish to show oneself is in constant conflict with the desire to hide oneself from the analyst's disgust. For instance, in a typical case, a patient may blush shamefacedly on her way to the couch, but once recumbent, may defiantly expose herself both physically and psychologically; once up, she takes a shameful flight to the door. The inherent humiliation of being a patient is often grossly intensified in these cases.

Having discussed whether the woman is analyzable, and having discussed the deep shames that suffuse the feminine psyche, I now need to consider whether the pathologically shameful patient can be treated successfully through psychoanalysis. The built-in shames of the analytic situation would seem to militate against this possibility; but the curious fact is that because shame is ubiquitous and existential and can thus be "shared" with the analyst and stimulate his empathic reaction, the condition lends itself uniquely to analysis.

There may, of course, be crises that may put the alliance to severe tests. Under conditions of acute shame during the analysis, the patient's personality may be temporarily disrupted, the regression may be swift, and within minutes one may be confronted by what looks and sounds like a screaming toddler. At such times, shame and paranoia are closely interlinked, and the hostility directed toward the analyst may be extreme. At such times, the man behind the couch becomes a part, as Erikson (1950) puts it, of the "dark continent":

> ...an area of the body which can be magically dominated and effectively invaded by those who would attack one's power of autonomy and who

would designate as evil those products of the bowels which were felt to be all right when they were being passed. This basic sense of doubt in whatever one has left behind forms a substratum for later and more verbal forms of compulsive doubting; *this finds its adult expression in paranoiac fears concerning hidden persecutors and secret persecutions threatening from behind and from within the behind* [p. 224; my italics].

There is an experience of a loss of self-control and, what is more, of foreign overcontrol by the analyst, bringing with it doubt and shame. Quite normal adults, seemingly mature and unneurotic, can display a sensitivity concerning a possibly shameful "loss of face" and a fear of being attacked "from behind." This is amplified in the type of neurotic woman I have been discussing and may become a haunting dread in the recumbent psychoanalytic setup. "Loss of face" and "fear of attack from behind" become critical aspects in the psychoanalysis of shame, and must be dealt with both at the beginning of the analysis and at its conclusion.

Wallace (1963) has suggested that the analytic posture, on the couch, tends to lead inevitably to a focus on guilt because of the auditory nature of the transaction, which also explains why shame was so prominent in Freud's early patients when he was visible, as contrasted with later on when he withdrew behind the couch.

Jacobson was on the whole somewhat dubious about the strict dichotomy expressed by Piers and Singer (1953) who considered shame to be basically a tension between the ego and the ego ideal, shame anxiety had to do with shortcomings in reaching a desired goal, and the unconscious shame threat related to abandonment; whereas guilt related to tensions between the ego and superego, guilt anxiety was specifically concerned with transgression, and the unconscious guilt threat came from castration. She agreed with Hartmann and Loewenstein (1962) that one could not sharply differentiate the two systems — the ego ideal and the superego — and that the ego ideal was incorporated into the superego. Nevertheless, she thought that clinically there were good reasons for treating shame and guilt distinctively, although the workings of shame eventually entered into the workings of guilt. Here Jacobson carefully and systematically separated useful operations notions in the clinical context from their metapsychological significances. My experience is in keeping with this view: one should not multiply one's metapsychological entities beyond necessity, but clinically shame and guilt are "as chalk and cheese" in cases with severe shame reactions.

In the more recent literature, these two potent "drive controls" have been used in the creation of two seemingly separate worlds: a shame or other-directed culture generated by shame-provoking child-rearing techniques and a guilt or inner-directed culture generated by guilt-provoking child-rearing measures (Benedict, 1946).

Psychoanalysts, in general, judging from their everyday practice, would tend to accept the idea that the ego ideal is formed earlier than the superego, that shame antedates guilt, and that shame is linked more closely with preoedipal components and guilt with oedipal ones. They might also agree that shame has a more ravaging effect on the formation of identity and that "inferiorities" could eventually come to dominate the personality and increase the vulnerability to narcissistic hurt. However, they would regard it as an oversimplification to categorize shame as predominantly a self response and guilt as an ego response with a different status within structural theory. Today, both would be seen as essentially narcissistic disorders inclining to narcissistic types of transference. Bibring's (1953) emphasis on the ego in relation to self-esteem and its regulation has certainly helped to bring shame more fully into the clinical context of depression.

The two moral elements also express themselves differently. The language of shame tends to be more physiological with its wide range of autonomic reactions, and nearer to the expressive phase of the infantile preverbal psychosomatic state (Schur, 1960), whereas guilt is more psychologically communicative and less archaic in its expressiveness.

The contemporary analyst is on the whole wary of having too many metapsychological angels dancing on the tip of a structural pin and is in sympathy with any effort to reduce structural diversity to identity, to quote Meyerson (1930). Shame and guilt are seen as interweaving with each other sequentially through development as well as through psychoanalytic treatment; and Jacobson, Piers, and I have described shame-guilt cycles that are worked through in analysis so that increasing amounts of shame are transformed into guilt, which is then resolved within the framework of the transference neurosis. There is an implicit suggestion here that shame is less tractable to change, unless it is first transformed and brought within the ambience of guilt. The processes are overlapping. At any one time in the analysis, the self-observing ego can be dealing with transactions between shame and the ego ideal, between guilt and the workings of conscience, with blame at times projected outward and at times internalized. In a typical guilt-shame cycle (to be observed either in real life or in the analytic process), wrongdoing may lead to guilt feelings, to remorse, to fears of retaliation, to attempts at reparation, to compliant submission, to feelings of weakness and helplessness, to a sense of inferiority, to a lowering of self-esteem, to a narcissistic crisis, to the "fury of humiliation," to open aggressiveness, and finally to the reactivation of guilt.

Jacobson has described conditions when masturbation, for example, could take one of two ways within the person: through sadistic masturbatory fantasies into guilt, or through passive, masochistic fantasies into shame, with the one alternately defending against the other. The patient is able to differentiate the one experience from the other. The "strange feeling of helplessness" associated with shame is phenomenologically different from the "helplessness and hopelessness" typical of severe guilt with depression.

The Shame Syndromes

Although our psychoanalytic knowledge is lacking in this area, it is possible to classify tentatively some of the conditions met with in the psychoanalysis of women where shame appears to play an inordinate role, although, as one follows any particular case, the shame may move in one direction into inferiority feelings, identity problems, and paranoid concerns, and in the other direction into guilt, depression, and pathological obsessiveness. Because of this dynamic changeability, the syndromes to be described are far from clear-cut, diagnostically unstable, and frequently overlapping. This variability has often been associated with the feminine psyche, and one of the reasons for it can be attributed to the vulnerability of the woman's still emergent identity.

Since the earliest historical records, the female of the human species has been compelled to submerge her personality in the service of the male ego. This has led in many cultures and in many centuries to a stunting of emotional development and the evolution of a pseudoidentity, characterized by such negative attributes as maso-

chism, self-denial, self-abasement, submissiveness, nonasser-
tiveness, servility, undue deference, shyness, oversensitivity, undue
modesty, shamefulness, and frailty ("Frailty, thy name is woman!").
This assumed identity, reinforced by every cultural device known to
man, gradually took on the character of a universal entity, the elements of which were marked by inferiority. As women in developed
countries were emancipated politically, socially, sexually, repro-
ductively, and economically, a new identity began to evolve that was
no longer determined to the same degree by masculine preferences
and assessments. The birth of the new identity has not been without
its pains. One cannot "pour new wine into old bottles" without
creating specific vulnerabilities to conflict, so that identity problems
have beset the new woman to the point that identity diffusion is a
growing menace accompanying emancipation. The young female
especially is often caught between the old and new identities and
very easily develops a sense of wrongness about her growing aspirations and achievements. She is often challenged to remember where
she has come from biologically and historically, and she is still confronted with the brute facts of her anatomy as if it hung like a mill-
stone around her psyche. Her physiology is also brought forward as
evidence of her inherent sensitivity, instability, and vulnerability.
Her constitution has long been regarded as inferior, although it was
difficult to explain why she so frequently outlived her masculine
counterpart.

Taking all these factors into consideration, one can classify the
shame syndromes as constitutional, physical and psychocultural.[5]

[5]One should mention a minor shame syndrome that occurs most frequently in
female adolescents and female patients in regression — the development of a grudge
following a humiliating experience with a close female friend (in an overt or covert
homosexual relationship) or following a "humiliating" interpretation in analysis.
The deep underlying conflicts of passivity, dependence, and submissiveness are at
oral fixation points to which regression occurs. The response patterns oscillate between paranoid-antihomosexual feelings (the grudge reaction), depressive-
masochistic feelings (the sulk reaction), obsessive preoccupations with the grudge,
and phobic avoidance of the grudge provoker.

A patient may drop out or threaten to drop out of analysis because of a grudge
against the analyst or relapse into a sulky silence for days or weeks. (In Melanie
Klein's terms, a splitting of introjects leads to the paranoid position as a regressive
defense against the depressive position.) Patients with this proclivity (and it includes
feminine males) follow a narcissistic line of development that indicates difficulty in
regulating self-esteem and in tolerating any withdrawal of narcissistic supplies. The
libido attached to the ego ideal takes largely a narcissistic and homosexual form. In

1. The constitutional syndromes are characterized by hypersensitivity, hyperreactivity, hyperallergy, which may eventually manifest themselves in erythrophobia, marked social anxiety, phobic reactions, paranoid developments, and depression.

2. The physical syndromes have their origin in handicaps, such as hearing difficulties, and physical stigmata that make for feelings of inferiority and difference. Once again, the syndrome is characterized by shyness and withdrawal, inferiority feelings, paranoid thinking, and proneness to depression.

3. The psychocultural syndromes are typically seen in shame inhibitions with a life history starting in a timid infancy, exaggerated stranger reaction during the toddler phase, extreme shyness and prudishness in the latency girl, sometimes coupled with school phobia and a marked constriction of personality in the adult woman with massive difficulties in the sexual and aggressive areas. Second, shame is predominant in the adolescent struggling with frightening biopsychological developments, physical awkwardness, and scarifying acne. Third, there is the type I depression with a great deal of shame and very little guilt (Anthony, 1975), which shows a cyclical development related to increases and reductions in the feelings of self-esteem. The psychopathology is mainly preoedipal and based on a marked symbiotic tie with the omnipotent, need-satisfying mother; the crucial problem has to do with discrepancies between the ego and the ego ideal, with resulting eruptions of shame, humiliation, inferiority, inadequacy, weakness, and ego helplessness. The object relations are narcissistic, orality is striking, and dependency is extreme. The mother, in turn, tends to be sadistic, disparaging, reproachful, and deflating. Such parenting has the effect of invading and pervading the entire personality, fixating it on a preoedipal level. The "identity theme" (Lichtenstein, 1961) imprinted on the girl is one of shame, its profile having the following characteristics: a narcissistic personality not unlike that of the mother; a preponderance of shame and inferiority over guilt reactions; paranoid fears of exposure associated with a paralyzing self-consciousness and a past history of humiliations, disappointments, and disillusionments; the presence of marked ambivalence and

---

analytic treatment, interpretation is often understood in demeaning terms, and transference is complicated by the projected image of the analyst as a shaming agent. The condition has been discussed by Wixen (1971).

dependency conflicts; severe regressive ego and superego pathology often resulting in a failure to establish self and object constancy, in alternations of acting out with compulsive behavior, sadism with masochism, and heterosexuality with homosexuality; an apparently endless searching for new objects, new selves, with consequently little or no experience of continuity or consistency; a setting up of situations that culminate in disappointments and states of "empty" depression. Diagnostically, these patients often present as narcissistic character disorders with obsessional, paranoid, and depressive features. The syndrome can be observed through several generations, suggesting a cycle of narcissistic deprivation that clinically injures the vulnerable ones in each generation. Jacobson has described similar depressive-paranoid syndromes and shame-guilt-inferiority in adult women, but the conditions are not limited to women.

The Psychoanalysis of the Shame Syndromes

According to Levin (1971): "When psychoanalysis is successful, it results, among other things, in a progressive alleviation of shame. In order to achieve this result to an optimum degree, it is necessary to analyse carefully the numerous reactions in which shame is involved." Levin goes on to remark that the analysis of shame is "often overlooked or inadequately executed" (p. 355); and with this I am strongly in agreement, especially in relation to the psychoanalysis of women.

Levin (1971) agrees with Aristotle and others that shame is a function of both constitutional and environmental factors, and it undergoes variations in its conflict structure throughout the course of development. Earlier on, in the preschool stage, it is mainly associated with performance: the control of bowel and bladder, the capacity for autonomous behavior in self-care procedures, and the learning of elementary skills in school. As the individual approaches adolescence, the shame may center on some deficiency, real or supposed, in the body,. and embarrassments may circulate from one organ to another. As with anxiety, depression, and guilt, shame provokes its own defensive strategies, such as avoidance of the shaming situations or embarrassing exposures; massive withdrawal from social contact, especially those associated with sexual shame; identification with shamers as a cover for weak and impotent feelings; shame turned against the self, leading to exaggerations of defects and inferiorities, the projection of shameful feelings onto others, and a whole range of countershame maneuvers. When shame is internalized, feelings of shame, like feelings of guilt, will make their appearance without an external provocation, so that strong mechanisms of repression may be utilized to deal with this "unconscious" shame. Levin makes the interesting suggestion that individuals may become "criminals from a sense of shame" (p. 355), just as there are those who may become "criminals from a sense of guilt" (Freud, 1916).

Apart from Levin, no other analyst has dealt in any detail with the psychoanalysis of shame; it is therefore relevant to summarize his techniques.

1. The psychoanalysis of shame is, to a large extent, an ego and ego ideal analysis.

2. The analysis of the shame defenses varies with the phase of treatment; certain conscious shames stimulated by the analytic situation may have to be dealt with before the unconscious, repressed shames can be released.

3. It is important for the analyst to work within the levels of shame tolerance of the patient; otherwise the patient may be overwhelmed by the humiliation and embarrassment so that his withdrawal tendencies may be reinforced.

4. Much of the analysis of shame is conducted in relation to the transference: unconscious shame anxieties rapidly become linked to the person of the analyst in the transference.

5. The analysis of resistance must also be conducted with extreme tact: for example, if the analyst calls attention to the blocking created by the patient's primary shame, this may precipitate intense secondary shame of being an "analytic failure." In such hypersensitive individuals, even the gentlest comment may be understood as scarifying criticism.

6. The motives that bring a patient with a shame syndrome into analysis are many: he may be envious of those who seem to be free of shame and aspire to become like them; or he may wish to develop defiant attitudes or countershames and shock others, rather than be put down by them; or he may wish to be "cured" of his excessive shame in order to indulge in gratifying behavior, which he currently

regards as indiscreet.

7. As the analysis progresses, a patient may attempt (as with Freud's cases) to recapture past traumatic instances of shame and may focus almost entirely on these to the exclusion of current shames. As with other flights into the past or present, the defensive purpose has to be carefully explored.

8. With the successful analysis of shame, many unconscious shameful thoughts and feelings and impulses are brought back into consciousness, particularly those having to do with sexual shames, and thus a more satisfactory sexual adjustment may be attained. Furthermore, the patient's characteristic secretiveness may give place to greater openness once his anticipated expectations of rejection are not fulfilled.

It will be seen that Levin's approach adds greatly to the earlier work of Freud. Its limitations are that it does not link the analysis of paranoia and depression with the analysis of shame, or the analysis of shame with the analysis of guilt, although he does mention the obsessiveness and shyness, the hypersensitivity to criticism, the constitutional limitation of the ego to avoid shame through normal defensive measures, and, superimposed upon all these, the effects of excessive shaming during childhood. Such patients become so ashamed of being ashamed that a circular reaction results that is comparable to a negative therapeutic reaction. Dropping out of treatment at such time is not unusual. Not only are these patients ashamed of becoming ashamed, but they are fearful of becoming ashamed, and the mastery of these experiences is by no means easy even with the help of psychoanalysis.

It is interesting that of the clinical vignettes offered by Levin, the main ones have to do with women, except for his opening case that he saw in a hospital. I too have seen male patients with shame reactions, but the majority of cases that I have had in analysis with shame syndromes have been women.

Vignette 1

A woman in her mid-thirties, with schizoid-obsessional characteristics, was not only habitually very shy but from time to time overcome by crises of shame. For a long time, she was unable to look at me upon entering or leaving the office, and she warned me from the beginning that although she understood the "golden rule," there were many thoughts that came into her mind that she would never be able to reveal. She had kept secrets ever since she had been a little girl and she could not see herself changing the habits of a lifetime. The existing ego constriction had been heavily reinforced by a cultural overload of prohibitions. She could remember as an adolescent feeling highly embarrassed to look at her own body. There was still a further factor that complicated her shamefulness: as a small child, she had been seriously injured on the upper part of her trunk so that a scar ran right across her breast. Nakedness had always been an agonizing experience, and she was very surprised when her husband refused to take much notice of the stigma.

It took her six months to inform me that she sometimes picked her nose when she was alone and enjoyed rolling the contents between her fingers. She was convinced that I would no longer want to see her or feel the same toward her after this admission. Very gradually, other orifices were brought into shameful awareness, until her whole body was exposed for the cesspool she considered it was. She wondered how men, and I in particular, were able to stay in the same room with her when she had urine in her bladder, feces in her intestines, blood and mucus in her vagina, phlegm in her throat, spit in her mouth, sweat under her arms, and "stuff" in her nostrils. How was it possible for me not to be repulsed when she herself was so repulsed? "I am just made up of a lot of filthy holes, and the worst of them are between my legs. When I think of them, I want to hide myself and bury myself in the ground forever." Sex was unthinkable unless she anesthetized her mind and felt nothing of what was being done to her. As she dwelt on this matter with increasing preoccupation, her shame began to take on a borderline aspect and she was flooded with unconscious equations of urine, feces, milk, semen, babies, and penises. She was all, in her words, a "gooey mess." At times, she would scream with the pain of her shame and her conviction that I was deliberately shaming her. This was because I hated and despised women and thought them to be inferior. She felt as ashamed with me as she once had felt ashamed when she had been a little girl and thought that all the grownups were laughing at her. She had been the only girl among five siblings and they all teased her because she squatted down to urinate. She hated those things hanging from her brothers, as she now hated the thing hanging from the analyst. She hoped it would shrivel up and develop gangrene, and smell, and become a stinking hole that everyone would hate.

Much of the earlier part of the analysis concentrated on her shame and on her image of the analyst as a shaming agent who was doing to her what had been done to her when she was little. At times, deep unconscious shames would intermingle with conscious everyday shames that seemed to come her way with unfailing regularity. In the face of her primary shame, her genital deficiency, her otherwise quite attractive feminine attributes — a pleasing appearance, a well-developed figure, and beautiful long hair — were completely ignored and any reference to them was regarded as attempts at reassurance. About the middle phase of the analysis, the projective mechanisms became so active and intense that she resembled a paranoid psychotic, although there were no actual breaks with reality. She investigated my shame system to see if I suffered like she, and she wondered whether I was sensitive about my appearance, which she regarded as not too "appetizing"! She seemed to be torn between wanting to shame me and behaving shamelessly toward me. She threatened to masturbate on the couch and seemed to take sadistic pleasure in imagining how embarrassed I would be. She also warned me that she would take her clothes off and scream so that people would come running in and find me in a most compromising position. She could just imagine my face as I was caught in this shameful predicament. It would ruin my career and I would never be able to hold my head up again.

Nothing that she seemed to do or to say appeared to provoke the desired shame reactions in me, and outwardly I continued to accord her my habitual concern and consideration. Inwardly, I was feeling somewhat lost in the morass created by the patient, and inwardly I began to feel ashamed that I was not doing too well with her. This coincided with her own sense of shame at being an analytic failure: she was deficient in every respect — she was unable to free-associate, unable to bring dreams, unable to develop a transference neurosis, and unable to generate insights. She had enough professional knowledge to know what was lacking.

Shame in the countertransference is difficult to handle self-analytically since it seems to pull the professional carpet from under one's feet. It is hard to decide whom to blame or what to blame. Could it be lack of technique, lack of understanding, lack of empathy, lack of knowledge, or lack of analyzability?

The patient, as it were, sensed my predicament and began to misuse and abuse me in a very aggressive way. When I continued, somewhat impotently, to point out her hostility (that hardly needed pointing out at this stage), her tactics seemed to undergo a mutation. She began, at first mildly, to express sorrow for being such a difficult patient; tried to make amends for the injuries that she had done me; became remorseful at having "crucified" me; and gradually began to show clinical evidence of depression. I was aware that something remarkable had taken place, but could not in any way hold myself responsible for it. It almost looked as if she had run out of shame and had rushed headlong into guilt and depression, a cycle described by Jacobson (1964). The attacks on me almost ceased as she became increasingly solicitous for my well-being in the manner of a defensive reaction formation. With the development of the depression, the analysis took an entirely new route and began to assume more classical proportions. From then onward it became predominantly a guilt analysis.

Vignette 2

An erythrophobic syndrome has almost the contours of a classical psychoneurosis, in that it gives, on first impression, a phase circumscription. The patient's complaint was one of intense social anxiety accompanied by blushing. There was a striking constitutional history: she had been an irritable, colicky baby prone to allergic disorders. Each step of her development was marked by an intensification of the social anxiety: her stranger reactions were exaggerated, gastrointestinal upsets were frequent with all new social encounters, and she was liable to throw up whenever taken into public places. Her opening year at school was a disaster, and thereafter every year was memorably painful. Although hypersensitive in all her reactions, her skin was perhaps her most reactive organ: it blushed and flushed and sweated and broke out into unseemly "blotches." It was also peculiarly thin so that the underlying vascular structure was very easily visible. This led to her feeling that she was transparent, both physiologically and psychologically.

The early part of the analysis had to be conducted with great tact, since she responded vehemently to the least suggestion of criticism or what she took to be criticism. I was obliged to work strictly within the limits of her shamefulness. Her self image was compounded of a long list of inferiorities, which she traced back to infancy, and was further amplified by a strict religious upbringing that emphasized not guilt but shame. She was constantly encouraged by a somewhat fanatical mother to live up to and emulate the lives of the saints who were her main standards of behavior throughout her childhood and adolescence. She tried constantly to keep herself pure in thought, word, and deed; and she lived in terror that others would perceive her shortcomings in these areas. She prayed constantly for perfection, so that she would have nothing to hide and nothing to be ashamed of. Her mother's constant reproachfulness was an additional goad to the example of the immaculate virgin.

Eventually, her own virginity became a shame in itself, especially when she reached an age when most of her contemporaries had, as she put it quaintly, "lost their maidenhead." She decided that it was time for her to lose hers, even though the mere sight of a man brought her skin out in blushes. With much trepidation, she maneuvered herself into a sexual situation and was not only deflowered, but impregnated. The ensuing shame was intense. She was now "a fallen woman." She became even more than ever convinced that everyone around her was cognizant of her shamefulness.

In the early stage of the analysis, we focused alternately on the shames evoked by the analytic situation and on the shames that had punctuated her early development. She took to wearing dark glasses when coming for her sessions since this diminished her sense of exposure. She likened the first visit to her recent consultation with the gynecologist who, without any preparation, set her up in the lithotomy position with her legs straddled from stirrups, leaving her genital parts "wide open to the world." She was not only being brutally scrutinized but tied down, a fantasy that she had often had in the past. His look, she said, was "belittling," and she wondered whether he could tell from the appearance of the genital that she masturbated regularly. She felt sure that he was sadistically enjoying her embarrassment. She also tried to surmise how much of her body I could observe from behind the couch, adding, with some humor, that perhaps I had X-ray eyes and could see through her clothes and would know that her underpants were soiled and a little frayed. She knew that I was there to find out all the "shitty" things about her. I would soon discover that she had a complex about dirt, and that she spent a great deal of time compulsively cleaning house, predominantly with the thought that at any time her mother might walk in and accuse her of keeping a pigsty.

She identified herself with her father, whom she regarded as the oldest of her mother's children. Like her, he was a sad, passive, and defeated man; quiet, weak, and introverted; and someone with a sensitive skin like hers who constantly thought that the neighbors were watching him. He rarely spoke, and it was her mother who usually spoke for him. He was, she said in summary, the classical *nebbish!*

She brought a dream that she claimed epitomized her whole life. She was in a house, high on a cliff, and there were three of them in her room: herself, her husband, and a third person who was a woman from her navel upward, that is, she was half a woman and half a man. The three of them were having sex together, and the so-called woman was having fellatio with her husband. Suddenly, his penis came right off and was given to her by the woman, so that it became her penis. She walked to the window and looked out. She had not wanted to bring this dream to the analyst, because she knew that I would interpret it as her wish for a male organ, whereas, in actual fact, she hated the idea of "this fleshy little thing." She thought that she might have gone to the window to see who was looking in, but her immediate thought was that it was I and that I was disapproving the robbing of her husband's penis. The other woman must have been her mother who, she was sure, had castrated her father many years ago. The father's penis, by right, belonged to her, and it was her mother who was the phallic thief. Her behavior at the window also reminded her of her mother who was completely self-centered and always wanted to be the center of the stage. "Throughout my childhood, I was nothing better than a lady-in-waiting in the court of my queen-mother. I did not seem to mind it then, but now I hate her for having kept me perpetually in the background. She can still make me feel horribly ashamed, as if I had wet my pants, simply by looking in my direction." It was her mother who had made her the inhibited woman that she was. How I must despise her, she thought! She was a disrespectful daughter, a reluctant woman, an inadequate wife, a neglectful mother, a completely shallow and uninteresting person, and an untreatable patient. Some people might also call her an abominable Christian and the Church would certainly condemn her as a sinner. She could well understand my contempt, since she was at the other pole to the perfect woman that I would have liked on my couch. She reported that her husband intensified her shame by constantly criticizing her for being a "slob," and he sometimes refused to be seen in public with her. In this sense, he was exactly like her mother and her mother's attitudes ruled her life.

Her bodily consciousness was often intense. She had been over it in microscopic detail, even examining her vagina in a mirror, and every crevice seemed obnoxious and ugly. Her breasts, which had made her ashamed at puberty because they seemed too large, now made her ashamed because they looked too small.

At no time during the first two years of the analysis did she exhibit any feeling that could remotely be labeled guilt or remorse. She was constantly abusive to her parents, her husband, and her analyst, but said that she was only paying us all back for making her "a thing of shame." She dreamed that she stuck her tongue out at me, kicked me in the rump, pulled a gun on me, and knifed me in the groin. "I hate all men, and since you are the only one I have available, you have to suffer for the lot."

Her sessions were turning more and more into an ordeal. She felt disparaged, divided, disregarded, and was tempted to kill herself in a car crash on her way in. She saw herself as a miserable, inadequate creature, a worthy target for the analyst's shaming techniques. "Every day you make me face myself for what I am and the picture is truly horrible. I never realized how appropriate the expression was that one could die of shame."

Toward the beginning of the third year, she said one day, with great conviction, that she was slowly getting the impression that I did not despise her, and that I seemed to like her in spite of hearing what a rotten, nervous creature she was. She had also become aware that she had not been blushing of late, either to or from the couch, and that it was a long time since she had experienced "blotches." For the first time in her life, she had begun to think that she might even be likable. "It is as if God had said to me, 'Find at least one person in the whole of St. Louis who does not regard you as a shameful slob and I will save you.'"

Both her dreams and fantasies underwent a change: the analyst's wife was now constantly in the picture, prominent among both the nocturnal and daytime images, sometimes leaving for another country, sometimes dying, and sometimes meeting with a serious road accident. The patient was always there to take her place, clean up the house, and bake a cake to take to the funeral. She felt herself looking younger and more attractive and had the notion that the analyst was becoming physically interested in her. She had recently read *Fear of Flying,* and knew that analysts could be very susceptible to their more charming patients. She said that, for the first time, she was enjoying being a woman. It was a pity that I was too old for her, because she was sure that she could make me happy. She could not imagine how she could have been so angry with me for the previous two years. Some women did marry men old enough to be their fathers, and she had heard that a man could have a child even when he was in the nineties! Quoting Shaw, she said that with her beauty and his analyst's brains they could manufacture a truly prodigious infant. Instead of babbling, its first vocalizations would be interpretations!

This transitional phase lasted a few months during which her social anxiety almost disappeared to be replaced by specifically ana-lytic concerns. She worried when I traveled about the country by air because crashes were not infrequent; she had had a dream of my death from which she woke up crying. She wished that she could make amends for all the nasty things she had said for so long. She had come to love me very much and wanted me to live forever. If I persisted in wanting to live with my wife, she was ready to acquiesce so that nothing would upset me, increase my blood pressure, and shorten my existence. She realized now what a difficult patient she had been for me and asked forgiveness. What surprised her was that she no longer felt she was being watched and evaluated "like a piece of meat." She now hoped that I would be taking an interest in her ap-pearance, her clothes, and her thoughts. She wanted me to be en-grossed with her. In a dream following this session, she had me in bed with her, touching her hand, but as she was preparing to take hold of it, the door opened, and my wife stood there like an avenging angel. The dream reminded her of fantasies she used to have during adolescence of a family romance in which a stepfather (her own father conveniently having died) would seduce her whenever her mother left the house. In the fantasy she wanted her mother to know so that she would suffer. All those father feelings, she now had for the analyst, but they were much more tender. "I love you very, very much: I really do. I seem to have found a real father who thinks I am quite a girl!" She wondered whether it was possible for me to adopt her. She would not want any inheritance, only my love.

She was now able to laugh about her nervousness, her blushing, and her "blotches." "I have to realize that I have a sensitive skin and that I was born with it, and that I will die with it. I don't have to feel humiliated all the time just because of that. I don't have to feel paranoid every time someone stops and takes a look at me. They might even be admiring me."

Prior to termination, she had a dream of my death. She could not bring herself to look at me in the casket. She woke up sobbing and felt extremely depressed for the rest of the day. My wife, in the dream, had looked old and somewhat decrepit, and she had felt sorry for her. She even began to feel sorry for her mother, and remarked wryly that she, the "almighty she," had begun to develop a shame complex about growing old. "I told her that age was nothing to be ashamed of, but that if it became troublesome, she should have an anlaysis. I knew of a good analyst whom I could recommend without reservation! But of course I was joking. I would never let her take you away from me. After all she did that with my father."

By the end of the third year, the changes were dramatic; the analytic situation was no longer a shameful one; the analyst was no longer the shaming agent; her outer environment was no longer suffused with embarrassment; and her relationship with her parents and with her husband had become relatively benign. She felt that she could take it from there.

Vignette 3

Sullivan (1953) had suggested that the sense of safety is protected by the paranoid projection; that the patient needs to blame others, to feel himself persecuted, and to draw into his self-system anyone or anything that threatened his security. When shame is linked to this paranoid circuit, the patient is hyperalerted to minimal slights and reproaches. In general, adolescents are resistant to the analytic process, but adolescents suffering from a shame-paranoid syndrome became extremely difficult to contain within the analytic situation.

Helen was fifteen when she was presented as a candidate for

analysis. She was described as being extremely nervous and self-conscious; had the constant fear that everyone was looking at her; was unable to eat in front of other people; feared getting into a crowd; and imagined that everyone was out to harm her. She also had a number of nervous ticlike mannerisms and at times felt that her legs were too weak to support her. Her peer relations were uniformly bad; she not only mixed poorly, but appeared actively to dislike young people of her own age and experienced great difficulty in talking with them. Her mistrustfulness was persistent and pervasive; she suspected everyone, especially those who tried to be nice to her, since she regarded this as a sinister manipulation. She saw her father as weak and inconsequential, and her mother as a self-absorbed woman who had little time for her children and occupied herself writing novels. The family had been afflicted with mental disorder through several generations, and Helen's maternal aunt had gone through a similar "catatonic" phase when she was adolescent. The father was an eccentric, self-contained individual who had separated from the family when Helen was five years.

What was striking about Helen was not so much her suspiciousness, which was manifest, but her excruciating sense of shame. She said to me, "I have been ashamed since I was born. Everything was wrong with me from the beginning, and my parents did not make things better." She sat in a stiff uncooperative posture and warned me not to stare at her, or else she would leave immediately. She told me that she was afraid of losing control because she might kill someone. She did not think that she would get alone with me. "I don't like you; I don't like doctors; and, in fact, I don't like men. They make me feel stupid, as if I was a nothing." Her earliest memory was running into a spider's web, at the center of which was an enormous spider. She associated the memory with her mother, but could not tell why. Ever since, she had had a great fear of spiders.

She said that she found the treatment situation very unpleasant. She had a strong fear of being looked at and being "found out" by me. She had an equally strong desire to look at me and make me cringe. She insisted on keeping a safe distance from me. Since childhood, she had never allowed anyone to touch her. She could not bear the thought of anyone "slobbering" over her. She also talked of her fear of committing suicide, of going crazy, and of getting caught in a crowd.

During the early sessions, she was tense and apprehensive. She felt sure I was trying to get at her brains, and she hated my smugness and superiority. I made her feel even more inferior than she felt outside, even more inferior than she felt with her mother. She could hardly bring herself to speak because of what might come out.

Her dreams were generally horrifying; mostly of people being drowned. With drowning, you kept swallowing water until you could swallow no more, and then you swelled up and died. There were prolonged silences during the sessions, sometimes brought to an end with a remark, "I hate coming to see you." She continued to talk of death, of dying, of drowning, of being buried alive, and of killing someone. She thought they would not hang her because she was a juvenile but only put her in prison for about fifteen years.

She began to talk about her blushing and how bad she felt about it. She felt hot all the time she was in the office with me, and this had obviously to do with the way I made her feel ashamed. "You think yourself wonderful just because you're a doctor. I think you are very conceited: just about as conceited as my father."

In the next session, she once again brought two frightening dreams, one dealing with the drowned body of her mother floating in the water, and the other with a dog who was biting her. Then a man came up and started sticking pins into her. I commented that she was still experiencing me as a hurtful figure, taking over, as it were, from her mother.

Her moods alternated suddenly and without warning: she either flopped forward, blushing, in a posture of shame, or she sat stiffly, looking extremely suspicious. Her hate for me began to grow by leaps and bounds. She accused me of keeping notes about her and demanded to have them. She threw a book at me and laughed when I stopped to pick it up and replace it. She wanted me on my knees, scared and ashamed. She would like to kill me, just as she wanted to get rid of her mother and father. At one point, she asked me to get out of the room because my very presence offended her. I spoke to her quietly and encouragingly, and then did as she requested, telling her that I would come back in a few minutes to see whether she felt a little better. She seemed astonished at my compliance and, on looking back, this appeared to be a mutative point in the analysis. She had always come every day on time, but now she took to coming earlier and waiting for her appointment. She began to talk more freely and when I had to leave for a week, she asked whether she might write to me, but then added, mistrustfully, that they would probably open her letters and read what she said and then put her away in a mental hospital.

The drowning and murder dreams were becoming less frequent, and her almost built-in suspiciousness was replaced by sadness and self-reproachfulness. She said that she wished that she had never been born because life had been such an unhappy time for her. I suggested to her that she had many painful feelings buried deep inside her, as was indicated by her dreams, and that these came to the surface when she got upset with me. She should know, however, that I would be there when she needed me.

The next session was, at first, full of silent hate. After a while, she was able to reveal another dream in which she was drowning in a large bath and no one seemed to be around. I suggested that the dream might be a response to what had happened the summer before and was probably expressing doubts that she had about my trustworthiness. Once again I repeated that it was my aim to make her feel safer both with me and outside. Considering the extent of her shame and insecurity, I appreciated just how much personal courage it took for her to be able to leave her home and come by herself for her sessions. Rather than being reassured, she flared up at this and said that she could in no way believe what I was saying to her and that I was just playing at being a doctor. I could afford to gloat since I was not the one who was suffering. I admitted that I was certainly not suffering like her, but like everyone else in the world I too had experienced moments of shame, humiliation, and embarrassment and knew how painful it could be. It was because of this that I could share her feelings and perhaps help her to understand why they happened. She said, grudgingly, "I suppose so." For the next two sessions, she sat silently, but without shame and without suspicion. She appeared to be working something out within herself. When asked how she felt about coming, in the face of so much shame, she burst out angrily with the remark that she had always come for her sessions and that it was I who kept questioning her wish to come. Perhaps I did not want her to come. Perhaps I could not take her. I remarked sympathetically that she must have experienced that same sense of rejection at home when she was little and that she expected to be rejected once again.

She now seemed to be feeling very much "at home" in the session. She was sitting comfortably in her chair and was able to talk without affective storms disrupting her communicatons. She said that she wanted to talk about "deeper" things that she had never told to anybody else. She knew that she brought about a great deal of her own suffering in her everyday life by the provocative and crazy way in which she behaved. She compared coming to see me with a period of tutoring that she had received from her father, who was a schoolteacher. She had also gone to him every day, and every day had been a torture of shame and ignominy and humiliation. It had always ended in a big upheaval because neither of them could stand the tension. He would refer to her as mentally defective. "And you think that I am mentally insane."

Her resistance to treatment reached a new level. She said that there were things about herself that she could never reveal to anybody. She would sooner die. There was no one in the world that she could trust sufficiently to tell. I interposed as gently as I could: "Even someone who might want to help you with them?" She bristled with rage. "I am fed up with people trying to help me. The more they try, the more I hate them. The more you want to help me, the more dumb and crazy and useless you make me feel." She said that if she told me her secrets, she was afraid that she might have to kill me since there would be someone walking about in the world who knew all about her shameful life. I remarked that when one was fifteen, many things about one's body seemed to be shameful. For example, things to do with sex often made one feel embarrassed. She said quickly and in some confusion, "No not that!" and was then silent. After a while, she said, "I am not afraid of crowds anymore. I go to work and I feel alright. Yet you keep nagging me and digging into me when I come here. Even if you do cure me, how do I know that I shall like what I become?" I asked her what kept her coming now that she felt so much better, and she admitted that she no longer was afraid to come and now even wanted to come sometimes, "because you never know what's going to happen next. I want to get better and I want to come and see you, but there's like a big hole in the ground between us and if I told you some things I would just go into it and get covered up and *never* come out again."

Although I was inactive for the next few sessions, she kept up a barrage of accusations. "I hate you nagging me. You want to make me feel ashamed like my mother. You are just like my mother, always nagging until I feel I could kill her. You are both exactly alike." She was then lost in thought for a few minutes, and added, "But then you also put me down like my father and make me feel dumb. My mother makes me feel dirty and my father makes me feel dumb and you make me feel both." I echoed some of these thoughts, "You have now made me into something like your mother and father and you expect me to shame you as they once did, even though you never told them the things you were really ashamed about." She once again reiterated that she would almost certainly hate me if she told me her secrets, to which I replied that if it helped her to feel better, I would not mind being hated. She said at once, "I hate you for not minding being hated. I want you to feel hurt. I want you to be upset like I am upset. I want you to be ashamed like I am ashamed." She was again silent and then added, "But you never seem to feel ashamed at anything I say to you and I want to be like that. I don't want to hate everybody. I want to have friends. I want to feel happy."

She was now, in the second year, talking much more freely, spontaneously, and unselfconsciously. She even laughed at times, and the outbursts of violent rage had almost ceased. She was now working in the evenings to obtain money to help with her treatment. Toward the end of the second year, she said that she was more contented now than she had ever been in her life, adding with satisfaction, "I know I have surprised you. I am doing much better than you ever expected me to do. You thought I was going to be a hospital case." She was now sitting closer and on one occasion asked whether I would like to share an apple that she had brought with her. I said that I would like to share certain things with her that she still did not feel quite ready to share with me, but that the apple was a good beginning and that I would be glad to have half of it. She was able to smile at this and added humorously, "All in good time. You mustn't try and run before you can walk." She sounded like a schoolteacher and I, in turn, had to smile.

At the beginning of her third year, the question of a vacation break arose and I asked her whether she would like to have the name of someone she might call in case she needed to do so. She threw up her hands in horror. "What do you mean? I am not going to see any other doctor. I just got over being ashamed with you and you want me to go through all that again." I said somewhat soothingly that it was only a suggestion. "It had better be!" she said and then added with a teasing smile, "Better the devil you know—!" There was laughter on both sides.

The paranoid and shame reactions were now conspicuously absent, but the situation was still far from stable. For example, she missed several days and blamed me for confusing her about her appointments when I had only made a small change in the time of her sessions. She could still become very angry. "Nothing is ever right when I come to see you. Everything seems to go wrong. You still blame me for everything. You always did." I could sense that something was coming up that was taxing the good therapeutic partnership that had now been established. After one or two very silent sessions, she said that she wanted to tell me something and then never to see me again. When there was no response from me about this, she turned her chair around and talked quietly and rapidly to the wall. She said that sometimes she felt very nervous and would take a razor and cut her arms and legs until the blood came. It always seemed to be when she was having very angry feelings toward her mother. She sometimes thought of doing it to her mother, and once or twice she had thought of doing it to me. She wanted to see my blood flow. She wondered why men did not bleed every month like women. It made her feel like a pig. She thought that everyone in the street would know that blood was running down from her body and they would despise her. She could not bear for me to know that she was bleeding under her clothes. I would just throw up. She knew that her brother did not bleed, and she would like to cut him with a razor. I listened her out quietly and then remarked that I understood about her shameful feelings now and that I was glad that she was able to talk to me about them. Sometimes such feelings covered over other feelings that could also be very upsetting: not only that I might despise her as she despised herself or felt that others despised her, but that I would leave her. She said that sometimes she had felt that if she could kill somebody, she would never have to feel inferior again in her life. "My brain has always been slow because of what that woman [meaning her mother] did to me. She must have hurt me when I was coming out of her. That's what one book said. When I feel inferior, I feel that no one wants me and that I'd better be dead or else they'd better be dead. I can tell what people think of me because I can see it in their eyes."

Feeling much more confident about the relationship, I suggested that some of her aggressive feelings toward me were a coverup for warmer and more sexual feelings that she did not want to admit. She said, "I am afraid of loving and hating people. I just want people to be neutral and I just want to be neutral."

A little later, she informed me that her mother wanted to come and speak with me, but that she had vetoed this vehemently. "If she comes, I go. It's either her or me. I'm not going to share you with her. She's always taken everything away from me because she only loves herself. She never even wanted me to have lessons from my father." She said that when she was about ten years old, she became extremely religious and thought of God as a very kind person who would forgive everything. She soon realized that this was quite untrue and that He could be very cruel and punishing like her parents. He made her feel so ashamed that she could no longer go to confession. She knew that if she had died then, she would go to hell and the devils would all be laughing and jeering at her for the bad things that she did.

She had a strong feeling, too, that her mother never wanted her to be born and that she was ashamed of her, because she was such a peculiar baby. She wondered how it was that I could like her when she was so peculiar now. She wished she could be like me and like everybody, even when they were mean and hated everybody. She wanted her mother to die, but she could not think of living without her. She sometimes thought that I might die, and then she knew that she herself would have to die because she could not live without me. There was no one else who cared about her, even though she was peculiar. She recalled how much torture it had been for her to come and see me in the early days and how wounded she had always felt. She used to leave and walk down the street feeling that everyone was staring at her and could see that her face was red and hot.

She then said that she wanted to tell me something. When she was about three years old, she remembered playing a game with a little boy about a year older. She had forgotten all about it until just now. He did "very dirty things" to her and she could hardly bear to think about it. When she was about thirteen, she had played the same sort of game with another girl who was only seven. She had met her again a few months ago and when the girl had said to her,

"Do you remember the games we used to play?" Helen had been terrified and told her that she must never mention this to anybody else or else she would kill herself.

I said that it was now our secret and that we could talk about it between ourselves to try to understand why it had made her feel so very ashamed. She said that the little boy had tried to rub his "thing" into her and that sometimes she now tried to do the same thing with her finger. At this, she once again turned her chair around and faced the wall. I pointed out how difficult this must have been for her to tell me, but that it was a mark of our good friendship and that I realized now how much she trusted me. She said that she was sure that somewhere inside me I hated her now that I knew the dreadful things that she did. Most of the thoughts that she had about me now when she was at home were bad thoughts. She wanted to cut me and watch my blood flow, and she wanted me to cut her and make her bleed. She wanted us to be the same. She said that she had had a dream recently in which the man had been cut in half and his bottom half had disappeared. I suggested that she wanted my bottom half so that she would not need to bleed anymore, but that my bottom half would not be right for a girl and that her bottom half was just right for a girl and something that she might be very proud about. I pointed to the fact that she was one of the people in the world who could produce beautiful babies from inside their bodies, whereas my bottom half could never do that.

A little later she began to talk about playing with dolls when she was little and giving it up because it bored her. She now thought that she would like to adopt a baby and wondered whether I could arrange this for her. We could both look after the baby together. No one else need know about it, and it would be our secret. She could live in a cottage in the country, and I could come down and see her there and play with "our" baby.

She was once again talking about how much better she felt and that after her sessions she even ran down the street feeling very light as if all the badness had gone out of her. A year ago, she would have killed herself rather than let me know about this. This morning she had actually thought that she would visit her father again. She had been avoiding him for many months, feeling that she could not bear to be with him in the same room. Now she wanted to see him and see how he really looked. She said that she had forgotten to tell me a dream recently that had made her feel very sad. First of all, she recalled that while I was away on vacation, she had quite a number of nightmares in which she was running away from something horrible and was looking everywhere for me. This had happened again the other night. She added naïvely, "I often dream about anything that I want very much and that I can't get." I pointed out that this was the first time that she had admitted dreaming about me, looking for me in her dreams, and telling me that it was because she wanted me so much that she dreamed about me. She blushed at this, but kept silent. When she left, she was smiling broadly and in a very loving sort of way. I talked with her about the many secrets she had revealed to me and that we now shared together without feeling bad about them. She had managed to let these things out from inside herself without needing to cut herself symbolically with a razor.

The next day, after she had seen another patient leave the office, she admitted to feeling very jealous, even though she realized that I did see other people. She had been rethinking her thoughts about her parents. She was now aware that both her father and mother had their problems, and she even found herself feeling sorry for them. It was a funny sort of feeling, as if she was coming out from inside herself and looking at the people for the first time. I said to her, half-humorously, that if she continued like this, she would soon start feeling sorry even for me. She took this very seriously and said that she could never imagine feeling sorry for me. I was such an all-right sort of person so that nothing ever seemed to worry me or make me feel ashamed, even when she was being most horrible to me, hating me, and wanting to kill me. I remarked that we had indeed become close friends and understood each other much better and were not thinking wrong things about each other and certainly not imagining things about each other. She looked at me and smiled spontaneously, making a sudden contrast in my earlier image of her as a frozen, rigid, tense, and very disturbed girl, wracked with paranoid anxieties. In her present relaxed state, she was looking pretty and was certainly dressing herself much more attractively. When the session was over and it was time for her to leave, she showed increasing reluctance to go and attempted to maneuver in several ways to stay. She said that she could ask me now what I felt about her because she knew that it would be true and she knew that it would not hurt her. The confidence and trust in me were constantly growing factors.

Perhaps the most striking feature, however, was the emergence of her feminine psyche. In the course of her treatment she had ranged between severe paranoid reactions, intense shamefulness, feelings of inferiority, murderous rages, depressions, new remorsefulness, and a consciousness of herself as a person.

Discussion

It is perhaps the last case that most clearly highlights the elements of guilt, shame, and inferiority, together with paranoid and depressive reactions, that torment the phase of adolescence. What one observes in the psychoanalysis of such cases is the emergence of a more integrated moral system under the aegis of a more stable superego and ego. In the disturbed cases of the shame syndromes, one is initially confronted with the often gross immaturity of the psychic systems and their proneness to regressive processes, conducive, at times, to experiences not only of object loss but also of a sense of "the loss of the self."

We have seen fairly typical examples of the interplay between the basic ingredients of the shame syndromes, realizing that they are merely exaggerations of what one sees in the development of normal adolescents. From my experience, it would seem that the young woman in the making is especially susceptible to the development of these states, chiefly because of their basis in primary shame. Once the shame feelings have been worked through both in the context of the analytic situation and the analytic process, guilt and depression make their appearance, so that a sudden transformation often seems to take place in the clinical picture. This is especially apparent in two of the illustrations offered. The regulation of self-esteem is to be patiently managed so that elements of pride and superiority can emerge without danger of being narcissistically affronted. Gradually the shame that arises as a secondary reaction to forbidden instinctual strivings is integrated into the complex moral system. At all times during the analysis one sees the shame reactions oscillating between guilt and inferiority feelings. From the case histories presented, it is clear that Freud's view (1933) tracing the origin of inferiority feelings to erotic roots, to parental rejection, to conflicts between superego and ego may need to be expanded in the light of our present-day knowledge. The connection between the development of the moral system, identity, and narcissistic conflicts must be considered as the very special contribution made by Jacobson to our understanding of this complex field of personality development.

Epilogue

Having taken off from Freud's original ideas, I believe it is perhaps fitting to return finally to this cornucopian source. In his first draft on paranoia (1950 [1895], pp. 206–210), he touches on a set of mechanisms *in normal use* that become clinically abused under certain intolerable conditions in certain susceptible individuals, and he labeled these mechanisms "projections." Let us examine what he does with this concept. He takes, for example, the case of a man, a relative stranger, who puts his penis in a woman's hand and then leaves forever. The woman is about thirty and unmarried. As an apparent consequence, she develops a state of intermittent paranoia, lasting a few weeks at a time following which her insight gradually returns and she becomes neurotic but in touch with reality. Freud refers to this second state as "sexual," but today we would be inclined to diagnose it as depressive. The intermittence therefore takes this form:

1. A paranoid phase is initiated by excitement, presumably generated by the sexual memory of the seduction scene. As a result, her sexual wishes are intensified and lead, in this unmarried woman, to feelings of shame. What happens next is that her insight diminishes, and the mechanism of projection comes into play so that her shame is now known to the neighbors who are in a position to reproach her. This, however, she can reject as undeserved (especially as she has repressed the original sexual memory), and so she is able to keep her ego shame-free.

2. The equilibrium is unstable, and the repression is undone, bringing the sexual memory back into the forefront where it is now subjected to the mechanism of introjection, so that the shame is returned to the ego, to which it properly belongs, and she experiences the reproach from the inside and develops depression.

This paranoid-depressive cycle has, as Freud indicated, its normal counterpart (but whether there is an infantile counterpart still remains a moot question). It is important to note that the subject matter, as Freud puts it, remains unaffected: what is altered is the location of the matter. In treating his patient, Freud made use of "concentration hypnosis" (a transitional combination of hypnosis and free association, soon to be abandoned) and attempted to relocate the matter of shame from the outside to the inside. What he wanted was for the patient to make use of introjective rather than projective mechanisms, and to develop depression rather than paranoia, on the grounds, perhaps, that the former was less difficult to treat. As a consequence of this therapeutic maneuver, the patient dropped out of treatment, complaining that it upset her too much, drawing from Freud the expostulation of "defense!"

Today, with our more leisurely analytic procedure, we might be inclined to think that the patient knew her own level of tolerance better than the therapist. In the three vignettes offered in this presentation, the "relocation" takes place in every patient, but not before a year or two of analysis. Positive elements in the transference appeared to encourage each of the women to forego the less painful paranoid mode for the more painful depressive mode. It also became clear that the relocation was needed if the patients were to resume normal identity formation. It should be emphasized that not every case of depression develops this interesting oscillation or intermittence. It is a feature of the type I shame-depressions I described (Anthony, 1975), where serious narcissistic disorders exist not only in the patient but in the patient's mother and where the regulation of self-esteem becomes extremely faulty. The earliest history of such patients records them as mistrustful and suspicious, with a ready tendency either to blame others or to retreat into a megalomanic disregard of shame. Again, we should note that the classical case offered by Freud for discussion is that of a woman.

Once the projected shames are relocated in the ego, and type I shame-depression results, the next therapeutic maneuver lies in their transformation into a guilt-depression to be followed by the classical analysis of a guilt-neurosis.

The emergence of the feminine psyche in the male patient may also induce the same type of shame syndromes. Men in their forties (the period of life referred to by Victor Hugo as "the old age of youth") with extensive passive, narcissistic, masochistic, and feminine identifications overlying strong latent homosexual conflicts may show very similar characteristics in their development and in their analysis. They display a strong and persistent need to prove their masculinity by sexual, social, or intellectual performance: when they succeed in approaching their ideal standards, they are filled with pride; and when they fail, they wallow in shame. The reactions are often complicated by their life situations. If, for example, they are married, extramarital sexual prowess may lead them to feel ashamed of themselves, whereas impotence, often a cause of shame, may help to relieve the small amounts of guilt that occasionally disturb them. Strong superego guilt is rarely present; and since shame is less of a deterrent than guilt within the moral system, acting out becomes excessive, repetitious, and compulsive to the point of being ego-syntonic. Unlike the guilt system in operation, the shame system may at times stimulate pleasure, especially "in the telling." A patient may dwell on his sexual potency or polymorphism with almost loving detail. To some extent, this represents, in the analysis, a defiance of the external authority figure. The characterological aspects may be as unchangeable as those of the thirty-year-old woman, and the paucity of guilt has the same effect of prolonging the analysis until "relocation" occurs and the guilt cycle is brought into being. Until then, the personality has an "as if" quality about it that occasionally makes the analyst despair of the outcome. Nevertheless, one should add that the shame syndromes in both women and men are analyzable but take considerable time and patience.

The four basic questions Freud raised remain as open, as debatable, and as researchable as in his early, middle, and late days: are women fully analyzable? Is becoming a woman more difficult and complicated than becoming a man and subject to more upset? Are women more liable to become ashamed and men to become guilty? And are women more likely to develop shame syndromes than men?

References

Abraham, K. (1924), A short study of the development of the libido, viewed in the light of mental disorders. In: *Selected Papers on Psycho-Analysis*. London: Hogarth Press, 1949, pp. 418–501.

Anthony, E. J. (1975), Two contrasting types of adolescent depression and their treatment. In: *Depression and Human Existence,* ed. E. J. Anthony & T. Benedek. Boston: Little Brown, pp. 445–460.

Aristotle (350 B.C.), *Nichomachean Ethics*. London: Everyman's Library, 1866.

Benedek, T. F. (1956), Toward the biology of the depressive constellation. *J. Amer. Psychoanal. Assn.,* 4:389–427.

Benedict, R. (1946), *Patterns of Culture.* New York: Penguin Books.

Bibring, E. (1953), The mechanism of depression. In: *Affective Disorders,* ed. P. Greenacre. New York: International Universities Press, pp. 13–48.

Erikson, E. H. (1950), *Childhood and Society.* New York: Norton.

Freud, S. (1896), Further remarks on the neuro-psychoses of defence. *Standard Edition,* 3:159–185. London: Hogarth Press, 1962.

_____ (1900), The interpretation of dreams. *Standard Edition,* 4 & 5. London: Hogarth Press, 1957.

_____ (1916), Some character-types met with in psycho-analytic work. *Standard Edition,* 14:309–323. London: Hogarth Press, 1957.

_____ (1933), New introductory lectures on psycho-analysis. *Standard Edition,* 22:3–182. London: Hogarth Press, 1964.

_____ (1937), Analysis terminable and interminable. *Standard Edition,* 23:209–269. London: Hogarth Press, 1964.

_____ (1950 [1892–99]), Extracts from the Fliess papers. *Standard Edition,* 1:175–397. London: Hogarth Press, 1966.

Glover, E. (1932), A psycho-analytic approach to the classification of mental disorders. In: *On the Early Development of Mind.* New York: International Universities Press, 1956, pp. 161–186.

Hartmann, H. & Loewenstein, R. M. (1962), Notes on the superego. *The Psychoanalytic Study of the Child,* 17:42–81.

Jacobson, E. (1964), *The Self and the Object World.* New York: International Universities Press.

_____ (1971), *Depression.* New York: International Universities Press.

Kawabata, Y. (1958), *Thousand Cranes.* New York: Alfred A. Knopf.

Klein, M. (1948), *Contributions to Psycho-Analysis (1921–45).* London: Hogarth Press.

Levin, S. (1971), The psychoanalysis of shame. *Int. J. Psycho-Anal.,* 52:355–362.

Lichtenstein, H. (1961), Identity and sexuality: a study of their interrelationships in man. *J. Amer. Psychoanal. Assn.,* 9:179–260.

Mahler, M. S. (1966), Notes on the development of basic moods: the depressive affect in psychoanalysis. In: *Psychoanalysis—A General Psychology,* ed. R. M. Loewenstein, L. M. Newman, M. Schur, & A. J. Solnit. New York: International Universities Press, pp. 152–168.

Meyerson, E. (1930), *Identity and Reality.* New York: Macmillan.

Piaget, J. (1932), *The Moral Judgment of the Child.* London: Kegan Paul.

Piers, G. & Singer, M. (1953), *Shame and Guilt.* Springfield, Ill.: Charles C. Thomas.

Sartre, J. P. (1950), *Being and Nothingness,* tr. H. E. Barnes. New York: Washington Square Press.

Schur, M. (1960), Phylogenesis and ontogenesis of affect—and structure—formation and the phenomenon of repetition compulsion. *Int. J. Psycho-Anal.,* 41:275–287.

Sullivan, H. S. (1953), *The Interpersonal Theory of Psychiatry.* New York: Norton.

Wallace, L. (1963), The mechanism of shame. *Arch. Gen. Psychiat.,* 8:80–85.

Wixen, B. (1971), Grudges. *Psychoanal. Rev.,* 58:333–344.

10

SHAME AND GUILT
IN HUMAN NATURE

HELEN BLOCK LEWIS, PH.D.

Psychoanalysts often remark wistfully on the awkwardness of the term "object relations" in referring to people as objects. Object relations theory not only carries an awkward name, but its ambiguities reflect the difficulties which inevitably arose when Freud's clinical discoveries about the role of forbidden sexual wishes in psychopathology were fitted into an admittedly inadequate theoretical framework. Object relations theory represents an important intermediate step between the individualistic instinct theory that Freud chose as his theoretical foundation and a fully cultural or social theory of human nature.

My own work, which has focused on the affective states of shame and guilt in neurosis (1971) and on sex differences in superego functioning (1976), has pushed me into a theoretical framework in which the cultural or social nature of human nature is regarded as our species' unique biological "given." In this framework, the social nature of the human infant is a fundamental axiom. On this hypothesis, socialization proceeds not only from affectionate caretaking by the infant's "objects," but on the basis of biological "givens" which equip the infant to participate in these earliest affectionate exchanges. The infant is seen as not only helpless and dependent *physically*, but as powerful *socially*. He or she participates in affectionate exchanges and can "amplify the dimension of tenderness in the [caretaking] adult" (Rheingold, 1969, p. 781).

This last point, in particular, involves an extension of object relations theory. Object relations theory has tended to conceptualize the infant's behavior as "symbiotic," a term that implies the infant's dependency. The theory also has tended to conceptualize the infant only as requiring affection rather than as also capable of participating in the exchange of it from earliest life. A view of the infant's earliest psychic life as social makes it possible to hypothesize that shame and guilt are early universal affective states which function to maintain and repair lost affectional bonds. Shame and guilt are different modes of effecting reparation, not just differing "drive" controls. "Attachment," "stranger anxiety," and "separation anxiety" are the empirically observed states in infancy that are early forerunners of more cognitively developed states of shame and guilt.

The idea that shame and guilt are both very early affective states resembles Melanie Klein's (1957) concepts of the early "paranoid" and "depressive" positions. (Klein arrived at her concepts while pursuing Freud's hypothesis of a death instinct, while my concept rests on an "opposite" basis in humanity's innate sociability.) What is even more important is the fact that studies of infancy over the last three decades have discovered the infant to be an organized, competent being, biologically equipped to behave in social fashion.

In this essay I shall describe the odyssey by which my own clinical work pushed me to concentrate on the affective states of shame and guilt and sketch the theoretical difficulties I encountered when I attempted to fit my observations into Freud's theoretical framework. These difficulties, like object relations theory, have had their origin in the schism between Freud's clinical work and his metapsychology. I shall first outline briefly some of the scientific developments which suggest the idea that human beings are cultural or social animals by biological origin. All of these scientific developments were unavailable to Freud, although, ironically, some of them were stimulated by his work.

Cultural Nature of Human Beings

Everywhere anthropologists have looked, they have found human beings organized into a society ruled by cultural laws governing the interaction of its members. In this respect, human beings are unique on earth. These cultural laws, moreover, clearly invade every moment of an individual's experience from birth to burial ceremonies. Some anthropologists, notably La Barre (1954), have suggested that this human cultural order is *our* species' form of adaptive relationship to nature. We human beings have evolved from fur-bearing to culture-bearing animals as our means of survival. Although the actual content of these laws varies from culture to culture, all are systems of moral law which each of us imbibes along with our mother's milk. Each culture, moreover, has its own myths: primary process transformations by means of which each culture tries to justify or rationalize the injustices in its own prescriptions. At a time when anthropology had only just begun, Freud had had the insight that human beings are somehow acculturated "by nature." But because there was little field material available, he had to express his insight in what Lévi-Strauss (1968) calls a culture myth: the legend of *Totem and Taboo*.

Another gap in knowledge in Freud's time was the absence of a usable theory of instincts, a gap that has to be understood in the context of Darwin's evolutionary theory which at that time had just begun to capture scientific thought. Darwin's theory implied that human beings share with other animals the fact of an adaptive relationship to their natural environment. Human beings, along with other primates, have instincts which facilitate their adaptation to their surroundings and thus contribute to the preservation of their species. Darwin's revolutionary notion, however, also had an androcentric cast. As Elaine Morgan has shown, in her delightfully witty book, *The Descent of Woman* (1972), the prototype of human evolution from primate ancestors was Tarzan, the Mighty Hunter come down out of the trees with his big brain, opposable thumb, and extra cunning. The idea that evolutionary sequences could be guided by the needs of the female succoring her young was never even considered.

In Freud's day, however, the concept that human beings, like other organisms, had instincts was a progressive idea. Freud's choice of the sexual instinct as his focus of study was an inspired one, since, as he put it (1914), the sexual instinct somehow has to do not only with the individual's development, but with the preservation of the species: no one individual ever dies for lack of sex, but the species would. As I read this statement, many years after it was formulated, I can interpret it to mean that the sexual instinct is a social instinct. This formulation of the sexual instinct as the only social one can, in fact, have several levels of meaning. It can have the meaning which Freud gave it, or it can be put in a more modern idiom: the sex drive is the only drive which involves (although it does not always require) union with another individual for its consummation. The sex drive is thus uniquely social among animal drives. Freud's decision to concentrate his researches on its vicissitudes in individual development thus led to the profoundly useful concept that psychosocial and psychosexual development are interrelated, must be studied in tandem, and are both governed by primary process.

This hypothesis guided many of the studies in the developing sciences of anthropology and sociology, which were almost nonexistent at the turn of the twentieth century. It was also of tremendous influence in pointing the direction of psychological research on the mother-infant interaction, including the Harlows' work. Although the heavy impact of these studies has been a revulsion against the concept of instinct, Freud's theoretical views retained their original reliance on instincts. This reliance had been necessary if Darwinian materialism was to prevail over religious-minded idealism.

Freud's insistence on retaining instincts in his theory also had a more personal source in the nature of Freud's own career. The cleavage between Freud's clinical observations and his metapsychology can be interpreted as a reflection of the cleavage between Freud's early ambitions as a neurologist and his relatively late and reluctant entrance into a career as a practicing psychiatrist (Mannoni, 1971). Freud's first academic career as a neurologist had foundered on his being a Jew. It was, however, a career in which he had a heavy personal investment. Freud had some twenty publications in physiology and neurology between 1877 and 1897. When Freud went to Paris to study with Charcot, he brought with him the silver-staining technique for treating slides he had invented. (Charcot was not particularly interested.) When Freud left the experimental laboratory to enter clinical practice, it was without clinical experience except for what he had learned from Charcot. How tempting it must have been to replace the trusted concepts of experimental neurology, in which he excelled, with a metapsychology which also dealt in impulses and forces. It is amusing to note that in present-day academia, psychologists are still struggling to reconcile the values of the clinic with those of the laboratory.

The scientific world in which Freud made his psychological discoveries had only speculative views about human nature among which to choose. Speculative views of human nature as either benign or aggressive, moreover, carried uncomfortable moral and ethical implications. In this context, choosing the most limited set of inherited "givens" can avoid complicated ethical questions. So Freud chose as his theoretical base the tendency of nervous stimulation to "discharge" or seek rest, and then struggled with the job of fitting his clinical observations about the working of peoples' conscience into this secularized but very narrow framework.

One consequence of such a narrow base for human behavior was an inadequate theory of affects. Freud suggested that affects are similar to "inherited hysterical attacks" in that they express or discharge unconscious ideas in bodily form (Rapaport, 1953). In this view, affects are more primitive than ideas, a concept which, in turn, implies the superiority of reason over emotion. It is in this context that the more affectful, less "rational" form of superego experience, shame, is taken for granted as being a less developed mode of superego functioning than guilt.

Freud's gift for clinical observation, for the accurate formulation of what was happening in his patients' affective life and the means they used to conceal their feelings from themselves, was thus constantly being overshadowed by the intellectual demands of a Zeitgeist in which science meant having a system of principles like those in physics and chemistry (Holt, 1972). Freud was clearly countering his own shame about only making clinical observations when he apologized for the fact that his case histories sounded like short stories. So he wrote a "Project," then bravely set it aside (only to have his followers resurrect it). But the problem of human development remained, for Freud, the problem of how a primary, isolated energy system develops: how a primary narcissist is molded into a socialized human being.

Let us look briefly at Freud's (1914) concept of primary narcissism to see how he understood its workings. Reading the paper on narcissism, one is struck by the extent to which he felt himself to be on speculative ground. Central to the paper is the insistence on a distinction between ego instincts and sexual instincts, and a corollary distinction between ego libido and object libido.

Basic to Freud's speculative formulation of an antithesis between object libido and ego libido is his notion that the "sexual instincts are at the outset attached to the satisfaction of the ego-instincts" (p. 87). Freud further said, "a human being has originally

two sexual objects—himself and the woman who nurses him—
...we are postulating a primary narcissism in everyone, which may in some cases manifest itself in a dominating fashion in his object-choice" (p. 88). We note that Freud is speaking about the male model of human nature. When he compares females and males in their object choice, he concludes, "Complete object-love of the attachment type...is characteristic of the male." Women at puberty are, in contrast, more subject to an "intensification of their original narcissism....Strictly speaking, it is only themselves that such women love" (pp. 88–89) and this narcissistic quality is what gives women (and children and criminals) their charm!

This is not just another example of Freud's androcentric thinking. It also shows how Freud's androcentric thinking was intertwined with an individualistic concept of human nature. If we follow Freud's language for the moment, we say that a woman's first object choice and her narcissistic choice are of the same sex as herself, while a man's first choice and his narcissistic choice are of different sexes. It might have been argued from this only that men therefore have a harder time of it than women in the development of gender identity. Instead, in unconsciously androcentric thinking, Freud argued that men are (the superior sex in being) more loving than women. In fact, men do have gender identity problems more often than women (Stoller, 1968). All empirical studies as well as general observation also agree that men are more aggressive, more hostile, and less affectionate in their behavior than women (H. B. Lewis, 1976; Maccoby and Jacklin, 1974).

What Freud was describing when he picked up the fact that men have an opposite-sex first caretaker and women a same-sex first caretaker goes beyond gender identity to the conflict between men's social behavior, which is modeled after mother's nurturance, and their individualistic, competitive behavior, which, especially in an individualistic and competitive patriarchal society, is modeled after father's powers. This conflict is different for men and women, and it often becomes entangled with earlier problems of gender identity. The difficulty Freud got into with his concept of primary narcissism is thus a symptom of a deeper trouble our theory is in because we combine a formally individualistic theory of human nature (which we share with mechanistic learning theories) and a unique insistence, especially in our clinical writings, on the social-sexual dynamics of the human self.

The notion of very early "internalization" of "objects" or "part-objects" is not new in psychoanalytic theory. Melanie Klein (1957) postulated that six-month-old infants internalized "good me" and "bad me" as well as "good world" and "bad world." Benedek (1938) described the attitude of confident expectancy which arises in the infant from the gratifications of his or her needs. Spitz and Wolf (1949) showed how a loved-hated introject can be symbolized in the fecal play of maternally deprived infants under a year of age. Erikson (1950) derives basic trust from the fulfillment of "oral needs." But these early internalizations are still considered to be "narcissistic." I am suggesting that what happens is not a narcissistic internalization of good and bad into the ego, but rather that internalization is itself a social process, derived from an interaction between the infant's "given" social ego and the mother's more fully developed social ego.

Psychologists who study infancy today are by no means agreed among themselves on the question of innate human sociability, but enough evidence has accumulated for some to adopt the theoretical position that the human infant at birth is a social being. As Stone et al. (1973) put it, "Love is now an acceptable variable in the design of studies on infant behavior" (p. 6). Ainsworth and Wittig (1969), for example, have evidence that infants develop best when mothers and infants have "mutual delight" in each other's company. Hogan (1975) has offered a theoretical paper in which he assembles some of the evidence for the sociocentric nature of human infants. He suggests that human beings tend to "seek social interaction within a structured framework" (p. 537). Young children's ready adoption of social roles occurs in the service of these social interactions and demonstrates the innate willingness of children to comply with benign authority.

It is interesting that this conception of human infants as social beings has developed along with a growing awareness among researchers that infants are much better organized cognitively than had previously been known. William James's "big, buzzing, blooming confusion" of infancy turns out to be more a myth than a reality. On the contrary, human infants seem to be equipped with a "template" for social behavior.

Whatever his theoretical position with regard to human nature,

Freud's hypothesis that neurosis was the result of faulty psycho-sexual development which began in infancy was a major spur to empirical studies of the mother-infant interaction. The Harlows' (1963) experiments on monkeys, and Bowlby's ethological studies (1969–73) are only two examples. The Harlows' work required them to postulate the existence of an "affectional system" between mother and infant. Bowlby was also pushed by his observations to formulate the existence of a biologically given goal-corrected system of attachment between mother and infant to which the infant brings "releasers" of maternal care. Bowlby distinguished five innate releasers of mother's response: sucking, crying, smiling, following, and clinging. Robson (1967) added a sixth innate releaser, eye-to-eye contact. This built-in releaser of human affection reminds us that the presence of shame is often signaled by a failure of eye contact.

It is amusing and instructive to read Bowlby's summary of previous theories of how infants become attached to their mothers. The most widespread theory, which Freud shared with others, is that infants learn to love their mothers because their mothers feed them. This is what Bowlby calls the "cupboard love" theory of human nature. (It is the kind of view one would expect to find in a world dominated by the marketplace, and it is also a mechanistic view.) Of course, if mothers did not feed their babies and no one else did, the babies would die. But it is clear to any observer of infants and their mothers that babies do not love a mechanical feeder and baby-tender any more than Harlows' monkeys could really develop adequately with a cloth mother-surrogate. Something else is involved in babies' attachment to their mothers besides a quid pro quo. Quid pro quo theories of how infants come to love their mothers imply that infants are naturally individualistic and aggressive — out to get something from mother's source of supplies.

In contrast, Bowlby's theory of infant-mother attachment as an affectional system implies mutual advantage and cooperative functioning between mother and infant. Mutually affectionate feelings of joy and security accompany attachment; sorrowful, angry, and frightened feelings accompany separation and detachment. To this list of (social) affects may be appended the pride which cements attachment, and the shameful and guilty feelings which attempt to retrieve it. These feelings are biologically given to an innately social human being.

Recent advances in electronics and in techniques of videotaping have made possible the extremely refined study of neonate behavior. These studies have made clear that neonates are social in their responses. I shall cite only a few examples. Condon and Sander (1974) have demonstrated that neonates' body movements are synchronized with the patterns of adult speech around them. Simner (1971) demonstrated that two- to three-day-old infants are specifically responsive to the cries of other newborns. This study, moreover, came upon an unexpected sex difference: girl infants are even more responsive than boys to the sounds of other newborns' crying. Meltzoff and Moore (1977) have demonstrated that twelve- to twenty-one-day-old infants actually imitate adult manual gestures and such facial gestures as mouth opening, lip protrusion, and tongue protrusion.

There also is some evidence for the innateness of infant social responses (H. B. Lewis, 1976). Blind infants smile at three months (Freedman, 1964). Twin studies indicate that infant smiling is under genetic control (Freedman, 1965). Eibl-Eibesfeldt (1974) has shown that blind and deaf "thalidomide" babies, born without arms to touch their mothers, unable to see and hear their mothers, still smile at three months like normal infants. Even these severely deprived infants are not "narcissistic" but social beings.

Shame and Guilt versus "Primary Narcissism" in Neurosis

I turn now to some implications for the theory of neurosis of a view that human nature is social versus a view of it as narcissistic. My own observations about the central importance of shame and guilt in neurosis derived from my clinical work with patients and from my simultaneous, long-standing study in the laboratory of the cognitive style called *field dependence* (Witkin et al., 1954, 1962, 1968).

Although psychoanalysis began with Freud's unraveling of the way forbidden sexual longings create neurotic symptoms, close and systematic attention to the actual experiences of the psychic censorship have come relatively late in psychoanalytic thinking. When I set out to study the phenomenology of shame and guilt, I found an extensive literature on guilt and comparatively little on shame. For example, in the *Index of Psychoanalytic Writings* (Grinstein, 1966), there are 64 citations under the heading of guilt and only 8 under the heading of shame. I found guilt mainly conceptualized as an "irrational and unconscious" operating force (English and English, 1958). The concept of unconscious guilt itself tended to turn attention away from guilt as a psychic state. The literature also did not distinguish carefully between guilt and shame and, except for Tomkins (1963), subsumed shame under the category of guilt. The relatively small literature on shame was also concerned with it as a defense mechanism or an operating force. While I drew heavily on the observations of Piers and Singer (1953) and Lynd (1958), my book was the first attempt to study the phenomenology of shame and guilt, the two affective states which operate as psychic censors and within which "primary process" neurotic symptoms form.

In my clinical work, my attention was drawn to those few (but disturbing) cases for whom analysis had at first seemed successful but then turned out to have failed. In each of these "returned" patients, the superego was even more vicious than it had been before analysis began. Analysis had only increased the patient's vocabulary of self-derogation. It gradually became apparent to me that these patients were suffering from unanalyzed shame in the transference. In some instances, the unanalyzed shame was concealed by intractable guilt.

This focus on shame and guilt was developing along with the notion that shame and guilt might be affective states expressed in different cognitive styles, depending on different conditions of superego stress. For example, the relation of the self to transgression for which it is responsible (guilt) is very different from the relation of the self to another person in unrequited love (shame). Some clinical observations of field-dependent and field-independent patients confirmed the usefulness of distinguishing carefully between these affective states.

In clinical accounts of psychoanalytic work with neurotic patients (1958, 1959), I used field dependence as a "tracer element" for following characteristic behavior and transference phenomena during treatment. In particular, the patients' perceptual style focused attention on the manner and extent of individuation of the self from significant "others." A field-dependent patient was described as readily merging herself with the surround. She was self-effacing; when she was self-conscious, it was in an awkward and shy way. A field-independent patient, also a woman, was described as having an organized self which took the initiative in vigilantly defending her place in the field. Differences between field-dependent and field-independent patients were also traced in the organization of the self in dreams.

From observations of an embarrassed four-year-old child patient who "watched" me vigilantly and continuously, I suggested (1963) that shame functions particularly as a protection against the loss of self boundaries which is implicit in absorbed sexual fantasy, i.e., in states of longing for attachment. Shame functions as a sharp, in fact, painful reminder that fantasy experience of the other is vicarious. Shame brings into focal awareness both the self and the other, with the imagery that the other rejects the self. It thus helps to maintain the sense of separate identity, by making the self the focus of experience. This notion about the function of shame is similar to Lynd's (1958) description of how shame can spur the sense of identity. It also parallels Erikson's (1956) observation that shame is the opposite of autonomy, but with the emendation that it is the opposite of the autonomy of the *self* rather than of the ego. This formulation, while recognizing the apparent "narcissism" in shame, regards this narcissism as a phenomenon in which the self is experienced "at the quick" (to use Lynd's term), while the person is maintaining affectional ties.

Making a link between characteristics of the self and characteristic functioning of the superego was one step in a line of reasoning which supposed that the superego functioned differently in field-dependent and field-independent patients. A field-dependent mode of superego functioning would be shame; while a field-independent mode would be guilt. Both modes of superego functioning represent an equally developed superego. Both modes could also be associated with an equally severe or malfunctioning superego.

An empirical study undertaken to check these predictions was able to confirm them (Witkin et al., 1968).[1] Patients selected on the basis of their perceptual style, and their figure drawings, were placed in individual psychotherapy in "pairs" of matched groups, a field-dependent and a field-independent patient each with the same therapist. Transcripts of their first two psychotherapy sessions were scored (by a "blind" judge) according to the method developed by

[1]This study was supported by Grants M-628 and MH-05518 from the National Institutes of Health, U.S. Public Health Service.

Gottschalk and Gleser (1969) for affect implied in verbal productions. As predicted, the transcripts of field-dependent patients contained significantly more references to anxiety of "shame, humiliation, embarrassment, ridicule, and exposure of private details," than references to the anxiety of "guilt, fault, responsibility, being punished, scolded, or abused." The converse was true for field-independent patients.

We also made predictions about the direction of hostility which would be found in the "pairs" of transcripts. These predictions were based both upon the nature of shame and guilt and upon what differences might be expected between field-dependent and field-independent patients. Specifically, we found that field-independent patients were more prone to direct their hostility both outward and inward, while field-dependent patients were more prone to self-directed hostility. There was some evidence that, regardless of patient type, shame tended to be found in association with self-directed hostility, and that this association was particularly strong in field-dependent patients.

The success in predicting a connection between perceptual style and proneness to shame and guilt encouraged the formulation of the notion of a superego style, which in turn practically required a phenomenological[2] analysis of the two states.

From the theoretical standpoint, my hypothesis that returned patients were suffering from unanalyzed shame created no problem for Freud's concept that psychiatric symptoms form out of primary process transformations of strangulated affect. One could simply assume that one kind of affect, namely, shame, had been ignored. Similarly, the notion of a cognitive style is congruent with Freud's concept of pervasive defensive or characterological styles originally rooted in emotional conflict.

But the question of why shame should be so important and, paradoxically, so ignored led me into difficulties with Freud's metapsychology. In particular, his failure to distinguish between the ego and the self was troublesome. Both Hartmann (1950) and Jacobson (1954) clarified this error of Freud's. But Hartmann's correction, in which he proposed the concept of an autonomous or conflict-free

---

[2]Although I differ with existential psychoanalysts, e.g., Binswanger (1958), in my adherence to a materialist view of nature, my work has grown out of some of the same roots.

ego, deepened the commitment of psychoanalysis to an individual-istic concept of human nature. The very term "autonomous ego" has echoes of the Protestant ethic, with guilt rather than shame the most highly developed affective state. This hierarchical order of guilt and shame led, in turn, to difficulties in making theoretical sense out of the sex differences which exist, not only in cognitive style, but in superego style and in proneness to psychiatric illness. Even in a Hartmann-corrected framework, women, more prone to depression, hysteria, shame, and a field-dependent cognitive style, must be re-garded as having a lower-order superego. This difficulty, once again, has its origin in the schism between Freud's concept of pri-mary process transformations of strangulated affect and his meta-psychological system.

At about the same time that I suggested that some analytic fail-ures were the result of the neglect of shame, other analysts were also describing difficult patients, but in rather different conceptual terms. Specifically, Kohut (1971) conceptualized a group of difficult pa-tients as "narcissistic personalities," Kernberg (1975) described diffi-cult "borderline" or "narcissistic" patients, and Guntrip (1971) dealt with the "schizoid" problem. It is generally agreed that these narcis-sistic or schizoid personalities often surprise the analyst who has mis-taken them for the more familiar transference neurotics. It seems possible to me that what is so surprising about these patients is the force of their unanalyzed shame reactions for which analysts are in-sufficiently prepared because of the neglect of shame in psycho-analytic theory.

When I apply the concept of shame-prone superego mode to de-scriptions of narcissistic or schizoid personalities, I find it easy to equate the narcissistic personality with the shame-prone superego mode (1979b). Kohut, for example, tells us that the center of dis-turbance in narcissistic personalities is the deficient quality of their "self-objects." Guntrip describes the more seriously ill schizoid per-sonalities as uncertain about the basic reality and viability of the central core of selfhood. Kernberg describes narcissistic personalities as having "deficiencies for experiencing guilt feelings and feelings of concern for objects....Over-idealized object-images and com-ponents of the ego-ideal...interfere with their superego integration" (p. 35). All three authors appear to be concentrating on the defec-tive self and are dealing with people whose experiences have more to do with shame than guilt.

Kohut contrasts the transference neuroses with the narcissistic personalities as follows: in the former, castration anxiety is the leading source of discomfort, with fear of loss of object coming second, while in the narcissistic personality disturbance, this order is reversed, i.e., fear of loss of object comes first. As I have shown (1971, esp. chap. 1), following Piers and Singer (1953) and Erikson (1950), shame arises out of the fear of "loss of love" and rests primarily on anaclitic identifications, while guilt is the internalization of the castration threat and rests primarily on defensive identifications. I can thus easily translate Kohut's contrast between the transference neuroses and the narcissistic personality disturbances to say that the superego of narcissistic patients is shame-prone, while the superego of transference neuroses patients is guilt-prone.[3] "Narcissistic personality" differs in concept from "shame-prone superego mode" in that the former is a more pervasive characterological deficiency. Shame-prone people can and also do function in the guilt mode. Even more important, shame is a normal affective state, while narcissism is a "regressed" condition.

The phenomena of shame and of narcissism are clearly related in being specifically and directly about the *self*. Shame is an "implosion" or momentary destruction of the self; narcissism is love of the self. But narcissism is recognized, not only by psychoanalysts but also by folk wisdom, as a defense against hatred of the self or shame. Grace Stuart (1956), in her little book on narcissism, pointed out that in ancient Greek belief seeing one's own image was a forerunner or omen of death. In a collection of ancient writings on dreams (N. Lewis, 1976), we find that dreaming of looking at oneself in a mirror was considered a bad omen even in the earliest known "dreambook," the Egyptian Dreambook, which may date from as early as 2000 B.C. That narcissism is inverted self-hatred is thus intuitively understood; shame and narcissism have the closest connection and can readily be transformed one into the other, as in the symbolism of the mirror.

The question arises, however, whether to subsume shame under the category of narcissistic phenomena, as Kernberg and

---

[3]Since narcissistic personalities cut across more familiar diagnostic categories, often confusing us by at first appearing to be transference neuroses (Kernberg, 1975), this is clearly also a gross classification.

Kohut do, or to subsume narcissism under the category of shame, as I do. If we regard shame as a normal, fundamental human affect whose function it is to replace lost affectional ties, then narcissistic defenses are primary process transformations formed under the influence of shame and having its restorative function.

Like feelings of guilt, feelings of pride in success or shame of failure are the results of a social interaction. They rest on anaclitic identifications; these are made not only out of being fed but out of an interaction in which affection is exchanged. Feelings of pride and shame are not therefore ipso facto narcissistic. This is another way of saying that even the most "narcissistic" states of shame and pride, states in which the self is focal in experience, involve a relationship between the self and an internalized other in whose eyes one is proud or ashamed. People who look in a mirror with pleasure at their own reflection are sometimes only summoning the "mutual delight" of an internalized affectionate interaction. When they look at themselves with shame, people are also mourning a lost "mutual delight," in which the internalized other is still beloved, only the self is hated.

By assuming that shame and guilt are both derived from social interactions operating from earliest life, it is also possible to see how men and women might differ in their prevailing superego mode without regarding one mode as more advanced than the other. Specifically, women, on the basis of their unchanging, same-sex anaclitic identifications should be more prone to shame than men, while men are more prone to guilt (H. B. Lewis, 1979a).

The question also arises whether neglected shame can have so powerful an impact on the person as to be responsible for analytic failures. This is not only a theoretical question but an empirical one. A careful study of the phenomenology of shame and guilt suggests that people are often in a state of shame or guilt (or both) without being able to identify these feelings accurately. The primary process transformations formed under the influence of unidentified shame and guilt are, indeed, often florid psychiatric symptoms. Among these are states in which the self is depersonalized or estranged. Its bounadries are seriously disordered. As I have shown in great detail (1971) unanalyzed shame in the patient-therapist relationship is a particularly potent source of negative therapeutic reactions.

Most important for the technique of therapy, however, was the unexpected realization that the phenomenological attitude toward shame and guilt is itself therapeutic. Patients who grow accustomed to analyzing the primary process transformations which are formed under the press of a superego upheaval find themselves ready to resume life without therapy rather earlier than in a course of treatment without this focus. Especially with patients who have not formed the prior expectation that analysis should be a lengthy process I have found the period of treatment much abbreviated. This is an empirical observation which awaits confirmation in systematic study. It does, however, remind us that the treatment of psychiatric illness and the study of its origins are two distinct processes which should not be confounded.

Shame and Depression/Hysteria; Guilt and Obsession/Paranoia

There is some laboratory evidence to support the hypothesis that shame is a central component in depression and the hysterias and that guilt is more apparent in obsessional neurosis and paranoia. Smith (1972) studied seventy persons, forty men and thirty women, with a mean age of thirty-one years, all patients at a pastoral counseling center. Shame and guilt proneness were assessed by an Early Memories Test and a Shame-Guilt Test. As predicted, patients who were relatively shame-prone were more likely to be suffering from depression. This result held for both sexes, and was stronger for women. In addition, as predicted, shame-prone patients showed significantly more self-directed hostility. Smith also predicted and confirmed that depressed patients high on shame were more likely to be hysterical, while depressed patients high on guilt were more likely to be obsessive.

This is not to imply that guilt plays no role in depression. Blatt (1974), for example, found it necessary to differentiate between "anaclitic" and "introjective" depression, a distinction which has many similarities to the distinction between shame and guilt. It may be that there are different varieties of depressive experience, in which shame and guilt occur in different proportions.

Beck's (1967) study of the masochistic content of depressed patients' dreams showed the depressed patients as the "recipients of rejection, disappointment, of humiliation, or other similar circumstances" (p. 217). Beck also called attention to the negative expectations which characterize depressed people's cognitions. Depressed people have a negative self image which adds up to an image of helplessness. This characteristic self image is the same as the experience of the self in shame: the self is unable, helpless, powerless.

Of particular interest is the paradox in depression (Abramson and Sackeim, 1977) that depressed people feel helpless to affect their destiny at the same time that their (helpless) self seems to them the appropriate target of hostility. If they are, indeed, as helpless as they feel, logic dictates that they should not feel responsible (guilty) for that of which they are incapable. The paradox in depression may be solved if one realizes that depressed people are experiencing two simultaneous characteristics of shame: hatred of the (deficient) self, which is focal in awareness, and the helplessness of the self to change the vicarious experience of the other's feeling.

There is also empirical evidence for a connection between field dependence and depression (Witkin, 1965; Levenson and Neuringer, 1974), and for a connection between field independence and obsessional neurosis and paranoia (Witkin, 1965). Of particular interest is the finding (Levenson and Neuringer, 1974) that male psychiatric patients (N = 84) who committed suicide were more field-dependent than a matched group (N = 84) of nonsuicidal patients. Scores on the Picture Completion, Object Assembly, and Block Design subtests of the WAIS (which correlate highly with the Rod and Frame and Embedded Figures Test) were used as the measure of field dependence. The patients who committed suicide had significantly lower scores on the WAIS subtests (although they actually had somewhat higher IQ scores and had achieved a slightly higher level of education). Levenson and Neuringer (1974) interpret this finding as indicating that a person who commits suicide has a cognitive style which lacks the "problem-solving processes to reorient his relationship to his environment" (p. 184). This formulation, which is similar to Beck's formulation of the cognitive deficit in depression, is also congruent with the idea that depression reflects the helplessness of shame.

The pattern of known sex differences in proneness to mental illness corresponds to the pattern of sex differences in cognitive style: women are more field-dependent than men, and they are more prone to depression and the hysterias; men are more field-independent than women, and they are more prone to obsessional neurosis, addictions, sexual deviations (compulsions), and to schizophrenia

(H. B. Lewis, 1976, 1978). I am suggesting that men's greater proneness to guilt and women's greater proneness to shame are underlying factors in this network of connections.

Empirical studies which directly approach the question of superego sex differences are pitifully few. Gleser et al. (1961) have evidence that women show more shame anxiety than men in a five-minute verbal sample. Yale undergraduate women show more shame than guilt in a Gottschalk and Gleser (1969) five-minute verbal sample; men show more guilt than shame (Wolf, 1975).

Siebert (1965) compared 100 men and 100 women undergraduates, using a variety of paper-and-pencil tests to assess their experience of the superego and the ego ideal. In response to a question about how they manage when confronting temptation, women were more concerned with the opinions of significant others, while men experienced guilt as a more internalized force. When using metaphors to describe their conscience experiences, men used animal and natural force symbols to express the power of conscience, while women used more human symbolic representations. These findings suggest that women's conscience is a more personalized experience, while men's is more impersonal. In another study of sex difference in proneness to shame and guilt, Binder (1970) found that women are more shame-prone, while men are more guilt-prone, as measured by an assessment of early memories. Smith (1972), however, failed to obtain a significant sex difference either in scores on the Shame-Guilt Test or on the Early Memories Test. The question of women's greater proneness to shame clearly needs empirical work.

Clinical Examples

The clinical examples are intended to illustrate the phenomenology of shame and guilt, and the sequences in which the two superego states lead to different paths of symptom formation. My underlying premise is that symptom formation occurs when *both* shame and guilt cannot be discharged or "righted." The state which is to the forefront of the person's experience is one determinant of whether symptoms of depression/hysteria or obsession/paranoia will appear. The examples also illustrate how unanalyzed shame in the patient-therapist relationship increases symptoms.

One unexpected finding of our therapy study (Witkin et al.,

1968) was that field-dependent patients showed an increase in total guilt anxiety in their second psychotherapy session as compared to their first. It is possible to speculate that this increase in guilt may have been the result of (unconscious) hostility evoked against the therapist in connection with acute but unidentified shame. For example, one (field-dependent) patient, a man, put it this way:

P: . . . I'll tell you something. The last two times I been depressed when I left here. Not that — when I was talking I wasn't depressed. It's after I leave. That bothers me.
T: Have you wondered about that?
P: Yes.
T: What thoughts do you have?
P: I . . . I made a joke of it to my sister, that's all. But uh . . . [inaud.] laugh out of it. I said, I don't know what's the matter; this, this guy, he's so nosy [laugh].
T: Do you think that's the aspect of the situation that makes you depressed?
P: I don't know.
T: Well, I know you don't know, but I wondered if that's what you feel.
P: *I feel like an idiot sometimes. When I think what I told you . . .* m — m [pause]. But it has some bearing I suppose.

"I feel like an idiot sometimes when I think what I told you" is an excellent phenomenological description of shameful imagery of himself vis-à-vis the therapist. In the next communication he also describes the burst of hostility — entirely self-directed — which accompanies feeling like an idiot. He starts thinking, he says, "What the hell am I telling him now." But the patient's hostility is throttled by his own awareness that it is "unwarranted" — in other words, by the patient's own sense of justice or guilt. The outcome is a "joke" in which he ridicules himself (and the therapist) for being a nosy bastard. What the patient experiences consciously is being *depressed* after he leaves the session. This is a clear example of the affinity between undischarged shame feeling and depressed mood, as well as of the exacerbation of symptoms resulting from unanalyzed shame in the patient-therapist relationship.

Another patient, a (field-dependent) woman, said the following in retrospect about her first session:

P: [Slight laugh.] Last time, uh, when I first came in, I was uhm and I started talking to you, I was upset, but I didn't know about what. And uhm, I sort of felt I was on the verge of tears, but I didn't know why, therefore, I really didn't mention it because I felt ridiculous. There was no reason.

The patient clearly is aware that she felt ridiculous (ashamed) because she was on the verge of tears. But she also is trying to say that something about talking to the therapist evoked a threat of tears. This unknown threat might well be the feeling of humiliation which is evoked by being a patient—in this instance, a female patient in treatment with a male therapist.

This excerpt also illustrates the affinity between shame and diffuse anxiety. Since the target of hostility in shame is the self, and the self is not an easily specifiable object, shame is experienced as tension or diffuse anxiety (or being on the verge of tears) but not knowing about what. In our study (Witkin et al., 1968), we predicted and confirmed a connection between field dependence and diffuse anxiety. The connection between shame and diffuse anxiety also needs to be pursued systematically.

The lack of specific content in shame also makes it an "irrational" experience for which one has difficulty finding a "rational" place in life. So, for example, the same field-dependent patient who was on the verge of tears and ashamed of herself because it was so ridiculous puts her dilemma this way (the patient had entered treatment because of a facial tic or "twitches"):

P: [Laughs.] I think I'd be interested in—well, I—think if I could get rid of the twitches, I'd get rid of the feelings that go with it, you know. But uh I guess if I had these things and I didn't care whether I had them or not, I guess it wouldn't matter either. I don't know [slight laugh]. But I don't see how I couldn't care...you know?

The patient is clearly aware that if she didn't *care* about having tics, i.e., if she were not ashamed of them, she would be better off. But she doesn't see how she could manage not to be ashamed of them. Rationally, she is quite aware of the facts that she really need not be ashamed of them but also that her feelings are not so easily persuaded. The patient is thus expressing a frequent dilemma in shame reactions: they occur in spite of one's better judgment, and compound themselves by making us ashamed that we are ashamed.

Perhaps because it feels like so primitive and "irrational" a state, shame is connected to a specific defense of hiding or running away. It is a state in which the mechanism of denial is particularly apt to occur. Denial makes shame difficult for the person experiencing it to identify, even though there is a strong affective reaction. The person often does not know what has hit him or her (see above).

The same patient who felt like an idiot when he thought of what he told his therapist illustrates the wordlessness of a shame reaction in an excerpt from the transcript which came shortly before the patient had his burst of ridicule at himself and at his "nosy bastard" therapist. Patient and therapist were talking about the patient's difficulties in school, and the patient began to remark about the therapist's personal characteristics in what was clearly (to an observer) some state of envy. The patient described his own schoolwork as having been so difficult because one had to compete against "brilliant people." There was a very long pause.

T: What were you thinking?
P: Mm—nothing...that I can remember anyway.
T: Mm?
P: Nothing that I can remember. If I was thinking.
T: You looked sort of depressed. Is that the way you were feeling?
P: I was....I have been depressed for quite a while. I don't know what I ...[hm?] I don't know what I think when I [inaud.] like that. Sometime I just stare at something [pause]. Wake up eventually. I don't know what the heck happens in between [long pause].

Another kind of defense against shame appears to operate before any affective state is evoked. This defense, which is best described as bypassing shame feeling, does not obliterate the recognition of shame events, but appears to prevent the development of shame feeling. This bypassing of shame is accomplished by a distancing maneuver. The self views itself from the standpoint of the other, but without much affect. The person wonders what he would think of himself if he were in the position of the other. The content of the ideation in question concerns shame events, but without shame affect. Shame affect is bypassed and replaced by watching the self from a variety of viewpoints, including that of the other. The following excerpt from the transcript of a (field-independent) male patient who was shortly going to talk about masturbation illustrates the phenomenon of bypassing shame. The excerpt begins after a long pause.

T: What are you thinking?

P: I don't know. I have this feeling that there's something—mm, mm—I felt myself almost wince a second ago, and I was trying to think of what it is that I'm, you know. I was also thinking of what I would do if I were the therapist...and I had a patient facing me, mm, and uh just what significance I would give to each of his movements and the like. This is something that uh I didn't think about to my knowledge for some time—this is what would I do if I were the other [inaud.].

The patient has clearly shifted the position of the self into the position of the observer in an effort to ward off shame feeling. The primary process nature of his ideation is subtly expressed in his wondering what significance the observer would give to each of his "movements." Our knowledge that the patient is caught in a state of shame about masturbation makes his use of the term "movements" interpretable as a "concrete" (primary process) outcome of the conflict in which he is caught. The shift in position of the self to the position of the observer who observes the self also illustrates the "doubleness" of shame experience and its affinity for the development of "scenes in an internal theatre" (Breuer and Freud, 1893–95) in which the self and the other play out their roles.

The next transcript, of the opening of the first therapy session of a (field-independent) woman patient, illustrates the "thing" quality of guilt. The bothersome thing is that the patient cannot now decide "whose fault it is" that she does not have an orgasm during intercourse.

P: I don't know where to begin, uh, even when I had gone to Dr. —a lot of things were really bothering me. Now I don't feel so turbulent. I just think that whatever was bothering me then is still bothering me really. At the time I went to him it was a problem of sexual adjustment with my husband. I was married in June and it's no problem but, it doesn't bother me as much. I think it's taken a different form. I, I used to really resent him very much and I didn't like lovemaking and I still don't, but I don't think it's my fault so much anymore. The thing that made me, I don't think I was frigid, uhm, I said "maybe it was me" and now I think maybe it's not. Maybe it's both of us. And maybe it's him just as much and maybe it's not all me.

This excerpt also illustrates the relative lack of affect—the isolation of affect—which occurs in connection with an insoluble dilemma of "is it my fault or his fault?" Since the "problem" is apparently an objective one and involves the just apportionment of blame, acute affect which catches the self "at the quick" is absent in this guilty train of thought. As the patient puts it, she is not so "turbulent" now, although she is aware that at times she can be. The unconscious gratification of being in a morally elevated state sometimes keeps the state of guilt active beyond the time of expiation. "He who despises himself," wrote Nietzsche (1937), "thereby esteems himself as the despiser. . . . When we train our conscience, it kisses as it bites." The self, then, may be caught in its own unconscious pride in being guilty, thus prolonging guilt rather than discharging it.

In the next sequence the field-independent, male patient who had wondered what he would think of himself if he were the therapist opened the same session by telling of his "good feeling" in obeying his conscience. Very shortly afterward, he was in an inexorable state of guilt for defying his conscience. The concrete "problem" or guilty act was *not* getting out of bed when he should.

P: I won a small-sized battle yesterday. . . . I did as much work as I could and I went right and took the exam and mm and uh felt very good about it. . . . Funny, today I was here at about 2:30 just to make sure I wouldn't be late, and I was fairly anxious to get here today.

Although the patient was not directly saying so, he was so proud of his obeying his own conscience that he wanted to share with the therapist his good feeling over winning the "small-sized battle." The patient's use of the term "funny" (which would rate a shame anxiety score) represents his own registration of ("childish") pride in his (and the therapist's) achievement.

But on the morning of this session, the patient who had awakened early enough to go job-hunting, got out of bed and then said to himself: "What the hell. . . and then I got right back in bed and couldn't sleep but I refused to get out of bed again." In the wake of this transgression the patient began a characteristic tirade of guilty ideation not only about staying in bed, but about widely generalized faults:

P: And uh I think I've grown accustomed to this life of uh, getting up when I please, not working, having no responsibility other than school and perhaps the feeling of responsibility toward home, but I keep destroying all chances of getting a job.

The flow of his guilt could not be stopped by the therapist's intervention:

T: Mm, there must be a reason.

P: Yeah, no doubt. Uh, I don't know, it — I was thinking it's possible that I don't want additional responsibility — you know that, with having a job, but somehow that just seems like rationalization to me.

When one is in a state of guilt, benign explanations of the reasons for one's conduct seem like rationalizations!

A particularly instructive example of a sequence from shame into guilt and thence into paranoid ideation comes from the transcript of a field-independent male patient whose therapist had been interpreting (with some derision) the grandiosity of the patient's ego ideal. It is easy for an observer to be amused by another person's ego ideal and to evoke shame in the person whose ego ideal is under inspection, especially since it is difficult to spell out a rationale for one's own strivings.

The patient had entered treatment for chest pains which had no organic base. He connected his symptoms to an "ego ideal or something that I'm setting up." The patient had a characteristic way of describing his chest pains; he kept saying that he "receives" the pain. The patient had been arguing with the therapist that his ambitions were necessary and inevitable in his life circumstances. In the midst of their dispute about the wisdom of ambition, the therapist called the patient's attention to his peculiar mode of speech about the pains. The patient laughed (most likely with embarrassment, although he did not say so) and several times assured the therapist that he, the patient, *knew* no one was giving him his pains. At the end of this hour, the patient was suddenly moved to ask the therapist about the microphone in the room — in spite of the fact that the microphone had been discussed at the opening session of the therapy and this was now the third session.

The patient opened his next hour by telling the therapist, "I was sort of curious last week about that microphone." It developed, on questioning, that the patient had had a fantasy which he himself labeled as "weird," "illogical," and "improbable" — that the therapist had sent a copy of the transcript of the therapy session to the school where the patient studied. His exact words are important because they pick up the theme of sending and "receiving," which had been a particular focus of the patient's embarrassment and had evoked the patient's need to reassure the therapist that he, the patient, was not crazy, since he *knew* he was not "receiving" chest pains from anyone.

Here is the text of the primary process transformation in which the patient has a "weird" fantasy of the therapist's betrayal made necessary out of "duty."

P: Well, yeah, I just thought that maybe you were drawing severe conclusions and that someone should *know* about it at school. And some administrative officer should *know* about me. . .mm. And I was just wondering, 'cause no one's ever *known* that I sort of. . .ah. . .had funny ideas or what [laughs; inaud.]. Just a normal human being. . .and now. . .the picture's changed. I just thought that maybe uh I just thought that maybe you were sending them out of duty or something. . .some way [laughs; inaud.], some way 'cause what's gonna happen if he does do it though.

The patient's shame and anger had been evoked by the therapist's interpretation, but it is hostility which has no "rationale" since the therapist is benign. The patient is in a state of guilt vis-à-vis the therapist for the patient's own shame-rage. The outcome is a paranoid fantasy which is very compelling, in spite of the patient's better judgment. And the content of the fantasy concretizes *receiving* and *sending* information about the severe conclusions which the therapist must be drawing about the patient's peculiarities, and which the therapist is compelled to make *known* on pain of the therapist's being in a state of guilt toward the authorities who should be notified. In this fantasy, both patient and therapist are in an insoluble dilemma of guilt.

Using a computer model to simulate the linguistic behavior of a paranoid patient in a diagnostic interview, Colby (1977) appraised four theories of paranoia. He suggests that a shame-humiliation model is preferable to a homosexual, hostility, or homeostatic model. Although there is an apparent contradiction to my view that guilt is the more frequent state out of which paranoia forms, the discrepancy between Colby and myself is more apparent than real. Colby's suggestion is that the paranoid forestalls the threat of humiliation (detected as a shame signal) by a strategy of "blaming others for wrongdoing" to the self (p. 56). Although Colby does not use the word "guilt," blaming others for wrongdoing is perceiving them as guilty.

As I have shown (1971), a reanalysis of Freud's cases from the point of view of undischarged shame and guilt clearly supports the connection between shame and depression/hysteria and between guilt and obsessional neurosis. For example, the small fragment of practically verbatum account of conversation with Lucy R. about being in love with her employer reads (Breuer and Freud, 1893–95, p. 117):

'...were you ashamed of loving a man?' [Freud asked.] 'Oh no [came the answer from Lucy], I'm not unreasonably prudish. We're not responsible for our feelings, anyhow. It was so distressing to me only because he is my employer and I am in his service and live in his house. I don't feel the same complete independence towards him that I could towards anyone else. And then I am only a poor girl and he is such a rich man. . . . People would laugh at me if they had any idea of it.'

Lucy says that she is not ashamed and not guilty — as indeed in reason she need not be. She characteristically denies shame as we all automatically do. But she goes on to recite in detail the state of shame which results from an inequality of status. The Gottschalk-Gleser scoring of Lucy's description of her feelings would rate shame scores, especially the last sentence.

Dora, similarly, was in a state which Freud (1905) described as "mortification" at her father's betrayal of her. But neither Freud nor Dora had room in their cognitive systems for the humiliated fury which accompanies mortification at personal betrayal. Both agreed that her rage was "exaggerated" since neither her father nor Herr K. had "made a formal agreement in which she was treated as an object for barter" (Freud, 1905, p. 34). In this cognitive system, which Dora and Freud shared, the shame of personal betrayal does not have the same status as guilt for breaking a contract. Indeed, shame is "subjective," i.e., only about the self, whereas guilt is "objective," i.e., about events or things in the world.

In the case of the Rat-Man, Freud (1909, p. 159) tells us that the patient spontaneously began his free associations at his first session by speaking about "a friend...of whom he had an extraordinarily high opinion. He used...to go to him [his friend] when he was tormented by some criminal impulse, and ask him whether he despised him as a criminal. His friend used to give him moral support by assuring him that he [the patient] was a man of irreproachable conduct, and had probably been in the habit, from his youth onwards, of taking a dark view of his own life."

The Rat-Man's obsessions, which developed out of his chronic sense of guilt, were about terrible events for which he would be responsible (guilty). I have been able to show that each obsessional outbreak was actually stirred by some bypassed shame in his experience (1971).

Implications for Therapy

A social theory of human nature brings with it the corollary assumption that the superego functions not only for the sake of the individual's survival, but for the survival of his or her profoundest attachments. It is this characteristic which makes it possible for some people to sacrifice their lives in acts of principled heroism or martyrdom, rather than betray their superego.

A social concept of human nature also leaves room for a superego which adheres not only to an abstract sense of distributive justice but to a set of standards of personal dignity or worth which can symbolize a person's existence (Lynd, 1958), and the violation of which evokes shame. In contrast, an individualistic conception of human nature supposes that the superego evolves as a more or less painful internalization of the "social contract." The resulting value system has at its apex of development a system of abstract distributive justice (Kohlberg, 1968; Piaget, 1932), in which guilt is a higher-order affect than shame.

Converting shame and guilt from individual drive controls into affectionate bond controls conceptualizes the internalization process as itself a social one. Anaclitic and defensive identifications are both social processes which form the superego. A difference between the sexes in characteristic superego mode can be described without a hierarchical order.

Abandoning the notions of "primary narcissism" and "narcissistic personality" in favor of a concept of shame as a universal "given" for the maintenance of affectionate bonds also has a number of advantages for therapeutic technique. The first is a less pejorative atmosphere for the analysis of states of pride, triumphant pleasure, and shame. Adopting the viewpoint that shame is a normal state which accompanies the breaking of affectional bonds allows shame to take its place along with guilt as a universal, normal human state of being. Analyzing shame reactions in an atmosphere in which their natural function is taken for granted makes analytic work considerably easier. Pride and shame are, of course, states in which one is aware of an incongruity between the self's "subjective" reaction and "objective" circumstances. Ask yourself to explain to yourself or to someone else just what your *ego ideals* are, and unless you are a hopeless prig, you will see how quickly you become ashamed of your ego ideals, i.e., your "grandiosity." Because shame and pride involve strong affect, it can seem, for the moment, as if the ego was defective. Thus, Kohut (1971), in a footnote (p. 181), rather cavalierly dismisses the well-documented idea that shame results from a failure to meet ego ideals. He regards shame as a result of the flooding of the ego with "unneutralized exhibitionism." But what is flooded in shame is *not* the ego, but the self. If the ego were not simultaneously registering an awareness of an incongruity, there would be no shame. In recent years, I have been much impressed by the rational components in shame reactions which tell one that shame is *only* about the self, therefore about objectively "trivial" events.

Among the chief beneficiaries of this accepting atmosphere toward the reparative function of shame are likely to be depressed and hysterical women patients. Easser and Lesser (1965), in a careful study of hysterical personalities in psychoanalytic treatment, were unable to find "provocative, seductive, exhibitionistic" behavior commonly ascribed to these patients. They suggested that "the intellectualized, scientific, methodologically bound investigator has been more at ease in the study of patients characterized by rigid, intellectual, and defensive maneuvers, namely, obsessives" (p. 391). By the same token, shame-prone personalities may be harder to understand than guilt-prone personalities, especially because psychiatrists and psychoanalysts tend more often to be male and guilt-prone than female and shame-prone.

As Bowlby (1973) has suggested, failure to conceptualize separation anxiety as a "given" concomitant of the attachment system has made it seem that it is "childish," even babyish, to yearn for the presence of a loved figure or to be distressed during her [or his] absence" (p. 80). So perhaps the greatest therapeutic advantage to viewing shame and guilt as affectional bond controls is the emphasis placed on the patients' efforts to restore their lost attachments. Respect for this underlying motivation makes it easier for patients to become aware that even the most "narcissistic" or shameful distortions of the self are attempts at preserving the beloved figures in their lives.

References

Abramson, L. & Sackeim, H. (1977), A paradox in depression. *Psychol. Bull.,* 84:838–851.

Ainsworth, M. & Wittig, M. (1969), Attachment and exploratory behavior of one-year-olds in a strange situation. In: *Determinants of Infant Behavior,* ed. B. M. Foss. London: Methuen, vol. 4, pp. 111–136.

Beck, A. (1967), *Depression.* New York: Harper & Row.

Benedek, T. F. (1938), Adaptation to reality in early infancy. *Psychoanal. Quart.,* 7:200–215.

Binder, J. (1970), The relative proneness to shame or guilt as a dimension of character style. Unpublished dissertation, University of Michigan.

Binswanger, L. (1958), The case of Ellen West. In: *Existence,* ed. R. May, E. Angel, & H. Ellenberger. New York: Basic Books, pp. 237–364.

Blatt, S. (1974), Level of object representation in anaclitic and introjective depression. *The Psychoanalytic Study of the Child,* 29:107–157. New York: Basic Books.

Bowlby, J. (1969–73), *Attachment and Loss,* vols. 1 & 2. New York: Basic Books.

Breuer, J. & Freud, S. (1893–95), Studies on hysteria. *Standard Edition,* 2. London: Hogarth Press, 1955.

Colby, K. (1977), Appraisal of four psychological theories of paranoid phenomena. *J. Abnorm. Psychol.,* 86:54–59.

Condon, W. & Sander, L. (1974), Neonate movement is synchronized with adult speech. *Science,* 183:99–101.

Easser, B. R. & Lesser, S. R. (1965), Hysterical personality. *Psychoanal. Quart.,* 34:390–395.

Eibl-Eibesfeldt, I. (1974), *Love and Hate.* New York: Schocken Books.

English, H. B. & English, A. (1958), *A Comprehensive Dictionary of Psychological and Psychoanalytical Terms.* New York: David McKay.

Erikson, E. H. (1950), *Childhood and Society.* New York: Norton.

——— (1956), Identity and the life cycle. *J. Amer. Psychoanal. Assn.,* 4:56–121.

Freedman, D. A. (1964), Smiling in blind infants. *J. Child Psychiat. Psychol.,* 5: 171–184.

——— (1965), Hereditary control of early social behavior. In: *Determinants of Infant Behavior,* ed. B. M. Foss. New York: Wiley, vol. 3, pp. 149–159.

Freud, S. (1905), Fragment of an analysis of a case of hysteria. *Standard Edition,* 7:3–122. London: Hogarth Press, 1953.

——— (1909), Notes upon a case of ιobsessional neurosis. *Standard Edition,* 10: 3–149. London: Hogarth Press, 1955.

——— (1914), On narcissism. *Standard Edition,* 14:67–102. London: Hogarth Press, 1957.

Fromm, E. (1976), *Marx's Concept of Man.* New York: Frederick Ungar.

Gleser, G., Gottschalk, L., & Springer, K. (1961), An anxiety scale applicable to verbal samples. *Arch. Gen. Psychiat.,* 5:593–605.

Gottschalk, L. & Gleser, G. (1969), *The Measurement of Psychological States Through the Context.* Berkeley: University of California Press.

Grinstein, A. (1966), *The Index of Psychoanalytic Writings,* vol. 9. New York: International Universities Press.

Guntrip, H. (1971), *Psychoanalytic Theory, Therapy and the Self.* New York: Basic Books.

Harlow, H., Harlow, M., & Hansen, E. (1963), The maternal affectional system of rhesus monkeys. In: *Maternal Behavior in Mammals,* ed. H. Rheingold. New York: Wiley, pp. 254–281.

Hartmann, H. (1950), Comments on the psychoanalytic theory of the ego. *The Psychoanalytic Study of the Child,* 5:74–96.

Heider, F. (1958), *The Psychology of Interpersonal Relations.* New York: Wiley.

Hogan, R. (1975), Theoretical egocentrism and the problem of compliance. *Amer. Psychologist,* 27:533–540.

Holt, R. R. (1972), Freud's mechanistic and humanistic images of man. In: *Psychoanalysis and Contemporary Science,* ed. R. R. Holt & E. Peterfreund. New York: Macmillan, vol. 1, pp. 3–24.

Jacobson, E. (1954), The self and the object world. *The Psychoanalytic Study of the Child,* 9:75–127.

Kernberg, O. F. (1975), *Borderline Conditions and Pathological Narcissism.* New York: Jason Aronson.

Klein, M. (1957), *Envy and Gratitude.* London: Tavistock Publications.

Kohlberg, L. (1968), Moral development. In: *International Encyclopedia of the Social Sciences,* 10:483–490. New York: Macmillan.

Kohut, H. (1971), *The Analysis of the Self.* New York: International Universities Press.

La Barre, W. (1954), *The Human Animal.* Chicago: University of Chicago Press.

Lévi-Strauss, C. (1968), *The Savage Mind.* Chicago: University of Chicago Press.

Levenson, M. & Neuringer, C. (1974), Suicide and field dependency. *Omega,* 5: 181–185.

Lewis, H. B. (1958), Over-differentiation and under-individuation of the self. *Psychoanal. & Psychoanal. Rev.,* 45:2–24.

——— (1959), Organization of the self as reflected in manifest dreams. *Psychoanal. & Psychoanal. Rev.,* 46:21–35.

——— (1963), A case of watching as a defense against an oral incorporation fantasy. *Psychoanal. Rev.,* 50:68–80.

——— (1971), *Shame and Guilt in Neurosis.* New York: International Universities Press.

——— (1976), *Psychic War in Men and Women.* New York: New York University Press.

——— (1978), Sex differences in superego mode as related to sex differences in psychiatric illness. *Soc. Sci. Med.,* 12:199–205.

——— (1979a), Gender identity. *Bull. Menninger Clin.,* 43:145–160.

——— (1979b), "Narcissistic personality" or "shame-prone" superego mode? *Compr. Psychother.,* in press.

Lewis, N. (1976), *The Interpretation of Dreams and Portents.* Toronto: Samuels, Stevens, Hakkert.

Lynd, H. (1958), *On Shame and the Search for Identity.* New York: Harcourt, Brace.

Maccoby, E. & Jacklin, C. (1974), *The Psychology of Sex Differences.* Stanford: Stanford University Press.

Mannoni, O. (1971), *Freud.* New York: Pantheon Books.

Meltzoff, A. & Moore, M. K. (1977), Imitation of facial and nonfacial gestures. *Science,* 198:75–78.

Morgan, E. (1972), *The Descent of Women.* New York: Bantam Books.

Nietzsche, F. (1937), *The Philosophy of Nietzsche.* New York: Modern Library.

Piaget, J. (1932), *The Moral Judgment of the Child.* Glencoe, Ill.: Free Press.

Piers, G. & Singer, J. (1953), *Shame and Guilt.* Springfield, Ill.: Charles C Thomas.

Rapaport, D. (1953), The psychoanalytic theory of affects. In: *The Collected Papers of David Rapaport*, ed. M. M. Gil. New York: Basic Books, 1967, pp. 476–512.

Rheingold, H. (1969), The social and socializing infant. In: *Handbook of Socialization Theory and Research*, ed. D. Goslin. Chicago: Rand-McNally, pp. 779–790.

Robson, K. (1967), The role of eye-to-eye contact in maternal-infant attachment. *J. Child Psychiat. Psychol.*, 8:13–25.

Safer, J. (1975), The effects of sex and psychological differentiation on response to a stressful group situation. Unpublished doctoral dissertation, The New School of Social Research.

Siebert, L. (1965), Superego sex differences. Unpublished doctoral dissertation, University of Michigan.

Simner, A. (1971), Newborn response to the cry of another infant. *Develpm. Psychol.*, 5:136–150.

Smith, R. (1972), The relative proneness to shame or guilt as an indicator of defensive style. Unpublished doctoral dissertation, Northwestern University.

Spitz, R. A. & Wolf, K. (1949), Autoerotism. *The Psychoanalytic Study of the Child*, 3/4:85–120.

Stoller, R. (1968), *Sex and Gender*. New York: Jason Aronson.

Stone, L., Smith, H., & Murphy, L., eds. (1973), *The Competent Infant*. New York: Basic Books.

Stuart, G. (1956), *Narcissism*. London: Allen & Unwin.

Tomkins, S. (1963), *Affect, Imagery and Consciousness*, vol. 2. New York: Springer.

Witkin, H. (1965), Psychological differentiation and forms of pathology. *J. Abnorm. Psychol.*, 70:317–336.

—————— Dyk, R., Faterson, H., Goodenough, D., & Karp, S. (1962), *Psychological Differentiation*. New York: Wiley.

—————— Lewis, H., Hertzman, M., Machover, K., Meissner, P., & Wepner, S. (1954), *Personality Through Perception*. New York: Harper & Row.

—————— —————— & Weil, E. (1968), Affective reactions and patient-therapist interactions among more and less differentiated patients early in therapy. *J. Nerv. Ment. Dis.*, 146:193–208.

Wolf, L. (1975), Personal communication.

11

VARIETIES OF SPLITTING

NORBERT FREEDMAN, PH.D.

The issues inherent in splitting have received renewed attention in present-day psychoanalytic thinking, in part as the result of a shift in emphasis from oedipal triadic conflicts to narcissism and the early mother-infant dyad. The basic dilemma which gives rise to splitting was neatly summarized by Mahler (1968), who states, "The mother of our nurturance is also the mother of our frustration." The dilemma is one of maintaining incompatible ideas in consciousness. In later years, this dilemma is handled by repression. Repression is a most significant developmental achievement. It implies the ability to keep unwanted information out of consciousness on a more or less permanent basis, allowing an individual to sustain cohesiveness in human contacts. Before repression, there is splitting: the splitting of affects, of perceptions, and of object relationships — all efforts born in the first year of life to establish relatively constant structures.

In spite of the centrality of splitting, it is a troublesome concept. Asking what splits in splitting, Pruyser (1975) noted the many difficulties that the concept creates and suggested that it be "dumped" as scientifically untenable. There is, first of all, the issue of whether the phenomenon refers to an active process ("I am splitting") versus a passive process ("I am in a state of being split"). Then there is the problem of splitting as a normal developmental phenomenon, that is, the infant's attempt at classifying his or her environment (Mahler et al., 1975) as distinct from splitting as a defense of path-

This work, from the Unit for the Study of Clinical Communication, was supported in part by Grant MH-14383 and Grant MH-07336, National Institute of Mental Health. I express my gratitude to my colleague, Dr. Wilma Bucci, for her significant contribution in the psycholinguistic analysis of the data. Appreciation is also expressed to Mr. Peter Grand for his creative and diversified assistance.

ological process. There is also the wide range of phenomena which have been embraced by the term. Clearly, the concept needs definition and a charting out.

My attempt to define splitting and the levels and kinds of splitting will begin with a classification of the phenomena of splitting as an integrative failure. Developmental in conception, my approach will relate levels of splitting to levels of narcissistic organization. I will then describe the regulatory principles which may contribute to the attainment of cohesiveness. I advance the hypothesis that splitting can be understood as reflecting a crisis in the experience of the early body self, a crisis that reemerges in adult psychopathology.

To support my hypothesis I draw on the observations of three clinical groups: chronic schizophrenic patients, patients who may be termed borderline, and a group called narcissistically depressed.[1] Psychopathology is an accident of nature that highlights, in more extreme forms, aspects of splitting which can also be observed in the general population. All observations cited are based on audio- and video-recorded communicative behaviors of eight schizophrenic, eight borderline, and four narcissistically depressed patients. All were observed during the initial phase of a psychiatric treatment interview.

Toward a Classification of the Phenomena of Splitting

The task of classifying patterns and levels of splitting is similar to what we faced with the problem of symbiosis some fifteen years ago (Freedman, 1967). Symbiosis, the phenomena of fusion and mutuality during the first year of life, represented a significant discovery, but it also represents an oversimplification. We now know that there are many stages on the path toward individuation, many patterns of symbiotic constellation. Similarly, there are many patterns of integrative failure on the path toward attaining cohesiveness, and these require definition in developmental terms.

A state of splitting may be defined by polarities of incompatible experiences or mental aggregates which cannot be synthesized. They may be images, thought fragments, representations of self or others, or emotional states. Splitting always reflects a failure

---

[1]The empirical work was conducted by our research group consisting of Drs. Stanley Grand, Felix Barroso, Wilma Bucci, and the author. For a detailed description of the kinetic and linguistic findings, see Freedman et al. (1978a).

of synthesis and is indicative of a more or less incomplete experience of self. One kind of classification could be based on the kinds of phenomena which fail to attain synthesis. Thus, we can speak of an integrative failure in basic sensorimotor function, a failure in the integration in the representational world of self and objects, and a failure in the integration of affects. In view of the connection between splitting and the emerging sense of self, some writers have held that splitting may simply be arranged along a linear developmental progression, reflecting an increasing sense of personal cohesion. But splitting reflects a discontinuity and, hence, must be viewed as patterned. Lustman (1977) outlines a model for delineating patterns of splitting. This model includes the temporal aspect of what is being split and the extent to which mental aggregates are held in consciousness. Split experiences may occur simultaneously; they may occur alternatively, with some aspects temporarily excluded from awareness; and they may occur with one aspect more or less held permanently out of consciousness. Such an analysis would yield three constellations of splitting: fragmentation, oscillation, and depletion.

Pattern I: Fragmentation

The most molecular form of splitting is fragmentation, the disconnected and simultaneous experience of images, thought fragments, motor acts, contradicting verbalizations, and condensations — all fully depicted in Bleuler's (1911) description of the schizophrenic process. Fragmentation is a split of basic sensorimotor functions. It presupposes a profound absence of self-boundaries as the patient is struggling with a most rudimentary discrimination between inner and outer. Hence, the person experiences himself as being at the mercy of continually disrupting stimulation. I view fragmentation, not necessarily as a sign of schizophrenia, but as a particular ego state which is highlighted in schizophrenia. In fragmentation, both self and object representations are chaotic, and images represent part rather than whole objects, with attributes of persons interchangeable in kaleidoscopic fashion.

In fragmentation, there is a profound disruption of the associative process. As Werner and Kaplan (1967) termed it, "the distinction between referential objects and symbolic vehicles tends to dissolve so that both kinds of 'entities' occupy the same domain." This was also shown in our study on language, in which the most prevalent use of pronouns was "that's it," as if the person was saying, "Don't ask me what is on my mind." The basic pathology in fragmentation is not linguistic, but deals with issues which far antedate language acquisition: the organism's ongoing struggle to define the most rudimentary boundaries between inner and outer and to create some constancy guiding the attentional process. The current psychoanalytic conceptions of schizophrenia by Blatt and Wild (1976) and Grand et al. (1975) view the task of boundary definition as the central issue.

The difficulty both in the associative and attentional processes appears in the context of what Winnicott (1965) termed an unintegrated ego state, a stage before the individual has repudiated the not-me, so that there is at this very early stage no external factor. It implies an experience of unspeakable dread. The regressive anxiety is one of "falling to pieces," "falling forever," "having no relationship to the body," and "having no orientation." Such disorganizing anxiety is not always present. In a quiescent state, the patient has a sense of oneness where the "not-me" has not yet been repudiated by the "I." When, however, in any human interaction, the person is roused and is confronted with an external factor, at that point fragmentation as we see it in language or gesture emerges. The request to symbolize, then, signifies a disruption of the state of oneness, and the fragmented product which we observe in language or in gesture is thus a manifestation of this disruption.

These considerations provide a starting point not only for a definition of one form of splitting, but also for the conditions favoring its resolution. The patient, while communicating, continuously strives toward the re-creation of the quiescent state. It appears to be an implicit request for creating conditions of a holding environment (Modell, 1976) in which the flux of information may be regulated and titrated. It is this concept of holding, in its narrow and broader sense, which points to one important therapeutic avenue in the treatment of early narcissistic disorders.

Pattern 2: Oscillation

Another form of integrative failure is the pattern of oscillation or splitting proper which refers to incompatible representations of self or objects. These, unlike the simultaneous fragmentations that tend to occur in schizophrenia, occur alternatively or in sequence. The same object may be adored at one moment and despised the next. The sense of self may bask in grandiose delight, followed by self-disparagement. Or the social world may be divided into good and bad, as in the "good" and "bad" mother of Melanie Klein (1946). In this form of representational splitting there are no modulating appraisals, so that in one state there is a complete disavowal of the other. The incompatible states are experienced in successive alternation. This alternation is at the core of the clinical descriptions of the borderline state by Kernberg (1967) and Masterson (1976).

Our study disclosed a characteristic feature in the language of borderline patients: a retraction phenomenon—It-I—a break in conceptual scheme. It involves an oscillation between an affirmation of self and an inanimate nonself. This "It-I" retraction suggests a developmental paradigm: the developmental roots of the oscillation of the borderline patient may be prefigured by the child's struggle between the self and an inanimate environment. I say prefigured, not rooted, because all early developmental events only provide patterns upon which later events become grafted. One model is suggested by Winnicott's (1965) description of the conflict of the "I" and the repudiation of the "not-me." Winnicott describes the struggle as "First comes 'I' which includes 'everything else is not me.' Then comes 'I am, I exist, I gather experiences and enrich myself and have an introjective and projective interaction with the NOT-ME, the actual world of shared reality.'" Winnicott further notes that "the skin becomes the boundary between the me and the not-me. In other words, the psyche has come to live in the soma and an individual's psycho-somatic life has been initiated" (p. 61). Through an ongoing process of projection and introjection, boundaries are formed; oscillation may then be regarded as an active process of boundary construction.

The recognition that what may be at the core of splitting proper is the struggle to delineate the "not-me" illuminates the well-known prevalence of undistilled aggression and rage in borderline states. The salient affect here is not dread, but rage. The rage not only is a response to a detached or withholding caretaker, but arises out of the first awareness of helplessness and the loss of omnipotence. At that

point in time either infant or adult faces the total randomness of the
environment vis-à-vis his own actions, so that the possibility of
affecting the environment (the "not-me") rests strictly upon the action of the self. The rage that ensues from this confrontation with
helplessness forms the genesis of splitting.

The key to the resolution of splitting is the establishment of externality. The literature contains varying approaches which implicitly or explicitly are designed to achieve this effect. Kernberg's (1967)
use of confrontation is one example. Loewald's (1960) articulation of
differential tension states is a subtler approach. From the vantage
point of individuation and separation, what becomes important is
the creation of an experience of the "not-me." All this adds up to a
common theme. The resolution of splitting may be promoted by experiences of segregation and boundedness. This emphasis does not
negate the importance of an empathic holding context, but it does
point to the addition of a differentiating factor in clinical discourse.

Pattern 3: Depletion

In the subjective state of depletion, there is no obvious phenomenological split. The patient feels drained, empty, helpless, and often
bitter. Yet, in spite of the painful affects, there is a sense of self,
albeit a devalued self. In the depleted state, the patient is attempting to define the conditions of dissatisfaction and, in this sense,
the depressive experience marks the state of partially internalized experiences — the beginning of object constancy. But this state also
marks a split of a different sort, involving the cohesiveness of affective experiences in significant interactions.

The patient, in this depleted state, has accepted the idea that
there is only one object on whom to depend. Within this "container,"
the nature of splitting has to do with the struggle to recapture a lost
affective connection. Such a patient had at some point in development (perhaps preoedipal or archaic) established an affective connection to a partially internalized loved and hated object. This is
supported by the quality of such patients' language, in which not "it"
or "I" but "he" or "she" predominates. I suspect, along with Kohut
(1971), that the splitting off of the affective core is a disavowal of the
early grandiose self. There is the inner recognition, and even conviction, of the precious and adored self which remains unrecognized

by the environment, and which the patient cannot even claim for himself. The task of overcoming this state of narcissistic depletion requires the gradual reinfusion of some aspect of early bliss. It is noteworthy that the experiences which are dissociated in the depleted state are much more libidinal than aggressive; they deal with a yearning for or mirroring of one's self in the gleam of mother's eye.

These formulations define conditions which would favor the reintegration of the dissociated affective experiences. The integrative failure here may be traced to the patient's inability to use what is proffered. The patient's struggle deals with the adequate linking and representation of affectively meaningful experiences.

Summary: The Stages of Integrative Failure in the Development of Narcissism

The three forms of splitting clearly offer widely different pictures of symptomatology. Fragmentation, oscillation, and depletion define different forms of splitting manifest respectively in perception, in representation, and in affect and drive. In fragmentation, there is dread; in oscillation, diffuse rage and aggression; and in depletion, depressed affect.

The most comprehensive understanding of the three patterns of splitting is suggested by Winnicott's (1965) concept of ego integration. Like a prism, the different forms of split experiences are but a manifestation of integrative failure at each level of organization. Thus, in fragmentation, we deal with an unintegrated ego state with minimal boundaries; in oscillation, we deal with the failure to repudiate the "not-me" from the "me"; and in depletion, the failure to connect the "me" to the "you." From a structural point of view, the three stages may be viewed as marking the transition from a state of "oneness" to a state of "wholeness."

These conceptions have pointed the way toward different models for the conditions which favor integration, conditions which will be examined in the last two parts of this essay. The unintegrated fragmented state appears to call for conditions of holding and oneness. The struggle over the repudiation of the "not-me" calls for conditions of demarcation and contrast, permitting the experience of externality. The depleted state calls for experiences of connecting, permitting experiences of wholeness.

Self-Regulation — The Wisdom of the Body

The movements of the body (hand, feet, head, torso), as they accompany speech during a therapeutic session, exert a regulatory effect upon the experiences of self and, hence, under favorable conditions, may mediate the change from splitting to cohesiveness. My focus, then, is on those actions of the body that play a regulatory role in the experience of a more cohesive self. The study of body movements has a particular relevance to a consideration of narcissistic phenomena. Narcissism, by definition, implies a crisis involving the events of the first year of life, and subsequent developmental events are particularly prefigured by the events of that period. As analysts, we are confronted with treating our patients with a method which relies upon symbolizing, communicating about events, some of which had their onset at a time when verbal competence was not yet established. It is through our understanding of the early roots that we learn to harness these derivatives of early schemata in the treatment of narcissistic states of consciousness.

Freud (1915) found "in the efficacy of. . . muscular activity a basis for distinguishing between an 'outside' and an 'inside'" (p. 119). I would like to paraphrase this by noting that it is in the efficacy of muscular activity that we sustain, throughout life, the integrity of our self and object representations. I wish to make it clear that my emphasis on bodily action is not concerned with the study of body language, the transmission of unconscious signs, symbols, or wishes; nor is it concerned with an understanding of bodily action as it is reflected in the crystallization of defenses or the flow of excitation. Rather, it is concerned with a dichotomy of centrifugal or centripetal action which is gradually built up to define the boundaries of self and nonself. This view, in a sense, diverges from traditional formulations by both Freud and Piaget. While all observers agree upon the fundamental role of bodily actions in the first year of life, the significance of these actions is usually believed to diminish as more complex symbolic structures develop. I believe, on the other hand, that derivatives of the early developmental period persist and, indeed, have a regulatory role throughout life.

A similar viewpoint was expressed by Lichtenberg and Slap (1973) who studied the role of body self in the testing of reality. They sketch a line of development of the body self, and specify the criteria by which different phases may be used both to delineate the self and to test reality. While Lichtenberg and Slap describe the role of body self as an aggregate experience, I focus more narrowly on body-action sequences and specifically on forms of self-stimulation. From a cognitive point of view, self-stimulation is the young infant's mechanism for sorting out the contours of the self vis-à-vis the onrush of incoming stimulation. In the first year of life, attention, intention, discrimination, and the ability to represent are based on schemata brought about by the child's recurring use of eyes, hands, and mouth. Thus, the early roots in the formulation of the self and the different developmental levels in the formulation of the self-cohesiveness can be approached by considering, as Spitz (1965) does, the spatial situation in which the child finds himself.

First, there is crib space in which hand-to-mouth or hand-to-hand activity is predominant. At this stage, the child struggles with tracking, with the establishment of patterned perception, and with the exclusion of the irrelevant from that which is relevant. Bilateral self-touching is an important mediator by which tracking and screening are achieved. This appears to be a period in which mechanisms dealing with selection and exclusion are developed. The hands, moreover, are used to confirm the experience of a "me." In visual tracking, the child does not yet distinguish between his own locomotion and that of the external events. Out of sight, as Weiner and Elkind (1972) note, is literally out of existence. The outside and the inside are still one.

Second, there is a period which I call the period of playpen space, a phase in which the child attempts to achieve erect posture and locomotion. Here we find efforts toward integrating foot movements with hand activity. Indeed, we can observe a sequential pattern beginning with the discharge of random foot movements, followed by periods of quiescence and focused exploration by the hands. As a child begins to coordinate foot and hand movements, he becomes better equipped to explore the external world and to discriminate self from nonself. Indeed, the establishment of internal action sequences is a prerequisite for the establishment of externality. This, then, is a period of heightened self-boundary definition. Sequential bursts of activity of an aggressive nature are important experiences in the establishment of discrimination between self and nonself. The phenomenon of externality has been depicted by Brain

(1951) through the concept of dropableness, the primary quality which distinguishes a small object from a part of one's body.

In the third period, the playground period, the emergent sense of self also implies the as yet tentative appearance of internalized representation of objects. The child emerging from a sandbox, stroking himself as he cries, is treating himself as he had previously been treated. His hands become agents; his body becomes the recipient. There is a linking, then, between conceptual schemas, one dealing with doing and the other with being done to. The major task in this third period, then, is the establishment of links between self representations and object representations.

I have used this developmental model to pinpoint a line in the evolution of self-regulation as it is manifest in bodily actions. This model reflects the organism's early mode of coping with information and establishing different levels of self-cohesion. Thus, there are action sequences that lead to the reduction of information and the establishment of the "me"; action sequences that lead to the classification of information and the identification of the "not-me"; and the action sequences that lead to the internalized affective representation of the "you." The concept of the body musculature as a finely tuned regulating apparatus thus attains fuller form. The three developmentally defined activities in space articulate three patterns of muscular activity: shielding, contrasting, and retrieving. This model may serve as a springboard for the understanding of communication in adult discourse.

While regulating activities have their roots in childhood, they are called into play in adult discourse when there is a threat to the integrity of the self. They may be viewed as a kind of "wisdom of the body," which may have a particular relevance to patients suffering from integrative failures. In an effort to determine how shielding, contrasting, or retrieving may aid in the process of establishing cohesion in the schizophrenic, borderline, and depressed patients, I now turn to some of the observations made in a research study of video-recorded interviews of three patient groups, who were evaluated in terms of language and forms of bodily activity. A ten-minute sample of recorded behavior during a mental status examination formed the basis of observation.

Shielding Activity in Schizophrenia

The strategy of shielding during discourse refers to continuous bilateral forms of self-stimulation. The movements disregard speech rhythms and cut across pause or clause boundaries. The person maintains a relatively restrained posture, hands folded at the midline, head leaning forward. The motions give the appearance of a self-produced "white noise" and are apparently aimed at screening out unwanted signals.

From a developmental perspective, shielding is probably a derivative of that phase in infancy when the child engages in circulatory motions within the confines of the crib (crib space), and when the conquest of attention and tracking is mediated primarily by hands, eyes, and mouth. It is the stuckness of both hands around the mouth which sets the stage for visual tracking. It is the meeting of the hands and fingers at the midline at about six months of age which sets the stage for intentionality and pursuit (Adelson and Fraiberg, 1971).

Shielding in adult communication is inevitably linked with high states of arousal, and is particularly elicited when the person experiences a fragmentation of self. Sometimes this can be induced experimentally, as has been done by confronting subjects with stressful interview conditions. While shielding activity can be experimentally induced, in psychopathology it can be observed as a function of the deficits inherent in self-organization. Probably no other condition has such a profound loss of self-boundaries as that of the schizophrenic patient in a fragmented state. Chronic schizophrenic patients accompany their speech with continuous bilateral finger-to-hand motions, often lasting throughout the entire ten-minute period. These movements appeared to have a monotonic and stereotyped quality, cutting across pause and clause boundaries, and took place while the patients were sitting in a rigid posture, hands folded at the midline. These movements struck the observer as a caricature of the "meeting of the hands at the midline" at six months of age, and their function appeared to be similar.

Shielding activity seems to be a treatment that the schizophrenic patient provides for himself in the effort to cope with fragmentation. This corresponds with Grand et al.'s (1975) formulations concerning the role of self-stimulation in schizophrenia. The patient, confronted with intrusive sensations from within and without, cannot synthesize them, cannot symbolize (That's it!), and thus, through high-intensity repetitive sensory innervation, reestablishes the minimal condition of me-ness or oneness. Tactile self-stimulation here appears to block the regressive pull of fragmentation.

Contrasting Activity in Borderline States

Contrasting activity involves a sequence of distinct bodily adjustments. Contrasting involves an oscillation between two major motor acts, one of motor tension discharge, such as gross action of limb or torso where proprioceptive feedback predominates (foot kick or posture shift); and the other, discrete and patterned forms of self-stimulation by the hand of a body part (hair, cheek, neck). These are brief and have an instrumental quality. The innervation is predominantly tactile. Thus, a contrasting unit is an event sequence in which there is first the onset of a discharge movement within one second of a pause, followed by a lateralized body touch which terminates prior to the onset of speech. The contrasting unit is a true unit in that it involves the coordination of two motor acts occurring around a nonfluency.

The contrasting sequence, I suspect, has its ontogenetic roots during that period of infancy when the child struggles with locomotion and prehension (playpen space). Contrasting units emerge at any point of discourse when the adult speaker feels an encroachment upon his sense of self, when differentiations from the environment must be established and the self reaffirmed.

Three previous observations identified a contrasting unit as a major organizer of psychological activity: in a study of the associative monologue, contrasting was observed as preceding the emergence of new associations (Freedman and Bucci, 1980); in a study of listening behavior, contrasting was linked to the ability to receive information (Freedman et al., 1978a); and in a developmental study of communicative patterns of children from four to sixteen years of age, contrasting was observed as a relatively late developmental achievement appearing at about twelve years of age (Freedman, 1977). The contrasting unit, as a boundary-defining unit, obviously is relevant to the communication of borderline patients. Earlier I traced the oscillating representation of borderline patients to a crisis involving the repudiation of the "me" from the "not-me"; hence, borderline patients are continually engaged in a definition and redefinition of self-boundaries. Empirical observations of borderline patients indicate that the contrasting sequence — discharge act, pause, self-touch — is prevalent in borderline states, but absent in both schizophrenic and depressed conditions. We may speculate that the instrumental body touch occurring in rhythm, in pause, is the act within that sequence which affirms an external factor. The contrasting sequence would seem to be a very efficient way of establishing experiences of boundedness. Contrasting has been observed as an attribute of highly differentiated cognitive organization, yet borderline patients are disturbed and troubled people. This brings out one of the well-known clinical contradictions — that in borderline patients, one can observe, side by side, the most differentiated forms of activity and clear manifestations of regressive thought. In our research, we were, in fact, able to distinguish between true and abortive contrasting — true contrasting (i.e., the contrasting unit) and abortive contrasting (i.e., random foot activity). We evaluated the consequences of abortive and true contrasting as they may be manifest in the cohesiveness of language. It was during abortive contrasting that we could localize the presence of linguistic retractions and a break in syntactic structure. During true contrasting, language structure was integrated. These data support the idea that contrasting, as a patterned mode of self-regulation, has a demonstrable effect on the cohesiveness of articulated thought.

These observations, then, present a paradigm for the study of two distinct processes operating in the communication of the borderline patient — abortive attempts at contrasting manifest in random discharge acts, and true contrasting units manifest in a kinetic event sequence. I suspect that it is the discharge phase which defines the genesis of the splitting, and that it is the contrasting phase proper which defines the process by which internal dissonance may find resolution.

Retrieving Activity in Depressed States

The idea that during discouse there may be a specific form of regulating activity which promotes the retrieval of previously dissociated experience has more clinical than experimental evidence in its support. The general notion is that the innervation of specific sensory endings may create the kind of subjective state which promotes the recall of thoughts or feelings from the periphery of consciousness. Retrieving activity refers to continuous patterned movements of hands acting upon specific body parts, particularly those having highly sensitive nerve endings, e.g., lips, cheeks, neck, upper arm. These movements, moreover, have a stroking and soothing quality.

A scrutiny of both the structure and function of this form of activity indicates that the movements reflect an interaction of partially internalized systems. The hands are actors or agents playing upon the body as object or recipient. The sensory experience of the body surface takes precedence over fingertip stimulation. If one closes one's eyes and touches one's cheek, a sensation of being stroked is created. One might surmise that the gestures have their roots in what I term playground space, in which the child, while seeking support, touches himself as he once was touched by his caretaker.

Most references to this form of self-stimulation are of a clinical nature, and they seem to suggest affective or imagistic experiences which are retrieved rather than lexical memories. Gottschalk and Uliana (1977) systematically observed hand-to-mouth approximations in a patient during psychoanalysis and found that these movements were associated with the retrieval of "oral" memories.

Similarly, Mahl (1977) has noted that patterned continuous body touching may contribute to the retrieval of affective memory. Rangell (1953) has argued that hand-to-snout movements are linked to recovery of feelings of pleasure and self-esteem. If the narcissistically depleted patient, as I suggested earlier, has difficulties in acknowledging an unnamed feeling of bliss and in linking it to verbalization, then this form of self-stimulation may have a particular self-regulatory relevance. The communication of depression, then, entails a process of connecting and reconnecting, and the work of mourning is a process of overcoming psychic pain via symbolization.

The empirical observations of depressed patients are straightforward. The patients show minimal finger or hand motions, minimal foot movements, minimal discrete body touching or contrasting units. They do engage in continuous lateralized forms of self-stimulation, focusing mostly on cheeks, mouth, neck, upper arms, that is, areas with a great concentration of sensory nerve endings, and the quality of the movements are stroking and soothing. The movements occur throughout the interview, during verbalization and during pausing. About six weeks after the initial interview, the same patients showed a major reduction in depressive symptomatology, and with it, a substantial reduction in continuous body touching. One might say the work of overcoming depression had been accomplished.

In this section I have defined a developmental dimension of self-regulation applicable to narcissistic states. The line of development corresponds to the evolution of the integration of the self. At each stage, different forms of self-regulation appear to reflect attempts at repair at those moments of interaction when the cohesiveness of the self is threatened.

Following Lichtenberg and Slap's outline of the levels in the integration of the body self, I submit that shielding activity is a manifestation of high-threshold stimulation that facilitates the rudimentary discrimination of the "me." Contrasting is an activity creating conditions of boundedness and the discrimination of the "me" and "not-me." Retrieving is an activity that connects to or links with an affective core, facilitating the possibility of true dialogue. The issue was poetically stated by William James some 80 years ago: "One great splitting of the whole universe into two halves is made by each of us; . . . we all draw the line of division. . . in a different place . . . [but] we all call the two halves by the same names. . . 'me' and 'not-me'. . . [This] may be a moral riddle, but it is a fundamental psychological fact" (p. 289). Through various forms of self-regulation, the line is drawn differently depending upon the individual's level of integration.

On the Possibilities of Resolving Splits: Regulating Activity as Psychic Organizers

There is by now ample evidence that at least three kinds of splits can be distinguished: those having to do with fragmentation, oscillation, and depletion. The clinical phenomena described by Winnicott (1965), Kernberg (1967), and Kohut (1971) have objective counterparts in both motoric and linguistic structures. As was previously suggested, the self-regulating activity reflects a process of cumulative attainment of integration at successive levels of development.

Before I examine the conditions which contribute to synthesis, it is necessary to discuss the meaning of the research data as they have relevance to clinical practice. This most central issue concerns our representation of a patient's motor activity. What is the status of action? Is it a concrete muscular event; is it the depiction of a symbol; or is it a wish? Once we have arrived at a satisfactory understanding of the role of action in psychoanalysis, we can readdress the process by which a patient's action may lead to synthesis. And, finally, what is the contribution of the analyst's understanding of this process to an understanding of the mutative factors in treatment?

Regulating actions in psychoanalysis are either fact or fiction, but always metaphor. In the use of metaphor during treatment, we must always embody both the concrete patterning of events and their symbolic equivalents. If we look only at the behavior, we become concrete and mechanistic. If we look only at the symbolic equivalents, we lose the impact of sensory or tactile innervation. Thus, we are always searching for metaphors which embody both realms. In considering regulating actions in analytic patients, we can observe them on three levels: the actual behavior, the recall of behavior, and the representation of behavior in the imagery of dreams. There is, within the consciousness of every person, a set of self-regulating activities which define the boundaries of self and nonself.

The activities derived from our observations of self-regulators should be distinguished from Schafer's (1976) idea of action language. The action language approach to psychoanalysis asserts that all psychological processes can be regarded as some form of action, so that all events or experiences can be stated by a verb defining the nature of the action and by an adverb defining its mode. I refer, instead, to regulating activity as an organizing construct having the formal properties of shielding, contrasting, and retrieving, and which, like a catalyst, affects other psychic experiences.

Having broadened the perspective of action, I will reexamine the process by which the experience of action may contribute to synthesis. The basic proposition advanced here is that the clinical phenomenology of splitting, the integrative failures in perception, in object relationships, and in affect, have at their roots a crisis involving the experience of the early body self. Thus, if the patient reenacts derivatives of the early body self during discourse, then we can describe the conditions which may favor levels of reintegration of the self. However, our observational data suggest that we can be more specific. I view regulating actions as psychic organizers (Spitz, 1959), but this term is reserved to actions which implement self-nonself boundaries. Self-regulating as a psychic organizer derives its integrative functions from the fact that actions (a) entail sensorimotor innervation, (b) operate at the periphery of awareness, and (c) are self-initiated.

These regulating actions are the guiding structures which may facilitate shared meaning. They function within the context of crib space, playpen space, or playground space. In each of these scenarios of enactment, different processes represent different attempts toward cohesiveness. Not only does the structure of activity differ at any given level of organization, but, correspondingly, so does its function. Thus, we can observe conditions that create oneness, differentiation, and synthesis.

These observations of self-regulations can make a contribution to the issue of mutative factors in treatment. The concepts of object relations theory, transference, therapeutic object relationships, and holding environment are in the forefront of current thought. The therapeutic dyad is assumed to re-create for the patient, in one form or another, the symbolic equivalent of the earliest dialogue. There is, however, in the history of psychoanalytic thought, a tradition which implicates nontransference factors as mediators of change: insight, working through, causality connecting, and naming are all processes working under the umbrella of a transference relationship which the patient mobilizes in his effort toward integration. All these rely upon a highly developed cognitive apparatus and have their roots in the treatment of psychoneurotic disturbances. They do not direct themselves to the issues in narcissistic disturbances. Self-regulators, as psychic organizers, have their roots in infancy, and have an ongoing relevance to the understanding of narcissistic disorders.

Regulating Actions in Clinical Discourse

With these thoughts in mind, I shall sketch out some clinical vignettes collected by myself and my supervisees, which illustrate self-regulating actions. Each clinical sequence, as already mentioned, must be viewed as a metaphor, and it may appear either as actual behavior, as recall of behavior, or as imagery in dreams.

Shielding may be regarded as a metaphor for a beleaguered state. It involves the creation of boundaries, barriers, or walls under the threat of impending fragmentation. In that sense, it provides at least a momentary respite. One patient created a barrier by entering the office requesting that I turn on the air conditioner to create a hum. He then lay on the couch. "I wanted the hum to exclude all the noise outside. Are you paying attention to me? So what are we going to talk about? Nothing comes to my mind. [He makes finger and hand motions.] The gurgling in my stomach has subsided. I feel at peace now."

Another patient gives all the signs of being in a fragmented state. She starts by telling the therapist she feels "terribly split." "I try to get O. off to school. It lasts the whole morning. I am irritated by the carpenter working next door. The drill working up the street. I feel tremendous rage, terribly helpless, I can't do the bills, it is like death coming over me and I feel terribly at odds. Then around noontime, I get myself to have a cup of coffee. I stir the coffee end-lessly. I start to do some sewing and knitting. Gradually I don't hear the men working in the street. Peace comes over me."

The repetitive stirring of the coffee, the stereotyped motions of knitting, the continuous stroking of finger upon finger, and even the hum of the air conditioner to screen out noise are all maneuvers which help reestablish a feeling of oneness for the person in a frag-mented state. Shielding is only the first stage in achieving cohesion.

Contrasting is a metaphor for a state of consolidation. The event sequence — discharge, pause, consolidation — not only applies to the microscopic structure of a single sentence, but is the pattern which governs the events of the life of many a person in our society. There are moments of frantic activity, moments of pausing, and moments of consolidation. Contrasting involves not only the imple-mentation of rhythm, but the use of externality within the confines of the rhythm. (Only when touching occurs during a pause did we note more coherent language.)

One patient established the external factor by enacting such a sequence during the analytic hour. He kicked his legs as he recalled a shameful experience of sexual humiliation. (He was involved in a sadomasochistic struggle with a girlfriend.) He paused, touched the tweedy material of the couch, and then verbalized, "I don't care anymore about Eve beating me. I just wanted to feel the leather and tweed of her skirt, that there was someone out there." At that point, he proceeded to recall his mother's psychotic depression after his younger brother was born.

In this clinical example of contrasting, the touching of the tweed and the texture of the leather, action sequences are used to establish the external factor. Through this ordering of physical space, the person achieves a definition of the boundedness, not only of self, but of the environment as well. This action sequence defines a structure for the resolution of the sadomasochistic, introjective-projective oscillation. Aggression is reduced, and memory retrieval may begin.

Retrieval is a metaphor for a state of reconstruction. It involves the creation of an inner dialogue which is tinged with libidinal affect, and this promotes the widening of the filter of consciousness.

A vignette presented by George Mahl (1977) illustrates the phenomenon vividly. Mr. F. often used his hands to hold himself as he would hold and/or be held by a woman. At one time, as he was expressing sympathetic concern for his ailing grandmother, he wrapped his arms about his chest and held the sides of his chest between open hands. At another time, he embraced himself extremely tightly as he was reflecting upon a lost picture of his mother and sister embracing each other. He fell silent, and then he recalled the intimacy and sexual pleasure that was evident in the facial expressions of his mother and sister.

Although these examples do not involve stimulation of the oral zone, they have the properties of retrieval behavior. They invoke the enactment of partially internalized representation. Hence, they signify the development of a sense of self seeking gratification and self-esteem. They entail an activity leading to the reinternalization of appropriate affective cues. And, finally, the movements occur in the context of aggressive, and libidinal, sensual affect. As one of the by-products of my observations, I found that retrieval and reconstruction involve the nourishment by libidinal experiences. When the person is confronted with stark facts of aggression, splitting proper ensues.

The self-regulating actions may occur in dreams, and even in a single dream sequence. A dream reported by a supervisee contained three components: "I was rowing in a boat surrounded by bodies of water" (shielding); "I descended from the boat, walked up the steps and reach for a tree" (contrasting); "I ran toward the boy and he urinated in my face." The encounter with the boyfriend urinating in her face led to the retrieval of the memory which proved to be at the root of the psychic conflict. The analysis of this dream, according to action sequences, provides the analyst with critical markers. The possible value of such identifiable markers leads to the last topic of this discussion.

Regulating Actions and Their Relation to Psychoanalytic Technique

I believe, as did Freud, that one cannot lead a patient toward his own synthesis. We can, however, be acutely conscious of factors which favor synthesis. While we can ask patients to enact for us, the decision to act is theirs. We do not explicitly analyze the actions, for they usually occur at the periphery of consciousness. How then do these patterns of self-regulation vis-à-vis the object become part of the treatment process?

One way is to suggest a therapeutic stance — not interpretation, because that is too specific — which refers to the mode or context which is created for the patients. Just as there are different models for narcissistic organization, so there are different stances. Modell's (1976) "holding environment" or Kohut's (1971) emphasis on the reevocation of an adored self suggest a receiving or empathic stance. Sometimes there is too much empathy and not enough interpretation. Kernberg (1967), on the other hand, stressing the role of diffuse aggression in splitting, emphasized challenge and confrontation; and Loewald (1960), in his more subtle handling of the mourning and loss experience, emphasizes reconnecting and linking.

While we employ any or all of these basic stances with patients, there is usually a salient and dominant stance, and the appropriateness of the stance may be suggested not by ideology, but perhaps more importantly by how the patient is "treating himself," i.e., the wisdom of his body. The sensitive clinician can thus note that the manner in which the patient treats himself may indeed be the optimal condition for the manner in which he needs to be treated at that moment. The novice may use the patient's actions as a guide.

Implicit in what has been stated here is that each regulating action suggests a complementary mode of intervention. A complementary stance to shielding is empathic reflection. A complementary stance to contrasting is confrontation and discrimination. A complementary stance to retrieving is reconstruction and naming. These actions, then, are markers depicting a particular object relationship state and suggest a stance for intervention.

Naming, as Fenichel (1933) has suggested, is one of the most powerful aspects of analytic work. It always identifies the experience to be named "and something more." But before the naming can take place, there must be the recognition of a "me" and "not-me" and a "you." The actions depicting each of these attainments of personal identity thus are precursors for naming and analytic work. There is an analogy here to Kris's (1956) "good hour." Insight, he notes, may be preceded by many hours of turbulent confrontation. The naming of the appropriate affective experience may similarly be a consequence of the prior sorting out of the cohesiveness of the self vis-à-vis the object world.

Actions in the Transitional Process

This study has shown that different levels of integrative failures create different host conditions. Throughout, I have described the correlation between splitting and regulating actions, and indicated the mediating mechanisms which account for levels of integration. The understanding of the process of change lies in the recognition that the actions of the early body self sustain their impact throughout life. Moreover, these actions must always be seen as operating within the appropriate space, so that it is never the action or action image, but rather is the action in space which has its impact as a psychic organizer. It is the quality of experienced context that determines the integrated significance of the movement. In this sense movements have a dynamic impact and offer the possibility of a bridge from lower to higher levels of integration. Movements have the quality of transitionality: they depict a state, but at the same time they effect the means of overcoming that state.

An examination of the issues of splitting thus has therapeutic implications for the repair of splitting and the attainment of integration.

References

Adelson, E. & Fraiberg, S. (1971), Mouth and hand in the early development of blind infants. In: *Symposium on Oral Sensation and Perception*, ed. J. F. Bosma. Springfield, Ill.: Charles C Thomas, pp. 420–430.

Blatt, S. J. & Wild, C. M. (1976), *Schizophrenia*. New York: Academic Press.

Bleuler, E. (1911), *Dementia Praecox or the Group of Schizophrenias*. New York: International Universities Press, 1950.

Brain, W. R. (1951), *Mind, Perception and Science*. Oxford: Blackwell Scientific Publications.

Fenichel, O. (1933), Problems of psychoanalytic technique. In: *The Evolution of Psychoanalytic Technique*, ed. M. Bergmann & F. Hartman. New York: Basic Books, 1976, pp. 271–272.

Freedman, N. (1967), Varieties of symbiotic manifestations. Read at scientific meeting of Institute for Psychoanalytic Training and Research.

———— (1977), Hands, words, and mind. In: *Communicative Structures and Psychic Structures*, ed. N. Freedman & S. Grand. New York: Plenum Press, pp. 102–132.

———— Barroso, F., Bucci, W., & Grand, S. (1978a), The bodily manifestations of listening, *Psychoanalysis and Contemporary Thought*, 1:157–194.

———— Bucci, W. (1980), On kinesic filtering in associative monologue (in press).

———— ———— Barroso, F., & Grand, S. (1978b), Varieties of splitting. Read at Second National Conference on Body Language, City University of New York.

Freud, S. (1911), Formulations on the two principles of mental functioning. *Standard Edition*, 12:218–226. London: Hogarth Press, 1958.

———— (1915), Instincts and their vicissitudes. *Standard Edition*, 14:109–140. London: Hogarth Press, 1957.

Gottschalk, L. A. & Uliana, R. L. (1977), Further studies on the relationship of nonverbal behavior. In: *Communicative Structures and Psychic Structures*, ed. N. Freedman & S. Grand. New York: Plenum Press, pp. 311–330.

Grand, S., Freedman, N., Steingart, I., & Buchwald, C. (1975), Communicative behavior in schizophrenia. *J. Nerv. Ment. Dis.*, 161:293–306.

James, W. (1890), *The Principles of Psychology*. New York: Holt.

Kernberg, O. F. (1967), Borderline personality organization. *J. Amer. Psychoanal. Assn.*, 15:611–685.

Klein, M. (1946), Notes on some schizoid mechanisms. *Int. J. Psycho-Anal.*, 27:99–110.

Kohut, H. (1971), *The Analysis of the Self*. New York: International Universities Press.

Kris, E. (1956), On some vicissitudes of insight in psycho-analysis. *Int. J. Psycho-Anal.*, 37:445–455.

Lichtenberg, J. D. & Slap, J. W. (1973), Notes on the concept of splitting and the defense mechanism of the splitting of representations. *J. Amer. Psychoanal. Assn.*, 21:772–787.

Loewald, H. W. (1960), On the therapeutic action of psycho-analysis. *Int. J. Psycho-Anal.*, 41:16–33.

Lustman, J. (1977), On splitting. *The Psychoanalytic Study of the Child*, 32:119–154.

Mahl, G. F. (1977), Body movement, ideation, and verbalization during psychoanalysis. In: *Communicative Structures and Psychic Structures*, ed. N. Freedman & S.

Grand. New York: Plenum Press, pp. 291–310.

Mahler, M. S. (1968), *On Human Symbiosis and the Vicissitudes of Individuation*. New York: International Universities Press.

—————— Pine, F., & Bergman, A. (1975), *The Psychological Birth of the Human Infant*. New York: Basic Books.

Masterson, J. F. (1976), *Psychotherapy of the Borderline Adult*. New York: Brunner/Mazel.

Modell, A. (1976), "The holding environment" and the therapeutic action of psychoanalysis. *J. Amer. Psychoanal. Assn.*, 24:285–308.

Pruyser, P. W. (1975), What splits in splitting? *Bull. Menninger Clin.*, 39:1–46.

Rangell, L. (1953), Some remarks on the psychic significance of the snout or perioral region. Presented at the annual meeting of the American Psychoanalytic Association, Los Angeles, California.

Schafer, R. (1976), *A New Language for Psychoanalysis*. London: Yale University Press.

Spitz, R. A. (1959), *A Genetic Field Theory of Ego Formation*. New York: International Universities Press.

—————— (1965), *The First Year of Life*. New York: International Universities Press.

Weiner, I. B. & Elkind, D. (1972), *Child Development*. New York: Wiley.

Werner, H. & Kaplan, B. (1967), *Symbol Formation*. New York: Wiley.

Winnicott, D. W. (1965), *The Maturational Processes and the Facilitating Environment*. New York: International Universities Press.

12

THE REPETITION COMPULSION
AND OBJECT RELATIONS THEORY

Muriel Zimmerman, Ph.D.

Freud and many writers after him have discussed the repetition compulsion from different vantage points. In my view, its overriding importance and centrality in human life have never been sufficiently appreciated. I believe it to be the most important stumbling block in many people's lives, as well as the reason for the failure of a considerable number of analyses to achieve as much as we would wish. The early object relations of the infant and child form the roots of the repetition compulsion and also make for its intransigence.

Freud first discussed the repetition compulsion in 1914 and concluded, "The main instrument...for curbing the patient's compulsion to repeat and for turning it into a motive for remembering lies in the handling of the transference" (p. 154). I interpret and extend this to mean that the crucial psychodynamics of the early object relations (especially with the parents) are reenacted over and over again with the analyst in the transference. This must be interpreted and reinterpreted to increase insight and stimulate abreaction.

By the very fact of his writing *Beyond the Pleasure Principle* (1920), Freud indicates his increasing awareness of the significance of the repetition compulsion in human life. He said, "we shall find courage to assume that there really does exist in the mind a compulsion to repeat which over-rides the pleasure principle" (p. 22). "Enough is left unexplained to justify the hypothesis of a compulsion to repeat — something that seems more primitive, more elementary, more instinctual than the pleasure principle which it over-rides" (p. 23).

While I do not consider the repetition compulsion to be instinc-

I wish to express my thanks for many constructive suggestions to Dr. Ruth Lax and Dr. Carol Kaye.

tual, it remains one of the most puzzling and difficult phenomena for us to understand, in spite of the many attempts to do so. It interferes frequently with our desire to help patients to change their reactions and problem-solving "techniques" in basic life conflicts. Bibring (1943) described the repetition compulsion very well as: (1) "the expression of the 'inertia' of living matter, of the conservative trend to maintain and repeat intensive experiences"; (2) "a regulating mechanism, with the task of discharging tensions caused by traumatic experiences after they have been bound, in fractional amounts."

The repetition compulsion has many different possible etiologies.[1] This paper will focus on its genesis in early infant and childhood object relations[2] and their paramount importance in determining the basic life-style of the person.

I shall consider primarily the negative, painful, or traumatic experiences which are repeated, although it is theoretically conceivable that repetition compulsions might result from positive experiences. The specific *nature* of the parents, especially the one with whom the child identifies, as well as the quality of the interactions determine the child's later personality dynamics and behavior. The defense mechanisms that the parents use are especially important in deciding whether or not counterproductive repetition compulsions will develop. If the growing child *sees* constructive problem-solving or sublimative methods used by the parents, he or she will by identification (and because of the affectionate ties) try to react and behave similarly.

In attempting to explore the dynamics of the repetition compulsion within the context of object relations, I shall briefly look at the experience of birth, since we know very little about the experiences of uterine life. Rank and others have pointed out effectively just how traumatic birth can be for the infant as well as the mother. How does the infant master this trauma? Ideally, a warm, loving person holds the infant, feeds him or her, alleviates the discomforts, thus developing the foundations of future feelings about difficult life situa-

[1]"The aim of the compulsion to repeat is to carry out the very same act freed of its secret unconscious meaning, or with the opposite unconscious meaning. If, because of the continued effectiveness of the repressed, some part of the original impulse insinuates itself again into the repetition which was intended as an expiation, a third, fourth, or fifth repetition of the act may become necessary" (Fenichel, 1945, p. 154).

[2]I am using Kernberg's (1976) definition of object relations theory as "the psychoanalytic approach to the internalization of interpersonal relations, their contribution to normal and pathological ego and superego developments, and the mutual influences of intrapsychic and interpersonal object relations" (p. 56).

tions. There may be genetic factors unknown to us, which influence the infant's ability to master the first trauma of life. However, we do know a lot, especially from the work of Winnicott (1965), about the importance of all the nuances of the first handling of the child. No matter how satisfying the early environment is, the loving person is not always there for comforting. How will the infant handle the tensions or frustrations, or whatever adult word we give, for the infant's feeling of helplessness in this big, overwhelming, often "cold" world? Usually, the infant cries at the first discomfort. What does the mother or mother surrogate do? If she comes to help, naturally the child is learning something important and will repeat this behavior when the next discomfort is experienced. Crying behavior is instinctively based. If gratification results, it leads to repetition of a crying pattern which is different from that of the ungratified baby. This is obvious. Our problems begin when we try to understand the repetition of reactions or behaviors which do *not* bring satisfaction — which often bring worse suffering.

The infant interacts with the objects around him and this interaction becomes introjected. In later repetitions of the interactions, the infant tries to master or change the nature of the interaction. If the first "caretakers" were not giving enough, will the child spend the rest of his life trying to *make* them be giving? Will the child try to conquer the challenge of rejection in order to get what he or she wants or needs? There are many possible ways of handling early deprivation. Satisfactions may be found with people in other environments. The defense mechanisms may be used with greater or lesser success. The child who is genetically endowed may be more able to sublimate successfully and escape the need for psychological treatment later. However, many people are not endowed and cannot handle the scars of the early years and later will need treatment.

In some cases treatment can do enough to make life satisfactory in spite of the early negative internalizations. The specific defense mechanisms plus the nature of the other object relations in the life space of an individual may make this possible. However, quite frequently, a repetition compulsion (or series of compulsions) develops and carries over to the treatment itself, resulting in a negative therapeutic reaction. The individual may not be able to accept the fact that he can never get what he "really" wants from analysis. The adult may persist in wanting what the infant wanted and be continually disappointed. If there has been a fixation on problems in the early object relations, those internalized images cannot be erased. Sometimes they can be modified, but it is too difficult to make totally new gestalts, to reorganize our perceptions and problem-solving methods, with those early ineradicable images in us. They are central to the developing gestalts. What happens to the old scars? These introjects act like internal anchors to the past, becoming the core of subsequent internalizations. If these internalizations of the important objects in the earliest stages of life are negative, mastery becomes very difficult, if not impossible. In other words, it is the "immovability" of the early internal object relations which makes subsequent mastery less possible.

In 1933, Freud said that "from the moment at which a state of things that once has been attained is upset, an instinct arises to create it afresh and brings about phenomena which we can describe as a 'compulsion to repeat'" (p. 106). If the infant experienced pain in the interaction with the objects, he may repeat this in the attempt actively to master the traumas and eliminate the fear of the painful situations. Some children want to change the *nature* of the interaction with the object—to make the mother more loving, etc. Sometimes painful experiences are repeated not just to "master" them, but to conquer the unconquerable. This means more than mastering one's inner tensions. It also means *changing* the negative environmental stimulus. For example, a child may try over and over again to be loved by one who is incapable of giving love. In one sense this may imply an ego deficiency (inability to accept reality), but in another sense it may imply a kind of ego strength—perseverance.

These characteristics and defense mechanisms must also have been conveyed by the imagoes of the early caretaking people. Thus, the unconscious motivation for the repetition compulsion comes from the early internalizations because they form the infant's whole world. That's all he knows.

Sometimes a child makes a direct attempt to change the external world. These alloplastic reactions are not as common as we might wish. More often there are fixations on the early negative internalizations. These fixations occur because of the child's associations of the experience with painful affects and may become a subsequent stimulus for repetition compulsions. The pathological alloplastic reactions may be more common than healthy alloplastic ones (mastery) because of the infant's total dependence on the caretaking adults. This dependency makes the early negative internalizations "stick like glue," impelling some individuals to react to them unconsciously throughout their lives. Here, identification with the parent is particularly important. If, for example, a child was fixated on a given painful set of experiences inherent in having a rejecting mother, the child may perceive himself as living in a rejecting world. The introject of the denying mother may form the basis for many later perceptions of other people which are unrealistic. The individual often cannot control, and usually is unconscious of the meaning of, his actions.

Many writers have noted the attempt to *master* the trauma by repeating the old unsatisfactory patterns of reaction. There is no doubt that this is often the case. Whether or not mastery is attempted is closely connected with the activity-passivity balance in the personality. Frequently, in spite of constant repetitions, one cannot master but still suffers the same way. Why continue the same reaction? Some people experience pleasure in pain. This factor and other aspects of masochistic reactions contribute to the continuance of apparently unsatisfactory emotional and behavioral reactions. Often a masochistic *seeking* for repetitions of the early pattern of interaction with the mother dominates important adult object relations.

Whether the child exposed to a rejecting mother will develop a masochistic repetition compulsion; whether he or she will master the problem or develop constructive alloplastic reactions will depend on the total life situation (including genetic factors). Often there is a fear of developing new problem-solving techniques. People tend to continue the familiar and predictable, even if it is unpleasurable or painful.

Compulsively repeating that which makes one suffer feeds masochistic needs. Freud postulated that masochistic needs develop primarily as a result of the individual's need to atone for guilt feelings.

According to Berliner (1947), "If the masochist seeks pain..., it is not for the sake of pain itself, but because pain, unconsciously to him, represents the personal love object that once gave him pain" (p. 463). In people who develop severe repetition compulsions, the primal love objects were so deeply and rigidly internalized at an early level that they "set" the patterns for later reactions. The repressed rage which the child may have felt in response to not having his wishes fulfilled may also contribute to the adult's refusal to give up painful repetition compulsions. According to Reik (1941), the child wants to be loved because of his suffering. The sick child receives more attention or tenderness. Reik also says that masochism represents an attempt to bind anxiety.[3] The connection between the *masochism* and the *negative therapeutic reaction* has been demonstrated in numerous writings. For some people, whose masochism is due to unconscious sense of guilt, suffering is preferable to cure. It is difficult to understand this. Perhaps something went wrong in the transference relationship. In discussing "some of the genetic and dynamic determinants of the negative therapeutic reaction," Asch (1976) quotes Olinick who pointed to a special character defense against the regressive pull to symbiotic fusion—"an ambivalent identification with a depressed, preoedipal maternal love object" (p. 345). Asch thinks that the fear of a regressive pull toward fusion specifically with an early depressed maternal object is the main genetic basis for the negative therapeutic reaction. He indicates that the negative therapeutic reaction preserves the relationship with the object as well as the fantasy of infantile omnipotence in order to deal with the anxiety over separation, fear of success, etc.[4]

Whatever the specific causes of the repetition compulsion in a given individual, it certainly makes the analysis or therapy for that individual much more difficult and sometimes unsuccessful, as the following case illustrates.

A twenty-five-year-old woman, Mrs. A., came to me with complaints of depression, general malaise, and weight gain. She told me a story of extreme childhood deprivation, in an understated and at

---

[3]Reik also stresses that masochism "is no original drive but a secondary instinctual function" (p. 186). It springs from the denial that meets the sadistic instinctual impulse and it develops from the sadistic aggressive or defiant fantasy which replaces reality. *Training* of all kinds by the mother and threats of punishment in early childhood lead to masochism as "a late memorial to difficulties of adjustment to reality that proved unpleasant to the child. The sequence of yielding and defiance, punishment and instinctual satisfaction, then would be the echo of long forgotten difficulties of the education by the mother. At that time she most certainly would have been feared as the object from whom punishment and loss of love threatened" (p. 209).

[4]Gero (1936) claims that negative therapeutic reaction is usually found in depression.

times "humorous" way. I was struck by the way she talked. It was obviously *not* a schizoid inappropriateness, but rather seemed to be an attempt at "bravery." Her decision to seek professional help, although it certainly did not fit in with her family background, was precipitated by two traumas occurring within the space of two months. The first was the death of her father's mother, whom she had loved very much, and the second was the breakup of her very unhappy sadomasochistic marriage.

Mrs. A. was the oldest of six children in a lower-middle-class Italian Catholic family. According to her recollections, her mother was always out of the house or sleeping. Whatever caretaking she could remember had been given by her father. Her earliest memory was of returning from a brief hospitalization as a little girl, having been called for by her father, and finding her mother totally uninvolved, sleeping on the living room couch.

The general atmosphere in the house was unhappy and the parents alway seemed to be quarreling. When my patient was eight years old, her mother walked out on the family. Although the mother visited them periodically, there was no discussion of the children's living with her. The mother's leaving was sudden (thus particularly traumatic) with no "preparation" for the children.

The father took it for granted that his oldest daughter would be the new mother of the family. At the age of eight, she cooked, cleaned, washed, ironed, and mothered the younger children as well as going to school herself. The father was very strict and showed no appreciation for what she did. It became clear in the treatment that his fear of an incestuous relationship with his daughter was a strong determinant of this behavior. She spent most of her time trying to be the "good little wife and mother," always trying to please and extract some signs of love and never succeeding. She lived out her "oedipal" fantasies in a masochistically compulsive way. Her attempts to get love only met with rejection, yet she never stopped trying in a compulsively repetitive way. Her anger at the father for his lack of response and at the mother for leaving her was completely repressed, as was even her anger at all the responsibilities she had. She "used" reaction formation and was a model child. As this material was discussed in treatment, she always cried. There was and is much abreaction.

Whenever the mother visited the family, the young girl continued to try to win her love (as she still does to some extent).

The preoedipal relations with mother and father, as far as the memories permit reconstruction, involved more attention and care-taking from the father than the mother, who was always tired and annoyed by the duties of housekeeping and child rearing. This pat-tern of interaction—receiving care from the father and being re-jected by the mother—formed the basis of later attempts to seek love and protection in a masochistic way. She chose men who were as un-giving as her father and repetitively tried to "extract" love from them. She always expected rejection and abandonment from women. From the data I was able to obtain, the father appeared to have been more giving when the children were infants and his wife lived with them. After the mother left, he became more withdrawn. This put the child into a state of confusion in relation to both her parents. However, the negative feelings were always pushed away, and the fear of separation and rejection resulted in overcompliant behavior, which never accomplished its aims.

The separation anxiety, fear of loss, and the masochism, all came out clearly in the transference with me. Not only my vacation, but even a change of hour, had to be understood in terms of the mother's departure. The masochistic pattern was demonstrated by her interpreting any change of schedule as a rejection of her. Sim-ilarly, many interpretations were seen as "criticisms" by her. The masochism was central in her choice of a husband. He was both phy-sically and psychologically cruel to her, yet she stayed with him for three years, always hoping, as she had with her father, that if she were a good enough girl, he would love her at long last. After her divorce, her choices of men were better, but they still repeated the old patterns to a lesser degree. At present she has succeeded in mak-ing what seems to be a good object choice.

The extraordinary lack of mother-child interaction of a positive kind, and the child's reaching out to the father, who was more avail-able psychologically then even though he always left for work in the morning, set the pattern of a negative self image and constant fear of rejection. This fear in later years was accompanied by an intense need to please, which in turn led to a masochistic repetition compul-sion in adult life. Mrs. A. had to please everyone—her co-workers, friends, lovers, me.

The early negative self image was reinforced by the precipitating traumas. The loss of the grandmother stirred up the rage and sadness at the mother's departure from the home. Mixed with her mourning were guilt feelings, "as if" she had been the bad girl who "caused" mother's departure. The divorce, even though she was the one who wanted it, was another separation and loss and therefore stirred up some of the old feelings, which were mixed with feelings of great relief.

Thus, to sum up the aspects of the case which illustrate the main points of this paper: we see a "life-style" of compulsively repeating masochistic interactions with people which follow the pattern of her early relationships. Her defense mechanisms of denial and repression were a precise mirroring of the ways that both parents handled painful affects and experiences. She is gradually, in twice-a-week psychoanalytically oriented psychotherapy, gaining insight, abreacting, and attempting to change the old counterproductive repetitions. One obvious change is her mastery of the oral trauma to the extent that she lost 75 pounds, without discussion of dieting by me.

The need to repeat may interfere with psychological growth on all levels. The transitions in life from one developmental stage to another are often made extremely painful by the repetition of feelings and behavior of earlier stages which are then no longer appropriate to reality. This is especially true of adults who repeat the preoedipal and oedipal conflicts in many of their most important emotional relationships.

Although we cannot erase the early internalized images and interactions, especially if there has been a fixation, good treatment sometimes succeeds in sufficiently modifying a person's established patterns so that he or she can lead a happier and more productive life.

References

Asch, S. S. (1976), Varieties of negative therapeutic reaction and problems of technique. *J. Amer. Psychoanal. Assn.*, 24:383–407.

Berliner, B. (1947), On some psychodynamics of masochism. *Psychoanal. Quart.*, 16:459–471.

Bibring, E. (1943), The conception of the repetition compulsion. *Psychoanal. Quart.*, 12:486–519.

Fenichel, O. (1945), *The Psychoanalytic Theory of Neurosis.* New York: Norton.

Freud, S. (1914), Remembering, repeating and working-through. *Standard Edition*, 12:145–156. London: Hogarth Press, 1958.

—— (1920), Beyond the pleasure principle. *Standard Edition*, 18:3–64. London:

Hogarth Press, 1955.
_____ (1933), New introductory lectures on psycho-analysis. *Standard Edition,* 22:3–182. London: Hogarth Press, 1964.
Gero, G. (1936), The construction of depression. *Int. J. Psycho-Anal.,* 17:423–461.
Kernberg, O. F. (1976), *Object Relations Theory and Clinical Psychoanalysis.* New York: Jason Aronson.
Reik, T. (1941), *Masochism in Modern Man.* New York: Farrar, Straus.
Winnicott, D. W. (1965), *Maturational Processes and the Facilitating Environment.* New York: International Universities Press.

13
PROJECTION
From Projective Identification To Project

ANDRÉ GREEN, M.D.

TRANSLATED BY JACQUES HOUIS AND J. NAIMAN

The verb *to project,* the adjective *projective,* the nouns *projection* and *project* do not belong exclusively to the terminology of psychoanalysis. These terms are used in a number of other disciplines; ballistics, physics, geometry, architecture, and physiology all attribute their own specific meanings to projection. Even philosophy, thanks to Condillac, has a theory of projection, according to which "sensations, felt originally as simple modifications of the mental state, are then 'projected' outside of the self (that is to say, localized at points in space other than where the thinking subject imagines himself to be), and only then acquire the appearance of independent reality" (Lalande, 1951). This description brings us quickly to the heart of the problem: the relationship of projection to reality via the medium of appearance. Psychoanalytic theory, which is based on clinical experience, thanks to Freud, lays claim to the concept of projection by specifying it. It is regrettable, however, that Freud either abandoned the idea of clarifying this concept or destroyed the rough draft of the paper which was to have been included in the *metapsychology.* Since Freud, there has been no shortage of contributions to the theory of projection. The concept of *projective identification* has dominated the metapsychology of M. Klein (1957) and her pupils, most notably Bion (1967). For some time the writings of psychoanalysts have featured a term long considered the preserve of Sartre and his disciples and, even more recently, of molecular biology: the *project.*

Where, how, and why projection in light of these two concepts? •

301

Summary of Basic Facts and Fundamental Problems

A certain number of clinical and theoretical facts must be reviewed before Freud's work on projection can be examined (Laplanche and Pontalis, 1973).

1. Projection is linked to a primary defense mechanism fundamentally defined by the action of expelling, of casting out (to project = to spit, to vomit) something from within which is unpleasant, disagreeable, even intolerable, but which had previously been introjected.

2. Projection has the effect of placing outside (outside of the ego) something judged undesirable (or excessively desired), but which had arisen inside. The danger is thus externalized.

3. Projection by externalizing is a means of self-defense against the internal by means of a counterexcitation, which treats the instinctual drive (internal excitation) as if it were a perception (external excitation).

4. Projection, which is a universal and normal defense, can become pathological inasmuch as it entails a radical misreading of the instinctual drives found within the subject.

5. Via displacement of the subject's cathexes toward the exterior, projection leads to a knowledge of the object which, although greatly dependent on the subject's input and therefore a distorted perception of the object's reality, nevertheless allows for a real knowledge of the object's unconscious. Of course, this knowledge of the object's unconscious is acquired at a cost—a radical misreading of the subject's unconscious; but the detour via knowledge of the object does constitute, by way of reflection, an implicit yet concealed knowledge of the subject.

This basic summary brings up a number of fundamental problems:

1. Projection is solidly linked to introjection: the projected can only be what has already been introjected. Only that which has been swallowed can be vomited.

2. Projection raises the question of the distinction between inside and outside, that is to say, of the split which allows this distinction to be made. This split is twofold since it affects not only the division of the inner world from the outer world, but also the division of the inner world into conscious-preconscious on the one hand, and

unconscious on the other.

3. Projection is inextricably linked to perception. A *passage a la limite* allows a dimension of the id (the projected material) to be transformed into a dimension of the ego (that which is perceived by projection).

4. Closely related to paranoia, projection raises the question of the relationship between, on the one hand, the shifting of an excess not tolerated by the psychic apparatus, which periodically expels what it cannot master, and, on the other hand, the subject's radical misreading which is expressed in delusions.

5. Projection forces us to examine the relationship between the subject and the other. The other, as we have seen, is both known and unknown: unknown because he is visible only through the distorting mirror that is the subject's image of him; known because this image corresponds nevertheless to a certain reality. Freud (1937) acknowledged this when he said that every delusion contains a kernel of truth.

This implies that:

1. There is a homologous or isomorphic relationship between the subject and the object since a kernel of truth links both of them through the delusion.

2. This knowledge/lack of knowledge (misreading) relationship is the product of a *construction*. This construction is not only *in* the other's space, but is also *of* that space as the externalization of the subject's inner space. This construction is a *theoretical construct*, a theory of the object which refers back to the theory of the subject, as the theory of what is foreclosed within his *own* space.

Projection and Instinctual Drive

Let us return to a more down-to-earth metapsychology. When we link, as Freud did, projection to instinctual drive, we return to the most basic concept in psychoanalysis; the primordial and definitive distinction that Freud drew between internal and external excitation is the basis of metapsychology. The instinctual drive or internal excitation is that constant tension which cannot be eliminated and from which we cannot flee. The complexity and obscurity of this concept of instinctual drive stem from the fact that it joins an internal somatic source to an external psychic object. Thus the instinctual drive and its movement (and we know there are those who refuse to see any difference between the two) connect a source located in the depths of the body to an object outside of this body which alone is able to extinguish the fire located—if I may be forgiven this paradox—at its source. The instinctual drive is destined, therefore, to be projected—to the extent that it is only by becoming bound, in order to reach the object capable of satisfying its aim, that the instinctual drive *exits toward the object,* tracing the path that leads movement to the object, hence to its aim. This path is necessarily projective in that it is directed outward, where the object is located.[1] We know that this path is unavoidable because the subject lacks the object; it is not available to him. In an ideal situation, where the object becomes immediately available when it is needed, there is no projection because the subject is spared the path and only has to greet the object which anticipates his desires. I have called this an *ideal situation.* It is, in fact, the nucleus of what we call *idealization* of the object—an object which is never the cause of any frustration and, consequently, of any projection. There is nothing to project. The subject has no project (to use the word in its most ordinary sense), because the object has anticipated it.[2] There is also nothing to project, in the more restricted sense of the word, because there is no frustration; therefore there is no aggression, since aggression arises from the need to release tension, and without frustration there is no tension. We are well acquainted with the other side of this coin: the dependence on the feeding object, and the blockage of psychic activity that we encounter in transferences where the analyst is idealized. But this idealization is, as we know, a primitive defense, like projection,[3] because this ideal situation, like all ideal situations, cannot exist. Frustration is therefore inevitable and, as a conse-

[1]It must also be stressed that the movement by which the instinctual drive becomes bound, a forward movement, sets off its own reactive movement and engenders a reflection of the forward movement into its backward opposite. Alongside this movement, toward the outside, there is then, from the outset, a corresponding movement of return to the inside. The orientation is from the start both centrifugal and centripetal.

[2]In his studies of the mother-child relationship, Winnicott (1958) clearly described the developmental phase dominated by this problem, but which, for me, extends well beyond this phase.

[3]In fact, this idealization is itself a projection of the ego's idealization onto the object—at least in the Kleinian conception where the good, like the bad, is projected after denial.

quence, so is projection.

This brings me to the most basic form of projection where, after projection is a mode of the instinctual drive, the projected material is the undesirable, that is to say, the unpleasant, the intolerable. A question arises which the theory of projection finds difficult to answer: does this type of projection imply that the distinction between inside and outside has already been acquired? Freud addressed this problem by postulating the existence of a reality ego which distinguishes, from the start, between the ego and the outer world by detecting the internal or external origins of excitation. What seems essential to me, in this case, is the attempt to cast off, through a centrifugal movement, that part of the body where the tension is felt. This is less a projection than an *excorporation,* of which the motor discharge is the behavioral manifestation—cries, tears, motor agitation. Here, a discussion of whether or not the outside as such exists, seems of little importance to me. The outside, then, is the "out of" or the "outside of"—Get out, demons!—Leave my body! This initial action performs excorporation, exorcism.[4] In my opinion, one can speak of projection only when an object can receive the excorporated. A *projective plane* is then constituted which receives the projected material.

Before going any futher, let me reiterate that only what has been incorporated can be excorporated. This can happen retroactively. In other words, the good object is not experienced as good when pleasure is obtained from it. Rather, this pleasure is perceived as such when it is lacking, cruelly lacking, and its place is taken by the unpleasure of the lack, which is the lack of the pleasurable object, the lack of pleasure. The search for pleasure is therefore, in essence, the attempt to recover a lost pleasure. The possibility of pleasure—which I do not intend to deny—is always shadowed by its negative double, the nostalgia for the rediscovery of lost pleasure. Add to this orientation toward the past the project for the future: "Next time I'll keep it and I'll never lose it again." Such is the fantasy-promise of the object's return. Fidelity is sworn to it. Nevertheless, when the joy of rediscovery has passed, the threat of loss reappears. And the cycle begins again—incorporation, loss, desire, frustration,

---

[4]I note in passing that for Tausk (1933), the first projection takes place inside the body and corresponds to finding the object for the first time. One could validly agree that this point in time necessarily precedes preliminary expulsion.

aggression, excorporation.

But this view of things is far too simple. It accounts only for the centrifugal aspect of expulsive projection. If we generalize the hypothesis according to which any progressive movement is reflexive and creates its inverted double in the form of a retrogressive movement, we can see that the projective movement is accompanied by an introjective movement. In other words, the excorporation of something previously incorporated provokes a partial reincorporation of the excorporated. It is as if, whatever the effort to expel the bad, something were opposed to its loss, which in the final analysis remains a narcissistic amputation. The "beyond" of *Beyond the Pleasure Principle* (Freud, 1920) is at work here in the shape of a return to the previous state, be it unpleasant or even unbearable, where perhaps we find one of the earliest forms of primary masochism as well as one of the subject's first reflections.[5]

Later, when the object is cathected, when its existence (preceding its perception) is "experienced," the aim inhibition, which prevents both a complete erotic fusion with the object and its total destruction by the death instinct, will provide a structure for this retroaction. This dual reversal (into its opposite and against itself) constitutes, along with splitting, one of the fundamental structuring activities of the instinctual drive. Projection, as Braunschweig (1971) and Fain (1966), as well as myself, have shown, manifests itself then as a negation, or rather, a *diversion*, of the dual reversal.

Projective Identification

Projection begins when the object provides a surface for projection. This suggests the metaphor of the mirror. But before dealing with this very special object, I would like to consider the case of objects which do not provide a reflecting surface. Other less narcissistically cathected objects crop up, beside the breast and the mirror. This is where the Kleinian concept of projective identification comes in. According to Hanna Segal (1964), "Projective identification is the result of the projection of parts of the self into an object. It may result in

[5]It must be carefully stressed that this excorporation of the instinctual drive is the precondition of the ego's cathexis, this exclusion being the matrix for subsequent splitting and for the cathexis, in due time, of the object as a replica of the ego, but with the additional task of working through its loss.

the object being perceived as having acquired the characteristics of the projected parts of the self but it can also result in the self becoming identified with the object of its projection" (p. 105).

Rosenfeld (1969) delineated the functions of projective identification in the transference. It can be used (1) to communicate preverbal experiences, (2) to deny psychic reality by expelling bad parts of the ego, and (3) to control the body of the transference object.

Projective identification is a defense primarily triggered by primitive aggression. Whether it is due to frustration or envy, it reflects an omnipotent narcissistic position. It implies a premature splitting. It often leads to the establishment of a parasitic relationship in which the analyst replaces the patient's ego. Projective identification contributes to creating in the subject an absolute split between the inner and outer world.

The features I have just reviewed indicate that projection arises simultaneously with splitting. External projection onto an object creates the distinction between an inside (the ego), and an outside (the object), which are divided by the metaphorical barrier of the space that separates them and helps to make them distinct. At the same time, however, this separation is accompanied by its denial. The accompanying fusion takes the shape of the subject's identification with the parts projected onto the object, through a kind of return to sender. In sum, we are faced with the two accepted meanings of the term *to identify:* one meaning in which an object is identified *by* the projection, leading to a second meaning, identification *with* the object, as if the vacuum created by the expulsion were immediately filled by the projection's return.

Bion (1967) gives a metaphorical description of the processes involved in projective identification.[6] Everything happens as if the parts expelled from the ego carry not only the bad objects but also the ego's bad parts. Projected onto external objects, these parts rush into the objects and attempt to seize control of them. What follows is a struggle between the external objects perceived as real and those parasitized by the invasion, the former trying to both poison and master the latter. The world becomes a world of malevolent objects, of bizarre ghosts, hostile to the ego. Worse yet, the real objects para-

[6]The original concept of projective identification is reworked and greatly changed in Bion's subsequent works.

sitized by the fantasized bad ones which now control them are attracted to their former habitat and try to force their way back into the cradle of the ego where they were born. There follows a struggle against their intrusion and a desire actively to resist them. Once more we can detect the reciprocating motion at work, which gives us the alternating images of progression-projection and regression-introjection. This motion belonged to the internal sequence of the instinctual drive movement at its formation. It now shifts over into the field of interaction between the ego and the object.

This image, which is not unlike science fiction — and what is science fiction if not a delusional dream — paints a picture of projection in schizophrenia. As such it would seem to be worthy of attention; on the other hand, it is less satisfactory in addressing paranoia than Freud's conception, which seems more heuristically fertile.

Foreclosed Projection

Projective identification is midway between excorporation and projection. Excorporation, a primitive expulsion, seeks only to project as far as possible in a centrifugal way.[7] Where? Everywhere and nowhere. What is projected is not localized in any precise place; it infiltrates the surrounding space, giving it that affective tone characteristic of the persecutory experience. Unlike projective identification, excorporation dwells not *within* things but *between* them. In projective identification, on the contrary, a receptacle is needed: the analyst's body or the mother's, which allows itself to be more or less passively penetrated by the projected parts. This effusion of objects and narcissism greatly drains the ego, making it anemic. It results in a fragmentation affect which reflects the holes left behind by the projected and exiled parts of the ego. One might think that this loss in the ego would bring about a compensatory outpouring of the id's energies to fill the gap. But that would be tantamount to sending a new Trojan horse into the ego. The result is not an increase in energy capable of restoring the ego's narcissistic and object deficits. It is, rather, an excess of destructive energy, because of the instinctual defusion which would further increase the need to project

---

[7]Language forces me to use this imprecise word, since there is no center here. The desire to avoid a neologism led me not to use the more exact term *locofugal*.

outside and lock the ego in a struggle against the return of the repressed. It is what Freud calls the *repression of reality* in psychosis. The ego's negative hallucination is periodically filled with the products of projection and reconstitutes itself indefinitely.

The foregoing shows the extent to which the meanings Freud gave to projection differ. In his work on Schreber's autobiography, Freud (1911) gives two definitions which would appear contradictory:

1. "An internal perception is suppressed and, instead, its content, after undergoing a certain kind of distortion, enters consciousness in the form of an external perception" (p. 66). Let us note that this involves the effect of a repression followed by a distortion which allows access to consciousness, but only after a displacement which changes the internal perception into an external perception. It is then possible to say that *projection changes instinctual drive into perception.* This process is not limited to paranoia, however, since it also applies perfectly to phobia and to dream.

2. "It was incorrect to say that the perception which was suppressed internally is projected outwards; the truth is rather, as we now see, that what was abolished internally returns from without" (p. 71).

The change in definitions involves the difference between "repression" and "abolition" on the one hand, and, on the other, the distinction between projection from the inside toward the outside and the return of the abolished from the outside to the inside. It is a clear reversal in direction, centrifugal in the first case, centripetal in the second. Freud is specifying psychotic projection: the abolition that Lacan (1956) has called *foreclosure,* thereby eliminating the phase of centrifugal projection, and considering projection the return of projected material, no aspect of which allows us to think that the return was preceded by a departure. A synthetic definition would allow us to think of projection as an uninterrupted coming and going, the first phase of which is foreclosed in the paranoiac.

These considerations permit a breakdown of projective operations into their component parts:

Phase 0:   Foreclosed—I (a man) love him (a man).

Phase 1:   The verb turns into its opposite—I don't love him, I hate him.

Phase 2:   The subject and object trade places—I hate him. He hates me.

Phase 3:   Rationalization—I don't love him. I hate him because he's persecuting me.

Lacan's formulation prompts several comments:

1. Changing the verb into its opposite suggests that the coming and going, a bringing together (I love him), is turned into an estrangement (I hate him). *Aversion is the reversion of a desire perceived as a perversion* (i.e., homosexuality). In this connection, it should be noted that Freud's expression, "I love him," may lack precision. It would be better to say, "I want to be loved," which implies that the desire is initially a passive one, an active desire to be loved passively (and masochistically). The verb's reversal thus implies a switch from passivity to activity (I love him), and then into its opposite (I hate him), a double reversal.

2. The inversion of subject and object suggests an identification between the terms "I" and "he" which become interchangeable: "I am him"; "He is me." Strictly speaking, there is no actual reversal onto the person himself. In relation to "I hate him," "He hates me" becomes a primarily passive construction: "I am hated by him." This formula has the advantage of preserving the "I" of "I hate him." The shift to the "he" effects a shift to the object: "It is he who hates me." There is an almost imperceptible nuance in the difference between "I am hated by him" and "He hates me." This nuance, nevertheless, accounts for the change in the initiative inherent in the shift from the passive "I" to the active "he." A structure of exchange between the two split entities then takes over. The split between the "I" and the "he" is retained; the two terms are not confused but exchanged. Three possibilities emerge:

1. No splitting. I = he = everything = nothing.

2. The presence of a split, but with the possibility of substituting the split terms: Love/Hate, I/he, and exclusion of one of the two.

3. Splitting with coexistence of the two terms separated by the split, in spite of the contradiction. I love him and/or I hate him; I hate him and/or he hates me. Both are true. This is the path to splitting as it appears in fetishism.

The Other

By introducing the "he" we are brought to the issue of the other. The other is the nonego and the non-I: nonego insofar as it is what my ego refuses to be and casts out of itself; non-I insofar as it is distinct from my person and not to be confused with my identity. When Lacan says of the other that it is the "place of the truth,"* he is referring to this other which corresponds to the foreclosed part of the ego, and which, because of its object status, is able to arouse my wish and consequently reveal me to myself.

But these remarks remain limited in scope. They are complemented by Freud's work of 1922 which added considerably to the entire theory of projection. It is not true that projection restricts me to an absolute misreading of reality. Projection is a measure of knowledge and constitutes access to a certain truth. What is projected onto the other undeniably reveals something about him: something the object's ego mistakes but the projecting subject recognizes. Thus, Othello is not mistaken when he senses in Desdemona a certain attraction for Cassio. His own desire for Cassio is foreclosed. My conclusion is that projection can reveal something about the object, and that what is foreclosed is the projecting subject's wish. In the final analysis the other is none other than the subject's own unconscious. At this point, difficulties surface which had heretofore gone unnoticed.

If the "projector" (the one who projects) can, while attributing to the object his own wishes, arrive at a real knowledge of said object, projection cannot be completely dismissed, as it becomes a mode of knowledge. This brings to mind Clerambault's remark to a patient afflicted with delusional jealousy: "May it please God that it should be enough to be cuckolded in order not to be delusional!"* To admit this is to offer the hypothesis of a certain homology or isomorphism[8] between the I and the other, since the I's projection — which is constructed according to the I's unconscious, but foreclosed — has its true counterpart in the unconscious of the other. On the other hand, it also means setting up the option of either (a) knowing the self and considering the other unknowable, or (b) knowing the other and considering the self unknowable. Here, I am touching, on the question of the construction of the other's space. This construct is "theoretical" in much the same way as Freud's concept of sexual theory.

---

*The editors were unsuccessful in locating the sources referred to, in this instance as well as those subsequently marked by an asterisk.

[8]The geometric sense of the term is applicable.

The other exists; I cannot ignore his existence. But I can only know him though myself. At the same time I cannot know the space of the other within me. Nevertheless, if I can get to know the other—with a knowledge that is truthful even though projected, and even if by knowing him I mistake myself—it is in constituting his space that I construct my own at the same time.

It follows that the other's wish, which I adopt, becomes the basis for the division within myself. In other words, the unity acquired at great expense by the ego, through narcissistic cathexis, can be attained only by referring to the pairs persecuted/persecutor, ego/object, inside/outside, conscious/unconscious. The conjunction-disjunction—internal conscious ego/external other's unconscious—is reflected in the conjunction-disjunction—internal conscious ego/other's internal unconscious.

This process implies the functioning of a surface-to-surface relationship, since mirror reflection is at work here. This is a good time to recall that Freud defines the ego as the body's surface of projection; the other is its mirror.[9] The mirror established on the surface of the ego's projection is the meeting place for the body projected from within and the other's image from without. Both sides of this mirror would, in other words, reflect, creating an image the components of which belong as much to the inside as to the outside.

It is clear that this logic is contrary to the logic of psychoanalysis, which argues that knowledge of the other improves as the subject pushes back the limits of his own unconscious. My conclusion is that this factor of deception must be a characteristic of the logic of paranoia.

The Narcissistic Homoerotic Object and the Projective Screen

It may be that the solution to these theoretical difficulties is provided by Freud's (1911) study of the mechanisms of paranoia: "we can assert that the length of *the step back from sublimated homosexuality to narcissism* is a measure of the amount of *regression* characteristic of paranoia" (p. 72). The recognition of homosexuality in paranoia by

[9]Let us note, however, that this reflection is not the totality of the ego-other relationship, but its fascinating narcissistic component coexisting with an "objective" knowledge of the other. Nevertheless, this knowledge is subjugated in the projection-foreclosure for reasons I am about to go into.

post-Freudian authors has not always taken into account the relationship between *sublimated* homosexuality and narcissism. It is difficult to know precisely what Freud is trying to tell us here. It is not a question of perverse homosexuality but of a homosexuality which has been sublimated, that is to say, displaced, inhibited as to aim, and *desexualized*. The relationship between a sublimated homoerotic object and the subject's narcissism has not been worked out. It is their correspondence which allows the exchange between ego and other. The ego, especially in its ideal part, is formed by narcissistic cathexes which have effected the desexualization, the aim inhibition, and the displacement of sexual interests. It therefore corresponds exactly to the image of the other as a sublimated homoerotic object. It is understandable that the ego allows itself to be so easily fascinated by an object fashioned from the subject's own narcissistic desires.[10] Just as God made man in his own image, the paranoiac makes the object resemble himself. It was inevitable that we would turn to the idea of a mirror's surface — or even better and closer to Freud's theory — to a projector and screen. Narcissism allows the ego to be unified. In other words, the transition from ego instincts to narcissism occurs through the constitution of the ego's projective plane as a reflecting surface. The narcissistically cathected ego tries to become an object to the id by attempting a seduction. It takes on the characteristics of the ideal object. The narcissism gathers its energy from the desexualization of the instinctual drives which come from the id and which the ego appropriates. Since the purpose of this narcissistic seduction is for the ego to model itself after the ideal object, it seems logical that this reflected and reflecting (projected and projecting) narcissism will constitute a projection screen upon which a homologous image of the other will appear. The cathexis of the other will project onto him the image of the ego and, in turn, the other will project this image onto the ego, reinforcing its deception. In paranoia this cathexis bears the mark of homoeroticism, a unity of subject and object based on each having the same sexual appearance. We must add, however, that such a cathexis is sublimated and narcissistic. In other words, there is a relationship of narcissistic identification between the ego and the other through their mutual projections. This projective current is duplicated by an introjective cur-

---

[10]This is the essential difference between phobic projection, in which there is a shift of libidinal cathexis, and paranoid projection, in which there is a shift of narcissistic projection.

rent, the other absorbing the ego's projections and vice versa. To the projective screen on the surface of the ego corresponds another projective screen located outside of the ego in the mirror formed by the other. The situation is alienating in that neither the ego nor the other can locate each other because the image is constantly bouncing back and forth between the ego's internal mirror and the other's external mirror. When the paranoiac becomes aware of this, he no longer knows where he is, he is no longer sure of the efficacy of projection, the split loses its effectiveness, he depersonalizes.

In paranoia the other, the object of the wish, is the blank screen upon which the subject's interior film materializes. This "movie," encountering a surface capable of receiving its signs, distributes those features capable of reflecting to the projecting subject the structures of his narcissism. Here, adding to the outside corresponds to subtracting from within; as if the more we see outside, the blanker the internal screen. The more the other shows its signs, the more blank the subject becomes. Absolved of his wishes, he becomes a virgin surface passively receiving the other's messages. Henceforth, fascinated by the other in reality, his eye is glued to the screen without being able to tear itself away from it — to the extent that he can no longer distinguish between the eye of the camera and the image on the screen. His eye is *in* the image on the screen and is an integral part of the projected feature. It is the screen and the projection, all in one. This position is the opposite of the neurotic's who, although succumbing to fascination, nevertheless retains the ability to see himself seeing. His eye witnesses the spectacle precisely insofar as he sees himself with the eye of another who is *absent* from the spectacle.

Thus, the key to the enigma is in this narcissistic relationship. This conforms to the clinical data, since we are dealing with paranoid psychosis. It could be that things are additionally complicated by the fact that I attributed to paranoid projection the maintenance of the split, with both parties switching places. The split is not constituted by the screen since the screen is not recognized as such, but by the distinction effected between love and hate, as between I and he. In fact, it is not the whole eye which is projected; it is the bad eye, the one you have to get rid of — forbidden, passive, homosexual love; a narcissistic homosexual love which, because of its cathectic requirements, endangers maintenance of the ego's narcissism.

Because of foreclosure, however, the split remains totally unconscious and the projected material — the bad eye — stays glued to the fabric of the screen. This eye, rather than looking, is destined to be looked at. The alienation created by this relationship of narcissistic fascination stems from the fact that it involves cathexes belonging to the subject's being rather than to his having. One could say that "Someone is keeping an eye on him," provided that one supplements this expression with another which says, "He's got someone under his skin."

The narcissistic cathexis of the object must necessarily return to the ego, since it belongs to it. It is therefore not the ordinary return of repressed libidinal material, but is a reappropriation, as inevitable as it is undesirable — hence the intense struggle surrounding the projection's return from the outside. The narcissistic cathexis seeks to reenter its own home, while repression aims at closing the door. This is the essential difference between paranoid projection and phobia.

Finally, in this structure, paranoid projection specifies the role of homosexuality: it is foreclosed and narcissistic. Bak (1946) and Mallet (1966) have emphasized its link with masochism, which is not surprising when one considers the links between narcissism and masochism. Masochism itself undergoes an important transformation. By turning into its opposite, it shows itself in a clear sadism toward the object (I do not love him, I hate him.). What seems to me characteristic of paranoia, compared with the more regressive, schizoparanoid forms, is that sadism cathects a unified object which has boundaries identified by the subject and with which the subject identifies. Indeed, narcissistic and homoerotic cathexis provides sadism with a framework. Instead of the diffuse sadism of projective identification, we are dealing with a sadism that is concentrated and applied to a single object. Identification has replaced scattering. A single split has replaced multiple splits (fragmentation). Sadism seems to be a product of the rejection of primary masochism, the more advanced forms of which are expressed by a rejection of passivity. Sadism contributes to the formation of the ego as a unified entity, through the dominance it asserts over the object of its attentions. On the other hand, the reintegration of this sadism turns back into masochism to the extent that the ego is a victim of the superego's supervision. The split becomes internal between a resexualized superego, allied to the id, which persecutes the ego and leads to an ever-increasing alienation. The ego's response is the foreclosed projection of this masochism, now transformed into the object's sadism toward the subject: "He hates me," allowing for self-defense.

The formation of delusion deserves its name of *neoreality* because foreclosure radically rejects the subject's wish. The struggle is shifted into the real or, more specifically, into the *social reality* of ego and other, a struggle that opposes neoreality to the real which is subject to repression — repression of reality.

Two Versions of Primary Narcissism

We know that Freud (1920) gave contradictory versions of primary narcissism. Sometimes he refers to *absolute* primary narcissism as the reduction of tension to the zero level in accordance with the Nirvana principle; sometimes he refers to the result of the passage from auto-erotism to the subject's unification. In a previous work (1967), I defended certain hypotheses regarding the relationship of primary narcissism to the death instinct and the wish for nothing, nothingness, emptiness. I put forth the idea that the negative hallucination of the mother could provide a framework, an empty frame to be filled by object cathexes and ego cathexes. What I am now presenting is the *form* — and I stress this word — taken by the subject's cathexes and the object's cathexes in a relationship of narcissistic complementarity. The object here is modeled on the subject's unified narcissism: the ego and the other are in a relationship of mutual doubling; the one is the other's double. The split is in place, but the terms complement each other and change places, as they always must. Any other outcome is denied them. *Othello* can end only in Desdemona's murder and Othello's suicide; there is no alternative. In the final analysis, the subject's unity is always a fallacy. He oscillates between nothing, zero and the pair he forms with his double: the narcissistic homo-erotic object.

The role of the double (Green, 1970) becomes evident here. It is at once the same and the other, since it stretches resemblance to the point of identity, while preserving otherness through some minimal differences. Mallet (1966) has stressed the older brother's role in male paranoia. This role could be explained by the fact that such a brother is an intermediate imago between the subject and his father, favoring narcissistic identification and the homoerotic object choice. At the same time, the small difference separating the brothers is never eliminated, thus constantly frustrating the subject's wish to reach the narcissistically cathected double's enviable position. Such is the other, my fellowman, my brother. There must be a meta-psychological status for such a position.

We can view it as one of the variants encompassed by Winnicott's concept of the transitional object, a transition between the subject and the object perceived in its difference, between inside and outside, love and hate, the narcissistic and the object-related. Winnicott (1958) defined the transitional object as the first nonego possession, placing it more on the "having" side (*not-me possession*). In my opinion, the double belongs in the "being" category. It is the nonbeing of being, that which being cannot consent to being and cannot help but be. It seems evident that the double is essentially the first object with which the subject changes place. To move away from this compulsory and absolutely determined exchange to an exchange that takes difference into account, however, the double must be repressed (but acknowledged as such, therefore capable of being symbolized) and the field of exchange based on other objects which are not totally stamped with the seal of the subject's narcissism — though I do not think the subject ever frees himself from his narcissistic projection onto the object. This projection, however, no longer constitutes a screen because the eye has torn itself away and now considers its projections from the outside (enabling it to question their projective origin, whatever the value of projection as knowledge). In the transference, the analysand can, at the beginning, score a bull's eye by guessing the truth about his analyst. In the middle of analysis, the analysand is less interested in the projection's content than in its motivation, to the extent that this motivation refers him back to himself. At the end, the analysand arrives both at a real and at a truthful knowledge of the reality of his unconscious and of the being of his analyst. It is what will allow him to express his wish elsewhere, in the elaboration of his own project.

From Projective Identification to Project

We have moved from projective identification to project, if we accept that the wish is always a project. The air of existentialism emanating from this word should not prevent us from using it.[11] What I wish to

---

[11]It was already used by Castoriadis-Aulagnier (1968, 1975).

stress here is that each one of the phases has a corresponding phase belonging to a complementary series. To the *excorporation* of the beginning corresponds *incorporation:* the taking into the subject's body of the object which will be expelled. To Melanie Klein's *projective identification* corresponds *introjective identification,* defined by Segal (1964) as the result of the process by which "the object is introjected into the ego which then identifies with some or all of its characteristics" (p. 105). To *projection* corresponds *introjection.* To the *project* (wish) corresponds *identification.* Without exception, Freudian thought works in pairs. Such is the whole history of the transference which, in those fortunate cases where it can be and is analyzed, ends in the freed play of the wish outside of the transference substitutes of analyst and in identification with the analyzing function.

These pairs involve specific cathexes of erogenous zones. In my opinion, the incorporation-excorporation pair calls forth a primarily oral relationship. The introjective identification-projective identification pair implies the participation of the anal zone (or perhaps better, both oral and anal). The introjection-projection pair, so strongly marked by narcissism, brings into play the matrix of the phallic-narcissistic relationships, in its search for a complete homoerotic unity and mutuality.

In the various phases I have outlined, the pairing of object libido and narcissistic libido must be taken into consideration. The cathexis of erogenous zones concentrates a great quantity of libidinal cathexis in these areas, making these sites of exchange between inside and outside veritable foci. Beyond these erogenous zones, however, the body's surface is narcissistically cathected. As the mouth and anus, being poles of entry and exit, are libidinally cathected, so is the rest of the body's surface negatively cathected when these orifices close. The closed mouth and the contracted anus allow for the filling of the body cavity and an increase in tension at the periphery. In the phallic narcissistic position of paranoia, sublimated, desexualized homosexuality corresponds to the intense narcissistic cathexis of the body's surface, including the penis's, as cathexis of the phallic "shape." In extreme cases, this penis can become foreclosed in the real as an influencing machine. One could add that when the ego's constitution is primarily narcissistic, the other represents its phallic complement; and when the other is narcissistically cathected, the ego assumes the phallic function. Only the advent of castration and sexual differences introduces the dimension of both the oedipus complex and neurosis. In this regard, the real, which can be considered as existing from the beginning (see the reality ego of the beginning, in Freud), and which acquired definite structure during the anal phase, is formed in two stages: first, with the appearance of the oedipus complex (the two differences, between the sexes and between the generations), and then with the acquisition of the knowledge of the vagina after puberty. Sexual reality is the matrix of a real acquisition of the real. Without wanting to sound pedantic, I stress that this knowledge of the vagina is the precondition of genuine procreation, the effect of which is to increase the possibilities of exchange through the triangulation of the parental couple and the creation of sibling relationships. This progression is also seen in the evolution of the transference in neurotic patients.

We know that the evolution of the transference is marked by the interplay of resistances and interpretations. The analyst's interpretation is related to the patient's projections. It is nevertheless received, in the very early stages of analysis, as if it were a delusional interpretation. In the eyes — or rather, to the ears — of the analysand, the analyst reacts to his speech like a paranoiac who believes that all the messages he receives concern him, whereas nothing, in the language confined by social conventions, would allow for such egocentrism. I should note, however, that the abuse of the power of interpretation which takes the form of "interpreting everything" leads to the same result as projective defense in the patient: rationalization. The analyst rationalizes his inexact interpretations to salvage his power of interpretation.

The work of interpretation leads to displacement of the analyst's simulated and manifest paranoia as the analysand's silent and latent paranoia is recognized. Through *projective induction* and the analysis of projection, interpretation contributes to the gradual lifting of the split between conscious and unconscious, and to a better functioning of the relationship between internal and external reality. Moreover, the split must be maintained and preserved, failing which there would be confusion between subject and object, internal and external worlds. In other words, whereas interpretation extends the field of Eros, it leaves to Thanatos the task of delimiting the separations which are indispensable to maintaining the split. It should be made clear that this analysis of the split should lead, not to the simple in-

tellectual acceptance of the repressed, but to the affective acknowledgment of its reality. The "belief" which originally lulled the ego
into illusions about its reality to the detriment of that of the unconscious now becomes belief in the two-sidedness of the subject and in
the influence of the unconscious on the ego. But the completed analysis — even if it was imperfect — also leads to a belief, undoubtedly
limited but unquestionably effective, in the ego's potential for
change as it reacquires the strength it used to exhaust in counter-
cathexes. The split is therefore maintained, while a recognition is
affirmed of an external reality regulated by its own laws and an internal reality governed by the all-powerful wish. It might be helpful
here to recall that for Freud the result of analysis was the lifting of
the excessive sexualization of object relations and the shift of
cathexes to the social sphere, in the shape of sublimated activities.

Social Reality

One could then question the extent of the split between internal and
external reality, and determine the boundaries of analysis. This
question leads one to envisage the limits of interpretation in the non-
therapeutic applications of psychoanalysis.

It may be necessary to refine our distinctions. The distinction
between external and internal reality is basic yet vague. Internal
reality is not just the reality of the wish, it is also the reality of the
body as the place of need. External reality also is not so simple. I
propose a distinction, within external reality, between social reality
and physical reality. There would be two extremes: the reality of the
body and that of the physical world, which would connect, even
though one belongs to internal reality and the other to external reality; and two intermediate terms, the psychic reality of the wish and
social reality, which are closely interrelated.

Social reality would be subject to the reality of the wish as well
as to the specific order linking men in their struggle to master nature
and to satisfy their needs. Thus the objects of social reality would be
intrinsically double, to the extent that they are at once linked to the
world of the wish and external to it. Here the most difficult part remains: to recognize what in social reality obeys the laws of the realm
that corresponds to the physical world. The problem here may be
that the function of such a realm is to create a mimetic equivalent of

natural laws.

For psychoanalysts the fact that culture is based on wish does not require further proof. But culture is also something else; it implies a technological and political development somewhat independent of wish. This is one more ambiguity of the other. The other is the object of my wish, yet he exists as such, such as my wish will never be able to define him, to justify his existence. I cannot apprehend him, not only because he is the object of a never-fulfilled wish (which guarantees that the lack will have its inalienable space), but also because he exists out of my range. This distinction is the basis of the split between the object-related and the objective. It remains to be seen whether the objective can be an area of study for psychoanalysis when it goes beyond the objectivity of the wish. The extent to which Freud's position implies a difficult choice should be noted. A confirmed materialist, he believed profoundly in the world's objectivity. Yet he also believed in the unknowability of this object world because of the enormous impact of subjectivity on our judgments. Nothing in him, however, led to skepticism; rather, he was impelled to the tireless work of acquiring knowledge in order to attain the greatest possible objectivity in the knowledge of both the inner and the outer world. It should be noted that this position implies that nothing should be entirely subjective in our knowledge of reality or entirely objective either.

Since paranoia has occupied the center of this study of projection, I can hypothetically determine its place in culture as belonging to the realm of social reality. I would maintain that any active culture is based on an implicit paranoia. This paranoia is found in the split which allows the identity of a culture to be affirmed through the difference and rejection of another culture, insofar as it is considered foreign, other. At the same time the foreign culture is loaded with all the evils against which the active culture defends itself, through the considerable narcissistic cathexis effected by casting the other culture into outer darkness. The evil it refuses to recognize in itself, it denounces mercilessly in the other. Any active culture, just as in paranoia, also supposes a reinforcing of sublimated homosexual links among its members. Even so, this sublimation is relative — cultural activity results in a considerable resexualization of social relations, just as in paranoia.

Finally, another aspect of group psychology, the members of an

active culture have a tendency to substitute for their ego ideal the
feared object on the model of the primitive horde's all-powerful
father (Freud, 1921).[12] Today, when the gods are dead, the other as
seat of the truth is represented by the deification of the leader. Social
structures die and are reborn continually.

One wonders if the very condition of a culture's activity does
not reside in its paranoia, otherwise referred to as ideology or group
mysticism, according to Bion (1959). Messianism is part of the
ideology of any culture; it is supported by the idealizing relationship
it establishes with itself, justifying its demands with the claim that it
is only seeking the elimination of evil (a basic paranoid concern),
after which the golden age of shared beatitude will reign, and para-
dise lost will be rediscovered. This does not mean that I reject all
cultures indiscriminately, since I have in mind only those characteristics of social reality which belong to the realm of the wish; and I
have maintained, on the contrary, that the world of the wish is not
sufficient in and of itself to define a social reality which has its objective dimension. When Freud (1930) ends *Civilization and Its
Discontents* by referring to the possible destruction of the human race
and the resulting anxiety, he is not referring to neurotic anxiety but
to *Realangst,* fear in the face of real danger.

The task of psychoanalysts as a cultural group is to avoid this
alienating situation through continual analysis of our conflicts with
social reality, both with other psychoanalytic groups and within our
own group—to avoid the various divisions which split us into sub-
groups. This "permanent analysis" must pursue the dual task of going as far as possible within the limits of the analyzable, and
acknowledging the existence of the extra-analytic, according to Donnet's (1973) formula, as the objective dimension of being. This is yet
another impossible aspect of our profession, since it is the task of
each one of us to draw the shifting boundaries that guide our steps.

The greatest contribution of Denise Braunschweig's profound
"Psychoanalysis and Reality" (1971) may be that it shows us that
reality is not the real. Reality is what happens *in* the real, what is
shown by the painting on the white canvas, with its dramatic or
dramatized images, its forces, its tensions, its history and structure.
The real is something else; it is the empty frame, the white canvas or

[12]In societies where this relationship is less important, mutual identification is
dominant, which does not alter the validity of the above statement.

the projective screen, altogether different from what is happening *within* the frame and *on* the canvas. Where reality is dramatic, the real is neutral. Whether the planet rediscovers its mythical golden age or is blown up by its own destructiveness, the real could not care less. It will continue to exist in one form or another, whether or not there is anyone there to take cognizance of it, to laugh or cry about it.

References

Bak, R.C. (1946), Masochism in paranoia. *Psychoanal. Quart.,* 15:285–301.

Bion, W. R. (1959), *Experiences in Groups.* London: Tavistock.

_____ (1967), *Second Thoughts.* New York: Jason Aronson.

Braunschweig, D. (1971), Psychanalyse et realite. *Rev. Franç. Psychanal.,* 35: 655–800.

Castoriadis-Aulagnier, P. (1968), Demande et identification. *L'Inconscient,* 7:23–65.

_____ (1975), *La Violence de l'interpretation.* Paris: Presses Universitaires de France.

Donnet, J. L. (1973), Le divan bien tempere. *Nouv. Rev. Psychanal.,* 8:23–49.

_____ & Green, A. (1973), *L'enfant de ça: la psychose blanche.* Paris: Editions Minuilt.

Fain, M. (1966), Regression et psychosomatique. *Rev. Franç. Psychanal.,* 30:451–456.

Freud, S. (1910), Five lectures on psycho-analysis. *Standard Edition,* 11:3–56. London: Hogarth Press, 1957.

_____ (1911), Psycho-analytic notes on an autobiographical account of a case of paranoia. *Standard Edition,* 12:3–82. London: Hogarth Press, 1958.

_____ (1920), Beyond the pleasure principle. *Standard Edition,* 18:3–64. London: Hogarth Press, 1955.

_____ (1921), Group psychology and the analysis of the ego. *Standard Edition,* 18:67–143. London: Hogarth Press, 1955.

_____ (1922), Some neurotic mechanisms in jealousy, paranoia and homosexuality. *Standard Edition,* 18:221–232. London: Hogarth Press, 1955.

_____ (1930), Civilization and its discontents. *Standard Edition,* 21:59–145. London: Hogarth Press, 1961.

_____ (1937), Constructions in analysis. *Standard Edition,* 22:255–269. London: Hogarth Press, 1964.

Green, A. (1967), Le narcissism primaire: structure ou etat. *L'Inconscient,* 1:121–157; 2:89–116.

_____ (1969), The psychoanalytic nosography of psychoses. In: *Problems of Psychosis,* ed. P. Doucet & C. Laurin. Amsterdam: Excerpta Medica, 1969, p. 75.

_____ (1970), Repetition, difference, replication. *Rev. Franç. Psychanal.,* 34: 461–501.

_____ (1973), *Le Discours vivant.* Paris: Presses Universitaires de France.

_____ (1974), The double and the absent. In: *Psychoanalysis, Creativity and Literature;* ed. A. Roland. New York: Columbia University Press, 1978, pp. 271–292.

_____ (1975), The analyst, symbolization and absence in the analytic setting. *Int. J. Psycho-Anal.,* 56:1–22.

_____ (1977), The borderline concept. In: *Borderline Personality Disorders,* ed. P. Hartocollis. New York: International Universities Press, pp. 15–44.

Klein, M. (1957), *Envy and Gratitude.* New York: Basic Books.

Lacan, J. (1956), Response au commentaire de Jean Hyppolite sur *Verneinung* de Freud. *La Psychanalyse,* 1:46.

Lalande, A. (1951), *Vocabulaire technique et critique de la philosophie.* Paris: Presses Universitaires de France.

Laplanche, J. & Pontalis, J. B. (1973), *The Language of Psychoanalysis.* New York: Norton.

Mallet, J. (1966), Une theorie de la paranoia. *Rev. Franç. Psychanal.,* 30:63–68.

Rosenfeld, H. (1969), Contribution to the psychopathology of psychotic states. In: *Problems of Psychosis,* ed. P. Doucet & C. Lauvin. Amsterdam: Excerpta Medica, pp. 125–128.

Segal, H. (1964), *Introduction to the Work of Melanie Klein.* London: Heinemann.

Tausk, V. (1933), On the origin of the 'influencing machine' in schizophrenia. *Psychoanal. Quart.,* 2:519–556.

Winnicott, D. W. (1958), *Collected Papers.* New York: Basic Books.

14

ANTISOCIAL BEHAVIOR AND
PERSONALITY ORGANIZATION

Sidney J. Blatt, Ph.D. and Shula Shichman, M.A.

In this paper we shall examine the hypothesis that there are two different personality organizations associated with antisocial behavior
which closely parallel two basic forms of depression. In her formulations of depression, Edith Jacobson (1971) discussed a primary or endogenous depression, which is a consequence of early narcissistic injury, and depression which results from a harsh, punitive, critical
superego. These two types or sources of depression were elaborated
further by Blatt (1974) who articulated an anaclitic depression characterized by feelings of helplessness, weakness, depletion, and fears of
abandonment; and an introjective depression characterized by feelings of worthlessness, guilt, failure, and a fear of disapproval and cen-
sure. The basic hypothesis of this paper is that these two sources of depression are paralleled by two general personality styles which provide
a psychological context which can motivate delinquent behavior. Because antisocial behavior, particularly in adolescents, is often an expression of underlying despair and depression, the two sources of depression may provide a basis for distinguishing different forms of delinquency and contribute to a further understanding of the dynamics
of antisocial behavior — a topic that was of great interest to Jacobson,
who wrote her first paper on antisocial character formation (1930).

Review of Literature

Despite an extensive literature there still remains considerable ambiguity about the psychodynamics of delinquency. There is a lack of
clarity about essential aspects of delinquency such as definition,

We are indebted to Drs. Anthony LaBruzza, Howard Lerner, and Ira Levine
for their comments on this paper.

325

classification, and etiology. There is inconsistency in the terminology and in the description of various forms of delinquency; different terms are used for similar phenomena, and identical terminology is frequently used by various investigators for different entities. Some of the inconsistency in the literature is caused by the use of broad-ranging diagnostic categories based primarily on symptomatic expressions. Falstein (1958) commented,

> ...actually, delinquency is a commonly used nonpsychiatric nondynamic term comprising many conditions, varying in severity and duration, and derived from different levels of developmental structure and conflict. Much if not all of the confusion in the literature seems to be the result of diagnostic generalizations based on symptoms or on one-sided approaches to an understanding of the subject, resulting in plethora of etiological claims [p. 614].

Another source for the confusion in the field is the failure to keep a distinction between the legal and the clinical point of view. Rather than considering antisocial behavior as a possible symptomatic manifestation of some clinical disturbance, many authors use the term delinquency in a social-legal context. Katz (1972), for example, noted that "juvenile delinquency is not a psychiatric term but a legal one, which encompasses a wide variety of different personality structures" (p. 10).

There has been little comprehensive discussion of delinquency as a consequence of the interaction of multiple factors. Though there is general agreement that delinquency is not a unitary phenomenon, but rather involves several different personality structures, there have only been a few sporadic attempts to study systematically some of the clinical and dynamic issues of these phenomena. There is also consensus that there exist at least three different types of delinquency, but there is considerable variation in the terminology, description, dynamics, and etiology used to define and understand these types of delinquency.

Social Delinquency

The first type of delinquency is generally viewed as consisting of individuals who were raised in a sociocultural milieu which stands in opposition to the general society and its value system. The antisocial behavior in these individuals is a result of adherence to the values of a deviant culture or of identification with a criminal environment. This type of delinquency has often been referred to in the literature as "socialized" (McCord and McCord, 1964; M. F. Cohen, 1969), "sociopathic" (Van Tessel, 1966; Cromes, 1972), "subcultural" (Hezel, 1969; Stewart, 1972), "sociologic" (Szurek, 1942; Johnson, 1959) and "socialized-subcultural" (Hetherington et al., 1971).

Johnson (1959) presents a survey of some of the major explanations of subcultural, sociologic, or gang delinquency. Some suggest that the disorder is "traditional" and passed on from generation to generation. The theory of "social disorganization" maintains that sociologic delinquency develops in particular areas in large cities which are not only economically depressed but densely populated, highly mobile, without much sense of community definition and pride, and a cohesive social structure. The "social disorganization" or "cultural origin" theory is supported by a great deal of data, which demonstrate the continuity of delinquency within a delinquent tradition. Shaw and McKay (1931) and Hewitt and Jenkins (1946), for example, found that delinquent cultural tradition was likely to develop in "substandard homes" within lower socioeconomic areas of the city (Johnson, 1959, p. 581).

Johnson (1959) discusses how the adult world in these subcultures fails to present a clear-cut model of authority, and the child is unable to develop respect for any moral code. While there may be a unity in the moral codes in these subcultures, the values are incongruent with the larger society. Hirschberg (1954), for example, emphasizes how the sociologic delinquent is directly and consciously influenced by environmental factors to stand in opposition to more conventional values. A. K. Cohen (1955) discusses delinquency as developing because the delinquent's social world fails to provide any support for respecting the conventional legal order. He suggests that being reared in a society with standards different from middle-class conventions eventually leads to a sense of frustration and loss of self-esteem. The subculture rewards attack on the traditional middle-class system, and these rewards serve as a compensation for the frustration inherent in the differences between early life experiences and middle-class standards (Johnson, 1959). Thus, there are a number of dimensions that have been considered as etiological factors in social delinquency such as poverty, child abuse and neglect, lack of consistent supervision, adult anti-social role models, and clashes between social classes.

Neurotic Delinquency

Social or cultural delinquency stands in contrast to delinquency which is a symptomatic expression of psychological conflicts within the individual. The interplay of dynamic forces creates antisocial behavior as an enactment of conflicts and as an attempt to resolve these conflicts. These individuals experience strong guilt feelings, a sense of inferiority, anxiety, remorse, discomfort, and conflict about their antisocial activity. This type of delinquency has been referred to as "neurotic" (Van Tessel, 1966; Powell, 1967; Post, 1968; M. F. Cohen, 1969; Hezel, 1969; Cromes, 1972; Stewart, 1972), "acting-out neurotic" (McCord and McCord, 1964), "borderline neurotic" (Aichhorn, 1925), "The unconsciously driven delinquent" (Johnson, 1959), and the "neurotically disturbed" (Hetherington et al., 1971).

Neurotic delinquency has been discussed as involving a variety of phenomenological issues and etiological dynamics. Guilt, harshly punitive or excessively permissive parental attitudes, shame, and problems in sexual identification have all been suggested as major etiological and dynamic factors in this form of delinquency.

Guilt has been conceptualized as a central dynamic in neurotic delinquency. Freud (1923) comments, "In many criminals, . . . it is possible to detect a very powerful sense of guilt which existed before the crime" (p. 52). Alexander (1930) conceived of the need for self-punishment as a motive for delinquent acting out. According to Jones (1929) as well as Hill (1938), hate can be used to conceal a deeper layer of guilt. Anger and hate can be an attempt to deal with guilt or with the feelings of impotence it causes. Menninger (1938) saw some criminality as a form of masked self-destructiveness. Having yielded to aggressive impulses, these individuals are obliged to surrender in the end to their conscience and guilt and seek punishment. An overwhelming hate, developed in childhood, is expressed toward society at the price of intimidation by the conscience which forces the individual to seek punishment. In her description of the mechanism of identification with the aggressor, Anna Freud (1936) notes that a number of people remain arrested at the intermediate stage in the development of the superego. In this preliminary phase of moral development the ego introjects the authority's criticism and projects prohibited impulses outward. Indignation at someone else's transgression is the precursor of and substitute for guilt feelings. Others (e.g., W. Reich [in Fenichel, 1945a]; Klein, 1948; Eissler, 1949; A. K. Cohen, 1955) have discussed delinquency as an attempt to deny conscience. The neurotic delinquent cannot endure the self-punishment and the punitive superego and tries to escape by acting out his guilt feelings (Lampl-de Groot, 1949). Aichhorn (1925) saw guilt and the need for punishment as major determinants of aggressive behavior. Excessively severe and harsh authority figures foster aggression, hatred, and rebellion in the child, and these may give rise to delinquency. The neurotic delinquents are often victims of their own morality. They try to withdraw or to diminish severe superego and ego-ideal demands, but nevertheless the unconscious feelings of guilt are the motivating force behind the delinquency. Bilmes (1965) also viewed the delinquent act as an attempt to escape from conscience. The delinquents feel inadequate to meet the demands of their conscience and try to elude it by defiantly committing delinquent acts. The crime is an effort to gain relief from a sense of guilt by meeting the superego's demand for punishment. The delinquent attempts to nullify his conscience and to escape from it by punishing the environment with his violent activity. Katz (1972) also considers a rigid superego as one of the factors which may lead to delinquency by causing a pervasive sense of guilt and then seeking punishment as a way of relieving this guilt.

For many years antisocial behavior has been explained in terms of extreme feelings of guilt. Recently there has been interest in the etiological factors that lead to the development of a pathologically punitive superego which forces the individual to act out the guilt in antisocial behavior. As early as 1942, Szurek suggested that the parents unconsciously encourage the antisocial behavior of the child, which in turn satisfies aspects of the parents' sometimes unconscious needs. Johnson (1949) observed that antisocial adolescents rarely have a generalized superego weakness but rather lack adequate superego development in certain circumscribed areas of behavior, which she termed "superego lacunae." Often there is a correspondence between the child's superego defects and those of the parents. "The parents may find vicarious gratification of their own poorly-integrated forbidden impulses in the acting out of the child, through their unconscious permissiveness or inconsistency" which encourages and fosters acting out in the child (Johnson and Szurek, 1952, p. 324). The child's acting out also often provides "a channel for the hostile, destructive impulses of the parent. . . . The asocial impulses of the child may serve the two-fold purpose of allowing the parent vicarious gratification of forbidden impulses as well as expression of hostile, destructive impulses toward the child" (Johnson and Szurek, 1952, p. 238). Giffin et al. (1954) as well as Katz (cited by Falstein, 1958) discuss how children are more or less seduced into their antisocial behavior by the unconscious sanctioning of these activities by their parents. Scharfman and Clark (1967), in an empirical study of familial patterns of delinquent adolescent girls, found parental inconsistency, indifference to the girl's activities, and the mother, often overtly or covertly suggesting delinquent behavior to the child by her actions. This pattern often alternated with unpredictable, irrational, and violent criticism and punishment. The parents consciously objected to the delinquent activity of the girl, while unconsciously they provoked such behavior. In other families there was sexual and aggressive overstimulation, with the girl being exposed to primal scene experiences and parental promiscuity. Frequent violent scenes as well as actual incestuous experiences were commonplace.

The role of shame in juvenile delinquency has also been emphasized as an etiological factor by other investigators. Bilmes (1967) considered the adolescent culture as intrinsically a shame culture where shame can play an important role in provoking delinquency. Major problems in adolescence include achievement, pride, passivity, sexual identity, heterosexual relations, independence, and attaining a sense of self-respect. Failure in any one of these areas can result in humiliation and experiences of shame. Bilmes illustrates how certain social factors predispose the adolescent to experiences of shame: "Facets of contemporary life create in many adolescents a massive need to overcome an inner sense of inferiority, insignificance, and damaged self-esteem and pride. There is a constant and painful threat to their ego ideal and hence constant vulnerability to exposure and shame." A prevalent form of compensation for shame is an attempt to forge a heroic self image by assuming a delinquent role. In various groups of young people such as the alienated, hippies, dropouts, and drug abusers, Unwin (1970) notes a common pattern of depression which is a function of the ego ideal and feelings of shame, rather than of the superego and feelings of guilt. The depression is related to the disparity between the ideal self and the real self (Nicholi, 1967), and a result of a marked disparity between personal standards and performance (Solnit, 1969). Antisocial behavior is an attempt to escape inevitable disillusionment, shame, and depression.

Problems in sexual identification are often discussed as another factor in juvenile delinquency. Rosenfeld (1969) investigated the relationship between sexual identification and delinquency in adolescent boys and viewed the adolescent delinquency as a hypermasculine restitution for a faulty sexual identification. He found that delinquents displayed more unconscious femininity and more conscious masculinity than nondelinquents. Katz (1972) also considers the adolescent male as struggling against passivity, dependency, and a feminine identification by becoming hypermasculine and forming delinquent gangs. Falstein (1958) discusses how oral fixations with accompanying hostile envy and greed in male adolescents lead to strong feelings of being feminine or babyish. These are experienced by the adolescent as shameful homosexuality, which is denied in masculine protest and delinquent behavior. Hostility and defiance become ready defenses against strong passive wishes which are associated with passive, feminine attitudes. James et al. (1967) made a similar observation about delinquent adolescent girls who frequently have problems in feminine identification. Sexual acting out can be an attempt to prove their femininity, to be popular, accepted, or loved.

Psychopathic Delinquency

In addition to social and neurotic delinquency, a third type of individuals who become involved in antisocial activity do not come from a culturally deprived milieu and tend not to present conflicts around superego issues. Their antisocial behavior seems unrelated to dynamic intrapsychic struggles, but rather is a consequence of a unique personality syndrome of impulsivity and aggressiveness, with little capacity for empathy and emotional bonds. This form of delinquency, often labeled as "psychopathic," derives from a failure to internalize available social norms. This lack of socialization and an inability to be concerned about others are manifested in impulsiveness, assaultiveness, and a rebellious, antiauthority, amoral attitude (Hetherington et al., 1971). For many years the term "psychopathy" has been used in an undifferentiated and overinclusive fashion to identify all antisocial individuals. The term and its synonyms have become a "psychiatric wastebasket" (Robins, 1967). Despite theoretical and practical confusion about the concept "psychopathy," there is general agreement about the existence of a distinct psychopathic syndrome.

D. O. Lewis and Balla (1976, p. 41) summarize Cleckley's (1955) more precise definition of the diagnosis of psychopathy using criteria of an undisturbed formal intelligence, unexplained failures, absence of neurotic manifestations, persistent antisocial behavior, irresponsibility, inability to distinguish between truth and falsehood, inability to accept blame, failure to learn by experience, incapability for love, fantastic reactions to alcohol, lack of insight, shallow and impersonal responses to sexual life, and infrequent suicide but persistent patterns of self-defeat. McCord and McCord (1964) described the fundamental profile of the psychopath as asocial, breaking social mores, and clashing with society. The psychopath is driven by uncontrolled desires — absorbed in his own needs and ignoring the needs of others — and by an exaggerated craving for excitement and change. In his self-centered search for pleasure, the psychopath ignores restrictions of his culture. The psychopath is highly impulsive, and his life seems an endless series of unplanned acts. For him, the moment is the essence — it is a segment of time completely detached from the continuity of his life. The psychopath is often very aggressive and has learned few, if any, socialized ways of coping with frustration and delay. He feels little, if any, guilt; his conscience is undeveloped or defective. His capacity for love is warped; his emotional relationships, when present, are meager, fleeting, and designed to satisfy his own desires. In effect, he treats people callously, as means for his own pleasure; and he generally wards off close attachments. Bender (1947) sees the main defect of psychopathy as the inability to form relationships, to identify empathically, and share in the experiences of others. These individuals have difficulty in understanding emotional and social problems and in appreciating appropriate social behavior. The developmental process appears to be fixated at a very early stage; there is little satisfaction derived from human contact and interactions, little access to feelings of anxiety and guilt. The problems appear to be not an expression of superego defect but an impairment in the development of basic ego functions. Greenacre (1945, p. 495) included in the diagnosis of psychopathy all patients with evidence of repeated antisocial behavior but without neurotic or psychotic symptoms. The behavior of these patients is characterized by marked impulsivity and extreme irresponsibility, a highly labile emotionality, and only the most superficial of interpersonal relationships. They are impetuous, often appear to live only for the moment, have little foresight, act without goals or plans, and appear to be seemingly unconcerned for consequences for themselves and for others. The lack any realistic appreciation of time and any ability to gain from past experience.

Psychological tests have been helpful in distinguishing and describing the unique personality structure of the psychopath. Different tests reveal the psychopath as immature, isolated from human interactions, impoverished in his emotional life, unable to profit from experience, having low frustration tolerance, reacting to frustration with hostility and fury, unable to identify with others, unrestrained by guilt and/or empathy, impulsive and aggressive, with severe and early rejection and emotional deprivation being the probable cause of the disorder (McCord and McCord, 1964).

Delinquency and Personality Styles

The literature on delinquency suggests that in addition to a social delinquency, there are at least two different personality organizations associated with antisocial behavior patterns. These two distinct personality organizations derive from developmental disruptions at different phases of the life cycle, involve different psychological disturbances and dynamic conflicts, and require different therapeutic approaches. One type of personality style is organized around anaclitic issues of interpersonal relatedness and intimacy, while the other is organized around the dynamics of identity and self image. Antisocial behavior can result from either of these two personality styles, but the delinquency in each differs in etiology, personality organization, level of ego development, the quality of interpersonal relations, and the nature of object and self representations (Jacobson, 1964). While the manifest form and expression of the delinquency may be similar and may involve identical antisocial acts, the delinquent behavior will have different meanings for the individual.

It is important to note that these two different styles in delinquency are similar to two major issues that are dominant in depression — issues of oral neediness and issues of an excessively punitive, internalized standard and moral code (Blatt, 1974). Delinquency may in part be a defense against profound experiences of dysphoria and depression as well as an externalization or an enactment of painful affect states related to neglect and deprivation, and/or severely critical, judgmental parental figures. Theories of depression may serve to clarify further some of the dynamic issues associated with the two character styles in delinquency.

Delinquency and Depression

The fact that at least some forms of delinquency are related to and are expressions of underlying depression was emphasized by Aichhorn (1925), Anna Freud (1936), Fenichel (1945b), Eissler (1949), Blos (1957), Falstein (1958), Kaufman et al. (1959), Burks and Harrison (1962), Toolan (1962), Chwast (1967), Glaser (1967), Scharfman and Clark (1967), Spiegel (1967), Unwin (1970), Lesse (1974), and many others. Greenson (cited by Kanzer, 1957) even suggested the term "impulsive depressives" in alluding to cases of delinquents with a depressive core. Fenichel (1945b) views most impulsive acts as a way of avoiding depression. Anna Freud (1936) draws a parallel between the superego arrest in "ruthless" individuals who have identified with the aggressor and the superego arrest in melancholia. Superego impairment may be expressed either in an external aggressive projection of guilt or in introjection as an important precursor in the development of melancholia. Eissler (1949) notes that when delinquents are prevented from indulging in delinquent acts, they become depressed, stuporous, or develop a panic reaction. The clinical examples presented by Aichhorn (1925) illustrate well the depression which often underlies many delinquent acts. Aichhorn, in fact, comments that delinquency can be a way in which an adolescent tries to escape from melancholia. For Falstein (1958), the heart of delinquency is a basic depressive core which is covered over by defensive layers. Toolan (1962, 1974) claims that depression is expressed in adolescence by various forms of behavioral problems such as acting out and delinquency. These attempts to avoid or mask depressive affect are often precipitated by intense reactions to loss of an object or of a state of well-being. Toolan also states that whether these losses will result in depression or delinquency depends on the developmental level of the individual when the loss is first experienced. The concept of masked depression implies that the experience of depression may be hidden from the individual himself, as well as an observer, by numerous façades including adolescent bravado and delinquency. Glaser (1967) and Lesse (1974) point out that depressive elements may be covered by multiple masks, among which are behavior problems, acting out, antisocial patterns, and delinquency. Glaser (1967) presents several cases demonstrating that delinquent behavior can be the presenting symptom of a masked depression. Chwast (1967) also suggests that depression can be hidden behind symptoms such as anger, acting out, and delinquency. In his study of the clinical records of 121 delinquents (ages seven to sixteen), he found that delinquents tend to be more rather than less depressed: 78 percent of the delinquents were somewhat depressed and 46 percent were substantially or predominantly depressed. Chwast concludes that there is a large depressive component in the personality structure of delinquents and that the antisocial acting out can be a means of filling a sense of emptiness, a way of attempting to cope with demanding situations in the absence of inner resources because of psychological impoverishment. The delinquent act is perceived by Chwast as a way of warding off depression. Thus, there is theoretical as well as considerable clinical and empirical evidence which points to the relationship between some forms of delinquent behavior and depression. Further understanding of delinquency may be gained by a careful consideration of issues of depression and their possible expression in delinquent behavior.

Anaclitic and Introjective Personality Styles

In a theoretical and clinical analysis of depression, Blatt (1974) introduced a developmental model of depression which differentiated an anaclitic and an introjective dimension of depression. These two sources of depression seem to reflect and express two general personality styles which result in differences in the experiential world, cognitive style, modes of defense and adaptation, interpersonal relations, and levels of object representation. The anaclitic personality is characterized by concerns with issues of interpersonal intimacy, whereas the introjective personality is characterized by preoccupations with issues of identity and self-worth. In both anaclitic and introjective personalities there may be impairment in the process of internalization and in the development of object representation, but the impairment derives from and involves different developmental issues and can lead to different forms of psychopathology.

Psychopathology of the Anaclitic Personality Style

Psychopathology within the anaclitic personality focuses on the basic relationship with the caretaking person, and there are dominant fears of abandonment and of being unloved. The psychopathology is

> ...primarily oral in nature and related to early childhood reactions to narcissistic injury, loss of love, and the fear of impoverishment and starvation....The primary feelings in anaclitic [psychopathology] are helplessness, weakness, depletion, and being unloved. There are intense wishes to be soothed and cared for, helped, fed, and protected. There are cries for love and of hunger, oral cravings, difficulty tolerating delay and postponement, and a desperation to find satisfaction and peace.... There are fears and apprehensions of being abandoned, and there is a sense of helplessness in being unable to find gratification and comfort.... Object relationships are primarily incorporative,...consuming, relatively undifferentiated, based on need gratification, and at the symbiotic and early substages of separation and individuation....The object is valued only for its capacity to provide need gratification. A sense of well-being derives from a continual supply of love and assurance. When an object is unable to provide these supplies, feelings of being unloved and helpless are stimulated. With support and need gratification, a temporary sense of comfort is achieved, but satisfaction and gratification are experienced as emanating only from the object (Jacobson, 1971). Thus, there is an inordinate fear of abandonment and an excessive vulnerability to object loss...and a difficulty expressing anger and rage for fear of destroying the object as a source of satisfaction [Blatt, 1974, pp. 115–116].

There is a preoccupation with frustration and gratification in the representation of the object. There are experiences of either blissful union or of utter depletion, depending on the direct availability of the object. There is relatively little internalization of the experiences of gratification or of the object providing the satisfaction. Thus, there is a constant demand for the visible and physical presence of objects. Separation and object loss are dealt with by primitive defenses such as denial and a frantic search for substitutes. The representation of objects is primarily in terms of action sequences. Because of an impairment in the process of internalization and limited levels of object representations, there is a need to maintain direct, physical, sensory, need-gratifying contact with the object. Because of this impairment in object representation there is a vulnerability to profound feelings of loneliness (Blatt, 1974).

Anaclitic Delinquency. An anaclitic personality organization can result in depression and/or antisocial behavior focused around oral neediness. This form of delinquency develops from fears of abandonment and experiences of neglect. Its origin is in early emotional deprivation, maternal neglect, or critical interruption in the continuity of caretaking relationships. These painful early experiences leave the individual with unfilled anaclitic strivings which may be expressed in various antisocial activities.

Many investigators have pointed to the crucial role that emotional deprivation plays in setting the stage for the appearance of both depression and delinquency. Both depression and antisocial behavior may have anaclitic antecedents engendered by early severe disturbances in parent-child relationships. Healy and Bronner (1936) established the etiological importance of severe disruptions in the early lives of delinquents such as: separation from parents, loss of affection, prolonged absence or death of parents, repeated change in foster homes, institutional life, etc. Such childhood background either disrupts or provides little opportunity for the development of personal attachment. Emotional deprivation experienced by these children appears to be related to the development of a psychopathic personality — one variant of anaclitic delinquency (Partridge, 1928; Knight, 1933; Field, 1940; Haller, 1942; Jenkins and Hewitt, 1944; Friedlander, 1947; Rabinovitch, 1950; Bowlby, 1952; Jenkins, 1960).

Bender (1947) discusses deprivation in the infantile period and critical breaks in the continuity of close personal relationships as responsible for the development of a psychopathic syndrome. A study of fifty-seven antisocial young children (Rexford, 1959) revealed that children who suffered from very disturbed early relationships with their parents and from emotionally and physically depriving environments were the most traumatized and difficult to treat because of their very limited capacity for object relations and their tenuous grasp of reality. Burks and Harrison (1962) in a study of aggressive children concluded that an understanding of some aggressive behavior is enhanced when it is viewed as a means of avoiding feelings of depression. This is particularly true in children who suffered deprivations and rejection in their early years (Newell, 1934, 1936; Levy, 1937; Symonds, 1939; Wolberg, 1944; Schachtel and Levi, 1945; B. Lewis, 1954; Bowlby et al., 1956). These children are characterized by their difficulty in forming lasting object relationships. The "deprived child" syndrome is a result of lack of mothering, either because of prolonged separation at a crucial age, or because the mother was unsatisfying. These children have the hallmarks of the psychopath: empty interpersonal relationships, hedonistic impulsivity, and a lack of guilt. Burks and Harrison (1962) discuss these characteristics as a form of self-protection against feelings of deprivation. The character structure of these aggressive children is similar to the character style of some depressed patients. Burks and Harrison see these children as utilizing aggressive behavior as a device to avoid recognition of their helplessness, powerlessness, and cravings for affection, all of which are central issues in the anaclitic form of depression. Katz (1972) and D. O. Lewis and Balla (1976) also discuss deprivation, neglect, psychological abuse, and cruelty as contributing to delinquency. The child has not developed meaningful object relations and is angry at the experiences of deprivation. People are just things for him, and therefore it is difficult to be considerate of others.

Disruptions of the early mother-child relationship play a central role in the formation of delinquency. Friedlander (1949) discusses how any interference with the establishment of a firm mother-child relationship and with consistent handling of primitive instinctual drives will hinder the process of ego development. Early separations as well as disinterest and personality defects in the mother which cause inconsistent, neglectful, and rejecting care-giving can lead to disturbances in ego development and impairments in the establishment of object relationships in the child. Delinquency may be the reaction to this disruption in development. Impaired ego and super-ego development results in impulsive behavior dominated by the pleasure principle, with little capacity for delay and planning. Anna Freud (1949) considers disruption of the mother-infant relationship as the important factor in delinquency. In situations "where the mother is either absent, neglectful, or emotionally unstable and ambivalent, and therefore fails to be a steady source of satisfaction, or in cases where the care of the infant is insufficient, impersonal, or given by frequently changing figures," the development of adequate interpersonal relationship is impaired. These early deprivations result in a blunting of libidinal development, which leads to an even further impairment in the capacity to contain destructive urges. This aggressiveness and this destructiveness are important components of delinquency. Most of the delinquent children studied by Schwartz (1968) at the Hampstead Child-Therapy Clinic had experienced a serious disruption of the mother-child relations. Schwartz explains the acting out of these delinquent children as a reaching out for new objects, a search for new objects, a search for a love object that would restore the original sense of well-being with the mother that was lost early in childhood.

The loss of a parent figure is repeatedly found in predelinquent children. Kaufman (1955) discusses depression, following the trauma of losing a parent, as the core of delinquency. Each of the cases presented by Aichhorn in *Wayward Youth* had a history of parental loss, often occurring in a traumatic fashion. Scharfman and Clark (1967) identified a pattern commonly found in the histories of delinquent girls which included parent loss through death, desertion, and/or divorce. Bowlby and Parks (1970) stress how early and premature separation from the mother causes antisocial character formation. They point out that prolonged or repeated disruptions of the mother-child bond during the first years of life are known to be especially frequent in individuals later diagnosed as psychopathic personalities.

Studies of children brought up in institutions indicate that they can be emotionally underprivileged, have little feeling for interpersonal relationships, are asocial, and have little anxiety or guilt (Becker, 1941). They often have features of infantilism, apathy, intellectual retardation, and an inability to form object relations (Goldfarb, 1945). Bender (1947) found the most severe type of psychopathy in children who had been raised in institutions for the first two to three years of their life. Thus, numerous reports consider the various forms of deprivation (neglect and rejection, unstable and unsatisfying mother figure, separation and loss, institutional life) during the early formative childhood period as leading to delinquency and/or depression. These impairments in early object relations lead to later development of anaclitic depression and delinquency.

Another issue which is prominent in the anaclitic personality is orality; its role in antisocial behavior has been discussed by various investigators. Fenichel (1945a) describes persons with fixations on oral types of regulation of self-esteem — dependent on external supplies, on being loved, on getting — as reacting to frustration with violence. Their primary conflict is between a tendency to take by violence what was not given to them, and a tendency to repress all aggressiveness out of fear of losing love. They view people, not as individuals, but as deliverers of supply and therefore interchangeable and of no significance as individuals in their own right. If the necessary supplies are missing, they become depressed and many of the impulsive acts serve as attempts to fill the emptiness and avoid this depression. Fenichel concludes that fixations on the oral type of self-esteem regulation form the dispositional basis for impulsive acting out, depression, and addiction. Falstein (1958) also discusses unfilled intensified oral needs in delinquents. The future delinquent is unable to express hostility directly toward the perceived depriving mother who fails to satisfy adequately the oral needs. Instead he expresses the rage toward the larger social group.

There is considerable evidence that some forms of antisocial behavior are a consequence of deprivation of anaclitic needs. The phenomenology, dynamics, and etiology of some delinquents indicate that there is a constellation of delinquency which can be conceptualized as an anaclitic delinquency. This conceptualization emphasizes the severe frustration and the profound impairment of the infant-mother relationship as the etiological factor of the antisocial behavior in anaclitic delinquency.

Clearly, there are forms of antisocial delinquent behavior which express a desperate need to fill unsatisfied oral cravings. These longings can be expressed in multiple forms, such as stealing supplies as replacement for love; achieving contact, warmth, and closeness in promiscuous sexual behavior (Hollender, 1970); substance abuse such as drugs (Lidz et al., 1976), alcohol or food to fill a bottomless void; and assaulting people because of rage over feelings of deprivation and frustration. The concept of an anaclitic personality provides meaning not only for these apparently meaningless and self-destructive acts, but also for understanding the most severe form of antisocial behavior—the psychopath.

The characteristics of the psychopath can be understood as a consequence of severe disruption in early caretaking relationships and as a grotesque and exaggerated expression of unfulfilled anaclitic needs. The psychopath is an extreme form or variant of anaclitic delinquency. Because of a failure to achieve a sense of closeness and interpersonal relatedness in early childhood, the psychopath is emotionally shallow and unable to identify with others and be considerate of them. His impaired capacity to experience empathy and emotional bonds limits the psychopath's ability to exist in a mutual interpersonal matrix and to experience anxiety, guilt, or shame. Because of inconsistent caring early in childhood, the psychopath is intolerant of delay and postponement and reacts to frustration with impulsivity and rage. His caretaking experiences were unpredictable, and he experienced little consistency or pattern in the way needs were satisfied. Therefore, his capacity to experience, understand, and utilize time is disturbed. All life is in the present, and there is little trust or sense of the future. One impetuous act follows upon the other in a search for sensation and stimulation to replace a barren emptiness and loneliness.

Some of the clinical issues involved in anaclitic delinquency are exemplified in the following case reports.

An Anaclitic Delinquent Male. A.B., a sixteen-year-old, single, white male, was referred for psychiatric hospitalization following an extended history of delinquency, which included breaking and entering, stealing and truancy. He had been involved in these activities for about three years prior to hospitalization. A. also had endocrinological difficulties which resulted in significant interference with his physical growth. He appeared considerably younger than his age; his stature was significantly shorter than normal; and he looked prepubescent. Behind his superficial bravado a frightened child seemed to be hiding.

A.'s mother was the only child of divorced parents. She left school at the age of sixteen to marry A.'s father because she was pregnant. Having been considered bright, she felt frustrated that she could not finish high school and continue her studies in college. A.'s father believed that his wife's pregnancy before marriage was a means she used to escape from her mother. But this possibly contrived attempt to achieve separation failed, and Mrs. B. was unable to establish an independent life — her mother visited her daily and constantly intruded into her married life.

Mr. B. was the youngest of three siblings. He established his own business and has remained in it for fifteen years. He married his wife, whom he had met in high school, immediately after finishing school. Their marital relationship was poor and, after ten years of marriage, ended in divorce. Both parents have had serious problems with alcohol abuse; Mrs. B. seemed to have a more severe alcohol problem and became intoxicated whenever faced with difficulties in living.

A. was the second of three children. After the birth of her first child, the mother did not want any more children; A. thus was unplanned and unwanted. When he was born Mrs. B. considered A. to be extremely ugly because "he had no neck, and his hair grew straight up." As soon as she brought him home from the hospital, she cut off his hair. The mother was incapable of showing affection to any of her children, and this was especially true with A. Family members reported that she always disliked and rejected A. and was very harsh to him.

At the age of two and a half years A. was diagnosed as having serious endocrinological problems requiring frequent hospitalization. A.'s earliest memory had to do with his medical difficulties at age five when he became delirious and thought that martians were coming. One of the consequences of his endocrinological difficulties and serious allergies was severe dietary restrictions which A.'s father recalled as having been very difficult for his son. Because of his severe allergies he was also forbidden to eat chocolate.

During his early childhood A. was frequently left with his aunt. She was the oldest of the father's siblings and had played a mothering role for Mr. B. when he had been a child and this extended even into his adulthood. She also often assumed primary responsibility for A.'s care, giving him the affection and nurturance he did not receive from his own parents. Several times each week, A.'s mother left him with the aunt while taking the other two children with her. At one point Mrs. B. even asked the aunt to adopt A., but the aunt refused because she already had children of her own. The aunt considered A. a lovable, warm child until the age of five, when he began taking candy, small items, and change from her home. His stealing coincided with the beginning of his mother's amphetamine and alcohol abuse. He apparently continued stealing money from relatives until the age of about thirteen, when he began breaking and entering homes in the neighborhood.

Mr. B. spent little time at home during A.'s early years because he was busy establishing his business or was often getting drunk. The father had severe problems in expressing emotion and in relating to others, claiming to have had special difficulties in understanding and communicating with A. He realized that he had not established a good father-son relationship with A. and attributed this failure to A.'s frequent hospitalizations and endocrinological difficulties.

In school A. first became a discipline problem in the fourth grade, when he was described as hyperactive. Between the ages of five to eight A.'s parents separated frequently, the father and the mother alternately leaving the home. When A. was eight his parents were finally divorced. The court awarded custody of the children to the father because the mother was considered incapable of taking care of them. He also did not want them and thought of them as a burden, but agreed to take them because they needed a home. For six months following the divorce, the children were cared for by their aunt and their paternal grandparents. The father then began a relationship with a woman who moved into their home with her daughters. A. and his sisters did not get along with this woman, and during this time A.'s father began to drink more heavily.

In the first three and a half years following the divorce, A. had very little contact with his mother, seeing her occasionally on weekends. When finally the conflict between A. and the woman his father was living with became intolerable to the father, A. was sent to live with his mother who was sober at the time. His young sister followed him shortly, as she had become very depressed. She would spend a great deal of time in her room crying. The mother soon began drinking again, and the two children were often left on their own. A. and his sister had many friends—who were described as "some of the worst kinds in town." They often came over to visit with

A. and his sister when there were no adults around the house. While living with his mother, A. began stealing and Mr. B. claimed that the mother took her children into stores to help her shoplift. Urged by his sister and mother, Mr. B. brought the children back into his home. Shortly afterward, A.'s younger sister ran away and was gone for two months.

A. often left the father's home to stay with his mother where he became involved in numerous incidents of breaking and entering. His usual pattern was to skip school with a classmate, go to a good neighborhood with better homes and enter a house, looking solely for money. They would then leave without damaging the property and without stealing anything of value. A. explained that he committed these thefts simply to get money, and apparently some of the money he stole went toward the purchase of motorbikes. Riding a motorbike became A.'s favorite pastime. His father, however, believed that A. stole money primarily to support his marihuana use. When A. was 15, his father had moved out of his own home into the house of a new girlfriend, and the court awarded temporary custody of A. to the paternal aunt. A. stayed with his aunt until he became a truancy problem and was returned to his father's home, where the situation had improved somewhat since the father's new girlfriend had moved in.

Eventually A. was caught breaking and entering. The court and the probation officer recommended psychiatric hospitalization. On admission, and during his hospitalization, there was no evidence of thought disorder, hallucinations, or delusional thinking. He seemed appropriate in his relations with peers on the clinical unit; however, he had serious difficulties in his relationships with staff members. He strongly resisted accepting authority figures, particularly females, and responded by defying any type of limit-setting. For example, he brought marihuana into the hospital and refused to participate in the hospital activities program. His defiance eventually reached the point at which it became necessary to use seclusion to control his behavior. His unwillingness to maintain the dietary restrictions demanded by his medical difficulties caused serious problems. At times his defiance of these restrictions seemed to have self-destructive intent. He maintained a massive denial of his medical problems, his disrupted family, and his personal difficulties, insisting that his problems were only legal and would be resolved if he could only find a job. He had difficulties discussing his feelings generally but especially those toward his father, whom he saw as distant and unapproachable when sober and as unpredictable and sometimes violent when intoxicated. A. appeared to be very angry and hostile toward his father but unable to acknowledge his rage directly. Interestingly enough, A. was quite fond and protective of his mother and liked to be with her and to take care of her when she was intoxicated.

A. had strong depressive feelings which were primarily anaclitic in nature. They originated in his highly traumatic and severely deprived early experiences. In his chaotic family situation he never experienced certainty and continuity. He alternated living with his mother, father, and aunt since early childhood. He never developed communication, understanding, or a sense of relatedness with any of them. His whole life was a saga of severe deprivation, rejection, and neglect, which began with his unwanted birth and continued throughout his early years when he had neither a constant home nor stable parental figures. His hunger for love, concern, and a consistently caring figure left him vulnerable to feelings of depression. His delinquency was a manifestation of this depression and of his unsatisfied anaclitic needs. His breaking and entering were desperate attempts to find satisfaction for his cravings for the love and concern he had never known.

An Anaclitic Delinquent Female. C., a sixteen-year-old, white, single, female high-school student, physically and socially precocious, presented a strikingly attractive appearance. C. had engaged in multiple delinquent behavior, including school truancy, running away from home, drug abuse, and prostitution since the age of twelve. She became progressively sad, anxious, scared, and confused as her delinquent behavior became more intense. Finally, she was referred for psychiatric hospitalization.

C.'s father grew up in a family with extreme marital tension. His mother pressured her children to accomplish a great deal and achieve high status. C.'s father maintained an enmeshed relationship with his own mother. He assumed a great deal of responsibility for her care, even though she was outspoken in her disapproval of his marriage. C.'s mother was from an immigrant family. Her father died at age fifty after a protracted illness. His death, one year prior to C.'s birth, provoked a prolonged and severe mourning reaction in the mother. C. has an older brother who had a history of school difficulties and violent outbursts and who had been in psychotherapy for these difficulties. C. grew up in an essentially enmeshed family where generational boundaries were diffuse and relationships were erotized, particularly with her father and brother. The family appeared to have been at war for many years. The characteristic interactional style of the family was hostile-dependent and the predominant affect in the family members was anger.

C.'s birth coincided with the anniversary of her maternal grandfather's death. The pregnancy had been complicated by her mother's lumbar disc problem which necessitated her spending the last six months of her pregnancy and the first three months after the delivery in bed. C.'s mother also had had a postpartum depression. C. knew that her mother had been very sick and depressed after she was born, and recalled that her mother had a lot of physical problems throughout C.'s childhood. C. also remembered her parents constantly fighting, her father coming home after working long hours and finding fault with everything mother did or said.

C.'s parents disagreed about the onset of her problems, her mother stating that she had difficulties in school virtually from the start, while her father maintained that no real problems had been apparent until C. was about thirteen, when she first began running away from home. According to C., the battle with her parents began when she was about eleven or twelve, and was precipitated by her becoming increasingly uncomfortable in her intense relationship with her father in which she was "Daddy's little girl" and "his little hostess for his friends." She had fond memories of her relationships with her father from ages six to ten. She liked to be outdoors with him, especially when her mother and brother did not take part in the outings. When C. was about eleven, disagreements and arguments developed with her parents, especially her father. The parents attempted to impose restrictions on her going out, dating, visiting with boys in her room with the door closed, smoking, using drugs, dressing up, and wearing makeup. C.'s explanation for these difficulties with her father was that he refused to accept the fact that she was not his little girl anymore, and he continually attempted to tell her "how to live, how to dress, and what to do." C. became increasingly involved in activities outside the home. At home she fought with her brother whom she described as "jealous of my popularity" and as hating her because she "took his parents away" from him. C.'s truancy and contentiousness at home escalated; when she was thirteen, she and her father engaged in a physical fight when led to C.'s leaving home, getting arrested and admitted to the hospital.

After a brief crisis intervention, C. and her family were referred for family therapy. C. felt that she served as the vehicle for her parents to get into treatment since all the sessions focused around their marital relationship. C. dropped out of the family therapy, but her parents continued. At that time C. decided that her mother could never protect her from her brother and father and that they could not continue to live together. She asked her mother to get a divorce from her father and then the two of them, C. and her mother, could live together. This was only one example of C.'s many attempts to split her family in order to gain her own gratification, finding it difficult to share her mother's attention with others. When her brother left home, C.'s behavior became more problematic, and the arguments with her father intensified, focusing around C.'s sexuality, provocative dress and behavior, with father calling her "a whore." She became increasingly involved in prostitution, which culminated in her current hospitalization when she became extremely fearful that her life was being threatened by a pimp. According to C., her experiments with drugs and prostitution gave her a sense of independence and control over her own life, and distance from her parents. Her involvements with friends much older than herself served as substitutes for her parents whom she denounced as incompetent and intrusive and with whom she felt deeply disappointed.

Several times during her hospitalization C. went AWOL, each incident occurring after an experience of separation and loss. The first was precipitated by her parents' vacation plans which she tried to thwart. The second and third elopement from the hospital occurred around the therapist's vacation. Several weeks before the therapist's vacation, C. became increasingly depressed and broke up with her boyfriend. Shortly before the therapist was to leave on vacation, C. ran away from the hospital. She returned after the therapist had left. Following the therapist's return from vacation, C. again ran away from the hospital and stayed away from the hospital about as long as her therapist had been on vacation. When she returned, C. began to talk about her needs to be loved and hugged, and about feeling compelled to run when she felt abandoned and alone. In a poignant moment she stated simply, "I just wanted to be held and loved." C. struggled with the impulse to flee when her needs became overwhelming or when she feared rejection or abandonment. In her struggle to deal with the feelings of loneliness and abandonment, she attempted to gain a false sense of independence, control, and autonomy.

In psychotherapy, after an initial period of mistrust, withdrawal, and superficiality, C. gradually began to talk about her sense of worthlessness, her poor self-esteem, and her feelings of depression. This was related to her experiments with drugs and prostitution prior to hospitalization. The more she became aware of her craving for maternal care and her anguish in having to share her mother with others, the more C. experienced depression with some suicidal ideation. She articulated feelings of sadness and increasingly tried to hurt herself.

C. was very impulsive, needy, and childlike, and initially she desperately defended against recognizing her deep desires to be taken care of and her profound dependency needs. Instead she displayed a counter-dependent posture and used denial, avoidance, and flight as defense mechanisms against her desperate anaclitic needs. The anaclitic personality structure underlying C.'s multiple antisocial activities seems clear. Serious deprivation of nurturance during her early childhood resulted in a sense of neediness. The lack of consistent caring by her mother left C. with a profound sense of longing, which she attempted to satisfy by her acting-out behavior, especially her promiscuity. In her involvement in prostitution she denied her feelings of loss and abandonment by her parents, while at the same time seeking to be taken care of by men. The sexual body contact supplied her with a sense of being held and with the illusion of intimacy and closeness for which she desperately longed. C.'s hostility against her parents — engendered by her experiences of deprivation by her mother and seductiveness by her father — contributed to her need for the stimulation of drugs and sexual contact. C.'s low frustration tolerance and her inability to delay gratification caused her to become enraged and suspicious when her needs were not immediately met. Whenever she felt pain, sadness, or disappointment, she attempted to run away both literally and metaphorically — to drugs and promiscuity. Her acting out also contained elements of the wish to punish and shame her parents, and constituted an inept attempt to achieve a separation from the family and to deny her feelings of loss. C.'s mature and natural autonomy from her family had been thwarted by the family's inability to provide an adequate holding environment. Her intense ambivalence around separation seemed to be one of the major determinants of her antisocial behavior.

Psychopathology of the Introjective Personality Style

The predominant issues of psychopathology in the introjective style no longer involve oral needs but rather involve issues of sexual identification, of the phallic-urethral phase and its consolidation, and the resolution of the oedipal conflict. As discussed previously (Blatt, 1974), concerns in the introjective style are primarily about feelings of

...being unworthy, unlovable rather than unloved, guilty, and having failed to live up to expectations and standards. . . . There are exceedingly high ideals (Jacobson, 1953), an overly harsh superego, a keen sense of morality and commitment, and a constant self-scrutiny and evaluation. There is guilt over temptations or thoughts of transgression (often related to oedipal issues) or the sense that one has failed to live up to the expectations and will be disapproved of and criticized. There are extensive demands for perfection, a proclivity to assume blame and responsibility, and feelings of helplessness to achieve approval, acceptance, and recognition. Intense, overstated standards are often attributed to external figures, and there is a constant concern about disapproval and punishment. Ambivalent and hostile feelings toward the object are difficult to express because of fears of losing the object's love. There are struggles to compensate by overachieving in order to win approval and recognition, but there is usually little lasting satisfaction. The presence of an object is important, not so much to provide need gratification, but to offer approval and acceptance. Libidinal concerns are primarily at the phallic-oedipal level and related to the development of the superego, the processes of sexual identification, and the beginning phases of the oedipal conflict. The parents' conscious and unconscious attitudes and feelings about themselves and their child. . . have important effects on the child's conscious and unconscious feelings about himself and his strivings [pp. 177–178].

In the psychopathology of the introjective personality organization defenses are no longer a simple denial or a desperate seeking of immediate need gratification, but rather involve obsessive-compulsive mechanisms and defenses associated with the phallic-urethral phase of development.

> [A] major defense. . .is introjection or identification with the aggressor, with a proclivity to assume responsibility and blame and to be harsh and critical toward the self. . .the cathexis of and involvement with the object persist independent of frustration and gratification. There are concerns about receiving love and approval from the object, and there are also concerns about the object's response to and acceptance of one's feelings of love for the object. The relationship is highly ambivalent, and the person is unable to resolve and integrate the contradictory feelings. There are attempts to retain the object and its potential love and approval through introjection, and the struggles which originally were between the person and the ambivalently loved object come to exist primarily within the person (Freud, 1917). The representations of the object are more differentiated, but are based on repetitive, drive-laden interactions with the object and on distorted, exaggerated, and contradictory part properties and features of the object. Since these representations are usually based on the ambivalent, hostile, and aggressive aspects of the object relationship, the internalizations result in feelings of doubt, self-criticism, and guilt. The continual negative self-judgments and guilt, as well as the exaggerated and overstated representations, serve to maintain contact with the object in a vivid and hypercathected way [Blatt, 1974, pp. 118–119].

Psychopathology within the introjective style involves a fragmented, pictorial, concrete, and contradictory concept of the object. Representations are still limited in scope, literal, and depictive. The content of the representations is often ambivalent, and there is an alternation between hostile, aggressive, overidealized, and idyllic features. There is not an intense need for immediate and direct physical contact with the object, but there is a need for continued experiences with the object, or aspects of the object, in order to support and maintain the representation of the object. The presence of guilt indicates that object representations are on a somewhat higher level because guilt requires some differentiated and reflective sense of self and some appreciation of causality both in assuming responsibility for an event and in considering ways of separation and atonement. In the introjective character the developmental task is to resolve the contradictions and ambivalence inherent in the separate and fragmented representations based on extreme and overstated features. These disparate elements must be integrated into a higher-level representation which resolves the ambivalence and integrates the isolated and contradictory fragments into a cohesive representation.

Introjective Delinquency. Delinquency can develop out of the preoccupations and concerns of the introjective personality with issues of self-worth, moral standards, superego, sexual identity, and identification. Delinquency, with a focus on themes related to the superego and ego ideal, can take the place of a neurosis; as we have noted earlier, this has been discussed as "neurotic delinquency." Thus antisocial activity can serve as a defense against and an externalization of difficulties associated with the broad issues of self concept and self image. The delinquency in the introjective personality is an expression of underlying conflicts around worthlessness, guilt, and shame, much as anaclitic delinquency is an expression of underlying conflicts around the deprivation of oral, narcissistic needs.

In contrast to anaclitic delinquency which develops from abandonment and neglect during the oral phase, introjective delinquency develops from a markedly ambivalent, demanding, depreciatory, and hostile parent-child relationship during the phallic-urethral phase. The relationship allows the child neither to develop positive self representations nor to enter fully into the oedipal phase and achieve an adequate oedipal resolution. At a time when the child is seeking to establish a sense of identification with his parents, he is also internalizing a wide range of conscious and unconscious values, including the parents' attitudes toward the child. Harsh, judgmental, critical, punitive demands of the parents are ambivalently internalized as part of the child's emerging identity. The standards are subsequently directed against the self, so that the adolescent's antisocial behavior is both a defiance of these standards and at the same time a seeking for punishment and retribution for the temptations to transgress. The search for punishment and the self-destructive activity have been considered as manifestations of powerful, primitive, superego introjects, and they are both part of introjective delinquency and introjective depression. The punitive agent, however, is externalized in delinquency, whereas it is internalized in depression. Aichhorn (1925) discussed the impairment of the ego ideal and of guilt as the bases for some forms of delinquency. An unconscious sense of guilt, closely linked with the oedipus complex, can become a primary motivating force for delinquency. The antisocial act is an effort to gain relief from a sense of guilt by dramatically violating the limits set by moral standards and at the same time inviting punishment in order to meet the superego's demands. The delinquent also attempts to escape from his conscience by identifying with the aggressor and punishing the environment with his violent activity.

Excessive, intense, and rigidly held parental moral codes suggest that there are conflicts within the parents around unconscious temptations to violate these standards. The areas of the child's impaired superego development reflect similar superego defects in the parents. The parents are conflicted about their own wishes to transgress moral rules and therefore feel both hostility and unconscious excitement toward the child for his being the embodiment of their own unconscious drives. The parents' unresolved conflicts may be expressed in their inconsistent discipline; their intense criticism alternates with moments of excessive permissiveness which encourage the antisocial activity of the child. Thus, the rigidity and instability of parental standards as well as the child's recognition of the parents' unconscious wishes provide the stage and the climate for the child to begin to consider the violation of the overstated and extreme moral code of the parents. The parents' conflicts also leave the child with rigid, severe, and conflict-laden moral standards. Without adequate internalization of modulating positive feelings of acceptance and respect, the child can also be left with a seriously impaired sense of self-worth and with inferiority feelings, both of which contribute to his poor self image and to his experience of shame.

The phallic-urethral and oedipal phases of development are the periods in which the child initially establishes a sense of sexual identity and begins to assume appropriate sex-role behavior within the family matrix. The child seeks to establish a primary identity with the same-sex parent and to initiate an appropriate intimate relationship with the other parent. The response of the opposite-sex parent can serve to facilitate the emerging sexual identity of the child. Since sexual identity is an integral part of psychological development in the phallic-urethral and oedipal phases, the antisocial activity of introjective delinquency often also involves sexual behavior. The introjective delinquent's sexuality, however, is not primarily a seeking of contact, but is an exaggerated attempt to state a poorly defined and vulnerable sexual identity. These struggles with sexual identity, initially disrupted in the phallic-urethral and oedipal phases, are stimulated once again with the upsurge in puberty. The developmental struggle with identity and appropriate intimate behavior in the phallic-urethral and oedipal phases are reexperienced in even bolder form in adolescence ("deferred action" [Freud, 1918, 1950]) when the culture demands a fuller definition of sexual identity and appropriate sex-role behavior. The stages in adolescent development which Erikson (1950) defined as identity and intimacy are partly recapitulations and consolidations of issues initially begun in the phallic-urethral and oedipal phases.

Even though the overt antisocial behavior may be the same in anaclitic and introjective delinquency, its motivation and meaning differ. A variety of antisocial acts can be expressions of profound doubts about self-worth and sexual identity. Stealing, for example, can be related to issues of sexual identity or status within a peer culture, a desire to possess forbidden objects, or a seeking of punishment, rather than a search for oral supplies or a clinging to objects for safety and security. Sexual promiscuity can be an attempt to affirm a tenuous sexual identity, rather than a seeking of warmth, closeness, affection, and body contact (Hollender, 1970). Substance abuse, such as alcoholism, drugs, or even food, may be a defiance of social standards or a retreat from the pressures of constantly having to achieve or prove one's self-worth rather than a seeking to fill an inner void. Truancy from school or running away from home can be a way of escaping inferiority feelings or excessive and unattainable demands and standards as well as an attempt to gain recognition, rather than express the wish to be sought after and to know that significant people care about one and seek one's return.

An Introjective Delinquent Female. D., a tall, thin, attractive, mature-appearing, seventeen-year-old, white, single female high school senior, had been hospitalized several times for severe drug abuse and antisocial behavior. Her history of drug abuse dated back to sixth grade when she lost interest in schoolwork. She began to dress sloppily and "to hang around with kids" from lower socioeconomic groups. She started sniffing glue because "I didn't want to know what was going on, I was sick of the fights with my parents, I was always under attack." A few months later she switched to "grass," feeling "tired of being told by everybody what to do. I was not worth being given a reason. I was hurt and wanted to numb out." Using Cannabis gave her a sense of respect in her peer group. She used it several times each week and obtained the money for its purchase by stealing from her parents. At the end of sixth grade she had her first sexual experience with a boy she met occasionally on the beach. Thereafter she became increasingly promiscuous. She started using amphetamines, thinking that it would make it possible for her to "accept anything and do anything." Amphetamines made her feel more capable and amiable. She recalled that even her parents commented on the favorable change in her. Toward the end of that year she became increasingly paranoid and anxious and had to use barbiturates to counter the effect of the amphetamines. She soon started to combine amphetamines with heroin, taking amphetamines in the morning and heroin at night. The use of heroin became heavier and, in order to obtain money, she "did everything except prostitution." She would steal from parents and friends, break into apartments of "speed friends," and engage in promiscuous sexual behavior. Somehow her parents never became aware of her intensive drug use until about a year later when she left home to live with an older man who was an amphetamine dealer. When she returned home after a few days, she told her parents that she had used only hash and they did not place any restrictions on her activities. She continued in her drug abuse and promiscuity and began to use cocaine in order to enjoy sex more fully. Her attendance at school was sporadic, and she returned to it only when her father threatened to send her to jail. She also entered outpatient therapy at a drug clinic "to get cleaned up." Eventually she was expelled from school because of her drug abuse. She then left home to join a drug addict who, after a few days, threw her out. She went to a drug clinic for two months, but pretended to be clean, giving false urine tests. She left home once again and stayed with a "junkie friend" who had been in jail for armed assault. She was taken home by the police and hospitalized for several months. Subsequent to her discharge from the hospital, she entered a methadone program. She moved into her aunt's apartment and was happy there, feeling for the first time a part of a real family. But she continued to take drugs, drank heavily, and started stealing, until finally her aunt asked her to leave the house. She was hospitalized once again.

D. came from an Irish family that had come into considerable wealth rather recently. The father was the youngest of nine children of a very caring, strong mother and a cruel, alcoholic father. The father built up an extensive and highly successful business, though he had only a high school education. Despite his remarkable success, he never achieved a stable sense of self-worth and continually remained vulnerable to criticism from his wife and others, feeling impotent and seeking approval and support.

D.'s mother often had a strange appearance and dressed in outlandish and inappropriate ways. Though she did remarkably well in high school, she did not go on to college because her parents lacked sufficient funds to support her. She was married shortly after graduation from high school to a man she described in idyllic terms. He was killed in an airplane accident shortly after their marriage, and his death left her profoundly depressed. It required years for her to get over her sorrow and grief. Several years after the death of her first husband, she met D.'s father. The relationship was tempestuous from the start, and they have had constant arguments and fights throughout their marriage. She used her critical comments and sarcasm to depreciate her children and her husband, especially by comparing him with her "perfect first husband." The mother was described by the hospital staff as having psychotic features. At times her speech was illogical, and she seemed to have a fluid and unstable sense of her self and others. She appeared very narcissistic, constantly demanding attention and gifts. She repeatedly insisted on being the center of the family and on her husband and children attending instantly to her needs. Both parents have had serious personal difficulties over the years, and both drank heavily at the end of each day. While the father's problems seemed to diminish after he began psychotherapy, the mother continued to become increasingly bizarre and depressed.

D. was born five years after the parents married. The parents argued about whether to have a child; the mother did not want one, but was "forced into it" by her husband. She claimed to have cared for D., but it was actually the maternal grandmother who assumed responsibility for much of the child's care, while the mother sat and read a book or slept. The mother wanted D. to be a "soft-spoken fairy princess," but instead D. was a sturdy, gurgly, active child. The mother would buy D. toys for little girls and dress her in frilly girls' clothes and expect her to sit and play quietly, but D. wanted to run around and play more active games. She never played with dolls but preferred boys' games and was considered a tomboy. One of D.'s earliest memories was how her mother made her sit and play piano, beginning around the age of four, and hit her on the knuckles with a ruler for incorrect notes.

D. was gregarious, enjoyed being with people, and spent much of her time playing with other children — to the annoyance of her mother, who considered herself above the rest of the neighbors and constantly tried to restrain D. from playing with other children in the neighborhood. D. went to a private school because her mother thought it was the proper thing to do. D. would have preferred to stay at home and be with her friends. In her neighborhood she felt embarrassed in front of the other kids because of her parents' wealth, and at school she did not feel accepted because her parents were considered snobbish and *nouveaux riches.* D. was an average student and always felt that she did not live up to her parents' expectations. Her academic achievements were significantly less than those of other members of the family. D. was also ashamed of her inability to produce anything for the school newspaper, and her parents kept commenting about it. Things that D. excelled in, such as gym and athletics, did not meet with her mother's approval. Nor did her parents approve of any of D.'s friends, whom they considered to be of lower intelligence and social background. They constantly criticized D. for her selection of friends, but D. continued to meet them secretly. D. had her menarche at the age of ten. She did not confide in her mother because she was afraid of her criticism. Instead she learned the preliminary facts from her girlfriends. D. felt different because of her early puberty and reacted in tough and rough behavior, assuming the role of a leader in her class.

The parents first noticed a change in D. when she was eight yeas old, following her brother's birth. Her mother had bleeding during the pregnancy and had to have a Caesarean section. D. was frightened that her mother would die. After her brother's birth, the mother spent a great deal of time with the baby, and D. felt she was "sort of forgotten about" for a while. The mother spent every minute with her son, effectively excluding everyone else from her life. She became involved in what her husband described as a "bizarre love relationship with her son." D. reacted to this by becoming frustrated, anxious, and overtly hostile. She was totally alienated and refused to participate in family life, often leaving the dinner table whenever she did not like something. She became sullen and quiet, spending increasing time alone in her room, often taunting and teasing her brother cruelly. The brother's birth apparently complicated an already difficult pattern of family interaction. The parents were unable to pay attention to D. Both D. and her mother competed for the father's attention; and whenever he wanted to show affection to D., the mother intruded and demanded that she come first. The father tried to find compensation in D., for the irrational behavior of his wife, but his interest in his daughter only enraged his wife all the more. D., in turn, tried to use her father to get even with her mother, especially when the mother showered her attention on her son. It was shortly after the birth of the brother that D.'s involvement with drugs began.

Behind a tough façade, D. seemed to be a little girl struggling desperately for some acknowledgment that she was worthwhile. The central theme of her life was the attempt, repeated again and again, to run away from a painful reality—a boundary-diffused family; an unavailable, overdemanding mother supported by an inconsistent father; a feeling that she never met parental expectations and was subjected to a constant sense of disapproval. D. indicated that quite early in her life she felt trapped and surrounded by her mother's wish that she become someone special. In effect, the mother wanted D. to fulfill her own frustrated aspirations. D. was naturally active, and her goals and behavior never met her mother's definition of an ideal girl or woman. D. felt that she was always on the verge of being criticized, rebuked, or punished. This fear was augmented by her perception of utter inconsistency in her mother's motives and standards. She was never quite sure what she was expected to do next. She was only aware that whatever she did usually provoked her mother's criticism and anger and charges of insubordination and deviancy. She was convinced that she was evil, destructive, and sinful. D. conveyed a strong sense of having been thwarted at almost every attempt to achieve a sense of individuality. She seemed to have had to struggle to break free of her mother's rejection, intrusive attacks, and criticism in order to find some sense of self-esteem and self-worth.

Both parents were extremely moralistic and had a very clear and rigid sense of right and wrong. Their behavior, however, was often quite inconsistent with their demands. D. was aware that she was often used by her parents in their marital battles. Both parents indirectly encouraged aspects of D.'s antisocial behavior which they then used as a weapon against each other. The confusion, anger, and ambiguity of values in her parents caused considerable turmoil for D. She dealt with these difficulties by isolation of affect, intellectualization, and other obsessive defenses through which she sought to find meaning for the frightening, jumbled relationships in the family and her own confused feelings and thoughts. Throughout her preadolescence she felt that she had to go "underground" in order to define herself and do the things she wanted to do. Her street experiences and drug involvement were, in many ways, her attempt to separate from her mother and establish a more clearly defined image of herself as a separate person, capable of independent action and judgment—even if those actions were labeled as deviant and malicious. The mother offered her little as a positive figure for identification. D. viewed her mother as disturbed, phony, aggressive, and inconsistent.

D. was concerned and confused about her own identity and her own values. She was frightened by the intimacy of therapy and was frightened that the therapist would impose his values on her. She continually focused on her need to be independent of any control or direction. Gradually she was able to begin to take actions based on a better defined, internal sense of direction. She began to set her own limits, rather than fighting against the possibility that others would set limits for her. Throughout the treatment, the therapist reported that he did not feel a need to provide D. with a maternal holding environment; rather, he felt a need to provide her with a context in which she could come to establish some identity and achieve some reasonable sense of limits and directions for her activities and interests.

Independent psychological testing revealed that D.'s severe delinquency covered over an inner life dominated by depression, rejection, loneliness, and a seething anger. What superficially appeared as thoughtless antisocial behavior and interpersonal blandness was a defense against the pain, fear, and the expectation of criticism and punishment. Rather than allowing herself any outward display of tenderness and warmth, D. appeared defiant and tough. She was frightened of forming relationships because she fully expected to be hurt or abandoned in the long run. To prevent this, she either isolated herself or hurt the other person, much as she felt she had been hurt in the past. Many of her Rorschach responses suggested a poignant loneliness; for example, she saw an old house in which no one was at home and which had been abandoned out in the woods. The major theme, however, throughout the projective testing was D.'s concept of herself as a poisonous, viperous monster who will contaminate, destroy, or injure anyone with whom she has close contact. Her Rorschach was dominated by a vast array of vampires, snakes, and biting predatory animals. Her self concept seemed to be epitomized by her percept of a bear trap, baited with a piece of meat, waiting to close around anyone who put pressure on it. D. felt herself to be quite evil and black-hearted and passively expected whatever punishment the world would mete out for her recurrent "crimes." She feared and expected severe and harsh punishment to come from some external source. She seemed to have established a life-style based on a recurring cycle of transgressions or provocative acts, followed by punishment, followed by more angry transgressions. Her two modes of relating seemed to be either as a criminal being punished or as a sly, seductive con-artist who would eventually betray any trust placed in her. Hostile and aggressive impulses frequently became merged with sexual impulses, and her expressions of affection were likely to take on a derisive, hostile flavor. For example, in a Rorschach response she told of two pigs sticking their tongues out at each other, but later suggested that perhaps the pigs might be kissing. Thus what appeared as tenderness and warmth may also involve considerable destructive, aggressive impulses.

Discussion

There are a number of observations which support our distinction between anaclitic and introjective forms of delinquency. Anna Freud (1949), for example, differentiated between social maladjustment based on early disturbance of object love and other forms of social maladjustment which derive from later realms of child's development. According to Anna Freud, the first type of social maladjustment is based on early disturbances of the development of object love and the consequent weakening in the later development of ego and superego functions. Other forms of social maladjustment are based on conflicts in the development and resolution of the oedipus complex. These social maladjustments are, in their content, nearer to the neurotic and may be best understood as developmental failures which appear later in the development of the child. Aichhorn (1925) distinguished between two groups of delinquency: dissocial delinquents who showed no evidence of neurotic conflict and whose struggle with the environment derives from serious frustrations of early libidinal needs, and delinquency due to neurotic conflicts. Aichhorn also differentiated between two kinds of hate in delinquency: an open hate which is the result of a loss of love because of parental repudiation, and a concealed hate which arises when the child feels that he is not loved for his own sake but is a replacement for parental self-fulfillment either within themselves or in their spouse. Aichhorn further drew a distinction between aggressive behavior determined by a lack of affection in the early environment and aggression determined by unconscious guilt and a need for punishment. In general, Aichhorn distinguished between uninhibited, primitive delinquents who have little or no guilt and delinquents who have intense, repressed guilt and are struggling with strong demands of a primitive superego. These distinctions are consistent with our formulations of an anaclitic and an introjective delinquency. Burks and Harrison (1962) likewise distinguish between aggressive antisocial behavior as a way of avoiding depressive loneliness and aggression which placates feelings of guilt.

Blos (1957) differentiated between two types of female delinquents: one has intense ties to the preoedipal mother, and the other struggles with the early phases of the oedipal complex. These two types of delinquents may commit similar offenses, but the dynamics and character structure of these two forms of delinquency are different and can be conceptualized along the anaclitic and introjective dimensions. Female delinquency based on a regression to the preoedipal mother is more anaclitic in nature. This type of delinquent girl has failed to achieve a liberation from a dependency upon her mother and uses heterosexuality to protect herself against a regressive pull toward mother. Severe deprivation and/or overstimulation result in a potential regression toward the preoedipal mother. Blos also discusses a second type of delinquent female which is more introjective in quality. There is a prevailing oedipal struggle which has never reached sufficient resolution to result in an adequate degree of internalization. This type of delinquent girl not only experiences an oedipal defeat at the hands of a distant, cruel, or absent father, but in addition she also shares in her mother's dissatisfaction with her husband. This ambivalent bond between mother and daughter based on a hostile or negative identification forges a destructive relationship between them. The girl's delinquent behavior is motivated by a need for the constant possession of a partner who serves as a fantasy replacement for oedipal defeat and a basis on which she can compete with the mother who has hated, rejected, or ridiculed the father. In her heterosexual delinquency, the girl expresses her desire to be sexually needed, wanted, and used.

In summary, the distinction between anaclitic and introjective delinquency provides a theoretical model for understanding the dynamics of antisocial behavior. It enables us to consider delinquency not simply as defiance of social order but as a consequence of impaired development and the establishment of particular structures of personality organization.

Psychopathology of the anaclitic character style involves an immature personality organization in which there is impaired capacity to tolerate delay and frustration. Antisocial behavior in this personality organization can be conceptualized as an anaclitic delinquency which serves to ward off feelings of helplessness and depletion, to avoid wishes to be cared for, loved, fed, and protected, and to struggle with fears of being abandoned, and an urgency to fill an inner emptiness and oral cravings. Antisocial behavior in this context can also be a way of expressing a rage about deprivation and neglect. The origin of this type of delinquency is an early emotional deprivation which leaves the individual with serious frustration of anaclitic strivings and with profoundly damaged object relations.

In the treatment of delinquent adolescents, the antisocial nature of their symptoms often distracts therapists, parents, teachers, and the adolescents themselves from recognizing and responding to the underlying feelings of depression. Glaser (1967) has discussed how the delinquent behavior masking the depression frequently becomes the focus of treatment. Spiegel (1967) stressed the importance of responding to the depression behind the rage and the delinquent act. The success of psychotherapy with delinquents depends on the therapist's "seeking, reaching out for the underlying depression... in terms of the primal experiences of abandonment by the beloved" (p. 600). It is essential in the treatment of anaclitic delinquency that the adolescent come to recognize that his delinquent acts are expressions of rage over profound feelings of neglect, rejection, and abandonment as well as a seeking of replacements for feeling unloved, unfed, and unwanted. Psychotherapy with anaclitic delinquency necessitates an articulation of the deprived anaclitic needs and the underlying anaclitic depressive experiences. Since acknowledgment of these experiences is difficult, the patient will probably try to avoid recognizing these threatening aspects of his inner world by resorting to further delinquent behavior. Patients frequently can come to know and experience these painful affects and memories only gradually, and the therapist must be prepared for sudden onrushes of intense depressive affect and episodes of angry and defensive antisocial behavior. The therapist must be aware of the disrupted and difficult early life experiences of these patients and provide them with a constructive, consistent relationship which will increasingly enable them to gain perspective on their feelings about early deprivations.

The internalization of aspects of the therapeutic relationship provides the basis on which the patient can begin to develop increased tolerance for delay and postpone gratification without experiencing intense rage. In the therapeutic relationship, the patient can begin to develop a sense of interpersonal relatedness, a sense of concern and sharing, leading to the development of the capacity for empathy. He can come to know and tolerate painful as well as pleasurable affects. Anxiety, guilt, and shame can become signal affects. The patient can reflect on feelings rather than seek to avoid and discharge distressing affects. As the patient comes to recognize and know the intensity of his depression related to the early deprivation of anaclitic needs, and as he begins to develop a therapeutic alliance and integrate aspects of the therapeutic relationship, the need for discharge through antisocial behavior may diminish. Transference issues in therapy will focus upon themes of dependability, affection, love, and concern, particularly provoked by experiences of separation and loss. The patient will demand to be loved, taken care of, and fed. The therapist's concerns for the patient and the dependability of the relationship will be tested frequently. Experiences of frustration and deprivation, particularly related to separation and loss, will provoke anger and rage.

Psychopathology of the introjective character style is organized mainly around issues of guilt and self image; it involves feelings of worthlessness, guilt, and having failed to live up to expectations and standards. Antisocial behavior in this personality organization can be conceptualized as an introjective delinquency which serves as a defense against and as an externalization of inner conflicts mainly associated with oedipal issues. The antisocial behavior can serve as a means of avoiding feelings of depression around issues of self-worth and guilt as well as inviting punishment for superego transgressions.

These neurotic conflicts and the depressive elements of introjective delinquency are the major issues that must be dealt with in psychotherapy. As discussed by Aichhorn (1925), the therapist and other constructive significant figures in the environment can become important alternatives for the parents who failed to provide the adolescent with an adequate basis for identification. The therapist and other significant people are an essential part of the therapeutic process because they provide the delinquent adolescent with alternate figures with whom they can establish meaningful identifications. These identifications are essential if the adolescent is to develop a self-definition, a sense of self-worth, an effective moral code, and appropriate and realistic personal standards and aspirations. The therapeutic process with introjective delinquents follows the basic principles of psychotherapy with neurotic patients, but, as with anaclitic delinquents, it is essential to be mindful of the underlying introjective depressive issues.

References

Aichhorn, A. (1925), *Wayward Youth.* New York: Meridian Books, 1955.

Alexander, F. (1930), The neurotic character. *Int. J. Psycho-Anal.,* 11:292–311.

Becker, M. (1941), Psychopathic personality. Dissertation, New York School of Social Work.

Bender, L. (1947), Psychopathic behavior disorders in children. In: *Handbook of Correctional Psychology,* ed. R. M. Lindner & R. V. Seliger. New York: Philosophical Library, pp. 360–377.

Bilmes, M. (1967), Shame and delinquency. *Contemp. Psychoanal.,* 3:113–132.

Blatt, S. J. (1974), Levels of object representations in anaclitic and introjective depression. *The Psychoanalytic Study of the Child,* 29:107–157.

Blos, P. (1957), Preoedipal factors in the etiology of female delinquency. *The Psychoanalytic Study of the Child,* 12:229–249.

Bowlby, J. (1952), *Maternal Care and Mental Health.* Geneva: World Health Organization.

———— Ainsworth, M., Boston, M., & Rosenbluth, D. (1956), The effects of mother-child separation. *Brit. J. Med. Psychol.,* 29:211–247.

———— & Parks, C. M. (1970), Separation and loss within the family. In: *The Child in His Family,* ed. E. J. Anthony & C. Koupernick. New York: Wiley, pp. 197–216.

Burks, H. L. & Harrison, S. I. (1962), Aggressive behavior as a means of avoiding depression. *Amer. J. Orthopsychiat.,* 32:416–422.

Chwast, J. (1967), Depressive reactions as manifested among adolescent delinquents. *Amer. J. Psychother.,* 21:575–584.

Cleckley, H. M. (1955), *The Mask of Sanity.* St. Louis: Mosby.

Cohen, A. K. (1955), *Delinquent Boys.* New York: Free Press.

Cohen, M. F. (1969), An investigation of the cooperative response in three types of delinquents. *Diss. Abstr.,* 29(12-B), 4840.

Cromes, G. F. (1972), The effect of group therapy experience on juvenile offenders relative to their classification as neurotic or sociopathic. *Diss. Abstr.,* 32(9-B), 5435.

Eissler, K. R. (1949), Some problems of delinquency. In: *Searchlights on Delinquency,* ed. K. R. Eissler. New York: International Universities Press, pp. 3–25.

Erikson, E. H. (1950), *Childhood and Society.* New York: Norton.

Falstein, E. (1958), The psychodynamics of male adolescent delinquency. *Amer. J. Orthopsychiat.,* 38:613–626.

Fenichel, O. (1945a), *The Psychoanalytic Theory of Neurosis.* New York: Norton.

———— (1945b), Neurotic acting out. *Psychoanal. Rev.,* 32:197–206.

Field, M. (1940), Maternal attitudes found in 25 cases of children with primary behavior disorder. *Amer. J. Orthopsychiat.,* 10:293–311.

Freud, A. (1936), *The Ego and the Mechanisms of Defense.* New York: International Universities Press, 1946.

———— (1949), Certain types and stages of social maladjustment. In: *Searchlights on Delinquency,* ed. K. R. Eissler. New York: International Universities Press, pp. 193–204.

Freud, S. (1917), Mourning and melancholia. *Standard Edition,* 14:243–258. London: Hogarth Press, 1957.

———— (1918), From the history of an infantile neurosis. *Standard Edition,* 17:3–123. London: Hogarth Press, 1955.

———— (1923), The ego and the id. *Standard Edition,* 19:3–66. London: Hogarth Press, 1961.

———— (1950 [1895]), Project for a scientific psychology. *Standard Edition,* 1:283–397. London: Hogarth Press, 1966.

Friedlander, K. (1947), *The Psycho-Analytical Approach to Juvenile Dellinquency.* New York: International Universities Press.

———— (1949), Latent delinquency and ego development. In: *Searchlights on Delinquency,* ed. K. R. Eissler. New York: International Universities Press, pp. 205–215.

Giffin, M. E., Johnson, A. M., & Litin, E. M. (1954), Specific factors determining antisocial acting out. *Amer. J. Orthopsychiat.,* 24:668–684.

Glaser, K. (1967), Masked depression in children and adolescents. *Amer. J. Psychother.,* 21:565–574.

Goldfarb, W. (1945), Effects of psychological deprivation in infancy and subsequent stimulation. *Amer. J. Psychiat.,* 102:18–33.

Greenacre, P. (1945), Conscience in the psychopath. *Amer. J. Orthopsychiat.,* 15:495–509.

Haller, B. L. (1942), Some factors related to the adjustment of psychopaths on parole from a state hospital. *Smith Coll. Stud. Soc. Wk.,* 13:193–194.

Healy, W. & Bronner, A. F. (1936), *New Light on Delinquency and Its Treatment*. New Haven: Yale University Press.

Hetherington, E. M., Stuwie, R. J., & Ridberg, E. H. (1971), Patterns of family interaction and child-rearing attitudes related to three dimensions of juvenile delinquency. *J. Abnorm. Psychol.*, 78:160–176.

Hewitt, C. E. & Jenkins, R. L. (1946), *Fundamental Patterns of Maladjustment*. Springfield, Ill.: State of Illinois.

Hezel, J. D. (1969), Some personality correlates of dimensions of delinquency. *Diss. Abstr.*, 8-B, 3087.

Hill, L. B. (1938), The use of hostility as defense. *Psychoanal. Quart.*, 7:254–264.

Hirschberg, C. (1954), Sociologic delinquency. Read at the San Francisco meeting of the American Medical Association.

Hollender, M. (1970), The need or wish to be held. *Arch. Gen. Psychiat.*, 22:445–453.

Jacobson, E. (1930), Beitrag zur asozialen Charakterbildung. *Int. Z. Psychoanal.*, 16:210–235.

——— (1953), Contribution to the metapsychology of cyclothymic depression. In: *Affective Disorders*, ed. P. Greenacre. New York: International Universities Press, pp. 49–83.

——— (1964), *The Self and the Object World*. New York: International Universities Press.

——— (1971), *Depression*. New York: International Universities Press.

James, S. L., Obson, F., & Oetting, E. R. (1967), Treatment for delinquent girls. *Commun. Ment. Hlth J.*, 3:377–381.

Jenkins, R. L. (1960), The psychopathic or antisocial personality. *J. Nerv. Ment. Dis.*, 131:318–334.

——— & Hewitt, L. (1944), Types of personality structure in child guidance clinics. *Amer. J. Orthopsychiat.*, 14:84–94.

Johnson, A. M. (1949), Sanctions for superego lacunae of adolescents. In: *Searchlights on Delinquency*, ed. K. R. Eissler. New York: International Universities Press, pp. 225–245.

——— (1959), Juvenile delinquency. In: *American Handbook of Psychiatry*, ed. S. Arieti. New York: Basic Books, vol. 1, pp. 840–856.

——— & Szurek, S. A. (1952), The genesis of antisocial acting out in children and adults. *Psychoanal. Quart.*, 21:323–342.

Jones, E. (1929), Fear, guilt and hate. *Int. J. Psycho-Anal.*, 10:383–397.

Kanzer, M. (1957), Panel report: Acting out and its relations to impulse disorders. *J. Amer. Psychoanal. Assn.*, 5:136–145.

Katz, P. (1972), Patients in the development of juvenile delinquency. *Corrective Psychiat. & J. Soc. Ther.*, 18(2):10–18.

Kaufman, I. (1955), Three basic sources for predelinquent character. *Nerv. Child*, 11:12–15.

——— Makkay, E., & Zilbach, J. (1959), The impact of adolescence on girls with delinquent character formation. *Amer. J. Orthopsychiat.*, 29:130–143.

Klein, M. (1948), *Contributions to Psycho-Analysis*. London: Hogarth Press.

Knight, E. M. (1933), A descriptive comparison of markedly aggressive and submissive children. *Smith Coll. Stud. Soc. Wk*, 4:168–169.

Lampl-de Groot, J. (1949), Neurotics, delinquents and ideal-formation. In: *Searchlights on Delinquency*, ed. K. R. Eissler. New York: International Universities Press, pp. 246–255.

Lesse, S. (1974), Depressive equivalents and the multivariant masks of depression.

In: *Masked Depression,* ed. S. Lesse. New York: Jason Aronson, pp. 3–23.

Levy, M. (1937), Primary affect hunger. *Amer. J. Psychiat.,* 94:643–652.

Lewis, B. (1954), *Deprived Children.* London: Oxford University Press.

Lewis, D. O. & Balla D. A. (1976), *Delinquency and Psychopathology.* New York: Grune & Stratton.

Lidz, T., Lidz, R. W., & Rubenstein, R. (1976), An anaclitic syndrome in adolescent amphetamine addicts. *The Psychoanalytic Study of the Child.* 31:317–348.

McCord, W. & McCord, J. (1964), *The Psychopath.* Princeton: D. van Norstrand.

Menninger, K. A. (1938), Criminal behavior as a form of masked self-destructiveness. *Bull. Menninger Clin.,* 2:1–7.

Newell, H. W. (1934), The psychodynamics of maternal rejection. *Amer. J. Orthopsychiat.,* 4:387–401.

———— (1936), A further study of maternal rejection. *Amer. J. Orthopsychiat.,* 6:576–589.

Nicholi, A. M. (1967), Harvard dropouts. *Amer. J. Psychiat.,* 124:651–658.

Partridge, G. E. (1928), A study of 50 cases of psychopathic personality. *Amer. J. Psychiat.,* 7:953–973.

Post, B. N. (1968), Responsivity of two types of institutionalized delinquents to social reinforcement. *Diss. Abstr.,* 29(1-B), 377.

Powell, T. J. (1967), Passive aims in two types of adolescent delinquents. *Diss. Abstr.,* 27(12-A), 4346.

Rabinovitch, R. (1950), Psychopathic delinquent children — 1949 Round Table. *Amer. J. Orthopsychiat.,* 20:233–265.

Rexford, E. N. (1959), Antisocial young children and their families. In: *Dynamic Psychopathology in Childhood,* ed. L. Jessner & E. Pavenstedt. New York: Grune & Stratton, pp. 181–221.

Robins, E. (1967), Antisocial and dyssocial personality disorders. In: *Comprehensive Textbook of Psychiatry,* ed. A. M. Freedman & H. I. Kaplan. Baltimore: Williams & Willkins, pp. 951–958.

Rosenfeld, H. M. (1969), Delinquent acting out in adolescent males and the task of sexual identification. *Smith Coll. Stud. Soc. Wk,* 40:1–29.

Schachtel, A. H. & Levi, M. B. (1945), Character structure of day nursery children as seen through the Rorschach. *Amer. J. Orthopsychiat.,* 15:213–222.

Scharfman, M. A. & Clark, R. W. (1967), Delinquent adolescent girls. *Arch. Gen. Psychiat.,* 17:441–447.

Schwartz, H. (1968), Contribution to symposium on acting out. *Int. J. Psycho-Anal.,* 49:179–181.

Shaw, C. R. & McKay, H. D. (1931), Social factors in juvenile delinquency. National Commission on Law Observance and Enforcement, 2. Report on the causes of crime, GPO, Washington, D.C.

Solnit, A. J. (1969), Youth unrest. *Amer. J. Psychiat.,* 125:1145–1159.

Spiegel, R. (1967), Anger and acting out. *Amer. J. Psychother.,* 21:597–606.

Stewart, D. J. (1972), Effects of social reinforcement on dependency and aggressive responses of psychopathic neurotic and subcultural delinquents. *J. Abnorm. Psychol.,* 79:76–83.

Symonds, P. M. (1939), *The Psychology of Parent-Child Relations.* New York: Appleton-Century.

Szurek, S. A. (1942), Notes on the genesis of psychopathic personality trends. *Psychiatry,* 5:1–6.

Toolan, J. M. (1962), Depression in children and adolescents. *Amer. J. Orthopsychiat.,* 32:404–415.

———— (1974), Masked depression in children and adolescents. In: *Masked Depression,* ed. S. Lesse. New York: Jason Aronson, pp. 141–164.

Unwin, J. R. (1970), Depression in alienated youth. *Canad. Psychiat. Assn. J.,* 15:83–86.

Van Tessel, E. G. (1966), Taking the role of the other in psychopathy. *Diss. Abstr.,* 27(3–4), 974.

Wolberg, L. (1944), The character structure of the rejected child. *Nerv. Child,* 3:74–88.

15

THE CONFLICT OF POWER AND ACHIEVEMENT IN DEPRESSION

SAMUEL SLIPP, M.D.

Edith Jacobson's clinical and theoretical contributions to the understanding and treatment of depressive disorders represent a major development in the growth of psychoanalysis. Her work opened the path for further investigations in ego psychology, object relations, and the psychology of the self. Jacobson's work is built on the firm foundation of previous psychoanalytic studies to which she has added her own unique contributions. Depression was one of the first areas that led to the exploration of ego psychology and object relations in psychoanalysis. Abraham (1911) noted unconscious hostility toward a lost love object, and Freud (1917) considered that the lost love object was incorporated into the patient's ego so that the hostility to the object turned against one's self. Splitting of the lost love object in depression was first reported by Rado (1927), with the good parent incorporated in the superego punishing the bad parent incorporated in the ego. Deutsch (1933) emphasized the maintenance of object relations. The persecuting parent incorporated in the superego was preserved through the ego's self-devaluation in order to gain forgiveness. Gero (1936) stressed that insufficient differentiation between the self and object representations resulted in depressives establishing symbiotic love relationships. Bibring (1953) stated that the conflict in the patient's ego was between the excessively high aspirations and the awareness of its helplessness to live up to these standards. The depressive's reaction to frustration was helplessness, which Bibring believed resulted from repeated experiences of helplessness during childhood. Jacobson extended the work of Bibring, but reemphasized the role of aggression. The conflict, according to her, is between the wishful self image, which contains these high standards for achievement, and the image of the failing self. When the patient is unable to achieve these high goals, frustration, helplessness, and rage result. This aggression is turned against the failing self, causing loss of self-esteem and depression.

Jacobson further developed the concepts of self and object images, particularly their lack of differentiation in depression and schizophrenia. The normal individual has a realistic self image, which correctly mirrors the assets and limitations of his or her bodily and mental self. Jacobson (1971) astutely notes that even in normal individuals, the stability of the self image remains dependent upon identification not only with past objects but with current groups in one's environment, i.e., social, vocational, national, racial, religious, and ideological groups. She describes how a group of newly arrived female inmates in a Nazi jail responded to the trauma of imprisonment. The dehumanizing circumstances undermined their former identifications upon which their self images were based, and they struggled against identifying with the degraded criminal image that was forced upon them. The struggle between accepting and undoing this identification resulted in depersonalization. The establishment of a group by inmates with the attitudes and values that encouraged intellectual work, cleanliness, and sharing prevented degradation of their self images by providing another reference group for identification. In her clinical case material, Jacobson fully recognized the importance of current, ongoing object relations — the effect of one individual upon another. In her theoretical work, she emphasized intrapsychic factors, the importance of affects and fantasies.

The theoretical position which I shall develop is in many respects an outgrowth of Jacobson's work, but stresses object relations. It is consistent with her clinical case material and views the intrapsychic and interpersonal determinants as interactive and interdependent. I consider aggression to be important, but do not see it as an isolated entity. It always occurs in relation to significant objects. I regard the ego's ways of handling aggression in depression as being aimed at preserving object relations.

Freud's original theory concerning the origin of psychopathology was founded on disturbed object relations, the result of interpersonal trauma. His seduction theory was based on the histories of patients who remembered having been seduced as children. The emotions arising from this trauma were so morally unacceptable that they were repressed together with the memory of the event and found expression in somatic symptoms. The symptom in turn symbolically represented the trauma and was used to manipulate and control object relations. Here both interpersonal and intrapsychic factors were interrelated, emotions always occurred in relation to objects, and the patient was seen as being affected by and affecting others. When Freud later discovered that these memories of childhood seduction were fantasies and not fact, his theoretical foundation became questionable. Freud resolved his dilemma by considering that infantile sexual fantasies could distort reality, and the etiology was not an actual interpersonal trauma. Thus, intrapsychic fantasies and emotional factors were emphasized over interpersonal and reality considerations. Another alternative was open to Freud, which he did not choose. Seduction need not be a single and actual physical event, but could be a style of relating, an interpersonal power maneuver to manipulate another person. Had Freud not abandoned the seduction theory but reformulated it in this manner, an interactive and interdependent theory combining intrapsychic and interpersonal factors would have remained. The patient would have continued to be viewed in the context of his environment.

In recent years object relations have again emerged as increasingly important, particularly in the work of the English school of psychoanalysis. An inborn object-seeking propensity has been noted by psychoanalytic investigators such as Balint (1953), Bowlby (1958), Escalona (1953), Provence and Lipton (1952), and Suttie (1952). Interaction with significant others has been found necessary for growth and development of the ego during infancy. Mahler and Furer (1968) subdivided infantile development in terms of object relationships. The autistic phase (from birth to three months), the symbiotic phase (to eighteen months), and the separation-individuation phase (from one to three years of age). During the symbiotic phase the mental representations of the self and mother are fused as a defense against the infant's helplessness. Separateness is denied in order ·to sustain a sense of magical control over the mother to insure survival. During the separation-individuation phase, the mother is no longer perceived as a part object, and a gradual differentiation of the mental images of self and other occurs. At the end of the symbiotic phase, the infant achieves a stable mental representation of the mother and can evoke her image when she is absent. Mahler (1964) noted that object permanence (in Piaget's sense) develops after the first year, while object constancy (in Hartmann's sense) occurs around two to three years of age. A harmonious relationship between mother and infant has been found experimentally by Piaget (1937) and Bell (1969) as well as clinically by Spitz (1945) to be a precondition for the development of object permanence.

Jacobson (1967) has employed this object relations framework and considers that the adult schizophrenic is fixated at the symbiotic phase, tending to regress to an undifferentiated state with merging of self and object mental representations. Although she recognizes constitutional and environmental factors in schizophrenia, such as deprivation or overstimulation by the mother, Jacobson explains the lack of establishment of object and self constancy as due to insufficient neutralization of aggression. I offered another explanation which combines both intrapsychic and interpersonal factors and views them as being mutually interdependent and interactive. I have called this theoretical formulation the "symbiotic survival pattern" (1973), because the fixation is at the symbiotic phase and has the purpose of survival.

In terms of the symbiotic survival pattern, the schizophrenic patient's fixation at the symbiotic phase is due not simply to intrapsychic fixation occurring during infancy, but to a continuing form of relationship within his family and with others. The family of the schizophrenic is involved in an overly close, symbiotic relationship in which each person's self-esteem and survival are felt to be dependent upon the others. Each member needs to control the others' feelings, thoughts, and behavior; and at the same time each feels controlled by his sense of responsibility for the self-esteem and survival of the others. This symbiotic relationship reinforces the child's preoperational, primary process thinking of magical control over relationships instead of offering an opposing reality essential for the development of secondary thought processes. Piaget (1927, 1937) found that in preoperational thinking, the child employs the concept of magical participation. The objects' coming and going are seen as a function of the child's physical action schema, wishes (efficacy), or their temporal sequences (phenomenalism). The infant does not perceive objects as having a separate and independent existence; thus, the infant feels part of and in magical control over the object's existence. The symbiotic pattern in the family reinforces this ego-centric, primary process form of cognition in the area of object relations instead of helping to resolve it. Object constancy does not occur, since the child still views objects as surviving in response to his behavior and wishes and as not having a stable identity over time despite contextual changes. The result is that the child's capacity for symbolic representation of reality remains constricted, and his cognitive processes remain preoperational, imagistic, and concrete (metaphoric).

The research studies of families of schizophrenics by Lidz et al. (1965) and Wynne et al. (1958) confirm the finding that family interaction is overly close and symbiotically binding. Family members are excessively sensitive to one another at the expense of individual identity. These findings have been validated further by the experimental laboratory studies of family interaction at the National Institute of Mental Health by Reiss (1971), who found families of schizophrenics overly sensitive to one another's response; he termed this pattern "consensus sensitive." In another form of laboratory research on symbiotic relatedness, Silverman et al. (1975) used tachistoscopic subliminal stimulation experiments. They found that the thought processes of male schizophrenics improve when they were given symbiotic merging messages with mother. This finding has been repeatedly replicated by others; and Cohen (1977) noted an improvement in the thought processes of female schizophrenics who were given symbiotic messages of merging with father. In these experiments, aggressive messages against mother increased the degree of thought disorder. The symbiosis can thus be viewed not only as pathogenic, but also as a learned interpersonal defense against destructive aggressive impulses that threaten relationships and hence survival.

The lack of internal differentiation between self and object images seems to be the result of an internalization of the symbiotic family relationship. Because of fluid ego boundaries between self and others, the internalized object relations are externalized through projective identification onto others. The other is then induced to recreate the original symbiotic relationship stemming from the family. This explanation not only is consistent with research findings and clinical material, but it has a high degree of internal consistency. The individual members of the family have succeeded in denying aggression, which threatens object relations and survival. Thus, symbiotic fusion occurs in schizophrenia to protect the self and object images from destruction. In depression, on the other hand, self-punishment is used to safeguard the powerful object upon whom survival depends.

In depressive phenomena, Jacobson (1971) extensively explores object relations in her case studies, but her theory emphasizes primarily intrapsychic processes. Jacobson develops the concept of power relations more fully than previous psychoanalytic investigators, but she attributes the strength of the powerful parental image to omnipotent fantasies arising within the child and does not relate it to the reality of the parental characteristics. This intrapsychic process is accomplished through splitting, with division of the object into a powerful "godlike" parent incorporated in the superego, and a deflated worthless parent incorporated in the self image. She also views the child's helplessness as stemming from the intrapsychic operation of idealization of the self, with the child being unable to live up to the excessively high standards that he sets up for himself.

My theoretical formulation, which combines both intrapsychic and interpersonal factors, is based on Freud's original theoretical construction in which he saw the individual in the context of his environment. This intrapsychic-interpersonal theory of depression (Slipp, 1976) stems from direct observations of families of depressed individuals. In these families, there were indeed real pressures for achievement which were not due only to the child's narcissistic distortion of reality. In addition, my theory explains where the child learns to incorporate the values and standards that become his goals. My clinical observations also were corroborated in the research studies of families of depressives by Lewis et al. (1976), who found that the family power structure was in reality of a dominant-submissive nature. One parent was powerful and the other parent deflated and weak, a factor that reinforced the child's intrapsychic process of splitting. In this instance, reality, being consistent with the intrapsychic fantasy, contributed to the child's fixation. I see the situation as follows:

The depressive individual as a child was exposed in the family to a double-bind over achievement. Usually one parent is dominant and overtly pressures the child for achievement. Through projective identification, this parent lives vicariously through the child's social achievement to enhance his or her own self-esteem. The child internalizes these goals, which become part of his good, achieving self image (which Jacobson terms the wishful self image). The child cannot function autonomously, because he is responsible for this parent's self-worth. This parent is the more powerful one in the family, affecting the child's sense of security and survival. The child fears abandonment if he does not achieve the goals set for him. This parent exploits the child's achievement for his or her own narcissistic enhancement with others, such as neighbors or friends, but the child is not emotionally gratified. Instead, the child's achievement either is taken for granted, or is never enough; or it is assumed that the next time the child will fail. Since the dominant parent withholds gratification, the child remains dependent for external validation and proof of his value and being loved. The child is thus controlled and prevented from becoming independent and strong. The parent's withholding of gratification for achievement also conveys a covert and unconscious message for the child to fail. The dominant parent's attitude stems from competitive and jealous strivings toward the child. The other parent is usually submissive, depressed, and regards himself or herself as a failure, but does provide nurturance and warmth to the child. Usually the dominant parent pressures the child for achievements in order to compensate for the submissive parent's lack of achievement. In submitting to the pressure for achievement, the child becomes an ally of the dominant parent, thereby further demeaning the submissive parent. By not achieving, the child protects the submissive parent, thereby safeguarding his continued narcissistic gratification.

A double introjection and incorporation of the actual parents occurs, which reinforces the intrapsychic process of splitting into strong and weak parental images. The dominant withholding parent (Jacobson's punitive and powerful parental image) becomes part of the superego, while the submissive warm parent (Jacobson's deflated, bad, worthless parental image) becomes part of the nonachieving bad self image (Jacobson's failing self image). The bad self image is also reinforced by the covert message to fail from the dominant parent. The child feels trapped by this double-bind over achievement. It is a no-win dilemma — if he wins, he loses; and if he loses, he loses. The result is a negative cognitive set, with a pervasive sense of helplessness and hopelessness. Compliance with the message to succeed brings not gratification from the dominant parent, but only a threat of abandonment by the submissive parent. The child's social achievement only enhances the dominant parent's prestige, resulting in the child's feeling exploited, deprived, demeaned, and enraged. However, the child feels compelled to gratify this parent's needs, since he feels too guilty and unworthy about his own needs. His parents are dependent upon him for their sense of worth, and his own self-esteem remains dependent upon them. Thus a form of symbiotic relationship evolves, in which the child cannot function independently to achieve an autonomous and realistic self image. Depressives equate autonomy with being alone and abandoned. Since the child is not prepared to function independently, he cannot openly express his rage at being exploited and trapped in this bind because this would threaten his relationship with both parents and hence his survival. Yet, without conscious awareness, anger can be released in some ways that still preserve object relationships. One is intrapsychically through self-punishment, an autoplastic magical maneuver. The other is interpersonally, when the child induces others to act out an oppositional type of symbiosis. This is an alloplastic maneuver, involving projective identification.

Intrapsychically, during the depressive episode, self-punishment represents an undoing of rage toward the dominant parent and a plea for atonement and reconciliation. The dominant parental image incorporated in the superego punishes the nonachieving bad self image in the ego. The patient hopes the punitive parental image will thereby change to the good parental image and reunite with the good self image to sustain his or her self-esteem. This formulation is in line with previous psychoanalytic theory, except that the dominant parent image is substituted for Rado's "good" parent, Deutsch's "persecutory" parent, and Jacobson's "powerful and punitive" parental image. In depression, the patient's primary identification is with the failing, bad self image, while in mania the patient identifies with the punitive, dominant parental image and externalizes his rage through projective identification of the bad self image onto others who are demeaned and punished.

The interpersonal maneuver involves externalization, acting out, and recapitulation of the symbiotic relationship with the dominant parent, but it has an oppositional quality. The patient induces significant others to expect gratification from him; then by partial compliance and rebellion, he frustrates them by withholding. This is a repetition of the original compromise solution to the double-bind over achievement. By partial compliance with both succeed and fail messages, he does not risk abandonment. He is not too successful, yet not a failure. He plays brinksmanship. By rebelling sufficiently through passive-aggressive means, he subtly defeats himself and the dominant parent, thereby expressing his anger and preserving some autonomy. This autonomy is always reactive and oppositional; he needs to be a counterpuncher, fighting back against the demands of the dominant other. Thus, the patient can frustrate the dominant parent's pressure for achievement and rob him or her of the spoils of success. The patient can deny responsibility for his failure, portraying himself as the victim of circumstances, thereby withholding gratification and frustrating the exploitation of his success. In addition, having complied with the fail message and been masochistic, the patient feels he is entitled to and can demand emotional support and love.

This type of interpersonal maneuver can occur only when some fluidity of ego boundaries between self and object and a degree of intrapsychic merging between self and object images exist. In depression, the degree of symbiotic fusion of self and other images is not as great as in schizophrenia. Although the object image is maintained as separate and whole, both self and object images seem to be linked together as a gestalt. This gestalt appears to be an internalization of the oppositional symbiotic relationship experienced with the family. This takes the form of the dominant, bad parent linked to the helpless, bad self. This relationship is then externalized and the other induced through projective identification to acting it out interpersonally.

There is a growing literature on countertransference reactions to borderline patients (see, e.g., Kernberg, 1975). The patient attempts to induce in the analyst certain countertransference responses through projective identification which re-create the internalized object relations stemming from childhood. In these instances the patient may flip back and forth between the parental and self images. I found that this form of interaction was not limited to the borderline patient, but was important in the interaction of families of depressives and characteristic of the depressive's relationships with others. In depression, the patient projects the dominant par-

ental image onto another, while he identifies with the worthless bad
self image. In mania, a reversal occurs, with projection of the bad
self image onto the other, and the patient identifying with the punitive bad parental image.

This process was noted by Arieti (1959) who said that the depressive views himself as worthless, helpless, and dependent, and
transfers onto others the image of the "dominant other." Jacobson
(1971, chap. 12) describes a woman patient who behaved submissively and masochistically, thereby trying to coerce Jacobson into
fitting the patient's superego image of the all-powerful parent. When
the analyst's show of love and value for the patient was not enough,
which it could not be, the patient viewed the analyst as the withholding, punitive, and sadistic object. The patient then attempted to
provoke the analyst's anger, in order to externalize and manipulate
the environment to fit her own internalized object relations. Jacobson describes another woman patient, a borderline depressive, who
identified with a lover onto whom the patient projected her own high
standards. The lover then served as a measure for the patient's self
worth. One can view this as the patient having identified with the
dominant parental image and projected her wishful, good self image
onto the lover, whom she was expected to achieve just as the patient
had for her dominant parent. The patient did to another what had
been done to her. Jacobson also discusses the case of Mr. W., who
projected the rebellious bad self image as well as the punitive bad
parental images onto others and induced them to act out. Mr. W.
encouraged a boy to act out and then lived vicariously through the
boy's bad conduct. The patient sent this boy for psychotherapy, but
later betrayed him by informing the boy's therapist and parents of
the boy's bad behavior and suggesting that the boy be punished.
Thus, the entire internalized conflict within the patient was projected onto and acted out interpersonally by two individuals. The
boy served as a container for projective identification of the bad self,
and his therapist and parents acted out the punitive, bad parental
images of the patient.

In summary, this paper stresses that the actual family interaction of the depressive with his parents reinforces the intrapsychic
process of splitting, since the characteristics of the parents fit the split
internalized images and do not present an opposing reality. One
parent is indeed the powerful, angry one who compulsively pres-

sures for achievement, while the other parent is weak, submissive, and deflated yet narcissistically gratifying. A double introjection and incorporation of these actual parents occur, with the dominant parent becoming part of the superego and the submissive parent part of the bad self image. The dominant parent uses projective identification and lives vicariously through the child's achievements to enhance his or her own self-worth. The child identifies with these excessively high goals for achievement and fears rejection unless he succeeds. The powerful parent maintains his or her position of control by withholding gratification from the child, who is thus kept dependent and bound for a sense of worth. Withholding gratification for achievement also communicates the covert message that the patient should not become too successful and independent lest he invoke this parent's jealousy and lose love. This fail message is also bolstered by the submissive parent, who is demeaned as a failure by the dominant parent, and thus threatens abandonment if the patient succeeds. The patient is caught up in a double-bind over achievement. If he fails, he loses love; and if he succeeds, he loses love. Because of the no-win dilemma, he feels helpless and hopeless. In addition, he feels responsible for his parents' self-esteem and remains dependent upon them for his own worth. Thus, he cannot differentiate and achieve autonomy. An oppositional symbiotic relationship evolves which allows for the indirect expression of rage yet sustains object relations and preserves some autonomy. This relationship becomes internalized, and others are induced through projective identification into acting out the dominant parental image. The patient may stimulate others into expecting that he will perform and gratify them. Then, through self-defeating maneuvers, the patient covertly rebels and withholds gratification. This melodrama of brinksmanship manifests itself in the depressive's work, love, and the analytic relationships. It re-creates the compromise solution that the child evolved in relation to the parental double-bind in order not to be totally submissive and helpless.

Either failure to achieve or loss of the dominant object relationship may result in decompensation. During the depressive episode, intrapsychic punishment of the failing bad self image by the dominant parental image represents a plea for forgiveness and love to preserve self-worth. The paradoxical situation where success and not failure precipitates a decompensation can be explained by the injunction against success being broken. Success means emancipation from control by the dominant parental image. Since the patient is still dependent for self-worth upon this relationship, independence represents abandonment. The patient may revert back to a masochistic and submissive position to restore power to the dominant parental image, thereby sustaining this internalized object relationship. These same dynamics may create resistance to change during psychoanalytic treatment as the patient grows toward independence. As he grows stronger and more successful, he may feel the analyst will abandon him precipitously or some catastrophe will occur. By being aware of the internalized parental conflict over power and achievement, the analyst can help the patient work these issues through to a successful outcome.

References

Abraham, K. (1911), Notes on the psycho-analytical investigation of manic-depressive insanity and allied conditions. In: *Selected Papers on Psycho-Analysis.* New York: Basic Books, 1953, pp. 137–156.

Arieti, S. (1959), Manic-depressive psychosis. In: *American Handbook of Psychiatry,* ed. S. Arieti. New York: Basic Books, vol. 1, pp. 419–454.

Balint, M. (1953), *Primary Love and Psychoanalytic Technique.* New York: Liveright.

Bell, S. M. (1969), The development of the concept of object as related to infant-mother attachment. Unpublished doctoral thesis, Johns Hopkins University.

Bibring, E. (1953), The mechanism of depression. In: *Affective Disorders,* ed. P. Greenacre. New York: International Universities Press, pp. 13–48.

Bowlby, J. (1958), The nature of the child's tie to his mother. *Int. J. Psycho-Anal.,* 39:350–373.

Cohen, R. O. (1977), The effect of four subliminal merging stimuli on the manifest psychopathology of schizophrenic woman. Unpublished doctoral thesis, Teachers College, Columbia University.

Deutsch, H. (1933), Psychologie der manisch-depressiven Zustände, insbesondere der chronischen Hypomanie. *Int. Z. Psychoanal.,* 19:358–371.

Escalona, S. K. (1953), Emotional development in the first year of life. In: *Problems of Infancy and Childhood,* ed. M. J. E. Senn. New York: Josiah Macy Jr. Foundation, pp. 11–92.

Gero, G. (1936), The construction of depression. *Int. J. Psycho-Anal.,* 17:423–461.

Freud, S. (1917), Mourning and melancholia. *Standard Edition,* 14:237–258. London: Hogarth Press, 1957.

Jacobson, E. (1967), *Psychotic Conflict and Reality.* New York: International Universities Press.

——— (1971), *Depression.* New York: International Universities Press.

Kernberg, O. F. (1975), *Borderline Conditions and Pathological Narcissism.* New York: Jason Aronson.

Lewis, J. M., Beavers, W. R., Gossett, J. T., & Phillips, V. A. (1976), *No Single Thread.* New York: Brunner/Mazel.

Lidz, T., Fleck, S., & Cornelison, A. R. (1965), *Schizophrenia and the Family.* New York: International Universities Press.

Mahler, M. S. (1964), On the significance of the normal separation-individuation phase. In: *Drives, Affects, Behavior,* ed. M. Schur. New York: International Universities Press, vol. 2, pp. 161–169.

_____ & Furer, M. (1968), *On Human Symbiosis and the Vicissitudes of Individuation.* New York: International Universities Press, chaps. 1 and 2.

Piaget, J. (1927), Realism and the origin of the idea of participation. In: *The Child's Conception of the World.* Paterson, N.J.: Littlefield Adams, 1963, pp. 123–168.

_____ (1937), *The Construction of Reality in the Child.* New York: Basic Books, 1954.

Provence, S. & Lipton, R. C. (1952), *Infants in Institutions.* New York: International Universities Press.

Rado, S. (1927), The problem of melancholia. *Int. J. Psycho-Anal.,* 9:420–438.

Reiss, D. (1971), Varieties of consensual experience: III. *J. Nerv. Ment. Dis.,* 152:73–95.

Silverman, L. H., Levinson, P., Mendelsohn E., Roseann Ungaro, B. A., & Bronstein, A. A. (1975), A clinical application of subliminal psychodynamic activation. *J. Nerv. Ment. Dis.,* 161:379–392.

Slipp, S. (1973), The symbiotic survival pattern. *Fam. Proc.,* 12:377–398.

_____ (1976), An intrapsychic-interpersonal theory of depression. *J. Amer. Acad. Psychoanal.,* 4:389–409.

Spitz, R. A. (1945), Hospitalism. *The Psychoanalytic Study of the Child,* 1:53–74.

Suttie, I. (1952), *The Origins of Love and Hate.* New York: Julian.

Wynne, L. C., Ryckoff, I., Day, J., & Hirsch, S. (1958), Pseudomutuality in the family relations of schizophrenics. *Psychiatry,* 21:205–220.

16

RECONSTRUCTION REVISITED

The Question of the Reconstruction

of Mental Functioning

During the Earliest Months of Life

DAVID L. RUBINFINE, M.D.

It should be axiomatic that all theories and "reconstructions" of the first year of life must be subjected to the most stringent control measures and fulfill these minimal requirements:

1. Such theories should, at worst, not conflict with the data of direct infant observation; and, at best, help to organize and explain such data.
2. They should not violate psychobiological probability.
3. They should operate with the minimum number of basic assumptions necessary (law of parsimony).

Glover (1947) has suggested that by using the concepts of drive, memory trace, mobility of energy, and affect, we can account for a good part of the mental life of the infant.

Assuming a mental apparatus modeled on a reflex arc with afferent, central, and efferent pathways, we can speak of a central locus in which drive tensions accumulate, activating and gradually expanding a system of primitive memory traces which are records of perceptual experiences of inner and outer sensory stimulation. With the concept of affect we can describe the infant's state of feelings that accompany the accumulation and discharge of drive tension. With the activation and reactivation of such primordial memory traces of drive need and drive discharge we can assume that the earliest mental mechanism is regression; i.e., when cathexis is withdrawn from these traces, primitive consciousness regresses in the direction of sleep. Let us also assume that the drive energy or cathexis is distributed over all of the infant's experiences which occur as the drive reaches threshold intensity and is discharged.

There are no discriminatory judgments possible in this primitive arrangement, i.e., no distinction between tactile, gustatory, visual, acoustic, olfactory, and labyrinthine experience, so that experience is global and diffuse. There is only one connection. These perceptions are organized around the experience of drive tension and drive discharge. This is essentially what we call the drive organization of memory and is characterized by the peculiarity that each such trace can represent the entire drive and drive discharge experience. If the cathexis of all these traces is transferred to one element, it is raised to hallucinatory intensity. This requires the assumption of (1) mobility of cathectic energy and (2) equivalence of all these primordial memory traces. What is implied when we speak of the achievement of perceptual identity? Is it the successful effort to reconstitute in the mind the exact experience of the drive discharge situation? This seems highly improbable because displacement or substitute formation would be impossible. The characteristic of such perceptual representations is that there is an accumulation of memory traces that are equivalent. Any one of them may appear in a dream, but there is no guarantee that a recurrent increase in drive tension will ever represent itself in the same image. To achieve perceptual identity, the thing perceived need not be the same as the original; it is important only that it be a concrete aspect of it. This is what we mean by primary process.

Freud, in his original topographical approach, assumed that the mental apparatus was continuously activated by movements of drive energy. However, his original system was based on the study of the dreams and neuroses of adults, which presupposed an organized preconscious system (secondary process thought relationships). This is not so in the infant. Mental activity at this stage of development consists of a series of dynamic, energic sequences representing and recording the flow and ebb of excitation. On this basis it is possible to infer that the earliest disorders of mental functioning must be disorders of excitation and discharge without fixed psychic content. These disorders, it seems to me, would consist of disturbances of affect, of organ innervations, and of mostly uncoordinated motor discharges, of sleep and of feeding and other gastrointestinal disturbances. They are due not to conflict but to stress (as in distress).

The earliest mechanisms for dealing with mental tension would be thresholds and, before the establishment of a rudimentary preconcious system, regression and reflexion of instinct or drive.

Disturbances of function and development could be clinically subdivided into inhibitions or exaggerations of function. The somatic manifestations of frustration or "damming up" of excitations would vary with the source of the drive and the zonal channels of stimulation and discharge; e.g., interference with oral, gastrointestinal, and skin functions, which carry the main load of libidinal excitation, and with motor activities, which carry the burden of the reactive responses (aggression and withdrawal).

It seems to me that such early disorders of excitation and discharge are a breeding ground for psychosomatic disturbances and the psychoses. Incidentally, we can infer three developmental stages of psychic stress:

1. Stress existing at a time when the ego is not yet organized. The stress is due to frustration of need, and accumulated tension or chronic pain.

2. Stresses that occur when the ego is more organized and employs specific defense mechanisms which are primarily regulated by anxiety. Here stress is largely due to clashes with the environment (objects).

3. Stresses that occur with the consolidation of the superego, where conflict is regulated by guilt and endopsychic conflict is the main psychic stress. Repression has been established and there is a clear demarcation between inner and outer, self and others, and conscious and unconscious.

In this scheme object relations and boundaries develop as follows:

The earliest phase would inevitably be what we term "primary identification." That is the stage of object relations in which no distinction is made between self and objects.

The second phase is carried by three major mechanisms: projection, introjection, and displacement, through the operation of which boundaries are gradually established. These mechanisms are superseded by the normal obsessional mechanisms of childhood which consolidate boundaries. We assume, furthermore, that when boundaries are firmly established, these mechanisms have yielded their primacy to identification and that stable mental object representations have developed.

In the primary phase, mental representations consist of transient ideation of a pictorial sensory or imaginal type. In the second phase, symbolic thinking would predominate; and in the third phase, with the firm establishment of waking consciousness and secondary process, conceptual thinking would predominate.

It now becomes necessary to tackle some problems having to do with the dynamics, economics, and structure of consciousness. Developmentally, according to Freud, consciousness to begin with perceives stimuli only from the environment. Internally it can only register tension and tension-release signals (unpleasure and pleasure). Gradually a set of signals (memory systems) develop which can be perceived by consciousness. At first these memory systems are drive organized. There are two ways in which an image (idea) can reach consciousness:

1. When the idea or impulse is the end result of one of a series of displacements and condensations. In this manner the idea in question via transfer of cathectic charge reaches an especially high degree of intensity and forces attention to itself. When this occurs in an adult, we see either a dream or, in waking life, a symptom, a slip, an obsession, or a delusion. Because of the imperious nature of these condensations and displacements and the intensity of the cathexis involved, the image (idea) commands attention, i.e., it intrudes into consciousness.

2. A preconscious train of thought achieves consciousness by the application of a charge of attention cathexis. We call such cathexis hypercathexis becaue it is an addition from the sense-organ consciousness to the drive cathexis of ideas.

There is a distinct and qualitative difference between these two mental processes. On the one hand, we have a passive registration by consciousness of an image, idea, or train of thought due to its intensity of charge; on the other, an active apparatus of consciousness which deploys hypercathexis.

The importance of this distinction is that dream consciousness, the primitive consciousness of the infant, and the altered or defective consciousness of the schizophrenic patient and the patient with an organic brain syndrome are all characterized by a deficiency of hypercathectic energy. Thus, stimuli reach consciousness either by way of the generation of a sufficient degree or intensity of unpleasure, or by attaining a sufficient intensity of drive cathexis by displacement and condensation.

The other pathway to consciousness (i.e., via hypercathexis) is especially important for the psychology of conceptual thinking and of secondary process. This is because whenever there is an active application of a charge of hypercathexis, it serves to integrate ideas, by creating thought relationships, i.e., by distributing the drive cathexis of the wish over a wide range of associations, thereby binding the excitation and inhibiting its mobility. A familiar example of this effect of application of hypercathexis is seen in secondary elaboration or revision, which works to create orderly and systematic connections.

It is my contention that the infant must have achieved a developmental level in which consciousness has at its disposal hypercathexis or attentional energy which can be actively deployed before an experience can be "constructed," i.e., achieve thought connections and relationships, so that it can produce derivatives. Only an apparatus that registers and organizes perceptual material from the inner and outer world can "construct" experience that can be tackled analytically and "reconstructed." This conclusion is hinted at as early as chapter 7 of *The Interpretation of Dreams* (and possibly even earlier, in *Studies on Hysteria*):

> A train of thought that has been set going like this in the preconscious may either cease spontaneously or persist. We picture the first of these outcomes as implying that the energy attaching to the train of thought is diffused along all the associative paths that radiate from it; this energy sets the whole network of thoughts into a state of excitation which lasts for a certain time and then dies away as the excitation in search of discharge becomes transformed into a quiescent cathexis [Freud, 1900, p. 594].

The key word in this sentence is "quiescent." It means *bound* as contrasted to freely mobile. The process of binding creates structure and requires work (as in the work required in analysis to overcome resistance). The result is that the energy is bound to a network of thought relationships and is no longer freely displaceable. This is the binding work of attention cathexis or hypercathexis and can be recognized in such formulations as "where id was there ego shall be" or "making the unconscious conscious."

These concepts are vital to the creation of a psychoanalytic learning theory. To illustrate this one cannot find a better point of attack than the process of working through. A derivative of an unconscious guilt or anxiety system appears in the patient's dreams or free associations and is interpreted. It is talked about, investigated both historically and in the transference so that the hypercathexis that is deployed by consciousness to the interpretation spreads from it to a network of thought and feeling connections creating structure. As the system is tracked in all its different forms and disguises, the newly established connections are consolidated and will remain available to the patient throughout his life. He will in a sense remember them forever, and it will require very little work to re-create them in consciousness. However, unless these derivatives and their unconscious substrata are hypercathected, they will disappear and the underlying systems will reappear in another costume, in the form of a symptom or acting out. What I mean here is that any concrete, perceptual aspect of the unconscious substrata may reappear (perceptual identity). Obviously, then, tension or excitation that is fully discharged does not lead to the formation of structure.

These considerations have significant consequences for the theory of repression. Consider the following passage from *The Interpretation of Dreams:*

> This effortless and regular avoidance by the psychical process of the memory of anything that had once been distressing affords us the prototype and first example of *psychical* repression. . . . If the perception reappears, the movement will at once be repeated (a movement of flight, it may be) till the perception has disappeared once more. In this case, no inclination will remain to recathect the perception of the source of pain, either hallucinatorily or in any other way [p. 600].

The "effortless" avoidance (in infancy) to which Freud alludes is, I believe, a consequence, not so much of a highly developed repressive mechanism but of the absence or unavailability of hypercathexis. The painful stimulus becomes fleetingly conscious only by forcing itself upon the passive and diffuse sense-organ consciousness because its intensity has exceeded a threshold or stimulus barrier — the withdrawal is a precursor of denial. If the painful stimulus, however, is so intense that it persists, there are consequences for later development (Rubinfine, 1962).

Writing about a theory of consciousness (Rubinfine, 1973), I chose to regard conflict as a given and attempted to investigate the effects of alterations of consciousness on the mental representations of conflict. For this purpose I examined data from patients with organic disturbances of consciousness and schizophrenia.

At that time I had not yet grasped the role of hypercathexis in the creation of thought connections and relationships, or of the meaning of "binding." So, in addressing the issue of why in organically brain-damaged patients remote memories were often available and lucid as compared to memories of percepts registered in the recent past, I concluded that memories of recent percepts are registered and stored in a diffuse, clouded state of consciousness, and that attempted recall occurs in this same altered state. On the other hand, remote memories formed prior to the onset of illness were registered and stored in a focused, waking state of consciousness. Hence these remote memories are delivered intact and encapsulated in the same state of consciousness in which they were registered. What I had not then been able to conceptualize is that in the organically damaged patient, in the schizophrenic patient, and in the infant, there is very little available hypercathexis. As a result, there is no creation of thought relationships, no integration or synthesis, no binding, and hence no structure formation.

Recall is not only unreliable but often impossible. In the infant this is what Freud (1915) called *primal repression:* "We have reason to assume that there is a *primal repression,* a first phase of repression, which consists in the psychical. . . representative of the instinct being denied entrance into consciousness. With this a *fixation* is established; the representative in question persists unaltered from then onwards" (p. 148).

Freud distinguished this first phase of repression from repression proper; he tagged these earliest repressions with the term fixations. The meaning of the term primal repression has always been unclear and has been, I believe, misunderstood.

This concept seems to me to be viable only if we assume a stage in infant development in which consciousness is not yet crystallized and in which hypercathexes are not yet available to be actively deployed. There are no organized preconscious systems; and, in fact, the psyche of the infant is undifferentiated. The stimuli arising from within are not distinguished from those impinging from the external world. Should a painful stimulus reach consciousness momentarily, it does so because of its intensity. Having once dimly evoked unpleasure, the mental apparatus withdraws from it. Such a percept remains isolated and fixed. Without hypercathexis no ideational connections or relationships are formed, as a result of which the amorphous trace is unable to transfer its cathexis by displacement to later layers of ideational derivatives.

These primordial repressed elements cannot be "reconstructed" because the infant did not have the means to "construct" them at the time of their occurrence. For this reason they are not available for analytic exploration. I believe that these primordia reside in the id, while later drive representations and the stimuli which connect with them have at some point achieved a hypercathectic organization and been repressed into the unconscious ego. These repressed ideational elements, being able to transfer their cathexes to day residues and other preconscious thoughts, thus are amenable to analytic investigation. They were constructed and can therefore be reconstructed.

In the decade since I wrote on reconstruction (Rubinfine, 1967) I have repeatedly been haunted by a section of a paper Freud wrote late in his life on "Constructions in Analysis" (1937). I have always felt it was significant that Freud chose to use the term *constructions* rather than *reconstructions*, implying by this choice the possibility that what we offer the patient is a plausible theory or hunch about what might have happened at such and such a time in his life rather than an actual re-creation of the past events (in this connection, see Kris, 1956).

I have returned to these passages over and over again, feeling that each time I had missed an extremely significant theoretical inference that might help explain the nature and function of our constructions of the earliest months of life. I shall offer some quotes from this paper and intersperse them with commentaries of my own, hoping thereby to throw some light on this issue.

> Only one point requires investigation and explanation. The path that starts from the analyst's construction ought to end in the patient's recollection; but it does not always lead so far. Quite often we do not succeed in bringing the patient to recollect what has been repressed. Instead of that, if the analysis is carried out correctly, we produce in him an assured conviction of the truth of the construction which achieves the

same therapeutic result as a recaptured memory. The problem of what the circumstances are in which this occurs and of how it is possible that what appears to be an incomplete substitute should nevertheless produce a complete result—all of this is matter for a later enquiry.

I shall conclude this brief paper with a few remarks which open up a wider perspective. I have been struck by the manner in which, in certain analyses, the communication of an obviously apt construction has evoked in patients a surprising and at first incomprehensible phenomenon. They have had lively recollections called up in them—which they themselves have described as 'ultra-clear' [*überdeutlich*]—but what they have recollected has not been the event that was the subject of the construction but details relating to that subject. For instance, they have recollected with abnormal sharpness the faces of the people involved in the construction or the rooms in which something of the sort might have happened, or, a step further away, the furniture in such rooms—on the subject of which the construction had naturally no possibility of any knowledge. This has occurred both in dreams immediately after the construction had been put forward and in waking states resembling phantasies. These recollections have themselves led to nothing further [pp. 265-266].

Can we assume that these related details that are "recollected" are the products of secondary elaboration—i.e., the result of the construction being invested with hypercathexis? This hypothesis has many strong arguments in its favor—and I shall attempt to review the antecedents in Freud's work which seem to me to lead to it. In their "Preliminary Communication" Breuer and Freud (1893–95) wrote:

The second group of conditions [i.e., which prevent memories of trauma from being abreacted] are determined, not by the content of the memories but by the psychical states in which the patient received the experiences in question. For we find, under hypnosis, among the causes of hysterical symptoms ideas...whose persistence is due to the fact that they originated during the prevalence of severely paralysing affects, such as fright, or during positively abnormal psychical states, such as the semi-hypnotic twilight states of day-dreaming, auto-hypnosis, and so on.... Both of these groups of conditions, however, have in common the fact that the *psychical* traumas... *cannot be disposed of by being worked over by means of association* [p. 11; my italics].

Our observations have often taught us that a memory of this kind which had hitherto provoked attacks, ceases to be able to do so after the process of reaction [abreaction] and *associative correction have been applied to it under hypnosis* [p. 15; my italics].

Although the language is that of the earliest abreaction theories, the meaning has relevance for us now. What Freud and Breuer assumed is that bringing the events (memories, etc.) into consciousness by deployment of attention cathexis (hypercathexis) creates associative connections and hence binds these ideas so they are now conceptually organized and not drive organized — thus they are no longer subject to primary processes and their energy or cathexis is not displaceable, as it must be for symptom formation (i.e., they become resistant to regression). This is a secondary process and hence describes the building of structure. The cathexes are quiescent or bound and no longer striving for discharge. The idea also is no longer isolated, and hence its cathexis is not freely displaceable.

These recollections have themselves led to nothing further and it has seemed plausible to regard them as the product of compromise. The 'upward drive' of the repressed, stirred into activity by the putting forward of the construction, has striven to carry the important memory-traces into consciousness; but a resistance has succeeded, not, it is true, in *stopping* that movement, but in *displacing* it on to adjacent objects of minor significance [Freud, 1937, p. 266].

Let us suppose that in dealing with the developmental events of earliest infancy and childhood we are dealing not with discrete actual events (from the viewpoint of the infant) but rather with a constellation of drive impulse and sensations associated with the experiences of satisfaction and/or frustration; these were laid down in loosely organized memory traces in which any one trace can represent the whole experience, i.e., carry the entire charge of cathexis. In this setting we have then the drive impulses relating to a zone (oral) with all of the perceptions and sensations both primary and reactive to gratification or delay in which perceptions and sensations of self, object, and discharge are loosely organized around the drive.

Let us also suppose that something has gone awry in this relatively unorganized constellation; perhaps excessive frustration for whatever cause, and that the result is an excess of anxiety-rage due to sustained or recurrent experiences of prolonged tension and pain. This state to which the infant becomes fixated will of course have profound effects on his subsequent ego development; e.g., on the degree of investment of the frustrating object with sadism as well as on the capacity to control and master anxiety. The result is a serious interference with the development of reality testing, which depends so much on the capacity for delay and detour and is possible only when object constancy has been achieved.

The question then is: can we in any way accurately reconstruct the traumatic event or events that produced this particular fixation and its subsequent anxious and sadistic fantasy systems?

I do not believe we can, particularly since there is no way — given the primary process, wish-fulfillment organization of the psyche at the time of the trauma — that the reconstruction can correspond to an organized, structured memory that is repressed; rather, the reconstruction can mesh with an affective state. That is, the construction resonates with an ancient ego state that is less ideational than it is affective in quality (and especially since at this time perceptual identity is the goal of ideation — i.e., the cathexis of any concrete aspect of a global, amorphous, diffuse equivalency of primordial memory traces).

What the construction does, however, is provide a structured substitute for the event. If this substitute does indeed make connections with the infantile fixated affective state, it is *then hypercathected* and as a result establishes thought connections with the ancient affective state and thus achieves a binding effect, i.e., becomes resistant to regression. Certain inferences emerge from this position:

1. The hallucinations and delusions of psychotic individuals are driven by these primitive, zonal, affective organizations, regulated by anxiety generated from stress rather than conflict. They are precipitates of these early fixated ego states, their content, ideational and affective, resulting from faulty or failed attempts at secondary elaboration (restitution) which draw upon memorial perceptual data from later levels of development.

2. Our constructions resemble delusions, but benign ones that we attempt to build up during treatment — substituting them for the failed efforts at secondary elaboration which are doomed because the inherent ego defect· is a disturbance in consciousness with consequent deficiency of available hypercathexis. The analyst, by adding an additional charge of hypercathexis via the construction, attempts to instigate the formation of psychic structure. He or she provides an anchor around which thought connections and relationship systems can form.

The delusions of patients appear to me to be the equivalents of the constructions which we build up in the course of an analytic treatment — attempts at
explanation and cure, though it is true that these, under the conditions of a
psychosis, can do no more than replace the fragment of reality that is being
disavowed in the present by another fragment that had already been
disavowed in the remote past. It will be the task of each individual investigation to reveal the intimate connections between the material of the
present disavowal and that of the original repression [Freud, 1937, p. 268].

What I am saying here is that we engage with the patient in the
production of a creative fiction, which provides a core for an autobiography. The better the quality of the creative fiction, the better it
works.

Perhaps the most significant theoretical inference from these
considerations is that under *no* circumstances are we ever justified in
using our creative fictional "constructions" about origins of
pathology in the first year of the life to serve as data for theorizing
about early psychological development. This, it seems to me, is the
major flaw of those theoretical systems that go beyond basic mental
concepts in constructing models for that era.

Even when our creative fictional constructions do indeed
ameliorate severe psychopathology, we should distinguish between
the results of suggestion (inexact interpretation) and etiological
propositions. For even had we been actually witness to the hypothesized events in the infancy of our patients, we would still be constructing fiction — since what we "remember" for the patient and the
actual impact of the events in question are quite disparate at best —
and we shall never know how accurate or distant from actuality our
fiction is.

In support of this thesis it is well to remind ourselves that Freud
concluded from his studies of screen memories that when dealing
with earliest childhood memories, we uncover not a genuine
memory trace, but a later *revision* of it.

Out of a number of childhood memories of significant experiences, all of
them of similar distinctness and clarity, there will be some scenes which,
when they are tested (for instance by the recollections of adults), turn out
to have been falsified. Not that they are complete inventions; they are
false in the sense that they have shifted an event to a place where it did
not occur . . . or that they have merged two people into one or substituted
one for the other, or the scenes as a whole give signs of being combina-

tions of two separate experiences....It may indeed be questioned whether we have any memories at all *from* our childhood: memories *relating to* our childhood may be all that we possess. Our childhood memories show us our earliest years not as they were but as they appeared at the later periods when the memories were aroused. In these periods of arousal, the childhood memories did not, as people are accustomed to say, *emerge;* they were *formed* at this time [Freud, 1899, p. 321f].

Finally, I would like to make a guess about what Freud meant when he stated that these primal repressions are fixations. I believe that he was struggling with clinical experiences of coming up against the wall of what later theoreticians called "constitution" and then use as an explanation for failed cases. These earliest experiences leave something that cannot be analyzed or reconstructed—something that seems at times like a given, an aspect of apparatus. These things hover as a backdrop over everything we do. If we are alert to them and think about them, we might be able to find words to describe them and then to elaborate some creative (fictional?) hunches about how they happened. We may convey these hunches to our patients, and they could then begin the difficult journey to a new kind of organization. This is the essence of "construction."

References

Breuer, J. & Freud, S. (1893–95), Studies on hysteria. *Standard Edition*, 2. London: Hogarth Press, 1955.

Freud, S. (1899), Screen memories. *Standard Edition*, 3:301–322. London: Hogarth Press, 1962.

———— (1900), The interpretation of dreams. *Standard Edition*, 4 & 5. London: Hogarth Press, 1953.

———— (1915), Repression. *Standard Edition*, 14:141–158. London: Hogarth Press, 1957.

———— (1937), Constructions in analysis. *Standard Edition*, 23:255–269. London: Hogarth Press, 1964.

Glover, E. (1947), *Basic Mental Concepts*. London: Imago Publishing Co.

Kris, E. (1956), The recovery of childhood memories in psychoanalysis. *The Psychoanalytic Study of the Child,* 11:54–89.

Rubinfine, D. L. (1962), Maternal stimulation, psychic structure, and early object relations. *The Psychoanalytic Study of the Child,* 17:265–282.

———— (1967), Notes on a theory of reconstruction. *Brit. J. Med. Psychol.,* 40:195–206.

———— (1973), Notes toward a theory of consciousness. *Int. J. Psychoanal. Psychother.,* 2:391–410.

17

OBJECT RELATIONS, DEFICIENCY STATES, AND THE ACQUISITION OF PSYCHIC STRUCTURE

PETER L. GIOVACCHINI, M.D.

For the past two decades, psychoanalysts have been giving increasing attention to patients whom Freud (1914b) would have considered to be examples of narcissistic neuroses and therefore untreatable by the conventional psychoanalytic procedure. This point need not be belabored. In the last several years, many psychoanalysts have concentrated on the treatment of patients who, for the most part, have been labeled borderline personalities or narcissistic character neuroses, terms which distinguish them from the florid psychotic as well as the classical psychoneurotic patient.

I have discussed the diagnostic issues elsewhere (Giovacchini, 1979). Here I shall state only my belief that those psychoanalysts who first became involved clinically with these patients (Boyer and Giovacchini, 1967; Giovacchini, 1975; Guntrip, 1969; Jacobson, 1954a, 1954b; Khan, 1960; Modell, 1968; Searles, 1965; Winnicott, 1958) did not realize the subtle complexities of the psychopathology facing them. The patient's emotional distress could not be understood in terms of clashing intrapsychic forces. Rather, the ego had to be viewed in greater detail. Hartmann's (1950) formulation of the self, Sandler and Rosenblatt's (1962) description of the self representation, and Erikson's (1959) clinical approach to identity problems alongside Freud's (1914b) classical formulation of narcissism have helped many of us construct a conceptual scaffold that enabled us to deal with these patients in a psychoanalytic frame of reference.

Jacobson (1954b) was one of the first analysts to stress the importance of object relations in healthy development and psychopathology. In her longitudinal observations Mahler (1968) empha-

sized the importance of the early symbiotic stage. To many clinicians, it has become obvious that the therapeutic interaction
somehow has to recapitulate the subtle nuances of primitive developmental stages. Can something occur within the analysis that corrects
ego defects or fills the ego lacunae that are typical of characterological psychopathology?

These questions are restatements of the more general question
— one that Freud (1914b, 1915a, 1915b) believed he had answered —
as to whether psychoanalysis is a method that is useful for the treatment of patients suffering from structural problems. Focusing on
early object relationships and ego subsystems enables us to treat a
far wider range of patients by psychoanalysis than Freud thought
possible. This is well known. The mechanisms that are responsible
for therapeutic resolution, however, are imperfectly understood.

Many of us, when we began practice, faced a dilemma because
we wanted to make analysis our chief therapeutic modality, but our
patients rarely suffered from psychoneuroses. Not having had previous experience or instruction about patients suffering from ego
defects, we did not know how to proceed. We soon learned that
transference occurs, but we soon encountered vast unexplored areas
of primitive mental states that had to be understood. Experience
with regressed states of patients suffering from emotional maldevelopment has taught us much about the growth-producing elements of
early object relationships. Much of what we learned in our secluded
interactions with patients has not yet been articulated. I propose to
make explicit some of my clinical experiences and conclusions.

Analysts who treat severely disturbed patients generally agree
that eventually a transference regression occurs in which the patient
fuses with the therapist. This represents the recapitulation of the
symbiotic phase of development. Apparently this stage has important implications for treatment and psychic development, and this is
understandable inasmuch as this is a phase during which ego boundaries are formed and object relationships are established. The study
of the patient-analyst fusion can help us formulate some principles
about the acquisition of psychic structure, primarily how mental
representations are formed.

Deficit, Defense, and Adaptation

From many clinical discussions with colleagues, I have learned that patients suffering from structural deficits can be especially frustrating in a psychoanalytic treatment relationship. The problem often takes the form of the question: how can a therapist analyze material that is basically an accurate appraisal of the patient's mental capacities?

Many borderline patients experience intense and painful feelings of inadequacy. They incessantly complain about themselves during sessions. Analysts attempt to locate the adaptive and transference elements in this material, but as they place the patient's attitudes about the self alongside behavior, achievement, and the quality of object relations, they find it difficult to maintain an analytic perspective. Seemingly, there is nothing to analyze because the patient apparently is revealing structural deficits; and when the patient states that he is inadequate, he is not defending himself against powerful overwhelming impulses that he is afraid will get out of control, or responding masochistically and submissively to the cruel admonitions of a harsh superego. On the contrary, he is, in fact, inadequate. The analyst, whose *modus operandi* involves viewing the patient's material as fantasy products with adaptive defensive significance, finds himself in a quandary when confronted with what the patient is convincing him to be a realistic self-appraisal. This can lead to specific countertransference impasses, but I will discuss these later.

Before the analyst abandons the situation as hopeless, there are several possible outcomes that can preserve the analysis and allow the analytic process to continue to unfold. These require that the analyst steadfastly maintains an analytic orientation, which, in essence, is designed to convert a structural defect into a transference transaction. Later it will have to be converted into a defensive adaptation which extends beyond the transference relationship.

In order to continue functioning as an analyst, the therapist of these patients may have to focus more strenuously on transference elements than would be necessary for less primitively fixated patients. The analyst may have to rely heavily on his countertransference responses in order to be able to locate how the patient's material subtly introduces infantile elements in the therapist-patient relationship. I prefer to phrase it as introducing the transference rather than referring to the almost ubiquitous mechanism of projection in the production of transference because many patients have not achieved levels of psychic structuralization that are required for the establishment of even such a primitive defense as projection.

Many analysts confess feeling irritated after having listened to the patient's self-deprecations with the same monotonous regularity month after month. Unfortunately, discomfort often causes them to terminate treatment. Another alternative is to wonder what other factors, beyond feeling confused about how to respond to the patient's material analytically, are involved in producing our reactions. Our natural tendency is to believe that it is self-evident that a person would react to the patient's constantly humbling and attacking himself with annoyance, but is this attitude really justified? Perhaps the majority of therapists would feel somewhat uncomfortable, but other elements intrinsic to the patient's psychopathology also have something to do with our responses.

The psychoanalytic viewpoint emphasizes that everything the patient brings to us is, in some way, significant. It may not be immediately apparent or even relevant, but from an unconscious viewpoint it has meaning. A person who is constantly emphasizing his infirmities must have some purpose in exposing his vulnerability and torment. Keeping this point in mind — and it is often difficult to do so — may lead to the obvious conclusion that the patient is trying to manipulate us. He might want to feel in control and self-protectively withdraw from us because, inasmuch as he feels inadequate, he is terrified of a close emotional relationship with the analyst that he would otherwise be inevitably drawn into. These motivations are legitimate subjects of analysis as they represent transference interactions.

I do not mean to imply that the exposure of basic structural defects invariably signifies that the patient is being manipulatively controlling or withdrawing from an involvement with an external object, the analyst. Other factors may be involved, but from an analytic viewpoint what seems to be simply a description of the lack of the patient's capacities also incorporates defensive and adaptive features or it acquires such a meaning during the course of analysis. *To the extent that an ego defect becomes a defensive adaptation during treatment, the analytic process is a setting in which psychic elements are structuralized.* The analytic interaction promotes structuralization. I will present a clinical vignette to illustrate what I consider to be these broad issues.

Mr. R., a thirty-five-year-old businessman, had lost his job because of his firm's general cutbacks. He could fairly easily find other employment, but his previous job was unique in that he could remain isolated in an office and never had to come in contact with the public or even fellow employees since he was able to confine his activities to keeping records and devising marketing systems. Nothing comparable was available to him in other positions; he would have to have some human contact, minimal as it might be.

He desperately sought therapy because he was overcome by waves of anxiety, bordering on panic. He lamented and protested that he could never become involved with people, because he knew that he was a "babe in the woods," totally inept, painfully shy, and utterly incapable of conducting himself as a mature adult, with competence and worthy of respect. In his work, he had been insulated, and at home his wife protected him. There was no social life, and he did not have or want friends.

For the first six months, he spent most of his sessions experiencing intense anxiety, usually reaching a peak when he would sob convulsively. Sometimes he became quite noisy and cried loudly. All of this was accompanied by writhing on the couch and kicking his feet. When he spoke, he emphasized his ineptness and his lack of sophistication. He did not "know" how to relate in an adult world. Often, he felt "drained" and attributed this to his poorly endowed weak constitution. This was frequently followed by a long series of images. He described the pictures that flashed through his mind, and he might continue throughout the remainder of the session in this visual mode. He would associate to the images, but he was so concretely oriented that I could not perceive their meaning or how they were related to the transference.

I am presenting this material in an abbreviated fashion because I want to restrict myself to the question of ego deficits and adaptation. It is apparent that he was emphasizing how defective he felt and how he lacked the capabilities required to master the exigencies of the external world. The persistent quality of his self-depreciation, sometimes bordering on self-castigation, the intensity of his anxiety, and his concrete visual imagery all seemed to work against the maintenance of the analytic perspective.

What I found to be most distressing was the never-changing quality of his anxiety. There was no relief. Each session he reported feeling worse, never better. I noted that I was beginning to resent him, his constant and increasing distress. I then realized that he was trying and succeeding in making me feel as he did. He was manipulating me by permeating the consultation room with his tension, and at the same time he had hindered my analytic functioning and maintained distance. This must have been a recapitulation of a defensive adaptation to infantile trauma as well as a frank display of inherent ego defects.

Viewing the patient's psychic state in this manner—as representing the repetition of infantile reactions—established a transference focus. I did not believe that my responses were the outcome of his projections. Projective mechanisms, primitive as they are, were beyond the capacity of his primitive developmental organization. Rather than projecting, he was trying to avoid contact, and this itself could be considered transference since he was protecting himself against me in the same way as he did against infantile objects. *This is a unique characteristic of the transference of primitively fixated patients — the transference of early preobject psychic states which antedate projection.*

The course of the analysis—or rather, the analysis was permitted to have a course, once I understood the patient in what, in essence, is an analytic fashion. I interpreted the adaptive features of his material as he was defensively withdrawing and manipulating me, and he became less intense and better able to get in touch with other parts of himself.

Formation of Psychic Structure

It is biologically consistent to view the psyche as progressing from a global amorphous state to a multifunctioning discrete organization with well-defined boundaries. Various ego subsystems, such as the perceptual, integrative, and executive, are well developed and the self representation is clearly delineated. If structuralization has occurred in a salutory fashion, there is a secure sense of autonomy; self-esteem is high, and the ego relates to the outer world with confidence and mastery.

Mr. R. demonstrated the ultimate antithesis of these qualities of a well-structured ego. Even more striking was his inability to retain any experiences from the outer world that might be potentially helpful. He complained about not being able to remember what he read or to learn anything that might help him in his social or vocational life. His difficulties were related to deficits and defects in structure which have to be examined from a developmental perspective.

The psychic processes that lead to the structuralization of memory traces and introjects are particularly pertinent. Since the symbiotic phase seems to be so crucial both for healthy development and for the formation of psychopathology, it is important to study the developmental process in terms of psychic events occurring during the symbiotic and postsymbiotic phases.

The clinician might also ask about the significance of presymbiotic phases, and here distinctions between maturation and development became important. Hartmann (1939) neatly divided structuralizing processes into two interrelated categories, those emanating from innate biological factors known as maturational processes and those that are primarily due to interactions with the external world referred to as developmental processes. The former are responsible for physical growth, and the latter for emotional development, but one cannot occur without the other.

During the presymbiotic neonatal period, maturational factors are especially active. The central nervous system is still undergoing myelinization, feeding and sleeping rhythms are gradually being established, the perceptual system is beginning to be integrated, and a variety of biological functions become regulated. The function of the environment is to provide nurture and protective shelter as well as to respond smoothly to the needs of various sensory modalities so that innate maturational processes can optimally progress. At this time, the mother's primary function is to maintain the infant's equilibrium and to provide what Winnicott (1955) called a holding environment. The neonate has little capacity to incorporate elements of the environment into his psyche because the latter is still too rudimentary.

During the following phase, the symbiotic stage, the situation changes (Giovacchini, 1972a). Under optimal circumstances, the infant's needs are immediately met. The mother is so in tune with her child that she almost instinctively responds to whatever he might require. This interaction is so smooth and appropriate that it has a grace and rhythm of its own. The mother's response and the infant's needs are congruent. As a result of this congruence, the child need not be aware that he is separate from the mother. This is a state of symbiosis, and he develops the belief that the source of nurture comes from within himself. He can omnipotently care for himself.

What I have just written is, of course, blatantly untrue. The child does not "believe that the source of nurture comes from within himself" or that he "can omnipotently care for himself." Winnicott (1953) emphasized that the infant has the "illusion" that he is his own source of gratification, but both Winnicott and I are using metaphors. At most, the infant experiences a state of comfort which is the outcome of the reestablishment of homeostatic equilibrium. Inasmuch as satisfaction immediately follows need, there must be very little if any distress, and biological requirements can be felt as pleasant or, at least, as nondisruptive. Because of these gratifying circumstances and the mother-child undifferentiation, the infant does not yet distinguish between inside and outside. For the adult observer, this could be elaborated into the belief that the child feels fused with the mother and self-sufficient.

In terms of psychic structure, the good mothering interaction leads to the endopsychic registration of a state that Winnicott called the transitional phenomenon, which, I believe, is important for the later ability to form introjects and to acquire adaptive techniques.

How can this endopsychic registration be viewed more precisely? Are we dealing with the formation of introjects or memory traces? Most likely neither are formed if we are to confine ourselves to the symbiotic stage. The construction of introjects or memory traces requires the ability to perceive the outside world in a somewhat organized way, which is beyond the capacity of a symbiotic orientation. Still, the continuing sequence of need satisfaction causes some structuralizing change to occur.

I asked Winnicott whether it would be consistent with his views to conceptualize the endopsychic structure that underlies the transitional phenomenon as a nurturing or functional modality. Since the child experiences needs followed by satisfaction and psychic equilibrium, the nurturing experience becomes fixed in the psyche as a registration. Winnicott agreed that it could be so considered. Now, we must explore the development of this functional modality.

The functional modality is a psychic structure which is not the outcome of introjective and projective processes and which develops in a relatively amorphous ego organization. It is the residual of biological gratification. As long as gratification continues, it can be sustained; in energic terms, it is periodically cathected. Once a need arises, this functional modality is activated and then the child receives the product or experience that he requires. At this stage, he operates as a self-contained unit not recognizing his dependence on the outside world. From another viewpoint, he does not have sufficient discrimination to locate the source of nurture. He can only perceive, in a nondescript fashion, states of tension or lack of tension. The latter, adultomorphically, are referred to as states of frustration or satisfaction.

The functional modality, though actually supported by the mother's ministrations, becomes a fixed part of the psyche, a rudimentary ego system that operates as a *nurturing matrix*. No matter how undeveloped the infant's capacity for object relations, this matrix receives reinforcement from the external world, and its continued existence within the psyche depends upon a moderately successful mothering relationship. I wish to emphasize again, however, that this is a modality or matrix and not a maternal introject that carries the mothering function within itself. It is a more primitive structure than an introject and requires periodic cathexis which the infant cannot really supply, although Winnicott (1953) believes the child has the illusion that he can. The consequences of maldevelopment or relative absence of this functional modality or nurturing matrix are enormous and have great significance for the occurrence of psychopathology based upon characterological malformation and ego deficits.

To maintain a developmental focus, the emergence from the symbiotic phase, Mahler's (1968) "hatching" stage, introduces features that are significant for the maintenance and further development of the nurturing modality. When I say matrix, I am again indulging in metaphor, but in view of what I am about to discuss, I find it a useful metaphor.

The dissolution of symbiotic fusion brings the child into the domain of object relations. At first he relates to rudimentary part objects; these characterize the earliest organization of the perception of the outer world. The ego achieves the capacity to incorporate various aspects of experiences that are recognized as coming from outside the self. This process can best be described in terms of a progression. Disturbances in this sequence involve the symbiotic nurturing matrix and are characteristic of specific types of psychopathology.

The progression of the ego's ability to make elements of the outside world part of itself is responsible for the acquisition of psychic structure. The initially relatively amorphous ego becomes organized into various subsystems as memory traces are firmly retained and transformed into stable introjects, which are eventually assimilated as the adaptations that make up the ego's executive system.

External percepts form memory traces. At first, they can be retained only with the reinforcement of the presence of the percept. Piaget (1923) investigated this early stage and included it in his first phase, the sensorimotor phase, of the hierarchy of thought operations. Simply stated, if the stimulus ceases, there is no response, nor is there any trace of the previous response. The latter is rapidly extinguished. There are types of psychopathology that are, to a large measure, fixated at this level. *Some patients are unable to retain memory traces without outside reinforcement.*

Once the ego is sufficiently integrated so that it can retain a mental representation of an external object without the object actually being present, further perceptual discrimination occurs. The psyche now recognizes that nurture comes from outside the self, a distinction that could not be made in the previous, symbiotic, phase. The surrounding world has become fairly distinct from the inner world of the psyche, and external objects, as part objects, are discriminated in terms of their function, that is, their propensity to gratify instinctual needs. These functional part objects are also taken into the psyche and become established as introjects.

The concept of the introject was formulated by Ferenczi (1909), who viewed it as an essential element of psychic structure. I would go a step further and postulate a continuum between the introject and the memory trace. The psyche, in the postsymbiotic phase, begins by incorporating external objects as mental representations. These can be called memory traces, and the infant probably registers primarily a visual construct. In the next stage, once this construct is relatively well fixed in the psyche, the functional aspects of the external object are added to the internal percept. We then have an introject, a combination of a memory trace and an accompanying modality that has been instrumental in gratifying basic needs. The addition of the introject to the psyche represents a structural accretion, but the ego is still relatively helpless and dependent.

The introject has discrete boundaries. It does not enable the child to gratify instinctual impulses, but he has become able to turn to outside sources when inner needs press for satisfaction. The ego has memories of nurturing experiences and this leads to confidence and self-esteem that provides a setting in which further structuralization can occur.

To proceed with a graphic continuum, the next step involves structures formed during the symbiotic phase. The nurturing modality or matrix can now receive reinforcement from the introject, such as the maternal introject, rather than having to rely upon the actual gratifying experience. As structuralization continues, the introject loses its discrete boundaries; and, with the functional modality that is the outcome of the transitional phenomenon, it becomes an integral part of the ego. The nurturing function is amalgamated into the ego's executive system and becomes an adaptive technique that contributes to the final sense of autonomy. Still, in this early postsymbiotic stage, the child first becomes aware that he is dependent upon the outside world.

To repeat this formulation in energic terms which do not necessarily require a psychoeconomic tension-discharge hypothesis: the introject cathects the nurturing matrix. This promotes a feeling of some independence because immediate satisfaction from the outside world is no longer required. The child has confidence that he will be taken care of, and he is developing some techniques to seek his own gratification. The cathected functional modality enables him to turn to external objects, who, he expects, will meet his needs. This is a measurably more secure position than one in which the infant has to rely on someone else's intuitively sensing and responding to his inner tension.

These processes can be further understood from another viewpoint. The functional modality is an endopsychic registration which crystallizes from the successful mothering experience. As stated, inner needs, by being immediately met, do not reach disruptive intensity. These satisfied needs, in a sense, are the content of the matrix. They can be considered as forming a matrix or a grid, which is a mental construct of a biological impulse. Thus, this matrix is, because of its drive derivation, at the physiological end of a spectrum that ranges from instinctual bodily activity to subtle, sophisticated, secondary process thinking. The postsymbiotic stage of part-object relationships and introjects is partially directed to the outer world. The introjects's functional modality initially belonged to an external object and, unlike the symbiotic matrix, has less of a drive component. The integration of the drive-oriented symbiotic structure with the functional aspects of the introjects brings together biological and experiential factors. The interaction with the environment, by forming introjects and activating an early endopsychic registration of a functional modality, leads to psychic structure and the establishment of adaptive techniques.

These abstract formulations by themselves are meaningless. I find them useful, however, because they are the outcome of experiences with patients suffering from severe psychopathology. Ego defects can be understood in terms of disturbances of the developmental process associated with stages immediately preceding and following symbiotic fusion. The early interactions characteristic of these primitive stages are recapitulated in the transference. The presence or absence of psychic structure is also reflected in the identity sense. How the patient views himself or how he defends himself against basic structural defects is voiced in his self-assessment and becomes a dominant theme in his material and symptomatology.

Some ego defects create therapeutic situations which may put the analyst in a difficult position unless he is aware of how the patient is manipulating the analytic ambience. Even being aware of what is happening may not help much. In these instances, subtle and potentially disruptive countertransference factors may be operating, which confuse both analyst and patient. Ego defects dominate the clinical setting, and the analyst feels the same futility, despair, and inadequacy as the patient feels.

Psychoanalytic Paradox, Vulnerability, and Countertransference Sensitivity

All clinicians have dealt with patients who are difficult to treat. In this section, I wish to examine these difficulties in terms of the patient's defective ego structure and how it can disrupt the maintenance of an analytic relationship. Of course, countertransference factors are involved, and these will also be examined, but, in contrast to an approach that focuses primarily on countertransference (Giovacchini, 1972b), I will here emphasize the patient's psychic structure. These patients have an exceptional ability to produce what I refer to as an *analytic paradox.*

The following clinical examples are typical of the analytic paradox. The propensity to create such paradoxes seems to be characteristic of patients suffering from the lack of the ability to form and maintain mental representations.

Mrs. D., a depressed woman in her late twenties, wistfully complained that she could not feel lonely in the consultation room. The analytic setting did not permit her to do so. She felt my constant presence, sometimes as soothing and sometimes as pervasively intrusive. In any case, she and I agreed, a fundamental factor of the analytic task is to create a setting in which the patient can get in touch with parts of the self and feelings. This occurs in the transference context. The patient needed to experience me in order to project onto or fuse with me, but this required me to be psychically there. The primal loneliness she had to locate and reexperience precluded my presence. In this instance, this referred to my actual presence. She was unable to sustain a fantasy that I was gone.

At first, this situation seemed puzzling. It was easy to understand that, in view of some fixation on primitive symbiotic levels, she would not be able to hold an internal construct of the analyst without his presence, but here we are discussing the need *not* to have such a mental representation of the analyst. *It gradually became apparent that on the one hand, she could not cathect a mental representation without reinforcement of the external object; on the other, she could not decathect a mental representation without the disappearance of the external object.* The analyst's presence would be intrusive, and she could not re-create the primal state of fundamental isolation. To state it otherwise, there was something intrinsic to the analytic setting that worked in opposition to her reliving infantile psychic states which would have been essential features of therapeutic regression.

The second example refers to Mr. R., the businessman discussed earlier. He seemed to be operating at a higher level of ego integration than that of the depressed woman, but this was not really the case. He complained that the analytic atmosphere somehow interfered with his capacity to feel anger. At first, this seemed ludicrous since he was experiencing all kinds of explosive feelings. He cried and sobbed convulsively as he felt uncontrollable waves of anxiety, but in spite of all these volcanic affects he bitterly complained that I would not allow him to become angry at me. He lamented that my calmness, reason, and logic dissipated angry feelings. How could he become angry at a person who was benign and would explain his reactions, rather than respond with anger? In order to sustain anger he had to place such a feeling in an atmosphere that would be capable of generating it. Still, this struck me as strange, because, as stated, he was able to have overwhelming amounts of affect otherwise.

Again, the explanation of these apparent inconsistencies can be found in the patient's incapacity to form and maintain certain psychic structures. His volcanic eruptions during sessions were not object-directed. He was displaying the manifestations of ego disintegration and its accompanying internal panic. He was reacting at a primitive level; and as far as the external world was concerned, he could deal with it by making it part of his chaos.

His emotions were as primitive as his regressed ego state. If feelings such as anger require an external object, that is, they have to be directed toward someone, then the person that is selected has to be an appropriate choice. This is also true of the analytic setting for such patients as Mr. R. These patients can view the therapist only in concrete terms, forming an endopsychic registration of him as he actually is, rather than making him consonant with their general ego organization. They need to reduce him to the level of the regressed ego state and its accompanying affects. For Mr. R., primitive anger had to be directed toward an external object that would be similar and indistinguishable from early infantile traumatic objects. He could not transform me into such an object, since he could only take me in as an analyst because his mental representation of me depended upon external reinforcement. He did not have the flexibility to manipulate his perceptions. Consequently, he could not feel anger toward me, but he needed to bring anger into the transference as an essential feature of his regression. I would have to become an appropriate object of his infantile past. Then I would no longer be an analyst, but as an analyst he could not make me congruent with the level of organization of his affects.

Such patients' inflexible perceptions and their construction of an evanescent mental representation restrict the range of transference relations. To repeat, if the analyst could somehow change himself sufficiently so that his corresponding mental representation could be cathected with infantile feelings, then the analytic setting would have achieved the purpose of facilitating transference regression. However, the analyst would have to obliterate all elements of his analytic identity to achieve this; so there would, in effect, be no analysis. To remain an analyst interferes with the establishment of transference, because the patient's ego defects do not permit more than a single, rigid view of external objects, thus precluding simultaneous multiple views of the therapist, which are a prerequisite for the formation of an analyzable transference. This constitutes an analytic paradox.

This phenomenon emphasizes pathology in the formation and retention of mental representations. During presymbiotic and symbiotic phases, inner sensations rather than external stimuli are more apt to become permanently registered in the psyche. Even though these infants supposedly do not yet discriminate between inside and outside, they are better able to react to internal stimuli. This is self-evident, because internal stimuli represent needs or tension states that require responses. In the later postsymbiotic phase, the mental representation has to be reinforced. In regard to psychic representations of bodily needs, reinforcement is self-created, in that these needs are periodically awakened. Needs are not, of course, constantly felt, but they are periodically cathected and this leads to the consolidation of what we can call a psychic registration of an instinctual impulse. Such a psychic structure would be simply an upward hierarchical extension, a structuralization, of an initially physiological process. This occurs during the natural course of emotional development.

The nurturing modality, Winnicott's transitional phenomenon, is a psychic structure that begins to be formed as a psychological representation of an inner need. However, it is more than that; *it is the mentational registration of a need that has been met.* To achieve permanence and autonomy, it has to receive reinforcement from both the inner and the outer world. The former will continue because of biological rhythms, but supplies from the outside can be capricious. Without outer cathexis, inner cathexis is experienced as disruptive, and whatever mental construct is formed does not smoothly become incorporated into the psyche and lead to the acquisition of adaptive techniques. This is a restatement of the familiar thesis that frustration leads to developmental arrest rather than progression. What I am emphasizing is that the vicissitudes involved in the formation of this first mental construct have an important bearing on the formation of the postsymbiotic introjects, which, in turn, serve as a source of cathexis that can lead to the stabilization of a function as well as the construction of self and object representations. The synthesis of the identity sense is dependent upon the outcome of these interactions. In treatment, the problems that have interfered with these structuralizing processes create specific tensions and manifest themselves in analytic paradoxes.

While experiencing such analytic paradoxes, patients feel especially vulnerable. In treatment, they require a particular surrounding world and external objects that will permit them to experience feelings and parts of the self so that these can be synthesized and integrated to form higher psychic structures. Because of their early fixations, these egos make use of such primitive defenses as splitting. Affects and parts of the self remain dissociated from each other, and the course of emotional development is hampered. This lack of organization leads to feelings of inadequacy and helplessness which, alongside the psychoanalytic paradox, cause specific therapeutic responses and technical problems.

Mr. R. was beset with intense feelings of helplessness and vulnerability and, as discussed, presented me with an analytic paradox inasmuch as he could not get in touch with his rage. During the sessions, he continued feeling dispirited. To be somewhat dramatic, it seemed as if his ego were being torn apart as he writhed and sobbed on my couch. Still, he looked forward to his sessions or, at least, he indicated that he needed them and, in a curious fashion, he felt relief for some time after each interview.

Patients who present emotional storms in treatment often succeed in ridding themselves of their tension and perhaps leaving hateful and destructive parts of the self in the consultation room. What this patient displayed appeared to be different. Mr. R. was exhibiting all the signs of psychic collapse.

Again, the distinction between a defect — in this instance, ego disintegration — and a defensive adaptation becomes blurred. The concept of a structural hierarchy is indispensable. Successive layers of the psyche are arranged in increasing degrees of organization. A particular level of the ego is better organized than those below it and less structured than those above it. This structural sequence may involve a continuum from the id to the ego or, in operational terms, from primary to secondary process. The spectrum could also be temporally arranged, from developmental levels characteristic of early ego states to more integrated and differentiated psychic organizations found in later stages. What might be a state of disorganization, when compared to a more advanced level, may be a state of organization and may function as a defensive adaptation in regard to a lower-level ego state.

The intensity of Mr. R.'s behavior at first defied my efforts to see anything in it but psychic collapse. Its integrative features were elusive. Still, he came to his sessions and felt better afterward. If he were simply experiencing primitive states of disintegration, he should have felt exhausted and depleted, and perhaps even have become psychotic. The purposeless kicking and screaming of a tantrum do not achieve equilibrium and cohesiveness.

Mr. R.'s material was striking in its copious production of images. Freud (1914a) wrote about the behavioral repetition of psychic events. Instead of remembering, the patient repeats. Behavior labeled acting out replaces free association. Mr. R., in a similar fashion, produced visual images in the same way as Freud described some patients as acting out. I had the feeling that Mr. R. was getting relief through these images, even though I found it difficult to understand them in terms of content.

For example, Mr. R. once saw penises and breasts. They were disconnected and floating around in some sort of collage. From this, he jumped to images of toy sailboats, and then he suddenly burst into a paroxysm of screaming and crying. He was truly suffering, rather than melodramatically and histrionically emoting. He was in a spasm and his neck muscles were a mass of knots. His face was beet red. I was especially curious about his thoughts and feelings that might account for his intense suffering. As usual, he was totally devoid of any associations that might give me some clue as to the unconscious forces that might explain his apparent disintegration.

I was reminded of Freud's experience (Breuer and Freud, 1893–95) when he was beginning to abandon hypnosis for the pressure technique, which finally led to the formulation of the fundamental rule (Freud, 1912, 1913). At first, patients said nothing came to mind, but as Freud continued to insist that this was impossible or that something would occur, they finally admitted that they had had some thoughts which they suppressed even the first time he applied pressure to their foreheads or held their heads in his hands. Unlike Freud's patients, this patient never revealed any associations, at least not at the time he saw images and was in the throes of affective upheavals.

Pondering further about Freud's experiments on therapeutic method brings us back to the reliving of traumatic events in hypnosis and abreaction. During hypnosis, Breuer brought his famous patient, Anna O., back to the situation when specific symptoms first developed. In her trance, she would describe the scene and react with intense feelings. Breuer called this "chimney-sweeping" and the "talking cure." Yet, a careful reading of the *Studies on Hysteria* uncovers practically nothing about the content of Anna O.'s associations that is in any way significantly different from the way my patient reacted to his images. Anna O., according to Breuer, described concrete events and discharged considerable tension at the same time, but her descriptions would not have enabled a modern analyst to make inferences about the unconscious factors that determined the etiological chains. Many of her symptoms can be interpreted in terms of familiar symbols, but the validity of our conclusions would be highly questionable. They would, at best, be imaginatively speculative.

I am reminded of Anna O.'s hallucination of snakes coming out of the wall, snakes that were around her father's bed and coming toward her. At the same time, the snakes became part of her body. Her fingers were transformed into snakes and the nails became small death heads. Mr. R. saw images of breasts and penises surrounding him, which threatened to engulf him. I believe that the clinician can infer that somehow my patient's visual images, similar to Anna O.'s hallucination, referred to a traumatic incident. He did not react at the time, only later when he pictured the seemingly innocuous toy sailboats. The first image appeared to have been frightening, but it did not seem to upset him. He was overcome with tension and intense feelings of vulnerability only after the peaceful scene of the pool. In view of the relief he obtained from the outbursts, I began to wonder whether I was witnessing something similar to Breuer's description of abreaction.

Mr. R. spent some time talking about other subjects as well as describing pictures. His verbal products by themselves seemed as concrete as his description of images. He described memories of past events in obsessive detail. In spite of such detail, it was very difficult for me to remember what he described. Presumably everything was given equal importance and, from the listener's viewpoint, his "discussions" were difficult to cathect even when their content was striking and dramatic. The contrast between his explosive reactions to images and his monotonous recounting of endless details in nonvisual communications was remarkable. However, shortly after he reported the breasts and penises and sailboat images, I was able to recall some memories he had talked about several months earlier. I now concluded that these were introductory associations to them.

He had discussed a potentially tragic incident that had occurred when he was very young. He was vague as to when it had happened or whether he had actually remembered it. Perhaps someone in the family told him about it. At first, he stated he was eighteen months old, a toddler, when he had this experience. This would make it highly improbable that he could recall it, but then he said that possibly he was three years old. He described the following incidents. There was a small fountain in the yard of his home, a replica of the one in Brussels, of a young boy urinating. A neighbor, most likely a four- or five-year-old boy, climbed the enclosing fence, since he was not allowed there, and put a piece of wood with a small sail into the pool. The patient's parents called their son to come into the house. The neighbor child was frightened on hearing their voices and since he was trespassing, he hid in the bushes. The patient was so absorbed in this floating piece of wood that he either did not hear or ignored the parents' calling him. Instead of responding, he leaned forward to touch the boat. He lost his balance and fell face first into the pool. Apparently, he panicked and thrashed around, but was not able to pull himself out. He started drowning. The parents, angry at his not responding, went outside and found him struggling in the pool, swallowing more and more water. They stood there watching him, completely immobilized, unable to do anything to save him. The neighbor boy, hiding in the bushes and anxiously watching this scene, could no longer stand it. In spite of his fear of exposing his trespassing, he finally rushed to the pool and pulled the drowning child out of it. Then he ran out of the yard as fast as he could. The parents continued to be paralyzed and did not move toward the patient. He lay on the ground, coughing and spluttering and trying to regain his breath. His parents did not touch him or thank the neighbor, nor did they remove the dangerous fountain.

The apparently disconnected outburst now made sense. He was gripped in the throes of the terror of annihilation and both sets of images related to some aspect of the inner catastrophe that was overwhelming him. They also had transference connections.

Breasts and penises, among other meanings, fundamentally represented mother and father. They also signified the external world, a world which surrounded him totally and threatened to engulf him. He had emphasized how these breasts and penises were moving toward him. He had on other occasions concentrated on breast sucking and fellatio fantasies, but these were unpleasant and frightening associations. He reported sucking his lips and was obsessed with the thought that they were grotesquely large. Actually, I had never seen him suck his lips, but after he reported these images, I recalled the many occasions when he spent most of the session talking about fellatio fantasies and his preoccupations with his mouth and lips.

He was breast-fed for the first two months of his life, but he did not interpret this as meaning that his mother was devoted to nurturing him. Apparently very soon after she started nursing him, she developed a breast abscess. He was weaned abruptly. Later when he was seven months old, she left him for four months. To this day, he did not know why and even though he had asked, he was never given a definite answer.

As he spoke of the pool incident, his anxiety was focused on how completely surrounded he felt. During the session, he relived the terror of suffocation. He had a very specific emphasis that is not particularly unique for a drowning person, but in view of his material I believe it is noteworthy. He experienced the external world as coming closer and closer and finally filling him up completely through his mouth. During months filled with anxiety, he often gagged. He compared his feelings to those of geese being force-fed so that they would develop fatty necrosis of the liver to produce *paté de foie gras*. He thought of drowning in the pool in the same way as having penises and breasts stuffed in his mouth and choking him to death. He carefully distinguished that he would be choked from within as his body was invaded, rather than his throat being constricted and crushed from the outside. This seemed to be related to the intensely traumatic impact of the memory of his accident.

The parent's inability to help also intensified the effects of nearly drowning. Their impotence and noninvolvement must have augmented his helpless vulnerability immensely. He was terrified. His parents simply watched him, being either unwilling or unable to do anything to help him.

In my office, he relived this terror and was able to bring it into the transference, making his feelings fit the analytic setting. I did not know at the time what was happening, but this helped the transference focus to develop rather than hindering it. As the parents, I was just watching him at the height of his vulnerability and terror, and, like them, I was unable or unwilling to do anything about it.

As I understood this material, I was able to handle it interpretatively. Even before I started interpreting it, however, Mr. R. was getting considerable relief. This may mean that in some ways he was similar to Anna O. The visual images referred to traumatic incidents, or, to be more precise, to traumatic factors in the infantile setting, and his affective upheavals had some resemblance to abreaction. This is only a comparison inasmuch as the therapeutic process is invariably more complex.

My initial reason for not responding was simply that I did not understand what was happening. I did not know that he was creating an important transference focus. He was constructing a setting within analysis similar to the infantile environment. I am not postulating a traumatic theory of neuroses, as Freud did in the early days of psychoanalysis. The patient referred to a traumatic event that supposedly had occurred, and his other images and outbursts presumably could be related to similar incidents, but I do not believe that it is the incident itself that is important. Rather, I find it easier to view the trauma he reported as a paradigm that reflects in a concrete, encapsulated form the general ambience that surrounded him. The images and the abreactive qualities of his associations do not require traumatic moments; they can be explained in terms of specific ego defects related to the inability to integrate and maintain mental representations. These led to specific countertransference difficulties, which I will now discuss.

At first, I found the patient's visual style fascinating, but as the sessions followed each other and I could not understand how his material fit into a transference context, I began feeling frustrated. I was very much aware of my need to make sufficient sense out of what he was saying so that I could formulate a transference interpretation. I was not even concerned about interpreting to him; I simply wanted interpretative understanding. Because of his imagery and concrete orientation, he seemed to be defying my attempts to gain insights.

The patient's verbal material was also frustrating in that it referred almost exclusively to external events and seldom, if ever, to thoughts or feeling. He seemed to immerse the consultation room with his past and current world, but his references to the inner world were sparse and infrequent. I found myself making judgments about the appropriateness or inappropriateness of the patient's perceptions and responses. I was becoming annoyed with some of his insensitive and selfish behavior, and was tempted to scold him for his rigidity, which often took the form of extreme parsimony. I believe I could have precipitated a transference psychosis if I had given in to my inclination.

I was able to restrain myself because I could recall other, similar experiences and therefore understood some of the inner disruption I felt which could have induced me to do something that might have been psychoanalytically disastrous. This disruption was in part due to the patient's having to keep me in his outer world. This need is perfectly reasonable in view of his structural defects and difficulties in constructing a stable inner world, but, at the time, it was far from apparent. As an analyst, I saw my role as that of the investigator of mental processes. He did not permit me to do this. Consequently, I felt frustrated at my inability to function as I thought an analyst should. I also felt angry and guilty. Rather than blaming myself, I found it easier to blame the patient. Consequently, I developed critical feelings as to how he related to the outer world, the world in which he was confining me. *If the patient does not allow the analyst to explore his mind, then the analyst can easily be seduced to divert his attention to the patient's behavior.* This was especially so with Mr. R., because he complained about everything, his mother-in-law, wife, children, job, and the joylessness of his life.

A case that was presented to me at a staff conference came to mind and helped me manage my propensity to become managerial and judgmental. As stated, I now believe I could have caused a transference psychosis, as occurred in the case of Mr. X. He was a recently graduated lawyer in his late twenties who had been engaged to be married since he was in college. As he achieved professional status, his social circle expanded. He met many attractive young ladies and gradually was becoming emotionally detached from his fiancée. Still, he did not want to break the engagement, partly because he felt guilty, but primarily because he was afraid of losing what represented an anchor, a point of stability. Without her, he might be alone. He might not be able to attach himself to someone else, and it was very important for his psychic stability that he have a continuous heterosexual object relationship. The therapist was struck by the patient's ambivalence, but there was no material during the sessions that would have indicated he was having any conflict. On the contrary, he dated many girls, but made no effort to do anything about his engagement. He blithely talked about having lost all feelings for his fiancée, but he continued seeing her and even having sexual intercourse with her. He seemed perfectly happy with this arrangement and willing to continue in this manner indefinitely.

The therapist felt differently. He felt inundated by the patient's copious descriptions of everyday activities and the lack of material that could give him insights into the transference. Mr. X. did not complain, as Mr. R. did. Instead, he constantly bragged of how well he was doing. He was displaying compensatory narcissistic defenses, and he had no feelings for others, especially not for his fiancée.

This is the point at which the therapist broke in. He "confronted" the patient with his narcissistic defenses and exploitations. He stressed that Mr. X. had no consideration for other people and, in all fairness, should make a clean break with his fiancée. As it stood now, Mr. X. was interfering with her opportunities of forming a relationship that would lead somewhere, and in terms of treatment, Mr. X. was acting out in an immature and dependent fashion that should be worked through rather than discharged in action. The patient seemed moved by what he heard. He took stock of himself and as discreetly as possible terminated the engagement. He indicated that he had achieved considerable emotional maturity by curtailing his acting out. The therapeutic relationship was pleasant and Mr. X. concluded that he was well enough to terminate. The therapist agreed, believing that they had achieved a successful outcome.

Six months later the patient returned. He was grateful for his first course of treatment, but several situations led him to believe that he was not as secure as he thought he was, so they resumed the treatment relationship. His material was now quite different. He emphasized his feelings of inadequacy, how helpless and left out he felt. He revealed that his mother never had any real interest in him. She used him, since he was a bright and attractive child, to enhance herself. Her concern was reserved for his younger sister; in any argument between them, she would side with the sister.

During the sessions the patient began to experience waves of anger, at first diffuse, and then directed toward the therapist. He lamented that the therapist cared nothing about him; he cared only for his other patients. Mr. X. became increasingly agitated as his feelings intensified. To be brief, he finally became paranoid, believing that the therapist hated him sufficiently that he wanted to kill him. He felt terrified and persecuted to a bizarre delusional degree. For example, according to Mr. X., the therapist had been in collusion with the C.I.A. in order to smear him and get him fired from his government job.

He was no longer able to function in his daily life and had to be hospitalized. His relatives decided he should go to a private sanatorium in a distant city. Apparently, this was a wise choice because as the director of the sanatorium informed the department of the hospital where the therapist worked, the patient made a symptomatic recovery and is now gainfully employed in that city.

I was asked to review this material in order to help clarify the genesis of the transference psychosis. I realize that I have written this in a fashion that leads to some rather obvious conclusions, but this presentation has been organized to highlight them. The material presented at the staff conference was not so arranged or presented. I had to ask many questions to obtain all this information.

If we consider the reality of the therapeutic relationship, then the patient's paranoid orientation cannot be evaluated as a transference psychosis. The therapist did, indeed, respond exactly as the patient felt that his mother would have when the therapist admonished Mr. X. for being unfair to his fiancée. This was disguised as part of the working-through process, but nevertheless the therapist had abandoned the analytic stance and had become judgmental and dictatorial. His concern with someone else, the fiancée, rather than the patient, was a replication of the infantile past. When the patient accused the therapist in a paranoid fashion, he was supported by the reality of the relationship. True, the reality was submerged by a seemingly therapeutic interaction couched in such professional terms as emotional immaturity and working through. He achieved a pseudointegration that covered up his rage, but, after he had faced some traumatic events in his daily life, it broke down. He was able to reintegrate in another city, considerably distant from that of his former therapist.

As mentioned, my recalling this patient helped me suppress my inclination to be critical of Mr. R. *To generalize, I believe it is quite possible that most instances of transference psychosis are due to some error by the analyst, an error in which the analyst has unwittingly let himself be cast in a role that duplicates that of some significant traumatizing person of the infantile past.*

In the case of Mr. R., I was able not to intrude into his extra-analytic life, and the relief he obtained from his affective upheavals was connected with defensive adaptations and the traumatic elements of infancy. This needs to be discussed further in the context of his structural defects.

Psychic Integration, Mental Representation, and Therapeutic Factors

I believe that Mr. R. is typical of a large group of patients suffering from ego defects. Because of certain characteristics that manifested themselves in analysis as a peculiar, perhaps bizarre, mode of communication, he revealed basic aspects of early development more easily than some other patients with similar structural problems. These defects or, more precisely, this maldevelopment gives us considerable information about the formation of psychic structures.

Mr. R.'s predominant use of visual imagery is especially interesting and revealing. We do not yet know precisely whether the infant reacts earlier to light stimuli or to sounds, although by now there is pretty good evidence that the earlier reaction is to *sound* (Brazelton and Als, 1979; Terhune, 1979). Nevertheless, it seems reasonable to assume that the first structured mental representations are prominently visually oriented. As they develop further, earlier kinesthetic and visual elements become integrated with auditory percepts, finally culminating in verbal thought. Freud (1915b) described this quite simply as a progression from the thing (visual) representation to the word (auditory) representation.

In regressed states, Mr. R. did not integrate the thing representation with the word representation. These were temporally separated in his analytic sessions. He had problems in structuring a cohesive mental representation. At best, he had what could be called *part mental representations* in that one set of representations was characterized by thing cathexes (visual images) and another by word cathexes, as depicted in dull, monotonous, intellectualized verbalizations. Both visual and auditory modalities were fixated at early postsymbiotic levels and did not undergo confluence as occurs during the course of psychic development and integration.

The expression I have just coined, part mental representation, has to be distinguished from a part-object representation. These early post symbiotic mental representations are representations of part objects, but they are also part mental representations inasmuch as various sensory modalities are not integrated within them.

The difficulties Mr. R. had in effecting this synthesis of modalities stemmed from problems in forming and holding a mental representation within the psyche. As a result, the earlier symbiotic nurturing matrix did not receive sustenance from mental representations and did not continue to develop.

To restate this less abstractly, the patient had little security that his needs would be met and did not form an endopsychic registration of a satisfying nurturing experience. Later, because of this lack, he could not integrate and maintain percepts of the outer world that would enhance his earlier satisfactions and lead to their further development, that is, the experience of higher levels of gratification. This would have been accomplished by the gradual achievement of autonomy, more complex and sophisticated perceptions, higher levels of integration, and the acquisition of adaptive techniques. In summary, the comparative lack of development of a psychic structure that embodies experiences of satisfaction results in the imperfect integration and maintenance of later, potentially gratifying interactions with the outer world, which in turn, in a reciprocal fashion, hinder the progressive development of this initial satisfaction. The latter does not achieve the capacity to master inner requirements and experience pleasure.

Mr. R. was anhedonic and terrified of new experiences. He required a completely unchangeable and predictable environment.

His symptoms developed when he was no longer shielded from the external world. Clearly, he could not integrate new experiences. In terms of the above, he could not take in mental representations.

Mr. R. felt completely helpless and totally inept. He believed, as do so many patients with ego defects, that he did not have the adaptive technique to master inner needs and problems in his surrounding environment. Conceptually, this can be linked to the lack of mutual reinforcement of the nurturing matrix and early mental representations. Introjects do not form, and the range of adaptation is narrow.

For the purpose of this paper, it is not necessary to give detailed descriptions of the early nurturing relationship as it was reconstructed in the transference. I shall mention only two aspects of the maternal interaction that are especially pertinent. First, his mother was frequently absent during the first year of his life. She was there during the symbiotic phase, and then she was absent for the next four months. Presumably, she was hospitalized because of an emotional disturbance or a physical illness; Mr. R. did not know. Second, he realized that his mother would relate to him only if he were completely helpless. He noted that she directed her attention to his children when they were infants and would not acknowledge them later when they showed signs of self-sufficiency. Even when she tried to respond to his children's needs, she did it so clumsily that instead of soothing she agitated them. Most likely she had reacted to him in the same fashion, which would make it understandable that he had found it difficult to internalize a gratifying experience.

The therapeutic task can be broadly viewed in terms of resolution and structuralization. This is true of any analysis, but with patients such as Mr. R., these processes refer to specific interactions. We are still dealing with interpretation of the transference, but as different types of psychopathology have their unique manifestations, the technical handling of this particular variety of ego defect has its own specific features.

The treatment began to develop a focus when visual images could be linked to verbal productions. The patient was dealing with particular themes, but this was far from apparent. He did not seem to make any sense. His material appeared to be completely disjointed. This can be understood as being due to the fragmented nature of his mental representations. When his verbal material was placed alongside its corresponding visual representation, his material became meaningful. The analytic task consisted of making this juxtaposition, which can be viewed as an integrative task. More specifically, the analyst helped integrate mental representations by bringing the visual and verbal modality, the thing and word cathexis, together. Then the patient's affective explosions, his abreactions, were supplied with content that could be interpreted.

Mr. R. was able to comprehend that he could relate to me only if he were helpless. His helplessness and vulnerability directed him to traumatic situations in which he felt he would perish as the outside world simply stood by passively, impotent, and unable to rescue him. The childhood memory of his parents' ineptness as he nearly drowned in a pool helped me understand his terror, but the important fact was that he was reliving the same situation in the transference. He had rendered me inept and unable to help him. This has all the elements of the repetition compulsion.

However, he was reacting to more than a situation. He was creating in my consultation room the ambience of the infantile past with all its terror and feelings of vulnerability. He had brought into the analysis his fearful reactions to the external world from which he was no longer as protected, an external world that he viewed as he did his infantile world. This constitutes transference.

My countertransference feelings of helplessness (the patient having succeeded in getting me to identity with his parents) helped me see some purpose and organization in his material. I want to emphasize a distinction that I briefly referred to at the beginning of this paper: that my feelings were the outcome of my making an identification and not a result of the patient's projections. The patient had not yet achieved sufficient psychic structure so that he could project. Nevertheless, I finally concluded that he was revealing to me a basic ego state that could not hold and integrate mental representations. My interpretations highlighted his despair about my inability to protect and rescue him from an external world that he perceived as inundating him. I did not need to pull together actively his images of enclosing breasts and penises and his telling me about the pool incident. He was able to do this himself after I had made such interpretations. Later in the analysis he was able to project his helplessness onto me.

As he became capable of synthesizing mental representations, his fixations were loosened and emotional development resumed. He could then view me from different perspectives and even feel angry at me. He also expressed many other feelings—dependence, envy, rivalry, and even affectionate and homosexual impulses. His visual images disappeared completely, and he freely associated as other patients do.

Mr. R.'s symptoms were dramatic and bizarre, but I believe that the problems he presented are far more common than is generally assumed. More precisely, patients suffering from ego defects that are the outcome of a relative lack of psychic structure are not rarely found in psychoanalytic consultation rooms. The transference relationship permits the reliving of infantile interactions and the reexperiencing of fundamental states of terror. These, when understood, can lead to the unblocking of a developmental drive and the acquisition of psychic structure. The analytic setting has an intrinsic structure which provides the patient's material with an organization that makes it comprehensible and subject to interpretation.

Summary

In order to treat a patient suffering from ego defects that are chiefly the outcome of a lack of psychic structure, the symbiotic and post-symbiotic stages have to be understood in considerable detail. In this paper, I investigate the formation and maintenance of symbiotic structures and post symbiotic mental representations. These later developed mental representations help structuralize earlier symbiotic endopsychic registrations further. The final outcome of a continuum from mental representations to introjects and their subsequent amalgamation into the ego system is the acquisition of adaptive techniques. Until now, little work has been done to understand presymbiotic stages in a similarly detailed fashion.

I discuss a patient whose material consisted of visual images followed by abreactive types of affective explosions. These were reflections of his inability to integrate various sensory modalities into his mental representations. I have, however, seen the preponderant use of visual imagery in other patients who did not have similar defects. Some highly concretely oriented patients present pictures instead of words; other patients, obsessionals, defensively separate sensory elements. My patient, in contrast, did not have sufficient structure to integrate different sensory modalities.

In spite of this patient's lack of psychic structure, it was possible to work with him in a transference context. Actually, it would be difficult to think of treating him in any other context. Interpretation led to the integration of visual and verbal representations and the acquisition of insight which helped separate his current environment from the traumatic infantile past that he had externalized into it.

I believe that this patient is typical of a large group of patients who are increasingly finding their way to analysts' offices. Their symptoms may not be as striking as those of this patient, but they suffer from similar problems in forming and maintaining mental representations. The analytic interaction has proven to be a structuralizing experience.

References

Brazelton, T. B. & Als, H. (1979), Four early stages in the development of mother-infant interaction. *The Psychoanalytic Study of the Child,* 34:349–369.

Breuer, J. & Freud, S. (1893–95), Studies on hysteria. *Standard Edition,* 2:1–310. London: Hogarth Press, 1955.

Boyer, L. B. & Giovacchini, P. L. (1967), *Psychoanalytic Treatment of Characterological and Schizophrenic Disorders.* New York: Jason Aronson.

Erikson, E. H. (1959), *Identity and the Life Cycle* [*Psychol. Issues,* Monogr. 1]. New York: International Universities Press.

Ferenczi, S. (1909), Introjection and transference. In: *Sex in Psychoanalysis.* New York: Dover, 1960, pp. 30–79.

Freud, S. (1912), The dynamics of transference. *Standard Edition,* 12:97–108. London: Hogarth Press, 1958.

_____ (1913), On beginning the treatment. *Standard Edition,* 12:121–145. London: Hogarth Press, 1958.

_____ (1914a), Remembering, repeating and working-through. *Standard Edition,* 12:145–156. London: Hogarth Press, 1958.

_____ (1914b), On narcissism. *Standard Edition,* 14:67–102. London: Hogarth Press, 1958.

_____ (1915a), Instincts and their vicissitudes. *Standard Edition,* 14:109–141. London: Hogarth Press, 1957.

_____ (1915b), The unconscious. *Standard Edition,* 14:159–215. London: Hogarth Press, 1957.

Giovacchini, P. L. (1972a), The symbiotic phase. In: *Tactics and Techniques in Psychoanalytic Therapy I,* ed. P. L. Giovacchini. New York: Jason Aronson, pp. 137–169.

_____ (1972b), Technical difficulties in treating some characterological disorders. In: *Psychoanalysis of Character Disorders.* New York: Jason Aronson, pp. 327–340.

_____ (1975), Self projections in the narcissistic transference. *Int. J. Psychoanal. Psychother.,* 4:142–167.

_____ (1979), *The Psychoanalysis of Primitive Mental States.* New York: Jason Aronson.

Guntrip, H. (1969), *Schizoid Phenomena, Object Relations and the Self.* New York: International Universities Press.

Hartmann, H. (1939), *Ego Psychology and the Problem of Adaptation.* New York: International Universities Press, 1958.

———— (1950), Comments on the psychoanalytic theory of the ego. *The Psychoanalytic Study of the Child,* 5:74–96.

Jacobson, E. (1954a), Contribution to the metapsychology of psychotic identifications. *J. Amer. Psychoanal. Assn.,* 2:239–262.

———— (1954b), The self and the object world. *The Psychoanalytic Study of the Child,* 9:75–127.

Khan, M. M. (1960), Clinical aspects of the schizoid personality. *Int. J. Psycho-Anal.,* 41:430–437.

Mahler, M. S. (1968), *On Human Symbiosis and the Vicissitudes of Individuation.* New York: International Universities Press.

Modell, A. (1968), *Object Love and Reality.* New York: International Universities Press.

Piaget, J. (1923), *The Language and Thought of the Child.* London: Routledge and Kegan Paul, 1932.

Sandler, J. & Rosenblatt, B. (1962), The concept of the representational world. *The Psychoanalytic Study of the Child,* 17:128–145.

Searles, H. S. (1965), *Collected Papers on Schizophrenia and Related Subjects.* New York: International Universities Press.

Terhune, C. B. (1979), The role of hearing in early ego organization. *The Psychoanalytic Study of the Child,* 34:371–383.

Winnicott, D. W. (1953), Transitional objects and transitional phenomena. *Int. J. Psycho-Anal.,* 34:89–97.

———— (1955), Metapsychological and clinical aspects of regression within the psycho-analytic setup. *Int. J. Psycho-Anal.,* 36:16–26.

———— (1958), *Collected Papers.* London: Tavistock.

18

TRANSFERENCE AND COUNTERTRANSFERENCE

An Examination from the Point of View
of Internalized Object Relations

VAMIK D. VOLKAN, M.D.

In the introduction to *The Self and the Object World,* Edith Jacobson (1964) tells how the treatment and supervision of the increasing number of borderline, psychotic, and "severely narcissistic neurotic" patients who turned to psychoanalysis for help led her to reexamine the process of regression. This process points to a grave deterioration of superego and ego functions, as might be expected. She emphasizes further the deterioration of object relations and the dissolution of those essential identifications on which the experience of one's personal identity is founded. Her study not only was a major contribution to the clarification of the concepts of ego, self, and self representations, but also demonstrated the reciprocal effects of the structural differentiation of id, ego, and superego, and the process of developing an integrated self representation, identity, and the corresponding integrated internalized object world.

Jacobson's work stimulated further interest in severely regressed patients who had been considered poor candidates for psychoanalysis proper or psychoanalytic psychotherapy. Consideration of the vicissitudes of their object relations in the preoedipal phase, and the relationship of their object relations to drive aspects of that phase, led to a systematization of stages (Kernberg, 1972, 1976a) in which object relations are internalized, and integrated self and object relations ultimately achieved. These in turn facilitate the consolidation of ego, superego, and id as definite intrapsychic structures and further the integration of ego identity. In proposing that the basic building blocks of intrapsychic structure are units of internalized object relations that reflect interpersonal relations fused with drive investments, Kernberg was especially influenced by Jacobson's work, giving attention also to the theoretical contributions of Mahler, Hartmann, and Erikson, and the clinical observations of Melanie Klein and her school. It then became possible to examine personality organization from a new hierarchical point of view. On a high level, where the integration of self representations and the internalized object world have been achieved, the ego relies on repression and related defense mechanisms to ward off unacceptable drive derivatives. Nevertheless, in a situation in which self and object representations are not integrated, primitive splitting of opposing representational units along with their connected drive derivatives is the main defense mechanism, one aided by other primitive defenses.

I shall examine the manifestations of transference-countertransference phenomena that appear in the analytic treatment of patients who use primitive splitting and related mechanisms as their main defense against anxiety, and who activate unintegrated self and object images in the therapeutic setting. I shall also compare some typical aspects of the transference-countertransference axis of such patients with those of neurotic patients whose functioning reflects a high level of personality organization.

The Theory of Internalized Object Relations

Since psychoanalysts do not altogether agree on what is involved in the theory of internalized object relations, I shall describe how I apply its principles. Kernberg (1976b), in his foreword to my book, suggests that the theory of object relations may be divided into three categories. The first and broadest definition is concerned with the internalization of interpersonal relations. Inasmuch as such internalizations are preserved within the patient's mental structures, the quality of his present interpersonal relationships can be best understood in the light of those that were generated by his early life experience. Kernberg also refers to the views of the English school, especially Melanie Klein and Fairbairn who adhere to a particularly restricted definition of object relations and occupy the other end of the spectrum. Kernberg (1966) himself offered a third definition of the psychoanalytic theory of object relations, one that represents a middle ground. Subsequently (1976), I attempted to examine in systematic fashion its clinical correlates.

Following the contributions of Jacobson (1964) and Mahler (1963, 1968), Kernberg stresses the bipolar building up of self and object images that reflect the original relationship between the infant and his mother, and the subsequent development of dyadic, triadic, and multiple internal and external interpersonal relations in general. In his early interaction with the mothering person, the infant acquires his orientation to extrauterine life. The stimuli, pleasurable or unpleasurable, impinging upon him lead to an ever-increasing number of memory traces of the two types through the inborn and autonomous (Hartmann, 1939) perceptive faculty of the primitive ego. From these memory traces the individual forms in a bipolar way what Mahler (1968) calls "memory islands," which contain "pleasurable-good" or "painful-bad" stimuli not yet allocated either to the self or to the not-self. The repeated experiences the infant has with the need-satisfying (and need-denying) outside sources nevertheless continue to strengthen the infant's vague affective discrimination between "self" and "not-self." He forms self and object *images,* at first undifferentiated, from the perceptions associated with these experiences. Consistent and more or less realistic endopsychic representations—a "more enduring schema" (Moore and Fine, 1968) of multiple images—of the object world and of the self gradually develop out of these images. During this gradual process,

> Libido and aggression are continuously turned from the love object to the self and vice versa, or also from one object to the other, while self and object images as well as images of different objects undergo temporary fusions and separate and join again. Simultaneously, there is a tendency to cathect one such composite image unit with libido only, while all the aggression is directed to another one, until ambivalence can be tolerated [Jacobson, 1964, p. 44].

These continually occurring cathectic shifts and changes, Jacobson further indicated, are reflected in introjective and projective mechanisms. These mechanisms are based on the child's unconscious fantasies of incorporation and ejection of the love object, and exist at least throughout the first year of life.

Kernberg (1976a), whose theory of internalized object relations

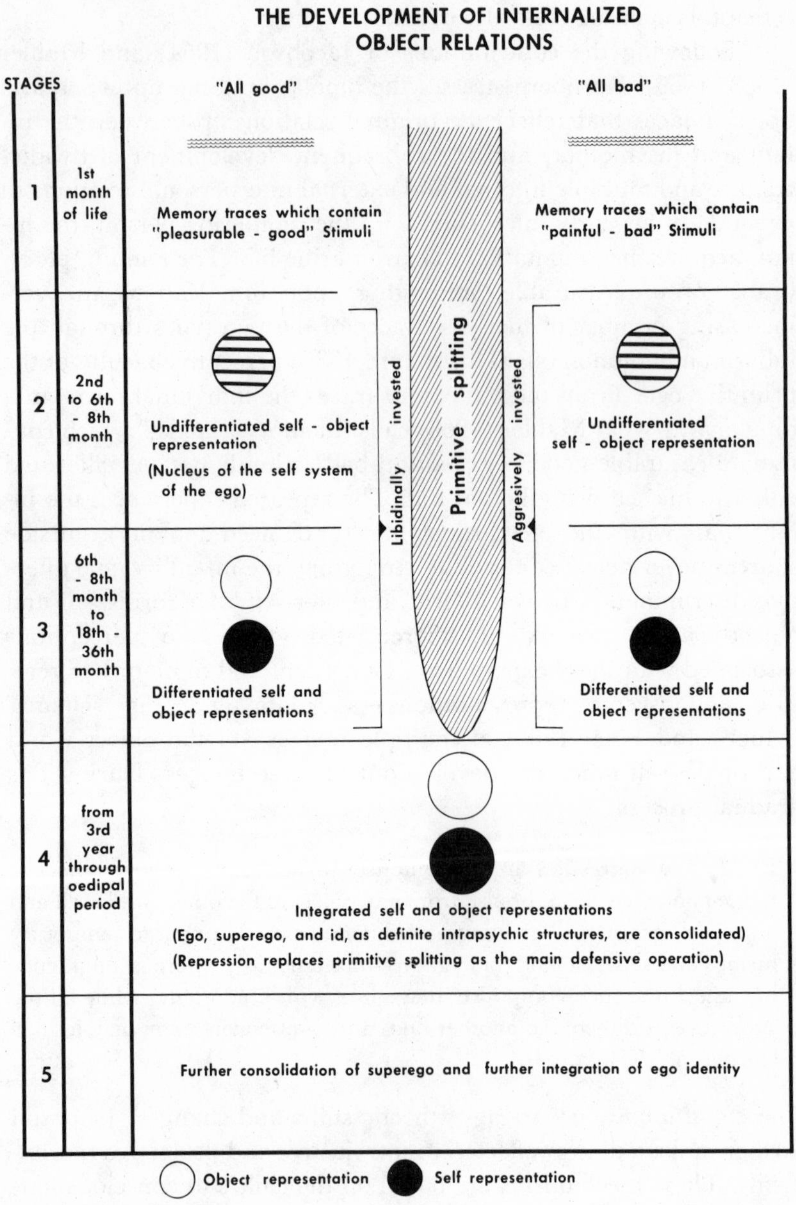

THE DEVELOPMENT OF INTERNALIZED
OBJECT RELATIONS

STAGES		"All good"			"All bad"

STAGE 1 — 1st month of life

"All good": Memory traces which contain "pleasurable - good" Stimuli

"All bad": Memory traces which contain "painful - bad" Stimuli

STAGE 2 — 2nd to 6th - 8th month

"All good": Undifferentiated self - object representation (Nucleus of the self system of the ego)

Libidinally invested | Primitive splitting | Aggresively invested

"All bad": Undifferentiated self - object representation

STAGE 3 — 6th - 8th month to 18th - 36th month

"All good": Differentiated self and object representations

"All bad": Differentiated self and object representations

STAGE 4 — from 3rd year through oedipal period

Integrated self and object representations
(Ego, superego, and id, as definite intrapsychic structures, are consolidated)
(Repression replaces primitive splitting as the main defensive operation)

STAGE 5

Further consolidation of superego and further integration of ego identity

○ Object representation   ● Self representation

FIGURE 1

treats both self representations and object representations as theoretical affective-cognitive structures, distinguished five stages in the gradual process to which Jacobson had referred. These stages reflect a process whereby undifferentiated bipolar self and object images are first differentiated and then integrated, when "good" and "bad" image units are put together. Figure 1 presents a graphic schema summarizing the stages outlined by Kernberg. Emphasis on the bipolar development of self and object representations and on the maintenance of such bipolarity until the integration of "good" and "bad" representations becomes possible — usually in the third year of life — justifies the use of the term splitting to indicate the separation of opposite representations.

I have consistently used the adjective *primitive* before splitting in this connection (1975, 1976) to differentiate this phenomenon in a primitive phase of the developmental process from the higher-level splitting that can be seen in fetishism and pathological grief (Freud, 1927, 1940) in those who have achieved a high level of personality organization. Specifically, primitive splitting is the separation of self and object images or representations, whereas higher-level splitting involves the splitting of ego functions to give two contrary reactions to the conflict at issue. Since the theory of internalized object relations takes into account the way in which "good" and "bad" self and object constellations are invested with libidinal and aggressive drives, the term *primitive splitting* refers to the separation of representational units along affective lines according to the investment of opposing drive derivatives.

Primitive splitting reflects at the outset the primitive ego's inability to integrate. With the gradual achievement of integrative capacity, primitive splitting is used less often, and it is ultimately abandoned for all practical purposes when circumstances are normal. In some situations, however, the separation of representations may be more and more resorted to since it can be used as a defensive measure, chiefly to prevent the internalized "good" relationship to the mother from becoming contaminated with "bad" experiences with her. Some adults continue primitive splitting as their dominant defense mechanism (Kernberg, 1967). There are many reasons for this, including so-called constitutional factors, which refer to inborn psychological foundations as well as to the nature of mutuality between the infant and mothering person, and also include early experience with excessive frustration that has given the "bad" unit an excessive load of contamination with aggressive drive derivatives. It then becomes difficult to mend the split; instead of integrating the "good" units the individual tries to maintain with these "bad" ones that are excessively invested with aggression, he finds it necessary to keep them apart. In other words, primitive splitting is used as a defense against conflicts of object relations that reflect the primitive anxiety of losing one's "good" representational units. A group of investigators (Berkowitz et al., 1974; Shapiro et al., 1975, 1977; Zinner and Shapiro, 1972) demonstrated the role of the family in perpetuating the use of primitive splitting as a defense. I have indicated (1976, 1981) how the mother's perception of her child as omnipotently "special" became part of a child's developing self concept, but could not be integrated with other self concepts of a small child. Like Cambor (1969), I have also referred to the persistent use of pathological splitting by those who experienced "multiple mothering" in infancy and childhood (1979).

The Contrast Between Structural Theory (and Structural Conflicts) and the Theory of Internalized Object Relations and Object Relations Conflicts

The original "good" self-object representation that is inwardly maintained becomes the nucleus of the ego (Kernberg, 1976a), although the role of certain primary functions of the organism commonly called autonomous ego functions — which include perception and memory — are clearly involved in the formation of self and object images. I use the concept of the nucleus of the ego in the sense that Freud (1923) used it, rather than in the sense of primary autonomous apparatus (Hartmann, 1939). The fully differentiated and fully formed ego does not come into existence, however, until "good" and "bad" self representations, as well as "good" and "bad" object representations, unite — until, in other words, the primitive splitting is mended. It is the developing integrative processes, along with the development of more mature cognition and affect, that reduce the utilization of primitive splitting. This occurs in normal development when the child arrives at the oedipal period, when the maturing ego can push unintegrated and unacceptable parts of his primitive internalized object relations into the id by means of repression. Van der Waals (1952), Kernberg (1976), and I (1979) have shown that the repressed portion of the id is not a pure id, but an "ego id." Moreover, the mending of representational units brings about the "loss" of "good" images, and in reaction to this loss a new set of images — *idealized* ones — develops. The coalescence of these idealized images into the superego, which derives from earlier excessively bad images, externalized and reinternalized, integrates the superego and tames its ferocity.

To summarize, the achievement of a stage in which opposing self and object representations are integrated begins the full differentiation of id, ego, and superego throughout the oedipal period; thus the psychopathology stemming from this period can be best understood, theoretically speaking, from the structural point of view. In recent years, the psychoanalytic literature has increasingly implied that the structural theory falls short of providing a full understanding of the psychopathology that stems from conflicts in the preoedipal period. The vicissitudes and complications of internalized object relations in this period are dominant and can be better explained by a theory that refers to self and object affective representational units as "theoretical structures" (Volkan and Akhtar, 1979).

A reciprocal influence is at work between the theoretical structures of self and object images or representations, and the theoretical structures of id, ego, and superego. Initiation of the former set begins with the help of autonomous aspects of the primitive ego, while it is the development of the self system and its differentiation from the internalized object world that bring about full separation of the ego from other related structures (Jacobson, 1964).

The "oedipal-preoedipal dilemma" referred to by Greenspan (1977) needs to be further examined since it indeed poses some unanswered questions such as the one Greenspan asks: how can a *regressive* preoedipal conflict situation be distinguished from a *pure* preoedipal situation? Even in referring to a surface clinical picture, some writers apply structural theory when such a picture appears in persons who have attained a differentiated id, ego, and superego; and apply the theory of object relations when such a picture appears in those who are stuck in their development of an integrated self representation and an integrated internalized object world. Socarides's (1978) explanation of homosexuality is an example of this; he differentiates this clinical picture when it is oedipal from its counterpart that reflects a conflict of object relations.

Although Dorpat (1976) does not use the same model of object relations that I use here, he contributes to the idea that conflicts from the preoedipal phase cannot be fully understood by applying the structural theory alone. Referring to Gedo and Goldberg's (1973) hierarchical model of the mind, Dorpat states that it is not only useful but necessary to apply different models and theories to the study of different developmental phases as well as to the examination of psychopathology of different developmental phases. We may use the tripartite model of ego, id, and superego to understand neuroses and high-level character disturbances in which conflicts center predominantly around oedipal problems; but we may need another model for the understanding of conflicts of object relationships. The content — that is, the wishes, prohibitions, and injunctions of the two opposing parts of the conflict — may not differentiate the structural from the object relations conflict. Dorpat refers to a *crucial* difference between the two; in the former, the person experiences the tendencies in conflict as aspects of himself, or is at least capable of doing so, if some aspect of the conflict is unconscious. He owns both the prohibitions, values, and injunctions with which he is struggling, and the aggressive, sexual, or other strivings with which they have come into collision. The opponents are generated within himself. Dorpat explains: "In the object relations conflict, the subject experiences the conflict as being between his own wishes and his representations (e.g., introjects) of another person's values, prohibitions, or injunctions" (p. 870).

In accordance with these formulations, I shall argue that there are important differences in the transference-countertransference phenomena of patients undergoing psychoanalytic treatment for structural conflict and those whose therapy focuses on conflicts of object relations. An understanding of these differences from both a clinical and a theoretical point of view reinforces the propriety of using different models for different levels of psychopathology. Object relations conflicts are here understood in specific reference to the theory of internalized object relations I have been discussing. Such conflicts take place between certain units of self and object representations that are contaminated with certain drive derivatives, and other, contradictory, or opposite units of self and object representations that are under the influence of their respective drive derivatives.

Transference Phenomena and the Theory of Internalized Object Relations

The usual understanding of transference as the displacement of behavior and feelings originally directed toward significant figures of one's childhood, and the usual view of transference neurosis as the displacement of infantile conflicts — between drives and defenses against drives — to the analyst may be inadequate to describe the state of affairs existing between the patient and the significant other (the analyst) when the patient activates many split-off self and object representations in a highly distorted way during his treatment. Anna Freud (1965) noted that the psychoanalyst trying to treat a psychotic patient has much in common with the child analyst; not all the relations transferred by the child in analysis are of the sort in which the analyst becomes cathected with libido or aggression. Many are due to externalization, "to processes in which the analyst is used to represent one or the other part of the patient's personality structure" (p. 41). Although she makes no reference to object relations conflicts in the sense described here, her view of differing kinds of transference is well taken. Her statement about "one or the other part of the patient's personality structure," when understood to include unintegrated self and object images or representations, enhances our understanding of what it is that is externalized onto or into the analyst.

The patient in ordinary transference neurosis also activates aspects of his infantile self and aspects of parental objects; but, as Kernberg (1976a) states, activated aspects of the infant self are linked to or integrated with the patient's infantile self in general, and activated aspects of the parental objects are in turn linked to or integrated with the parental figures as experienced in infancy and childhood. Such linking or integration of what is activated with the rest of the self and object representations does not occur in purely pre-oedipal transference types. Dorpat (1976) referred to such types in general as "narcissistic." Although this is accurate, the application of the theory of internalized object relations gives us greater specificity about the types of preoedipal transference than the use of the general term *narcissistic* can provide, as I shall attempt to show. The transference manifestations of the patient without integrated self and object representations reflect the externalization and subsequent reinternalization of split self and object representations.

In this statement I use the term *externalization* as Novick and Kelly (1970) and Berg (1977) use it, and differentiate it from projection proper. Projection is used to defend against a specific drive derivative directed against an object. In treating neurotic patients we are entirely familiar with transference projections exhibited side by side with transference displacements. The patient directs a drive derivative onto his analyst; he subjectively allocates it to the analyst, while the patient experiences himself as the object of that drive derivative.

Externalization is an earlier defense mechanism, one pertaining to aspects of the self as well as to aspects of internalized objects. It is used here similarly to Melanie Klein's (1946) term projective identification. She described projective identification as "a combination of splitting off parts of the self and projecting them on to another person" (p. 108). It appears when the child faces the extremely difficult task of integrating the various dissonant components of his developing self representations as well as the internalized object world. Some aspects are "valued through both the child's own pleasure and, more importantly, the parents' response to one or another aspect of himself. Those aspects which are not so valued may become dystonic. Their retention within the self representation will lead to a narcissistic pain such as humiliation. . . . One solution is to *externalize* that aspect of himself" (Novick and Kelly, p. 83).

I believe, as Berg (1977) does, that all patients of the purely preoedipal type, once they are in treatment, include their analyst in their constant effort to externalize and reinternalize, making their analyst first one split-off image and then another, while adopting for themselves one self image after another, and so on. Although this process can be clearly seen in lower-level types of patients, it may be rather hidden—at least initially—in those nearing stage 4 (see fig. 1). In patients functioning at stage 2, externalization and reinternalization are further complicated because certain self and object images may fuse with one another and separate, only to fuse again.

To summarize, externalization and reinternalization of self and object images dominate in all preoedipal types, but the variety of such externalization and reinternalization depends on the degree to which the patient has an integrated self identity and total object representations. Kernberg's systematization of the stages of development is useful for the theoretical grasp of the different manifestations such patients exhibit.

Kernberg (1967) described the borderline personality organization that reflects the phase in which self representations are differentiated from the representations of objects, but primitive splitting remains in full force as a defense (see fig. 1, stage 3). The transference manifestation reflecting this state can be called *primitively split transference*. I have discussed (1976) the circumstances in which, because of primitive splitting, the therapist can sense the presence in his office of four rather than two players, since the patient's "good" self and object representations are present as well as his "bad" self and object representations. Operation *below* the level of the borderline personality organization, where self and object representations are not differentiated from each other, induces transference manifestations described in the literature by such different terms as *transference psychosis* (Rosenfeld, 1954; Searles, 1963); *symbiotic* (Mahler, 1963); *psychosis* — and possible *transitional object relatedness* (Modell, 1968). Distortions in the transference are gross, and the patient's reality-testing ability relative to what the therapist represents to him seldom functions. The therapist as an external object, as well as the target of the patient's externalization, merges with other object and self images.

Although primitively split transference is related to a well-formed mechanism of primitive splitting, the primitive splitting that occurs in transference psychosis on the level of stage 2 is not an effective defense. Shifts of self and object images, mostly but not always undifferentiated, follow one another in quick succession (see fig. 2). The fusion of self and object images can itself be used as a defense, as can be seen in the murderous rage against a needed object that would induce conflict giving rise to primitive anxiety. This anxiety would in turn be handled by the patient's fusing his angry part with the image of the target part of the object. But now such a fusion would lead to anxiety concerning self annihilation. This, in turn, could be handled by the refusion of self and object representations, and such a cycle would continue (Volkan and Akhtar, 1979).

Operation *above* the borderline level, when primitive splitting is overcome, produces the classical *transference neurosis* during analytic treatment. Recent psychoanalytic writings also mention *narcissistic transference*, but not in the sense in which Freud described the withdrawal of the psychotic individual and his unrelatedness to the analyst. The term *narcissistic transference* refers today to the transference

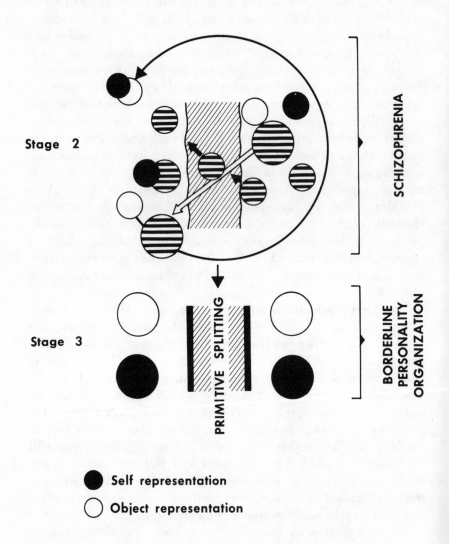

Stage 2

Stage 3

SCHIZOPHRENIA

BORDERLINE
PERSONALITY
ORGANIZATION

PRIMITIVE SPLITTING

● Self representation
○ Object representation

FIGURE 2

manifestations of the patient with narcissistic personality disorder. The nature of this personality organization has led to the formulations of what are basically two schools, one championed by Kernberg (1975), the other by Kohut (1971). From the viewpoint of internalized object relations Kernberg describes such patients as having a grandiose self — to borrow a term from Kohut — which is a condensation of the *real* self, reflecting the specialness of the child reinforced by early experiences, with the images of the ideal self and ideal object. The grandiose self develops when self integration takes a pathological turn.

In this sense, a narcissistic organization falls between borderline and neurotic (or character pathology on a high level). In the narcissistic organization, primitive splitting also affects the transference. The grandiose self is split off from underlying devalued self and object images as well as from devalued external objects. In the narcissistic transference, the patient behaves as though he were the world's greatest inhabitant and as though it were the analyst's task to adore him. When he realizes that the analyst is not adoring him, the patient scorns the analyst altogether. The typical countertransference at this stage of the treatment is boredom (Kohut, 1971; Modell, 1975; Volkan, 1979b), inasmuch as in the stage the patient's grandiose self forbids him to acknowledge his analyst's existence in any role other than that of a worshiper — or a worthless being.

Once the narcissistic patient is in analytic treatment, however, one can expect him to manifest primitively split transferences in his regression. The same is true for the borderline patient, who, once in analytic treatment, may manifest a transference psychosis prior to a reorganization. Transference manifestations reflecting the reactivation of fantastic internalized object relations will prevail in all preoedipal types until the patient can tolerate ambivalence in his relationships and until he can achieve an integrated self concept and an integrated internalized object world.

In accordance with the views of Boyer (1967) and others, I have suggested (1976) that one of the most important initial goals of work with such patients is to help them to differentiate in piecemeal fashion the representation of the analyst from the archaic and unintegrated self and object images. The analyst's representation then becomes a new object (Loewald, 1960) or what Giovacchini (1972) refers to as "an analytic introject." When such an introject is as-

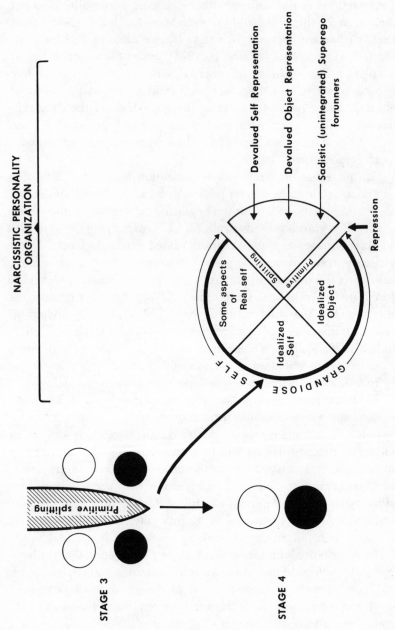

FIGURE 3

similated into the patient's self system as analytic functions and attitudes, the patient's integrative ego functions are enriched. The assimilation of the representation of the analyst can be used to mend primitive splitting and to provide a graft over the images that have been split or fragmented, and glue to hold them together.

Clinical Manifestations of Transference and Countertransference in Preoedipal and Oedipal Types

A statement made by Novick and Kelly (1970) in their comparison of projection proper and externalization may shed light not only on the nature of transference but also on the analyst's emotional response (an aspect of countertransference) to the transference. These investigators always see "some degree of fit" in projection; what is projected always has somewhere a basis of reality, they believe. That is, the patient hangs his projections on some real event—a canceled therapy session, for example—and the projection of hostile impulses will always have some core of truth. This is particularly clear in the analysis of a child. I am in agreement (1979a), however, with Novick and Kelly that there may be very little fit between externalized dystonic ("bad") representations and reality; indeed, there may be no observable fit at all.

Analysts usually are more familiar with and more tolerant of a patient's transference projections and transference displacements than of his transference externalizations. First, if we are to assume that the analyst functioned on a neurotic level or with high-level character pathology before his training analysis, we expect him to have become familiar with his own transference projections and his analyst's reactions to them. Thus he "learns" through identification how to be subject to these projections and to remain in the therapeutic position. Such tolerance is part of his professional identity.

Once a patient's analysis is under way and the transference neurosis is manifested, we can follow in the usual analytic setting the transference projections as they are anchored in some real event. For example, a neurotic patient of mine had a dominant mother who had customarily denigrated her husband. The father was accordingly perceived as ineffectual, and in spite of his considerable professional accomplishments my patient considered *himself* to be ineffectual as well. His analysis revealed that this identification with the *degraded* image of his father also had been a defensive maneuver to deal with castration anxiety. As his analysis advanced, memories that showed other aspects of his father as a stronger man surfaced. This new development went hand in hand with his transference displacement onto me of his attitudes and feelings toward this stronger father. As might have been expected, they were accompanied by references to castration anxiety. In other words, to see his father as stronger was to expect castration at his hands — through transference neurosis, at the hands of the "stronger" analyst. His references to this were initially tentative, and his view of me as a castrator did not induce in me any particularly strong emotional response since my experience as an analyst had made me familiar in the course of my professional development and practice with being considered a castrator at some time or other by neurotic patients.

One day this patient, while lying on the couch at this stage of his analysis, calmly told me how amazed he was to recognize the pattern of the radiator grill in my office. He said that his father, who had been a mechanic, had made grills and had made a beautiful one exactly like mine for his own office. The patient thus acknowledged his father's manual skills and made him appear a strong man. After a deep silence the patient suddenly broke into a loud outburst of hostility toward me in which he cursed and raved. He made it clear that during the silence he had felt fear of me, thinking that I could hurt him and take advantage of him. His outburst was in the service of warding off my attack. Since he was usually obsessional and polite, his hostility took me by surprise, and I am sure I presented the appearance of someone under attack, having a quickened heartbeat and the sudden sweat of alarm. Regardless of this natural human response, my emotions did not lose their signaling functions; thus I was able to think through the patient's use of the radiator grill as a means of displacing behavior originally directed toward his father-castrator. His outburst was a protective maneuver against his projection of his own murderous impulses onto me. Moreover, it protected him from the possibility of homosexual surrender to his father. The reality of the grill in my office and its actual or fancied resemblance to the one in the office of his father gave an *anchoring point* for the interaction that took place between us. Within seconds I was in command of my counteremotions. I chose not to tell my patient about them since such knowledge on his part would burden him unnecessarily, but in due course the process was repeated and then was interpreted to him. This episode is but one example of many similar events that occur in our daily work.

I must emphasize that I do not equate this kind of counteremotion felt on one occasion with what we regard as a manifestation of a full-blown countertransference. I use it here simply as a microscopic example of a collection of such events, the macroscopic correlate of which is the full-blown countertransference reaction to the transference of a patient.

The analyst who is the subject of externalizations may lack the advantage of having an observable anchoring point in reality which precipitates or accompanies such processes; he is more at the mercy of what is attributed to him by his patient. He will, however, come to understand more of what is going on as the therapeutic process advances, and as he gains secondary process understanding of the affect-laden sensations he experiences as the recipient of his patient's split-off self and object representations. Even so, his countertransference responses are more likely to be generally unfamiliar to the analyst dealing with a patient who externalizes. It is likely that his training analysis, outside of relatively brief periods of extreme regression which seldom escaped the attention of his observing ego, has not provided him enough opportunity to identify with his analyst as he handles such externalization.

Most of us feel comfortable in the treatment situation when we see a low-level behavior pattern such as a hallucination in a patient, unless this behavior is accompanied by an emotion such as hostility directed toward us. One reason we can feel comfortable is that our own "normal" behavior pattern is so far removed from the observably "crazy" pattern of the patient. We do not identify ourselves with the patient experiencing what is beyond the range of our usual way of life. But to be a target for the externalization of the patient's representational units that are connected with untamed affects is something altogether different. Some therapists cannot "regress in the service of the other" — to use Olinick's phrase (1969) — when deep regression is required. Accordingly, some psychoanalytic therapists may be unsuited for treating borderline or schizophrenic patients in analytic ways that require their own regression, accompanied by an observing and therapeutic ego, in order to develop fully a therapeutic relationship that parallels the child-mother interaction. Long experience with such patients, under supervision, can, however, give the therapist familiarity with, tolerance of, and the ability to use such externalizations therapeutically. I would not advise anyone to undertake such therapies without first having had considerable supervised experience with them. I recall almost literally choking when working early in my analytic psychotherapy with a severe borderline patient whose behavior suddenly filled me with unbearable "bad" feelings; I felt it necessary for my survival that I flee into the fresh air and sunshine, and I could hardly wait for her to depart. It is not surprising that this patient's first remembered childhood dream was of her mother's feeding her oatmeal and choking her with it. During the hour in which I felt choked I had become her helpless self representation, and, identifying with the "bad" mother representation, my patient had choked me/her. Were such interaction to occur now, I expect that my emotional response would be tamer because I am now familiar with such externalizations. I would still feel it intensely if I were sufficiently regressed to accept her externalization, but I doubt that I would lose my objectivity. Moreover, I would find a suitable way to utilize my emotional reaction in the treatment process. After accepting her externalizations long enough for her to realize that I could tolerate them, so that in her identification with the analytic introject such tolerance could be assimilated by her, I would tell her, if she had enough ego function to enable her to grasp my interpretation, that she wanted me to have a firsthand experience of the intrusive mother. As this microscopic example suggests, I use my countertransference responses more readily and openly in therapy with patients who activate unmended self and object representations. Countertransference can more readily become a part of the therapeutic process in such cases than in the case of a patient with a structural conflict.

Thus far I have described countertransference as the analyst's response to his patient's transference. In practice, of course, we deal with a "totalistic" (Kernberg, 1965) form of countertransference which includes the analyst's total emotional reaction to the patient. Other factors over and beyond a response to the patient's transference influence how we feel about our patients. I agree with Giovacchini (1975) that analysts may have *common* factors influencing their countertransferences since certain characterological features may be expected in persons who have chosen to be psychoanalysts. For example, Olinick (1969) suggests that those who choose the psychoanalytic approach to patients, and those who can regress in the service of the other, may typically be influenced by rescue fantasies of their own childhood which were uniquely directed to a depressive mother.

In comparing the countertransference responses to a patient who has conflicts of object relations with those that occur to the patient with structural conflicts, I do not suggest that the countertransference problems in the treatment of neurotic patients may not be — on occasion — difficult ones. We all know how prolonged issues of countertransference toward the patient who is at the neurotic level can bring about an unwelcome stalemate. However, they differ from those typically experienced toward the patient who activates unmended split self and object images and the affects associated with them.

When a split transference or a transference psychosis is established, it is not enough for the analyst to think that "now a 'good' representation is being externalized onto me, and then a 'bad' one." Each such dominant representation has its own developmental history and collections of affective experiences related to it and, accordingly, a specific context which the analyst must understand. Although they are ultimately to be interpreted to the patient, what counts initially with such patients is not to make genetic interpretations of context, but to make an interpretation of the same context in current terms, as it appears between the patient and his analyst, with careful consideration being given to the eventual basic aim of helping the patient to integrate the split-off representation and to advance toward a more realistic self concept and a more realistic internalized object world. The psychoanalyst's examination of the countertransference will yield important clues to the understanding of the specific context of the patient's image units as they are being externalized onto the analyst.

Let me explain my meaning from a practical point of view. During the past year I have been psychoanalytically treating a young woman who declares that she is in communication with many spirits from another world. These are both good and bad spirits, and the patient sometimes feels them within herself. On occasion I am invested with them. This patient's self concept is accordingly fragmented and aligned in two opposing camps; sometimes she is an omnipotent savior; at other times she feels that she is dead. She is now a woman, then a man, and so on. The genetic aspects of her psychopathology refer to the circumstances of her having been adopted as a newborn baby into a household in which a young man had died. The family was unable to grieve for him, and when the young man's sister aborted in the fifth month of her pregnancy, the patient was adopted, given the feminine version of the young man's name, and viewed as his reincarnation. Thus she was perceived by important others in her early life as half dead, half alive; half male, half female. The incompatible aspects of her self concept could not be integrated (mended) with her other self concepts as a little girl. My appreciation in analysis of how it had been for her as a child in this family was connected with the externalizations she made onto me. I felt numb and dead when the "dead" unit was in me, and enlivened and saved by her when her early mother's object representation was in me. My affective countertransference responses began to make sense as I learned more about her history and the details of her life.

There is yet another difference between the transference-countertransference phenomena in the treatment of a neurotic patient and that of a patient with conflicts in object relations. The notion that the neurotic transference is strongest at the time the patient enters treatment, and that a real relationship comes about at the end of the treatment, is erroneous. Anna Freud (1954), addressing this issue, states that the neurotic patient enters analysis with an attitude toward his analyst that is based on reality, but that this becomes secondary as the full-blown transference neurosis develops. When this is worked through, the figure of the analyst can emerge once again, but "to the extent to which the patient has a healthy part of his personality, his real relationship to the analyst is never wholly submerged" (p. 373). I can add here that the same comment can appropriately be made about countertransference. This description cannot, however, be applied when one takes into treatment those patients who activate primitive internalized object relations. In such cases, transference distortions may be extreme at the beginning of the treatment, and accordingly may induce "unfamiliar" and intense emotional responses in the analyst at the outset, bringing about a situation unlike that in which the transference-countertransference axis develops step by step in work with a neurotic individual.

Summary

Structural theory is still the best instrument for understanding the psychopathology of patients with fully differentiated id, ego, and superego, and for success in handling transference-countertransference manifestations in their treatment. I argue that this theory is not very useful, however, when applied to the treatment of patients whose dominant psychopathology reflects the reactivation of internalized object relations. I summarize the theory of internalized object relations and examine transference-countertransference phenomena, applying this theory to the treatment of patients with an unintegrated self concept and an unintegrated internalized object world.

References

Berg, M. D. (1977), The externalizing transference. *Int. J. Psycho-Anal.*, 58:235–244.

Berkowitz, D. A., Shapiro, R. L., Zinner, J., & Shapiro, E. R. (1974), Concurrent family treatment of narcissistic disorders in adolescence. *Int. J. Psychoanal. Psychother.*, 3:379–396.

Boyer, L. B. (1967), Office treatment of schizophrenic patients. In: *Psychoanalytic Treatment of Characterological and Schizophrenic Disorders*, ed. L. B. Boyer & P. L. Giovacchini. New York: Science House, pp. 143–188.

Cambor, C. G. (1969), Preoedipal factors in superego development. *Psychoanal. Quart.*, 38:81–96.

Dorpat, T. L. (1976), Structural conflict and object relations conflict. *J. Amer. Psychoanal. Assn.*, 24:855–874.

Freud, A. (1954), The widening scope of indications for psychoanalysis. *The Writings of Anna Freud*, 4:356–376. New York: International Universities Press, 1968.

_____ (1965), *Normality and Pathology in Childhood. The Writings of Anna Freud*, 6. New York: International Universities Press.

Freud, S. (1923), The ego and the id. *Standard Edition*, 19:3–66. London: Hogarth Press, 1961.

_____ (1927), Fetishism. *Standard Edition*, 21:149–157. London: Hogarth Press, 1961.

_____ (1940), Splitting of the ego in the process of defence. *Standard Edition*, 23:271–278. London: Hogarth Press, 1964.

Gedo, J. E. & Goldberg, A. (1973), *Models of the Mind*. Chicago: University of Chicago Press.

Giovacchini, P. L. (1972), Interpretation and definition of the analytic setting. In: *Tactics and Techniques in Psychoanalytic Therapy*, ed. P. L. Giovacchini. New York: Science House, vol. 1, pp. 291–304.

_____ (1975), Various aspects of the analytic process. In: *Tactics and Techniques in Psychoanalytic Therapy*, ed. P. L. Giovacchini. New York: Jason Aronson, vol. 2, pp. 5-94.

Greenspan, S. I. (1977), The oedipal-preoedipal dilemma. *Int. Rev. Psycho-Anal.*, 4: 381-391.

Hartmann, H. (1939), *Ego Psychology and the Problem of Adaptation.* New York: International Universities Press, 1958.

Jacobson, E. (1964), *The Self and the Object World.* New York: International Universities Press.

Kernberg, O. F. (1965), Notes on countertransference. *J. Amer. Psychoanal. Assn.*, 13:38-56.

———— (1966), Structural derivatives of object relationships. *Int. J. Psycho-Anal.*, 236-253.

———— (1967), Borderline personality organization. *J. Amer. Psychoanal. Assn.*, 15:641-685.

———— (1972), Early ego integration and object relations. *Ann. N.Y. Acad. Sci.*, 193:233-247.

———— (1975), *Borderline Conditions and Pathological Narcissism.* New York: Jason Aronson.

———— (1976a), *Object Relations Theory and Clinical Psychoanalysis.* New York: Jason Aronson.

———— (1976b), Foreword, *Primitive Internalized Object Relations,* by V. D. Volkan. New York: International Universities Press.

Klein, M. (1946), Notes on some schizoid mechanisms. *Int. J. Psycho-Anal.*, 27: 99-110.

Kohut, H. (1971), *The Analysis of the Self.* New York: International Universities Press.

Loewald, H. W. (1960), On the therapeutic action of psycho-analysis. *Int. J. Psycho-Anal.*, 41:16-33.

Mahler, M. S. (1963), Thoughts about development and individuation. *The Psychoanalytic Study of the Child,* 18:307-324.

———— (1968), *On Human Symbiosis and the Vicissitudes of Individuation.* New York: International Universities Press.

Modell, A. H. (1968), *Object Love and Reality.* New York: International Universities Press.

———— (1975), A narcissistic defense against affects and the illusion of self-sufficiency. *Int. J. Psycho-Anal.*, 56:275-282.

Moore, R. E. & Fine, R. D. (1968), *A Glossary of Psychoanalytic Terms and Concepts.* New York: American Psychoanalytic Association.

Novick, J. & Kelly, K. (1970), Projection and externalization. *The Psychoanalytic Study of the Child,* 25:69-95.

Olinick, S. L. (1969), On empathy and regression in the service of the other. *Brit. J. Med. Psychol.,* 42:41-49.

Rosenfeld, H. (1954), Considerations regarding the psycho-analytic approach to acute and chronic schizophrenia. *Int. J. Psycho-Anal.,* 35:135-140.

Searles, H. F. (1963), Transference psychosis in the psychotherapy of chronic schizophrenia. *Int. J. Psycho-Anal.,* 44:249-281.

Shapiro, E. R., Shapiro, R. L., Zinner, J., & Berkowitz, D. A. (1977), The borderline ego and the working alliance. *Int. J. Psycho-Anal.,* 58:77-87.

———— Zinner, J., Shapiro, R. L., & Berkowitz, D. A. (1975), The influence of family experience on borderline personality development. *Int. Rev. Psycho-Anal.,* 2:399-411.

Socarides, C. W. (1978), *Homosexuality*. New York: Jason Aronson.

van der Waals, H. G. (1952), Discussion of: The mutual influences in the development of ego and id. *The Psychoanalytic Study of the Child*, 7:66–68.

Volkan, V. D. (1975), Cosmic laughter. In: *Tactics and Techniques in Psychoanalytic Therapy*, ed. P. L. Giovacchini. New York: Jason Aronson, vol. 2, pp. 427–440.

_____ (1976), *Primitive Internalized Object Relations*. New York: International Universities Press.

_____ (1979a), *Cyprus — War and Adaptation*. Charlottesville: University Press of Virginia.

_____ (1979b), The "glass bubble" of the narcissistic patient. In: *Advances in Psychotherapy of the Borderline Patient*, ed. J. LeBoit & A. Capponi. New York: Jason Aronson, pp. 405–431.

_____ (1981), Immortal Atatürk. *The Psychoanalytic Study of Society*, ed. W. Munsterberger & L. B. Boyer. New York: Psychohistory Press.

_____ & Akhtar, S. (1979), The symptoms of schizophrenia. In: *Integrating Ego Psychology and Object Relations Theory*, ed. L. Saretsky. G. D. Goldman, & D. S. Milman. Dubuque, Iowa: Kendall/Hunt, pp. 270–285.

Zinner, J. & Shapiro, R. L. (1972), Projective identification as a mode of perception and behavior in families of adolescents. *Int. J. Psycho-Anal.*, 53:523–530.

Part III
APPLICATIONS

19

SELF, OTHER, AND FREE ASSOCIATION

Some Experimental Observations

PETER H. KNAPP, M.D. and ANN SKENDALL TEELE, PH.D.

A patient, who had worked for some time in the mental health field, decided to undertake psychoanalysis, and came for his first hour. Lying down on the couch, he said wryly: "Welcome to my analysis." He was condensing many years of introspective struggle and also, so it developed, issuing a warning that in the different struggle ahead, he would not easily relinquish the reins.

Another patient, of a more familiar kind, frequently appeared to be so immersed in his associations that the analyst's interventions came as an intrusion, jarring him out of a near dream; yet in that same dreamlike state he would be aware of the faintest stirring from the chair behind him. He was simultaneously lost in his own thoughts and in exquisite touch with the other person in the room.

Free association, as these fragments emphasize, is a dual process of self-observation and intense interaction with another. The term has an additional duality: it refers to the contents reported and to the act of reporting. In both of these dualities, the self and the other, as actual individuals and as actors in the script which is unfolded, play complex and changing roles. Free association has much to contribute to our knowledge of the external realities and internal representations of the self and its key object relationships, which were thrust into the center of psychoanalytic thought by Edith Jacobson (1964). Several authors, particularly Kubie (1959) and Bellak (1961), have urged a crucial role for it in psychoanalytic research; yet except for a few studies, notably those of Colby (1960, 1961), little systematic attention has been paid to free association.

Our own approach to the topic has been two-pronged—experimental and clinical. In this paper we deal with some experimental observations and attempt to construct a model for relating them to clinical findings.

Overview

In the experiment, described more fully elsewhere (Knapp et al., 1979), we used paid volunteer subjects, young males recruited by newspaper advertisement. These were characteristic volunteers, some of them students, some of them marginally employed, eager for the pay, mildly curious, mildly or even moderately neurotic. Because of our interest in psychosomatic investigation, we selected six subjects in good physical health and seven with mild bronchial asthma. After a screening interview with the psychologist (A.S.T.) they were instructed briefly about free association and gave formal consent to take part in a study which included psychological and physiological measurements and audiovisual recording. They then came back for three sessions, in which they spoke as spontaneously as possible for half an hour. They were semirecumbent and had EKG leads attached to their arms and chest. A silent clinical observer (P.H.K.) was behind them. He intervened only, in predesigned fashion nondirectively, when blocking stopped the flow of associations. After each session both investigators conducted an independent brief inquiry, asking subjects for their reactions.

Before and after each session we also required each subject to draw two human figures and then an animal. This maneuver, used in an earlier study (Knapp and Bahnson, 1963), was specifically designed to elicit information about aspects of the SELF and experience of the OTHER. (To promote clarity we use the following conventions: "SELF" and "OTHER" refer respectively to the actual subject/patient and clinical listener; "self" and "other(s)" refer to the report of the subject about himself and about other figures in his life, including, at times, the listener as well.) Our initial supposition was that two-person drawings would reflect conscious or preconscious self-other representations, whereas animal drawings would represent more unconscious projective self images.

We assessed these drawings using the sophistication of body concept scale of Witkin et al. (1962) and scales of our own, which rated sophistication of animal form, as well as the degree of differentiation and level of interaction between the two humans. From these scales we derived a composite rating of "maturity." Our subjects were widely distributed along this dimension. It is of interest that this rating differentiated asthmatic from comparison subjects; the psychosomatic group, according to our operational criteria, was significantly less mature.

Free-associative communication showed a similar range. Some subjects were at ease almost at once in the situation, fluent and expressive, though showing brief periods of resistance. Indeed, some transient blocking and difficulty in maintaining the flow of associations, as well as other manifestations of distress at the demands of the task, were virtually invariant. Again the simplest index of such resistance, sheer verbal productivity, distinguished asthmatic from comparison subjects. The psychosomatic group had significantly more difficulty in mastering the free-associative task.

Less easily quantifiable, but equally striking, were the manifestations of transference to the clinical listener. The ways in which he was involved, the roles attributed to him, and the externalized attitudes expressed through him varied widely but could be detected in all the protocols.

Another feature, carried over from the clinical situation (Knapp, 1974), was periodic shifting in the associative focus of our subjects. An individual may focus on different periods of time, from remote past to immediate present. There is also variation in what we call *associative mode*. That term refers to categories of content used by a speaker as he addresses the task of free association. Our current classification of these modes is as follows:

NAR: This is the familiar mode, a narrative account of the subject's experience involving himself and other persons.

DIR: Direct reference to the experiment (or therapy) or direct engagement of the experimenter (or therapist) in dispute, questions, or other forms of conversation.

NEUT: Discourse on neutral topics, such as news events, general theory, or factual happenings, unrelated either to the subject's personal experience or the experiment.

DRM: Report of a dream, rare in the experimental situation (at least without suggestive stimulation to produce dreaming, as was done in an experiment by Fisher [1953]).

PRI: Private, primitive, sensory or fantasy experience, usually occurring as an intrusion, that is, sensory awareness of details in the immediate environment, or of bodily sensations, or of imagery or fantasy.

Using this system, we independently divided our free-associative sessions into segments and found a high degree of agreement between two observers — better than p < .01 using the Kappa statistic of Cohen (1960).

Among the modes, NAR tends to be predominant, in both clinical and experimental productions. The other modes are less frequent, although they recur in a somewhat rhythmic fashion. They interrupt a subject's narrative, and at times, one or the other of them may assume prominence, in ways that reflect vicissitudes of the associative relationship and the emotions it engenders. Thus we can systematically observe not only the contents reported but the act of reporting.

Such observations, along with detailed study of pictorial content, supplemented the quantitative measures of "maturity" and fluency. They lent clinical support to the finding of group differences. Comparison subjects, by and large, had observable neurotic conflicts, but with one or two exceptions these were relatively mild. Asthmatics, on the other hand, tended to have primitive and deepseated character pathology.

We now present material from a comparison subject and from an asthmatic for detailed scrutiny as evidence for our view. We then study the interplay in two contrasting individuals of SELF and OTHER as real figures, as well as self and other as inner representations.

Case Material

The Songwriter

This subject was a twenty-one-year-old, single, male whose label in the study came from his long-standing ambitions in the field of music. The initial history, taken by the psychologist, revealed that the subject was a college dropout, at present not regularly employed, living on welfare, playing intermittently in a band made up of fellow musicians with whom he lived. He had heard of the experiment through a friend and volunteered for it partly out of financial need and partly out of interest.

He was the younger of two sons, raised by an apparently stable lower-middle-class family in the eastern United States. He described his father as "easygoing," a factory foreman. His mother worked for the same firm. Apparently his parents had a close relationship; he said, "they still make out on the couch after 30 years." The subject reported that he had had some intimate relationships with women but had drifted away from them, not wanting to become "too dependent." Friends told him that he was "always looking for a mother."

His interest in music had been fostered, ostensibly, by piano lessons which he first began at age eight. It also seemed related to his only sibling, a brother four years older. The brother had taken up guitar playing as a teenager and still loved music, although he had renounced it for a more conventional career of college, marriage, and job as a caseworker in a welfare office. The subject spoke of rivalry with his brother, but said he had "given that up" because he "never liked competition." He added that if he had continued on at college he probably would have majored in psychology, his brother's field. His lifelong interest in music was marked by evidence of conflict. He felt he should start working at it seriously, but that at present he was drifting. He spoke articulately about the different forms of music and their meaning for him, including a special interest in composing not only melodies but lyrics. He was particularly proud of a song having the theme: "Even when you don't see him, the blind man is still blind."

He appeared relaxed and articulate. He stated that he was a profuse dreamer and enjoyed his dreams.

His only illness of significance had been an obscure period of twitching of his arms at age twelve. At that time had had been seen by a neurologist. An EEG had been reported to be negative. He had been given Valium, which he took intermittently for a year. He himself related the problem to school pressures and his concerns over competition. Although the symptom had abated, he reported that it still recurred occasionally when he was tense. He had no other major neurotic or other symptoms. Like many of our volunteer subjects, he acknowledged casual use of drugs, mostly marijuana; he had also taken "speed" and LSD, although rarely. He reported that he had had one "bad trip," but he did not elaborate on the experience.

The first free-associative session started with a brief comment about the situation and then an easy move into the NAR mode and a discussion of his profession. The following is a verbatim quotation of approximately the first two minutes. The marginal notation indicates our categorization of the mode (and temporal focus) by the method just outlined.

> Do I get grades or anything [laughs] I guess —
> Uh I suppose most people say they have   DIR (immediate)
> nothing to say or anything [chuckles]. I won't
> disappoint you.

> I'll start off by talking about the band that I was
> in. I'm a musician and I play piano and
> guitar — the piano a lot longer. I've been playing
> for about twelve years. I consider myself uh to
> play music rather than to be a musician. I con-
> sider it just a — another tongue, just an extension
> of my — an extension of myself, my person-   NAR — work & self
> ality — all related. Everything I do is related to   (current)
> what I think and feel, so I mean I won't go into —
> I don't think anyone's born a musician. I don't
> think it's really innate at all. I think — uh — like I
> said — it's just an extension of my feelings and uh
> personality.

> And as far as the band I was in — uh — inevitably I
> hope to get in a band where we could accept each
> other for — for what each other is worth, get into   NAR — work & social
> each other's feelings and emotions, which is   (future)
> pretty — uh — that's pretty difficult if — if no one's
> willing to — to give and take equally.

> Which was — which was the main problem with
> this band I was in. We were all pretty self-
> centered and everyone was out for themself, and   NAR — work & social
> there wasn't enough — there wasn't enough look-   (past; adult)
> ing after each other, acceptance of each other in
> the house.

(We note that he starts by saying that he in essence wants to please and to introspect, although he is ambivalent about both. He then talks of the wish to reveal his most important self, symbolically located in the world of music, which is his "tongue. . . an extension of myself." At the same time he speaks of wanting closeness, at the manifest level to others in his band. We suspect the early influence of transference attitudes.)

He went on to talk about music, expressing himself in a somewhat idiosyncratic set of near clichés, using phrases such as "it's a long road to the field of dreams." Again there were subtle overtones suggesting transference: he spoke of trying to find "reality and happiness" but of fearing too great dependency — translatable as a fear of too great an attachment to the experimenter in a parental, even maternal role. The subject said, "I could easily get caught up in a situation and not even thinking that I had other things I want to do."

The main material in this first session dealt with his ticlike illness at age twelve. He described twitching, "doing things by fours," apparently an obsessive-compulsive need to count, repeat, and control his behavior. There is more than a hint of masturbatory issues: he went on to talk about "bodily freedom," envying blacks as they dance. Some of the dangers connected with this then appeared; he spoke about a "bad trip, when everything kept unraveling," accompanied by a sense of fusing with everyone around him. In the session itself he temporarily lost the thread of his discourse.

He then described a sense of "rebirth"; it had occurred during his teens, and through it he had learned to express his conflicts through music. The session ended with another burst of his curiously clichélike language, which again hinted at covert attitudes, as he said, "You can always learn more if your eyes are open and your ears are open." (The ambiguity of the pronoun "you" suggests the translation: "we can learn from each other.")

His drawings were relatively sophisticated both in their form and in the human interactions he depicted. Before this first session he drew two humans shown in figure 1. He described them as follows:

You and — uh — me. [Thoughts?] Well it was the first thing that came into my head. I was mostly thinking about the experiment while I was drawing out how it's all related to what the topic's supposed to be. [Anything else?] Just thinking how we both ended up right here at the same time for some reason whatever that reason might be.

The sketch is subtle: it shows a female figure, who recurs in several of his subsequent drawings, presumably the psychologist (A.S.T.).

FIGURE 1
Songwriter's Two-Person Drawing (day 1, before the session)

The other figure is only partial: arms holding a clipboard, a view of himself using the actual experimental clipboard. On it he is drawing the same figure and the same arms holding a clipboard, on which there is a still more miniscule representation of the same scene. It is a creative rendition of the endless mirroring that is introspection.

He followed this by drawing an animal (fig. 2), which he described as follows:

> Uh—I'm just thinking of names—I haven't really come across any yet— [laughs]. I draw horrible [laughs]! A dog I came across in the park yesterday—but you wouldn't know it. I drew him like Lon Chaney. He looked almost human in the face—a really pretty dog. Just stuck out in my mind because I stopped to look at him yesterday [laughs]. He looks horrible there—like the wolfman or like Lon Chaney.

The tendency to draw relatively simple creatures but to link them to humans in one or another way persisted in almost all of his animal drawings.

After this first associative session he drew two male figures followed by a small cat, which he said was likely to be hit by a child.

His second free-associative session began with a veiled confession of difficulty in telling his feelings, by way of describing conflict with two girls. He went on to say he felt pressured and hinted at hidden surges of anger. From events between the two sessions he recalled an account of being held up by two black muggers after leaving a supermarket. This theme of attack and aggression interwove itself with wishes to conform and to rebel. The latter were violent but masked. He recalled fear that a girlfriend had been killed in an accident or burned in a fire some months ago. He spoke of a sense of unreality in a bus station after working on a night shift, seeing all the conventional jobholders going to work, "all their suits, all their briefcases."

He closed with deeply disguised hostility, giving a brief account in the NEUT mode about the "corrupt political scene," in which the populace with manipulated by "Nixons, or Hitlers, or Stalins."

In inquiry after the session he said he felt better today; it had been "a lot of fun," although he immediately added that he had felt "frustrated" and "angry," even "hopeless" because he "kept coming on to new things more and more." To the psychologist he added that he had more and more thoughts during the session but had been

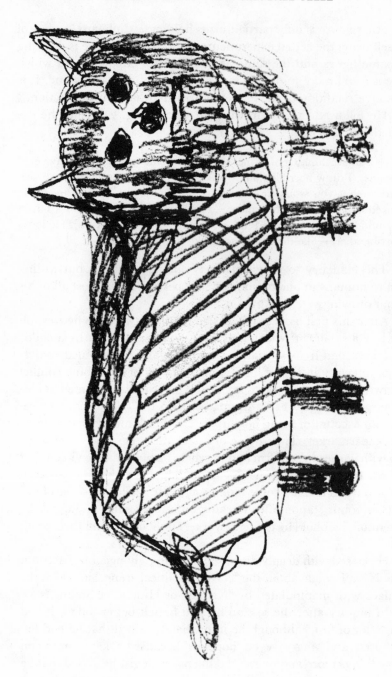

FIGURE 2
Songwriter's Animal Drawing (day 1, before the session)

FIGURE 3
Songwriter's Animal Drawing (day 2, before the session)

bothered by feeling "cut off" at the end of it, wondering whether the listener had been "not interested, just treating me as an experiment."

Drawings before this session were those of a girl and young man who, he said, had "incredible energy." His animal drawing was again conventional, a large "fat cat" which, he stated explicitly, was drawn from behind. This is shown in figure 3.

After the session he produced a witty representation of the experiment itself (fig. 4): two humans who, he stated, were "me and Dr. K" (the listener). The clipboard was now in the hands of the experimenter, as it in fact had been during free association. The subject himself was a diminutive figure, pinned behind a board, almost as if in stocks. There was a suggestion of reversal of roles, in that he seemed to be above and behind, peering at the experimenter.

He followed this by a picture of a giraffe, remarking "it takes a long time for food to get to his stomach."

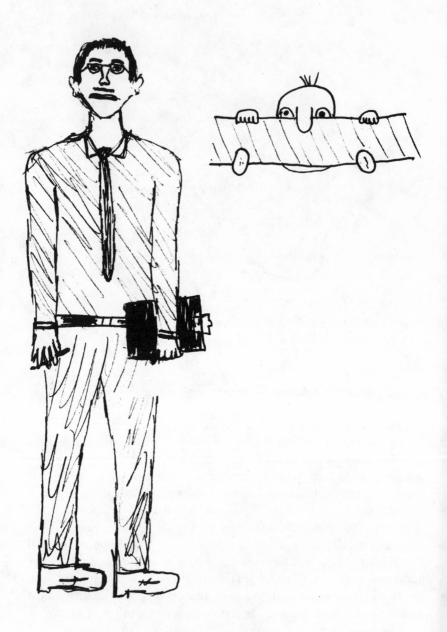

FIGURE 4
Songwriter's Two-Person Drawing (day 2, after the session)

He began the third and last free-associative session by saying that he had gotten a conventional haircut, wondering obliquely whether it would be approved. Then he talked directly about the experiment. He had been puzzling over the question of whether he really did have more feelings than he was aware of as he took the routine adjective checklist tests before these sessions.

He switched briefly to the neutral mode thinking of the current hot spell which made the nights uncomfortable. Going back to himself he said that he enjoyed sleeping in the heat. At this point he had his only intrusion of primitive material: he looked at the design on the electric fan in the room and imagined it as a dragonfly. (The image suggests a reference both to himself and to another person, a fantasy both threatening and exciting.)

This led to memories of feeling crippled, wearing glasses; yet he was better off than those who are blind, toward whom he feels guilty. The major theme of control over aggression again came to the fore: he recalled his aged aunt who, in senility, had become uncontrollably profane. "Eighty years of frustration came out...in waves." Immediately following this recollection was an anxious speculation: he had heard that rage can cause cancer and death.

He ended debating the issue of whether he should get some professional help for his indecisiveness and anxiety. This course had its own dangers. Virtually his last statement was: "Suddenly I'm a blank, aware of the camera, careful not to expose myself....I should take more chances but I am staying with old familiar ways."

In the inquiry after this session he continued his closing theme, saying that the experience had been "good and bad." He had experienced "frustration from fighting with myself." He felt that he might like to talk to someone further, "having walked out the last two days feeling really good." On the other hand, he was "tired of talking." On this inconclusive note he ended, saying that he "hoped everything works out well with the experiment."

On the third day, before the session, he drew a "girl and guy" (fig. 5); the latter was grotesque and wearing a shirt covered with "yin-yang" symbols. The subject mentioned that it could "represent everything."

Before the session, he drew a pelican, saying that he was intrigued by its mouth. After the session, he again drew male and female humans whom he described as two of his idols, the baseball

FIGURE 5
Songwriter's Two-Person Drawing (day 3, before the session)

player Willy Mays and the actress Ali McGraw. The word "giant" was emblazoned on the man's shirt. He said, "He's energetic; she's exciting to look at."

His final animal drawing was a "canyon sparrow" in a deep V-shaped crevice (fig. 6). It was one of the few drawings in our series that contained any overt representation of the physical environment surrounding the creature drawn. Its ambiguity is interesting in view of his ambivalence about ending this encounter: the sparrow might be flying in or out of the canyon.

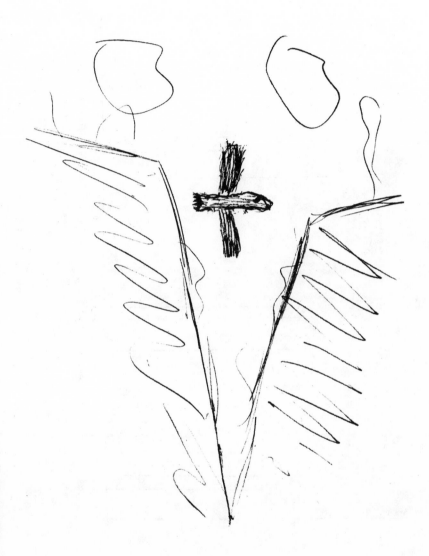

FIGURE 6
Songwriter's Animal Drawing (day 3, after the session)

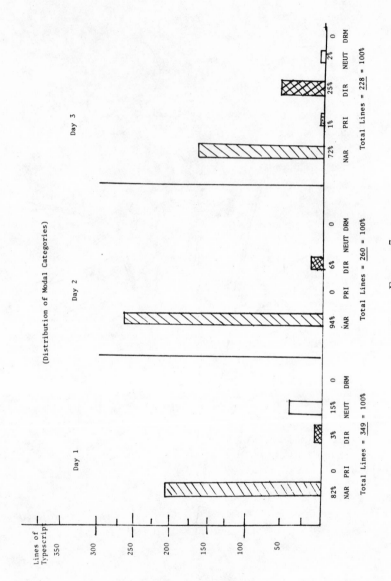

FIGURE 7
Songwriter's Associative Modes

It is possible to chart the total proportion of lines devoted to various modes of associative focus in each session. Figure 7 reveals a gradual increase in references to the direct experimental situation, along with a decline in the narrative mode. We note that the only intrusion of primitive material was the brief image of the dragonfly (mentioned in describing his third session).

A diagnostic impression of this subject can be derived from the two aspects of his data which we have mentioned: what he expresses about himself, and how.

The *content* reveals a clear neurotic structure. This is marked by two competing preconscious systems of self representation. The first centers around the schema of himself as aggressive and rebellious and is dramatically illustrated by his early drawing of a "horrible dog...wolfman." More indirectly it is reflected in the recollections of a girl being destroyed by a fire, and of his senile aunt, losing control, pouring out frustration and rage. Despite their indirect nature these elements lead in turn to fantasies of attack, mutilation, and death. The result is retreat to a second position, passive and conciliatory. He cuts off his hair in order to conform, pins himself behind a board in his drawing of the associative situation (fig. 4). Along with the ebb and flow of aggression there is a more hidden libidinal ambivalence, in which concerns about exposure, and especially looking, are prominent. He wants to show off and be admired for his art; and he has conflictual voyeuristic preoccupations, appearing in his drawing (e.g., figs. 1 and 2), as well as in his initial allusion to his parents "making out" on the couch, and more obliquely in the theme of the man who is blind "even when you don't see him." He seems to find it safest to remain small and dependent, though his hidden urges continuously tempt him away from this stance. His conflict in life is epitomized by his final drawing of a canyon sparrow entering, or leaving, a vast crevice.

The form of his communication is fluent and easy. He engages the experimenters with immediacy and directly represents himself and them and their mutual involvement. However, this involvement remains largely in the background, subordinated to the task of supplying associative material, fueled by his wishes not only to comply but to see himself. The organization of his self-other representations is hierarchical. His male-female two-person drawings represent energetic images of an ideal self (Willy Mays) and an attractive woman (Ali McGraw); but they also express two sides of himself. This internal structure becomes even clearer when he draws the robust, if humorous and grotesque young man wearing a "yin-yang" shirt (fig. 5). A rapidly oscillating self-other organization in the actual associative situation reveals itself in his language, as he shifts rapidly back and forth between representing himself and representing another, particularly in his use of the inherently ambiguous pronoun "you": for example, "You always learn more if your eyes are open and your ears are open."

He shows, then, well-defined neurotic structure; it rapidly pervades the free-associative situation and takes on elements of transference, which become clear over the course of the three experimental sessions.

However, he does not lose himself. There is no sense of confusion or of being overwhelmed. Rather, these alternate views are organized by what we must conclude is a predominantly effective sense of himself. Although somewhat uneasy, he has a positive core in which his self representation is differentiated from others, leaving him free to display and report about inner selves and others to an actual outer OTHER, with whom he is able to interact in an essentially trusting and friendly way.

The Astrologer

This subject was a twenty-eight-year-old, single, white male who had adopted the profession of astrology as a way to earn a living and to maintain precarious contact with people. He had taken part in numerous other experimental studies involving asthma. He claimed that these had been "picky" and "mechanical," because of his feelings about his illness. He believed his illness was not "physiological" but "emotional."

He had had asthma as well as hay fever as long as he could remember. Both were relieved by medicines, particularly adrenergic drugs. However, the side effects of these, he said, were worse than the disease, so that he took them as seldom as possible. He described his asthma as precipitated by dust or dampness, other extremes of climate, and "sleeping in strange places." The disorder had tended to improve steadily since early adolescence, a fact which he attributed to a regimen of running.

His only other medical condition was an undescended testicle, corrected surgically at age twenty-six. He described himself as "hypochondriacal," believing that he suffered from every disease which he heard described.

His father had died when he was eighteen of a heart attack. He described him as domineering, their relationship as marked by conflict and argument. The death had come at Christmastime, just after the patient had gotten himself ejected from college and lost a girlfriend. As he spoke of this, he smiled inappropriately, reinforcing an impression of odd emotional reactions and possibly minimally distorted thought processes. Shortly after the father's death he had had a brief period of outpatient psychotherapy. He said that he had wanted to be judged as "crazy" so that he could avoid responsibility. The treatment lasted only a month. After that he "ran away" to the West Coast. He remained there for several years, then returned to finish college, but again left, this time for six years.

His mother was a teacher of dyslexic children. He described her as "excessive in all things; she makes me feel very conservative, spends money wildly, goes overboard a lot."

A brother, twenty-three years old, was in charge of a day-care center. The subject said that he and his brother did not get along well, that the brother took after the mother's side of the family and was "passive," which the subject found upsetting. A sister, twenty-one yeas old, lives with a boyfriend and resembles the subject, taking after the father: "wild, crazy people, emotional, breaking out, doing strange things."

He described himself as "a rotten little kid, spoiled, bad-tempered and stubborn." He recalled frequent battles with his mother in which he would seize something, for example a lamppost, and the mother would drag him away from it. He felt that she had put constant pressure on him for good marks, to which he had reacted by becoming a borderline student, hating regimentation, and an occasional truant, forging letters to excuse his absences. He always enjoyed sports. Although for the most part isolated, as one of the few Jews in a Catholic neighborhood, he made a sort of social mark by athletic prowess, playing on a hockey team and getting a scholarship in school, and later taking part in sports in college.

After finishing college, which had been interrupted by his wanderings, he planned to be a playwright, but gave that up as "unpractical." He wandered again. On his travels he had intermittent relationships with girls, which he described as "taking tragic turns, like a Greek drama." He had too much "hubris," he stated, which led him into problems with domineering women. He would break up with them, then react "with madness," immersing himself in isolated fantasy, aided by absorption in television.

Gradually he developed an interest in astrology; he enjoyed counseling people, and evidently was seeking some stability for himself in the process. He ascribed his return to Boston as due to "lunar forces." He had become "too mystical" and wanted to be in "the real world." At the time of the experiment he was living at his mother's, but with a girlfriend, who had returned with him from the West. His current feeling was that he needed a stable, mature life and was moving toward it, though still unsure of his present social or professional commitments.

His performance in the free-associative situation contrasted markedly with that of the Songwriter. He was slow, halting, and distressed, particularly at the start. He began:

[Pause 15 sec.] Chilly in here [pause 5 sec.]. Feels very strange to be in a raised chair here in this position in the center of the room. Very much the focus of attention while lying down. Monitored with a camera. Not, I suppose, an ideal situation for free-flowing — uh — talk [pause 15 sec.].　　DIR (immediate)

George Washington, Madison, Jefferson — whitewash [pause 15 sec.].[1]　　PRI (immediate)

It's — uh — difficult to let things flow. The whole situation seems to be one of restraints and measurements [pause 20 sec.].　　DIR (immediate)

Light and shadows, tapes and wires, and shoes [humming; pause 20 sec.]. And black and white [pause 13 sec.].　　PRI (immediate)

Hospital and doctors, patients, medicine, drugs,

[1]This jumbled intrusion was a mocking reference to one part of the experiment which involved reading aloud from a history textbook.

smells, nurses [pause 13 sec.]. Not moving. Water,   DIR (immediate)
time clock, electricity [pause 30 sec.].

Tired, sleeping, inactivity, cold morning, breathing   PRI (immediate)
badly.

The Scientific American. Tired eyes, yawning, no
coffee. Manipulation, Subjects. Experiments. Cold   DIR (immediate)
[pause 10 sec.]. Sanitary [pause 23 sec.].

Experimenter: Where are your thoughts now?

Into the corners of the room trying to get out.   DIR (immediate)

Difficulties. Stoppage. Blockage. Muscular tightness.   PRI (immediate)

He remained focused largely on the experiment, or, alternately, on intrusive primitive imagery, in which perceptual and bodily sensations were mixed. He had some fragmented memories, not relating to clearly defined persons. These contained hints of violent impulses, as in a typical fragmentary sequence: "Criminal destruction...dogs eating garbage...throwing rocks." Alternating with these were feelings of passivity: "Dizzy...retreating, fading, fading away. Losing touch. Misery."

The outstanding feature was his inability to escape from awareness of the experiment. "It's difficult to say something without any reference at all, without any starting point, without anything to go from or start from or go to."

His distress was so great that in the routine inquiry immediately after the free-associative session the experimenter moved into an unplanned quasi-clinical style, in an effort to ease almost unverbalizable difficulties with the task. The subject, amplifying his conflictual experience, said, "If I really say, o.k., I'm not going to think about anything, then there's nobody here to say anything, 'cause I'm not here 'cause I'm not thinking about it."

As the experimenter empathized with this feeling of near paralysis, the subject went on: "I get my energy by bumping my head against the wall and fighting the situation...straining against it." The experimenter remarked on his irritability over the task. Yes, he said, "Tapes and cameras...made me feel I'm going to give you that information and I don't want to give you that information." He added that it had to do with helplessness and veiled panic, a sense of being "trapped," making it harder to breathe, a sense of being strapped down" (although there had been no actual physical restraint). Asked to elaborate, he said it was a matter of "not understanding what I'm supposed to do....I know a laser beam is not going to come down from the ceiling, but tilting back gives me the feeling of falling back into a dream."

His drawings revealed a different aspect of his detached and isolated sense of self. On the screening day he drew two stick figures, saying that they "could be anybody or anything....One has a beard and nose...my attempt to make them male and female." For an animal he drew a cat, which he said was "like my cat." "Cats are efficient, not as easy to pet as dogs, much more vicious, especially female cats."

On the first free association day he described his initial two-person drawing (fig. 8) as Sun and Moon.

> My major thought was to do something different than last time and having to have two, the first division I thought about was the sun and the moon....Seems like someone in kindergarten could have done better with half a crayon.

He followed this by drawing, for an animal, a "fish with eyebrows." Again he showed a tendency to amend his drawings, as if to provide greater definition: he put a spout in the fish's back and asked, "Whales are mammals, aren't they?"

After this first associative session he drew two shapeless figures, whom he called Mr. and Mrs. Potato. Then he drew a bizarre animal (fig. 9), of which he said:

> It's sort of a conglomerate. I drew the body first. I had vague intentions of kitty cat, duck, rabbit, somewhere along those lines, but the head got completely out of — uh context...it could be a duck, it could be a bunny rabbit, it could be — oh — some kind of mutation. The tail looks a little bit like a squirrel...a lot of times — uh — I make doodles or drawings of half human, half animal and different combinations of animals....I've always liked centaurs very much. Can you show me the drawing again? A weasel — a definite weasel — it's a weasel head. The shape of the head also reminds me of a dinosaur...it might have been a beak at one time.

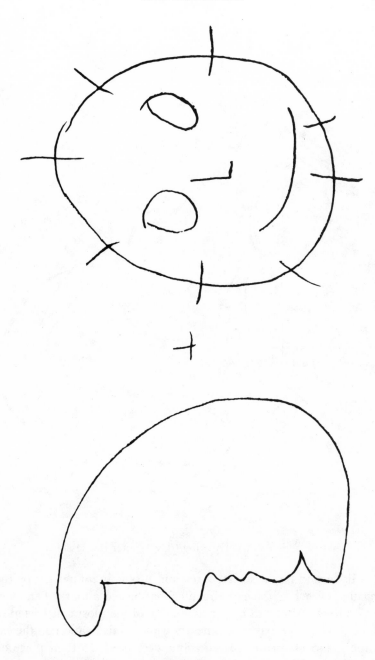

FIGURE 8
Astrologer's Two-Person Drawing (day 1, before the session)

FIGURE 9
Astrologer's Animal Drawing (day 1, after the session)

His second free-associative session, probably influenced by the clinical approach of the experimenter, he showed a marked change. He was freer. Although he remained one of the most constricted of our subjects, his verbal output nearly tripled. His fixation on the experiment and his primitive intrusions decreased. In their place he plunged into the past and gave scattered memories of his earlier years, starting out with a brief allusion to his "grandfather holding court." Persons emerged in a fragmentary way: grandparents, an uncle, cousins on the West Coast. Alone of our thirteen subjects, he explicitly and repeatedly mentioned odors in his association, using the word "smells" eleven times, recalling blossoms, cut grass, the tangy smell of winter, his grandfather's spray on trees, the odor of leather.

These associations seemed to epitomize longings, both erotized and dangerous; for example, he spoke of "heavy air," too much oxygen, and "gasping for breath." Again aggressive themes wove their way into the discourse: a dead whale hacked up, pushing a cousin into the water, the dangers of getting hit.

In the inquiry he stated that things had gone "a little better. . . . I decided rather than just sit here like a vegetable and not give myself any direction, I would point myself in a certain direction and see if I could. It seemed a little easier that way. . . . I think of the past and all of a sudden it comes up and hits me. . . . It's hard to separate it."

His drawings again had a remote, stylized quality. Before the associative session, he drew two people in saint and devil costumes, and a composite bird sitting on a tree branch. After the session, he drew two "esoteric" people, again almost stick figures, the one on the left resembling a bumblebee, the one on the right being only a head and feet. This was followed by a "motorized bird" which might be "an eagle, a hawk, or a falcon."

On the final free-associative day he was again more fluent, largely in the narrative mode except at the very end when he expressed immediate discomfort. Once more there was an abundance of perceptual references, particularly to smells. Twice again he mentioned garbage. There were by now no allusions to the experimenter and not many to actual other persons, though slightly more than in previous sessions. He recalled driving across the country, struggling with snow, alone, but also fishing with his father and brother. Two summer vacation memories were striking. One involved swimming, diving for clams and getting caught between someone's legs, unable to breathe. Another was being stalled in summer traffic, surrounded by noise, a congested yet barren scene, feeling both crowded in and isolated. He seemed to be talking of diffuse urges for closeness and dual fears of either having too much or of being separated. He elaborated on a fleeting mention from previous sessions of building up his strength, feeling good working in the post office, lifting mail sacks, and especially running.

At the end sensitivity to loss reflected itself covertly. He spoke of writing a letter to a friend named Peter (the name of the listener). This led to vivid memories and anticipations of hay fever, the misery of sneezing and itching, and the need to go to a doctor, feeling miserable and ridiculous. "It's a pain in the ass, the whole thing."

Again in the inquiry he remarked on how readily he could get lost in his recollections: "Suddenly I'll be in the car driving...it's like plugging into a daydream...like driving...your mind does very strange things." He felt the experiment had been interesting but "too detached." The experimenter wondered whether he might want to continue to talk to someone. He expressed some interest, but again spoke about the fear connected with "opening up."

His final drawings were of interest. Before the session, he again drew fragmentary stick figures which he labeled male and female. Once more both his animal drawings were birds, the last one a peculiar heraldic falcon, shown in figure 10. He had wanted to go in "the direction of the heraldic.... Usually they have them standing with the bird facing front, and the head is turned and you get like the beaks of the bird."

He described his final two-person drawing (fig. 11) as follows:

> I just usually draw two people, usually male and female, but there usually isn't too much happening between them, so I thought I would try to draw two people together....I was specifically thinking of one particular thing, which was a sculpture by Henry Moore, which is Mother and Child which is in very simple shapes, no features, of a mother and a baby.

Figure 12 charts his total productivity and its distrubution, session by session in the various modes of associational focus. We note his marked constriction compared to the previous subject, who was average in productivity in our group of subjects. We also see the Astrologer's sharp shift from total absorption, in the immediate situation, to almost total avoidance of it.

To summarize and formulate: this was a lonely, isolated man, attached ambivalently to his mother. We are less sure about his relationship to his father, knowing only that he evidently fought stubbornly against him. His personal and professional identities were

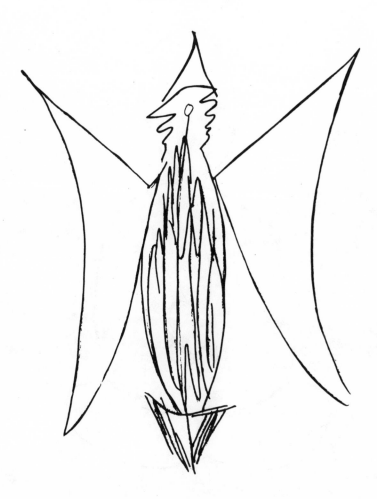

FIGURE 10
Astrologer's Animal Drawing (day 3, after the session)

unformed; he seemed to be attempting to solve them by helping others resolve their life problems via outer astrological signs.

His confusions colored his verbalized self representations. During the first free-associative session these could only be inferred from fragments, in which violent urges were counterposed to a sense of being sickly and weak. In his second session, after an unplanned intervention by the experimenter, the subject revealed more, a diffuse, vague self and patchy hints of others, his grandfather and family

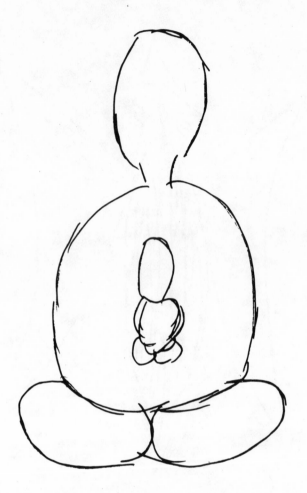

FIGURE 11
Astrologer's Two-Person Drawing (day 3, after the session)

members emerging as if the subject were riffling through the family album about which he spoke. Again images of aggression, some directly toward persons, others more internal and anal in coloration, via his references to slime, dirt, and garbage, were interwoven with positively toned erotic images, not clearly emerging as memories of people but rather as sensations, particularly odors, in almost Proustian style. A little more clarity emerged in the third session, which involved some incidents with particular individuals, although mostly

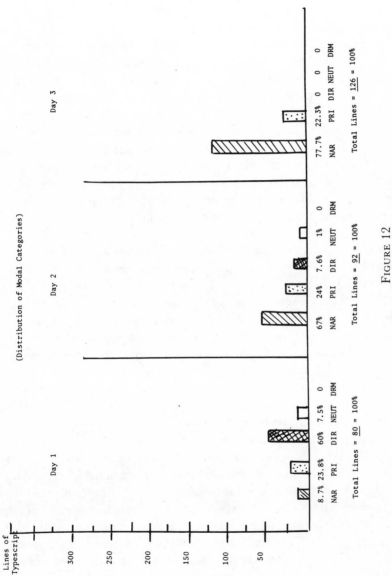

FIGURE 12
Astrologer's Associative Modes

he conveyed a sense of aloneness. Along with this was a lifelong struggle for self-sufficiency and strength, centered around hard physical work and running. His defensive efforts, however, seemed unable to overcome a sense of helplessness and a lack of control; he was either trapped and suffocated or abandoned. As the sessions came to the end, he thought of writing a friend named Peter and had intensified recollections of his illness.

Explicit representations in his drawings confirmed the sense of confusion about himself and others. He drew detached "humanoid" figures interacting minimally with one another, and almost arbitrarily seemed to introduce features at the last moment "to make them male and female." His animals at the healthiest seemed to be derivatives of aggressive females. For the most part they were disorganized presexual images, epitomized by the symmetrical heraldic falcon and the conglomerate creature finally labeled a dinosaur.

His deeper self-in-action, revealed by his responses to the free-associative situation, showed a sense of passivity. He felt forced, controlled, unable to introspect, struggling to define himself by "fighting against the situation." To let go raised the danger of losing control, "falling back into a dream." Initially he could not escape awareness of the experiment—and presumably just behind that the experimenter. As he became more comfortable, he swung to the opposite extreme and plunged into fragmentary memories from the past, isolating himself, almost totally avoiding the immediate situation. His free-associative behavior supports the interpretation of his words and drawings that he lacked a well-defined and usable sense of self, able to perceive and interact with a clearly apperceived OTHER.

Thus he provides clear evidence of a deep pregenital character disturbance. We can only speculate about its relationship to asthma. Conflict between the emotions of primitive yearning and primitive rage, and a parallel conflict between interpersonal fantasies of taking in and of expelling, have been described in other asthmatics (Knapp, 1960). The Astrologer felt that his illness had strong "psychological" components and that he had gained some control over it by his massive efforts at exercise. Wider psychosomatic implications of this contrast between asthmatic and nonasthmatic subjects are discussed elsewhere (Knapp et al., 1979). Here we wish to underline the clarity with which our present approach highlights self-other confusion. It permeated his free-associative performance, stood out dramatically in his drawing of a composite monster and in his final two-person drawing. This mother-child pair showed a figure inside a figure, the ultimate in incorporation and fusion.

Discussion

The inner world of self and key others, or human objects, is central to psychoanalytic understanding of behavior. Yet its study is beset by complexities, for it comprises a multiplicity of levels derived from multiple sources.

"Others" include many persons, stemming from current life and from the recent and remote past, ultimately traceable to composite archaic imagoes. Self representations, although in one sense part of a single individual, are almost as varied; many component partial selves are discernible, also coming originally from those same imagoes, parts of the individual's early internal world.

Psychological testing can be aimed at one or another level with some precision, but at the expense of richness. Clinical psychoanalytic material reveals a wide range of self-other images and derivatives; but so far it has not been accompanied by methods for sorting and specifying these accurately. Our effort is to fill this gap by a combined approach, striving to achieve both precision and depth.

Basically such an approach must be characterized as *projective*. However, that blanket term itself requires specification. It will be useful to distinguish four interrelated kinds of projective processes: (1) projective construction; (2) projective apperception; (3) projective attribution; and (4) projective externalization. The first two are intended as limited terms, derived from psychological testing. Projective construction, in this usage, refers to the production of aspects of one's self experience by some activity, such as the figure drawings employed in this study. Projective apperception refers to perceiving and describing such aspects in a relatively unstructured external stimulus, such as a Rorschach inkblot or TAT card. The two terms overlap. Construction is projective activity *de novo;* apperception is shaped by a stimulus but involves the activity of description.

Attribution and externalization are used as more general terms to designate two differing aspects of projection as these are encountered clinically and as they are evoked by the relatively un-structured free-associative situation. Projective attribution refers to ascription of qualities to another which are recalled or derived from a past figure (the silent listener felt to be cold and indifferent, like the father).[2] Projective externalization refers to ascription of qualities to another which are felt or feared to be part of one's self (the silent listener attacked for being cold and mocking, those qualities being an unwitting, repudiated part of one's own stance toward the world.) Clearly, there are interrelationships between attributions and externalizations: attribution in a transference context is projection on-to the listener of remembered qualities from past figures; but these same qualities, at a deeper level, are often found to be parts of the self; at perhaps the deepest level, in the most remote past, they, in fact, had their origins in early figures outside the subject.

The psychological test methods used here rely upon construction. However, they also involve varying degrees of attribution and externalization, which are not always easy to disentangle. To do so requires careful analysis of both content and form, what is drawn and how.

The content of drawings, we assume, reflects images or schemata of the self and others. Insofar as these derive from varied and progressively more inferential psychic strata, they become less clear, and often—as with many symbols, in art or in dreams—they pose the problem of who is who. To disentangle their ambiguity we use various cues—explicit language, as when the Songwriter said of figure 1, "This is you and me"; implicit language, as when the Astrologer described figure 11 as a mother and child. The evidence becomes more and more contextual, including such matters as posi-tioning of the figures and the relative emphasis accorded them pic-torially or in subsequent verbal description; for example, in figure 5 the man with the yin-yang shirt was larger than the ambiguous female figure behind him, the center of attention pictorially and ver-bally, and almost certainly represented the self.

[2]In this usage "projective attribution" occupies a conceptual borderline, having features of displacement as well as projection. Some aspects of transference are best described as displacement of a subject's feelings or impulses from earlier targets; some are best described as projection of a subject's attitudes, fantasies, and percep-tions about his internalized early figures onto a current undifferentiated stimulus object (the "blank screen").

Cues pointing toward a clear separation of self from another, and toward meaningful interaction between the two, provide crucial evidence of separation-individuation in the core of the personality. The "mother and child" (fig. 11) or even the "sun and moon" (fig. 8) of the Astrologer represent extremes, on the one hand of fusion and on the other of isolation. We recall that the Astrologer also drew stick figures, adding sexually differentiating features at the last minute, almost as an afterthought. All of these drawings of his were relatively static. They differ from those of the Songwriter, with their "incredible energy," and their explicit portrayal of human interaction. We might note that the interaction, in several of the Songwriter's constructions, was with a member of the experimental team. This tendency to bring the immediate, here-and-now relationship into the drawing task was more common in our comparison subjects than in our psychosomatic patients. It seems to reflect a capacity for open spontaneous involvement, an indicator of psychological health.

Portrayal of a separate self and interaction between persons obviously does not imply absence of complexity. The clipboard in the "you and I" drawing of the Songwriter suggests levels of introspection and shared viewing. The yin-yang shirt on the young man in figure 5, which could "represent everything," appears to symbolize multiple partial identifications, but also suggests that these are hierarchically organized within a predominantly masculine self system.

Animal drawings, as we used them, elicited a single representation; we assumed that this would be a disguised version of self. At times contextual evidence appeared to bear out this assumption, as in the Songwriter's dog which was also a "wolfman" (fig. 2). Animal drawings often provided various alternating, reasonably coherent versions of the self. The contrasting dog and cat images of the Songwriter resembled those of other comparatively well-organized subjects. By contrast, other subjects, like the Astrologer, produced images that were primitive and chaotic, suggesting far less coherence of identity, less clear emergence of a dominant self organization.

These features characterize the Astrologer's hybrid monster (fig. 9) and his heraldic falcon (fig. 10). The outlines of the latter were both jagged and symmetrical, so that it was difficult to distinguish up from down, front from rear. It was hard to say how much these drawings represented conflicting parts of the self and how much images of self mixed with others. Confirmation of such primitive confusion came from the "mother and child" (fig. 11) of the Astrologer. Elsewhere we show another drawing of a fused pair of human figures, also constructed by one of our asthmatic subjects (Knapp et al., 1979).

The argument has already moved toward considering not merely the "what" but the "how" of these contructions. We must consider both skill and will, ability of the subject to perform, and his disposition to collaborate. Ability, or skill, involves factors of aptitude and inhibition, largely lying beyond the scope of our inquiry, although they may in part reflect the maturational features that have been our major concern. Goodenough's work (1926) suggests that as children advance in chronological age they produce increasing richness of detail in the Draw-a-Person test. This is congruent with the way a composite estimate of "maturity" appeared to detect "psychological age" in our sample of young adults, and to differentiate our comparison subjects from our more primitive asthmatics.

Disposition to collaborate, or will, was overtly a less important factor in these experimentally produced drawings; they were part of a task to be completed for pay. Overt refusal would have meant canceling the experimental contract. Covert manifestations of resistance did appear in verbalized disparagement by subjects of the experiment or of their own performance, for instance, the Astrologer's apologetic comment, "Seems like someone in kindergarten could have done better."

In apperceptive projective tests conflicts over performance, revealed by time delay or constriction of productivity, may become prominent. The Rorschach, for instance, uses these features as regular measurements. A task for the future will be to supplement our current figure drawings by simplified repeatable apperceptive stimuli.

Free association, in many ways, complemented figure drawings. Self and other representations, less directly elicited, formed a more elaborate tapestry within the flow of associations. Here, too, not only what is said, but how, becomes crucial. Content is illuminated by the form of the communicative interaction.

Within the content one readily sees multiple levels. A manifest self is displayed in the recall of conscious experiences, including those involving other persons. At times these include the present and listening OTHER. The roles, interactions, and attendant emotions combine to allow inferences about various preconscious selves and others, figures of identification and parental surrogates. The number of symbolic transformations and displacements rapidly becomes extensive. As we are led to more pervasive, "deeper" configurations of self and other, we soon face the same question of who is who. Transference projections, in particular, make for difficulties in distinguishing between attribution and externalization.

The form of free association does not immediately solve these difficulties; but an approach toward some answers emerges from examining its systematic regularities. The first set of these falls under the general rubric of resistance. Early in the history of psychoanalysis clinical intuition recognized the importance not only of what was spoken but of what was left unspoken, and the tensions revealed during the process of speaking. In the present study and also in a subsequent replication involving thirty subjects (Ross et al., 1979) sheer time and bulk of verbalization demonstrated that a significant majority as asthmatics were more constricted than healthy comparison subjects.

Obviously one would want to go beyond these relatively crude indices in the search for meanings conveyed by the formal aspects of free association. Not only the sum of silences but their rhythm and context provide information, as Weisman (1955), among others, has remarked. Additional data are provided by verbal and nonverbal glosses indicating distress or ease with the task, as well as awareness of the listener or of the speaker's own observing self. Still more informative, we believe, are the shifts and apparent discontinuities in temporal focus and what we call the modes or categories of discourse. The tendency to range backward and forward in time, and between reality, fantasy, and direct encounter in the consulting room, is a hallmark of the "good" associative session, to use Kris's term (1956).

A further word may clarify the role of these modal categories in various forms of communication. Ordinary discourse generally contains a substantial amount of direct, action-oriented language, aimed at eliciting specific listener counteraction (our DIR mode). Subtle rules govern sharing of the "floor" and the amount of self absorption which is acceptable (Duncan and Fiske, 1978). Thus varying amounts of recounting of personal experience (our NAR mode) occur, along with a mixture of impersonal statements (our NEUT mode). A switch to predominantly personal narrative generally characterizes adoption of a "client" role, particularly in free association. The instruction to report one's total mental contents provides a powerful impetus toward the inner monologue which dominates so much of human experience, filled as it is with various partial selves and inner others.

As the associative process continues, the OTHER, silent and invisible, engenders the peculiar tensions of this situation. Undefined by feedback responses, he becomes a projective target for externalizations and attributions, a catalyst mobilizing split-off selves and others from the past. Concomitant emotions intensify and exert pressure for expression in the present. Experimentally as well as clinically we see a periodic return toward direct engagement. But now this may be dangerous. Often it is postponed or realized only partially and symbolically by way of private or primitive imagery, ostensibly neutral material, or sometimes, a reported dream.

The Songwriter showed this pattern: predominant personal narrative, gradually interspersed with bits of neutral material (the anti-Nixon diatribe) along with one primitive intrusion, and as the sessions went on by increasing direct interchange with the OTHER.

At times, of course, the intensified influence of the situation, and implicitly the OTHER, is manifest immediately and so overpowering as to make free association almost impossible. That was the impasse faced by the Astrologer until quasi-clinical experimental intervention allowed him to take refuge in almost uninterrupted personal narrative.

Clearly, such observations are only the beginning of systematic and rigorous treatment of free association. Decoding depends upon combined scrutiny of content and form, the report and the act of reporting.

It is worth examining further these two aspects — the report and the act of reporting. From a phylogenetic and entogenetic viewpoint, communicative activity precedes clear linguistic content, as can be seen in the babbling of infants long before one-word sentences appear. Neuropsychological evidence suggests that lower brain centers play a role in initiating speech and in regulating alternate selection and uttering of words (Martindale, 1977). An extensive linguistic argument now states that speech is primarily action, making use of semantic and syntactic elements to attain its end (Austin, 1962;

Schafer, 1976). Such a line of reasoning supports the psychoanalytic argument that motives instigate and guide cognitive processes. Without entering here into the linguistic and metalinguistic issues involved, we would simply suggest that for language as a whole active urges precede and shape precise verbal content. In free association, then, the varieties of self and other which emerge with relative clarity must be seen as products of a less obvious, unverbalizable self-in-action. Further, such a self-in-action, in this communicative context, is inevitably acting on, toward, with the OTHER.

Philosophically one could argue that in the beginning this was inevitably so, that psychic life began in an interpersonal context. To do so would be to side with those students of relationships and development who believe that the earliest and deepest psychological structures are outgrowths of an essentially social unit, for example, Fairbairn (1952), Bowlby (1960), Sander (1964, 1976), Balint (1968), Mahler (1968), and many others.

Rather than pursue that argument in detail here, we would close by suggesting a model of some aspects of the free-associative situation. Figure 13 depicts SELF and OTHER in a transactional feedback relationship. It posits phenomenological outer layers, in which various representations of self and other can be discerned. As these reach the focus of attention, they move toward potential explicit description in words. The model also proposes a hidden motivational core of self-in-action-with-others. By that we mean a core of schemata involving selves inexorably linked to the important human figures around them. The various types of feedback interchange are too complex to indicate fully in this diagram. They exist between all levels within the SELF and in subtle ways between SELF and OTHERS. For instance, Jacobson (1953) describes beautifully how a depressed subject may force himself to maintain an idealized image of someone he needs, raging at his inner self image, lest he direct the rage outward and lose the attachment.

These schemata are also inexorably linked to bodily processes. Thus by necessity the latter have aims and objects, as in the psychoanalytic concept of instinctual drive. However, the model tries to avoid a disembodied connection of aim and object to mechanical "forces." Instead it stresses their mutual organization in primordial protosymbolic self systems—which have strivings, intention, will. The term "schemactive core" and the compound word "otherself"

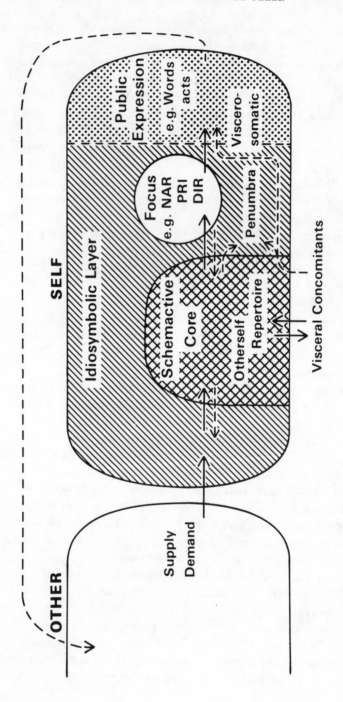

FIGURE 13
OTHER-SELF: General Model

represent steps toward bridging familiar semantic disjunctions, gaps between "mind" and "body," "will" and "determinism," which plague our theories of human nature (Knapp, 1976).

In terms of our present formulations, the core of figure 13 is the projector; the surrounding psychological areas are projected contents. In these contents we can distinguish a focus, moving toward conscious expression, and a penumbra containing available preconscious elements, waiting, as it were, in the wings. The focus in free-associative discourse may move like a spotlight from one to another mode in dynamic patterns like those we have described. Viscissitudes of this associative flow, along with the symbolic relationships that can be discerned in it, permit inferences about the state of the core, its relative organization or disorganization, its stability or conflict.

This model can depict the initial behavior of our contrasting research subjects. They exemplify two common—though by no means the only two—configurations encountered in free association. Initially the Songwriter gave a characteristic report of his life activities in what we call the NAR mode. After an initial marginal comment on the experimenter—wondering whether he would "grade" the subject—the focus was predominantly on self. The OTHER, as listener, remained unobtrusive, part of the penumbra of discourse. We may infer that he exerted definite influence on it, for example, as the subject talked about getting into a situation with colleagues "where we could accept each other for what each other is worth, get into each other's feelings and emotions, which is pretty difficult." We have cited evidence that his unverbalized "otherself" consisted primarily of a satisfying, trust-inspiring schemactive core in which an active nucleus of self was defined and separated out from a surrounding background of other. Figure 14 depicts this situation in terms of the model we have proposed.

Throughout the course of the three sessions, we recall, ambivalent desire for close communication about his hidden preoccupations intensified. As it did so, the OTHER intermittently emerged from the shadows, so to speak, and became more prominent in the associations. At the same time evidence accumulated of a self suffering from conflict and guilt over aggressive and libidinal impulses. These conflicts themselves gained public expression, both in the subjects' free-associative report, and in his drawings, particularly the

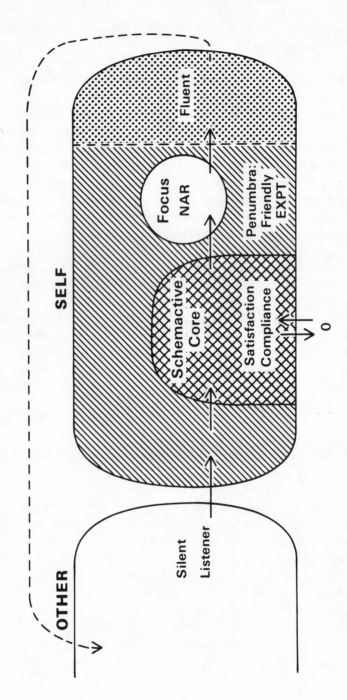

FIGURE 14
OTHER-SELF: Songwriter

witty representation of himself peering over a board from above and behind the experimenter, literally turning the tables on him.

The Astrologer presented a contrasting picture. Initially he could not withdraw his attention from the experiment and the experimenter. They largely filled his focal awareness, while in the background was a self feeling inadequate and angry. Aided by his own responses to careful questioning after the session, we may infer that his "otherself" core consisted of frustrating, confused "schemactive" contents, himself locked in a struggle with and poorly separated from a demanding, resented, feared, ungiving, unclear person-world. The intensity of intra- and interpersonal conflict spilled over to activate mild wheezing. Diagrammatically we may depict his free-associative field as in figure 15.

The subsequent course, after the postsession intervention, was to shift his focus to the narrative mode. The swing is complete. The OTHER was almost totally excluded, though remaining, we suspect, as a powerful hidden presence, threatening to engulf the subject, an inference supported by his final drawing of the "mother and child," a dramatic portrayal of quasi-symbiotic fusion.

Future Implications

As presented so far the experimental approach has been largely of heuristic value. Experimental data themselves have been scrutinized as though by a clinician. The reader might well ask: is there justification for using such a cumbersome collection and laborious study of quasi-clinical material, which has inevitable interpretive uncertainties, indeed, compounded by its relatively limited clinical scope? Such questioning prompts a final word about the potential research contributions of this method.

The free-associative task, like a projective test, forces an individual to reveal important facets of his inner self. It rapidly and inexorably exposes both important interpersonal behavioral patterns and their defensive modulation; thus it is a unique psychodynamic probe. It can be employed in a relatively economical fashion for psychoanalytically based investigation of different classes of individuals. We used it in this way to test hypotheses about trait and state differences between a normal and a psychosomatic population. The approach could equally well study other groups having various

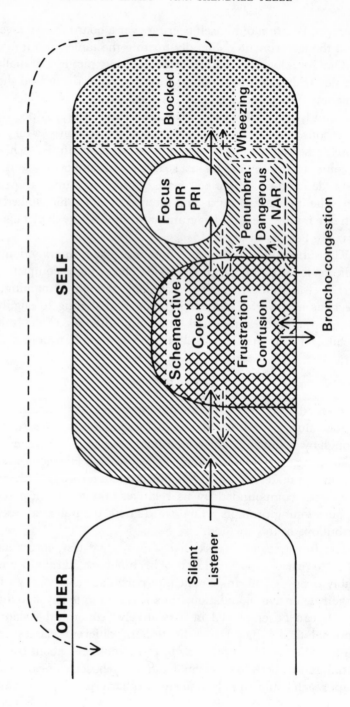

FIGURE 15

OTHER-SELF: Astrologer

symptomatic, characterological, or sociological features.

Second, it permits application of concomitant investigative tools to freely associating subjects, such as the testing and measurements which we used. Obviously one could combine it with other methods, psychological, physiological, or neuropsychological, most of which would constitute a gross intrusion into the clinical psychoanalytic situation.

A third and related possibility is to extend the relatively brief experimental contact described here so as to allow gradations of intensity in the relationship, as well as to permit experimentally chosen psychoanalytic interventions, an approach begun by Colby (1960, 1961). The dramatic effect on the Astrologer of an inadvertent reassuring intervention between his first and second free-associative sessions testifies to the potential power of such planned activity.

In short, although experimental free association cannot supply the infinitely deeper and richer context of actual psychoanalysis, it provides opportunities for comprehensive, accurate recording, and for controlled study of crucial psychoanalytic phenomena.

By combining the clinical and experimental approaches, we can aim at a further goal, namely, more precise knowledge of the nature and range of communicative and linguistic processes subsumed under the term free association. One can study the associations of large numbers of subjects, relatively free from the influence that inevitably results from prolonged contact with a therapist, possibly speaking under different instructional "sets"; and one can compare these with the wide variety of associative patterns encountered in clinical situations. We need a taxonomy of free association, and of the processes underlying it. These include, according to the argument in this paper, a taxonomy of core self-other fantasies, inferred from both the form and content of associations.

Such an enterprise calls for further study of the structures of language, thought, and emotion revealed by free association and of the ways in which we make inferences from surface to "deeper" processes. This effort has led us to construct the model presented here of important interpersonal aspects of the free-associative process. Such a model, of course, raises a multitude of questions. To mention only some: how does activity of the OTHER impinge on and reach the "schemactive" core? What is the relationship of such a proposed core to the biological centers of drive and emotion as these are currently understood? What are the relationships between apperceptive-evaluative aspects of psychic life and effector-expressive aspects? How do the unverbalizable schemata of the core deploy and employ more clearly representable psychic contents? How do attentional processes develop, and what is their relationship to various levels of consciousness?

Clearly, we are dealing with some of the central issues addressed by Freud's successive models of the psychic apparatus. An overriding problem is the gap between phenomenological observations and dynamic explanations. Seen more precisely and in a historical context, this gap reflects different conceptual levels dealt with by psychoanalysis. Its clinical theory has to do with interpersonal relationships, in all their conflict-ridden variety, and with their inner representations in imagery and fantasy. The general theory of psychoanalysis deals with dynamic forces, using progressively more abstract terms, many deriving from Freud's heritage in the biological science of his time.

Present-day psychoanalysis is intrigued by formulations of the self and others, which were in the forefront of the seminal work by Edith Jacobson (1964). These have not yet been satisfactorily integrated with concepts of instinct and ego, although there are urgent needs for defining interrelationships between the two conceptual realms. For instance, Kernberg (1976) stresses the abnormal strength of aggression in borderline patients; Kohut (1977) emphasizes the incomplete development of "self" in narcissistic disturbances, which lead to inevitable ego distortions, attributing both of these features to faulty emancipation from important human objects.

Such formulations might be sharpened with the aid of a model such as ours. Material like that obtained from the Astrologer might test derivative hypotheses, for example, about the relationship between primitive aggression and fusion of self and others. We do not suggest that we have solutions to the major conceptual problems facing psychoanalysis, but we offer an approach that may be helpful in moving toward solutions.

References

Austin, J. L. (1962), *How to Do Things With Words*. New York: Oxford University Press.

Balint, M. (1968), *The Basic Fault.* London: Tavistock Publications.

Bellak, L. (1961), Free association, conceptual and clinical aspects. *Int. J. Psycho-Anal.,* 42:9–20.

Bowlby, J. (1960), Separation anxiety. *Int. J. Psycho-Anal.,* 41:89–113.

Cohen, J. A. (1960), A coefficient of agreement for nominal scales. *Psychol. Measmt.,* 20:37–46.

Colby, K. M. (1960), Experiment on the effects of an observer's presence on the imago system. *Behav. Sci.,* 5:216–232.

_____ (1961), On the greater amplifying power of causal-correlative over interrogative inputs on free association in an experimental psychoanalytic situation. *J. Nerv. Ment. Dis.,* 133:233–239.

Duncan, S., Jr. & Fiske, D. W. (1978), Dynamic patterning in conversation. *Amer. Scientist,* 67:90–98.

Fairbairn, W. R. D. (1952), *An Object Relations Theory of the Personality.* New York: Basic Books.

Fisher, C. (1953), Studies on the nature of suggestion: I. *J. Amer. Psychoanal. Assn.,* 1:222–255.

Goodenough, F. (1926), *The Measurement of Intelligence by Drawings.* Yonkers, N.Y.: World Books.

Jacobson, E. (1953), Contribution to the metapsychology of cyclothymic depression. In: *Affective Disorders,* ed. P. Greenacre. New York: International Universities Press, pp. 49–83.

_____ (1964), *The Self and the Object World.* New York: International Universities Press.

Kernberg, O. F. (1976), *Object Relations Theory and Clinical Psychoanalysis.* New York: Jason Aronson.

Knapp, P. H. (1960), Acute bronchial asthma: II. *Psychosom. Med.,* 22:88–105.

_____ (1974), Segmentation and structure in psychoanalysis. *J. Amer. Psychoanal. Assn.,* 23:13–36.

_____ (1976), The mysterious "split." In: *Consciousness and the Brain,* ed. G. Globus, G. Maxwell, & I. Savodniko. New York: Plenum, pp. 33–70.

_____ & Bahnson, C. B. (1963), The emotional field. *Psychosom. Med.,* 25: 438–460.

_____ Teele, A. S., & Vachon, L. (1979), Experimental free association and psychophysiological function in bronchial asthma. *Psychosom. Med.* (in press).

Kohut, H. (1977), *The Restoration of the Self.* New York: International Universities Press.

Kris, E. (1956), On some vicissitudes of insight in psycho-analysis. *Int. J. Psycho-Anal.,* 37:445–455.

Kubie, L. S. (1959), Psychoanalysis and scientific method. In: *Psychoanalysis, Scientific Method and Philosophy,* ed. S. Hook. New York: New York University Press, pp. 55–77.

Mahler, M. S. (1968), *On Human Symbiosis and the Vicissitudes of Individuation.* New York: International Universities Press.

Martindale, C. (1977), Syntactic and semantic correlates in Giles de la Tourettes syndrome. *Brain and Language,* 4:231–247.

Ross, R., Knapp, P. H., & Vachon, L. (1979), Speech and stress in mild asthmatics. *Psychosom. Med.,* 41:77.

Sander, L. W. (1964), Adaptive relationships in early mother-child relationships. *J. Amer. Acad. Child Psychiat.,* 3:231–264.

———— (1976), Regulation of exchange in the infant caretaker system. In: *Communicative Structures and Psychic Structures,* ed. N. Freedman & S. Grand. New York: Plenum, pp. 13–34.

Schafer, R. (1976), *A New Language for Psychoanalysis.* New Haven: Yale University Press.

Weisman, A. D. (1955), Silence and psychotherapy. *Psychiatry,* 18:241–260.

Witkin, H. A., Dyk, R. B., Faterson, H. F., Goodenough, D. R., & Karp, S. A. (1962), *Psychological Differentiation.* New York: Wiley.

20

THE CORE CONFLICTUAL
RELATIONSHIP THEME

A Demonstration of Reliable Clinical Inference
by the Method of Mismatched Cases

Frederic J. Levine, Ph.D. and Lester Luborsky, Ph.D.

The well-known difficulty of making reliable judgments of major psychoanalytic concepts from clinical data has been termed by Seitz (1966) "the consensus problem in psychoanalytic research." In fact, there has often been an inverse relationship between the consensus that could be obtained and the importance of the concept to be judged. At the extreme, "very exact answers to questions [i.e., answers about which there is near-perfect agreement] can often be given if the subjects with which we deal are very small in relation to ourselves and to all things that matter to us" (Waelder, 1962, p. 259). It is usually possible to obtain adequate agreement among observers if rather severe restrictions are applied to the data, as, for example, when the observers are asked to rate material on predetermined checklists of possible meanings, as in the study by Bellak and Smith (1956). However, such procedures are very different from the analyst's usual mode of listening to and understanding the patient. When the analyst's usual mode is employed, as was done in the major study of consensus by Seitz and his group (1966), agreement is not obtained. Moreover, in the light of our experiences with a new method, it seems likely that Seitz's method was not adequate to the

This study was supported in part by USPHS Research Grant MH 15442 and Research Scientist Award MH 40710 to Dr. Luborsky.

The authors wish to express their appreciation to Drs. Harold Sackeim and Donald P. Spence, who encouraged the use of the method of mismatched cases, and to Mr. Paul Christoph and Mrs. Marjorie Cohen for help in executing the study.

job of evaluating the consensus or lack of consensus which could be achieved. We shall describe this new method of abstracting a core conflictual relationship theme from patients' psychotherapy sessions. The method can assist clinical-quantitative research in psychoanalysis and psychotherapy by its reliable delineation of patterns of object relationships such as transference patterns.

The Method

Its Origin

The core conflictual relationship theme method is an outgrowth of the long search which one of us (Luborsky, 1977b) has been conducting to identify the curative factors in psychotherapy. Studies by the Penn psychotherapy research project (Auerbach et al., 1972; Luborsky et al., 1979; and others, e.g., Fiske et al., 1964), and an extensive literature review (Luborsky et al., 1975) have shown that although the majority of patients benefit from psychotherapy and psychoanalysis, it is clear that the outcome of *each* treatment venture is only slightly predictable from the initial characteristics of patient or therapist, the match between the two, or the type of treatment. Since the pretreatment measurements contribute only slightly to the predictability of the outcome, it was reasonable to explore the predictive power of data gathered from the patient-therapist interaction as they emerge in the course of treatment. To understand the groundwork for these interactions, it was necessary to work out ways of delineating the main themes which appear in the patient-therapist relationship during treatment.

The touchstone of our method is its focus on the patterns and vicissitudes of the patient's internalized images of his object relations as they emerge from "relationship episodes" — the patient's actual descriptions of outside-of-treatment relationship incidents or enactments of relationships to the therapist in the treatment sessions themselves. Research on content scoring for psychoanalytic sessions often consists of an attempt to catalogue the frequencies with which a predetermined list of themes occurs, e.g., Bellak and Smith (1956). By contrast, our method is based on the same basic inferential and interpretive processes used by the psychoanalytic clinician in drawing conclusions about the major conflictual theme, or the main transference pattern, in a patient's free associations. This theme is the one which is most redundant across many examples of the patient's relationships — the one which is most prevalent and special for the individual and appears with varying intensity in most of the patient's relationships. Guidelines are provided to the observer who by a clinical inference process evaluates these episodes in transcripts of sessions in order to identify an individually unique, pervasive, and hypervalent theme — the "core conflictual relationship theme" (CCRT). The first article on the method described the procedure and gave some examples of its results (Luborsky, 1977a).

This paper is aimed at taking up one of the remaining problems of the method — to develop ways of showing the agreement that is possible with it. After describing and illustrating our method, we shall present the agreement among individuals independently formulating the core conflictual relationship theme from a set of clinical data, including agreement based on using the same case ("matched") vs. different cases ("mismatched").

The Psychoanalytic Rationale of the Core Conflictual Relationship Theme

Beginning with Freud, analysts have been impressed with recurring conflictual patterns demonstrated by their patients. Freud (1914) described the compulsion to repeat which is evident in the transference and resistance. He considered the mechanisms of defense to be modes of reaction which are repeated throughout the person's life (1937). French and Wheeler (1963) put forward the idea of a single "nuclear conflict" in each patient. A similar concept is the "residual trauma" (Blos, 1941; Ekstein, 1956), a recurrent conflictual pattern which is evident throughout a person's life, and even after the analysis.

Jacobson (1954, 1964) has shown in rich and subtle detail how conflictual patterns have a particularly strong impact upon the formation of psychic representations of the self and objects:

> ...these images arise essentially from the memory traces of pleasurable and unpleasurable [infantile] experiences and are only gradually linked up with and corrected by...reality....The defects [in self and object images] caused by the work of repression may be filled in by screen elements, by distortions or embellishments produced by the elaborate maneuvers of the ego's defense system. Moreover, to the extent to which the

repressed fantasies that have remained cathected in the unconscious can find their way to the surface, they will lend the coloring of past infantile images to the self and object representations...our view of the world, and especially of the animate object world,...easily permits distortions by transference of infantile images onto other persons [1964, pp. 21–22].

In searching for a multifaceted theme that recurs, with variations, in all or most of an individual's object relations, we were following the path indicated by conceptions such as these. According to Arlow (1969), "in keeping with the synthetic function of the ego and the principle of multiple function, the traumatic events in the individual's life and the pathogenic conflicts that grow out of them are worked over defensively by the ego and incorporated into a *scheme of memories and patterns of fantasy...and as such exert a never-ending dynamic effect...on our responses to and appreciation of reality*" (p. 43f., our italics). By examining the patient's descriptions and enactments of relationships, we hoped to identify this unified, synthesized scheme, in the form of the central theme characterizing the patient's dealings with people.

Procedure

Several types of procedures are involved in this task: (1) sampling the cases and the psychotherapy sessions; (2) locating the examples of relationships; (3) identifying and describing the relationship patterns; (4) recording components of the main theme which are present in each description or enactment of an object relationship; and (5) assessing their strength or prominence in the particular episode.

1. *Sampling psychotherapy sessions.* From the tape recordings of psychoanalytically oriented psychotherapies of seventy-three patients in the Penn Psychotherapy Research Project, we focused on the seven patients who showed most improvement with treatment, and the eight who improved least. A sample of sessions was reviewed for each patient, two from early in the treatment and two more close to termination. The data were further reduced by using only the first twenty minutes of each session. This provided the raters with a substantial but manageable excerpt from the treatment.

2. *Locating "relationship episodes."* The next step was to identify, within the twenty-minute segments, *the present and past specifically described interactions with people,* both outside of the treatment and with the thera-

pist. Each such relationship episode was marked off on the transcript, the clarity of the episode was rated, and the "object" dealt with in the episode was identified. Focusing on these episodes highlighted the relationship behaviors that were of interest. Furthermore, the focus on interactions with specific people was supported by a previous study which had found that transference could be rated with more interjudge agreement when judges considered only delimited interactions with objects than when ratings were based on an entire therapy segment (Luborsky et al., 1973).

3. *Formulating the theme. a.* All relationship episodes for a given patient are inspected in sequence to find thematic consistencies. The inspection job is based on clinical judgment without preconceived focus or expectations because, "it must not be forgotten that the things one hears [in analysis] are for the most part things whose meaning is only recognized later on" (Freud, 1912, p. 112). Earlier episodes become more understandable to the judge after the later ones are studied; redundant themes within and across episodes gradually appear. It does not matter that a few episodes are opaque or do not seem to fit—our focus is on those whose themes repeat themselves; the redundancy of the theme is a mark of where the main conflict lies.

The statement of the theme formulation is guided by a simple structural format, and phrased in terms describing the manifest conflict at close to the level at which the patient sees it. In other words, these formulations are made at what Waelder (1962) called *the level of clinical interpretation*—the first level of inference beyond the concrete clinical data.

b. Without a structure to provide guidelines for the form of theme statements, they might differ considerably from judge to judge simply as an artifact of differences in style or syntax. In order to overcome this, each judge makes his independent theme formulation according to a standard format.

The theme structure can be described as a "tree"—the main trunk is composed of the wish, need, or intention expressed by the patient in his relationships, and the branches are the consequences the patient encounters or expects to meet for expressing the wish or trying to fulfill the wish (see table 1). The consequences are divided into two main types, external and internal; and for each of these, the main ones are listed in the order of the judge's estimate of their frequency.

TABLE 1

The Suggested Format for the
Core Conflictual Relationship Theme Formulation

Wish, Need, Intention*	Consequence*		
A. I wish from (object) but....	1. Negative external response	a. _____	
a. _____		b. _____	
b. _____		c. _____	
c. _____	2. Negative internal response	a. _____	
		b. _____	
		c. _____	
	3. Positive external response	a. _____	
		b. _____	
		c. _____	
	4. Positive internal response	a. _____	
		b. _____	
		c. _____	

*List each in order, with the most frequent first.

Four judges[1] participated in the initial theme formulation: each made his own theme statement, and these were then combined into a single "tree" by grafting on any unrepresented subthemes of the several judges. There was little difficulty in reaching agreement on this "tree."

c. The components of the theme are then scored for each of the relationship episodes. This can be done independently by other judges who rate the degree to which each component of the theme applies to each episode. These data can yield results which include both the overall frequencies of the theme and its components in the episodes throughout treatment; the separate frequencies for early versus late sessions, and such other special studies as frequencies for episodes in which the therapist is the object versus other episodes; and the effect of transference interpretations on the frequencies.

Findings

When the relationship episodes were abstracted according to this procedure, our expectations were confirmed. One main (branched)

[1]Richard Kluft, Frederic J. Levine, Thomas Wolman, and Lester Luborsky.

theme was indeed detected, characterizing each patient. There was considerable diversity among patients so that a given individual's theme was distinctive. The theme for each patient was similar across all types of objects, indicating that this method appears to tap a pervasive, prominent psychic structure. When material from early in treatment is compared with sessions near termination, the same theme is found in both, but there are often differences in emphasis: in the later sessions the theme becomes more focused and affectively involved in the relationship with the therapist. Finally, preliminary findings suggest that the patients who benefited most from treatment showed an improved sense of mastery of the same core conflict toward the end of therapy, but this did not occur in nonimprovers.

For illustrative purposes, capsule versions of a young male patient's relationship episodes are presented in table 2 — Mr. AL, who improved significantly in the course of treatment. Beside each episode are the theme components identified in it by each member of the research group. Table 3 presents the combined theme formulation derived by the four members of the clinical research group. Inspecting the theme components gives an impression of agreement; it is the job of this paper to try to specify the amount of agreement. The organization of theme components in table 3 is intended to convey the frequency of theme components — the most frequent ones are presented first. For Mr. AL, the most frequent theme is theme A: "I want to assert myself (to hold up my end), but I am rejected and dominated, and/or I go along with the person or I withdraw."

The Problem of Consensus

There has been little research in which independent clinical observers have agreed on formulating a main conflictual theme or transference pattern from the same set of data (Luborsky and Spence, 1978). This problem — apart from serving as a springboard for skepticism about the "scientific status" of psychoanalysis — does present a serious obstacle to systematic clinical-quantitative research.

A major attempt to tackle this issue was made by Seitz's (1966) study group in Chicago which sought commonalities among the members' formulations of clinical data: "The researchers continued for three years and then disbanded because of inability to make

TABLE 2

Mr. AL
Theme and Scores for Each Episode

Session 3 *Episode*	Rater	Wish Need Intent	External Response	Internal Response
1. Object: guy (roommate) Guy tried to dominate conversation. "It irritated me"; "I repressed everything and just sink back"; "now brooding" and "pissed off" — fantasies of putting him down.	LL	Ab* Aa	1a	2e
	FL	Ab Aa	1a 1b	2e, 2b, 2c 2f, 2N
	TW	Aa Ab	1a 1b	?
	RK	Aa Ab	1b 1a	2f, 2b, 2e 2d
2. Object: policeman "Cop comes up and tells her to sit right"; "they stood up to him"; "I got really anxious; I would have automatically obeyed."	LL	(Ab)	(1b)	2a, 2d
	FL	Aa	(1b)	2a, 2d
	TW	Aa′, Ab	(1b)	2a, 2d
	RK	Ab		2a, 2d
3. Object: weird guy "I'm friendly with people I don't want to be friendly with"; "Big weird guy comes around"; "I have choice of being mean or being a hypocrite"; "I don't want him around."	LL	Ac		2a
	FL	Ac Ad	1b	2a, 2e
	TW	Ac	1b	2a
	RK	Ab Ac		2a

TABLE 2 (continued)

Session 3 Episode	Rater	Wish Need Intent	External Response	Internal Response
4. Object: girl with "clap"	LL	Ac*		2a, (2d)
Girl who has been cooking dinners for me: "I really don't want to get involved with her sexually"—keep being too involved. "Hungry to have people around."	FL	Ac, Aa Ad		2a
	TW	Aa′, Ac	3N	2b, 4a
	RK	Ad, Ac		2b
5. Object: therapist (T)	LL	Aa		2b
"I have to prove myself. . .to come across to people and impress them—I think it is happening to me right now in here" with (T). "Typical of a situation when I start feeling better. . .more aware. . .alive. . . I get to a point where I want to go back, to close up again."	FL	Aa		2b, 4a
	TW	Aa	3b?	2b
	RK	Aa Ac		1b, 1N
6. Object: another T	LL	(Aa)		(2b)
"I have tendencies to retreat, like the sessions I had with Dr. A [previous T] when I was feeling pretty good."	FL	(Aa)		2b, 4a
	TW	Ad	1a	
	RK	Aa		4N, ?3N
7. Object: mother	LL	Aa	3a	2d
"I called home last night to talk to mother about money for the cycle [motorcycle]; I first thought of doing it behind their back as a shock and surprise to them." "I have ulterior motives. . .of impressing people"; "She thought I was old enough to make the decision for myself."	FL	Aa Ab		3a, 2f
	TW	Aa Aa′	3a 3b	4a
	RK	Aa Ab	3a 3N	4a

*Letters and numbers refer to scoring on table 3.

TABLE 3

The Research Judges' Combined Theme Formulation for Mr. AL

Wish	Consequence	
A. I want to assert myself (to hold up my end)*	1. Negative External Response	a. I am *rejected* (put down; can't get my view across)
		b. I am dominated.
	2. Negative Internal Response	a. I go along (I agree, etc.)
		b. I withdraw
		c. I get depressed
		d. I get scared (of being hurt)
		e. I get inappropriately angry
		f. I delay affective response
		N. I am helpless
	3. Positive External Response	a. I am given approval
		b. Structure is provided
		N. I get what I wish for
	4. Positive Internal Response	a. I feel in control
		b. I identify with the therapist
		N. I give myself a positive response

*These are similar or related versions of the wish:
a. To impress others by showing my strength (e.g., to get my opinion across and to convince others; to show competence and effectiveness).
a'. To prove self sexually; to show masculinity.
b. To put someone else down (usually someone who seems big in comparison, i.e., an authority.)
c. To not go along with others, and keep my distance from them.
d. To satisfy my indiscriminate hunger to be closer.
e. To obtain structure, that is, someone to tell me what to do.

progress in developing a reliable interpretive method" (p. 210). Seitz's evaluation of his project was: "Our results in this respect [i.e., in regard to consensus] are strongly negative" (p. 214). Seitz attributed the failure of his group to reach consensus primarily to "the various observers focusing upon different parts of a total picture. . . [with each therefore] only partly right" (p. 209). Although instructed to identify preconscious "focal conflicts, . . . instead, we found that participants often tended to interpret at levels deeper than the focal conflict in the preconscious, frequently singling out a specific *uncon*scious overdeterminant of the focal conflict and organizing an entire interpretive formulation around that particular dynamic trend" (p. 215). In other words, since all behavior is multiply determined and can be described at different metapsychological levels of analysis (Waelder, 1962), one important reason for lack of consensus is the difficulty in getting several observers consistently to use the same level of analysis and point of view at the same time.

One important test of the value of the core conflictual relationship theme method was whether it could succeed, where Seitz's group did not, and produce a meaningful consensus among different judges of the same clinical data. Our present attempt to make this test is the first with a large number of judges. It was conducted in a class of graduate students in clinical psychology — a relatively inexperienced group clinically, where lack of consensus would not have been surprising. It, therefore, constitutes a severe test of the method.

Method

1. The student judges were eighteen first-year graduate students. Most were in their early twenties, but a number were older. The majority had some basic patient-care experience as psychiatric aides, counselors, and the like; and all were treating one or two patients under supervision. About half the group had some personal psychotherapy.

The students participated in this project as part of a first course in principles of psychotherapy in which they had previously received instruction in basic tenets of psychoanalytic theory and an overview of the purpose, structure, and theory of therapy. They were told that we wished to explore the utility of the core conflictual theme format as a method of helping them to organize and begin to understand clinical data, and also that we wanted to compare their formulations with the theme statements that had been previously arrived at by the research group in its consideration of the same patient's material.

2. The procedure was as follows: the students were first asked to read and discuss in class a paper describing the CCRT concept and method, with cases illustrating the application of the method (Luborsky, 1977a). They were then given the transcript of the first twenty minutes of the third treatment session with Mr. AL (see tables 2 and 3). Seven relationship episodes were marked on the transcript (table 2), and the "object" for each episode was identified. Each student, working individually during a single ninety-minute class session, formulated a theme statement based on these seven episodes. (Two of the eighteen students did not follow the instructions correctly and were, therefore, dropped from the study.)

Time restrictions made it necessary to have the student judges base their formulations on an unusually limited amount of material (one session rather than four). In this way we could have a large number of judges simultaneously process the same set of data. However, in choosing this procedure we were, of necessity, setting up an exceptionally hard test of the method because such a small data base would probably increase the influence of random or transient factors on the material and thus make accurate formulation of the main pervasive theme more difficult. It would be expected to reduce the amount of agreement between the student judges and the combined research judges' formulation which was based on the material of four sessions.

3. The problem of accurately estimating the amount of consensus is a complex one. It required a second set of raters ("agreement judges") whose task it was to rate the agreement between the theme statements made by each of the sixteen student judges and the combined research judges' formulation (table 3). Separate comparisons were made for each of the elements of the theme—the "trunk" (wish) and each "branch" (consequence) of the "tree," and for major subthemes.

Table 4 summarizes the steps followed by the three types of judges involved. The *research judges* provide a single composite formulation which is compared in turn with each of the sixteen *student judges'* formulations. The comparison is made by the *agreement judges*. In those cases where the student judges' formulations were worded

TABLE 4

The Steps in the Reliability Study

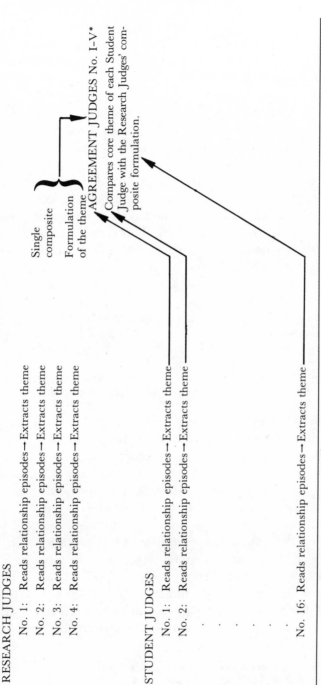

RESEARCH JUDGES

No. 1: Reads relationship episodes → Extracts theme
No. 2: Reads relationship episodes → Extracts theme
No. 3: Reads relationship episodes → Extracts theme
No. 4: Reads relationship episodes → Extracts theme

Single composite Formulation of the theme

AGREEMENT JUDGES No. I–V*

Compares core theme of each Student Judge with the Research Judges' composite formulation.

STUDENT JUDGES

No. 1: Reads relationship episodes → Extracts theme
No. 2: Reads relationship episodes → Extracts theme

· · · ·
· · · ·
· · · ·

No. 16: Reads relationship episodes → Extracts theme

*Two agreement judges (IV and V) repeated the comparison procedure three times, using three different researchers' formulations, Mr. AL and two mismatched cases.

identically with those of the combined research judges', it was obvious that agreement was present. However, the agreement judges' opinions were needed in other instances to decide whether there was the same substantive meaning, even though somewhat different language was used.

4. We needed to know of possible bias in the agreement judges — they might inflate the agreement just to be agreeable or vice versa. In order to control for such influence, and to determine whether there was significant agreement, two of the agreement judges compared the student judges' themes, not only with the combined research judges' formulation for patient Mr. AL, but also with theme statements that had been formulated by the research group from the protocols of two other patients. This is the approach we called "the method of matched vs. mismatched pairs." No more than chance similarities were expected between the student judges' themes and the two control formulations, not based on patient Mr. AL, i.e., the mismatched pairs. The agreement judges were not informed of the presence of such differences among the three combined research judges' formulations.

Findings: Comparisons of Sixteen Student Judges
With One Composite Formulation of the Research Judges

Table 5 shows the ratings by the five agreement judges[2] of the number of times each element of the research judges' composite formulation (table 3) appeared in the theme statements of the sixteen student judges. Included are only those cases in which the student placed the element in the same category as did the research judges (e.g., "I get scared" would be tabulated as agreement only if it is listed by both as a Negative Internal Consequence).

a. Reliability of agreement judges. Our first task was to determine whether the agreement judges' ratings were reliable. This would show whether it is actually possible to use judges to determine consensus among theme formulations made by several different individuals using this format. As can be seen in table 5, some agreement judges were consistently more ready than others to conclude

---

[2]The agreement judges were: Frederic J. Levine, Wendy Smolen, Yonna S. Levine, Deena Adler, Cheryl Biemer, and Victoria Handfield.

TABLE 5

Number of Agreements on Theme Elements Between Student
Judges (N = 16) and Composite Research Judges

	Element (from table 1)	I	II	III	IV	V
			Agreement Judges			
Wish (e.g., I wish	A	11	14	10	13	7
to assert self)	a	7	9	3	10	5
	a′	2	3	1	1	1
	b	3	3	2	2	0
	c	1	5	1	3	1
	d	2	5	1	6	0
	e	0	0	0	0	0
	A or a*	14	15	11	14	10
	None†	2	1	4	1	5
Consequences						
Neg. Ext.	a	5	5	5	6	5
("but...")	b	8	9	9	8	8
	a or b*	9	10	10	10	9
	None†	7	6	6	6	7
Neg. Int.	a	6	8	7	6	4
("but...")	b	8	10	9	10	9
	c	2	2	0	2	0
	d	7	9	3	10	3
	e	9	9	8	11	8
	f	4	3	0	3	0
	N	2	3	1	2	1
	a or b*	11	13	13	13	11
	None†	2	1	2	1	3
Pos. Ext.	a	5	7	5	6	1
("and...")	b	0	0	1	1	0
	N	4	5	4	5	5
	None†	8	6	7	7	11
Pos. Int.	a	5	4	2	4	0
("and...")	b	0	0	0	0	0
	N	2	7	2	4	0
	None†	9	7	12	9	16

*These are the numbers of students who included either or both of the indicated elements, which were the two most prominent ones in each category for the research group.

†Numbers of students showing *none* of the theme elements reported in each category by the research group.

that a given student judge agreed with the research judges' formulation, but nevertheless the total picture of which elements showed agreement and which did not was seen in very similar ways by all five agreement judges. When the agreement judges' ratings were intercorrelated, the correlations obtained ranged from .83 to .96, with an average intercorrelation for all agreement judges of .88.

Further evidence of the reliability of these judgments was garnered in an examination of the ratings of each student judge's theme by the agreement judges; this inspection clearly showed that all used the same qualitative criteria of similarity, but some agreement judges consistently were narrow and conservative,in comparing the two themes, while others consistently made judgments more broadly and inclusively—and that difference in orientation or "set" accounted for virtually all the variation among them in rating agreements. For example, for Wish element A, judge V rated seven cases as showing agreement, judge III also rated the same seven agreements, and added three more; judge I rated the same ten cases as showing agreement, plus one more; judge IV found the same eleven agreements, and added two others; and judge II saw agreements in all thirteen cases so rated by judge IV, and also an additional one.

b. Agreement for wishes vs. consequences. The large majority of student judges' theme statements included the same Wish element A that had been found most often by the researchers. When the second most prominent Wish element a was also considered, nearly all the students cited one or both of these alternatives (see table 5). The minor variant Wish elements made only rare and sporadic appearances in the students' formulations—which was, after all, to be expected since the student judges were instructed to pick out the *main* theme.

On the consequence side, there was greater variability, but again prominent areas of agreement occurred. About half of the students' theme statements included Negative External Consequence 1b, and about three fourths included either or both of the Negative Internal Consequences which were most prominent for the researchers (2a and 2b).

There was much less agreement about Positive Consequences. This is probably because the students rated session 3, an early point in the treatment when Mr. AL saw few positive outcomes for his interactions with people. (Inspection of the researchers' ratings of session 3, in table 2, shows that they, too, did not see many Positive Consequences in that particular session.)

It is noteworthy that, with each student judge free to choose his own way of formulating the theme, nine of the sixteen used the same word ("assert") for the major Wish element—a word chosen by the researchers as well.

c. *Agreement for judging matched pairs (from the same case) vs. mismatched pairs (from different cases).* Table 6 shows the ratings by agreement judges IV and V of the number of times the student judges' formulations contained the elements from the research judges' formulation for patient Mr. AL and from the two control formulations developed for other patients (here designated X and Y).

The student judges' formulations for Mr. AL showed some areas of greater agreement with the research judges' formulation for Mr. AL as compared with the control formulations, but there were also areas in which the student formulations contained many of the same elements as for the mismatched patients.

For the main Wish elements, the students' formulations were very significantly more similar to the research judges' formulation for Mr. AL than for the mismatched cases. For element A, X^2 was 14.35, with a probability of less than .001; for element a, X^2 was 8.9, with a probability less than .05; and for agreement on A or a, X^2 was 10.4, with probability less than .01.

For Negative External Consequences, there were no differences between agreements for Mr. AL vs. the control formulations. For all three patients the two main Negative External Consequences were, in essence, being rejected and being dominated by the object; consequently, there was an almost identical amount of agreement of the student judges' themes with all three of the research judges' formulations.

For the main Negative Internal Consequences, the picture was more consistent with expectations: for Consequence a, no difference was found, but on Negative Internal Consequence b, there was significantly more frequent agreement between the students' judgments and the research judges' formulation for Mr. AL than for the two control formulations.

Since very few positive consequences were rated in the early treatment hour seen by the students, comparisons on those variables

TABLE 6

Number of Agreements on Theme Elements for Student Judges and Composite of the Research Judges for a Correctly Matched (M) vs. Two Mismatched (MM) Cases

	Element	Agreement Judge IV M Mr. AL	MM Pt. X	MM Pt. Y	Agreement Judge V M Mr. AL	MM Pt. X	MM Pt. Y
Wish	A	13	0	8	7	0	5
	a	10	4	1	5	2	0
	a'	1	3	5	1	0	3
	b	2	2	0	0	0	0
	c	3			1		
	d	6			0		
	e	0			0		
	A or a*	14	4	8	10	2	5
	None†	1	9	5	5	14	9
Consequence							
Neg. Ext.	a	6	6	6	5	5	5
	b	8	10	9	8	9	8
	c		0			0	
	A or b*	10	11	11	9	10	9
	None†	6	5	4	7	6	3
Neg. Int.	a	6	9	3	4	6	3
	b	10	1	7	9	2	6
	c	2	0	2	0	0	1
	d	10	8	10	3	6	9
	e	11	10		8	9	
	f	3	1		0	0	
	N	2			1		
	a or b*	13	10	8	11	7	7
	None†	1	2	1	3	2	4
Post. Ext.	a	6	2		1	0	
	b	1	9		0	3	
	N	5	0		5	0	
	None†	7	6		11	13	
Pos. Int.	a	4	0		0	0	
	b	0	3		0	4	
	N	4			0		
	None†	9	13		16	12	

*Numbers of student judges including either or both of the two most prominent elements.

†Numbers of students showing none of the theme elements in the researchers' formulations in each category.

are not meaningful.[3]

Summary and Conclusions

The core conflictual relationship theme (CCRT) method is a system which uses the inferential techniques of the psychoanalytic psychotherapist to extract from the data of the treatment sessions a central conflictual theme pattern which is both clinically meaningful and also sufficiently reproducible and measurable to provide a basis for clinical-quantitative research. It seems to us that we have been able to obtain meaningful as well as substantially reliable results, precisely because this method uses the basic clinical inference process, but adds to it the guidance afforded by relationship episodes, a particular format for stating the theme, and the principle of searching for the most redundant theme.[4] The data presented here warrant these conclusions:

1. Even relatively inexperienced observers, in this case clinical psychology students, reliably agree with experienced observers (the composite research judges' formulation); for example, the five agreement judges going over the sixteen student judges' themes and comparing them with the composite research judges' formulation agreed with each other that the two groups of judgments agreed. The agreement judges' ratings were highly intercorrelated (the correlations ranging from .83 to .96 with an average of .88).

2. The agreement of the student judges with the composite of the research judges was greater for the Wish component than for the Consequence components. The agreement in this one instance was impressive; for example, for Mr. AL, with each student free to choose his own formulation of the theme, nine of the sixteen used the word "assert" as a Wish element, a word chosen by the researchers as well.

3. The new reliability procedure introduced in the study was the comparison of agreement on "same case" pairs vs. "mismatched"

---

[3]Seitz (1966) reported that judges found most consensus on "disturbing motives" and least on "defenses and solutions." This appears similar to our judges who showed more consensus on Wishes than on Consequences.

[4]In a later study we will use psychoanalysts as judges. This should provide a less difficult test of the method than did the use of student judges since analysts are highly practiced in clinical inference-making.

pairs, that is, student judges' theme statements based on Mr. AL vs. composite research judges' theme statements based on two different cases. For the main Wish element, the student judges were more in agreement with the research judges for Mr. AL (matched case) vs. the mismatched cases. The difference between matched and mismatched pairs for Consequences was inconsistent. For example, for the main Negative Internal Consequence, the expected differences appeared for correctly matched vs. mismatched pairs; for Negative External Consequences, the expected differences were not evident.

The studies done so far show (1) a single, central multifaceted relationship theme characterizes each individual. (2) The main theme has various subthemes, but, consistent with the synthetic function of the ego, it is essentially a unity. (3) The same theme is discovered both in early and late sessions, in patients who improve with treatment and in those who do not.

These findings strongly suggest that what has been uncovered is a pervasive psychic structure with a slow rate of change. Arlow (1969) states vividly the nature of this phenomenon, "The organization of these [conflictual] fantasies takes shape early in life and persists in this form with only minor variations throughout life. To borrow an analogy from literature, one would say that the plot line of the fantasy remains the same although the characters and the situations may vary" (p. 47). Jacobson (1964) appears to have been pointing to the same phenomenon even in the "normal" individual: "With full maturation and the achievement of instinctual mastery, the representations of the self and of the object world in general acquire a final, characteristic configuration . . . they have what may be called 'complementary' qualities which characterize a prominent aspect of his personality . . . these complementary qualities of his object and self representations reflect and define both his own identity and his *Weltbild;* i.e., his fundamental position in relation to himself and to the world" (p. 193).

Why has the core conflictual theme method been successful, where other attempts have failed, in obtaining consensus about the interpretation of clinical material? Undoubtedly the factors mentioned above—the use of episodes, the formulation format, and the redundancy principle—carry very important responsibility for this achievement. Also important, we think, is the clear emphasis on a specified level of inference—the experiential level—to be used in theme formulations. This greatly reduces the problem which Seitz (1966) encountered, that agreement tends to be weakened when several clinicians are asked to interpret a set of data because different clinicians are likely to use different levels of analysis.

Difficulties created by inconsistent and sometimes inappropriate use of the various levels of psychoanalytic analysis of data and theory occur with some frequency in the psychoanalytic literature (Slap and Levine, 1978), and especially in attempts to objectify psychoanalytic interpretations so that they may be studied by quantitative means (Levine, 1974). Our findings suggest that the core conflictual relationship theme method has avoided these difficulties by utilizing formulations that are approximately at what Waelder (1962) called the *level of clinical interpretation*. This is the first level of inference from the data of observation in which they are made "the subject of interpretation regarding their interconnections and their relationships with other behavior or conscious content" (p. 251). Along with the facts of observation themselves, Waelder considered the clinical interpretations to be "entirely indispensable, not only for the practice of psychoanalysis, but for any degree of understanding of it" (p. 252). All the more experience-distant levels of analysis were seen by Waelder as, at least to some degree, less necessary and certainly less central to the analyst's typical day-to-day ways of conceptualizing and understanding his patient's productions. The present effort at objectification then, unlike some others, is at a level of analysis "entirely indispensable...for...understanding."

This fact also makes the core conflictual relationship theme method a useful adjunct in formal classroom instruction in principles of psychotherapy. Beginning students often have difficulty making connections between their clinical experiences on the one hand and didactic presentations which are often couched at Waelder's more "dispensable" *level of clinical theory* ("theoretical concepts...such as repression, defense, return of the repressed, regression" [p. 252]). This method can be a useful illustration of the clinical inference process that seems both tangible and convincing, and therefore can help bridge the gap between theory and experience. Furthermore, constructing this formulation at a level close to the conscious experience of the patient is also a good approximation, for teaching purposes, of the type of clinical formulation which can be communicated to and understood by the patient.

Student reaction to this exercise was strongly positive—it was a highlight of the course. They felt that this procedure gave structure to their efforts to sort out and understand their patients' communications, and that it served as a concrete illustration of the inference process they had learned about (Freud, 1912). They stressed that this experientially oriented approach helped them to grasp the clinical material at a level akin to the patient's own viewpoint. They contrasted its pragmatic value with the more abstract genetic, dynamic, or structural formulations of psychopathology, and with the descriptive psychiatric viewpoint, all of which had been emphasized in their prior training.

Projected Lines of Development

Some aspects of our present method require refinement, improvement, simplification, or just further exploration:

—The method is now based upon free response—the judge formulates the wish and consequences components in whatever language he chooses. This has great advantages, as we have pointed out. We are now ready for the next step, which is a quantitative one; that is, to have independent judges go back to the individual relationship episodes and score the components of these. We would then be able to summarize the scores (both for frequency and intensity of each component) for each relationship episode, for each type of object, in each session, at each point in the treatment.

—We found that the agreement judges' ratings were strongly influenced by an irrelevant factor—individual tendencies or "sets" toward being broadly inclusive, versus narrow and precise, in readiness to judge that consensus is present. As a result of this, although our agreement judges all found the same *pattern* of consensus between the student judges and researchers, they differed widely among themselves in judging the *extent* of agreement; i.e., the number of student formulations in which the same element occurred as in the researchers' theme statement. More comprehensive instructions and training for agreement judges should be tried in future studies as methods for reducing this problem.

—We might profitably simplify the job of the agreement judges by asking the initial judge to report only the one or two most outstanding wishes and consequences—instead of the present method of asking for all possible wishes and consequences.

— The lack of discrimination on Negative External Consequences needs to be understood. It may be because some consequences are uniform across cases. In all three researcher formulations used here, based on three different cases (and also in the only other cases formulated to date), the main Negative External Consequences were rejection and domination by the object. It is, of course, possible that for some reason these are the major external consequences commonly feared by most people — in which case this part of the theme would not differentiate among people. However, we suspect that more refined analysis of these variables will yield a more adequate discrimination.

— A question sometimes raised about the core relationship theme is the degree to which it reflects the patient's response to the particular therapist with whom he is in treatment. The question is sometimes put as follows: "Such a uniform core relationship theme may appear because the patient brings up relationship incidents that tell his response to the particular therapist. How do you know that the core relationship theme would not be very different for a treatment with another therapist?" To examine this possibility, a Relationship Anecdotes Paradigm (RAP) Test has been developed. In this test the patient is asked to give an account of six to eight incidents in relationship to people in which he could recall some of what happened — some of what he said and the other person said, and what came of it. This Relationship Anecdotes Paradigm Test was given as part of the follow-up to a sample of the more versus less improved patients in the Penn psychotherapy project. Preliminary inspection of the data from the two approaches, one as part of the therapy, the other as part of the follow-up procedures administered by another person, showed the core relationship theme to be quite similar in both.

— The results of the core conflictual relationship theme method as applied to psychoanalysis and psychotherapy and the Relationship Anecdotes Paradigm Test should be related to other assessment devices. One of the most natural ones would be the Thematic Apperception Test (TAT) (Murray, 1938). The TAT, after all, was set up to estimate themes of many sorts. Even though its approach differs fundamentally from our own, it still would be of value to compare the two. The Thematic Apperception Test uses a preset list of categories and is based upon projective material; the core conflictual relationship theme method and the Relationship Anecdotes Paradigm Test method are based upon patients' accounts of actual relationship interactions. It would also be of value to compare the results with questionnaire approaches such as the Barrett-Lennard Relationship Inventory (1962) or the Horowitz (1979) Interpersonal Problems measure.

— Unless they are told otherwise, the agreement judges assume that they are judging a pair of these formulations by two different judges *for the same case.* Some studies of systematic variations in the instructions to the agreement judges ought to be tried. A more correct instruction should be given when mismatched cases are provided, e.g., "The theme that you are asked to judge may or may not be from the same case."

— A basic assumption in the core relationship theme method is that the job of the clinical judge can be simplified by providing him with the relationship episodes alone rather than the total session. This assumption should be further explored. The most natural beginning point would be to ask the clinical judges to provide the same type of themes based upon whole sessions. Other components that should be tested are the redundancy rule, and the format for presentation of the theme. The design could be that of a repeated evaluation of the same material with the successive alteration of one element of the method at a time.

— The aim of the core relationship theme method is to provide a clear delineation of the types of relationship themes. It would be valuable also to examine the relationship episodes for the maturity of the relationships. The system by Mayman (1967) or Blatt et al. (1976) would be useful for providing that information, or the set of rating scales by Pruitt (1979). Having both sets of data on each patient's relationships — type and maturity — we would be in a good position to relate the two to see whether they are, as they seem to be, two largely separable components of relationships.

— The core conflictual relationship themes apply to most relationship patterns. We have not yet investigated variants of the core conflictual relationship theme which might be specific to different types of objects, e.g., to each parent. To do this would require a comparison of an adequate sample of episodes for each type of object.

— Finally, what phenomenon from the psychoanalytic process is most likely to be related to the core relationship theme? By far the best candidate as a cognate is the main transference theme — the core relationship theme is probably a more exactly delineated version of the main transference theme. To relate these concepts more precisely from the same data is difficult since no empirical method now exists for identifying the main transference theme. We would have to fall back on doing the core relationship theme by our method and having the main transference theme described by the analyst in the usual clinical way, then work out a method for having agreement judges compare the two. Within the framework of the CCRT method, another procedure would be to compare the themes derived from relationship episodes with the therapist as object vs. from episodes dealing with other objects. Our data suggest a mirroring of themes with the therapist and other relationships which may imply a transference basis for the therapist themes. Even though such further research is not yet done, we are already satisfied with the usefulness of the core relationship theme method for some research and teaching aims.

References

Arlow, J. A. (1969), Fantasy, memory, and reality testing. *Psychoanal. Quart.*, 38:28–51.

Auerbach, A. H., Luborsky, L., & Johnson, M. (1972), Clinicians' predictions of psychotherapy outcome: A trial of a Prognostic Index. *Amer. J. Psychiat.*, 128:830–835.

Barrett-Lennard, G. T. (1962), Dimensions of therapist response as causal factors in therapeutic change. *Psychol. Monogr.*, 76:1–36.

Bellak, L. & Smith, M. B. (1956), An experimental exploration of the psychoanalytic process. *Psychoanal. Quart.*, 25:385–414.

Blatt, S. J., Brennels, C., Schimek, J., & Glick, M. (1976), Normal development and psychopathological impairment of the concept of the object on the Rorschach. *J. Abnorm. Psychol.*, 85:364–373.

Blos, P. (1941), *The Adolescent Personality.* New York & London: Appleton-Century-Crofts.

Ekstein, R. (1956), Psychoanalytic techniques. In: *Progress in Clinical Psychology,* ed. D. Brower & L. E. Abt. New York: Grune & Stratton, vol. 2, pp. 79–97.

Fiske, D. W., Cartwright, D. S., & Kirtner, W. L. (1964), Are psychotherapeutic changes predictable? *J. Abnorm. Soc. Psychol.*, 69:418–426.

French, T. & Wheeler, D. R. (1963), Hope and repudiation of hope in psychoanalytic therapy. *Int. J. Psycho-Anal.*, 44:304–316.

Freud, S. (1912), Recommendations to physicians practising psycho-analysis. *Standard Edition,* 12:111–120. London: Hogarth Press, 1958.

——— (1914), Remembering, repeating and working-through. *Standard Edition*, 12:145–156. London: Hogarth Press, 1958.

——— (1937), Analysis terminable and interminable. *Standard Edition*, 23:209–253. London: Hogarth Press, 1964.

Horowitz, L. (1979), On the cognitive structure of interpersonal problems treated in psychotherapy. *J. Consult. Clin. Psychol.*, 47:5–15.

Jacobson, E. (1954), The self and the object world. *The Psychoanalytic Study of the Child*, 9:75–127.

——— (1964), *The Self and the Object World.* New York: International Universities Press.

Levine, F. J. (1974), Review of: *Psychoanalytic Research: Three Approaches to the Experimental Study of Subliminal Processes,* ed. M. Mayman. *J. Philadelphia Assn. Psychoanal.*, 1:236–239.

Luborsky, L. (1977a), Measuring a pervasive psychic structure in psychotherapy. In: *Communicative Structures and Psychic Structures,* ed. N. Freedman & S. Grand. New York: Plenum Press, pp. 367–395.

——— (1977b), Curative factors in psychoanalytic and psychodynamic psychotherapies. In: *Psychiatry: Areas of Promise and Advancement,* ed. J. P. Brady, J. Mendels, M. T. Orne, & W. Rieger. New York: Spectrum, pp. 187–203. ·

——— Graff, H., Pulver, S., & Curtis, H. (1973), A clinical-quantitative examination of consensus on the concept of transference. *Arch. Gen. Psychiat.*, 29:69–75.

——— Mintz, J., Auerbach, A., Christoph, P., Bachrach, H., Todd, T., Johnson, M., Cohen, M., & O'Brien, C. P. (1979), Predicting the outcomes of psychotherapy. *Arch. Gen. Psychiat.*, 37:471–481.

——— Singer, B., & Luborsky, L. (1975), Comparative studies of psychotherapies. *Arch. Gen. Psychiat.*, 32:995–1008.

——— & Spence, D. (1978), Quantitative research in psychoanalytic therapy. In: *Handbook of Psychotherapy and Behavior Change* (rev. ed.), ed. S. L. Garfield & A. E. Bergin. New York: Wiley, pp. 331–368.

Mayman, M. (1967), Object-representations and object-relationships in Rorschach responses. *J. Proj. Tech. & Pers. Assessmnt.*, 3:17–24.

Murray, H. A. (1938), *Explorations in Personality.* New York: Oxford University Press.

Pruitt, D. (1979), Diagnosing borderline personality by the pattern of relationship deficits (in preparation).

Seitz, P. (1966), The consensus problem in psychoanalytic research. In: *Methods of Research in Psychotherapy,* ed. L. A. Gottschalk & A. H. Auerbach. New York: Appleton-Century-Crofts, pp. 209–225.

Slap, J. W. & Levine, F. J. (1978), On hybrid concepts in psychoanalysis. *Psychoanal. Quart.*, 47:499–523.

Waelder, R. (1962), Psychoanalysis, scientfic method, and philosophy. In: *Psychoanalysis: Observation, Theory, Application,* ed. S. A. Guttman. New York: International Universities Press, 1976, pp. 248–274.

21

NARCISSUS OF THE MYTH
An Essay on Narcissism and Victimization

STANLEY ROSENMAN, PH.D.

The legend of Narcissus is a story of repeated victimizations. The father, Cephisus, a river god, rapes and nearly drowns Liriope, a water nymph. He immediately abandons the pretty girl and the resulting offspring. Liriope's ambivalence to her child is manifested in her concern about whether Narcissus would have a long life. The prophet Tiresias (identifying with the imperious gods who had marred him for knowing too much) declares that Narcissus will live to old age "only if never he comes to know himself." Although Ovid claims the tale's outcome confirmed this prophecy, it is Narcissus' failure to become more aware of himself that causes him to succumb.

Not only does Cephisus mistreat Liriope; but the adulterous Jupiter betrays his wife, Hera. A chattering Echo thwarts Hera's efforts to discover the culprit and Hera punishes her: "The tongue which has deceived me shall make nothing but the poor/brief noises of the fewest words."

Narcissus, grown into handsome adolescence, now becomes the victimizer. He spends his days netting and killing deer. He elicits love from women and men only to reject them. "In that slender form was pride so cold that no youth, no maiden touched his heart." Narcissus intended to widen the gulf of prestigiousness between himself and those love-sick persons whose very existence depended upon another's love. Having himself, he needed no one else. To the infatuated Echo he spits out: "No, you must not touch — Go, take your hands away, may I be dead/Before you throw your fearful chains around me." And a mortified, grieving Echo dematerializes, leaving only her voice alive.

The way Narcissus betrays Echo, so he "played with all:/Girls of the river, women of the mountains, with boys and men. Until one boy, love-sick/And left behind, raised prayers to highest heaven:/'O may he love himself alone,' he cried/'And yet fail in that great love.'"[1] Nemesis responds to the curse, making Narcissus fall in love. But love's consummation was to be denied for it is his own image seen in the reflecting pool for which Narcissus yearns. And yearning, he wastes away. His body vanishes. In its place stands a "flower of gold with white brimmed petals."

The legend bears witness to the torment that the powerful inflict upon the powerless. The narcissistically injured seek revenge upon anyone fate puts in their hands. Narcissus is the victim at the end of a long series of victimizations initiated by the self-indulgent gods. Only when, in order to overcome his past traumas, he acts toward would-be lovers like a god himself—adored, imperious, and torturing, in short, invidious—is he struck down. The gods neither allow Narcissus to act out nor permit him to know himself. Thus he is destined to agonize exquisitely and die.

The gods symbolize the part objects incorporated by the idealizing child from parents who were themselves ill-used by their parents. And, in part, the gods represent a society seeking to siphon off the rage of its members toward the society—a rage which threatens its equilibrium—by enjoining discharge upon sacrificial victims. The gods mark their godliness by the inferior lot they mete out to mortals. They flaw the mortal and then punish him for his imperfection or for trying to undo that flaw. Narcissus has been set up to be a sacrificial victim. The gods insist that they be allowed to express their whims and jealousies by molesting lesser beings without being confronted. There is no reproach of Cephisus, Jupiter, Hera, and Nemesis for their malignant abuse of power. Instead the focus is on the moral failings of Narcissus, a youth struggling desperately to avoid yielding to the death drive and to prevent the dissolution of his personality—problems exacerbated by the turbulence of adolescence. Narcissus and Echo are left to destroy themselves in vain efforts to handle their sense of disesteem and ineffectuality in the

---

[1]Canon, Ovid's contemporary, elaborated upon the youth who fell in love with Narcissus. One day, Narcissus mockingly sends a sword to this most insistent suitor, Ameinius, after whom the river Ameinius was named. Having previously threatened suicide if Narcissus did not return his love, Ameinius stabs himself on Narcissus' threshold, calling on the gods to avenge his death.

tumultuous wake left by the reckless gods.

Victimizing is an interpersonal mode of behavior which uniquely feeds back to its agent that he is godly and special. It enables the agent to realize his distinct adequacy in comparison with the needy, depreciated victim. Power can be directly experienced by setting up victims to be derogated and weakened. The victimizer may free himself from debilitating systems — painful memories, toxic introjects, negative self images, horrendous imagery — by placing them in victims. The victimizer may reassure himself that he will not be reengulfed or invaded by the victim who is required to remain helpless and impotent. The victimizer joins with the "parent" gods by emulating them. He may ingratiate himself with the gods and their introjected representatives by bringing victims to their altars. The victimizer can discharge the rage that otherwise, turned against the self, corrodes a fragile sense of self-esteem and integrity. The victimizer may break out of life's dull routines by the excitement of stripping objects of their dignity and life. The agent may overcome his loneliness by cruelly imprinting his experiences upon the object, making them a permanent part of the latter. The agent thereby ensures companions who know what he underwent. The agent may disclose to the world his secret suffering at the hands of parents by making a public display of similar scenes. The pained scenes of infancy and childhood may be mastered by repeatedly and actively producing them so that each feature may be palpated and understood at length. Casting the object in the victim's role supplies the victimizer with that optimal distance for understanding his past.

In addition to these gains in self-esteem anticipated by the victimizer, he also trusts that the victimizing act will have a tonic impact upon (a) his reality-testing capacity as he interacts with the world in the victimizing act, (b) the self-representational structure by way of underscoring his uniqueness compared to the victim, and (c) the sense of social identity as he joins the victimizing group.

It is not only Narcissus, but also the folk who created the myth with its recurring mortifications as well as the fascinated reader through the centuries, who strive for discharge of the tensions of severely damaged self-esteem via terror, pity, and condescension — in essence, a vicarious victimizing.

The myth's basic motif of victimization is expressed in the following variations: (1) The subject mortifies a helpless object by intruding upon him. (2) The subject mortifies the object by rebuffing or abandoning him. The mortification is underscored by the subject's communication that he is perfectly self-contained or that he prefers others. These two themes have their counterparts in the victim's experience. (3) The individual is held in mortifying captivity by another person who violates his very being. (4) The individual pines in vain for the love of the object who is uncaring. This theme overlaps with the previous one insofar as such infatuation is experienced as a violation of the subject's self by the adored object. Because his inner entities are harsh or uncaring, the person is completely dependent on the object's reciprocating fondness. The myth's three corpses signify that the victim of narcissistic wounding experienced the hurt as the death of his spirit, eliminating any desire to live. The individual's very existence, his sense of self-worth, depend on attracting the unavailable other person. "I must have you or I'll die." (5) There is public exposure of the individual's mortified state, adding to the humiliation. (6) The subject seeks to harm the object who mortified him. Since the mortification felt like death, the subject feels justified in killing the noxious object. (7) If the individual does not revenge himself on the mortifying object, he must mutilate either another person or himself. (8) Only if the individual is lowly and destroys a superior or equal creature, must he perish by way of retaliation or guilt. (9) If the subject overreaches himself, other persons seek to set him down. (10) The gods seemingly transcend being subject to past victimization. Horrendous childhood events leave them relatively unscarred, but apparently on the covert condition that they may victimize mortals and lower gods with impunity.

What follows then is an illustration of Narcissus' acting both as subject and object of these themes of victimization.

The rape and near-drowning of Liriope initiate the person and the legend of Narcissus. The residue of this experience for Liriope is a basic feeling of vulnerability edged by terror, mortification, and rage. She has lost face and is given no replenishment by society. Nor can she turn within, for there is the creature implanted by the hated one. Her son is not only a reminder of the incident; in this tale of repeated reflections and echoes, he represents the abhorred rapist. The traumatic incident demands reenactment, with herself as the active agent, in order to discharge the unbearable tensions. The river god is not an available target, but his son is. Still, she is ambivalent: Narcissus is "so charming even as a baby,/That he inspired girls with thoughts of love."

Liriope's ambivalence toward her son is apparent in her asking Tiresias to determine her son's life-span. Tiresias grasps the threat of her evil passions to the boy's life. For it is Narcissus' destiny to be sacrificed in order to maintain Liriope's equilibrium. He is to be the vessel into which she can discharge her torturous affects.

Narcissus fails to experience the accurate identification of reflected images from his mother since she is unable to affirm empathically the infant's experiences. Narcissus is thereby forced to engage in a precocious predicting of the mother's mood. The mother has intruded on the baby's legitimate early experience of omnipotence (Winnicott, 1953). Had the mother's adaptation been good enough, the baby would not have become precociously aware of his dependence on the mother and would not have had to exploit whatever mental functions emerged for the purpose of self-defense (Freud, 1920; Khan, 1963a, 1963b). That Narcissus could be "loved" even as an infant by nymphs may imply that he worked at eliciting mothering at a very early stage.

Rather than the mother being the container of the baby's toxic affects, Narcissus is forced to be the depository for Liriope's tensions. The traumatized mother seeks to have the infant inundated by her own as well as his undischarged tensions, including futile yearning for affection. Narcissus' final act is to reexperience extreme despair in the presence of the adored but uncaring image—an act that provides cues to his earliest experiences. Bion (1963), in clarifying his container-contained concept, graphically describes the infant's early state:

> The infant suffering pangs of hunger and fear that it is dying, wracked by guilt and anxiety, and impaled by greed, messes itself and cries. The mother picks it up, feeds it and comforts it, and eventually the infant sleeps... the infant filled with painful lumps of faeces, guilt, fears of impending death, chunks of greed, meanness and urine, evacuates these bad objects into the breast that is not there. As it does so the good object turns the no-breast (mouth) into a breast, the faeces and urine into milk, the fears of impending death and anxiety into vitality and confidence, the greed and meanness into feelings of love and generosity, and the infant sucks its bad property, now translated into goodness, back again [p. 31].

Insufficient early love and caring push Narcissus toward a terminal state of extreme organismic distress. At the reflecting pool he reproduces the frequent trauma of his infancy caused by the mother's poor task performance in soothing the infant's anguish and fear of annihilation. Narcissus, as he wastes away, attests to his early lack of normal "confident expectation" of rescue from or gratification of affect hunger (Mahler, 1968). He is subject to repeated episodes of helplessness, withdrawal of cathexis, and futile crying—all badges of the manifest deficiency in his ego's effectiveness due to poor mothering (Hoffer, 1952; Kaplan, 1964). He reexperiences the reaction of hate and anxiety of his infancy. In the face of repeated and accumulated failures of mothering (Khan, 1963b), this state proved "far too strong a weapon in the hands of such a weak ego, it has become uncontrollable and...[threatens] to destroy its owner" (Riviere, 1936, p. 44).

Liriope's hypothesized negation during Narcissus' infancy is repeated during her son's adolescence. While the remotely commiserative nymphs all knew of the youth's desperate plight at the reflecting pool, there is no sign of a concerned Liriope rushing to his side. Similarly, when he began brewing trouble for himself by rejecting others, there is no mention of her making any effort to socialize him. It is likely that she is vicariously inflated via the youth's crude rebuff of others. He is doing to others what she wants done. Prompted by her damaged pride, forever needing victims to make her feel less ill-used and lowly, she has apparently trained the boy to be a crusher of others' pride. She lives in the grandiose self representation of Narcissus that is given expression by his haughty behavior.

Liriope has done more than simply condition Narcissus with rewards and punishments in order to motivate him to want others to experience themselves as feculent. She has shaped a personality structure which for its very equilibrium and discharge of insufferable tensions requires, as does her own, esteem-ravaged victims.

Narcissus' identification with Liriope remains rather total because his unattended needs were so chronically exigent. The introjection of and identification with Liriope permit him to imagine control over her, allow him to express anger safely and secretly, reduce the anxiety in viewing himself as helpless and hateful, and counteract the panic of separation from the mother. His separation anxiety suggests that the rapprochement phase has also gone awry. The actions of the legend may be seen as a dreamy replay of patterned incidents of his childhood: after leaving mother (Echo), mother (the image in the reflecting pool) removes herself despite his desperate cries. Implicitly she accuses him of having harmed her (killing deer, rebuffing Echo) by his independent actions (Mahler, 1968; Masterson, 1976).

The introjected image of mother as disdainful becomes the ideal object in the psyche of Narcissus. He fashions his ideal self after it. Imbued with self-feeling, these images converge to serve as the nucleus of the conscious representation of the self. This self image is employed to repress the counterpart image of the self as wretched, an image which in turn has ties to the split-off image of the mother as pitiable. Not only is this latter image of the self despised; since it holds the painful memories of helplessness at the hands of a maltreating mother, it is dreaded.

Nevertheless, this latter self image, carrying the burden of unhappy childhood memories, always threatens to become conscious. This sector of his being induces Narcissus to believe it is only the love wrested from an unloving object which has the power to take him from the state of being unworthy to being special. Thus this self image portends the reproduction of his childhood with himself as the subject currently in love with an indifferent object. The danger is checked by countercathecting aggression from the disdainful self-object representation of Narcissus-mother. As further defense, the infant-in-want image is thrust into the self structure of would-be lovers. They are not only rebuffed. Narcissus evokes in them feelings of inferiority as well as envy for the apparently self-contained godlike Narcissus. He becomes their ideal object. They are compelled to be mirror images of his derogated self. At the same time he replicates the relationship he had with his mother. This time he acts the role of the supercilious person inattentive to the pitiable objects even as they perish.

The early victimizing relationship with his mother, now internalized, is largely what Narcissus is. His inner world mirrors the frightening world of his infancy. He suffers the constant peril of being the helpless target of a deliberately discordant mother. With one part of him being his mother, the other part a baby, there is scarcely any resourceful, extant Narcissus who is for himself. His early world has been too traumatizing. Nor can he get himself together. The two self representations are separated by currents of anger, suspicion, and fear. The representation of self as needy infant is neither accepted nor nurtured nor helped to mature. On the contrary, it is used as a dumping ground for any negative quality the conscious self image experiences, thus becoming ever more abhorrent. The less conviction of a solid internal base there is, the more vaingloriously Narcissus behaves. The more conceitedly he acts, the more he generates dysphoric affects, i.e., self-directed aggression activating the frightening early memories of maternal hostility at his vulnerable self.

The self-directed hate is additionally fueled by Narcissus becoming a passive victim of defused, deneutralized instinctual forces. The released aggression stems from a spreading to the instinctual area of his failure to integrate the divided self representations (Mahler, 1968). The self-directed aggression further disrupts the boundary surrounding the self-representational structure. Thus he is unable to distinguish between himself, the object, and the relatively unassimilated introject. This confusion erupts at the reflecting pool.

Narcissus' victimization of objects provides relief, but it does not cultivate an integrated definition of self. He cannot quite find himself as he plays out mother mistreating the baby. It is as if there is mother and Echo or Ameinius, but Narcissus is not to be seen. This shaky self structure reveals another reason to play the victimizer. His acting as if he had it all together is fraudulent. Humiliating exposure is feared. To conquer this dread, he must break up the veneers of his victims, publicly exhibiting them as pathetic infants requiring the stroking of an external figure to live. It is they, not he, who are deceitful poseurs.

Narcissus' two chief victims are Echo and Ameinius. Echo's very name in this legend of reflections and reverberations suggests that she is a double, an alter ego for the chief characters of the legend. She symbolizes the proclivity for narcissistic regression after mortification. This throwback of her identity includes a remerger of the self image with the image of others. There is a consequent inability to relate except by way of imitative forms of identification. She also represents ambivalence in relationships. Thwarted in her yearning for affection, she jeers at others as she feels she has been jeered at.

Echo's life is a counterpart to that of Narcissus. Echo's mother as symbolized by Hera gave her poor mothering too: "babies who conspicuously engage in...peculiar and often rhythmic vocalizations without communicatory or expressive meaning...had mothers who were distant, or mothers who were singularly inept in comforting their babies" (Escalona and Heider, quoted by Kaplan, 1964, p. 415). Echo simulates Narcissus' overriding need to have the mother's love. The terror of being without this love ushers in denial. There is the effort to restore belief in the benignity of mother by believing that the child wronged her. Both Echo and Narcissus are punished by mothers who hope to make them feel the hurt and mortification that the mothers had undergone at the hands of their mates. Echo and Narcissus both respond to their mothers' desire to destroy the children by deferring to the wish. They are mortified by the mothers' rejection; consciousness is so painful, they escape to nonanimate forms of existence; Echo is transformed into rocks and a reflecting voice.

The condition for another person becoming an object of infatuation is that person's unwillingness to reciprocate the love. Thus, it is no accident that Echo chooses Narcissus. His scorn adds to his beauty. Echo also seeks an unhappy attachment like that of Hera's to Jupiter in order to beseech Hera for reconciliation. Echo and Narcissus have to cope not only with the difficulty of lost object relations, but with grief over the investment in grief, the waste of time and of life that went into being devoted to unrequited love. Each resorts to suicide as the only way to express anger at the unloving mother. Both are peculiarly involved with the primal scene, which in turn has a detrimental impact on their lives. Both have aspirations that go far beyond their station, e.g., Echo's tie with Jupiter, her voice disembodied like that of a god, Narcissus' flaunty derision of other persons. Echo's similarity to Narcissus of course helps determine the displacement of his self-hate to her.

Echo also doubles for Liriope. Both are pretty nymphs. Each has had sex with and a child by a deity. One legend states that Pan seduced Echo (Graves, 1955); another that Pan, unable to win her love, had her torn to pieces by the shepherds (Guirand, 1960). Echo is either trying to master this early trauma of sex with a childish father figure or else is demonstrating her part in provoking it by her cross-generational (nymphs were said to live 9,000 years) interest in a youth of sixteen. At any rate, the involvement with the father gods has led to misery for both females. Both are ambivalent mockers. (One marvels at Echo's creative use of her disability to communicate her crush to Narcissus.) Echo's similarity to Liriope facilitates her being a target of Narcissus' anger against his mother. The alikeness of the two nymphs also accounts for some of the vehemence in Narcissus' slight of Echo: "Let me be;/Death be my portion ere I yield to thee." He anticipates anew the anguish of being subject to the neglectful mother if he entered a relationship with Echo.

Ameinius is the love-sick youth who seeks a homosexual tie with Narcissus and, when scorned, commits suicide, calling on the gods for vengeance. He clearly represents the fury of the mortified victim, although he too turns part of it against the self. The neediness of Ameinius makes him especially repulsive to Narcissus, who rejects this aspect of himself. The homosexual theme, recurrent in the story, reemphasizes Narcissus' identification with his seductive, beautiful mother. It also hints at the heterosexual scarring of Narcissus by his mother's mistreatment.

That a river is named after Ameinius suggests his equivalence to Narcissus' father, a river god, and intimates the nature of Narcissus' involvement with his father: wrath at being abandoned, a yearning for the love of a strong man, and an effort to identify with the abandoning father by scorning other persons, as his father had done. Niederland (1956, 1957) contends that the river god who does not permit the hero to proceed is the father opposed to the son's journey of conquest. Narcissus' river demon performs an obstructive role by not aiding the mother to sustain a good environment for the child.

Narcissus' attitudes of derogation and selfishness lead him inexorably to the magic glade, which "no creature tame or wild, no bird...had e'er defiled." Narcissus' uniquely invidious message is that, unlike the viewer, particularly unlike the observer who has undergone a difficult childhood, he has successfully transformed the victimizing significant figures of his past into competent, concerned, internal entities who are responsive, give good guidance, aid him in adapting to reality, and help him master his drives, conflicts, and tensions. They worship him, and he reveres them. He basks in their presence. He beseeches the adored self-object externalized into the pool to return his devotion so that all will be in conformity with his proclaimed internal tableau. Narcissus covets adulation from his

audience for having attained an inner peace: like a god, he has transcended his anguished childhood.

Containing supportive inner entities, he will prove able to dis-
card all others. He qualifies to be his own good appraiser, fair judge,
and tender caretaker. He has audaciously sought to convince others
that he is the effective captain of a "team" in which all its members,
i.e., internal entities, work for the success of the whole. He boasts a
capacity to remain adaptively the same under stress.

Credence is to be given to his additional success in sculpting
and cultivating a progressing identity. His highly individualized and
coherent self-representational structure supposedly ensures continuity while directing him to paths which lead to growth. An ideal
process of identity formation, Narcissus professes, has found reflection in his subjective feeling of cohesive identity (Jacobson, 1964;
Lichtenstein, 1964). He pushes away the suspicion that his posture
of extreme self-possession hides the opposite: a self-pitying and forlorn creature who has not at all transcended the negative maternal
imprint.

The glade and its reflecting pool symbolize isolation and apart-
ness from man. Here the individual not only resides in his deepest
unconscious, he may gaze upon it. No "ruffling of constant
incidents" (Rousseau, quoted by Zweig, 1968) impedes the subject's
looking into the depths simultaneously with seeing his surface reflection. The secret pool surrounded by woods represents the chaste
mother's body and genitals. The symbol of the earliest source of life
activates the desire to remerge with the mother. The reflecting pool
reminds Narcissus of his defects, tempting him to go back to the initial warping moments and to redo them.

The pool's surface represents the boundary between the self
structure and the representation of others. Can Narcissus demonstrate that with the proclivity to regression, and while under the
stress of stimuli deprivation, this boundary has the caliber to hold
fast? Can he retain psychic integrity without being bonded to his
fellowman? Can he survive without a structure-supporting response
by companionable others? Does he have the know-how to pass this
trial: remaining adept at distinguishing reality from illusion, initial
sounds from echoes, and objects from reflections? That nothing animate has ever entered the glade suggests another test—can Narcissus maintain human consciousness despite severe pain? (On an-

other level Narcissus' retreat can be intrepreted as a drawing back from a world too abrasive and exploitive, but this theme is largely the response of the vulnerable-infant sector of the self. At this moment life for the beautiful adolescent gratifies his arrogant self.)

Narcissus fails the test. He is exposed as a sham, revealing the lack of any autonomy beyond the internalized relation of infant with tormenting mother. His identification with the powerful mother, as she appeared to the infant, was magical. Apparently he has not performed the psychological work that would have given him genuine strength and self-composure. Not only is his grandiosity mocked, his very mask of staunch identity has been torn. His presumption of internal tranquility corresponding to the calm of the glade is given the lie by the emergent specter. Essentially he whimpers for the image to tell him whether he is a lovable or naughty child. He surrenders power to the other to be his judge, even to decide whether he deserves to live. In short, he is now the infatuated one. The image taunts him, making him again feel unwanted. The corollary of his discovery that it is he with whom he is enamored is that one part of him hates him enough to kill him.

When he begins to realize that it is his own image with which he is taken, he cries: "What shall I do. Shall I be wooed or woo. Why woo at all? What I desire, I have, the very abundance of my riches beggars me." Yet this is the issue. He does not have it. Its qualities have not been integrated. He yearns not only for his ideal mirror image (Elkisch, 1957; Greenacre, 1960), but for the very idea of being whole. Death would be welcome because of the unity it promises: "we, so coupled, two in one must die."

He yields to the self-destructive desires that now come forth. "My sorrow saps my strength; no portion long/Of life is left; I perish tho so young/And death, which ends my grief is light to me." But he does want the image to watch his last hours. Before hastening his death by beating himself, he cries: "Oh stay, from him that loves you do not fly/Oh be it given, if not to touch, to see/And feel my madness and my misery." His cry to the image in the pool is directed to the mother. A nymph of the water, her beauty presumably resembles his: "Lovely was she and lovely what she bore." If he suffers enough, if he atones for what his father did by now being helpless in her power, surely she will relent.

The sudden loss of his hunting companions stimulated the

memories of absent maternal support. Also, since he joined with his hunting companions to net deer, that most feminine of beasts, he has lost the peer support on which he leaned in being independent of the mother. Without the group's buttressing, he slips into a strange state of consciousness in which he relives his early experiences. No one aids him during his final ordeal, reconfirming to Narcissus that his world wishes him dead.

Anger at the mordant mother is in evidence. The thwarted infant seeks revenge. The mother's image will also expire as he dies. Furthermore, Narcissus' pitiful story, the death of a loving infant made sport of by a jeering mother, will pass through the ages, he hopes, further disgracing Liriope. He implores the woods to take note of his state: "Oh woodlands wise, the lover's friendly screen, Has e'er a lover so tormented been?/Can you, whose lives through generations go/Remember one by loving brought so low?" (Of course, variations on these themes hold for the father, also a spirit of the water.) Narcissus' early death is an inevitable outcome of the hateful feelings directed by each sector of his self structure against the other, a relationship modeled on that with the mother.

The rage passing between the two components of his self structure raises questions as to the nature of the self-punitive affects that Narcissus experiences. Obviously he feels disquiet, not about loving himself too well but for having harmed would-be lovers. He has outraged the community and its gods. He has captured and probably killed deer. The introjected mother image condensed with the self seems to be a major source of the precursory guilt feeling. This image is readily externalized, e.g., at the spell-binding pool. Moreover, his Nemesis is a vengeful goddess who, like his mother, has been raped by a god and left with child (Tripp, 1970). The archaic superego trades heavily in derision, invidious comparisons, and invitations to act out in self-defeating ways. The self-destructive acting out diminishes the clear experience of guilt. Nemesis' persecution of Narcissus is another version of the infant being destroyed by the retributive mother. The affect that Narcissus experiences might best be described as a retaliatory anxiety admixed with elements of guilt, shame, and helplessness. Stripped of his pretensions, proud Narcissus is humbled. Mortification, combining with the other affects, reinforces the inward-turned aggression. This aggression takes the form of a self-detestation, which further dissolves his will to live. His talion punishment follows the fate he carefully arranged for his victims.

His self dissolving, spinning toward death, Narcissus nevertheless makes some restitutional efforts, though they are inadequate, to overcome the early psychic damage. Partly prompted by the wish to unfreeze the stultified pose which imprisons him (Waelder, 1930; Balint, 1952; Winnicott, 1954; Greenacre, 1960), he would revisit the infantile traumas, regressing to a primitive stage to start a new mode of adaptation. He would juxtapose the eerie horror show of his infancy with his now almost adult status and skills. At first in the glade, he could make the image disappear by rippling the water. He could slake his thirst, cool his body, rest, and leave. He could demonstrate to himself his ability to "purify" his own toxic state. He may thus have extirpated the bad mother introject that ennervates him. Its replacement could be the firm conviction of his own ability to be a warm, sympathetic figure for himself. However, the regressive forces overcome him. The glade which could erase his anguish insidiously becomes like the mother, removed and harsh, exacerbating his pain.

The enchanted, reflected surface of the quiet pool, set in the lonely glade locks its viewer into the ultimate contest between life and death forces. Even as his props are snapping, Narcissus creatively reproduces his life history. The different aspects of his psyche are perceived in new fashion. Narcissus endeavors to thrust into the pool's depth incursive representations of others which have disruptively settled into the self-representational structure. The youth, his foundations crumbling about him, labors grimly, if vainly, to use the pool to win back a solid core of genuine selfhood based on an understanding of his past.

Narcissistic hurt lingers over having his life determined by events transpiring when the person was not present to participate. The individual continues to claim a right to decide, although key events gave him no say. Narcissus attempts to undo that exclusion by transforming the past into the present, playing chords of the past, and, yet again, resounding them. The mode of his conception, in particular, has major significance for Narcissus' life. He re-creates it, seeking his life's motif: to be in mortifying captivity to another person who profanes the subject's essence. At the side of a pool, being subject and object, he lives out his many speculations about his father's role: feeling rebuffed and craving the unattainable woman, an inability to endure arousal by a teasing nymph, the arrogance that could not accept indifference. Narcissus also undergoes Liriope's terror, being prostrate in the hands of the homicidal god, and her possible hurt at the sharp abandonment. He reenacts the traumatic primal scene to which, though never observed, his life was forced to bear constant witness. With help from Echo's ineffective parroting of his laments, he reexperiences the mother's fruitless efforts to protect the child from the compulsion to do to him what the river god had done to her. He replays how the infant endured it.

Not only does the transfixing pool enable Narcissus to review his past life, it also facilitates a visualization of his current psychic structure. The mirroring surface can be equated with the boundary between the yearning-infantile self and the self that is combined with the fractionally assimilated, haughty mother (Eidelberg, 1959; Shengold, 1974). The two split sectors are in manifest confrontation. Narcissus can thus observe himself as a percipient observer might: his inner conflicts are made graphic, as are the thematic elements of his defenses. He can consciously experience the repressed yearning-infantile self. He has risked mobilizing his basic conflicts in order to understand and better integrate them into a functioning whole (Miller, 1948). Seeking to retrieve from the pool his lost sense of adequacy and the dissolving ego boundary, he looks at the mirror image in order to "make sure who, what, where he was, so that he may possibly hold on to his however fragmentary self-identity" (Elkisch, 1957, p. 242). To mature, he must scrutinize the mother's mirroring in order to reascertain that he is not the hated father. His self-boundary is strengthened by the mirror perception of himself in which he can perceive that his existence is separate from all others (Andreas-Salomé, 1921). Even his distress is partly employed in this forlorn effort to strengthen the representation of the self. That is, he marks the self by having unique and powerful feelings.

By surveying his psychic structure holistically and pictorially, Narcissus hopes to re-create his life. He cooperates with the pool's magic power to draw forth externalizing behavior (Weiss, 1947; Elkisch, 1957; Berg, 1977), especially that feature referred to as "release of the introject" (Bychowski, 1956a, 1956b; Coleman, 1956; Spotnitz, 1976). In part, the self-object image of the disdainful mother is thrust into the pool because in his changed psychological field Narcissus no longer possesses the energy to contain the introject (Bychowski, 1956a). Narcissus is also prompted by the wish to trim down to a unified self, eliminating the anxiety and confusion that accompany the split representation of the self as disdainful mother. By externalizing this image, he hopes that its very distance will allow him objectivity. A tangible confrontation with a distal object may generate more adaptive responses to the rejecting introject. (A related surmise is offered by Eisnitz [1969]: mirror dreams may be defenses against narcissistic mortification from the superego; the threatening part of the superego is split off and projected onto the mirror; omnipotent voyeurism then accomplishes the mastery of the projected image.)

Narcissus' desperate efforts to benefit from the threatening disintegration misfire. The reels of his life, which he had hoped to reedit successfully, project an ensnaring nightmare. He enters this arena with insufficient resources to profit from the personal upheaval. Forbidden self-knowledge by the envious gods, too long deluded about his ideal internal state with which he wanted to impress others, he begins, unpracticed and too readily disheartened, to achieve a genuine metamorphosis. The reparative process cannot stave off the flooding by the reactivated traumatic affects of his early life, particularly the catatonoid helplessness that follows from the turning of rage against the self (Stern, 1968).

The final scene of the legend conveys a second meaning. While the death drive wins out, it is forced to cede a "plant" life to Narcissus. He is transformed into a "flower of gold with white brimmed petals." The first syllable of "narcissus" is the same as that of "narcolepsy" and "narcotic"; Spotnitz and Resnikoff (1954) underscored the flower's narcotic and toxic qualities. The glade in which Narcissus meets with transmogrification has never before known animal or human, i.e., conscious life. Narcissus returns to a nonsentient vegetative existence. His tenuous hold on life is exposed. It rests on the condition that consciousness no longer torment him.

Awareness has proved too painful. To be unwanted by parents and by society; to be hounded by the gods; to have publicly disgraced his parents — but to be disgraced himself since they remain so much part of the self (Jacobson, 1954, 1964); to have his name used pejoratively through the ages as signifying self-focused and haughty; to have his superciliousness come crashing down around him; to be the public fool not knowing his shadow from another person, his real self from an image of an object, the reachable from the unattainable, and his beauty from effectuality; to be threatened by personal dissolution—how much better to slough off human distinctiveness or even animal life, and embrace being as a plant—confronted by these he yearns to lose his identity (Searles, 1960, 1966).

Discussion

The review of the myth of Narcissus permits the following conclusions:

1. Rather than loving himself too well, Narcissus and persons with similar narcissistic character neuroses are infatuated with an ideal self-object and abhor the components of the self that inevitably are discrepant with this ideal.

2. There is a split in the self structure of Narcissus, in contrast to Kernberg's (1975) contention that the self structure of the narcissistic character neurosis is a unitary structure.

3. This divided self structure requires victims upon whom to thrust the negative self. As a result of this frequent resort to projective identification, the person with this kind of narcissistic pathology feels surrounded by repulsive and hostile creatures. And he induces in them such feelings about themselves in order to confirm his picture of the world and to stabilize his own identity.

4. The trait of invidiousness, i.e., the regular evocation of an abrasive envy within the object, serves as a lynchpin in many individuals with pathological narcissism. Narcissus keenly counts his conquests; his pretense of indifference only adds to the envy he seeks to arouse.

5. The definition of narcissism as the libidinal cathexis of the self representation is inadequate in energic terms (Freud, 1914; Kaplan, 1964; Kohut, 1971; Kernberg, 1975). This definition also omits the structural, genetic, and dynamic aspects necessary to do justice to the data (Joffe and Sandler, 1967; Kligerman, cited by Segal, 1969).

6. The term "narcissism" has been used to describe quite different character traits (Hart, 1947; Pulver, 1970; Goldberg, 1974; Spruiell, 1974; Wangh, 1974; Stolorow, 1975). Narcissus is not on a level of primary narcissism, impulsively reaching for sensual gratification without seeing the object. Interestingly enough, Narcissus appears quite ascetic. Nor does he simply retreat, asking the world to leave him alone. The self-sufficiency of Narcissus is in the service of luring victims who will adore him. He exultantly counts his many conquests. The narcissistic yearnings are interwoven with destructive actions toward others.

7. The self-esteem system of the individual may be conceptualized as a defensive perimeter of the identity structure, signaling threats to the latter's steadiness.

8. Having a parent who intends the mortification of the subject increases the hostile component of the latter's narcissistic pathology.

9. The victimizer increases his chances of enhancing himself by victimizing acts if he belongs to a powerful collegial group with a shared, explicit, incontrovertible ideology authorizing the redress of past injustices by diminishing the target (Jacobson, 1959; Rosenman, 1977).

10. The personality structure of Narcissus which I have sketched suggests a compromise solution to the debate whether the self-hatred of the person with narcissistic pathology is mediated by the ego alone (Bibring, 1953) or by the superego (Beres, 1966). Rage is directed by two split self-object structures against each other. The disdainful self-object is pitted against the needy self. The self-object image of the self-mother, which leads to the loathing of the needy-infant self, is a somewhat differentiated part of the self representation, but at a stage considerably prior to the subsequent differentiation in which one sector of the self-mother image crystallizes into a part of a solid superego system and another sector into a metabolized part of the ego. The needy self seeks to undermine and expose the pretensions of the preening self. The needy self exults in the mortification of the preening self. Dostoyevsky's descriptions of the elation to be found in shameful exhibitions of the derogated self are unexcelled.

11. "Mirroring" is a concept with ambiguous features. The term alludes to an objective, noncoercive portrayal of the child to himself, an obvious aid to a helpful, reality-governed appraisal of what and where he is (Elkisch, 1957; Winnicott, 1967). Mirroring marks an actively approving response. The child is supplied with the desired reply to exhibitionistic displays (Kohut, 1971). Yet, mirroring may also convey that cold, impersonal withholding, or jibing reflection of the image in the magic pool.

The patient's narcissistic use of the analyst as a mirror may not simply be the compensatory effort to make up for deficient mirroring. The patient having suffered actively bad mirroring during childhood may render the object into a victimized mirror, e.g, a mere lifeless reflector of the patient. The patient digests the earlier traumas by repeating them with himself as the controlling, traumatic force.

12. Winnicott's (1960) concept of the false self fits Narcissus in-

sofar as the self as disdainful mother hides his true self and is imitative of mother. But Narcissus' false self is not submissive, socially pleasant, and mannered — all qualities ascribed by Winnicott to the false self. It does not devote itself to finding a way for the "true" self to live or to come into its own. The reflected image of the pool demonstrates that it would not be distressed if the needy-infant self died.

13. On one level, the Narcissus tale deals with narcotics, regression, and illusion. In this respect it contains a caution against thrusting oneself into identity-melting experiences without proper preparation or supportive guidance. It may be most heroic for a person to try to precipitate the crisis by seeking the isolation or chemical that will change the state of consciousness. The risk, possibly unconsciously the overriding desire, is that the person at the same time empties himself of resources. He leaves himself once more the infant helpless in the grip of malevolent, bigger-than-life apparitions. The now passive antihero trusts that the apparitions will do the work of metamorphosing themselves.

14. The Narcissus legend is marked by desperate infatuations. On the deepest level the infatuated person pleads to be delivered from blows and tensions threatening his life. He is to be helped to fend off the temptation to avoid anguish by diminishing consciousness. The would-be lover is to communicate the desire, redeeming in its effect, that the person live. The object is viewed as having the potential to confer gifts which serve to affirm the subject's existence.

On more advanced levels of the personality, the subject approaches the object with a split imagery of the self. The subject is therefore enjoining the object to demarcate the subject, to bind the divided perception of the self. The subject further trembles with hope that he will be defined by the powerful target of the infatuation as the good, able, mature self. The person takes on an identity provided by the object. The target of the infatuation has been converted into the subject's private reflecting pool. Joining the object in a dyad may lead to a proud, secure identity.

When the target of an infatuation is a competent person, that person may respond by also falling in love. On unconscious levels, he may be identifying with the infatuated object. The person who is the target of infatuation thrills to the fantasy of being the rescuer: the erstwhile ravaged object (unconsciously, the rescuer's needy self), now loved, begins to quell his powerful death instinct and to glow with life, to integrate the self-representational structures, and to brim with self-esteem.

15. Jacobson dealt with the role of hostility in the narcissistic personality disorder. She underscored the significance of idealizing trends for the individual's maturation. These trends evolve into ego ideal and superego structures, both of which then promote and direct the further maturation of the individual. At the same time, she stressed that narcissism cannot be considered apart from masochism, i.e., the potential for destructiveness and its currents in the dynamic inner world of the person. She pointed out that Freud's 1914 paper on narcissism, which preceded his dual drive theory, was confined to libidinal determinants. My description of Narcissus' regression at the magic pool follows closely Jacobson's presentation of internal object relations. She contends that a regression after a narcissistic wounding consists of an increased merging of self and object representations, dedifferentiation of energy, a defusion and deneutralization of libidinal and aggressive drives, and an increased primacy of the body ego with centripetal discharge. Thus, in a narcissistic regression, there is a relative dominance of the aggressive urges which cathect the somewhat merged images of self and other. Implied too is that to the extent that libido cathects the self representation in this narcissistic state, to that degree is undiluted aggression directed at the object.

In short, Jacobson anticipated the hypothesis set forth here: although denied by many theorists, destructive aggression, a distinctive urge of man, intermingles with and undergirds pathological narcissism.

References

Andreas-Salomé, L. (1921), The dual orientation of narcissism. *Psychoanal. Quart.,* 31:1-30, 1962.

Balint, M. (1952), New beginnings and the paranoid and depressive syndromes. *Int. J. Psycho-Anal.,* 33:214-224.

Beres, D. (1966), Superego and depression. In: *Psychoanalysis — A General Psychology,* ed. R. M. Loewenstein, L. M. Newman, M. Schur, & A. J. Solnit. New York: International Universities Press, pp. 479-498.

Berg, M. D. (1977), The externalizing transference. *Int. J. Psycho-Anal.,* 58:235-244.

Bibring, E. (1953), The mechanism of depression. In: *Affective Disorders,* ed. P. Greenacre. New York: International Universities Press, pp. 13-48.

Bion, W. R. (1963), *The Elements of Psycho-Analysis.* London: Heinemann.

Burstyn, B. (1977), The narcissistic course. In: *The Narcissistic Condition,* ed. M. C. Nelson. New York: Human Sciences, pp. 100-126.

Bychowski, G. (1956a), The ego and the introjects. *Psychoanal. Quart.*, 25:11–36.
_____ (1956b), Aspects and implications of introjection. *Psychoanal. Quart.*, 25: 530–548.
Coleman, M. (1956), Externalization of the toxic introject. *Psychoanal. Rev.*, 43: 235–242.
Eidelberg, L. (1959), The concept of narcissistic mortification. *Int. J. Psycho-Anal.*, 40:136–168.
Eisnitz, A. J. (1969), Narcissistic object choice, self-representation. *Int. J. Psycho-Anal.*, 50:15–25.
Elkisch, P. (1957), The psychological significance of the mirror. *J. Amer. Psychoanal. Assn.*, 5:235–244.
Freud, S. (1914), On narcissism. *Standard Edition*, 14:67–102. London: Hogarth Press, 1957.
_____ (1920), Beyond the pleasure principle. *Standard Edition*, 18:3–64. London: Hogarth Press, 1955.
Goldberg, A. I. (1974), On the prognosis and treatment of narcissism. *J. Amer. Psychoanal. Assn.*, 22:243–254.
Graves, R. (1955), *The Greek Myths*, 2 vols. Baltimore: Penguin Books.
Greenacre, P. (1960), Regression and fixation. *J. Amer. Psychoanal. Assn.*, 8: 703–723.
Guirand, F. (1960), Greek mythology. In: *Larousse Encyclopedia of Mythology*. New York: Prometheus, pp. 87–212.
Hart, H. H. (1947), Narcissistic equilibrium. *Int. J. Psycho-Anal.*, 28:106–114.
Hoffer, W. (1952), The mutual influences in the development of the ego and id: earliest stages. *The Psychoanalytic Study of the Child*, 7:31–41.
Jacobson, E. (1954), The self and the object world. *The Psychoanalytic Study of the Child*, 9:75–127.
_____ (1959), The "exceptions." *The Psychoanalytic Study of the Child*, 14:135–154.
_____ (1964), *The Self and the Object World*. New York: International Universities Press.
Joffe, W. G. & Sandler, J. (1967), Some conceptual problems involved in the consideration of disorders of narcissism. *J. Child. Psychother.*, 2:56–66.
Kaplan, S. (1964), A clinical contribution to the study of narcissism in infancy. *The Psychoanalytic Study of the Child*, 19:398–420.
Kernberg, O. F. (1975), *Borderline Conditions and Pathological Narcissism*. New York: Jason Aronson.
Khan, M. M. R. (1963a), Ego ideal, excitement, and the threat of annihilation. *J. Hillside Hosp.*, 12:195–217.
_____ (1963b), The concept of cumulative trauma. *The Psychoanalytic Study of the Child*, 18:286–306.
Kohut, H. (1971), *The Analysis of the Self*. New York: International Universities Press.
Lichtenstein, H. (1964), The role of narcissism in the emergence and maintenance of primary identity. *Int. J. Psycho-Anal.*, 45:49–56.
Mahler, M. S. (1968), *On Human Symbiosis and the Vicissitudes of Individuation*. New York: International Universities Press.
Masterson, J. F. (1976), *Psychotherapy of the Borderline Adult*. New York: Brunner.
Miller, M. L. (1948), Ego function in two types of dreams. *Psychoanal. Quart.*, 17:346–355.
Niederland, W. G. (1956), River symbolism: I. *Psychoanal. Quart.*, 25:469–505.

———— (1957), River symbolism: II. *Psychoanal. Quart.*, 25:50–75.

Ovid, *Metamorphoses*, tr. H. Gregory. New York: Viking, 1958. (Quotes from published translations by A. E. Watts and J. Miller were also used in this paper.)

Pulver, S. (1970), Narcissism. *J. Amer. Psychoanal. Assn.*, 18:319–341.

Riviere, J. (1936), On the genesis of psychical conflict in earliest infancy. In: *Developments in Psycho-Analysis*, ed. M. Klein, P. Heimann, S. Isaacs, & J. Riviere. London: Hogarth Press, 1952, pp. 37–66.

Rochlin, G. (1973), *Man's Aggression.* New York: Delta.

Rosenman, S. (1977), Psychoanalytic reflections on anti-Semitism. *J. Psychol. & Judaism*, 1:3–24.

Sandler, J., Holder, A., & Meers, D. (1963), The ego ideal and the ideal self. *The Psychoanalytic Study of the Child*, 13:139–159.

Searles, H. F. (1960), *The Nonhuman Environment in Normal Development and Schizophrenia.* New York: International Universities Press.

———— (1966), Concerning the development of an identity. *Psychoanal. Rev.*, 53: 7–30.

Segal, N. P. (1969), Panel report: Narcissistic resistance. *J. Amer. Psychoanal. Assn.*, 17:944–954.

Shengold, L. (1974), The metaphor of. the mirror. *J. Amer. Psychoanal. Assn.*, 22:97–115.

Spotnitz, H. (1976), *Psychotherapy of Preoedipal Conditions.* New York: Jason Aronson.

———— & Resnikoff, P. (1954), The myth of Narcissus. *Psychoanal. Rev.*, 41:173–181.

Spruiell, V. (1974), Theories of the treatment of narcissistic personalities. *J. Amer. Psychoanal. Assn.*, 22:268–278.

Stern, M. (1968), Fear of death and trauma. *Int. J. Psycho-Anal.*, 49:457–463.

Stolorow, R. (1975), Towards a functional definition of narcissism. *Int. J. Psycho-Anal.*, 56:179–185.

Tripp, E. (1970), *Crowell's Handbook of Classical Mythology.* New York: Crowell.

Waelder, R. (1930), The principle of multiple function. In: *Psychoanalysis: Observation, Theory, Application*, ed. S. A. Guttman. New York: International Universities Press, 1976, pp. 68–83.

Wangh, M. (1974), Concluding remarks on technique and prognosis in the treatment of narcissism. *J. Amer. Psychoanal. Assn.*, 22:307–309.

Weiss, E. (1947), Projection, extrajection, and objectivation. *Psychoanal. Quart.*, 16:357–377.

Winnicott, D. W. (1953), Transitional objects and transitional phenomena. In: *Collected Papers.* New York: Basic Books, 1958, pp. 229–242.

———— (1954), Metapsychological and clinical aspects of regression within the psycho-analytic set-up. In: *Collected Papers.* New York: Basic Books, 1958, pp. 278–294.

———— (1960), Ego distortion in terms of true and false self. In: *The Maturational Processes and the Facilitating Environment.* New York: International Universities Press, 1965, pp. 140–152.

———— (1967), Mirror-role mother and family in child development. In: *Playing and Reality.* London: Tavistock, 1971, pp. 111–118.

Zweig, P. (1968), *The Heresy of Self-Love.* New York: Basic Books.